Marguerite
YOURCENAR

JOSYANE SAVIGNEAU

Marguerite YOURCENAR

Inventing a Life

TRANSLATED BY
Joan E. Howard

THE UNIVERSITY OF CHICAGO PRESS

Chicago and London

JOSYANE SAVIGNEAU is editor of
"*Le Monde* des livres," Paris.

JOAN E. HOWARD is an independent scholar
and translator.

THE UNIVERSITY OF CHICAGO PRESS, Chicago 60637
THE UNIVERSITY OF CHICAGO PRESS, Ltd., London
© 1993 by The University of Chicago
All rights reserved. Published 1993
Printed in the United States of America
02 01 00 99 98 97 96 95 94 93   1 2 3 4 5
ISBN: 0-226-73544-3 (cloth)

Originally published as *Marguerite Yourcenar: L'Invention
d'une vie.* © 1990, Éditions Gallimard, Paris. The English
translation has been published with the support of the
French Ministry of Culture.

Library of Congress Cataloging-in-Publication Data

Savigneau, Josyane.
[Marguerite Yourcenar.   English]
Marguerite Yourcenar : inventing a life / Josyane Savigneau ;
translated by Joan E. Howard.
p.   cm.
Includes bibliographical references and index.
1. Yourcenar, Marguerite—Biography.   2. Authors, French—20th
century—Biography.   I. Title.
PQ2649.O8Z8713   1993
848'.91209—dc20   93-449
[B]   CIP

For Yannick Guillou

For Deirdre Wilson

CONTENTS

PART 4

FORKS IN THE ROAD

PART 5

THE NOMADIC ACADEMICIAN

APPENDIXES

ILLUSTRATIONS

TRANSLATOR'S FOREWORD

ENGLISH-SPEAKING READERS had their first chance to meet the world-renowned French author Marguerite Yourcenar through Arthur Goldhammer's elegant English translation of *With Open Eyes,* published in 1984.[1] A series of interviews with the late Matthieu Galey, one of France's foremost literary critics, *With Open Eyes* presents us with a woman whose uncanny capacity to speak, as her gardener Elliot McGarr once said, "like an open book" is matched only by her compassion and concern for humankind, indeed for all creatures on this planet.[2]

In *Marguerite Yourcenar: Inventing a Life,* winner of the Prix Femina, Josyane Savigneau introduces us to certain other sides of this author who wrote some of the most erudite and moving literary works of our century. She resists the temptation—and it must have been a strong one—to mythologize her already myth-enshrouded subject and depicts for us instead a woman whom she clearly admires but whose foibles and obsessions she does not pass over in silence. And it is thoroughly fitting, given Yourcenar's own predilection for irony, that strands of contradiction should be seen as the woof and the warp of her literary and personal life: As a twenty-six-year-old woman, Yourcenar made her first lasting mark on the literary world with the probing self-reflection of a young homosexual male, Alexis; and the most memorable protagonists of her artistic maturity—Hadrian, Zeno, Nathanael, Michel—were, similarly, masculine figures. Though she ardently loved her native tongue, as only the French perhaps are wont to, she lived half her life in New England. An avid and active seductress of women, who spent forty years virtually married to her most faithful conquest, Grace Frick, Yourcenar nonetheless fell hopelessly in love, both early and late in her life, with two young men who were unwilling, or unable, to return her affection in kind. Gleaned from a wealth of correspondence, daily diaries, interviews with persons who knew Yourcenar in various capacities

1. Matthieu Galey, *With Open Eyes,* trans. Arthur Goldhammer (Boston: Beacon Press, 1984).

2. See chapter 21, p. 433, below.

at different stages of her life, and the author's writing journals and published works, such are the strands of existence that, along with many others, are woven here into a pattern.

Editor of *"Le Monde* des livres," the literary pages of France's most influential newspaper, Josyane Savigneau first met Marguerite Yourcenar, on assignment, in 1984. What began as a professional relationship gradually turned into a friendship. And in June of 1987 Savigneau spent several days at Petite Plaisance with the woman whose life she was to chronicle. Her personal insight into that life thus enriches her nonetheless exhaustively documented text.

My own involvement with this project could not have been more serendipitous. Having recently finished a study of sacrifice in Yourcenar's theater and prose,[3] I contacted the University of Chicago Press in connection with the editing and translating service I had launched in the fall of 1990. When Penelope Kaiserlian, associate director at the press, wrote back to say that she might in fact be able to offer me some translation assignments, I was very pleased. When word came that Chicago had obtained, of all things, the American rights to Yourcenar's biography, I was astonished.

I had met Josyane Savigneau and discussed the biography with her in the fall of 1988 at a conference sponsored by the Société Internationale d'Etudes Yourcenariennes [International Society of Yourcenar Studies] in Tours, France. I had also spent three summers and occasional weekends at Petite Plaisance with Madame Yourcenar, whom I had interviewed during the summer of 1982 while doing research for my doctoral thesis. It surely seemed as if one of those "magnetic fields" that Marguerite Yourcenar often saw at work in her own life was exerting its pull on my behalf.[4] I could not have hoped for a more congenial project, or one that would have given me more pleasure.

Certain principles have guided my work, some of which it may be helpful for the reader to know at the outset. First of all, since this is the translation of Marguerite Yourcenar's biography, to be published in the country where she spent the greater part of her adult life, I have done my best to identify and include here the original English texts of any letters, daybook entries, journals, published works, or other documentary materials used by Savigneau. I have been able, for example, to read and cite from Jerry Wilson's notebooks and travel journals thanks to Jeannie Lunt, Madame Your-

---

3. Joan E. Howard, *From Violence to Vision: Sacrifice in the Works of Marguerite Yourcenar* (Carbondale: Southern Illinois University Press, 1992).

4. See chapter 17, p. 339, and p. 493, n. 22, below.

cenar's former assistant, now a trustee of her estate.[5] There are certain materials, however, that I have not been able to consult: most notably, the infamous postcard to Lucy Kyriakos that should have been sealed until 2037, a few letters, and two notes that Yourcenar wrote regarding the calendars kept first by Grace Frick, then by herself. Although Savigneau situates these items at Houghton Library of Harvard University, they were not available there during the time I spent working on this project. I have thus supplied my own translations in these instances.

Secondly, concerning the titles of books, essays, and short stories that were first published in languages other than English, I have provided on first reference the title in its original language followed by an English translation. If the work has been published in English, that translation appears in parentheses and is either italicized, in the case of books, or set within quotation marks, in the case of essays and short stories. Subsequent references, then, will generally be made to the English-language title of the work.[6] If I have been unable to find proof that a work has appeared in English translation,[7] then I provide an unitalicized English translation in brackets rather than parentheses on first mention in each chapter. Subsequent references in this event are to the title of the work in its original language.

Numbered documentary notes can be found at the back of this volume, preceding the index. These notes are Savigneau's unless otherwise indicated. The endnotes that I have inserted attempt to provide information to the English-speaking reader regarding French cultural figures or phenomena that may be unfamiliar. It is my hope that these notes will be numerous enough to be helpful and few enough not to be a nuisance.

Perhaps it should also be noted that this book, written, of course, by a Frenchwoman, occasionally offers a view of the United States to which many Americans may not subscribe. When Savigneau asserts, for example, that Yourcenar did not much care "for the very particular 'conviviality' of American universities," or, in referring to New York, speaks (in direct or indirect discourse?) of "the mixture of puritanism and megalomania that typified this people without a civilization," one senses a cultural complicity between French author and French reader from which one is perforce ex-

5. These materials had been kept at Petite Plaisance until Jeannie Lunt sent them to me in the spring of 1992, and they are now in the hands of Wilson's mother.

6. In certain instances, however, when it is a question, for example, of the publishing history of a given Yourcenar work within France, I will not follow this general rule.

7. In the case of books, I have consulted *Books in Print,* the *National Union Catalog,* and the *Library of Congress Catalog.*

cluded, even if one shares the opinion or attitude expressed. Although a certain French disdain for things American, born of historical circumstance, may account for such moments, the possibility cannot be ruled out that there exists within France, a nation so attached to its cultural and geographic patrimony, a perplexity of sorts regarding why on earth it was that this national treasure, this first *Immortelle,* should have chosen to live her life on unhallowed ground—which is to say, beyond the borders of France. In any event, and whatever the reasons, there can be no denying that she did so, nor that the most creative years of her life were spent here—inventing her heroes and inventing a life.

TRANSLATOR'S
ACKNOWLEDGMENTS

IT IS HARD TO IMAGINE that any book ever gets written or translated by one, unassisted individual. This one certainly did not, and I owe many debts. My thanks are due first to Penelope Kaiserlian, associate director of the University of Chicago Press, for her unerring advice, her support of my work and of this project, and her ready assistance at every stage along the way. Whitney Linder of the University of Chicago Press has also been a great help to me, always answering my questions speedily and thoroughly. Carolyn Cimon Williams edited the manuscript with exceptional care and intelligence.

The Florence Gould Foundation of New York made an invaluable contribution to this endeavor by awarding me a translation grant. I give thanks in particular to John R. Young, president of the Gould Foundation, for his interest in and generous financial support of this project.

I am indebted as well to several members of the staff at the Portsmouth (New Hampshire) Public Library: Kate Giordano, who tirelessly procured for me, by way of that amazing and wondrous institution that is interlibrary loan, a myriad of often obscure published tomes; Michael Huxtable, whose personal knowledge of music and professional knowledge of reference materials on many occasions saved me hours of research time; Nancy Noble and Holly Horne who always graciously headed me in the right direction, often coming up with ingenious ways to figure out how one might answer the peculiar kinds of questions I would regularly plague them with; and Richard Winslow III, Portsmouth's maritime historian.

At Dimond Library of the University of New Hampshire I was ably assited, as ever, by Linda Prillaman, Deborah Watson, and Deanna Wood. Elizabeth Falsey and the members of the staff at Houghton Library of Harvard University were all most helpful in guiding me through the Yourcenar collection and keeping me supplied with a steady stream of documents during my several days of research in Cambridge. Theodora B. Newlands, Librarian of Hartford College for Women, took an interest in this project and provided me not only with the answers to my questions but with quite a bit of interesting material about Grace Frick's tenure as academic dean at Hartford Junior College, now Hartford College for Women, as well.

Marguerite Yourcenar's energetic and efficient assistant, Jeannie Lunt, now a trustee of the Yourcenar estate, came to the rescue, as she has so many times before, with a wealth of documents unavailable anywhere else but at Petite Plaisance, for which I thank her most warmly. Dee Dee Wilson, Madame Yourcenar's ever-faithful friend and nurse, and a uniquely special person, provided help that only she could provide, having been there, for example, when Grace Frick died and her ashes were buried, and there, once again, when Marguerite Yourcenar herself passed away. I have been blessed these past ten years not only by the practical assistance but also by the friendship of Jeannie Lunt and Dee Dee Wilson, and for that there is no sufficient expression of gratitude.

I also thank Josyane Savigneau, who took time out from a demanding professional schedule to answer many questions, which wended their way slowly from Portsmouth to Paris and back. Without her collaboration my work would have been a good deal harder and the result of that work less concise than it is.

Last but the opposite of least, I am forever obliged to my friend and former colleague Claire-Lise Malarte-Feldman, who I thank God had the notion some fifteen years ago to pack her bags and leave France for the United States. From the beginning to the end of this project, I have turned to Claire-Lise with my thorniest translation problems. Never once did she fail to clarify matters where clarification was possible, or to tussle with a sentence or a phrase until it had surrendered all its secrets. During months of her life that were more trying than any human being should be called upon to bear, Claire-Lise gave many an hour of her time to helping me. Though there is no way to adequately thank her, if it were my place to do so, I would dedicate this book to Claire-Lise Malarte-Feldman.

AUTHOR'S
ACKNOWLEDGMENTS

I WOULD LIKE TO THANK everyone who has helped me undertake this project and carry it through, everyone whose contributions, knowledge, advice, and encouragement have made the existence of this book possible:

Dimitri T. Analis, Eugénio de Andrade, Gilles Andriveau, Dominique Aury, Silvia Baron-Supervielle, Patricia Baudoin, Ulrike Bergweiler, Jean-Paul Bertrand, Jean Blot, François Bott and the team at *"Le Monde* des livres,"* Philippe Boucher, Jean-Denis Bredin, Anna Cancogni, Philippe Catinchi, Jean Chalon, Jean-Loup Champion, Jacques Chancel, Florence Codman, Susan Cohen, Jean-Pierre Corteggiani, Stanley Crantson, André Delvaux, Alix De Weck, Helena and Constantine Dimaras, Gérard Dubuisson, Christian Dumais-Lvowski, Jean Eeckhout, Didier Eribon, Bernard de Fallois, Camillo Faverzani, William Fenton, Jacques Folch-Ribas, André Fontaine, André Fraigneau, Carlos Freire, Colette Gallimard, Wilhem Ganz, Anne Garréta, Jeannette Hadzinicoli, Houghton Library of Harvard University, Walter Kaiser, Anya Kayaloff, Christian Lahache, Jean Lambert, Antoine Lebègue, Yvan Leclerc, Nelly Liambey, Marguerite Liberaki, Durlin Lunt, David Lustbader, Diane de Margerie, Shirley and Elliott McGarr, Jean Mouton, Claude and Ivan Nabokov, Eugène Nicole, Heloïsa Novaes, Jean d'Ormesson, Alain Oulman (†), Bernard Pivot, Bertrand Poirot-Delpech, Charlotte Pomerantz-Marzani, Anne Quellennec, Dominique Rolin, Hélène de Saint-Hippolyte, Danièle Sallenave, Barbara Solonche-Lustbader, Louis Sonneville, Raphaël Sorin, Roger Straus, William Styron, Harold Taylor, Baron Egon de Vietinghoff, François Wasserfallen, and Dr. Robert Wilson.

René Hilsum, who is essentially at the origin of this book, since he was the one who, in 1929, published *Alexis ou Le Traité du vain combat (Alexis)*, died on 14 April 1990 in his ninety-fifth year. I had met him for the first time in 1986, with Marguerite Yourcenar, who had retained a great esteem and a certain affection for that brilliant man, full of charm and humor, whom all believed to be indestructible. He had lived through two wars and his own deportation, and had still kept his curiosity and taste for life intact. He welcomed me at his home, on several occasions, from the very beginning of my research through its later stages. He gave me access to his papers. He gathered his memories for me. Rediscovering the publisher's reflexes that were still very much a part of him despite his "retirement," he encouraged me to see this project through to the end. This book owes a lot to him, and, sadly, we won't be able to discuss it together.

This work also owes much to the insightful assistance of Jean-Pierre Dauphin and the archives personnel at Editions Gallimard; the archives personnel at Editions Grasset; Jean-Luc Pidoux-Payot, who gave me permission to consult and copy the archives at Plon; François Chapon, the head conservator of the Jacques Doucet Collection and Natalie Barney's literary executor.

I offer special thanks to:

Antoine Gallimard, for having urged me to undertake writing this book.

Marc Brossollet, Claude Gallimard, and Yannick Guillou, Yourcenar's literary executors, who had faith in me and made my research easier than it would otherwise have been.

Hector Bianciotti and Philippe Sollers, for their readings, their words of advice, and their support.

Eric Vigne for his attention and precision.

Jean E. Lunt and Deirdre Wilson, who took me in in Northeast Harbor, constantly helped me with my research there, and allowed me to work in Marguerite Yourcenar's house.

Georges de Crayencour, who provided me both his testimony and access to his personal papers.

I especially want to point out the exceptional quality of Valérie Cadet's documentation; this volume attests only partially to the precision, intelligence, and breadth of her work. Cadet also edited the book's notes, index, appendices, and bibliography.

Finally, I give very special thanks to Monique Nemer and Françoise Verny, who, purely out of friendship, were such tireless readers.

Marguerite
YOURCENAR

I NTRODUCTION

*It is amazing that the prospect of having
a biographer has caused no one to abandon the idea
of having a life.*
CIORAN

8 FEBRUARY 1986. For the third time, Marguerite Yourcenar found herself alone. Jerry had died on that morning in Paris, at the Laënnec Hospital—Jerry who was thirty-six years old, the traveling companion of those last six years, thanks to whom she had renewed ties, in a way, with her youth—Jerry who, if there existed an order of things, should have held her hand on the evening of the final passage, as she had held the hand of her father Michel, one day during the winter of 1929. Michel, the only witness of her childhood, her only link to the little Marguerite de Crayencour she once was, had died in Lausanne on 1 January 1929. She was not yet twenty-six. A French publisher had just accepted her first novel, *Alexis ou Le Traité du vain combat (Alexis)*, which would appear in November of the same year. A certain Marg Yourcenar—who would quickly go back to her given name, Marguerite—was beginning her life, alone. Michel de Crayencour, with the elegance he had always shown in her regard, discreetly withdrew, effacing as he did so his name, a name that bound Marguerite to another history and to a family that—no more than for Michel, the adventurous, unreasonable gentleman of letters—had no place for a "Yourcenar," for a free, nomadic, and studious woman, who created her own patronymic, however nearly perfect an anagram of Crayencour it may have been. Michel's death was a disappearance, not an abandonment. On the contrary, he had urged his daughter, one last time, to forge a self free from obligations, to make her own decisions for herself. And she was so busy doing this for years that Michel de Crayencour did not resume his place by her side until a very long time afterward, when she made him a character in one of her books.

Fifty years later, on 18 November 1979, just exactly half a century after the publication of *Alexis*, Grace Frick, for her part, did abandon her. She passed away after a heroic, twenty-year-long fight against cancer. The story of Grace we can tell in few words: they spent forty years together—Grace, with her maniacal sense of organization, her odd ways, her fits of rage; Grace, the American woman who had caused Yourcenar to live on "her" native soil and adopt her nationality; Grace the meticulous, the indignant, the elusive; Grace, who took with her into death the irreplaceable daily reflection on a life's work that she had rendered possible. At the dawn of that winter, four decades of existence shared collapsed into a bygone past. Nevertheless, she gave back to Marguerite a kind of freedom, the freedom to take up the wandering life once again, to come full circle before it was her turn to die, to get back to the existence of "before": traveling, be it alone (rarely) or with companions met by chance. In the end, there was only one companion left, it was the one that Grace had chosen for her, the young Jerry Wilson, who had come in October 1978 to Petite Plaisance with a French television crew.[1] A common origin, the American South, and their shared passion for the French language had caused them to strike up a close friendship, in just a few days' time. A declining Grace, who, without wanting to admit it, knew herself to be doomed, had recommended Jerry to Marguerite as a secretary.

Today, in 1986, as in 1929, as in 1979, but this time in the depths of a North American winter, of the interminable frozen winter of Maine, Jerry's death was more than a withdrawal, more than an abandonment; it was a desertion. Surviving Grace was a situation that Marguerite had had time to contemplate, whereas she'd had only a few months to come to terms with the incongruous idea of outliving Jerry, half a century her junior—the time since the confirmation of his illness, one he knew he was linked to by a lifestyle he refused to change. In only two brief months his AIDS had entered the phase that could only lead to rapid death. Marguerite spent those two months on the telephone. And like Grace, when the end was close at hand, Jerry hated her, knowing that she would survive him. Quite some time will pass before the similarities between Grace and Jerry will all have been thought out.

1986: MARGUERITE YOURCENAR was going on eighty-three years old. For the first time—she acknowledged it several weeks after Jerry's death, when she was regaining her strength—one thought was no longer abstract: "Living is very difficult; and suddenly I feel what I have never felt myself to be before: *old.*" Nevertheless, she readily spoke about old age. Her friends hardly dared to ask her questions, but journalists would sometimes be so bold. Thus, in Paris, in December 1984, she had responded to *Le Monde* with that sense of understatement that, for her, was not equivocation but a concern for accuracy: "When I get over an illness, I feel—not so much very old—but very close to the edge of things."[2] Then there had been "the horrible year of 1985 and its fatal shadows," as she wrote in a personal journal. And in September, there was the trouble with her heart and a quintuple coronary bypass operation at Massachusetts General Hospital in Boston. Nonetheless, the feeling of old age then did not come from her own illness, however exhausting it may have been. She felt extremely weak, but Jerry was still alive. He needed her. He needed an apartment in Paris, where he hoped to be treated. He needed to be well provided for. She could not have borne the thought of failing him. It was already more than enough to be so far away, to know that she would not be by his side at the final moment. With Jerry gone, death became, for the first time, a matter of indifference to her. She said as much one day, without mentioning Jerry, in front of her own gravestone, while in the presence of a young woman who was deeply distressed by the inscription on the small black slab in the Somesville cemetery: "Marguerite Yourcenar 1903–19 . . .": "I am not afraid of death. The moment, from now on, matters little to me. This has not always been the case. This inscription, which makes you sad, reassures and comforts me. All is in order. I am at peace. It could be in ten minutes, in six weeks, in several months, or several years . . . I seek neither to hasten nor to provoke, but I am ready. And I had them engrave the first two digits, 19 . . . , because I do not think the year 2000 is for me."

On 8 February 1986, she managed only to write down in her daybook "Jerry's death," and to note on the fifteenth of February "Jerry has been dead for a week." However, behind the woman overwhelmed by grief and age, there still lay an entire existence made up of tenacity, stubborn determination, and the certainty of being "someone." Marguerite Yourcenar did not disappear with Jerry Wilson, however much she may have wanted people to believe it. Behind that pose of the grande dame needing to cling to the certainty of one last passionate affection, Marguerite Yourcenar was keeping watch. She bore a strength that had triumphed over all the depressions; a will, spectacular to everyone else and unsuspected on her own part; a perseverance that had brought her this far, through the passions and the wounds, and that would see her to the end of the road, accompanying her in the strangeness of this new feeling, never experienced up until now: detachment.

Although Yourcenar would not have liked to hear it, since Jerry had become a pure and mythical figure of youth, the last sign of life in her eyes, reasons for surviving remained. One, at least, was writing. She had to get back to *Quoi? L'Eternité* [What? Eternity], the last volume of the family trilogy. *Le Tour de la prison* [This, Our Prison], an account of her last journeys, had been interrupted. Perhaps it would never be finished. *Quoi? L'Eternité*, however, had to be completed. She would stop in 1937, when she met Grace. Some of her friends thought she should go further—not in an attempt to forestall efforts on the part of biographers (Is it possible to do so, and, moreover, does one really want to?) but to give "her" version of the facts. The relative secrecy, if not the mystery, of her existence excited imaginations. Talking about the years with Grace Frick would not preclude a diversity of interpretations but would no doubt keep anyone from drifting into fantasy or fiction.

For the time being, Yourcenar had to let things take their course and honor the engagement scheduled, on 26 February in New York, for the presentation of the commander's insignia of the French Legion of Honor and the National Arts Club's Gold Medal. The photos of that evening give the impression of a woman grown frail, her skin transparent, who is slowly getting back on her feet in the world, emerging thinner and pale from a state of intense fatigue and mental anguish. But from snapshot to snapshot, the tired smile gives way to a kind of renewed energy, to a certain satisfaction with being there, with being honored and recognized—in a word, with single-handedly triumphing over herself.

A departure for Europe was scheduled for 20 April. The first stop, as so often before, was Amsterdam. Why make this trip? Was it only because traveling had been her most constant way of life? Was it a way of fighting old age, which threatened to win the struggle? Not necessarily. Staying put would have taken more energy than leaving. It would have meant getting down to work; being carried by the friendship and efficiency of Jeannie, her assistant, or Dee Dee, who was more than a nurse; abandoning the prospect of hearing French and speaking French, except upon the rare occasion of visits from friends; and, every day, writing, alone. It would have meant seeing *Quoi? L'Eternité* through to the end without a break; perhaps finishing *Le Tour de la prison.* Such strength as this she no longer had. Staying would have meant fighting old age, with the greatest possible resolve. She no longer believed that she could. Her way of accepting old age was neither to stay put nor to set off for places unknown, but to repeat the past. So she would take the trips once more that she had taken back in Grace's time and Jerry's. She would see Europe again, as well as England, to which she'd been attached since childhood and her stay there with Monsieur de Crayencour. She would go back to Morocco. She would spend several days in Bruges, in close touch with Zeno, Grace, and Jerry, and walk along the street where, in times past, she had walked the dog Valentine each day. The time for discovery had passed. It was no longer for her. Although, perhaps she would go to Nepal, a journey planned at the time of her 1985 trip to India with Jerry but canceled because of his illness. It surely seemed that in order to live right up to the end one had to travel right up to the end. There was no choice but to leave.

And what if death caught her by surprise during this journey? After all, it was she who had so often thought, so often said, so often written that one must not die unawares but, on the contrary, miss nothing of that ultimate experience, that final passage. She who wished to die with open eyes, to feel death stealing its way into her, to live her death somehow, felt from now on a kind of indifference. As she had said, she was ready. What difference did the date make, or the place, or the circumstances, just as long as she did not spend months on end depending on someone or other to take care of her? Perhaps death would even be, if not easier, at least more certain while traveling: there would not necessarily be a hospital within arm's reach where they would fight so fiercely to keep you alive. But, still, should one "pass on" accidentally, without realizing it? She never had thought so and still could not bring herself to accept it. She had performed that final rite of accompaniment, which for her served as a kind of belief in the absence of faith, with her father and with Grace, at whose bedside, when the time came and words could no longer reach her, the little music box played a Haydn arietta. Having already missed it with Jerry, she too would probably be deprived of this rite of passage. As she had begun her life at the hands of wet nurses and maids, she was going to end it at the hands of doctors and nurses; but they would be devoted, certainly, even loving, where Dee Dee was concerned. If she died at Petite Plaisance, neither attention, nor love, nor perfect care would be lacking.

Lacking, however, forever would be the community of language and culture that one needs in the final hour—the weight of a common past, even if it is only literary, of a common history. Whether she made up her mind to leave or resolved to stay, those who would gather at her deathbed would not speak "her" language. At best, they would have read her books in translation; at worst, they would not know them at all. She would thus no doubt be deprived of something that, beyond words, is shared; that, with a look, with a squeeze of the hand, allows one to "pass on the baton"—at least provisionally—guaranteeing a kind of survival at the moment before one gives way; something more than a memory in any case: the assurance that, come the next morning, someone would continue to keep her alive by taking care of what her life had been built on—her words and her life's work, which she liked to refer to, mischievously, as "the several books I have happened to write." Because of this uncertainty, indecision was not called for. She had to leave. She had to go away, to get back to what she had always been, a nomad, and to the wandering that competed with her literary work but that, alone, made it possible.

Travel, as her character the emperor Hadrian had said, "disrupts all habit and endlessly jolts each prejudice."[3] Wandering, rupture, death: was she not born beneath their sign, in that house in Brussels, now destroyed, as all the places where she stayed have been, except Petite Plaisance, that modest "country house" she was preparing to close up once again?

She set off.

"GONE ARE THE DAYS when we could enjoy *Hamlet* and not interest ourselves in Shakespeare: vulgar curiosity about biographical anecdotes is a characteristic of our time, increased tenfold by the methods of a press and media addressed to a public more and more incapable of reading. All of us tend to seek out not only the writer, who by definition expresses himself in his books, but also the individual, always necessarily manifold, contradictory, and changeable, hidden in some places and visible in others, and finally—perhaps more than the other two—the *persona*, that reflection or shadow which sometimes the man himself (as was the case with Mishima) projects as a defense or out of bravado, but behind which the human being of flesh and blood lived and died in that impenetrable mystery which is part of every life."[4] In the essay she devoted in 1981 to Mishima—*Mishima ou La Vision du vide* (*Mishima: A Vision of the Void*)—Yourcenar ironically questioned, right from the start, the pertinence of biographical investigation. She had often protested as well, in various interviews, against "the exaggeration of the 'personality cult' among writers nowadays."

As far as the analysis and judgment of her work are concerned, one can only share this point of view: the meaning of an *œuvre* that seeks to secure for itself a lasting place in time has more to do with how it is read than with the reasons for which it was written. Even so, one must take into account the distinction that Yourcenar makes between "writer," "individual," and "persona." Only then will the reader appreciate what distinguishes them from one another. It is not simply a question of indifference or a casual forgetfulness of facts and dates. In the difference between the person and the "persona," since the latter almost falls within the province of fiction, there resides a kind of creation in the first degree. And was it not precisely the "persona" of Marguerite Yourcenar—"that reflection or shadow which sometimes the man himself projects," as she expressed it—that required her to assert the insignificance of biography, even though she herself was currently occupied annotating, filing, and compiling, with an almost obsessive attention to detail, an inventory of the events, both great and minor, of her life? Accusing the biographical enterprise of insignificance under such circumstances surely seems like an ironic challenge issued to the researcher, summoned, as he or she is, to decipher information that is successively overabundant, incomplete, and contradictory.

Calmly assured that she already was—and would be even more so in the future—"the prey of biographers," as she wrote in a September 1977 letter to her nephew, Georges de Crayencour, she wanted to leave them the smallest possible amount of room for discovery and interpretation. "I am in a better position than anyone," she added in the same letter, "to know that biographers, even when they are not willfully malicious, almost always make mistakes, because all they possess regarding the people about whom they write is superficial knowledge." Continuing her defense, she then justified certain fragments of *Archives du Nord* [Archives from the Nord], the second volume of her family trilogy, specifically the passage concerning her father's desertion: "some author or other of biographies would one day have discovered those details in attempting to find out about my ascendants: I would rather be the one to present them myself, with the greatest humanity possible." Thus had Yourcenar decided to take the initiative. First, she revealed the materials needed to understand her genealogy, of which she underestimated neither the importance nor the strong appeal; secondly, she proposed an interpretation of it that could not fail to be authoritative, while branding any other reading illegitimate—or so she anticipated.

Thus, with a feigned solicitude that was not without a certain irony quite typical of her, she projected a constant concern with "helping" her future biographers. So it was that she retained copies of all the messages or letters addressed to her correspondents, both casual and close. She kept them in files, as she did nearly all the mail that she received. These files, for the most part, have been assembled in the United States and deposited at the Houghton Library of Harvard University. But Yourcenar decided to keep some of them sealed for a period of fifty years after her death, long enough to be transformed from memory to history.[5]

This arrangement has already been violated, since, in various colloquia devoted to Yourcenar, a more or less incomplete or distorted list of these papers has been mentioned. For this reason, it seems to me neither improper nor illegitimate to point out what I myself have discovered. So here is the

list of the sealed items, in the terms established by Yourcenar when she
sent them:

1938: Geneva, Lausanne, Beaune, Paris, Capri, Sorrento, Sierre, Lausanne, Paris: letters to Grace Frick.

1938: letter to Alice Parker informing her of a departure for Austria in
December 1938.

Fifty-odd pages of a personal diary covering the years 1935 to 1945.

A few notes taken between 1945 and 1954.

A short note from 1980.

Letters to Grace Frick, in 1939: Athens, Chalcis, Sierre, Lausanne,
Paris, Bordeaux.

1940: letters to Grace Frick, from whom Marguerite Yourcenar was frequently separated. New York, Hartford, Maine, and a few other places in
the United States.

1940: a short card to Lucy Kryiakos, never sent due to the addressee's
death. (Contrary to the instructions, this document is freely available at
Harvard. The text, in English, is innocuous, but ends with *Love,* a word
that, although it has a relatively banal connotation in English, is extremely
unusual from Yourcenar's pen in her correspondence. It is a sign of the
intimacy shared, before the war, with this young Greek woman.)

1979–1980: personal diaries in the form of letters addressed to Madame
Carayon (Yourcenar's proofreader and friend).

The personal papers (letters, notebooks) found in the house after her
death must be sealed for fifty years; the manuscripts and literary works in
progress must be taken over by her literary executors at Gallimard.

HOW CAN WE interpret this choice between what was immediately destined
to be made public and what it seemed prudent to set aside for future judgment? Was it a question of "hiding"—or, specifically, of "hiding oneself"?
Apparently not, for what seemed advisable to conceal from posterity was
purely and simply done away with. Yourcenar thus destroyed numerous
documents during the summer of 1987, which would turn out to be her
last one. She professed to be "tidying up." Her assistant and her nurse report
that she burned many papers in the fireplace. To anyone upset by this, she
would mockingly reply: "But I would have thought you'd be pleased that
I was taking the trouble to do this." Was she suddenly putting René Char's
recommendation into practice, that "a poet must leave traces of his passage,
not proof. Only traces make one dream"? Had she known of it, she would
likely have endorsed it, for it was by revealing only traces of herself that she
had become that distant, strange, intriguing persona that helped attract an

ever more numerous public to her books. However, by decisively getting rid of things, she was also giving in both to the urgent sense her life was coming to an end and, with unmistakable jubilation, to the permanent desire to cover her tracks, as she had always done, personally and professionally. There is no surer way to keep the investigator off important trails than to tamper with insignificant ones.

In Yourcenar's careful retention of papers, we can also see, and more simply (since one collection of letters at least, the ones she wrote to Frick, is quite clearly a collection of love letters), the wish that no one who had known her or been close to her should have access to or, even worse, publicize that amorous discourse, those intimate missives, which, no matter how great a writer one may be, are likely to resemble all other love letters in their naiveté, sentimentality, silliness, and indiscretion. Someone else will come up with the answer, in 2037. But one need only read the excerpts, for example, from the letters exchanged between Natalie Barney and Liane de Pougy at the time of their affair—particularly in Jean Chalon's *Portrait d'une séductrice* (*Portrait of a Seductress*), a book that Yourcenar knew well—in order to understand her reluctance or to gauge the uneasiness brought on, not by the revelation of an intimate relationship, but by the disclosure of its most private, most secret manifestation: the billet-doux.

Considering what Yourcenar made available, "without any restriction," one at first has the feeling, given the extent of those collections of letters so carefully catalogued by author, once or twice reproduced on India proof paper, photocopied, or recopied by hand (in Frick's writing most of the time) of being in the presence of all of the epistolary exchanges with an interlocutor, and that nothing here has been hidden from the researcher. Apparently proving that exhaustiveness: even answers to greeting cards, stereotypical and without importance, were kept. How remarkable this is for someone who ostensibly challenged the validity of biographical interest!

Both minutiae and abundance are deceptive, however: no sooner does one meet some of Yourcenar's correspondents and gain access to the originals of that supposedly exhaustive correspondence than one realizes that Yourcenar carefully reread the copies of her letters and sorted them out before sending them to Harvard—just as she reread the records Frick kept from day to day, sometimes annotating them. She did her best to anticipate and control interpretations of her life, just as she tried to restrict the field of critics and researchers, pointing them in certain directions, in the manifold notes, prefaces, bibliographies, comments, or other "reflections" that she added to her works.

She frequently played similar tricks with chronology. "I have always lacked a sense of time," she says in *Quoi? L'Eternité*. "Yes, I keep a journal, but very sporadically; sometimes twenty years go by between entries," she responded to a survey published in *Le Monde* on 9 July 1982. "I do it—for what I believe to be the most frequent reason—so as not to lose my footing entirely in 'that flowing stream.'[6] . . . I write everything down, when I do, in a most elliptical manner, almost in shorthand. Those texts are absolutely not meant to be published; all sincerity would vanish if one believed that they might be, and they would mean almost nothing handed over to a reader without commentary."

"Not losing her footing in that flowing stream" was a constant preoccupation for her. Was this the reason that Frick, at the end of some of those annual daybooks, prepared recapitulatory chronologies of Yourcenar's life, as if by this repetitive, almost obsessive, gesture she was helping to ward off the erosions of time? One can only wonder, nonetheless, what would have happened without the assistance of those records. For, despite their existence, the "Chronologie" [Chronology] that Yourcenar prepared for the Pléiade edition of her work—she is one of the rare authors ever included in this collection while still living, in 1982—is more than approximative.[7] It bears noting, moreover, that she did not sign it: the edition bears the heading "Foreword by the Author and Chronology" and not "Foreword and Chronology by the Author." Sometimes we have three different dates for the same fact: one from the Pléiade's "Chronologie," one from Frick's records, kept from day to day, and, alternatively, one given in the preface of a book. Such is the case for a trunk that was to become famous (it contained a fragment of the future *Mémoires d'Hadrien* [*Memoirs of Hadrian*]): the Pléiade edition informs us that the trunk, sent on from Switzerland where Yourcenar had left it before the war, reached her, in the United States, in 1948. In several interviews, Yourcenar situated the arrival of the trunk back in 1947. Finally, in the records that Frick and she kept from day to day, the date—certainly the right one—is 24 January 1949.

Amidst these confusions, how much was intentional? No doubt it was often a question of real indifference regarding chronological accuracy. Perhaps she also was playing a game with her interpreters and, specifically, with her biographers; perhaps she found it amusing to say "since this is the date that I give, it is therefore the correct one." In a similar vein, when someone would point out to Marguerite Yourcenar that she was using an erroneous quotation, she would retort: "No matter, it's better this way." Thus was she in the habit of transforming Cocteau's formula, "Man's time is folded and hidden in eternity,"[8] into something slightly different, which she still attributed to Cocteau: "Time is hidden and folded in eternity." And it was almost reluctantly that she consented in *La Voix des choses* [The Voice of Things] to cite what he had really written.

About her life, the only things that deeply interested her were those that could serve as pretexts for literary reconstruction. As familiar as she was with Gide's work, there can be no doubt that she pondered this passage from his *Journals*, dated 3 January 1892: "A man's life is his image.... This can therefore be said, which strikes me as a kind of reverse sincerity (on the part of the artist): Rather than recounting his life as he has lived it, he must live his life as he will recount it. In other words, the portrait of him formed by his life must identify itself with the ideal portrait he desires. And, in still simpler terms, he must be as he wishes to be."[9]

Reconstructing and reinterpreting her maternal and paternal ancestry, her childhood, and her adolescence fascinated her. "Autobiography!" she exclaimed in 1986 upon learning the subject of a colloquium on her work that would be held in Spain. "But one could say that none of my works is autobiographical [*Quoi? L'Eternité* was not yet finished] or that all of them are." From a real-life incident, she could compose a fiction—which is very common among writers—then reinterpret a moment of her life in light of that fiction, which is less so.

For all that, this biographical inquiry will not attempt to analyze or comment on the work itself—a project that would entail an entirely different method—but will confine itself to retracing an itinerary, one that bears an indisputably necessary relation to what was created, but one that is just as indisputably insufficient as an explanation of the latter. For Yourcenar every literary work was "fashioned ... out of a mixture of vision, memory, and act, of ideas and information received in the course of a lifetime from conversations or books, and the shavings of our own existence,"[10] as she indicated in the Postface of *Un Homme obscur* ("An Obscure Man"). She would probably have subscribed to what Frederic Prokosch said about his own book, *Voices: A Memoir:* "In *Voices* everything is true. Everything really took place. Faces, places, voices, everything was indeed there. But none of it all came back to life until the masks of memory were placed upon the faded faces, until the shadows of time began to lengthen on the uncertain landscapes."

For Yourcenar, the boundary between reality and fiction was more than blurred. She calmly avowed spending more time in the company of Zeno than with her friends, as well as "turning to him" sometimes for an opinion or advice. And she had written down the date of birth that she assigned to Zeno, 24 February, next to her mother's, which was also the twenty-fourth. It had pleased her to have Zeno born on the same day as her mother: approximation yet again, as revealed by family papers where Fernande de Cartier de Marchienne's date of birth is given as 23 February.

Writing a biography, and singularly Marguerite Yourcenar's, can only be, in the sense meant by Louis Aragon in *La Semaine sainte* (*Holy Week*), attempting to approximate "the truth of a lie." Not that this last term is meant to refer to a continually deliberate falsification; rather, it evokes the series of discrepancies and memory gaps, and, if truth be told, the fiction that is, if not every life, at least every look brought to bear on a life. "We lose track of everything, and of everyone, even ourselves," writes Yourcenar in "Reflections on the Composition of *Memoirs of Hadrian*." "The facts of my father's life are less known to me than those of the life of Hadrian. My own existence, if I had to write of it, would be reconstructed by me from externals, laboriously, as if it were the life of someone else: I should have to turn to letters, and to the recollections of others, in order to clarify such uncertain memories. What is ever left but crumbled walls, or masses of shade?"[11] Which amounts to saying that Aragon's expression can evidently be reversed and biography become, in all good faith, the lie of a truth, if interpretation does not subject itself to the facts, and if the facts themselves are not pursued beyond the falsely objective account of them that is given. But would one be so eager to take the risk, to reconstruct that singular itinerary, to discover what inspired that existence, if Marguerite Yourcenar had not ventured off the beaten paths into places forbidden, leaving traces of her passage—not wiped out, but at least partially hidden—or if her route did not wend its way to secret glades of freedom?

CERTAINLY, the "shadows of time" are not yet long enough upon Marguerite Yourcenar for any likeness to bring out with utmost definition all the nuances and contrasts of her life. First, as I have said, because the nearness of her death does not permit us to use all existing documents to confirm or invalidate any given hypothesis; thus, this work only seeks to propose certain avenues of inquiry whose validity others will be able to assess. Also because, for this biographer, the memory is still so vivid of a trust that sometimes bordered on confidential disclosure that to report certain things would have more to do with indiscretion than information. But at least one can attempt to sketch, for all those who never crossed her path, the silhouette of this woman who traversed the century a solitary figure—proud, sometimes aloof, often kindly—and who was able to attain a manner of serenity without ever giving in to indifference, eager to preserve until reaching the end of her road the subtle pleasures of everyday life, intellectual vigilance, and the enchantments of love.

PART 1

The Name beneath the Name

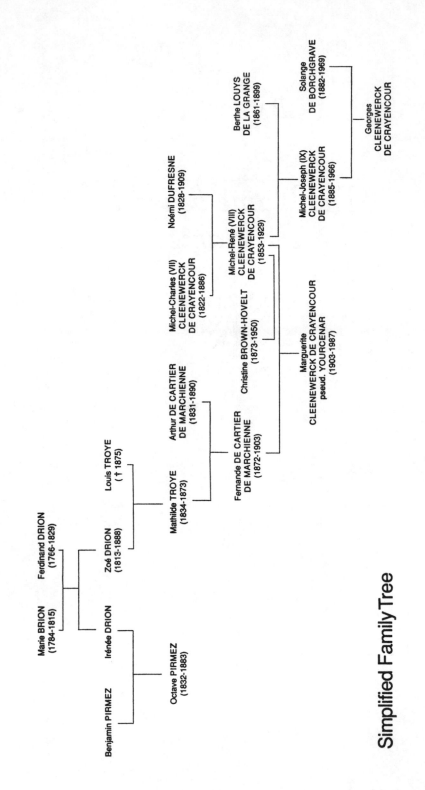

Simplified Family Tree

I

The Child and the Maidservants

IF THE HOUSEHOLD wasn't tense, it was at least busy and impatient, on 7 June 1903, in the opulent residence at 193 Avenue Louise in Brussels—a "house [that] was swallowed up by a high-rise some fifteen years ago," writes Yourcenar in *Souvenirs pieux* (*Dear Departed*). Madame de Crayencour, who had turned thirty-one several months earlier, on 23 February, was about to give birth to her first child. The young Fernande was descended from a Belgian family, the Cartiers de Marchienne. Marguerite Yourcenar devoted an entire book, *Dear Departed*—which bears this Zen text as an epigraph: "What did your face look like before your father and mother met?"—to retracing the course of this family. She briefly sums up its origins in the Pléiade "Chronologie": "Fernande de Cartier de Marchienne came from a very old family originating in Liège, which established itself during the seventeenth century in Hainaut, in the town of this same name. Her 'uncle,' or more accurately her parents' first cousin, both on the paternal side and on the maternal side, Octave Pirmez, a poet and novelist known as 'the solitary of Acoz,' was one of the outstanding essayists of nineteenth-century Belgium."[1] Yourcenar could not have failed to call attention to that literary ancestry, however modest it may have been.

FERNANDE had persuaded her husband to rent the house on Avenue Louise because, for her delivery, she preferred Brussels and her native land to Mont-Noir, the family estate of the Cleenewercks de Crayencour, in northern France near Saint-Jans-Cappel. The Crayencour "dynasty" is the subject of the second panel of Yourcenar's family triptych, *Le Labyrinthe du monde* [The Labyrinth of the World], but she evokes them briefly, as she does the Marchienne family, at the beginning of the Pléiade "Chronologie," while noting the fact of her own birth: "M. de Crayencour came from an old family of northern France. The cradle of that family seems to have been Caestre, near Cassel. Michel de Crayencour's ancestors had been rooted in Bailleul for several centuries, then his parents had settled in Lille shortly before his birth. His father, Michel-Charles, a rich landowner, had for a long time been a prefectoral councilor, then president of the prefectoral council of the département of the Nord. His mother, Noémi Dufresne, was the daughter of Amable Dufresne, presiding magistrate of Lille, himself the son of a notary from Béthune."[2]

ON AVENUE LOUISE, everything was set, as June began, for the arrival of the child. The servants—Aldegonde, Barbara, Azélie—were ready, awaiting the first labor pains to send someone for the doctor. Monsieur de Crayencour was not worried. He would be fifty years old two months later and had already been through the way births and deaths have of taking turns with one another in families. We'll never know whether he was happy or slightly annoyed at having to become a father for the second time. No doubt he was doing his best to look upon it all with a certain indifference. He did not get along well with the son that his first wife, Berthe, had given him. This seventeen-year-old boy—whose first name, like his own, was Michel, in accordance with family tradition—aroused in him nothing but distrust. He found him withdrawn, silently hostile, and had always felt as if he were an enemy. Monsieur de Crayencour had behind him a life of extravagance and adventures that his son, silently but conspicuously, condemned. He had promenaded his carefree elegance over nearly all of Europe, from gaming table to gallant soirée, and "settling down" was hardly in his nature. Nevertheless, he had complied with the wishes of Fernande, who saw maternity as the only way to really be a woman.

This banal situation, the apparent beginning of a "city romance," would not merit our attention if it were not at the origin of Yourcenar's destiny.[3] For things happened just as, in her darkest hours, Fernande had feared they would. Yourcenar told the story in detail in *Dear Departed,* an account recreated some seventy years after her birth and after much cross-checking of sources. During her childhood, this moment was never brought up, and Fernande, rarely mentioned, was only referred to as "Marguerite's mother."

At eight o'clock on Monday morning, 8 June 1903, at the end of a night of intense suffering, Fernande brought into the world a little girl, who was named Marguerite Antoinette Jeanne Marie Ghislaine.

> The pretty room looked like the scene of a crime. Barbara, wholly occupied with the orders that the nurse was giving her, had but a timid glance to spare for the ashen face of the woman in the bed, knees bent, feet extending from the sheet and supported by a pillow. The child, already separated from its mother, was wailing in a basket, covered with a blanket. A heated argument had just erupted between Monsieur and the doctor, whose hands and cheeks were trembling. Monsieur was calling him a butcher. Azélie skillfully

intervened to silence the barely suppressed outbursts of the two men. Monsieur the doctor was exhausted and would do well to go home and rest. This was not the first time that she, Azélie, had assisted at a difficult birth. Monsieur savagely ordered Barbara to show the doctor out. . . .

With the help of Aldegonde, who was called to the rescue, the women restored to chaos a semblance of order. The sheets soiled with the blood and wastes of the birth were rolled in a ball and brought to the washhouse. The viscous and sacred residues of all births, which every adult has some trouble imagining himself to have been furnished with, ended up being burned in the kitchen fire. The newborn was bathed. It was a robust little girl whose head was covered with black down resembling mouse fur.[4]

After a slight improvement, the state of Fernande's health declined, and in spite of the treatment she received from a new doctor, she died, during the evening of 18 June, of puerperal fever and peritonitis. Her death was probably registered the next day, since it is the date of 19 June that appears on her *souvenir pieux,* a small mourning card bearing prayers and personal sentiments that can be placed between the pages of a missal. During those few days, when she had understood that she would not survive, Fernande had the time to make a recommendation to her husband in the presence of her sister, Mademoiselle Jeanne—"the invalid aunt" whom Marguerite would talk about frequently—and the German governess, always referred to as "Fräulein," but to whom, nonetheless, the little girl just born owed her first name (her name was Margareta): "If the little one ever wants to become a nun, don't anyone prevent her." "Monsieur de C. never told me about this, and Jeanne had the discretion to avoid mentioning it," comments Yourcenar.[5] She adds, "It was otherwise with Fräulein. Each time I prepared to spend several days visiting the woman I knew as Aunt Jeanne, Mademoiselle Fräulein would tirelessly repeat to me my mother's last words, which made the poor old German woman, whose caresses and boisterous teasing I had already found irritating, unbearable to me. From the age of seven or eight, it seemed to me that this mother of whom I knew almost nothing, whose picture my father had never shown me (Mademoiselle Jeanne did have a photograph of my mother, along with many others, on her piano, but she hardly took the trouble to draw my attention to it), encroached unduly on my life and liberty, trying to push me too obviously in a particular direction. The idea of entering a convent appealed very little to me, but I would doubtless have been just as rebellious if I had known that on her deathbed she had planned my future marriage or named the school I was to attend. Why were all these people interfering? I balked, imperceptibly, resisting like a dog that turns its head when shown a collar."[6]

The photographs of Fernande on her deathbed, which Yourcenar only saw as an adult (she always maintained that she never saw a picture of her mother before the age of thirty-five), show her stomach deformed by the infection, just as swollen as if she had not yet given birth. Monsieur de Crayencour found himself a widower for the second time in four years. And judging from what one can assume about the death of his first wife, Berthe, and of her sister Gabrielle, deaths most likely due to abortion procedures, he was twice a widower for reasons linked to procreation. "I have stated elsewhere that Berthe's death shook Michel without grieving him," Yourcenar observes. "After closely examining what little I know of the facts, I assume him to have been at least deeply distressed. In any event, he seems to have returned to Mont-Noir with the intention of staying there for good, which, in his case, seems like an admission of defeat."[7]

Berthe was a woman who liked to take risks. Her son, for his part, thinks that, more than anything else, she submitted to her husband's will, but, given his style, one suspects that conventional imagery wins out over reality: "I was fourteen at the time, and could taste all the bitterness of my misfortune. I was losing a good and gentle mother who cherished me tenderly . . . ," relates Michel-Fernand-Joseph. "How many times did I see great tears well up on the lids of her large black eyes when she would leave me to follow the incessant peregrinations of my father . . . Goodby, my little man, she would say to me choking back a sigh."[8]

Yourcenar, on the contrary, imagines and recreates a Berthe who is capricious like her husband. The facts do not contradict her. Adventurous, an excellent horsewoman, she had followed Monsieur de Crayencour across Europe and had not hesitated, one day when funds were low, to take a job along with him in a circus, earning what they needed to continue on their way. "In Vienna the three travelers [Michel, Berthe, and Gabrielle] were short of money once again," writes Yourcenar. "If one goes by Michel, it was being broke that time that made them decide to head back toward the West, trailing after a circus in which they performed feats of horsemanship and helped out with taking care of the horses. I tend, rather, to suspect that the appeal of the sawdust, of the red velvet dressing rooms, of the chestnut-brown horses, their tails swaying with flourish to the band's brassy blare, and the smell of sweat and wildcats all had something to do with it. Renoir, Degas, and Manet loved them, too."[9]

On the other hand, "poor Fernande," as her daughter sometimes calls her, a gentle and a somewhat timid woman, shielded herself; she did not take any chances. She liked traveling more for the dreams it inspired than for adventure: "The somewhat insipid style of these daydreams," Yourcenar remarks, "does not prevent them from embodying something essential: the need for love, which Fernande envelops in clouds of literature, and the need for sexual satisfaction, which she does not acknowledge."[10]

Yourcenar evoked, in both *Dear Departed* and *Archives du Nord,* what had led Michel de Crayencour on 8 November 1900, at the age of forty-seven, to marry the young Fernande, who was twenty-eight years old and the bearer of a "tender solicitude for a man who had endured certain trials of which she was not unaware."[11] This does not mean that she understood them. Here is how she sums up their three years of life together:

> There is something moving about those words of consolation and those promises made by one fragile human being to another, whose wounds were poorly healed. The promises were kept to the extent that it was in Fernande to keep them. The future . . . lasted a little bit longer than three years. . . . Three years of a slow waltz across Europe, which was this time a Europe of museums, royal parks, mountain meanderings, and paths in the forest; three years of conversation and reading, of love as well, and a happiness undoubtedly marked here and there by misunderstandings and arguments between this quickly angered man and this woman quickly hurt. But happiness just the same, since Michel had written on the back of the young woman's death announcement that, instead of crying because she was no longer, one should be gladdened by the fact that she had been. He added, with dubious praise, that she "always tried to do her best." . . . If the past had not been abolished, at least it had faded momentarily. One cannot say that three years of near happiness beside a different young woman, in a light that had changed, in a state of intimacy filled as with the music of Schumann, were nothing for a man of forty-six [*sic*] who had much and violently lived.[12]

This "near happiness," though it had not been born of a reciprocal passion, or precisely because it had not been born of such a passion, could have lasted years if the fragile Fernande had not fallen victim to what she feared above all else: dying in childbirth.

Monsieur de Crayencour, for his part, could not tell which was worse, the sorrow, the awkward position he was in, or the weariness, when he went back to Mont-Noir at the end of July, with little Marguerite and the nurse Azélie. "A gentleman dressed all in black, whom the porters and ticket collector had no trouble recognizing as Monsieur de C., got off a train at Lille and took the local to Bailleul, where Madame Noémi's horses and their driver, Achille, were waiting for him," Yourcenar writes. "Monsieur de C. had the basset hound Trier on a leash, one of the relics of Fernande, who had bought the dog in Germany during their engagement trip. Walking behind him were two ladies, the objects of his solicitude, also dressed in black, whom the employees of the little railway station soon recognized as household servants. One was Barbe, or Barbra, as I shall call her later on. . . . The other was the nurse, Madame Azélie. . . . Madame Azélie was carrying the little one in her arms, nestled on a pillow that was covered in white; to be safer, the infant was tied to it by great satin knots."[13]

The prospect of having both to put up with his mother, Noémi, and to watch over the child, whom he was duty-bound to help along, was hardly comforting to Michel—especially in this "château," which he never managed to like despite the country charm of its setting. "The 'château' where I spent the summer months," Yourcenar wrote later, "from 1903, the year of my birth, until 1912, was a small brick manor house, built with a great many superadded turrets, in that Louis XIII style so cherished during the Romantic era. The date 1824 was engraved on the façade. . . . Though the buildings themselves were mediocre, the view from the terrace was very beautiful, and very beautiful as well were the great sloping pastures and the woods."[14] According to Georges de Crayencour, the château of Mont-Noir was built in 1815 by Charles-Augustin Cleenewerck. It was at the insistence of the latter's wife that the patronymic de Crayencour was officially appended to the family name, following a judgment rendered by the court of Hazebrouck on 19 June 1858.[15] This name, as is customary, was that of a property belonging to the Cleenewerck family.

In one of the first letters that she sent to her half nephew Georges de Crayencour, at Christmastime in 1966, Yourcenar evokes the château of Mont-Noir, reconstructed much later in *Quoi? L'Eternité* [What? Eternity].[16] According to legend, the place boasted an unlikely procession of rooms:

> One gets the impression that Mont-Noir had a hundred rooms (as ancient Thebes had a hundred doors!). I have sometimes thought about it since then and have never been able to count more than thirty or so. If you cheated a little and added the little caretaker's house, which still exists, the stable, which later became a garage, and the laundry where I washed my fat lamb every Saturday, then you could come up with about forty rooms at the very most. Such are the accretions of legend. . . .

"Much could also be said about the people who lived under that roof," Yourcenar continues, addressing her half nephew:

> from your redoubtable great-grandmother—"Madame Cleenewerck"—as your grandfather liked to call her, to the servants, the coachman Achille, the gardener Hector, the cook Julienne, Great Madeleine and Little Madeleine, and the butler/valet Joseph, who used to drink what was left over in the wine bottles, singing popular songs of the time—or songs that had been popular

ten years earlier ("Brave ol' General Boulanger"). All these people and a few more besides lived in the basements, the great, dark kitchen with all its shining copper, the milk house, where stoneware pots stood full of salted butter, and the "common room" with its big round table, located just beneath the masters' dining room and more cheerful than the latter.

This sums up at least part of the decor, which I recorded with the eyes of a very little girl, shortly before the time your mother made her first visit to Mont-Noir. Most people who speak of the past do so either in a joking, superior tone, as if excusing themselves for having known such an "outmoded" state of affairs, or else nostalgically, seeing everything through rose-colored glasses. Both attitudes are mistaken: there were things to take and things to leave in that life at Mont-Noir, as is the case everywhere else. . . . The rest is for the book that I shall write perhaps one day.[17]

Noémi ("Madame Cleenewerck") loved only the boy they kept calling "Little Michel" (even though he was a tall young man)—Marguerite's half brother, whom she always called Michel-Joseph.[18] "The mistress of the manor, born Noémi Dufresne to an important family of the Lille bourgeoisie, who was rather appalled by her son's financial extravagance and wastefulness (she had also had two daughters, both of whom died tragically), soon called together a family council over which she presided with the guidance of her notaries . . . in an attempt to safeguard for her one and only grandson, Michel Fernand, his rightful share of the family wealth. These precautions, it would seem, had very little effect; Noémi died on 16 April 1909. What arrangements, good or bad, had she succeeded at making? Were they respected?"[19]

Georges de Crayencour, son of "Little Michel," says today that his half aunt, Marguerite Yourcenar, painted an accusatory portrait of Noémi that was "unjust and excessively negative." And indeed, Yourcenar was not tender toward Noémi: "And now let us turn our attention to that abyss of small-mindedness: Noémi," she wrote in *Archives du Nord.* "I only knew her as an eighty-year-old, hunched and ponderous with age, coming and going in the hallways of Mont-Noir as, in a story by Walter De la Mare, Seaton's unforgettable aunt roams about her empty house, having become in the eyes of the children who watch her the stocky incarnation of Death, or, even worse, of Evil. But the prosaic Noémi was not the type to terrify. . . . That old woman, who had feared death all her life, died alone at Mont-Noir when her heart gave out. 'Her heart?' a country neighbor cried facetiously. 'And yet she never used it much.'"[20]

Yourcenar instinctively—and also, no doubt, intentionally—assumed her father's animosity toward his mother, a woman who, he said, had never loved him. To this must be added how much she herself felt Noémi's ample displeasure at having her as a granddaughter, and even more at having her stay at Mont-Noir. In Yourcenar's view, Noémi "hardly knew that she would die one day; she knew that her parents would die and that she would inherit from them. . . . No one ever told her that things deserve to be loved in and of themselves, apart from us, their uncertain possessors. . . . She was virtuous in the ignobly narrow sense that was given to this word at the time, when it was used in its feminine form as if virtue for a woman concerned only a slit in the body. Monsieur de C. would not be cheated on. Was she chaste? Her sheets alone could answer this question. Perhaps that robust wife had ardent desires that Michel-Charles knew how to satisfy, or, on the contrary (I tend toward this alternative, for no fulfilled woman is shrewish), perhaps a certain poverty of temperament, or a lack of curiosity or imagination, or else the pieces of advice that Alexandrine-Joséphine must have given her turned her away from the 'illicit' pleasures, and even from the pleasures permitted."[21] In view of these lines, it is not surprising that Yourcenar felt very little attraction to such a conception of "virtue" or that, much later, she chose to appropriate this word for her own purposes, giving it a less conventional, more Roman, definition.

MONSIEUR DE CRAYENCOUR, annoyed by the inevitable cohabitation with his mother, however provisional, burdened with a baby that Noémi did not even want to see, had a hard time imagining his future. He certainly had no idea then that he would one day take an interest in his daughter, that she would revive his taste for study and literature, or that what was starting there, at Mont-Noir, was the singular itinerary of an exceptional woman. He would not have dared to dream that Marguerite might follow his own personal bent, at least as far as his nomadism—"one is always better off somewhere else"—and his solitary freedom were concerned. And yet she did, adding on, of course, a form of conjugality as well as fierce persistence with respect to her work that he might have deemed excessive. Monsieur de Crayencour had turned dissipation into art. His daughter would find out that in order to leave behind a literary *œuvre*, which would very soon become her one and only real preoccupation, she had to restrain herself, or at least accept being restrained.

REGARDING YOURCENAR'S childhood years, we have hardly anything beyond her own account, particularly in *Quoi? L'Eternité*, the last volume of her family trilogy. There is so little, first, because the age at which she died, eighty-four, precludes an abundance of witnesses; then, because she lived alone with her father; because they moved frequently and traveled a lot; and because she never went to school, being taught only by tutors. Thus there are none of those notebooks, attesting to a precocious taste for literature or history, that give a reassuring sense of early inclinations rediscovered; nor are there any of those schoolmates so precious to biographers, and so loquacious about all the little details, sometimes embellished, sometimes tarnished by time, but that still provide colors for the portrait of a child at the time of her first social experience. She herself "long believed that [she] had few childhood memories." "I mean by that memories from before the age of seven," she writes in *Quoi? L'Eternité.* "But I was wrong: I suppose rather that, until now, I rarely gave them the chance to rise to the surface."[22]

In attempting to make her way back up the stream of those first distant memories, Yourcenar recalled those flower-filled meadows of the century's beginning, for which we now feel such nostalgia. "A spray of poppies, three stray cornflowers move us," she confided at the end of her life, "whereas back then there was a profusion, an inundation of color, as in that painting by Monet where a woman is lost in the poppies."

She also remembered the animals: the nanny-goat whose horns had been gilded by Michel, her father; the lamb; and the basset hound Trier, the dog Fernande had picked out, who had traveled with the young married couple during their brief conjugal life, and who, at Mont-Noir, watched over the cradle of the motherless baby. She had a harder time recalling objects and playthings, with the exception, perhaps, of an ordinary doll, which, like all children, she preferred to "rich people's toys": "All one winter, a ten-cent doll, a baby made of Celluloid, taught me about motherhood. Whether by chance or premonition, I called it André, which two men who would be dear to me were named, though my emotions with respect to them were not at all motherly."[23]

Nonetheless, since we must not forget that Yourcenar never really took an interest in her personal life except to reconstruct it as a literary object, we must approach the "information" contained in the family trilogy with utmost caution. What's more, when Yourcenar would speak of *Quoi? L'Eternité,* she called it "my novel"—a way of warning those yet uninformed that recreating "real life," the brute facts, was by no means her intention. Most of the characters whose portraits she paints in *Quoi? L'Eternité* were, no doubt, charming, interesting, or even fascinating to her as a child. Even though, according to her, children have practically no interest whatsoever in adults.

The total indifference [of children] to certain facts, the ardent passion that erupts in other instances, would be less extraordinary than we imagine if we could accept to a greater degree the obscure presence in children of an adult personality, and of an already individualized consciousness, before orders force them into step or customs turn them into dullards. I am fighting here, almost desperately, not just to evoke only those memories that are entirely my own, but also to avoid any mawkish image of childhood, at one moment falsely tender, as irritating as a toothache, at another moment gently condescending. Children, by instinct, do not communicate with adults; very quickly, what grown-ups tell them seems false, or at least without importance.[24]

The people who accompanied her or crossed her path during childhood were never really loved by Marguerite Yourcenar until she made them into characters, figures halfway between reality and fiction—even before assigning them a place in her literary universe—and then began to describe them, to write them into being. She said so, often, laying special emphasis on the case of her father, although he is probably the one for whom this is least true, deep down, so thoroughly did she share with him her formative years. We must not, however, overestimate the importance of this father, as too many have, saying that he was "the man of her life." For those with a penchant for psychoanalytic cliché, there had to be a man who, for her, "hid" all the others; otherwise she would not have decided to live with a woman.

It is clear that, for years, the characters in the books Yourcenar wrote, Hadrian or Zeno, did conceal the memory of Monsieur de Crayencour. He made his presence felt again when she made him a protagonist in *Archives du Nord.*

It would be equally wise to refrain from making Monsieur de Crayencour a "new father"—a nonexistent term then—one who paid passionate attention to the newborn, then to the little girl's progress. This image, however, was reinforced by family legend, as Georges de Crayencour reports: "Little Marguerite's father, God knows why, foresaw in her every gift. An intelligent, eclectic, and rich man, he seems to have wanted to console himself for his great sorrows, or in any case for what one would normally consider to be such, by dedicating himself to the intellectual awakening of his little girl, now the center of the world for him. One of his nieces by marriage, an aunt of mine, who was a brilliant, good, and independent woman, added that he was a man of great innate kindness and blindly generous. They lived, he and his daughter, as in some kind of passion, 'staring into each other's eyes,' troubled by the slightest moments of presence or absence. The son from his first marriage was too different from him and, he assumed, from her."[25]

This idyllic vision was greatly tempered by Yourcenar herself: when she was still a little girl of only three, Monsieur de Crayencour was fifty-three years old, and he did not intend that the way of life he had chosen for himself should be turned upside-down by a child. Judging her "robust" (as Yourcenar pointed out on numerous occasions; yet she would say later on that her health had always been fragile), he took her with him to the south of France, where he liked to spend the winter months on account of the climate and the casinos. But there, as at Mont-Noir or in the family's "handsome townhouse" at 26 Rue Marais in Lille, where the child and he spent the winters of 1903 and 1904, he saw little of Marguerite, leaving her in the hands of the duly trained members of the household staff. "Michel did not really change his life for the child. I am not saying that he made a lot of sacrifices for her; nevertheless, he came home in the evening a little earlier than he would have had she not been there," writes Yourcenar in her preliminary notes to *Quoi? L'Eternité*.[26]

One of the rare witnesses to Yourcenar's early childhood who is still living is Baron Egon de Vietinghoff, whose family holds an important place in Yourcenar's life, or at least in her mental universe. He is a painter and consequently not in the habit, himself, of reconstituting everything in language. Thus there are many more gaps in his memory than in that of his first playmate, in 1905 and 1906, on the magnificent Dutch beach of Scheveningen. "We spent a summer together, perhaps two, but I only remember one clearly," says he whom Yourcenar later refers to as "my first boy friend"[27] or as "the son of Alexis." (His father had been one of the models for the main character in Yourcenar's first novel, *Alexis ou Le Traité du vain combat* [*Alexis*].)

Egon and his family are at the heart of Yourcenar's *œuvre*, but she delighted in sowing confusion. Not satisfied with concealing their patronymic, as she had to at least for the works of pure fiction, she even switched the names so that the father was referred to by his son's first name. Baron Egon de Vietinghoff is the son of Conrad de Vietinghoff, a musician, and his wife Jeanne, who, according to Yourcenar, was the great love of her father's life, and who came to be conceived of by her as a kind of ideal mother. Conrad de Vietinghoff is called Egon in *Quoi? L'Eternité* (while Egon, his son, becomes Clément). Jeanne, one of the book's crucial characters, is called Madame de Reval but appears with her authentic first name. Nevertheless, she was already present in *Dear Departed* and *Archives du Nord* as Monique. On only one occasion does she appear in her fully authentic identity, in a text from 1929 entitled "En mémoire de Diotime: Jeanne de Vietinghoff" ("In Memory of Diotima: Jeanne de Vietinghoff"), which was reprinted in the collection of essays *Le Temps, ce grand sculpteur* (*That Mighty Sculptor, Time*).[28]

Jeanne, Egon's mother, and Fernande, the mother of Yourcenar, had met at a boarding school run by the Sisters of the Sacred Heart in Brussels. Fernande had been captivated by the young Dutch baroness whose mother sent her to a Francophone boarding school for the purpose of perfecting her French. No sooner did Jeanne arrive than Fernande's highly superior scholastic record began to deteriorate. Her governess, Fräulein, "believed it to be the result of an infatuation, which is tantamount to saying a love affair," comments Yourcenar.[29] The relations between Jeanne and Fernande were of great interest to Yourcenar during the course of her research into her family origins. "I know that I am liable to be accused of omission or innuendo if I fail to mention the role that sensuality may have played in that love," she observed in *Dear Departed.* "But the question in itself is pointless: all our passions are sensual. At the very most, we may wonder to what extent that sensuality was translated into action. . . . Physical intimacy between two persons of the same sex is too much a part of the behavior of the species to have been excluded from even the most straitlaced boarding schools of the past. . . . Sensuality is not presented as culpable; it is vaguely felt to be unclean and, in an case, incompatible with good breeding. It is not inconceivable, however, that two passionate adolescents—overstepping, consciously or not, those strong arguments concerning feminine nature— might have discovered sensual pleasure, or at least a presage of it, in a kiss, in the suggestion of a caress, less plausibly in the complete union of bodies. It is not impossible, but it is doubtful."[30]

She returns to the subject in *Quoi? L'Eternité:* "Former governesses' toothless lips long whispered that a passionate friendship existed between the two students. In any case, they shared a warm, caressing intimacy. It is one of the miracles of youth to be able to discover—without the help of models, murmured secrets, or forbidden books, thanks to a profound carnal knowledge that is within us all for as long as we have not been taught to fear it or deny it—all the secrets that eroticism is believed to possess, though most of the time it possesses nothing but an imitation of them. But the gossip of old Fräuleins is too little proof that such an illumination of the senses occurred: we shall never know if Jeanne and Fernande experienced it or even caught a glimpse of it together."[31]

In any event, the nature of the adolescent relations between Jeanne and Fernande is only of anecdotal interest. The questions Yourcenar poses on the subject are valuable primarily for what she says about a first brush with the erotic that is natural, unconcerned with sexes or norms, and also because this reflection is occasioned by her two "mothers," one real, the other an ideal.

Whatever the case may be, then, Jeanne and Fernande had promised to assist one another and vowed that if one should pass away prematurely, the other would watch over her children. So when Jeanne learned, only in 1905, about Fernande's death, she immediately wrote to Monsieur de Crayencour:

> Monsieur, I cannot keep myself from trembling as I write to you.
>
> I learned only very recently about the death of Fernande, who was one of my best friends. You no doubt barely remember me: I was maid of honor at your wedding, and I only met you on that day.
>
> I in turn got married just a few months later, in Dresden, to a Balt, and, as such, a Russian subject. We lived for about two years in Kurland, where his family resides, then in Saint Petersburg, and after that in Germany. The announcement, if one was sent, never reached me. It was not until I came back to Holland that I learned from my mother the circumstances of Fernande's death, and the fact that she left you with a little girl. When Fernande wrote me to say that she was pregnant, I myself was as well. We promised each other reciprocally, in the event of an accident, to watch over our children. It would be pointless and pretentious of me to propose to take her mother's place in the eyes of the little one; I feel this more strongly than ever, now that I myself have two sons. But perhaps I can help you a little, when you would like me to, with the task of raising a child, a task so burdensome for a widower.
>
> Perhaps you know that, in the woods of Scheveningue,[32] my mother owns a big house where we spend the summer months. There is a cottage in the garden for guests; nowadays, it is almost always empty, as my mother rarely entertains. It would be a joy for her and for me if you agreed to stay there for part of the summer with the little one and the person who takes care of her. You would be in a friendly milieu, and the fresh sea air would do the child good. My husband, who concurs with me about everything, would also be happy to have you. He is very busy with his musical career, and requests that you excuse him in advance for being frequently absent."[33]

"This was how we found ourselves, she and I, two youngsters of the same age, on the beach at Scheveningen," Egon de Vietinghoff recalls.[34] "There are still a few photographs from that time. I am kissing her hand. I remember that she was not shy, not unsociable, and if I ventured to kiss her hand, then it was probably because she had shown some interest in me and friendship, as children sometimes do among themselves. We were more like temporary playmates for a summer or two than real childhood friends. Strangely, however, something very strong had stayed with us. We discovered this in our old age.

"I only realized much later that Marguerite was very attached to my mother, even though they saw each other rarely. I then learned that she had seen my mother again at the end of her life. My mother didn't talk about her much with me, and not at that time. I was in France and I was preoccupied with many things. I was married then to someone that my mother would not have chosen. She would undoubtedly have preferred Marguerite. I don't believe my mother knew how important she had become in Marguerite's life. She was very modest and did not take any notice of the influence that she might have. She wrote a few books, but she was much more exceptional than those little works. She also had an extraordinary moral strength. She died of cancer of the liver, when we, both Marguerite and I, were just slightly older than twenty. I believe it was in 1925, but I am no longer quite sure of all that.

"Despite the pseudonym, I realized from the time of Marguerite Yourcenar's first books, my mother having told me that Marguerite wanted to become a writer, that she was the little girl I had known. Moreover, my brother's name was Alexis, the title of her first novel, which is perhaps, though I cannot confirm it, part of the story of my father. It's possible, as Marguerite thought, that there was a love affair between her father—whom I absolutely do not remember—and my mother. But I don't have a single piece of information that would enable me to make a judgment.

"I followed Marguerite's career—now she was Marguerite Yourcenar— by way of her books, but I did not make myself known to her. I have no idea why. I only wrote to her, at my son's urging, when I was seventy years old. I then discovered that I felt close to her. I wrote her some rather intimate letters, love letters almost. In her responses, she never committed herself. For me, she was "Marguerite, Soror." And *Anna, soror* . . . ("Anna, Soror . . ."), as it happens, is one of my favorite books of hers. She, for her part, never said anything about her life. She never spoke to me about Grace Frick, and I did not know that she lived with a woman. When we saw each other again, in 1983, we were eighty years old. I told her that we would have been better off if we had married. She laughed. And, when you get right down to it, she was right. As authoritarian as she struck me as being, it wouldn't have worked."[35]

Yourcenar recalls that conversation in *Quoi? L'Eternité,* and, responding to her friend and translator Walter Kaiser, who had put forth the hypothesis that she might be Egon's sister ("no . . . the dates aren't right"), she concludes: "Thus . . . today we strive to give meaning to what has none, to explain, if we can, this very thin, yet magic, bond between two beings whose lives so briefly touched at the beginning of their days." [36]

THIS "BEGINNING of their days," both for her and for little Egon, represented, according to Yourcenar, the years that gave rise to the love between Jeanne and Monsieur de Crayencour. Egon himself claims he didn't notice anything and merely renders a laconic "It's quite possible." Could it be that this man who took too much interest in his mother wanted to forget something that perhaps disrupted his childhood? He doesn't think so, asserting only that "the recollection has not stayed with [him]." Yourcenar, who had spoken with Egon about that period to nourish her account in *Quoi? L'Eternité*, complained of the "bad memory" of her childhood friend and wondered if he didn't want quite simply to hide what he thought from her. The only thing she was forgetting was that Egon, unlike her, had not spent part of his existence reinventing that story.

As a means of recreating the beginning of her own life, Yourcenar liked to describe photographs. She does so in her three "family" volumes, most notably in *Quoi? L'Eternité*. Nevertheless, she did not include in her final manuscript—and there is reason to be sorry she didn't—a rather beautiful passage from her preliminary notes, on photographs and memory: "Hadrian and Zeno are still seen through well-defined structures; aggregates of flesh and bone, of acts and memories they had or that I gave them. I do not do as good a job sketching my own. Here, it is too early to speak of memory. No precise recollection of things will emerge from the immensity of what has been forgotten until about my thirteenth year. But I do possess photographs. Let's see what I can learn from them.

"I see a little human creature, a few months old, sprawled out naked on a sheepskin, hideously swathed so you cannot, for certain, make out its sex. The child is healthy, of the white race, as they say."

She next describes a photo, placing it around 1906, in which she is sitting in an armchair, wearing a dress made of broderie anglaise: "the blue eyes are wide open, not yet partially covered by the eyelids as they will be three-quarters of a century later—eyelids too long swollen by traces of allergy and sinusitis, imparting thus to the aged face a look that is somehow vaguely Asian." There follows a minutely detailed examination of a photograph that shows the right hand of a willful, stubborn little girl clutching an old doll, a puppet of some kind in rather bad shape. "When I think of what she must have put up with (from relatives, photographers) in order to keep it with her," Yourcenar comments, "I admire the loyalty of that good, if somewhat fierce, little woman to her clown." "During the party given in my honor last year at Mont-Noir," she adds (she wrote this in 1981, the party having taken place at the end of 1980), "someone came up with the charming idea of having a little girl about four years old offer me flowers ... Let us not stoop to the level of the sentimental chromo."

There follows, in the preliminary writings of *Quoi? L'Eternité*, an unfinished sentence: "since, unfortunately, it [this little parcel of life] came into the world—that desire of Fernande's cost the poor woman dearly."[37] Yet again, one observes that, for Yourcenar, no discourse on the subject of Fernande can come to an end.

Marguerite Yourcenar regularly claimed, greatly scandalizing some, that she never missed her mother. It would, therefore, be hard to imagine her providing details of the feelings she had as a motherless child. "I believe the lack was absolutely nil," she insisted in 1979 in response to a question posed by Bernard Pivot, during a television interview. "For, after all, it is impossible, unless you have an extremely romantic character, to be enamored of, or moved by, a person you have never seen."[38] She no doubt did not miss Fernande, since she had never been there, and since Monsieur de Crayencour had fostered no sentimentality regarding her absence. Surely, as she willingly repeated during her old age, life is "always much more fleeting, much more fluid than one is usually inclined to say afterward, when reconstructing it from memory."[39] But that is it precisely; Yourcenar, reconstituting her childhood, had had the chance to gauge to what extent a mother—of Fernande's social class and generation—could have been a hindrance, another obstacle to surmount in her quest for freedom. And she was not prepared to make concessions regarding the so-called "lack of a mother figure."

If, in the limbo of early childhood, Yourcenar loved someone like a mother, it was the woman who tucked her into bed, who bathed her, and who taught her the first gestures of life, her nursemaid Barbe, who was twenty years old when she was born in 1903. However, in *Quoi? L'Eternité*, for the first time, she invents a symbolic mother for herself, Jeanne. And we're surprised, less by this dream of a mother than by the secret so untypically shared. Having looked at some old photographs, having conversed with Egon, Yourcenar recalls, in what she admits is a rather hazy way, an afternoon on the beach at Scheveningen. She and Egon, each one equipped with a rake, a shovel, and a pail, were amusing themselves, at something of a distance from their parents.

> The little girl, a bit clumsy, tripped on her spade, fell, and scraped her knee slightly, then stayed sitting on the ground neither screaming nor crying,

already vaguely occupied by a little crab running on the sand. . . . Returning Axel [Alexis, Egon's younger brother] to the nursemaids' attentive care, Jeanne got up, took the two older children by the hand, and headed with them slowly toward the sea.

To the little girl, it seemed that the long white skirt and the long white scarf beat like wings in the wind. But the reddish-brown photographs are hazy: I shall never know if that white skirt and that helping hand were not my nursemaid's. Perhaps it is because I want that walk to have been some kind of abduction far away from the little, known, domestic world, an adoption of sorts, that I have chosen to imagine that lovely face bent over me, that voice gentler than Barbe's, and the clasp of those light, intelligent fingers.[40]

Little Marguerite's feelings were much more confused—as Yourcenar admitted—than the reconstruction that led her to write in *Quoi? L'Eternité*: "I was not the daughter of Marie [her father's younger sister, whom, people told her, she resembled]; nor was I the daughter of Fernande; she was too faraway, too fragile, too long lost in the mists of memory. I was more the daughter of Jeanne," and "I would no doubt be very different from what I am, if Jeanne, from a distance, had not molded me."[41] But from the time of that brief holiday—when she lived for the first time with a woman who was neither her maidservant nor one of her female relatives—she had without a doubt noticed that Jeanne's attitude was vastly different from that of the nursemaids, who were paid to take care of children. "Jeanne adjusted her pace to the children's, stopping here and there to let them gather shells."[42] Even when they carried out their duties with kindness, with a kind of warmth or even tenderness sometimes, as was the case with Barbe, the nursemaids could not provide the attention, the patience, or the thoughtfulness of someone who has borne a child, or chosen to raise one simply out of love.

The substitution of Jeanne for Fernande in Yourcenar's mental universe sheds a different light on the questions she posed regarding their adolescent affections. Perhaps she needed their love for one another to be real so that she, Marguerite, could forge an origin for her life. That there was probably nothing to it, as she admits, only highlights the ever-present gap between reality and what should be the truth. A whole lifetime of writing to fill that gap was beginning.

2

"I don't know whether I loved that tall gentleman or not"

"I DON'T KNOW whether I loved that tall gentleman or not. He was affectionate without making a fuss, he never addressed me reprovingly, but sometimes he did so with a big smile," Yourcenar writes in *Quoi? L'Eternité.*[1] In the photographs that show him with his daughter, Michel looks like an old man, deeply marked by age at fifty. There is nothing left of the man she describes in *Archives du Nord,* basing her description on a photo captioned "Michel at the age of thirty-seven": "This very young-looking personage does not give the impression of vigor and alacrity that emerges from the portraits of his maturity; he was still weak, at that stage that for so many young beings precedes and makes way, inexplicably, for strength. Nor is this a portrait of the assiduous high liver at the fashionable spots. The eyes are dreamy; a cigarette dangles from the long-fingered hand adorned with a signet ring; the hand, too, seems to dream. Unexplained melancholy and incertitude emanate from this face and this body. It is the image of a Saint-Loup back when he still worried about Rachel, or about Monsieur d'Amercoeur."[2]

But for the little girl, he was "the grown-up around whom revolved the mechanism of life"; "my two nursemaids and the nuns who, at Mont-Noir, were beginning to teach me to read," she adds, "had made no bones about letting me know that I would see changes when my father died: I would wear a black woolen dress and an apron at a boarding school run by good sisters; there would be lots of praying and few treats; I would be forbidden to have with me Monsieur Trier of the crooked paws; and, when I disobeyed, I would be rapped on the fingers with a ruler. 'And don't expect your half brother to spend a cent on you.' My father's death did not worry me much, since I didn't really know what death was, and most little children believe that grown-ups are immortal." Thus does Yourcenar assert that, in the evening, she would fight off sleep, waiting for her father to come home, immediately going on to say: "Much later, I was sometimes reminded of those nights when, as a woman, I would stay up late waiting for someone."[3] This is certainly accurate. But it is no doubt just as true that, starting from the more recent memory of her nights spent waiting up as an adult, she found buried—or simply reinvented—those evenings spent waiting for the first man who counted in her life and who, like others later on, had a nocturnal life apart from her. And then, while making the journey back to her childhood, the grande dame probably encountered—confusedly, amid the twists and turns of memory—Proust, whose work she had spent so much time reading: those "shifting and confused gusts of memory" of the child alone in the night, on which he dwells at the beginning of *Du côté de chez Swann* (*Swann's Way*); the long time spent waiting, in his case, for his mother, for "the moment in which I heard her climb the stairs, and then caught the sound of her garden dress of blue muslin, from which hung little tassels of plaited straw, rustling along the double-doored corridor." Proust himself also links the child's anxious night watch to the amorous anxiety that he ascribes to Swann, for whom "a similar anguish had been the bane of his life for many years."[4]

Between the conventional discourse that portrays Monsieur de Crayencour as the man to be reckoned with in Yourcenar's life and her own effort to remain at a distance while writing her family trilogy, one encounters certain difficulties in attempting to form a clear idea of the relations between this father and his daughter. During early childhood, they were rather distant. "He renounced neither women, nor gambling (no one would ask as much), nor sumptuously dissipating what was left of his fortune," writes Yourcenar. "No doubt there was a strong attachment," she acknowledges. "As there is when one is raising a puppy. Or a kitten that has lost its mother. But Michel was not one of those fathers who are always picking up their children to hold them in their arms. I cannot recall a kiss (in 24 years) other than the friendly, routine kisses on both cheeks in the morning, and then, again, with a bit more solemnity, at night. This was as far as French families went back then in displaying affection. Nor do I recall ever having sat in his lap (except for the day I got a sunburn, when he lulled me to sleep)."[5]

She returns to the subject in *Quoi? L'Eternité* to underscore that any real manifestations of physical affection came—but for Jeanne, "who was not often there"—from her nursemaid, Barbe. "During my very early childhood, she had borne me that unconsciously sensual passion that so many women feel for very young children. I remember, at around age two or three, being lifted out of my little cot and having my entire body covered with warm kisses, revealing contours of my flesh unknown to me before and giving me, so to speak, a form. I believe there is an innate sexuality of childhood, but those wholly tactile sensations were not yet infused with eroticism: my senses had sprouted neither buds nor leaves. Later on, those effusions ceased, but affectionate kisses were not rare.[6]

Thus does Yourcenar date her first great sorrow back to the departure of Barbe. "My first wrenching separation was caused not by the death of Fernande but by the departure of my nurse," she writes in *Dear Departed.*[7] Barbe, who was not without charm, in the flush of her twentieth year, had perhaps had "a few carnal contacts" with Monsieur de Crayencour, Marguerite suggests, "despite the latter's disdain for love relations with subordinates."[8] In any case, she was too sensible to dream of a mistress's role. But her taste for men and a desire to add a little something to her nonetheless generous salary inspired her to frequent hotels of somewhat ill repute, in the Principality [Monaco] in winter, during the seasonal stay in Paris, and sometimes in Brussels."[9]

While she went to visit the "gentlemen," Barbe left Marguerite in a movie theater, with the complicity of an usherette. No doubt judging this too dangerous, and exhibiting a curious sense of responsibility, she quite simply decided to take the child with her "to the house of assignation."[10] After only two or three of these expeditions, an anonymous letter arrived at Mont-Noir denouncing Barbe. Monsieur de Crayencour decided to dismiss her.

In 1910, Barbara Aerst therefore left the service of the de Crayencour family. But no one had alerted the child that she was leaving. One morning, they took her on an "excursion" without Barbe, which struck her as being rather odd. When she got back, Barbe had disappeared. Monsieur de Crayencour lied about the reasons for her banishment, claiming that Barbe's family had called her back home. And he enjoined his daughter "not to cry so loudly."[11] Marguerite immediately knew that she was being lied to. To her sorrow thus was added indignation. "Over the days that followed," Yourcenar writes in *Quoi? L'Eternité,* "I sent Barbe badly spelled postcards asking her to come back. After a lengthy interval, she responded with a little affectionate letter telling me of her marriage to a farmer from Hasselt. I had grown accustomed to her absence, but an enormous weight bore down on me: I had been lied to. From then on, I could no longer place complete trust in anyone, not even Michel."[12] Barbe and Marguerite kept writing to one another until 1920; Yourcenar was then seventeen years old and Barbe was thirty-seven.

From the time she was seven years old, Marguerite de Crayencour was a curious little person. She remembers herself as "docile," having no fits of anger, no childhood tantrums. Such is not entirely her half nephew's opinion: "As one might suspect given the absorbed attentions of her father, then well into his fifties, her character was somewhat akin to that of only children, who are inevitably a bit spoiled from certain points of view. If a rainstorm prevented her from frolicking about in the garden, she would sometimes stand with her forehead pressed against the windowpane, ceaselessly chanting: 'Why's it rainin'? Don' want it to rain: why's it rainin'? Don' wan it to rain ... etc.' Which more than likely had the effect, among other things, of making her father feel sorry for her and irritating her half brother; let's not even speak of what her grandmother had to say."[13]

It's a safe bet that she had already understood that, when it gets right down to it, you can only count on yourself. And that you had to learn, in every situation, to be self-sufficient, since questions of propriety could break up, without any explanation, the relationship between a child and the woman who, from the time of her birth, had served as her mother. As Yourcenar observed, "morals count for more than laws, and social conventions for more than morals."[14] Barbe's departure, experienced no doubt as an inexplicable abandonment that the silence surrounding her intensified, is one of the key moments of Yourcenar's childhood. It is also where we find the first traces of her writing, in a note to Aunt Jeanne de Cartier de Marchienne (in 1909 or 1910 according to Yourcenar): "In Bailleul, 8 July: I am impatiently waiting for the weather to be nice to come to Coq-sur-Mer." And to the same she wrote, regarding the dog Trier's death, shortly before the departure of Barbe: "My Dear Aunt, I write to say that I am very sad, because my poor Trier has died." "For all intents and purposes, that is my first literary composition; I could just as well have stopped right there," comments Yourcenar.[15]

The absence, not of Fernande, but of a mother, however painful it may have been at certain times—as the child's sorrow at Barbe's departure and the effort of the elderly woman writing *Quoi? L'Eternité* to "adopt" Jeanne, more than having herself adopted by her, attest—did, nonetheless, spare Marguerite from the insipid education that little girls of that era typically received. Among those close to her, people were highly shocked that a future wife and mother should be learning neither to embroider nor to play "mommy" with her doll, and in their estimation, Marguerite "did not have a childhood." "She did not own any toys, or so I've been told" reports Georges de Crayencour. "One day when she was visiting my family, she was struck dumb with astonishment on entering the playroom. On the other hand, she knew how to recite and liked nothing better than to read dictation exercises aloud to the other children or to teach them lines of poetry, though no one had the slightest desire to participate." It is false to say that Marguerite had no toys. But it is true, as we have seen from the time of her earliest childhood, that she set little store by them and could only remember, later on, her doll André, because of the men she loved as a grown woman, and a mock grotto off Lourdes that lit up, because she had hated it.

She very quickly had the feeling she was different, "important, even very important," she confided with an absence of false modesty that we cannot but be grateful for. And one has only to look at photographs of her at the age of six or seven to realize that it is not a matter of an adult's retrospective commentary. One can already see what everyone would notice upon first meeting Marguerite Yourcenar, at whatever stage of her life: the back and head held very straight, a sensuous mouth, adept at the provocative smile, eyes so blue as to be nearly transparent, sometimes ironic and mischievous, but sometimes extremely cold as well, a certain charm and an unmistakable haughtiness—in short, a natural authority. At that early age, Marguerite had a passion for learning to read, then for reading, and Monsieur de Crayencour, a cultured man with a diploma in law, an "officier d'Académie" who had his own passion for literature, very soon realized that he was dealing with a remarkable child.[16] Great credit is due him for not scoffing at Marguerite's desires on account of her gender. Nevertheless, it is surprising to see a man of his generation neglect his son to such an extent and take an interest, as he was nearing sixty, in the concerns of a little girl.

It is true that his son Michel, as we know, rejected everything he stood for, hated everything he loved, disapproved of the choices he made, beginning with his lack of interest in observing the tradition of the family fortune. At the age of twenty-one, in 1906, Michel went so far as to adopt the Belgian nationality, which his father found intolerable. "The fact that his son, choosing to belong to a neutral country, should have opted for Belgium," Yourcenar points out in *Quoi? L'Eternité*, "infuriated [the elder] Michel, who would not have been pleased to be reminded that two successive desertions had forced him to take up residence on the other side of the border when Berthe was pregnant with their son, thus preparing the way for the option that struck him as so scandalous."[17] Yourcenar told the story of her father's two desertions in *Archives du Nord*, with a benevolent neutrality that would doubtless have scandalized her half brother. Monsieur de Crayencour's first desertion—he had joined the French army in January 1873—took place in August 1874 owing to a gambling debt that his father refused to cover, thus exposing him to the threat of prosecution. He went over to England, where he fell in love with a woman named Maud. After several months, he returned to France and to his regiment. "When he got back, he was demoted, and the ceremony held to tear off his stripes, which he later compared, offhandedly, to a tooth extraction, was no doubt more painful than he admitted afterward."[18]

But "Michel's nights were spent in London."[19] And, probably in March 1878, according to Yourcenar, "for the second time, the young noncommissioned officer lay his carefully folded uniform in a drawer, cast a last glance at his shiny breastplate, high up in a closet, dressed up in civvies, and discreetly left the district. He was not unaware that these actions would consummate his split not only with the army, but also with his family and with France, to which, without an amnesty, he would not be able to return before the age of forty-five."[20]

To her half nephew, Georges de Crayencour, who criticized her, upon reading *Archives du Nord,* for elaborating on those two episodes, Yourcenar responded that, though a precise accounting of the facts and what motivated them did not put Michel in the clear, it did make his conduct understandable: "You tell me that, without chipping corners off the truth, you would have tread more lightly through certain episodes in 'Michel's' life that strike you as being rather scandalous. But that's impossible. Everything is of a piece, so much so that everything had to be said and said completely, in such a way that the reader may understand the human emotions behind the facts. If I had simply said, in just a few words, that Michel had deserted twice, then we both—I as much as you—would naturally be terribly embarrassed by that revelation. When, on the contrary, one looks closely at the circumstances, one gains a better understanding."[21]

"Little Michel," his son, was scandalized, of course, by this kind of behavior. According to the young Marguerite, the only thing that had brought these two men together, for a time, was their common interest in automobiles. "For the moment, gasoline and space intoxicated Michel; already a good rider, he found he also had a talent for driving. . . . This new infatuation even brought him closer to his son, who was crazy about race cars. Michel-Joseph, who drove as if charging headlong, respected in his father, now become a companion, the deft, audacious driver. . . . A shared toy caused Michel-Joseph to forget momentarily that the birth, rather late in his father's life, of a half sister from a second marriage had, as the snickering dowager—he was her favorite—said, financially 'cut him in two.' Michel stopped remembering that Fernande could not bear this sullen, brutal boy and that he did not even go to his own mother's bedside when she lay dying. This last reproach is unfair, as I have said elsewhere. Berthe's tragic and unexplained death was much more likely to inhibit than to move a fifteen-year-old boy.

"But that passion for machines would pass as everything passes."[22]

Georges de Crayencour, for his part, does not believe that even this moment of truce occurred between his father and his grandfather. "Living his own idle, elegant youth, he [young Michel] had a passion for one sport during childhood: the automobile, and his father (who was not very fond of all that!) owned an extremely handsome model. That vehicle, which his father did not appreciate as much, was no doubt a bit frightening for the little sister, but it was the object of the big brother's most careful attentions."[23]

In Yourcenar's judgment, "Michel had lived free without even devising a theory of freedom for himself; his son had made a great show of opting for order, a large family, an apparently unblemished social surface, and the kind of Catholicism that exhibits itself at the eleven-o'clock mass."[24] Since his son was irremediably from another world, with a different philosophy of life, a different moral code, which to Monsieur de Crayencour appeared to epitomize the same conventionality, the same bourgeois mentality that he had spent his life fleeing, then why shouldn't the little girl, so avid to learn and understand, be his true heir, heir to his splits and his freedom, to his independent spirit, to his knowledge, to his well-to-do cosmopolitanism, and to his nonconformism? It had been her lot to escape a mother's love, which tended to keep daughters on the side of tradition and passivity. Did this make her less of a woman? Monsieur de Crayencour did not concern himself with this question. He would not have known how to define what a woman was supposed to be. Fernande or Berthe? A good girl or a rebel with an unpredictable temper? Antigone, Phaedra, Marguerite de Navarre, or the Princesse de Clèves? Monsieur de Crayencour, so full of biased notions where the women he loved, or at least seduced, were concerned—they owed him their allegiance and had to respect his freedom—did not think in these terms when he reflected on the future of his daughter. "This man who continually repeated that nothing human should be alien to us, viewed age and sex as merely secondary contingencies in the matter of literary creation. Problems that at a later date would leave my critics perplexed were not problems for him," writes Yourcenar in *Dear Departed*.[25] If she so desired, he would help her become a free person. She would be an extension of him. She would follow and prolong him, accomplishing what he had not been able to finish himself. It would not be enough for her to break with the "lineage" as he had done by neglecting all the duties incumbent on a good family's son—she would not concern herself with looking after the patrimony and seeing that it prospered, or with perpetuating the name. She would be someone, that is to say someone different, radically. As she confided to Bernard Pivot, the "As a child, I yearned for glory" that she attributes to Alexis in her first novel was one of the realities of her own childhood.[26] With a certain deliberate grandiosity and a time-worn lyric form, her first poems, later on, would bear traces of this yearning for solitary radiance, which had been born very early:

> *Glory! Hail to you, whom I love and await*
> *You who lead the choir of universal Voices,*
> *Inspire in my mind the fine, shining verses![27]*

Or again:

> *O, Winds! Carry me away to the fiercest heights,*
> *To the loftiest summits of triumph to come!*
> *Carry me, Gust, carry me, Gales!*
> *Already dawn invades the dark firmament:*
> *To the land of pride, to the land of conquests,*
> *O, Winds! Carry me![28]*

These "yearned-for stormy winds" do not by any means blow with a remarkable formal modernity, but the overall design, for a very young girl of the beginning of this century, does not lack subversive grandeur.

This feeling of importance and difference, which her poems expressed later on, is what emerges most forcefully from the years 1909 to 1911. This precludes us from suspecting that it might be a re-creation after the fact—in other words, a fiction. By contrast, what led up to the split between Monsieur de Crayencour and Jeanne, and the split itself—which Yourcenar situates in the spring of 1909 and which takes up an entire chapter of *Quoi? L'Eternité*—is so profoundly inspired, as we shall see, by the last years of Yourcenar's own life (the very time she was writing *Quoi? L'Eternité*), that we can hardly give her credit for remembering it.[29] For one thing, at the time of that split—if indeed it occurred—Yourcenar was only six years old. For another, her father was not the kind of man to confide in his daughter regarding such a matter, as she has stated on numerous occasions. Nor was Egon de Vietinghoff of any help to her in recreating the relations between Monsieur de Crayencour and his mother, Jeanne. But none of this prevented Yourcenar, when she recounted this episode, from describing her father's attitude in detail—with more lucidity, for that matter, than affection. He was a man who remained, with regard to the women he loved, profoundly steeped in the prejudices of his sex and his generation. With her, there is always a play between truth and reality.

What is certain is that, beginning in the spring of 1909, Marguerite no longer saw Jeanne. Thus she could become mythical, a model, the one whom "Michel, despite his many resentments, had not ceased to hold up for me as a perfect image of womanhood," Yourcenar writes in *Quoi? L'Eternité*.[30] From afar, Jeanne could begin to take on real importance in her life. Yourcenar would not see her until some fifteen years later, during the twenties, shortly before she died. In 1929, Yourcenar wrote a "tribute" to Jeanne de Vietinghoff, which was published in *La Revue Mondiale*.[31] In it, she paints the portrait of a woman endowed with "a heart of genius." "I have neglected to say how beautiful she herself was," writes Yourcenar toward the end of her text. "She was still almost young when she died, before the trials of old age came, which she did not fear. Much more than her writing, it is her life which gives me the impression of perfection. . . . Had Jeanne de Vietinghoff written nothing, her character would be no less lofty. Only, many of us would never have known it. It is the way of the world that the rarest virtues of a person always remain the secret of someone else. . . . Life on earth, which she loved so much, was for her only the visible side of life eternal. No doubt she accepted death as a night darker than the others, but one which would be followed by a more shining dawn. One would like to believe she was not mistaken. One would like to believe that the dissolution in the tomb did not arrest such a rare development; one would like to believe that death, for such souls, is merely one further step." [32]

Where everything else is concerned, those years remain as if enshrouded in a nebula. They take up no more than a few lines in the Pléiade's "Chronologie." We know that Yourcenar made her first communion in 1910, at Mont-Noir, an event she reconstructs rather cursorily in *Quoi? L'Eternité*, and not without a certain offhandedness: "I was a few weeks short of seven years old. It was the era of early first communions. I had had some instruction from the good sisters of the Free School of Saint-Jans-Cappel, to which the parish priest's brief catechism did not add much. I was especially advised not to brush my teeth on the morning of the big day; of course there was no question but that one should be fasting. But I found part of an apple on my bedside table and nibbled away at it without thinking. I made the mistake of telling the priest about it one day, and he nearly had a fit. I was the only one receiving communion that particular morning. There is a faded snapshot of me in a white dress and white veil, which Barbe liked to call a bride's veil; this at first made me laugh, and then cry, because I thought I was being made fun of." [33]

She is even more laconic regarding her half brother's marriage that same year, with Solange de Borchgrave, only bringing it up incidentally: "The Belgian marriage, which was a normal enough result [of Michel-Joseph's adoption of Belgian nationality], was no doubt less brilliant than the interested party had anticipated. . . . What Michel never knew was that this marriage had been engineered by an abbot who traveled in fashionable circles and frequented Madame de Marcigny, who, for her part, found it difficult to abide that twenty-four-year-old boy dragging his heels in her Parisian salon."[34]

In any case, another event took place in April 1909—the death of Noémi, her father's mother—whose importance, it seems, Yourcenar did not fully appreciate. It was nonetheless Noémi's death that made way for the exclusive tête-à-tête between the little girl and her father, a bond at once distant and strong that would truly forge her personality. One part of the "family chapter" had definitely come to a close with her grandmother's death, which would enable Marguerite's father to sell Mont-Noir, an act looked upon with such reproach, even today, by the entire family.

When Noémi died, Marguerite had just discovered Paris, where she and her father went for several short stays between 1909 and 1911. The beginning of another life was in view. Early childhood, in its relative passivity, was over. In 1911, Marguerite was eight years old. She knew perfectly well how to read, and she also wrote properly, as we saw in the messages to her Aunt Jeanne, whom she visited quite often, in Brussels, in 1911. But what she calls her "studies" did not really begin until the move to Paris, and even then, there was no going to school—"I was quite certain that I had never set foot in any school, and I had absolutely no desire to do so"[35]—no encounter with the rigidity of collective discipline, no submission to the authority of the "school mistresses," no experience of forced coexistence with other children one's own age or of that confrontation that, sometimes for the better, sometimes for the worse, forges or disintegrates self-consciousness.

3
Early Lessons

PUTTING ASIDE the escapades in Paris, Yourcenar's young existence was still quite traditional for a child of her background and
era. It was with the sale of Mont-Noir in 1912 that her life and
that of Monsieur de Crayencour began to change, slipping further and further away from the family and conventional models. They took up residence
in Paris, first in the seventeenth arrondissement, on Rue Anatole de la
Forge, then at 15 Avenue d'Antin (which today is Avenue Franklin D. Roo-
sevelt). "The main building overlooking a courtyard planted with box-
woods has disappeared," Yourcenar points out in the Pléiade "Chronologie," underscoring yet again that none of the places where she lived subsists
in its original state. Marguerite was nine years old and had a new maid,
Camille, who was with her until she reached adulthood. A teacher came to
give her the basic instruction that little girls her age were receiving in
school. But she was learning still more, she says later, by visiting the museums of Paris, sometimes with her father, by going to matinée performances
of classical theater, and, above all, by reading. Unlike the other little girls of
her generation, even those who were socially privileged, as she was, Yourcenar was not restricted to reading books *ad usum puellarum.* Monsieur de
Crayencour, himself a great reader, loaned her the books that he himself
read and reread: better Tolstoy than the Comtesse de Ségur.[1]

In that same year, 1912, Monsieur de Crayencour bought a villa in
Westende, on the Belgian coast. It would be his summer residence, in 1912,
1913, and 1914. His son, who also spent some of the summer months there,
remembered that very beautiful house: "It had been built and furnished in
a particularly luxurious and considered fashion. . . . Much of the furniture,
which was often specially adapted to the shape of the rooms, was made of
amaranth wood, a kind of mahogony with purple highlights. Attention to
detail had been carried to such an extent that, for both the building and
the furniture, the sunflower had served as a decorative 'leitmotif'; even the
Chantilly lace curtains that graced all the windows and some of the em-
bossed velvet draperies, painted by hand, featured that sunflower."[2]

In Westende, Monsieur de Crayencour lived a luxurious life of diversion, from which Marguerite was not always excluded, as is shown by a photograph of her in a little girl's ball gown. It would be a mistake to imagine her as excessively studious. This would have exasperated her father who, from the time when she was six years old, would repeat to her one of his favorite precepts: "to know things well is to free oneself of them." Nevertheless, this is one of the rare sayings of Monsieur de Crayencour that Yourcenar contested energetically. As if by chance, it comes from Fernande. "[S]he took as her motto a thought that she had gleaned from some book or other: 'To know things well is to free oneself of them,'" writes Yourcenar in *Dear Departed.* "She later passed on her fondness for it to Monsieur de C., who allowed it to pervade his thinking. I have often taken exception to it. To know things well is . . . to correct the flat, conventional, and summary image that we form of objects we have never examined closely. In its most profound sense, however, the phrase touches on certain basic truths. Yet in order to make them truly our own, we must be satisfied in body and soul. Fernande was far from satisfied."[3]

In 1914, while the de Crayencours were spending the summer in their house at Westende, the First World War broke out. "The Westende villa would be destroyed by a bombardment," confided Yourcenar much later. Yet another house disappears. Yourcenar remembers having heard, for the first time, the alarm bells of the little Flemish villages ringing all day long. Monsieur de Crayencour decided that they must leave immediately. The road to Lille and Paris being cut off, they embarked for England: "probably between the twelfth and the fifteenth of August," Grace Frick would subsequently note, in one of her innumerable chronologies of Yourcenar's life. "The decision was made to take a few suitcases and leave the rest in order to travel to Ostende on foot, since the honorable little tramway was no longer functioning. We left in the middle of the night, so as to reach the port during the early hours of dawn. . . . At my age, I confused the face of war with that of adventure. I still remember that precipitous flight as a nighttime outing."[4]

When she disembarked at Dover, Marguerite did not yet know that she was setting foot on the soil of what was to become one of her "homelands," "one of those countries in which one is instinctively at ease with oneself."[5] It would be the longest time she ever spent there—fourteen months. Her father, for his part, no doubt encountered there the memory of Maud, for whom he had twice deserted the army. Yourcenar would spend, she tells us, "a half-childish, half-adolescent" year in a house flanked by a little garden on the outskirts of London, equally distant from Putney Common and

Richmond Park. It was an "almost idyllic year," despite the presence of her half brother whose relations with his father—so tense that the two men sometimes nearly came to blows—made for an oppressive atmosphere.

Marguerite enjoyed herself equally, whether taking long pony rides or discovering London, its museums, and its monuments. She saw a statue of Hadrian for the first time. And in *Quoi? L'Eternité* she dates her first sexual, but not amorous, discoveries back to that period in London. The first involved a woman, young Yolande, who had crossed over to England with the de Crayencours, having been unable to get back to her family. Yolande and Marguerite had to share a bed, beginning with the first night, in London, in the hotel at Charing Cross.

> I have no desire to mention here a small fact that is supposedly obscene, but what follows corroborates in advance the opinion I hold today on that so highly controversial subject of the awakening of the senses, our future tyrants. Lying that night in Yolande's narrow bed, the only one available to us, an instinct, a premonition of intermittent desires experienced and satisfied later in the course of my life, allowed me to discover right away the posture and the movements needed by two women who love one another. Proust talked about the heart's intermittencies. Who will talk about those of the senses, particularly about those desires that the ignorant assume to be either so thoroughly against nature as to be always artificially acquired or else, on the contrary, inscribed in the flesh of certain persons like a nefarious and permanent fate? My own would not really awaken until years later, then in turn, and for years at a time, disappear to the point of being forgotten. Though a bit callous, Yolande admonished me kindly:
> "I've been told it was bad to do those things."
> "Really?" I said.
> And turning away without protest, I stretched out and fell asleep on the edge of the bed.[6]

The second "discovery" involved a man, whom she refers to as "Cousin X" in *Quoi? L'Eternité*, and who indulged himself in some fondling, the meaning of which was not entirely clear to her. She was no more shocked at the time than she was years later:

> I vaguely sensed that, for him, something had happened. But I had been neither alarmed, nor offended, much less bullied or hurt. If I record here this episode that would be so easy to conceal, it is in order to voice my disagreement with the hysteria provoked nowadays by any contact, however slight, between an adult and a child who is not yet—or just barely—pubescent. When violence, sadism (even with no immediately obvious link to sexuality), or carnal appetites out of control wreak themselves on a defenseless

being, it is atrocious, and it can often distort or inhibit a life, to say nothing of destroying that of the adult, so often falsely accused. It cannot be proven, on the contrary, that an initiation to certain aspects of sensual interplay is always harmful; it can be a way to save some time. I went to sleep happy that I had been found pretty, moved by the knowledge that the meager protuberances on my chest were already called breasts, and also satisfied to know a little bit more about what a man is.[7]

And leave it to Yourcenar to add, revealing in the crook of a sentence—as she so often does in this final book she wrote—one of the keys to her love life: "If my somnolent senses had not reacted, or hardly had, perhaps it is because sensual pleasure, of which I did not yet have anything more than a very vague idea, was still indissolubly linked for me to the idea of beauty: it was inseparable from the smooth torsos of Greek statues, from the golden skin of Da Vinci's Bacchus, from the young Russian dancer stretched out on a cast-off scarf. We were nowhere near the target: Cousin X was not handsome."[8]

FROM THIS British sojourn, Yourcenar was not limited to a few memories of outings and a foretaste of the pleasures of the flesh. It would have been stupid not to take advantage of her stay in England by beginning to study English. So she took a stab at it, along with her father, who also set about introducing her to Latin. Who came up with the idea that she should learn these languages? Against all who viewed her studies as the fruit of a paternal intention—including her half nephew—Yourcenar always maintained that it was her decision. She stressed this to the point of reprimanding and correcting those who made contrary assertions, without cease or amiability. We have various pieces of evidence today proving her strange insistence on rectifying what would appear to be minor details, notably a letter addressed to the Club français du livre [French Book Club], which had published an appendix to an edition of *Alexis* "an anonymous biographical postface": "When I think that this biographer, who is writing about me while I am alive and who could so easily have obtained accurate information from me, is so frequently mistaken," writes Yourcenar, "it is in a state of gloom that I wonder what to think of Hadrian's chroniclers, who wrote of him from a distance of at least half a century. . . . It is fortunate that our own actions and deeds will never be recorded in anything more than the footnotes of history."[9] "It is not true," she adds, that Michel "pushed his daughter toward the study of ancient literatures. His great merit consisted of not pushing her toward anything. On the contrary, it was the little twelve-year-old girl's passion for the classical languages that reawakened in the man who was by then sixty years old the penchants and interests of an earlier time; he went back to Latin and Greek because Marguerite was learning them."[10]

What could be the reason for such a relentless attempt to reinstate biographical "truth," when we already know how casually Yourcenar made use of such "truth" in other contexts? Could it be that her "persona" was a source of concern? Could she have wished to make it known that, in a sense, it was she who led the way in this strange father-daughter couple, and that Michel deferred, when she was still very young, to her authority?

As for the study of English, a language that Michel handled elegantly, Yourcenar indicates in her preliminary notes for *Quoi? L'Eternité* that she began it with some difficulty. With her father, she read through an English translation of Marcus Aurelius once, in an effort both to acquaint herself with Marcus Aurelius and to gain some practice in English. "But that reading improved neither the accent nor the vocabulary of the pupil, and Michel ended up throwing that manual of wisdom and moderation at her." Seventy-three years later, in 1987, the last year of Yourcenar's life, her vocabulary was impeccable, but her accent, despite a lengthy stay in the United States, would still have been unbearable to Monsieur de Crayencour. Though she had become an American citizen, Yourcenar had long since given up making the slightest effort to improve it.

Despite those sometimes "perilous" pedagogical sessions and the surprising interest that he showed in his daughter, Monsieur de Crayencour, who was "so little the father in the foolish or tyrannical sense of the word,"[11] began to grow tired of that "English year." Like many others, he had believed that the war would only last a few months, and he could ill imagine launching into a second year of "family exile." He was decidedly bored, without a woman, or nearly so. "For the first time since he had been widowed once again, Michel was without a woman; but the game of love was no doubt of less interest to him than it had been in former times. Nonetheless, there was a lady who emerged on certain days to join us outside the London tube."[12] It was Christine Hovelt, who would become his third and last wife.

On 11 September 1915, he obtained a safe-conduct to return to his Parisian residence with his daughter, who was twelve years old. "Marguerite's father planted what he scarcely still referred to as his family there (with a good allowance for his son) and took off, with his daughter, for Paris," writes his grandson Georges de Crayencour. "This consummated the nearly total split between Michel-René [the father] and Michel-Fernand [the son]."[13] At the end of her life, Yourcenar still possessed the safe-conduct that allowed them to return to France. Two photos, hardly discolored by time, were stapled to it. One shows "Michel, his high collar, his closely cropped hair, his imposing corsair's mustache belied by kind eyes." On the other appears Yourcenar who comments in *Quoi? L'Eternité:* "As for me, I am rigged out in a dress from the summer before, too small for me now. My hair, which looks unkempt, is still tied back at the temple with a limp bow; though my face betrays my awkward age, the eyes are determined and brave." And she adds: "I had just reached puberty, without even noticing. The maids gave me a supply of thick, carefully stitched linen bands, telling me that this was how it was, every month, for all women. I didn't go beyond that explanation."[14] Nor would Yourcenar ever go any further in reflecting on that moment in a girl's life when it is customary to tell her she has now become a woman, since she can from then on procreate. Was she indifferent to her body or prudish? I tend to doubt it. Her silence stemmed more likely from the vague sense of a feminine fate that must have been rather distasteful for her, as was everything she could not control, and that hardly seemed worthy of reflection.

BACK IN PARIS, in the fall of 1915, Monsieur de Crayencour again took up the dissipated life he was fond of, but money problems became more and more pressing. He thus devoted less time to his daughter who, in the apartment on Avenue d'Antin, which she remembered as being very badly heated in the winter, began studying Greek with a tutor and Italian on her own. For her, "what can truly be called a sense of the adventure of the mind dates back to that particular time," when she was twelve or thirteen years old. Like many adolescents, she wrote poetry.[15] Above all, she kept reading avidly, sharing more and more often the books that her father would read, which scandalized "the family." The family in this case was Monsieur de Crayencour's "sister-in-law," who sometimes showed up at the Avenue d'Antin residence. (In fact, she was the second wife of Paul de Sacy, whose first wife had been Marie, Michel de Crayencour's younger sister. Marie had been killed on the day of a wild boar hunt by a bullet ricocheting off a tree.) On Yourcenar's work table could thus be found Huysmans, D'Annunzio, Tolstoy, "an interlinear edition of one of Plato's dialogues, a work of Virgil." Of course, "it is known that Latin defies the limits of decency, and Greek, no doubt, does too."[16] As for Michel, "he reads too many foreign authors" in his sister-in-law's opinion: Shakespeare and Goethe, for example. It was the last straw, in the family's judgment, when Michel had his daughter read *Au-dessus de la mêlée* (*Above the Battle*) by Romain Rolland, which had become his bedside reading: "That Swiss who has the nerve to judge France!"

the sister-in-law raged. "At that time, Romain Rolland was quite often assumed to be Swiss, it being hard for upstanding people to imagine that a Frenchman could dishonor himself by straightforwardly attempting to sort out the respective obligations of France and of Germany. That book, which Michel had given me to read, and which was my first experience of thinking that went against the current, had become for him an anchor on that sea of lies into which journalists, who had either been bought or who themselves were caught up in the same mass hysteria they were fueling all around them, had plunged great nations. He liked France a little better because one Frenchman at least, a courageous and vilified one, was trying to look at this chaos of imposture face on."[17]

All of this was in the logic of what Yourcenar characterizes as Michel's "political awakening," "in May 1871, at the time of the suppression of the Commune." "That book, which would haunt Michel all his life, did not turn him into a man of the Left; it saved him from being a man of the Right."[18] Yourcenar would recall the aftereffects of that reading several times during her life, notably in letters to Jean Guéhenno and Gabriel Germain: "What you have told me about Romain Rolland," she writes to Guéhenno, "brings me closer to that writer, who was so great in spite of certain shortcomings (who is without them?) and around whom there arose such an unfair conspiracy of silence. He played a great role in my education: at the age of twelve, I would listen in the evening to my father reading *Jean-Christophe* (*John Christopher*); at fourteen, in the darkened Paris of 1917, he handed me *Above the Battle*, and this is one of the things for which I am most thankful to him."[19] "As for Romain Rolland," she confided to Germain, "I am still infinitely grateful to my father, who had me read ... *Above the Battle*, a breath of pure air, which he had been intoxicated by, in the atmosphere of the Great War's stifling chauvinism. A bit later, some of his biographies, which seem to me today excessively hagiographic and somewhat timid, and even certain passages from *John Christopher*, became reserves of energy and courage for me. This must be weighed against a public-meeting rhetoric that we no longer put up with."[20]

That "first experience of thinking that went against the current" would have a lasting influence on Yourcenar. So, too, would the first manifestation of her spiritual freedom. Monsieur de Crayencour consulted her to find out if she wanted to be confirmed. She indicated that she had no wish to, and he decided not to force her. At the age of thirteen, Marguerite de Crayencour had decidedly put childhood behind her, and very nearly adolescence as well.

IN PARIS, while Marguerite pursued a half-solitary education, read, and took walks with Camille, Monsieur de Crayencour, indefatigably, gambled. And he lost a lot, it seems, since his financial situation became more and more worrisome. Two excessively cold winters and incessant money problems were too much to bear for an aging Monsieur de Crayencour. In November of 1917, when the interminable war was finally on the verge of ending, he decided to leave the capital for the south of France. Only an occasional trip and the last months of his existence, almost twelve years later, would take him away from there.

From the moment he arrived, he spent most of his time gambling, in an attempt to regain his fortune. Thus, this was a period when Marguerite was often "left to herself," as she says in the Pléiade's "Chronologie."[21] She continued taking courses—whose programs corresponded to those of the lycée, which she did not attend—with "sporadic private tutors." If no one but her father had been at the source of her penchant for studying, she could quite easily have given up the effort in those circumstances. Such was not at all the case—on the contrary.

Yourcenar has never had very much to say about her conversations with her father during those years when one could talk to her entirely as if she were an adult. It was a period of great financial uncertainty for Monsieur de Crayencour, who was this time really broke. So his worries took up all of his attention, leaving little time free for Marguerite. Nevertheless, it was during this moment of apparent separation that the knot of incomparable complicity uniting daughter and father until the latter's death was tied. And perhaps this was precisely because Monsieur de Crayencour felt that finally his daughter was fully autonomous, because she did not cast him any silent looks of reprobation, which could not have failed—since he had very little taste for anything resembling a feeling of guilt—to distance him from the young woman. Marguerite asked no questions, showed no concern, and did not seem to wait anxiously when he did not come home at night before she went to bed.

Thus, while the hours they spent together were not hours of intimacy, they bore the marks of real closeness. The two took long hikes in the back-country of Provence, of which Michel was particularly fond. They lived in Menton, Saint-Roman, and Monte Carlo, where the Villa Loretta on Boulevard d'Italie would be their primary residence between 1920 and 1928. We don't know what kinds of things were said during those walks. It is unlikely, however, that money problems were mentioned. Marguerite certainly did not take it upon herself to ask questions. "He [Michel] would be alone with his thoughts, at her side, as she would be alone, with her thoughts, next to him," she observes in the preliminary notes for *Quoi? L'Eternité.*[22] Monsieur de Crayencour, nonetheless, must have inquired into the adolescent's progress with her studies. In 1918, notably, she had instructors of Greek and mathematics, her reading of Plato, she says, having inspired her to study mathematics.

But she considers that "her true intellectual nourishment came from reading." She read voraciously, while Michel, between one sinecure and another, learned Russian. When together, they liked to read aloud: Virgil in Latin, Homer in Greek; Ibsen, Nietzsche, and Selma Lagerlöf, whom Yourcenar considered all her life "a writer of genius."[23] "He sometimes read to me, from Chateaubriand," she would tell Galey.

> And he read me Maeterlinck, including *Le Trésor des humbles* (*The Treasure of the Humble*), from which I acquired a taste for mysticism that has been growing ever since. . . . [T]he historical novels of Merezhkovski . . . or Tolstoy. I also read Shakespeare . . . Racine, La Bruyère, and the rest. . . . On the other hand, my father didn't read much Balzac. Though it may appear arrogant to say so, I would even go so far as to suggest that it was I who forced him to read a part of nineteenth-century French literature. For example, I was the one who said, "Let's read *La Chartreuse de Parme* (*The Charterhouse of Parma*)."
>
> We read together a great deal, out loud. We passed the book back and forth. I would read, and when I became tired my father would spell me. He read very well, far better than I: he put much more of himself into the characters. . . . We read some French writers too, such as Saint-Simon. My father particularly liked the seventeenth-century writers. I read almost all of Saint-Simon with him. He introduced me to whole crowds of humanity.[24]

Although no one quite knows why—perhaps she had more of a need for "external validation" than she thought—Marguerite took the first part of the examination for a secondary-school degree in Greek and Latin as an independent candidate, in Nice on 9 July 1919. We have her diploma, which was issued by the Aix-Marseilles district on 29 May 1920, bearing the indication "pass." She never said whether or not she presented herself for the second part of the examination, and there is no trace of another diploma. The grade of passing could hardly have encouraged her, and one can easily imagine her pride not wanting to expose itself anew to a possible "affront." It is therefore surprising to find her asserting, in the Pléiade's "Chronologie," on the subject of the twenties, that "a plan to earn an Arts degree having been quickly rejected, those years were also, and above all, the years of my discovery of Italy." How could one enroll at the university without a full diploma from secondary school?

When one knows the route taken by Yourcenar, one cannot help but wonder why she, who so often kept things hidden, brings to light in the Pléiade's "Chronologie" her attempt, only partially successful, at a diploma and the impossible project of a university degree. Did she wish to make manifest a sudden, highly fleeting, temptation to join the ranks of those who follow the norm or, at least where her diploma was concerned, to show an interest in measuring herself against that norm? Was she seeking the socialization she had been deprived of by her lack of schooling? If it is technically possible to imagine these motives for the adolescent Yourcenar's unexpected confrontation with the "exam," at the time, it is hard to see why she would return to and perpetuate an inconsistent account so many years later. Unless, quite simply, she had forgotten—indeed, perhaps, never known—that she could not undertake a university degree with an incomplete diploma from secondary school. Or else, perhaps it is a question of one of those "pseudomemories" that people end up believing even though they aren't real. The hypothesis of pressure from the family seems highly unlikely: Marguerite had already learned how to live by her own wits, in that autarchical manner that would constitute her strength and allow her to resist, even at a very old age, the pressure and possessive desires of those around her. What is more, she would deny ever having had any interest in teaching. Nonetheless, in her future life, if one reads her correspondence over the years, especially with young writers seeking advice, one cannot fail to notice Yourcenar's pronounced pedagogical streak, pronounced to the point where it occasionally seems that this woman who never stepped foot in a school was almost a caricature of the Third Republic schoolmistress.

We find traces of this characteristic trait in her correspondence with young authors or aspiring writers, as is illustrated by the following four-point program addressed to a young woman of twenty-six who had asked for some tips. Its pedantry verges on the comical:

> 1. Work. One must learn the art of writing: this involves saying what one thinks and what one feels as clearly and as forcefully as possible. Do exercises: make yourself describe, precisely and completely, a painting in a museum, a scene in the street; relate a conversation you participated in; sort out your ideas on a subject important to you and put them down in writing. Never write more than a few pages at a time; write and rewrite until you have exactly what you want and have eliminated what is artificial or superfluous.

2. Learn to think; educate yourself. One can never read too much, see too much, or give too much thought to things. Devise for yourself an extensive and disinterested reading program (that is to say, without any immediate intention of putting your reading to use as a writer). Let one work lead to, and inform, the next. Do not leave out any field until you know exactly what you want to delve into more deeply for the time being.

3. Learn to see and hear everything around you, from the smallest kitchen utensil to the stars, from a barking dog to the voice of the wind.

4. Devote little thought to yourself, and none to the nonsense of success or glory. Ask yourself why you want to write.

(And number the pages of your letters, and put your address on the inside. Envelopes get lost. This is all part of the trade.)[25]

When it comes right down to it, her brief detour toward the "institution of the university"—secondary-school degrees were issued by the university back then—was perhaps nothing more than a way to put off a very serious decision. Or rather, it was a way of demonstrating that she had not taken lightly the important decision marking 1919, the year she turned sixteen. Whatever the family might think or have to say, adding thus to the opprobrium of financial ruin brought on by her father, Marguerite de Crayencour would join the vaguely disreputable group of traveling acrobats and bohemians of all kinds, as her grandmother Noémi would undoubtedly have muttered: she would be a writer. In 1919, she had already devoted most of her year, far more than to studying for her diploma, to writing a number of poems and composing a drama in verse, *Icare* [Icarus], which would become *Le Jardin des Chimères* [The Garden of the Chimeras], a text "full of the poetic clichés that are inevitable in the case of a child who has read too much," Yourcenar would comment. She would call it "ambitious" during her interviews with Matthieu Galey. "The cut of the poem was greatly influenced by Victor Hugo, almost to the point of plagiarism, and there was an epigraph consisting of two beautiful lines from Desportes, the best lines in that very slim volume: Heaven was his desire, the sea his sepulchre. / Is there a more beautiful design or a more sumptuous tomb?

"Not bad choosing for a girl of sixteen. Except for this there was nothing; the poem consisted of Icarus's reveries. There was, though, one rather good, and rather touching, scene—my first portrait of an old man—depicting Daedalus conversing with Death."[26]

"Regarding *Le Jardin des Chimères*," she would also confide to one of her correspondents, "a naive work but one that already went further [than the following collection, *Les Dieux ne sont pas morts* (The Gods Are Not Dead)];

it has surprised me to discover to what an extent the themes that would concern me later on and still concern me today are to be found there. One develops, let us hope so at least, but what is deep down does not change." [27] "I still value that little poem, though it is so awkward, as a first step, because it grazed the surface of a certain number of important themes to which I would later return," she wrote to another correspondent. [28]

Michel was not a man to oppose his daughter's wishes, especially since he too had dreamed of being a writer. "During the time of his involvement with Jeanne" he had translated, from the English version, *The Labyrinth of the World* by the Moravian writer Comenius. "He worked furiously on that translation of Comenius, whom he sometimes found exciting, sometimes insipid," she wrote in *Quoi? L'Eternité.* [29] "The same Michel who had composed a few poems, sometimes good ones, and had, with only one exception, thrown them in the wastebasket before finishing them, who had even undertaken, after Fernande's death, a starkly realistic novel abandoned at the end of the first chapter—which he later gave to me to transform into a short story, provided I put my own name on it—finally forced himself to follow through on a literary task to the end. He realized for the first time that manipulating words, feeling the weight of them, exploring their meaning, is a way of making love, especially when what one is writing is inspired by someone, or destined for someone." [30]

At Mercure de France, to which Michel brought the manuscript, "Vallette protested that nothing was done without the recommendation of the reading committee. Besides, it was a sure bet that this Comenius, whom no one knew in France, except perhaps one or two specialists, would be a dead loss." [31] The work was finally published in Lille, at the author's expense, and half of the five hundred copies printed were sent to Jeanne. "When he was in his seventies, [Michel] received from the Ministry of Culture of Czechoslovakia, by then a nation, an elegant and eloquent letter thanking him for having translated into French that masterpiece by a Czech patriot. He was as delighted by this as he would have been to see a tree believed dead growing green again." [32] It would even appear that the young Yourcenar contemplated working on that translation for a time, since the "By-the-Same-Author" page in *Les Dieux ne sont pas morts* indicates "In Progress: *The Labyrinth of the World* by Comenius (1623), translation." The plan was not carried out, but Yourcenar did give this title to her family trilogy, in homage, it seems, to her father rather than to Comenius. Although it is amusing—if not highly significant, who knows?—that she chose this title, and thus this particular reference, for retracing the history of those who, often without knowing it, "molded" her: Comenius, during the seventeenth century, was not only a "Czech patriot" but also, and notably, a great reformer of pedagogy.

So Michel, seeing that his daughter had firmly decided to accomplish what for him had been no more than a hazy dream, could only encourage her, push her, and help her out with all the means at his disposal. "For the young writer," Yourcenar wrote "he was an admirable literary adviser, completely disdainful of all the momentary trends and imbued with the best traditions of French language and literature." While he was surely an adviser, he was not an imperious, dominating mentor: it bears repeating that Monsieur de Crayencour and his daughter did not live in a state of mutual devotion. Christine Brown-Hovelt's arrival on the scene, in 1920, took place at just the right moment to prove it. She was the woman he had spent time with in London during 1915, and he had no doubt seen her since then, intermittently. But in 1920, she moved to Monte Carlo, which would lead Barbe, the former maid, to think that Monsieur de Crayencour had married her. Thus did she write in her last letter to Yourcenar, on 1 May 1920: "I am very happy that my little Marguerite has not forgotten me before setting off on her trip to Switzerland. I also hope that it will be a fine trip for your father and his new wife. I find him very brave to have taken on a third wife. At least he will be able to judge whether there is a difference between French women, Belgian women, and English women."[33]

Monsieur de Crayencour would not, in fact, marry Christine Brown-Hovelt until 25 October 1926, in Monte Carlo. She was fifty-three years old and he was seventy-three. Yourcenar maintained that she encouraged him: "I was the one (I was twenty-two) who advised Michel to marry her in October 1926 (two years and three months before his death), when the idea suddenly came to him to do it 'because it would please her,'" she would confide to her half nephew.[34]

Curiously, however, Christine de Crayencour, formerly Christine Brown-Hovelt, does not appear once in the "Chronologie" of the Pléiade. No part of the account given there of the twenties bears any trace of even a temporary life as a threesome, and the notion of a tête-à-tête, at once secret and complicitous, between the father and the now-adult daughter is perpetuated. Christine Brown-Hovelt had a distinct talent as a miniaturist, and Yourcenar always kept the miniatures Christine had made for her based on childhood photographs. But she was far from having the intelligence to hold the attention of her stepdaughter—who, for that matter, would have hated being referred to in this way. In the thirties, nonetheless, Yourcenar would continue to have her own room in her stepmother's Lausanne apartment, and during the Second World War, when Christine was destitute, Yourcenar, despite the precarity of her own situation in the United States, did the best she could to help her out financially, as she did until her death in Pau, in 1950.

Despite all this, and even though she dedicated her *Pindare* [Pindar], published by Grasset in 1932, "To my dearest Christine de Crayencour, in memory of happy days in Italy and in Provence"[35]—Yourcenar would claim that she had not had anything more than the politely neutral relations with Christine that a daughter emerging from adolescence should have with her father's wife. The dedication in *Pindare,* according to her, was just "a simple courtesy." She only let her irritation show when relating, in *Archives du Nord,* how, at the bedside of her dying father, Christine, a "sentimental and conventional Englishwoman," had insisted, against even Michel's wishes, that they notify his son, Michel-Joseph.[36]

In general, Yourcenar never talked about the feelings she had regarding her father's conquests, with the exception of Jeanne, the one she had "chosen." Should we conclude, then, that she was indifferent about them most of the time? Perhaps. At the very least, she made an effort at indifference, refusing to enter into games of sentiment that would have struck her as degrading. And then, Monsieur de Crayencour was not a man to look favorably on feelings of possessiveness or sentimental territorial wars. We have seen how he and his daughter were always careful to avoid the kind of chatty intimacy that both parties would probably have deemed unseemly. Shared secrets, thus, were out of the question, or nearly. Should we see a shadow of regret in this brief remark from the preliminary notes for *Quoi? L'Eternité:* "she would be the one who listened (not his confidante, but that is of little importance)"? Nothing really authorizes us to; it is, rather, an observation, along the lines of what she said during her conversation with Bernard Pivot in 1979. She claimed to know the emperor Hadrian, "about whom we have a great deal of documented information," better than her own father and challenged "the misbelief of people who always think that the family is something one is excessively close to": "Let's look at things closely for a moment. A father is a man who had you as a daughter, in my case, when he was forty-five years old [he was fifty]. Let's say that I began observing him when I myself was seven. . . . His entire youth was behind him. I had to reconstruct it from his accounts, which, happily, were rather plentiful. Then . . . the mere fact of being a daughter distorts the situation with regard to this personage: he was 'my' father. And we are not sufficiently aware that this father is a gentleman who has his own life, his own adventures, his own woes. He may be a very good father, but he does not consist entirely of his paternity. Indeed, there are many other things that we easily forget."[37]

During that year, 1920, Monsieur de Crayencour without a doubt paid attention to, and was interested in, his seventeen-year-old adolescent in a way that he could not have suspected when, sad and alone, he had returned to Mont-Noir with a baby in 1903. Yourcenar, for her part, admired that man "perpetually absent without leave," with a kind of admiration that would soon become reciprocal. With the composition, in 1919, of *Icare*, Yourcenar's literary activities had taken such a serious turn that Monsieur de Crayencour could not look upon her work as a series of adolescent distractions. With *Icare* barely finished, she started working on a second collection of poems. It was *Les Dieux ne sont pas morts*, of which several pieces had been written prior to *Le Jardin des Chimères*, and which would be completed when she was eighteen, in 1921. After the fact, she would judge it "inferior to the first," "since the poems in it were . . . in fact lifted straight out of my schoolgirl's copybook," as she said to Matthieu Galey. "These poems contained overtones of just about all the poets of the late nineteenth century. Of course artists must learn their trade just like anyone else, but at least musicians practice their scales in their own rooms and don't bother anyone outside the family, while young writers sometimes publish too soon. It would have been better, I think, to have thrown those early works in the wastebasket."[38]

But those stylistic exercises, full of grandiosity and lyricism, saturated with references to antiquity, copied, it seems, from the worst of Alfred de Vigny, attest, early on, to her certitude that she was a writer, and, as we have seen, to her desire for distinction and glory:

> *Be solemn. Scorning every slavish chain,*
> *Withdraw from what is evil, vile, and hideous.*
> *Rigorously sculpt your ideal.*
> *Working, be unmindful of the crowd's hollow cries,*
> *And hold fast, in these times when all respect is crumbling,*
> *To a serene love of Beauty.*[39]

Or, again:

> *Like those dreamers envied by your pride,*
> *Force Fate to crown your life.*
> *The world is great enough for your greatest desire.*
> *Climb, your eyes fixed on heights supreme*
> *Where still in splendor gleams the ancient diadem,*
> *Which only the victor can seize.*[40]

Clearly, the work offers more biographical than literary interest, as Yourcenar, happily, realized: "If I do not include these two works [*Le Jardin des Chimères* and *Les Dieux ne sont pas morts*] on the list of my books, it is because I view them as the first efforts of a child; they could, one day perhaps, be of interest to critics attempting to evaluate my complete *œuvre*, if such critics there be, but they are certainly not—especially *Les Dieux ne sont pas morts*—of any value for the general public." [41] "As regards the juvenilia," she confided to another correspondent, "*Le Jardin des Chimères*, written at the age of sixteen and published at the author's expense when I was eighteen, and *Les Dieux ne sont pas morts*, containing poems written during and after my fourteenth year, and which was published at the author's expense when I was nineteen, they are not worth reading. . . . With the exception of two or three poems that seem to me to capture something childlike rather gracefully, in the manner of the rondeaus of a very young musician ("Limpide source" [Limpid Spring] . . . "Eté" [Summer] . . .), everything is tortuous, jigsawed, and pompous. Adolescence is the time when we force ourselves to be something we are not, something more than what we are. Such ambitions are necessary, but they are not without awkwardness or pretension. The only curious thing is that, having realized how poor those poems were, I pulped them as early as 1925, but afterward—in 1930, and sometimes later on—I relentlessly worked on those pieces, or variations of them, as one compels oneself to play a piece of music until one has executed it more or less properly." [42]

If we cannot take Yourcenar to task for pieces we would be more inclined to call versified than poetic, and which she herself deemed insipid, we can wonder why that young girl smitten with literature deliberately chose her models in the stuffiest corners of the nineteenth century and why she was unaware, or so it seems, of the formidable poetic revolution that was going on around her: *Alcools* (*Alcools*) appeared in 1913 and Surrealism was coming to life. [43] Perhaps we must see this incongruity as the consequence of a certain provincialism or, more appropriately still, of a life so far removed from the society of others that only the "classical" texts with which Michel had been nourished found their way into her hands.

Whatever the case may be, in 1920, Yourcenar had not yet reached the stage of self-criticism that would lead her to abandon those first compositions, condemned, to destruction: she dreamed of seeing her literary stammerings in print. Her father, only too happy to help, undertook to make arrangements with publishers. It was at this time that Monsieur de Crayencour and Marguerite, who wanted to select a pen name for herself, spent an evening playing with the letters of their patronymic. They eventually happened on a nearly perfect anagram—there is only one C missing—of Crayencour: Yourcenar, "for the pleasure of the Y," she would say. It most likely was also for the mystery of this name with the ring of a password. The former Marguerite de Crayencour would take it as her legal name when she became an American citizen. As for the first name, it would become "Marg," for ten years or so: at the time, Yourcenar must have liked that indeterminacy.

Regarding the question of a publisher, their choice seems to have fallen on Perrin. (They may have written to other houses, though no evidence to this effect has yet come to light.) But in the files at Plon, which include those of Perrin, now a member of the same group of publishers, several letters have been found. One of them, written in the firm hand of an adult, proposes a poetry collection "of about 200 pages," and inquires as to price and how long publication would take.[44] The letter is signed "M. de Crayencour." Quite naturally, the response is addressed to "Monsieur," as well it should have been: a handwriting comparison attests that it was indeed Monsieur de Crayencour who wrote the letter. At the end of the month of September, with yet no news of the manuscript, Monsieur de Crayencour posted a new letter—typed, but signed in his hand—to the publisher:

Sir,

On the date of 5 August last, I had the honor of sending you (by registered mail), consequently to your letter of 2 August, a manuscript, "Le Jardin des Chimères" (under the pseudonym of Marg Yourcenar). That work was to have been submitted to the approval of your Reading Committee, in view of a printing the terms of which we were negotiating.

Since that time, that is to say for nearly two months, I have been without news of that mailing.

Since I have a portfolio containing a certain number of separate poems, I would be of a mind to publish only, for the moment, La Légende Dramatique d'Icare [The Dramatic Legend of Icarus], which is already part of the manuscript I sent to you, setting aside the other poems in the same mailing for a book that I would like to have published in a few months, adding to them the new poems, which would then make up, along with the old ones, a volume of about 300 pages. I would prefer this method to the immediate production of a work that might be criticized for lacking unity.

La Légende Dramatique d'Icare would nonetheless be produced under the title "Jardin des Chimères" and would constitute a slim volume of about 80 pages.

I shall be grateful for your letting me know what decision has been made by your Reading Committee and trust you will accept my sincerest good wishes.[45]

On 4 October, when the publisher had made a favorable response, Michel answered with a handwritten letter, signed "Marguerite de Crayencour"!

I have just received your letter of 2 October and am deeply affected by the flattering words of approval that you were so kind as to express to me regarding my manuscript.

I thank you for being so kind as to undertake the publication of "La Légende d'Icare," and I am in agreement with you that it would be best to use a very wide printing format in order to avoid the appearance of a brochure.

I would be infinitely grateful to you for being so kind as to see to this work as soon as possible. It goes without saying that I accept your conditions with respect to price and defer to your judgment regarding choice of paper and typesetting.

Please return to me the poems that follow "La Légende d'Icare." When I shall have rounded out their number, I would like to have them published in a volume entitled "L'Epée et le Miroir" [The Sword and the Mirror].

At present, I am working on a dramatic poem that will be called "Irène aux Cygnes blancs" [Irene of the White Swans]. I will be honored to submit these two manuscripts to you when they are completed, and I hope that they will meet with the gracious welcome accorded by you to my first work.

Please accept, as I thank you once again, my sincerest good wishes.

Marguerite de Crayencour

P.S. I have chosen as my pseudonym Marg Yourcenar, which is, as you can see, an anagram of my real name.

Villa Loretta
Boulevard d'Italie
Monte Carlo

I believe it is customary to pay half the price in advance. Having rounded off the sum, I send you a check for two thousand francs to be credited to my account.[46]

So the game played by father and daughter went this far—to the point of mixing up their signatures. We can surely imagine Michel de Crayencour distinctly relishing the act of signing that strange feminine name, "Marguerite Yourcenar," thus peering into a future of such fame as he would not have dared conceive. But we cannot impute this incident solely to the curious delights of role confusion—though confusion, nonetheless, there must have been. We must also take into account the simple practicality of Monsieur de Crayencour's intervention. His calligraphic style of writing was more serious-looking, firmer, and, in a word, more adult. Yourcenar herself at that time had a charmingly childish penmanship, or nearly so, which would soon become a very personal handwriting style, not much like the norm of upstrokes and downstrokes she must have been taught, even if she hadn't learned to write in a schoolroom, and against which, yet again, she must have calmly rebelled.

Finally then, the text was accepted, and it was at Perrin in 1921 that the first work of Marguerite de Crayencour—become an eighteen-year-old writer of indecipherable gender, a certain Marg Yourcenar—appeared, at the author's expense (thus Michel de Crayencour's), under the title *Le Jardin des Chimères*. Exactly sixty years later, in 1981, a woman of seventy-eight, Marguerite Yourcenar, would be the first person of "the sex" to be invested as a member of the Académie Française, beneath the dome at Quai Conti.

4

I, the Undersigned,
Marguerite Yourcenar

THE SECOND BOOK of the young Mademoiselle de Crayencour, who as yet was a writer only where her plans and fondest wishes were concerned, was also published at Michel de Crayencour's expense. Despite few reactions to *Le Jardin des Chimères*, Yourcenar had been encouraged to persist in her literary endeavors by the words of a man for whom she had much admiration: Rabindranath Tagore, a symbolic figure of the Orient, which already fascinated her. "It was in 1921," she would write to a journalist long afterward. "I was eighteen years old; I had just published at my own expense—or, rather, an overly enthusiastic father had just published—my first poem, a slim volume entitled *Le Jardin des Chimères*, and I had sent it to Rabindranath Tagore, among other personalities. The other personalities, as far as I can remember, did not respond. Tagore responded immediately, inviting me to spend a season in Shantiniketan. I later learned that he often extended such invitations to young Westerners who contacted him. As you can well imagine, I was terribly tempted but did not have the personal means of taking that long journey. I wonder today how greatly my life and my thinking would be different from what they are now if I had gone. I kept those two letters that Tagore had kindly sent me for a long time; they were lost, like so many other things, in the disaster of 1939–1945."[1]

Les Dieux ne sont pas morts came out in 1922 at Sansot. As *Pindare* would be as well, it was dedicated to the woman who would become her father's third wife four years later—*To my cherished friend Christine Hovelt*—in one of those surges of adolescent affection that one rues later on, when one is clearly aware that the recipient was not the person one had imagined.

The Pléiade's "Chronologie" asserts, after the fact and somewhat hastily, that from 1921 on the author was known only by the name of Yourcenar. To the two or three years following it dates a work that would never see the light of day intact but that can be considered as the matrix of Yourcenar's *œuvre*. What she planned was a very long novel, *Remous* [Crosscurrents], recounting the intermingled stories of several families over the course of some four centuries.[2]

She attests to writing five hundred pages of the book in four years, in a disorganized, "somewhat haphazard" way, then throwing everything out except for three fragments. During the entire first stage of her life as a writer—before World War II—Yourcenar would destroy an abundance of preliminary drafts. She incidentally explains this radical behavior, born of rigid standards self-imposed by a twenty-year-old writer and little by little abandoned—indeed, perhaps too thoroughly abandoned, in her old age— digressing somewhat from a passage in *Dear Departed* concerning Octave Pirmez, her writerly ancestor: "I [have shown disdain for] his fervent desire to reveal only what he deemed best in himself: when I was twenty, I would have understood this. At that age, my ambition was to remain the anonymous author (or one known at most by a name and by two perhaps disputed dates) of five or six sonnets that might win the admiration of half a dozen people in any generation. It was not long before I gave up thinking this way.... Nevertheless, compared with the unhealthy exhibitionism of our own day, Octave's reserve, though likewise unhealthy, is appealing to me."[3]

AFTER REWORKING, the *Remous* texts that had been saved would subsequently constitute the collection of novellas, *La Mort conduit l'attelage* [Death Drives the Cart][4] (in 1934): "a few years later, having taken up a 'literary career,' as it were, it occurred to me to rescue at least some parts of that earlier, abandoned work. Thus it was that the story called 'Anna, soror ...' appeared in 1935 [*sic*] in the collection of three novellas entitled *Death Drives the Cart....* To give them at least the appearance of some unity, I chose to call them respectively 'After Dürer,' 'After El Greco,' and 'After Rembrandt.'"[5]

But this little book did not mark the limit of their destiny. The first story, *D'après Dürer* [After Dürer], bore the seed of *L'Œuvre au noir* (*The Abyss*). The second, *D'après Greco* [After El Greco], would reappear with almost no modification in 1981 under the title *Anna, soror....* And from the third, *D'après Rembrandt* [After Rembrandt], two stories would emerge, *Un Homme obscur* ("An Obscure Man") and *Une Belle Matinée* ("A Lovely Morning"), which were entirely redone between 1979 and 1981.[6] Moreover, the intention to reconstruct family history, in *Remous,* on the basis of genealogical documents read for the first time by Yourcenar in 1921 would find more than an echo in *Dear Departed* and *Archives du Nord,* the first two volumes of the trilogy entitled *Le Labyrinthe du monde,* volumes "built around the story of several families from northern France and Belgium during the nineteenth century and delving back sometimes into a much more distant ancestry."[7]

Yourcenar considered that her literary destiny was anchored in what she referred to throughout her life as the "projects of my twentieth year," and which in fact were formed, though still hazily, in "overflowing reveries" between the ages of nineteen and twenty-four.[8] Was she anxious to situate, *a posteriori,* her work's unity and origin somewhere, in this initial implosion, as it were, from which everything proceeded? Surely not. On the contrary, she would be quite irritated, in her old age, by the emphasis placed on her propensity to endlessly revise the books written previously and claimed "to have rewritten much less than people say." Thus, to Jacques Chancel, who was discussing how much pleasure she took in "redoing and starting all over again," she retorted: "That depends; one must be leery of generalizations. There are works, for instance, like *Le Coup de grâce (Coup de Grâce)* or *Alexis,* that have never been altered, except in the case of their misuse of the subjunctive, or certain details of grammar that did not strike me as entirely felicitous. . . . Other books have been revised because they were begun when I was much too young. This, I believe, is a particularly curious feature of my writing. At the age of twenty, I had foreseen some four or five of my books, and I had started scribbling on a great deal of paper. At that time, of course, I had taken on a burden that I was not able to carry."[9]

Nonetheless, as early as *Les Dieux ne sont pas morts,* although in the form of nebulae, the galaxy of Yourcenar's works was already in place. Her incessant labors of re-creation would explore that galaxy to the point of obsession, playing with its depth, its expansion, its contraction, its development, or its accuracy. In what is at least a large portion of her work, Yourcenar developed—"inflected," one might say in a language that she would have deemed delinquent—the "madness" of her visionary youth. Thus did she create "upon her own former self," in an almost autarchical manner, spending her life forgetting in order to rediscover, revise, rethink, remodel.

She often expressed—in her correspondence, her prefaces or postfaces, or during interviews—this particular need not to abandon her characters, to invent a future for them, a more "rounded-out" destiny. "The further I go, the more that particular madness that consists of doing old books over again strikes me as great wisdom," she would write in her "Carnets de notes de *L'Œuvre au noir*" [Reflections on the Composition of *The Abyss*]. "Every writer only carries within him a certain number of beings. Rather than representing the latter in the guise of new characters, which would hardly be anything but old characters with different first names, I have been more inclined to deepen, develop, and nourish those beings with whom I was already in the habit of living, getting to know them better as I have learned more about life and improving on a world that was already my own. 'I have never been able to understand how one could have enough of any beloved,'[10] I have Hadrian say, speaking of his loves. Nor have I ever believed that I could have enough of any character I had created. I am not yet through watching them live. They will have surprises in store for me until the end of my days." [11]

One hesitates, of course, in the face of the banal metaphor "literary children" for a writer's creations. But here, one cannot help noticing to what an extent the model is implicitly that of a strange sort of Bildungsroman whose protagonists are at once the narrator/author and her characters.

That singular fictional family, which we shall refrain, at least by way of paraleipsis, from deeming substitutional, was born of a time span so lengthy as to challenge haste's approximation or urgency's neglect and to pleasure in the kinds of successions that establish a lineage: Yourcenar would willingly use the term "geology" to refer to the "sedimentation" of a being, the length of time necessary for him or her to reach maturity. Slowness and aging, to the extent that they entail maturation rather than stagnation, were constant objects of reflection and observation for her. She always preferred to "shooting stars"—even more so in politics than in literature—those that last: "Hadrian wasn't flashy," she would say, evoking the hero of the book that made her famous. "That's one of the things I like about him. He was above all clear-headed and always open-minded about worlds different from his own." [12]

YOURCENAR'S literary precocity and her taste for erudition did not, however, cause her to become suddenly sedentary. It is well known how fully she shared the incurable nomadism of her father, who took pleasure in repeating, "That's nothing to worry about! Who gives a damn? We're not from these parts, and in any case, tomorrow we're clearing out." In 1914, the conditions of what she took for a jaunt—which was instead a term of exile in London—as well as her age, had not allowed her to get to know Great Britain well. But in 1922, the year of her first stay in Venice with her father, she would begin exploring Italy with a passion and continued to the whole decade long—alone, in the company of Michel, or in that of other, as yet imprecise, companions.

About her travels, of course, she would only reveal what pertained to her work. Consider her visit, for example, still in 1922, to Milan and Verona, where she witnessed the march on Rome (an impetus for her novel *Denier du rêve* [*A Coin in Nine Hands*]):

It is always a serious moment when a young mind once unconcerned with politics suddenly discovers that injustice and calculated interests poorly understood are passing back and forth before one on the streets of a city, impressively decked out in capes and uniforms, or are sitting at a café in the guise of upstanding bourgeois who don't take sides. For me, 1922 was one of those milestones, and the place where revelation occurred was Venice and Verona. . . . The surge of liberal fervor that preceded the Risorgimento in Italy is one of the finest, most extraordinary, episodes of the century. . . . One has a more difficult time accepting that what followed was the bourgeois Savoy monarchy . . . or that the disorder from which reforms should have emerged gave way to fascist saber rattling and ended up with Hitler barking angrily in Naples (I hear him still) between two rows of eagles made of imitation stone, with rats devouring carcasses in the Ardeatine Caves, Ciano shot to death in his armchair, and the bodies of the Romagnese dictator and his mistress hung up by their feet in a garage.[13]

She would frequently evoke her first stay in Rome in 1924—the only time her father accompanied her—and their discovery of the Villa Adriana. "This lovely spot is today desacralized by imprudent renovations and by the dubious statues one finds here and there on the grounds arbitrarily grouped beneath patched-up porticos, to say nothing of the presence of a refreshment stand and parking lot two steps away from the great wall designed by Piranesi. We miss the old Villa of Count Fede, the way it still was during my adolescence, with its long walkway lined with cypress trees, a Praetorian Guard leading step by step to the silent domain of the shadows; in April it was haunted by the cuckoo's cry, in August by the screeching of cicadas, but the last time I was there, I heard, primarily, transistor radios."[14]

It was upon that first visit to one of the emperor Hadrian's habitats that she decided to undertake what, twenty-seven years later, would become her first great public success, *Memoirs of Hadrian.*

ABOUT FLORENCE she says nothing except that she went there in 1923, accompanied by her father. On the other hand, she recounted at length to Grace Frick—who tells the story in the process of drawing up one of her chronologies of Yourcenar's life[15]—her arrival in Naples in the spring of 1925 and her first visit to Castel Sant'Elmo, where she would set the action of "Anna, Soror . . . ." Her father joined her there and saw Naples for the first time. It was Yourcenar, from then on, who would introduce Monsieur de Crayencour to new sights. He was nearly seventy-two years old, he was tired, he was weak, and, this time, he really was totally bankrupt.

She showed him the strange Pietà of the Sant'Anna dei Lombardi church about which she would speak all her life as of a violent and lasting impression. She describes this in "Anna, Soror . . ." during the Maundy Thursday

scene, one of the compelling episodes of this story of incestuous love between the two main characters, Anna and her brother Miguel, who, writes
Yourcenar, "[o]n these last days of Lent ... were struggling against the
exhaustion caused by prolonged abstinence." [16]

In the postface written in 1981 for the Pléiade edition of her prose works,
Yourcenar would say that she had essentially written "Anna, Soror ..."
"in several weeks" during that spring of 1925, and "immediately upon the
return" from her visit to Naples.

> [T]hat perhaps explains why the love affair of the brother and sister takes
> place and reaches its climax during Holy Week. Even more than by the antiq-
> uities in its museum or the frescoes of the Villa of the Mysteries at Pompeii
> (which it has been my fate to love from one end of my life to the other), I was
> spellbound in Naples by the grinding poverty and liveliness of the popular
> quarters, and by the austere beauty or faded splendor of the churches, some
> of which have since been badly damaged or completely destroyed by the
> bombings of 1944—like the little church of San Giovanni a Mare, where I
> depict Anna opening the coffin of Miguel. I visited Castel Sant'Elmo, where
> I cause my characters to live, and the Certosa next door, where I imagine
> Don Alvaro finishing his life. I had passed through a few of the small, deso-
> late villages of the Basilicata, in one of which I situated the semi-seigneurial,
> semi-rustic building where Valentina and her children come for the grape
> harvest; and the ruins seen by Miguel as if in a dream are unquestionably
> those of Paestum. Never was a novel's creation more directly inspired by the
> locales in which it is placed. [17]

In the fall, Yourcenar, who stayed in Naples after her father's departure,
"sold grapes in the street," reports Frick, then came back to Rome where
she would spend three months, until Christmas. She had just turned
twenty-two and, when she described the dying Valentina, in "Anna, Soror
... ," she was speaking of the woman whom she already knew she had
decided not to be: "Valentina's life had been one long drifting into silence." [18]
And at the same time, she was marking out the limits, by way of literary
mediation, of what would be from then on the field of her desires and her
choices: "Throughout those few weeks, even while continuing to make the
habitual gestures and to carry on the habitual relationships of existence, I
lived uninterruptedly within those two bodies and those two souls, slipping
from Anna into Miguel and from Miguel into Anna. . . . I was twenty-one,
precisely the age at which Anna has her passionate affair, yet I entered into
a worn-out, aged Anna or into a declining Don Alvaro without the slightest
difficulty. At that time my sexual experience remained fairly limited; that of
real passion lay just around the corner; but nonetheless the love of Anna
and Miguel burned within me." [19]

YOURCENAR DECIDED to extend the range of her reading, which was already considerable, though very much centered on fictional literature, on the one hand, and Greco-Roman antiquity, on the other. She first moved in the direction of contemporary history, socialist and anarchist theorists, then nineteenth-century German and English philosophers and poets, and, finally, the Orient. For the first time, she read translations of Indian and Far Eastern texts. She continued, furthermore, to apply herself to the study of mathematics, which she considered a thoroughly salutary discipline, perhaps even an indispensible one for what she had resolved to accomplish with respect to her intellectual training.

So when Christmastime came, she returned to France and joined her father in Monte Carlo, where he was residing with Christine Hovelt. Some might well be surprised to find such a very young woman of that era traveling, perhaps not alone, but in any case without a "chaperone." That historical moment still wavered between the nineteenth and the twentieth centuries, despite the irrevocable fracture of the First World War. There was still a kind of oscillation between the modes of conduct dominant in each of the two centuries, which Yourcenar summed up perfectly in *Dear Departed:* "Wherever one goes, falsehood reigns. In the twentieth century, which is crude, garish, and loud, it most frequently takes the form of imposture; in the nineteenth century, a more subdued age, it took the form of hypocrisy."[20]

Thus during those years, in which the nineteenth century was fading into the distance, while there had not yet appeared on the horizon what would often make the twentieth century rather grotesque in its frantic pursuit of different brands of "liberation"—which bear the same relation to freedom that the swimming pool bears to the ocean—Yourcenar, for her part, chose to assert her independence. And she would continue to—without proclamations, without ostentation, but without ever deviating from the exercise of her own will. She always attempted to judge as accurately as possible the limits of her sphere and her latitude for movement.

According to the Pléiade's "Chronologie," Monsieur de Crayencour set up residence in Switzerland in 1926, seeking medical treatment. He was seventy-three years old, and he knew that from then on he would suffer from cancer. Yourcenar claims that she went with him to Switzerland and hardly left this country while he was still alive. This is false: in 1926, Monsieur de Crayencour was still in the south of France, except perhaps for sporadic trips to Switzerland where he was treated. He married Christine Hovelt in Monte Carlo on 25 October 1926, and he did not move to Switzerland until the late spring of 1927, to escape the heat of a Mediterranean summer. In early 1927, he spent a great deal of his time taking walks with his daughter. They took excursions together to the backcountry villages "between two crises at the baccarat table or roulette wheel." They went as far as Menton, sometimes even as far as the Italian Riviera. Some days, they would take off on long walks, generally of ten kilometers or so, with the exceptional hike of fifteen or seventeen kilometers. When they were too tired to return on foot, they would take a taxi or a horse-drawn carriage, asking the driver or the coachman to go as slowly as possible, so they could soak up the scenery.

At the same time, Yourcenar, who was keeping relatively close track of what was being published—as she would do throughout her life, denying it all the while, with a curious coquetry—was tempted by the success of certain biographies that were being written for a popular readership, such as the ones appearing at Grasset. She decided to devote one to Pindar because, as she would say in the dedication she wrote for Grace Frick in June 1938, "she thought she knew Greek." She started working immediately and, at the end of 1926 or the beginning of the following year, she went to Paris to offer her manuscript to Grasset: it would in fact be published by this house, but not until 1932.

Nonetheless, we can indeed situate the real beginning of Yourcenar's literary career in 1926. After the publication in *L'Humanité*, thanks to Henri Barbusse's intervention, of an article bearing the stamp, in her opinion, "of a still-juvenile radicalism," "L'Homme couvert de dieux" [The Man Covered with Gods] (unfortunately titled "L'Homme" [Man] as the result of an error on the part of the newspaper's editing staff), she would alternate regularly between books and periodical pieces, until the beginning of the war. The article in question, rather ponderously allegorical, is of no great interest. But from that time on she would not cease to ply her writer's trade. Since she was never receptive to the social game played by French writers, or to frequenting the literary circles of Paris (at least after the war), or to flinging herself into the race for prizes, she was sometimes taken for an amiable dilettante who hardly saw writing as a profession. The fierceness of her disputes with publishers proves that nothing was further from the truth. And in 1927, right after she had settled herself at the Hôtel Bellevue et Belvédère in Glion-sur-Montreux, Switzerland, she wrote to her former maid Camille on 19 June: "I brought my typewriter with me and I'm 'tapping away' at my articles all day long, when I'm not out for a walk."[21]

Worth remembering from 1927 and 1928 are a short story, "Kâli décapitée" ("Kali Beheaded"), which appeared in the *Revue Européenne* and was the first piece based on her readings of Far Eastern authors,[22] and especially the highly polemical "Diagnostic de l'Europe" [European Diagnosis] (which would appear in 1929 in the *Revue de Genève*).[23] The latter text, which has not been republished in any of her essay collections, not even in the posthumous *En pèlerin et en étranger* [Like a Pilgrim, Like a Stranger], is fascinating. "Diagnostic de l'Europe" resembles *La Défaite de la pensée* [The Defeat of Thought][24] before the fact, clearly peremptory, as the reasoning of a young woman twenty-four years old can be. Undoubtedly, it was influenced by Paul Valéry and the famous incipit of *Variété I* ("The Crisis of the Mind"): "We later civilizations . . . we too now know that we are mortal."[25] That influence is acknowledged by Yourcenar: "Valéry is the first one from whom, when I was twenty years old, I learned that there existed a method. And he will probably be the last poet to make us feel the almost sacred beauty of form."[26] She was also quite accurately portrayed by Edmond Jaloux, *Nouvelles Littéraires'* influential critic, who would refer to this text in the article he wrote about *Alexis:* "I only knew of Madame Marguerite Yourcenar from a fine study in historical philosophy that appeared in the interesting *Revue de Genève* called 'Diagnostic de l'Europe,' a rather pessimistic study, with a typically 'Valéryan' pessimism. But Madame Marguerite Yourcenar, after having revealed Europe's serious condition, gave us a no less vivid picture of the charm of that condition; thus, they say, do the Japanese eat fish that are more or less alive, watching as their death throes take on the most beautiful colors before their eyes. Europe, for Madame Yourcenar, makes a similarly rich phosphorescent display that one cannot quite describe, a display that charms her and that is already the finery of decomposition. Her study struck me. Since reading *Alexis ou Le Traité du vain combat,* I am not so sure of its truth. I have the impression that Madame Marguerite Yourcenar takes personal pleasure in the ideas of culmination and decline and that she turned her attention to the old age of our world with the very same eyes that gazed upon the youth of her hero."[27]

Many years later, toward the end of her life, Yourcenar herself would return to that text of her youth in a few sentences handwritten on the first page of the review in which it had been published: "The predictions were wrong because I imagined that an era of discipline was coming next; on the contrary, it was a much more total chaos that proved true."[28] Actually, the description she made then of that chaos, however accurate it may be, is relatively conventional and attests to a less refined sense of analysis than in her first text, where "Valéryan pessimism" was coupled with a kind of aesthetic delectation, and a subtle taste for the provocative, that prevented one from viewing this piece as nothing more than an aggrieved lamentation. In other, more brutal words, she was young.

OVER THE COURSE of the summer of 1928, the state of Monsieur de Crayencour's health seemed to improve, if we can trust the news relayed by Yourcenar to her former maid Camille: "My father is much better." It was also in that postcard that the matter of the visit of her half brother Michel, accompanied by his wife Solange, was raised, a visit that Yourcenar would subsequently deny or forget.[29] During that same period, between August 1927 and September 1928 (and she did not cease to travel, since she went to Austria and since Frick notes, as always in one of her "chronologies," "perhaps the first visit to Innsbruck," one of Zeno's locales) she composed the first work that she would really recognize as her own to the extent of letting it be republished with very few corrections: *Alexis ou Le Traité du vain combat,* whose Gidean title echoes *Le Traité du vain désir* (*The Treatise of Vain Desire*). She began it on 31 August 1927 and finished on 17 September 1928.

With regard to this book, she claims to have been influenced by Rilke and Schnitzler more than Gide and does not even mention Roger Martin du Gard.[30] All of which allows her to consciously lay claim to the first two while producing a text where what appears, instead, are traces of the second two authors. According to Yourcenar, *Alexis* is "the story of a young musician from an aristocratic, poor family, fighting against tendencies assumed to be abnormal and reprehensible, who ends up leaving his young wife, whom he nonetheless loves and with whom he has just had a son, to reclaim a kind of freedom he cannot live without."[31] This short novel is a long letter in which Alexis, explaining to his wife Monique why he is leaving her—he prefers the pleasure men give him—explores the "difference that exists between external conformity and inner morality."[32] A long while later, Yourcenar would explain, in one of her interviews with Matthieu Galey, why it had been important for her, in *Alexis,* to distinguish between pleasure and love:

"In *Alexis,* though, I think I introduced the distinction mainly in reaction to the clichéd French notion of love, which I felt, and still feel, did not ring true. The French have in a sense stylized love, created a certain style of love, a certain form. And having done that, they proceeded to believe in what they had invented, they forced themselves to love in a particular way when they would have experienced it in an entirely different way had there not been all that literature behind them. In my view, it's only in France that La Rochefoucauld could have said 'there are many people who, had they never heard of love, would never have felt it.' I don't think that such a statement makes any sense here [in the United States] and perhaps in many other parts of the world."[33]

Her incurable penchant for self-commentary will cause her to justify, in a preface, the style she chose for this subject and text, "that spare, almost abstract language, both circumspect and precise," that one might otherwise impute to pusillanimity, or to a case of the literary shivers:

> The writer who endeavors to present the story of Alexis honestly, eliminating from his language formulae which are supposedly decorous but in reality are the semi-timorous or semi-licentious formulae of cheap literature, has little choice except between two or three modes of expression more or less inadequate and often unacceptable. The scientific terminology recently formulated and doomed to become outmoded with the theories that support it . . . go[es] against the chief aim of literature, which is individuality of expression. Obscenity, a literary mode which has always had its adherents, is a defensible shock treatment if one has to force a prudish or indifferent public to face what it does not want to look at or what, as the result of too prolonged a habit, it can no longer see. . . . Yet such a brutal solution remains an external solution: the hypocritical reader tends to accept the unseemly word as a form of the picturesque. . . . The brutality of language conceals the banality of thought and, with certain major exceptions, is indistinguishable from a kind of conformism.
>
> A third solution may offer itself to the writer: the use of that spare, almost abstract language, both circumspect and precise, which in France has for centuries served preachers, moralists, and often novelists in the classical period as well, as a vehicle for discussing what was termed at that time "the aberrations of the senses." This traditional style for the examination of conscience lends itself so well to the formulation of innumerable nuances of judgment on a subject which is by its nature as complex as life itself that a Bourdaloue or a Massillon resorted to it for the expression of indignation or censure, and a Laclos for licentiousness or voluptuousness. By its very discretion, this decanted language has seemed to me especially appropriate for the pensive, scrupulous deliberations of Alexis.[34]

"A shocking topic at the time and from the pen of a young woman," Yourcenar would comment. To build *Alexis,* she used both a recent personal experience[35] and the memory of what she had assumed were the amorous preferences of Conrad, Jeanne's husband. It should be noted that the first name, Monique, given to the wife of Alexis, would be precisely the one used by Yourcenar to designate Jeanne de Vietinghoff, in *Dear Departed* and *Archives du Nord.* The latter woman would not be reunited with her real first name, Jeanne, until *Quoi? L'Eternité.* Egon de Vietinghoff, Jeanne and Conrad's son, makes no other comment, for his part, on the tastes of his father—a professional musician like Alexis—beyond his habitual "It's possible." But he does point out that Alexis was the first name of his brother (who became Axel in *Quoi? L'Eternité*). As for Yourcenar, she refers, in her 1963 preface, to Virgil's second eclogue regarding her choice of a first name, which is clearly not incompatible.

What was that "recent personal experience" of which we also find a trace in *Quoi? L'Eternité*? She relates in that book an altercation between her father and the character she calls Egon. Monsieur de Crayencour takes his interlocutor to task, not because of his homosexuality, but because of the fact that the latter considers such behavior an exceptional adventure. She does not conceal having had "only the vaguest of notions regarding the conversation between the two men during those days" but maintains she was "well placed" to attribute to Michel those remarks about the overall innocuousness of homosexual choices: "He used more or less the same terms with me twenty years later, on a bench in Antibes where we sat looking at the sea. . . . On the beach at Scheveningue,[36] around 1905, that young man of thirty must have seemed to him just about as ignorant of the ways of the world as a twenty-year-old youth disturbed by an encounter with a young stranger who struck her as being different from other men. . . . He merely cautioned me against a tendency to dramatize life. . . . There was no sequel to the conversation in Antibes. In both cases, Michel had tried to calm a troubled mind or heart by pointing out that nothing is truly strange or unacceptable. He was not sharing personal secrets (Michel never confided in anyone); he was testifying."[37]

There are two possible interpretations of this anecdote. Either Yourcenar is disguising words pronounced on the subject of her own homosexual desires ("homosexual" being a term she never used: "too medical," she said)—and it was well within the temperament of Michel de Crayencour to point out to his daughter that she was not thereby experiencing anything exceptional—or else Yourcenar is telling the truth when she speaks of a "friend," and she had just fallen in love with a man who preferred men, which would happen to her several times over the course of her life. It is not certain, however, that Yourcenar ever brought up her taste for women in front of her father. Intimate matters, as she reiterated time and again, had little place in their dealings with one another. And since *Quoi? L'Eternité* is a book in which she clearly states how she came to have a taste for women—there being, thus, little reason for her to conceal the conversation's real subject—we can let the friend hypothesis stand. It is even more likely since the idea of unburdening herself of a painful personal situation by transmuting it into fiction was well within Yourcenar's modus operandi. She would do so again.

As the writing of *Alexis* progressed, Yourcenar would read a few pages to Michel, "a good listener who was capable of entering immediately into that character's inner life, so different from his own."[38] The account of Alexis's marriage even reminded Michel of a novel begun and abandoned, which he resuscitated for his daughter:

> These made up the first chapter of a novel, begun around 1904, which he had not developed any further. With the exception of a translation and some poems, it was the only literary work he ever undertook. . . . I was quite taken with the true-to-life tone of this story, which had no literary pretensions. . . . He suggested that I publish his tale under my own name. This offer, unusual if one thinks about it, was typical of the sort of free and easy intimacy that prevailed between us. I refused, for the simple reason that I was not the author of those pages. He insisted. . . .
>
> The playful scheme tempted me. Michel found nothing incongruous about attributing this story to my pen . . . , any more than he was surprised to see me writing Alexis's intimate thoughts. This man, who continually repeated that nothing human should be alien to us, viewed age and sex as merely secondary contingencies in the matter of literary creation. Problems that at a later date would leave my critics perplexed were not problems for him. . . . [T]he story was sent off to a journal, which rejected it after the usual delay, then to another, which accepted it; but by that time, my father was dead. The piece was published a year later and received a modest literary prize, an outcome that would have amused Michel but also would have pleased him.[39]

Just the same, it was surely a curious relationship that this father and daughter shared in which both of them would sign on the other's behalf, the first one writing to a publisher in the name of the second, the second one signing a text that was written by the first.

WHEN YOURCENAR finished *Alexis,* her father was very ill. He knew that he was going to die, that the cancer had spread throughout his body. He would have just enough time to read his daughter's first novel before his death, on 12 January 1929 in Lausanne: "My father did read the manuscript before he died," Yourcenar would tell Matthieu Galey. "He never discussed it with me, but I found a slip of paper stuck in the pages of the last book he opened, the letters of Alain-Fournier to Jacques Rivière. On it he had written, 'I've never read anything as limpid as *Alexis.*' You can imagine how happy I was! That final message contained all the friendship and understanding that my father and I shared."[40] In *Quoi? L'Eternité,* Yourcenar returns to this episode and changes the qualifying adjective in a significant way: "Michel read *Alexis* on his deathbed and noted in the margin of that short narrative that there was nothing 'more pure,' a comment that still moves me today, but which shows to what an extent the word 'pure' became on the lips of Michel something other than what it is for most fathers."[41] Was it pure or was it limpid? Was it a comment on the content or the form?

In addition to her accounts in *Archives du Nord,* Yourcenar would recall Michel's final months for Galey: "I took care of him, not very well, mind you," she told him, "because at the age of twenty-four a young woman has her own concerns, her own preoccupations, and is a mere novice when it comes to sickness and death. . . . At the age of twenty-four one still has far too much confidence in life.[42] But in the end I was with him: I saw him die. That taught me one lesson right off the bat, that he had lived a fine, successful life, when someone judging from outside might say that it had been a mad life of missed opportunities.

"I felt this immediately. I was old enough to judge. And he, too, felt it. He felt that his life had been very full."[43]

IN HER NOTEBOOK of preliminary writings for *Quoi? L'Eternité,* Yourcenar painted a portrait of Michel, capturing him, with successive brushstrokes, over all the years they shared. She relates this anecdote, among others: "One fine day while watching me read: 'If you died, I would take your books, your clothes, whatever is yours, and fill up a dinghy with everything; then I'd tow that dinghy out behind another boat and sink it all on the open sea.' I was eighteen years old. My imagination was struck by that violent image, that Viking's sacrifice. But his thoughts were already somewhere else."[44]

There is no question but that Michel de Crayencour was the first architect of Yourcenar's literary career. This should not give us license, however, to augment his influence, as there is always a tendency to do. He had the intelligence to accompany that remarkable child rather than attempt to mold her. No doubt he had a secret admiration, at the end of his life, for what she was in the process of becoming. And even if it is only what we might call one of life's "chance" occurrences, Michel de Crayencour's death, just before his daughter's first real book appeared, was like a sign. He disappeared at precisely the moment at which she became a writer, which is to say, absolutely herself.

It was at the moment when he was going to die that Yourcenar would see Michel cry remembering Jeanne, just as she had seen "tears overflow onto Madame de Reval's gray cheeks when pronouncing the name of that man who had been out of her life for so many years, and who continued to want nothing to do with her." It was thus that she became convinced of their mutual love, for, she adds, "memories rarely burn for such a long time unless, between two beings, there has been some kind of carnal complicity." [45]

Yourcenar dates her final break with her half brother to that period, for the notable reason that he did not attend his father's burial service:

> In January 1929, I wrote him from Lausanne to call him to his dying father's bedside. I was wrong to do so: Michel had asked me not to do anything of the kind. . . . Michel-Joseph responded that, involved as he was in building himself a house on the outskirts of Brussels, he could not put his hands on the money for this trip; besides which, in the midst of such a rigorous winter, and on the morning of a snowstorm, his wife had gone into hysterics at the thought of traveling to Switzerland. The facts of the matter were that this defender of all the finest family traditions was afraid he would have to foot a share of the expenses entailed by the long illness and funeral of a father who died poor and by whom he believed he had been wronged. [46]

Nonetheless, she had entrusted her financial interests to this brother whom she could barely stand; her funds were partially invested by him in a real estate venture that would completely fall apart in the great economic crisis of that year, aggravating the animosity between them, as she reports in *Archives du Nord*:

> The winds of the American crisis were already causing the European house of cards to teeter. The real estate investment bank collapsed. . . . The hotel caved in too, at least metaphorically. . . . I did what I should have done two years before: I appealed for help to an old French jurist who had already, in other circumstances, rescued Michel from some tight spots; with the help of one of his Belgian colleagues, he recuperated approximately half of the loan that had been granted to the hotelkeepers now in default. I decided that that sum, prudently nibbled away at, would be enough to afford me ten or twelve years of luxurious freedom. After that? We would see when the time came. . . . That decision, which I congratulate myself for having made, carried me through, with a thin safety margin, to September 1939. Living off the income from funds invested in Belgium and managed by my half brother, I would have continued to be more or less linked to a family with which I had nothing in common and to the country of my birth, my mother's country, which, in its present guise at least, was completely foreign to me. That nearly total financial debacle restored me to myself. [47]

Georges de Crayencour, for his part, believes that Yourcenar's account, as always when she speaks of her half brother, is unjust and partial. With regard to his father, Georges might, of course, fail to be very objective; but it is no less to be doubted that there is something deeply perfidious, on

Yourcenar's part, about imputing to her half brother the consequences of a convulsion that, in 1929, shook the most canny financiers. Moreover, in this passage from *Archives du Nord,* in which she settles her accounts with her half brother a bit rudely and with no excess of concern for nuance, Yourcenar herself tones down her account, recollecting a conversation with Michel-Joseph in Brussels in 1929, the last time they saw each other,[48] says she, when he accompanied her to the Midi Station:

> He envied me my freedom, which, for that matter, he exaggerated; life quickly sees to it that new ties are forged to replace those one believes one has undone; whatever one does and wherever one goes, walls go up around us and by our own efforts; they are shelters at first, and soon prisons. But these truths were not clear to me either at that time. That man who had willed himself to counter what his father had been felt that he had exhausted his allotment of choices in one fell swoop. "What can one do? I've created a family for myself; I can't strangle all those people." We both agreed that such a means of starting over would only have been suitable for Sultan Murad.[49] But, for the first time, I sensed in that man an instinct for freedom not so different from my own, just as his taste for genealogy counterbalanced my interest in history. It wasn't merely with respect to the arch of our eyebrows or the color of our eyes that we resembled one another.[50]

Shortly before Monsieur de Crayencour's death, Yourcenar had sent the manuscript of *Alexis,* signed Marg Yourcenar, to Gallimard, who turned it down.[51] No documents revealing what motivated that decision have been found. Perhaps the length of the work—more a short story than a novella, even less a novel—did not conform to the "editorial policy" existing at that time. So she offered it to a small house, Sans Pareil, that she admired for having published the Surrealists and whose director was the thirty-three-year old René Hilsum. As is often the case, Yourcenar's memory and that of other witnesses are in conflict here. She always maintained that she had not sent her text to Sans Pareil until after her father's death. Hilsum, whose memory did not seem to be failing and who enjoyed telling the story of his "discovery" of Marguerite Yourcenar (he died on 14 April 1990, in his ninety-fifth year), asserted to the contrary that she had been late responding to him when he had wanted to meet her to discuss this manuscript because, she said, she was at her dying father's bedside.

As Hilsum pointed out, "this uncertainty about the dates, which involves a few weeks, changes nothing essential with regard to the affair." "No doubt it was because of the strange name that she had made up, Marg Yourcenar, that I always had a clear recollection of the *Alexis* episode. And then what came to pass in Marguerite Yourcenar's career led me to tell the tale a few times. The manuscript arrived in the mail and was read by Louis Martin-Chauffier, who worked with me. His comment was: 'It is a remarkable, very interesting text, somewhat influenced by Gide.' Then we pondered over this 'Marg Yourcenar.' A pseudonym, without a doubt. But who was hiding behind it? A man or a woman? We tended to think it was a man, for one does not escape the stereotype of the 'woman's novel' or of 'feminine writing,' and *Alexis* did not fall within the province of either one. I wonder how on earth I managed to write to her using neither 'Monsieur' nor 'Madame.' Unfortunately, neither she nor I kept those first letters. When I wrote to her to say that I was interested in her short story—it really is a short story, when you get right down to it—she was in Lausanne. She answered me, explaining that she was a woman, that her first name was Marguerite, that Yourcenar was an anagram of her name, and that she did not wish to publish under her family name, Crayencour.

"The first time we met, I pointed out to her that this pseudonym was a bit mysterious. She responded to the effect that she did not consider that to be a drawback."[52] And she was right, for this exotic-sounding patronymic that calls to mind faraway places unknown, this name that strikes one as the very sign of something strange, played a part in the fascination that Marguerite Yourcenar would elicit, which goes beyond her work, bordering sometimes on fetishism. Marguerite de Crayencour, a good French writer, could not have become a star, indeed a myth. Marguerite Yourcenar could.

Hilsum, despite the sixty-some-odd years that had passed since his first interview with Yourcenar, recalled "very accurately her arrival in the offices of Editions Sans Pareil, on Rue Kléber at that time. Physically, she was astonishing. Rather more interesting than beautiful, to my eyes. Extraordinarily seductive, however. The first thing one noticed was her intelligence, which blazed, before she even spoke, in her eyes. She struck me even then as impressive. She was twenty-six years old, and I was thirty-four."[53]

With the first, modest sum brought in by her work as a writer, one hundred fifty francs, Yourcenar wanted to "splurge." She bought herself a blue Lalique vase, which she would keep all her life. It survived all the moves, the precipitous departures, and forgetfulness—a symbolic witness to her recognition as a writer: "what I had written was worth a little money, and was considered work, not a pastime," she confided.

To Jacques Chancel who asked her if she was aware of the position she held as a writer, she would confirm having been so on only one specific occasion in her life, at the time of the publication of *Alexis*, "which, all in all, was my first book; the first book that I had finished, that had a cover and a certain number of pages, whose advance copy I had gone to pick up from my publisher, the excellent René Hilsum. It was in November—on a fine, cold day in Paris . . . , I walked down the Champs-Elysées. I got to Place Vendôme, where I was going for I'm not quite sure what reason, and I said to myself: 'Now, just think! There are several hundred at least, perhaps several thousand, French writers one more or less remembers. So now I've done it, and I feel like I'm among them, somewhere in the crowd.' On that day, yes, I was conscious of being a writer. I believe that was the only day of my life when that idea preoccupied me."[54]

RELEASED AT THE END of November 1929, *Alexis* had the good luck to be noticed by Edmond Jaloux, with whom Yourcenar kept up friendly relations afterward. "Her novel surprised me, in the manner of a revelation," he wrote at that time.

> The revelation of a great new talent. Not that it was perfect. Far from it, even. Her book is hardly more than a preface—a long preface to a book that has not been written—but that preface is a fine one. Nonetheless, it lets you down. The novel ends when the action begins. It serves as a meticulous preliminary to a series of deeds that it purports to explain but that it does not explain. . . . It would behoove one to enter into the physical side of the subject, and Marguerite Yourcenar is loath to do so. She prefers an abstract style—which is the authentic French style, that of the highest tradition. . . . Madame Yourcenar's Alexis thus resembles Thomas de Quincey and Chateaubriand, Pierre Loti and Barrès, and he calls to mind . . . the traits of André Gide's Michel. . . . What is particularly fine about *Alexis ou Le Traité du vain combat* (a rather too Gidean title in my opinion) is the timbre of the style and, I would almost go so far as to say, of the voice. The voice is low and deep, and soft of modulation; it is tender and harsh at the same time, descending to the deepest depths of conscience and stirring feelings in us that only great writers have so thoroughly aroused, making itself heard, amid the din of contemporary literature, with all the assurance of its highly pure tone, despite its almost faraway resonance. . . . Where his race, his predispositions, and his character are concerned, Alexis Géra often recalls Malte Laurids Brigge: Rainer Maria Rilke's influence on Madame Yourcenar must have been considerable, moreover; some of her thoughts were clearly inspired by him. . . . The book's conclusion is fully supported throughout the entire book; only the experiential details pertaining to the marriage of Monique and Alexis and to their separation lack clarity. We suspect more than we see, but I quite believe the author wanted it this way.
>
> Certain pages of *Alexis* remind one of Benjamin Constant, owing as much to the icy music of the style as to the depth of inner observation. One out of every three sentences would be worthy of citing and remembering; to say that the psychological power of this brief volume sometimes equals that of our great, hallowed works is to give you an idea of its richness.[55]

"Saturated though it is by the influence of Gide in its inspiration, its style, and its form, this book is nonetheless remarkable," judged Paul Morand, for his part, on the pages of the *Courrier Littéraire*. "This little, pithy book should be given a choice spot in the library, between Helvétius and the author of *Les Nourritures terrestres (Fruits of the Earth)*."[56] "Most astonishing," he adds, "is that this is the work of a woman, who has succeeded at identifying herself with her subject so completely that *Alexis* truly is the confession of a man fallen victim to his penchants, so completely that there is not one line of this lucid, discreet, and thus all the more pathetic, confession that does not ring admirably true." This is a comment that would be addressed to Yourcenar her whole life long, as much by men as by women, and to which, not without a certain testiness, she would tirelessly offer the same response. For example, in the postface of "Anna, Soror . . . ," she evokes "that indifference to sex which is, I believe, that of all creators in the presence of their creations," and points out in a note: "One might cite here the experience Flaubert recounts to Louise Colet in a letter written at the time of the composition of *Madame Bovary*: 'Today, for example, both a man and a woman, a lover and a mistress at the same time, I rode on horseback through a forest beneath the yellow leaves of an autumn afternoon, and I was the horses, the leaves, the wind, the words they spoke, and the red sun which closed their eyelids brimming with love.'"[57]

Alexis received this recognition from the critics, which was far from nothing for a twenty-six-year-old novelist, but it did not achieve what we could even call a succès d'estime among the general public: "That text met with absolutely no success," said Hilsum. "A first book, by someone unknown, with that impossible name . . . Unlikely. It came as no surprise. Moreover, if *Alexis* was not a bad book, I did not think it was the seed of an *œuvre*. I saw no signs to that effect."

One finds in that book, notably, beyond certain literary influences, some savory passages on the subject of the public's lack of understanding (a theme that would continue to be dear to Yourcenar, but that she would subsequently reserve for conversations rather than her books): "You do not read the newspapers, but mutual friends will have told you that I enjoy what is called success—which is to say nothing more than that many people praise me without having heard me and some without having understood me."[58]

"Nevertheless, I am happy to have published that text," Hilsum insisted, "and not only in light of what Marguerite Yourcenar became. Besides which, *Alexis* marked the last year that Sans Pareil flourished. I am sure that if I had kept my firm, Marguerite Yourcenar would have continued to publish with me. She never forgot me, and we always had, if not intimate relations, at least very privileged ones."

MARG YOURCENAR was quite proud of this first real book that, finally, gave her a genuine right to this name born of her and her father, but that broke with all other family ties. Rereading it in 1963, at which time she wrote her preface, Yourcenar, who had expected to find it terribly dated, was surprised that it "possess[ed] a sort of relevance":

> [E]xcept in matters concerning a few infelicities of style, this little book has been left as it was. There are two reasons for this, which at first glance may seem contradictory: one is the highly personal character of a confession strictly limited to a milieu, a time, and a land now vanished from maps; a confession, moreover, impregnated with the old-fashioned atmosphere of Central (and essentially French) Europe, in which the slightest detail could not have been changed without transforming the acoustics of the book. The second reason, in contrast, is the fact that this story, judging from the reactions it continues to provoke, seems to possess a sort of relevance, and even usefulness, for some people.[59]

Ten years after *Alexis* appeared, on the occasion of a lecture on the then still-limited *œuvre* of Marguerite Yourcenar given in Brussels, the Catholic essayist Gonzague Truc invoked the character Alexis in terms that are at the very least ambiguous, in which a fierce moralism pierces through an apparent display of admiration:

> Several years ago, Madame Yourcenar published, at "Sans Pareil," one of those bold publishers that do not tend to last very long, a slim volume whose subject should have brought it widespread attention, had this subject not been treated with as much faithfulness as dignity. It was called *Alexis ou Le Traité du vain combat* and concerned a homosexual who could not manage to be cured. Many of you will be reminded, naturally, of the literature of Monsieur André Gide—to leave the matter there—but you will be mistaken. For Madame Yourcenar, both in her study and by virtue of her intentions, places herself well beyond and, I dare say, well above that other literature: if Monsieur André Gide had chosen to treat her subject, there would have been no question of a cure.
>
> By Madame Yourcenar, the scandalous material was manipulated with an incredible delicacy; and though her words, all decency and delicacy, seem foreign to a topic such as this one, they are, however, those that must be used. The drama, a real drama, was nuanced by imperceptible touches of a nonetheless profound and heartrending truth; the essence of that truth seemed just as present and perhaps more moving than in the unforgettable

analyses of Proust: a kind of fatal monstrosity, a natural perversion of the feelings and the organs, a sin or a fall that, though unacceptable, one had to accept, the pain and, in the end, the sterile, hard serenity born of a hideous choice.[60]

One could easily pass over the unforgettable Gonzague Truc's "analysis," but for this episode: In 1977, some forty years after Truc's comments, which one could well have thought classified once and for all as ridiculous, a young woman proposed a certain manuscript to Yourcenar, a "contemporary" response of sorts to Alexis's letter. In this piece, a rich Monique—an ardent devotee of Maseratis you can coax up to "two hundred forty kilometers an hour"—was still striving to "cure" Alexis and to make him undergo "homosexuality treatments." To begin with, Yourcenar expressed deep shock at her correspondent's attempt to commit this literary "abduction": "A character taken outright from another writer will never be lifelike or ductile in the hands of the appropriating novelist; he or she will always seem 'tacked on,' with the result that the impropriety involved in using such a character will be immediately recompensed by defeat of a literary order." But she was more critical of the woman's bad reading of her novel and of the way that Alexis was treated: "The real Monique de Géra would possess neither this sentimentalism (which is extremely irksome), nor this tendency to confuse 'success' in Alexis's musical career with a fulfillment of an entirely different order, dreamed of by a young musician who disdains any notion of 'glory'; she certainly would not possess this indelicate possessiveness that makes her try to 'cure' Alexis, instead of benevolently accepting him as he is, nor, above all, this naive confidence in psychoanalysis (do not forget that Freud was practicing in Vienna during her time). Dare I say that Monique becomes, in your hands, a character fit for women's romance magazines? In any event, it is less a question in *Alexis* of a minor case of sexual incompatibility (or quasi-incompatibility) between spouses than of the process undergone within the mind of a scrupulous and timid man slowly ridding himself of certain fears and certain prejudices peculiar to a moral code that he judges conventional. Even what you have called your novel, 'Un Garçon nommé Eros' [A Boy Named Eros], is the kind of 'catchy' title that would be enough to keep me from buying the book. Poor Alexis . . . He was so reserved, so austere really, so little the seducer, probably not even handsome."[61]

A close reading of the preface of *Alexis*, considered final since it is included in the Pléiade edition of Yourcenar's prose works, refutes in a radical way such interpretations as these, which are either stupid or delirious—or, as we have just seen, both at once. Here is how it ends: "Certain subjects are in the air at certain moments; they are also in the fabric of a life." If male homosexuality fascinated Yourcenar to the point of becoming an almost-always-present subject in her books, it clearly was not because she saw it as an aberration, much less an illness. Nor was it to conceal her love of women while speaking of it all the while, as she was so often mistakenly accused of doing. Nor did she dream of being a man—though men will never be convinced of this. No matter. The fact is that male homosexuality was indeed "in the fabric" of her life, particularly over the years that would follow the publication of *Alexis* and her father's death, those years of conquering nomadism during which, more than at any other stage of her existence, she would follow in the wandering footsteps of Michel de Crayencour.

PART 2

"The Wanderings"

5

Nomadism of the Heart and of the Mind

ONCE *ALEXIS* WAS PUBLISHED, Yourcenar went back to Lausanne, to write. She had a room in her stepmother's apartment. But she soon stopped staying there, preferring Lausanne's Hôtel Meurice for her stopovers between one trip and another. She was working on a novel, *La Nouvelle Eurydice* [The New Eurydice], on various articles, and on a short play, *Le Dialogue dans le marécage* [Dialogue on the Marsh].

However one interprets her quarrels with her half brother, one thing was still certain at the beginning of this decade, regarding Yourcenar's financial situation: it was quite precarious. She was not to be one of those heiresses who, never paying any mind to material concerns, can devote themselves to writing simply as a chosen pastime. Having been "saved from total ruin by a man of the law," as she would say, she decided to augment the small amount of money she had salvaged with the proceeds from the sale of nearly all her valuable possessions. As we have seen, she determined that by keeping an eye on her spending she could live off this modest sum for ten or twelve years: this period of guaranteed freedom seemed preferable to her to immediately seeking out security for the future, which certainly would have entailed other constraints.

We don't know how Yourcenar mourned her father's death. She always spoke and acted as if, during that year, 1929, the publication of her first novel had displaced the center of gravity of her concerns, compensating for the loss of the man who had been her constant, and nearly unique, interlocutor for twenty-six years. But she was not one to dwell for long on her distress. Much later, she would simply speak of her father's "return" to her daily existence, nearly fifty years after his death, when she undertook to tell the story of her family. Everything we know about her demonstrates that—except at the very end of her life, a period for which amnesty is granted in advance—she had little taste for brooding over her troubles, even less for seeing virtue in pain. This is even more so since she did not participate in the denegation of death—a phenomenon peculiar to the twentieth century. Monsieur de Crayencour's death came at the close of a life filled with pleasures and freedom. Yourcenar was certainly grieved by it. She did not plunge into despair. With a clarity of mind that would only seem brutal in the view of a vacuous pseudopropriety—and that was no doubt an utmost refinement of courtesy, thoroughly devoid of pointless rhetoric—she would be able to say to Galey: "[A]fter I shed tears over his death (which came when I was twenty-five), I confess that I almost forgot him for nearly thirty years. Which wouldn't have shocked or surprised my father, because a young person should forget and should live. It wasn't until much later that my father again occupied my thoughts for fairly long periods."[1]

Predominant during the year of 1930, when she was not absorbed by her work, was a feeling of boredom. She did not wish to talk with her stepmother, and she missed her conversations with her father. She missed their mutual, implicit understanding, their intellectual complicity, the readings they had shared. Besides which, and contrary to the legend that would be built up around her when she became famous, Yourcenar did not like solitude. Once she got up from her work table, she liked conversation, taking walks, having tea or a drink, in company with others. She liked listening, talking, seducing.

What seemed, thus, to be evolving was one of those slow and studious, rather colorless years, brightened only by the prospect of a few trips. But one day in Paris, at Editions Grasset, a young man opened "a cabinet in which were kept some manuscripts we had decided not to publish," he recalled, where he discovered Yourcenar's *Pindare*. That man's name was André Fraigneau, and he would play a key role in Yourcenar's career, but also in her private life. After studying at Montpellier, Fraigneau, who wanted to become a writer—and would—began working at Grasset, as an intern, during the summer of 1929.[2] "I was twenty-two years old," he recalls. "It was during the summer. Bernard Grasset was on vacation. When he got back, he asked who 'the new one' was that wrote clear reader's reports, and such short ones—some ten lines. I was pointed out to him. He hired me. In 1930, when I found the *Pindare* manuscript in the 'discards' cabinet, the name Yourcenar was not unknown to me. I had read *Alexis*. What I found in that biographical essay was talent and quality, the characteristics, even then, that would distinguish all the Marguerite Yourcenar works that I saw to publishing. I believed we had to publish this one. And I was convincing."[3]

But no one knew where Yourcenar was any more. The address in the south of France that appeared on the manuscript had long since been invalid. Editions Sans Pareil, which could have helped to find her, had disappeared. Thanks to René Hilsum, however, Fraigneau got an address in Lausanne. Yourcenar responded and came to Paris to meet him. "I no longer can say what time of year it was when this took place," Fraigneau admits today, "perhaps in summer, or in the fall." And since Yourcenar banished his name from the chronology of her life—for reasons that the thirties will elucidate—there is hardly any way of determining precisely the date of that first meeting at this point. To that first appointment, Yourcenar brought *La Nouvelle Eurydice*, her second novel, which Fraigneau decided to publish before *Pindare*. He would remain her editor throughout that whole decade and would relentlessly promote her to Bernard Grasset—who was sometimes concerned about sales that barely topped eight hundred copies. "As for *Pindare*," says Fraigneau, "she had almost forgotten about it. It was like an adolescent sin for her. But she was one of those people who attain maturity right away, in their first works."

It was thus that *La Nouvelle Eurydice* appeared in 1931 at Grasset. Yourcenar proved very severe with regard to this text: "too full of purely literary developments, [it] had neither the force nor the unity of tone of *Alexis.*"[4] "After *Alexis*," she related to Matthieu Galey,

> events in my life were such that I was unable immediately to begin writing again. Then I retraced my own steps, which was a mistake. Telling myself that the time had come to begin my career as a writer (how conventional youth is!), I wrote a bad novel—*La Nouvelle Eurydice*. This novel . . . has its loyal admirers, but I'm not one of them. I wanted to "do" a novel, and of course nothing came of it because I was then convinced that to be a genuine novelist one had to find a subject in reality and transform it into fiction. I had formed my own idea of what a novel ought to be: it needed episodes of this or that kind, a love interest, landscapes, this, that, and the other. You can imagine what a mess I got myself into! . . . It was an extremely "literary" work, and I intend that as a reproach.[5]

It was a text worthy of "reproach," to the point where she forbade its republication. "Nonetheless, that was a time when she had grace," comments Fraigneau, who by far prefers the prewar works to those that came after, which brought celebrity to Yourcenar.

La Nouvelle Eurydice presents one of those trios that Yourcenar had a liking for: a man—Stanislas, the narrator—and a couple, Thérèse and Emmanuel, who are friends of his. Stanislas falls in love with Thérèse. Thérèse keeps on loving Emmanuel, although he prefers men. It is true that this text does not have the force of *Alexis*, and that this second short novel is not as well executed as the first. Yourcenar had probably wanted to transpose more clearly in that book things she had sensed about the trio of Michel de Crayencour, Jeanne de Vietinghoff, and Conrad de Vietinghoff, but her effort to turn them into "literature" had somehow weakened the story. She had avoided neither literary pastiche, nor grandiloquence, nor peremptory simplifications: "right up to the end, Emmanuel and his wife had not ceased to be united, not only by tenderness, but by the thousand habits that intertwine two lives, the rest, after all, being only of passing significance."[6]

If there is pleasure to be had from acquainting oneself with this text, as a document, one can easily understand why Yourcenar had no desire to include it in the Pléiade edition of her prose works. It is nonetheless true that a certain taste, prevalent today, for "lesser masters," for dated texts, would perhaps cause some to say, as Fraigneau still maintains, that *La Nouvelle Eurydice* has a kind of grace. What remains to be seen is whether grace is, for everyone, a literary virtue.

In *La Revue de France,* in which one of the very first critical appraisals of the work appeared, Pierre Audiat—in a style very heavily marked by its era, but with such well-worn comments as would continue over time (wonder of wonders, the author is a woman!)—cannot sing enough praises:

> A novel swollen with mystery as the invisible wind swells the thin sail. It will no doubt be clear that we feel here a very particular joy in greeting the first great work of Madame M. Yourcenar. . . . To tell you the truth, if we did not publish a picture of the author at the same time we announced the appearance of her book, *La Nouvelle Eurydice,* people would refuse to believe that this author was a woman. It is impossible to detect in the story those often charming weaknesses . . . by which one identifies a feminine pen. The hand does not yield, it does not caress the paper; it is clasped by an iron gauntlet that obliges it to write with two fingers stretched taut, the little finger barely grazing the writing case. . . . The result is not impassiveness, but a lucidity that contrasts with the story's obscurity, entirely psychological, and which is one of the qualities of what we still call the "classical." Without going back as far as *Adolphe (Adolphe),*[7] which is eternally evoked in such cases, we must cite the influence of André Gide, which is visible here and almost palpable. . . . There are brilliant reflections, gemstones set handsomely in words, brief and striking evocations of a nature complicitous always with love and with death; and a painful echo of human anxiety.[8]

But other assessments are distinctly less enthusiastic: "Shall I shame myself by admitting it? I do not see what this story has in common with the myth of Orpheus," writes Louis de Mondadon in the review *Etudes.* "Nor, for that matter, is this the only point of obscurity. I defy the reader to see his way clearly through the labyrinth of sentimental complications into which he is dragged by the thousand tangled strands of this exaggeratedly detailed analysis."[9]

Edmond Jaloux, for his part, ponders over the negative responses provoked by the publication of the volume:

> The critics were hard on *La Nouvelle Eurydice*, and I am not exactly sure
> why. Did its both abstract and delicate form appear outmoded to certain
> of our colleagues? . . . Like Monsieur Jacques Chardonne, whom Madame
> Yourcenar reminds one of sometimes, she is even more of a moralist than a
> novelist, and her comments on her heroes' situation are almost always admi-
> rable. It is by virtue of those comments that she really situates them in life
> and in the action. . . .
>
> I have already called attention to this characteristic of Madame Margue-
> rite Yourcenar, when I spoke in this very place about *Alexis ou Le Traité du
> vain combat;* I found it again, more mature and more profound still, in *La
> Nouvelle Eurydice.* . . . The criticism that I could address to her is one that I
> would make regarding all works of this sort: it is that the commentary's qual-
> ity itself, the depth of the author's reflections, the intensity of the abstract
> analysis, shunts the characters into the background somewhat and that they
> often seem to be serving in a psychological experiment rather than being
> real, flesh-and-blood beings. But, after all, this defect is one that is inherent,
> inevitably, to this type of book. What needs to be said is that Madame Mar-
> guerite Yourcenar succeeds at writing works of lasting quality, in a tradition
> that is at once one of the most difficult and one of the purest.[10]

As for *Pindare*, written when she was twenty-three, serially published
almost in its entirety in 1931 in the review *Le Manuscrit Autographe*,[11] and
published as a book by Grasset also in 1931, Yourcenar was also harsh and
similarly forbade its inclusion in her complete works.[12] She faults its too
scholarly side—and its style as well, however—and a manner of assertion
lacking neither audacity nor haughtiness that is peculiar to "what one
thinks one knows when, in fact, one has hardly begun the process of learning," she would confide.

Pindare is the only work of Yourcenar's to which Jaloux did not devote
one of his "Esprit des livres" columns in *Les Nouvelles Littéraires*. He would,
however, say about this book, at the time of his review of *Feux* (*Fires*), that
it was an "excellent work." As Fraigneau—whose talent was also perceived
by Jaloux—explains, "Jaloux's reviews didn't 'sell,' as people would now
say, preoccupied as they are by nothing else, but they established reputa-
tions. Back then there were only two or three critics that counted, and Jaloux was the very first."

PINDARE, at least for the critic and the exegete—despite the reservations it
generated and its author's disavowal—is still more interesting, in many

ways, than *La Nouvelle Eurydice.* We find many more traces in this work of what was to be Yourcenar's universe, her thought, and even her style. We can glean a few aphorisms from *Pindare* that Yourcenar would be attached to all her life: "He was reaching the age where egoism is as much a virtue as it is a necessity," or else "Every life contains a failure, and glory, when it comes, only serves to call more attention to it."[13] We also find this innocuous sentence, which must be noted, even as early as *Pindare:* "The Greek race, which some imagine as eternally serene, was too intelligent not to have known sadness."[14] It's not the Greeks that matter here but the use of the word "race." For, later on, people accused Yourcenar of anti-Semitism based on her reference to the Jewish "race." Now, if the debate about Yourcenar's anti-Semitism remains pertinent, one can in no way deploy as an argument her use of the word "race." In keeping with practice current at the time, it was used for "people," in both her work and her private correspondence. She continued this throughout her whole life; *Pindare* was only the first example. Finally, in evoking Pindar's old age and his amorous passions late in life, the young woman that Yourcenar was when she wrote this book made some astonishingly premonitory remarks. Through Pindar, she sketched something of a self-portrait of the old woman that she would become: "At all stages of his life, one could glimpse a lively sensuality in Pindar. This is a positive quality. . . . That simple sensuality disciplined itself in art. . . . With age, as always, his rather haughty reserve diminished: a weakening will could no longer hold instinct in check. It is toward the end, in the formless writing on the final pages, that intimate tastes and torments are revealed. Regret: that remembrance of desire. . . . Let the reader not consider himself obliged to exhibit at this inappropriate juncture what few remaining principles he has. This taste for young beauty is a frequent one in those who are getting on in years."[15] She who had Alexis say "As a child, I yearned for glory"—and who would admit much later on to having spoken of herself in this way—ends her essay on Pindar with this sentence: "The only lesson we can learn from this life, so distant from our own, is that glory after all is nothing more than a temporary concession."[16]

AS FOR THAT "temporary concession," to which she did not yet have the latitude to aspire, no doubt Yourcenar would not have disdained it. And who could blame her? Thus she plied her writer's trade, in earnest and with conscientiousness. In 1932, *La Revue de France* published *Le Dialogue dans le marécage,* about which Yourcenar would say that it was written "at the latest in 1931, perhaps even as early as 1929."[17] "The little play that follows," she would say in the preface to the reedition of this text, in 1971, "owes its inspiration to an insignificant event that took place during the Italian Middle Ages, the story of a Sienese patrician, Pia Tolomei, relegated to an unhealthy château in Maremma by a jealous husband who left her there to die. This moving anecdote, an invented one of course, is known to us by way of the commentaries surrounding four rather cryptic verses that Dante devoted to it in Canto V of his *Purgatorio*."[18] "Unconsciously" inspired by her discovery of Japanese Nō plays, toward the end of the twenties, Yourcenar would say that she had encountered again upon rereading her play "a bit of the sensuality that is found everywhere throughout D'Annunzio, and, especially, a bit of the poignant, as if mumbled, emotion of Maeterlinck," on which her adolescence had been nourished.[19] But—as she had already pointed out in *Icare*—she would particularly insist that *Le Dialogue dans le marécage*, like "Sixtine" ("Sistine"),[20] another brief work written "in the same key during those years, and in which I tried to evoke in a few pages an aged Michelangelo, is above all the portrait of an old man, or at least of a man who has grown older."[21]

SHE STARTED writing *A Coin in Nine Hands* the same year, in Italy. Alongside it, she worked on recasting certain stories extracted from her long novel that would never see the light of day, *Remous*. The literary activities to which she was applying herself—no doubt less regularly than she would later on—did not prevent those years from being a nomadic time. Nomadism would be one of the constants of her life, and at that time, it was carried to its highest extreme, since she had no permanent address. Also included in those constants of her life is what she would have called, without any pejorative implication, "a certain dissipation": meaning alcohol (a little), men (no doubt a few), and women (a lot, beyond a doubt). When she was in Paris, she frequented the tea shops where women met, particularly the Thé Colombin, on Rue du Mont-Thabor, right next to her hotel, and the Wagram, located at 208 Rue de Rivoli. As for that period of "dissipation," she always maintained the highest degree of discretion, confiding only at the very end of her life her fascination for night life, red-light districts, and debauchery, which, until then, had only appeared in her work. Witnesses and photographs alone reveal how much she liked love and conquest.

She always laid claim, on the contrary, to her nomadism. She alluded to numerous trips to Italy and Austria. She frequently stayed in Vienna, for which she had a particular liking, and traveled up and down the Danube, between Vienna and Belgrade. It was also in Vienna that she met the Austrian philosopher Rudolf Kassner.[22] She had a great deal of respect and admiration for this scholar, a keen lover of travel, with a passion for theater and mythology. And she would be pleased to meet up with him again some twenty years later, in Sierre, Switzerland, where he had been residing since 1946. Her first meetings with the essayist and literary critic Charles Du Bos, a friend of Gide and Jacques Rivière, also date back to this period.[23] Having converted to Catholicism in 1927, Du Bos, the author of *Approximations* [Approximations], exchanged with Yourcenar during the final two years of his life, 1938 and 1939, a very interesting correspondence, centered on spiritual questions.

THESE WERE also the years of discovering Greece. André Fraigneau recalls that, while reading *Pindare*, he had been convinced that its author knew Greece well. Such was not at all the case. He had just discovered Greece himself. "Gaston Baissette[24] had just published his much-trumpeted *Hippocrate* [Hippocrates] at Grasset, and the same publisher was printing Marguerite Yourcenar's *Pindare*. The two young French writers were not familiar with the Greece of which they spoke, but they did so with such a prescience that I—just back from Athens, bedazzled and making my bedazzlement known (*Les Voyageurs transfigurés* [Travelers Transformed], Gallimard)—was astonished by it. I invited them to make the journey as Mario Meunier and the painter Salvat had invited me to. . . . One might say that we lived from then on only for Greece and through Greece, for months, to the point where we lost all feeling for the present and were living in that intermediary space of the Fabulous and the Everyday described in the immortal *Gradiva* (*Gradiva, a Pompeiian Fancy*)."[25] All three gave themselves over to the literary game of writing sketches based on this or that myth. Thus did each one develop a text evoking the myth of the Labyrinth. Yourcenar's, moreover, *Ariane et l'aventurier* [Ariane and the Adventurer], provided the point of departure for the play she would write during the mid-forties: *Qui n'a pas son Minotaure?* (*To Each His Minotaur*).

Fraigneau recommended Yourcenar to one of his Greek friends, André Embiricos, a writer and a psychoanalyst.[26] The first half of the thirties, therefore, brought about the appearance of the two Andrés, about whom Yourcenar would always maintain—without citing their surnames—that they were two men who counted in her existence. Beginning in 1932 and up until 1939, Yourcenar's life, as she herself has stated, was "centered on Greece," as much in the private domain as in her literary activity. She studied and worked on the Greek poet Constantine Cavafy with a Greek intellectual of her own age, Constantine Dimaras. "During that period," she confided, "I stayed in Greece for several months every year. As for the rest of the time, I would generally spend the winter or the spring in Paris—

though my stays were, of course, interrupted by various excursions—at the Hôtel Wagram." Those were the years during which "the very notion of myth itself played a truly essential role."[27] It was a notion that would nourish three of the works written during that period: *Fires, Nouvelles orientales* (*Oriental Tales*), and *Les Songes et les sorts* [Dreams and Destinies]. During that time, in 1935 and 1936, she published a few essays in *Le Voyage en Grèce*, a review to which Pierre Reverdy, François Mauriac, Roger Callois, and Roger Vitrac contributed.[28]

Yourcenar would say to one of her correspondents that Greece revealed to her "these four essential truths: That [this country] was the great event (perhaps the only great event) in the history of humanity. That this miracle was the product of a particular land, a particular sky; that passion, sensual ardor, and the most fervent vitality in all of its forms explain and nourish this miracle, and that the Greek equilibrium and wisdom of which we have heard so much are not the meager equilibrium nor the poor wisdom of professors; and finally, as follows from what precedes, at least in part, that Greek art, history, and literature are often badly taught."[29] But, as far as the works subsequent to that period are concerned, Yourcenar would sometimes show her irritation with the somewhat too hasty and systematic reference made by critics to her hellenism: "You are thoroughly correct in noting that my work is not, essentially, hellenic," she would write to a young student, "or is so only because all of the spiritual tendencies, if one searches carefully, can be found at the heart of hellenism. A certain 'classical' conception of my books is very widespread, and very naive. I very quickly recovered from any blind faith I might have had concerning Greece."[30]

BUT IN 1934, it was Italy that pervaded the two books appearing at Grasset—two books that served as proof, if such were needed, of Yourcenar's determination to show that her decision to be a writer was a radical and final one. First she published *A Coin in Nine Hands*, which she would entirely redo in 1959. *A Coin in Nine Hands* is the "half-realistic, half-symbolic story of an attempted anti-Fascist assassination in Rome in the year XI [1933] of the dictatorship. . . . [A] certain number of tragicomic characters, sometimes linked to the main drama, sometimes totally divorced from it, but almost all more or less consciously affected by the conflicts and slogans of their times, are grouped around three or four heroes of the central episode."[31] A coin circulates from one hand to another, thus linking the characters and episodes: "the ten-lira coin, . . . the symbol of contact between human beings each lost in his own passions and in his intrinsic solitude."[32]

For Yourcenar this novel's genesis could be traced back to her trips to

Rome during the twenties. It was linked, as well, to her association with Italian intellectuals. "Marcella," she would say to Matthieu Galey regarding the heroine of *A Coin in Nine Hands,* is "largely based on an Italian woman I knew at the time. . . . [S]everal of the novel's characters . . . were members of militant antifascist groups, and it was through them that I shared in the excitement and emotion of the moment." "I had a rather clear image of Italy," she continues further on, "but the problem was that I didn't know what details to use to convey that image. That's undoubtedly why I redid the book years later with the same details decanted or further developed. I saw fascism as something grotesque. I had seen the march on Rome: gentlemen of 'good family' sweating under their black shirts and beating people who didn't agree with them. It wasn't pleasant to look at. And I was never taken in by the claims of unanimous support. No country is ever fully in agreement with its government. It never happens. Rural people and workers weren't won over. They simply kept quiet."[33]

André Fraigneau does not conceal his indignation with regard to that "rewrite": "The first *Coin in Nine Hands* was absolutely not anti-Mussolini, as opposed to the one that is available today," he asserts. "At that time, Marguerite Yourcenar had no preoccupation whatsoever of that sort. She adapted very well to life in fascist Italy. It was after the Second World War that she was moved to give that novel a political coloration. For my part, I find the idea of rewriting a novel in order to reorient its meaning quite intolerable. Better to write another book. This is a way of going about things that I ill understand and object to." Fraigneau may be excessive in accusing the novel of departing from its forebear, for reasons that pertain to his "sympathies" during the war; but no doubt it is not false to say that the new version of *A Coin in Nine Hands* puts more emphasis on the political aspects of the plot than the first. Moreover, Yourcenar acknowledged this herself: "Like all the [other] themes in this book, [however, and perhaps more so,] the political one is reinforced and developed in the present version . . . ," she would point out in the preface of the 1959 version.

> The repercussions of the political drama on secondary characters are more deeply etched. . . .
> Perhaps no one will be surprised that political evil plays a bigger part in this version than it did in the older one, or that the *Denier du rêve* of 1959 is more bitter or more ironic than the one of 1934. Rereading the new parts of the book as though someone else had written them, however, I'm especially cognizant of the fact that the text is now both a little more scathing and a little less dark, that certain judgments about human nature are perhaps less cutting and yet less vague. . . . The feeling that the human story is even more

tragic, if that's possible, than we suspected a quarter of a century ago, but also more complicated, richer, sometimes simpler, and especially stranger than I had tried to depict it then—this was perhaps my strongest reason for rewriting the book.[34]

Jaloux saw in this work more a novelistic montage serving as a pretext for reflection than a primary concern with creating an accomplished piece of fiction:

> The event ["an assassination attempt mounted, in Rome, against a Chief of State"] plays no role in the novel of Mademoiselle Marguerite Yourcenar. The only things that count are ideas, at least the ideas that move beings to act, which is to say the passions, which are eternal. . . . As we make our way through the work, we have the feeling we're disturbing phantoms. Marguerite Yourcenar's characters are real, carved out of real flesh, but they themselves move in a world so troubled by fictions of the mind that they most often seem, to one another, like ghosts—even at those times when they are most specifically the victims of their exigent, ill, or wounded bodies. . . .
>
> This ensemble makes up a rare book that demands attention, that is of rich moral import, and that makes us live in a special world, at once tragically real and intellectually stylized, modern in its form and stripped bare in its conception of all the artful ploys of our time.[35]

In the review *Etudes,* Louis de Mondadon proves even more fierce than he had been for *La Nouvelle Eurydice:* "The perhaps symbolic characters imagined by Madame Yourcenar seek to extract themselves after a fashion from the realities into which I know not what absurd and cruel Demiurge plunged them. You would do likewise, I think, if your life, like theirs, were dull, gray, workaday, lacking any kind of ideal. In truth, the stories Madame Yourcenar tells us are very gloomy and pathetic ones. She felt obliged, in an attempt to spice things up, to sprinkle her account with ribald or irreligious touches: far from adding anything agreeable, this tactic only serves to heighten one's sense of mediocrity."[36]

IN 1934, *La Mort conduit l'attelage* also appeared, a collection of three narratives salvaged from *Remous,* that "immense novel—unrealizable and unrealized," first mapped out in 1921, then abandoned.[37] Yourcenar dedicated this book "to the memory of [her] father." The two critics previously cited remained faithful to their usual manner of reading Yourcenar. In the review *Etudes*—aligned, let it be recalled, with Catholicism—Mondadon displays total contempt, and expresses an unqualified blame: "So full of enigmas are

they that one would need to write a lengthy commentary in order to expli-
cate the three short stories in which Madame Yourcenar attempted, if I am
not mistaken, to symbolize, after the fashion of Dürer, Greco, and Rembrandt, various aspects of the irreligious and lascivious Renaissance. Engraved beneath its title, the book bears the image of a woman bestriding a
skeleton. It is more a question of guessing at than distinguishing the em-
blems she holds. Even her features are imprecise. The text corresponds to
this almost indecipherable frontpiece: what, in point of fact, is it all about?
Let the curious feel free to go find out; I am merely warning them that they
risk wasting their time. I would add that the revolting vices of one or another of the characters will require one's condemnation, even if one has
understood something."[38] Presumably, "the revolting vices" were homosexuality ("D'après Dürer") and incest ("D'après Greco"). For his part,
Jaloux writes "Madame Yourcenar feels wonderfully at ease, be it in certain
eras of the Middle Ages, be it at the beginning of the Renaissance."

> But [she] does not turn to the past for purposes of historical reconstruction.
> She has neither the soul of an archeologist, nor that of a paleographical archi-
> vist, nor that of a draper. And perhaps not precisely that of a psychologist.
> Her objective is to paint pictures of human life and to show us that those
> pictures are always the same, despite outward differences in custom or dress,
> and despite the multitude of forms that fanaticism, stupidity, and cruelty
> can take. . . .
>   The only thing for which I would criticize Madame Yourcenar is that her
> narrative sometimes lacks clarity. . . . *La Mort conduit l'attelage* is nonetheless
> a work of high value and one that further augments the interest we bear this
> author, such a personal one, and one in whom, at least, we encounter none
> of the literary fashions, nor the practices that are standard with so many
> writers.[39]

THAT YEAR, in the month of August, a young American woman made her
first trip to Europe with her uncle George La Rue. Both of them left Paris
for England at the end of the month. While her uncle departed again for
the United States, the young woman went to Germany. She would return
to the United States at the end of September, after having stopped in Paris
again. That thirty-one-year-old American was named Grace Frick. Her
path would not cross Marguerite Yourcenar's until nearly three years later.
And both of their lives would be radically changed.

In 1934, Yourcenar met lots of women. She enjoyed seducing them. She
could hardly stand to be resisted. She also sought to seduce men, as those
who saw her often over the course of that decade recall. She did so with less

success, though, which is not very surprising once one has seen the young man's look she had adopted for herself. And yet, she was in love with a man—in love as she had never been before, and would never be again, she thought. He was blond and very handsome, very much in keeping with her tastes. He was intelligent, and, no matter what he may say about it now—trying, as he does, to claim that she had "told herself stories"—he was the man of her life. It was her editor, the one who read over her work— "without changing anything," he says, "it was impeccable"—encouraged her, supported her, advised her: André Fraigneau.

6

The Impossible Passion

NINETEEN THIRTY-FIVE was a year of no publications other than occasional articles in periodicals. On the subject of which, we must note the appearance of a poem, in December, in the review *La Phalange*, edited by Jean Royère. It was "Le Poème du joug" ("Poem of the Yoke"), later included in *Les Charités d'Alcippe* (*The Alms of Alcippe*) (where it is assigned a date of 1936!).[1] In certain chronologies or studies of Yourcenar, the date of this publication is designated as 1939, which, once one knows the positions taken by *La Phalange* as of 1938, would clearly throw a completely different light on the contribution. The issue in which Yourcenar took part was dated 15 December 1935 and bears the heading: "*La Phalange*, 9th year. New series." It opens with the reprint of an article by Valery Larbaud, which had appeared in the same review in 1926. There follow an "Hommage à l'Italie" [Homage to Italy], with texts by Claude Farrère and Emile Male, and, under the "Phalange nouvelle" rubric, some poems, including Yourcenar's. It was on 15 January 1938 that the review took the subtitle "France-Italy-Spain" for the first time, and it was from then on that one regularly found texts of Franco and Mussolini in the table of contents. The last issue was dated "15 November 1938/January 1939." That number was entirely devoted to the poet Francis Jammes. Yourcenar had no part in it whatsoever.

If 1935 was an almost empty period in her literary career, it was, on the contrary, an extremely important time in the amorous life—perhaps it would be more accurate to say in the passional neurosis—of Marguerite Yourcenar. It was a year divided up between the image of André Fraigneau and a relationship—whose exact nature we do not know—with André Embiricos. Yourcenar took a long cruise with the latter André, during the summer, which brought them to Istanbul in July. During this voyage, she started writing *Fires*, which bears the trace of her impossible passion for Fraigneau, as well as *Oriental Tales*, which would not appear until 1938 at Gallimard, dedicated to Embiricos.

André Embiricos, who was born of a rich shipping family in 1901 and died in 1975, fascinated generations of young Greek intellectuals. The testimony of Dimitri T. Analis, a Greek poet established in Paris and writing in French, gives a faithful account of the attraction exercised by "that exceptional man, at once a Surrealist poet, a communist, a psychoanalyst, probably one of the first Greek psychoanalysts."[2] He belonged to a very sophisticated, also very conservative, family that was part of the same cosmopolitan and cultivated European "gentry" of the beginning of the century frequented by Yourcenar's father. "André Embiricos was an extremely fine-looking man," remembers Analis. "When I knew him, well after the Second World War, he wore a beard, as he does on most of his papers that we still have. But I remember a photograph from before the war, without the beard. This was how Marguerite Yourcenar knew him. The Slavic look he had inherited from his Russian grandmother was more pronounced on his clean-shaven face, just as his magnificent, light-colored eyes, shaped like almonds, stood out more. He had a very strange charm. The beauty of the Devil, somehow. He was linked to the Surrealists and, between the wars, published two works of Surrealist poetry. For a time, he practiced psychoanalysis; I even knew a woman who had been his patient. But his habit of advocating sexual freedom, and behavioral and spiritual freedom, caused a scandal at the time, just as his far-left political positions did. It was only because of his family's power that he never met with any trouble. After the war, he published mostly in avant-garde periodicals. But, as this decade of the eighties now draws to a close, part of his *œuvre* remains unpublished. He was a man who left his mark on several generations of intellectuals and creators, not only by virtue of what he wrote, but also by means of the support that he provided, to all of them, by his capacity for listening, advising, helping out. He was something of an éminence grise of Greek literature. You would usually find him in cafés. He spoke magnificently. With him, there was hardly any difference between spoken language and written language."

The nature of the relationship between Yourcenar and Embiricos still remains rather obscure. In addition to the summer cruise in 1935, she often sailed with him, either alone or in the company of friends they had in common, in search of islands nearly deserted, of still-virgin beaches. Both of them, throughout their lives, maintained a discretion regarding their relationship that bordered on mutism. According to Analis, "if you asked him questions about Marguerite Yourcenar, Embiricos immediately withdrew. His manner, on all occasions, was that of a perfect gentleman. Never would he have allowed himself to comment on their intimacy." Even though this "manner of a perfect gentleman" that is imputed to Embiricos may lead one to gather that he could have compromised a woman but that, in his elegance, he refused to do so, it really doesn't mean very much: assenting to utter no comments could quite simply signify that there was nothing to comment upon. As for Yourcenar, though she did not erase the name of Embiricos from the commentary on her life—unlike Fraigneau's—she too did not make any allusion, as was her wont, to a possible intimacy. To Jerry Wilson, who recorded it in a personal journal, she recounted only "long walks taken in the Greek countryside with the friend to whom she dedicated *Oriental Tales.*" "They would sometimes walk several kilometers, four or five, without meeting up with another living soul, with the exception, perhaps, of a peasant woman dressed in a goatskin." [3] At the time of Embiricos's death, Yourcenar would confine herself to mentioning, in a letter to a friend, that he had broken off all correspondence with her beginning in 1939.

Analis, carried away by his admiration for Embiricos, makes this man a bit too much the Pygmalion of Marguerite Yourcenar's intellectual and sensual "maturation." "Her writing, before meeting Embiricos, is beautiful, but it does not touch life. Marguerite Yourcenar, before Embiricos, has no feeling for the earth, or the sky. It is after their meeting, in all of her writing, that her sensuality explodes. It was he who made it possible for her to link together the materiality and the spirituality of life. He showed her, in Greece, the permanence of things. She found, with him, the path leading toward what she herself wanted to do. In *Memoirs of Hadrian,* the traces of that everyday Greece will appear. In Greece, Marguerite Yourcenar matured and Embiricos was the vector of that transformation. I believe that their relationship was intimate, and carnal, but that that was not the most important part. Embiricos was very free in his ideas, but of rather monogamous temperament and not at all, to my eyes, a 'womanizer.' I believe that he was looking for an exceptional woman, a kind of muse, and that Marguerite Yourcenar was able, for a moment, to play this role for him."

It is also to Embiricos's intellectual acknowledgment of Yourcenar that Fraigneau calls attention: "I believe that, above all, he appreciated her culture and her talent as a writer, that he marveled at her intelligence. He saw her, in fact, a lot more than I did, I who only met with her when she was more or less 'in transit,' in Paris, for a few weeks. Perhaps he tried to have an amorous relationship with her and perhaps he succeeded. If he tried, he undoubtedly succeeded, judging from the attitudes and diverse desires of Marguerite Yourcenar during those years." Fraigneau, who put Embiricos and Yourcenar in contact with one another, had, for his part as well, a great admiration for that man to whom he dedicated one of his books, *Les Voya-*

geurs transfigurés.[4] In another novel, *L'Amour vagabond* [Vagabond Love], he used Embiricos as a model; he is very recognizable behind Andréas Mavrodacos, the seductive son of a rich shipping magnate, the man whose voice, "with its deep timbre and its rolled *r*'s," possessed a strange calming power.[5] However, this does not keep Fraigneau, when one asks him whether Embiricos was indeed a communist, from being, as is his wont, acerbic: "Of course, like all the millionaires!"

Jeannette Hadzinicoli, who has translated and published Yourcenar in Greek, also thinks, for her part, that there was "something more than a loving friendship" between Embiricos and Yourcenar.[6] Nevertheless, she sees in him "a man who, certainly, had an enormous charm," but "someone much more frivolous" than Analis says he was. According to her, Embiricos is the man to whom Yourcenar refers in *Archives du Nord* when she evokes the story of a ring:

> Michel-Charles had kept for himself and had mounted in a ring an antique cameo of the purest style. . . . He bequeathed it to his son, who then gave it to me in honor of my fifteenth year. I wore it myself for seventeen years. . . . Around 1935, in one of those sudden impulses one must never regret, I gave it to a man I loved, or thought I loved. I am somewhat displeased with myself for having placed this beautiful object in the hands of an individual, hands from which, no doubt, it soon passed on to others, instead of assuring it the haven of a public or private collection—where, for that matter, it may have ended up. Must I say it, however? Perhaps I would never have parted with that masterpiece, if I had not discovered, a few days before giving it away, that a slight crack, due to some unknown blow, had appeared on the very edge of the onyx. Thus it now seemed to be less precious, imperceptibly damaged, perishable: this gave me a reason at the time to be a bit less attached to it. Today it would give me one to be attached to it a bit more.[7]

It is certainly not forbidden to read that crack quite metaphorically, and the regret at having relinquished an object—and a being—suddenly perceived as "imperceptibly damaged, perishable."

Only Constantine Dimaras, who himself also "greatly loved" Embiricos, gives no credence "at all to that love story between him and Marguerite." "But I am a rather bad witness," he points out. "However, knowing that she frequented women, if I had caught on to something intimate between Embiricos and her, I would have noticed it all the more. I had the feeling that, for her, the 'male chapter' was closed. I always thought that she had had a very violent shock, an impossible affair, something somewhere between love and sexuality, that had put her off from love with men." On this last point, Dimaras is certainly getting close to the truth: all of Yourcenar's sexuality, then no doubt her near-abstinence from sex for a long period, was determined, not so much perhaps by her passion for Fraigneau as by the stories she told herself about that passion, and what was transcribed in *Fires.*

For if the degree of her intimacy with Embiricos remains uncertain, with Fraigneau, on the other hand, things are very clear—painfully limpid. Yourcenar loved this man, who was four years her junior. He himself preferred boys. Had he let himself be seduced by someone of the other sex, he certainly would not have chosen a woman who looked like an ersatz young man. "Physically, I found her rather ugly," he says simply today. "I understand why she succeeded in attracting women who love women, but they must surely have been the only ones to see beauty in her. She, for her part, liked love; that much is obvious. She liked bars, alcohol, long conversations. She was constantly seeking to seduce. She tried with several of my friends. And then she had the odd habit of always thinking that such-and-such a person was making love with such-and-such another, who was simply a friend. This was all of great interest to her. As for me, I was something of a special case, even if, in hindsight, one can say that I was simply the 'object' of a passion she desired. It could have been someone other than me. She would send me poems, she wanted to see me often, when she was in Paris, which fortunately was not very frequently. She didn't enjoy herself in cities; there was something rather wild about her. I liked talking with her, of course. She was really intelligent and gifted. But she never became part of my private life, to say nothing of there having been an amorous relationship. She didn't know my friends. It was not through me that she met Cocteau, to whom I was very close. It was later. She never spent evenings with us. She never came with us to the Boeuf sur le toit.[8] I would see her in the afternoon, in those tea houses she was in the habit of going to in order to meet women. The area around her hotel was full of them. At the time, I told myself that she must have chosen her hotel for that reason. She was the very epitome of a woman who loves women. Nonetheless, I soon realized that she dreamed of being the mistress of men who love men. And she was persistent, as in everything else. I know that *Fires* is the result of her failure with me. She even wished to dedicate it to me. My being her editor made this impossible, so she dedicated the book to Hermes, so that he would deliver the message to me."

Did Yourcenar desire to be "the mistress of men who love men" several times throughout her life? It's more than probable. Must we thus conclude that she wanted to be a man? About this there is reason to be doubtful. For many men—and women, for that matter—every woman who loves women dreams of being a man, a cliché whose day should now be past, but one that dies hard. Certain lesbians detest homosexual men, others, on the contrary, enjoy their company. What is more rare, and what we find in Yourcenar, is this determination to have physical relations with men who are left sexually indifferent by women. More than a desire to appropriate a fantasized virility by way of transference, it is rather a way of imagining herself an absolute woman, recognized as such and yet loved as an individual, as a person, beyond the obligatory ritualizations and proprieties. To be loved by a homosexual man is to be "chosen," superlatively: a behavior that is thoroughly in keeping with megalomaniacal tendencies, tendencies obvious in the case of Marguerite Yourcenar. Having said this, through the twists and turns of the contradictory testimony regarding her love life and her sexual life during the thirties, we know nothing for certain about her physical relations with men, homosexual or not. On the other hand, with regard to her supposed desire to be a man, Yourcenar tried to explain herself in her interviews with Matthieu Galey. But the time had not yet come—and still has not come ten years later—when a truly free woman could assert that she had never had the slightest desire to be a member of the other sex. "Didn't you ever suffer from being a woman?" Galey asked her, apparently without laughing.

> YOURCENAR: Not in the slightest, and I never wanted to be a man, nor would I have wanted to be a woman had I been born a man. Besides, what would I have gained from being a man, other than the privilege of taking a somewhat more direct part in a number of wars? To be sure, it is just this sort of advancement that the future seems to hold in store for women too.
>
> GALEY: In the Mediterranean countries, where you lived for many years, didn't you ever feel that you were "creating a scandal"?
>
> YOURCENAR: Never, except perhaps once when I went swimming in the nude below the ruins of Selinunte and no doubt shocked several *contadini* who happened to pass by. But in the Mediterranean countries, you must remember, I was a foreigner, and people tolerated in foreigners what they would not tolerate in their own women.[9]

"In your books, however, you've always hidden behind men in giving your view of the world," he went on insistently.

"Hidden? The word offends me. In any event it isn't true of *Fires*, in which it is a woman who speaks all the time."[10]

Fires in fact appeared—after fragments had been published in *La Revue de France* in 1935—at Grasset in 1936. It consists of nine "lyrical prose pieces," inspired certainly by Greek myths—"Phaedra, or Despair," "Achilles, or the Lie," "Sappho, or Suicide," and so forth. But they are linked together by fragments that Yourcenar herself defined as forming a "notion of love." A short preface—which would disappear in subsequent editions, and which explicitly avows them to be transpositions of a personal experience—introduces them:

> You will find here neither a collection of poems nor a series of legends. The author has mixed together thoughts, which were for her theorems of passion, with narratives that illustrate, explain, demonstrate, and often mask them. Perhaps it is the case with this book as it is with certain buildings that have only one secret door and of which strangers know only an insurmountable wall. Behind this wall the most disturbing of costume balls is being given: the one where someone is disguised as HIMSELF. If the reader is meant to understand and love the order that this human architecture obeys, its colonnades will open like flowers for him all by themselves. If he does not hold the key of a similar experience, we can promise at the very most that he will glimpse, of the inner celebration or massacre, a few glimmers of torchlight through the cracks in the stones, a few cries, a few laughs for no reason, a few gusts of perhaps discordant music, and some broken hearts crashing.[11]

When the second edition appeared, at Plon, in 1957, the tone of this "foreword" had already changed considerably, but it does not deny that there was something of an alibi behind the transposition:

> This account of an inner crisis uses methods, sometimes toward different ends, that were also those of other poets in 1936, reshaping myths or legends—the deliberate transposition and the anachronistic detail having here as their purpose, not to make the past present, but to extinguish any notion of time. . . . Everywhere, what counts in myth or legend is their capacity to serve us as a touchstone, as an alibi if you will, or rather as a vehicle for taking a personal experience as far as possible, and, if one can, for going beyond it in the end.[12]

The third preface, finally, which Yourcenar wrote on the occasion of a new edition in 1967, puts the personal anecdote at an even greater remove, to the—apparent—advantage of a critical reflection on the form and the content. Though she reveals here Paul Valéry's influence on these texts, her adverse reaction to Giraudoux's "ingenious and Parisian Greece," and what she owes to certain methods of Jean Cocteau as well as to the work of some Surrealists, she concludes: "Through the dash and unconstraint of these sort of quasi-public confessions, certain passages in *Fires* seem to me to contain today truths glimpsed early on that needed a whole lifetime to be rediscovered and authenticated. For me, this masked ball was only a stage of awareness."[13]

IN NONE of her books did Yourcenar ever come so close to an open confession—nor to neurosis, for that matter. It is simple, leafing through *Fires*, to provide some examples, almost at random, whose pomposity—not to say grandiloquence—is revealing:

> *You could fall suddenly into the void the dead go to: I would be comforted if you would bequeath me your hands. Only your hands would continue to exist, detached from you, unexplainable like those of marble gods turned into the dust and the limestone of their own tomb. They would survive your actions, the wretched bodies they caressed. They would no longer serve as intermediaries between you and things: they themselves would be changed into things. Innocent again now, since you would no longer be there to turn them into your accomplices, sad like grey-hounds without masters, disconcerted like archangels to whom no god gives orders, your useless hands would rest on the lap of darkness. Your open hands incapable of giving or taking the slightest joy would have let me slump like a broken doll. I kiss the wrists of these indifferent hands you will no longer pull away from mine: I stroke the blue artery, the blood column that once spurted continuously like a fountain from the ground of your heart. With little sobs of contentment, I rest my head like a child between these palms filled with the stars, the crosses, the precipices of my previous fate.*[14]

Or, again: *"There is no sterile love. No precaution can avert it. When I leave you, I have deep within me my suffering like a sort of terrible offspring."*[15] *"The only horror is not to be used. Turn me into whatever you want, even a screen, even a metallic conductor."*[16]

FIRES OPENS with *"I hope this book will never be read."* Then there is one of the still-celebrated passages: *"Loneliness . . . I don't believe as they do, I don't live as they do, I don't love as they do . . . I will die as they die."* Then, *"Alcohol sobers me. After a few swallows of brandy, I no longer think of you."*[17] (Brandy was always Yourcenar's favorite form of alcohol—she didn't like whiskey. During the thirties, she regularly carried a flask of it about with her—to which Fraigneau attests—as in the last years of her life.)

Even in its most intimate section, *Fires* is not limited to a discourse on passion in general, or on the man whom we now know to be André Fraigneau. We already find Yourcenar affirming some of the choices she would make, particularly not to have a child: *"A child is a hostage. Life has you."*[18]

We also find in this collection the passage she was often asked to comment on, during the last decade of her life, at the time of her media celebrity: *"A heart is perhaps something unsavory. It's on the order of anatomy tables and butcher's stalls. I prefer your body."*[19] On the "Apostrophes" program that

Bernard Pivot devoted especially to her in 1979, she talked about that passage. Several times, she said how profoundly she objected to the notion, in her eyes "very French, literary, and romantic," of love. This was a subject she would go back over willingly, as often in her interviews with journalists as in her texts, her correspondence, or in private conversations. "We all believed that by talking about sex, about the body, things were going to get better, that we would head toward greater freedom. One sees today that such was not at all the case. In the end, there is nothing to be said about the body except that it exists." People hastened to hear only the first part of this last sentence—"there is nothing to be said about the body"—in order to comfort themselves with the idea that Yourcenar, the vague reincarnation—only slightly incarnate—of a long-ago Roman emperor, judged that it was urgent to ignore the body, not to be preoccupied by it. They would perhaps have been better advised to dwell on "except that it exists": it has its demands and its requirements to which one must consent. But engaging in a discourse on the subject of the body and thinking that this discourse alone can bring about more freedom is a myth. Such was, very clearly, Yourcenar's opinion at the end of her life. Such was also at just about the same time—but did she know it?—the opinion of Michel Foucault.

We can't be certain that in 1936, at the moment *Fires* was published, she was convinced of the pointlessness of talking about the body. Rather, she was going through the period to which she alludes in saying "we all believed that by talking about the body . . ."

The book's reception, if qualified, gave notice that she was becoming a writer people "follow": "Marguerite Yourcenar's book is uneven," wrote Émilie Noulet on the pages of *La Nouvelle Revue Française;* "but the parts that are beautiful shine with a hard and savage brilliance. It is not perfect, but always abundant. It bears witness to a somewhat showy richness, but to what is incontestably a writerly temperament."[20] Edmond Jaloux, for his part, praised the virtuosity of the mythological reorientation and concluded: "The purity of the style, of the images, inserts these thoughts in a tissue of words wherein the abstract vies in a curious way with the concrete. But it seems that this wealth of metaphors, of poetic visions, of gripping analogies serves the sole purpose of rendering bearable the work's fearsome central idea, which is that of despair."[21]

DURING THE YEAR 1936, we have no more than a very vague picture of her life—a rather troubled one then, according to her friends from that time. There are a few written traces, a few photographic documents. From 14 March through 25 April, she asked people to write to her in Paris at the

Hôtel Wagram, after which, she specified, beginning on 1 May, her "permanent address" would be the Meurice in Lausanne. In the spring, she made a trip to England, about which nothing is known, and another to Venice, from which we still have a photograph of her, in the company of an as yet unidentified woman. Finally she made it known that in August and September her address would be the Petit Palais in Athens and that she would not come back to Paris before November, where once again she would stay at the Wagram.

Constantine Dimaras, who translated the poems of Cavafy with Yourcenar, dates their collaboration back to that summer.[22] "Of course, I could be off by a year, it was so long ago," he acknowledges, "but it was not in 1939, as she maintained in the Pléiade's 'Chronologie.' I did not myself see Marguerite Yourcenar in Greece again after 1937. I even thought that she had not come back." (She did in fact go back there, and during 1939, notably at Easter time, for private, sentimental reasons.) "In 1939, in March, Gide came to Athens. And I remember very well that Marguerite was not there. Otherwise we would have invited them over together. Gide thought most highly of her. He was very categorical regarding her talent.

"For my part, I admired Marguerite. I enjoyed working with her very much. It lasted for an entire summer. She came to my house every day. My wife, Helena, and I both got along very well with her. But we were not part of her intimate circle. She lived in another group, a group of intellectuals and artists. We ourselves led a more bourgeois, more settled life. We met one another, Marguerite and I, one evening in 1935, I believe, by way of André Embiricos. I don't remember anymore how I happened to talk with her about Constantine Cavafy. In the years between 1930 and 1935 I had done a lot of work on him. I knew him as he was known by Athenian young people, when he left Alexandria for Athens. He was afflicted with cancer of the throat. He came to Athens to be operated on. We saw him a great deal, Helena and I. He then went back to Alexandria, where he died in 1933. I took a very active part in the first edition of his collected poetry. Cavafy himself printed his poems on loose sheets of paper and distributed them to his friends. It was only very late that he put collections together. After his death, a large amount of unpublished material came out, along with some poems of his youth. Cavafy was someone very important to me, and it was natural that, conversing with an intellectual, I would speak of him. Marguerite was fascinated by what I told her about this man and wanted, at once, to get to know his poetry. I was working in a bookstore for which I had a key in my possession. We went there, in the middle of the night. I took a copy of Cavafy and I started to translate the poems for her, as I read along, since she didn't know modern Greek. I no longer recall how the idea came into being for the two of us to collaborate on translating Cavafy's entire *œuvre,* a volume whose publication I had been involved in.

"So we spent all of one summer on it, which I still believe was the summer of 1936. Our collaboration was not always entirely peaceful. Marguerite Yourcenar, as I think everyone today is aware, was rather authoritarian. And stubborn. I, for my part, had some very specific ideas about what a translation should be. She did not share these ideas. My view of translation is not at all lenient. I don't like the idea of 'euphonious inaccuracies.' Marguerite, for her part, was solely concerned with what she thought sounded good in French. Much later, she proved that what she did was not 'translating,' when she published *La Couronne et la lyre* [The Crown and the Lyre]. What one finds in this book are French poems, adapted from Greek poems, but in no instance are they translated. This is not the case for Cavafy. It's really a translation. But our differences of opinion always revolved around this question. I would give her a word-for-word translation and she would 'arrange' things. Sometimes our discussions would heat up, each of us ardently defending his or her position. Then my wife would intervene. She would join us, in the sitting room where we had set ourselves up to work. And things would cool down. Marguerite's wish was to create something with style, in French. Of course, I had nothing against that. But I wanted the translation to be accurate. The translation of Cavafy that we composed, she and I, does not deviate too far from these principles. With the exception of a few places where she really insisted and I gave in. There exist other translations, in French, that are more faithful, but that are far from being of the same literary value. Having said this, Marguerite Yourcenar's translation does not really render the distinctive atmosphere of Cavafy's poetry. I still see it more as the work of a great French stylist than the work of a Greek poet."

Yourcenar said over and over again that, for her, writing or translating were identical acts. "In any event, it was very exciting to work with her. I can only congratulate myself for having had this privilege," Dimaras is eager to make clear. "Marguerite was someone. We were contemporaries, since she was born in 1903 and I in 1904. But she had already published several works. She had a higher 'standing' than I did. I respected her, not only because of that, but because she compelled respect in her own right. She had a very commanding presence, physically. It was not only women she wanted to conquer. She wanted to conquer, period. To seduce. She spoke magnificent French, but, at the time, she was not the only one. All the intellectuals spoke meticulous French."

In the article she published during the war, in May 1944, in the review *Fontaine* (from Algiers), Yourcenar notes, for her part, that the French translation of Cavafy's poems was finished in Athens in July 1939, at which time she was composing in part what would be the *Présentation critique de Constantin Cavafy* [Critical Introduction to Constantine Cavafy].

According to Yourcenar's account, "our evenings were spent making endless evaluations, which were only slightly disturbed by the threatening sounds of the Radio in the next room. I remember the exquisite, simple foods, which my collaborator, who remained in Greece, may himself recall as well upon occasion, during hunger's painful reveries; I can still see the bouquets of wild anemones that I bought every evening at shops lit by gas lamps; the barracks yard at the corner of the avenue, made more nocturnal by the presence of the trees, with soldiers dancing the Cretan dance of the swords to the high-pitched sound of a sorrowful flute, great white silhouettes that were already much like ghosts."[23]

Despite his uncertainties of memory, we can postulate that Dimaras is right to set a date of 1936 for the work they did together on Cavafy. For in 1937 Yourcenar was traveling with Grace Frick, whom she had just met, in Greece and in Italy, and made quite a short stay in Athens. During the summer of 1938, she was first in Paris, in July, then, in August, in Sorrento, Italy, where she finished *Coup de Grâce*. If she spent some time in Greece then, for a vacation—whose date and location, yet again, are a subject of dispute—it wasn't in Athens, and the stay was not sufficient to allow for undertaking a long intellectual project. During 1939 she made occasional trips to Greece. The only trace of a long stay in Athens is patently that of summer 1936, during which time she gave the Petit Palais as her address for the months of August and September.

This confusion of dates surfaces again regarding her relationship with Lucy Kyriakos, one of the women with whom Yourcenar had quite a long amorous liaison until her departure for New York in October 1939. Kyriakos, as photographs attest, was a very beautiful young woman, married to one of the Dimarases' cousins, and the mother of a little boy. She died at the very beginning of the war, in the bombardment of Janina. "Lucy was charming," Helena Dimaras recalls. "But neither she nor her husband were intellectuals. We did not realize until later that her relationship with Marguerite was more than a friendship. Lucy was one of those women who you can't imagine would think about having an affair with another woman."

But you could count on Yourcenar, at that time, to seduce women who were "least likely to cherish impassioned feelings for another of her sex," as Swann put it, with as little perceptiveness, regarding Odette de Crécy.[24] The memory of Lucy remained very vivid for Yourcenar, who, in certain years, underlined Saint Lucy's Day in her calendar, long after the war.[25] But did she see Kyriakos during the summer of 1936? Did she already know her? It is rather difficult to determine when they met. Yourcenar wrote on some photographs: "1934: Nelly Liambey, Lucy, M.Y., Athanase, in Agios Geórgios, Euboea." But on other photos, which are included in one of Yourcenar's albums called "Autobiography III" and which seem to be part of the same series, she noted: "Euboea 1938 at Mr. Athanase Chrystomanos's with Lucy and a sister and a cousin of Lucy's." The sole survivor of the men and women who appear in those photos is Nelly Liambey; she hasn't managed to date that vacation with certainty either. "I lean toward 1934," she says. She confirms that the photos were indeed taken on Euboea, at Athanase Chrystomanos's. But she also remembers another meeting with Yourcenar. "I no longer recall if it was in 1936, 1937, or even 1938. We happened to be staying at the same time, Marguerite and I, at a mutual friend's, for just two or three days. It was on Corfu. Our friend Lucy Kyriakos had rented a property on the island for the summer. It was an enchanting spot, with an enormous garden in a wild state, and a dilapidated house that people said was haunted, far from the city of Corfu. That property now belongs to the Club Méditerranée. Marguerite Yourcenar had come, I believe, for a few days. She arrived at the end of my stay, unless it was I, rather, who arrived at the end of hers. But I don't think we spent more than two or three days together in that city."[26]

If it was a matter of visiting for a few days, it could just as well have been in 1934 as in any of the years mentioned by Liambey, during which, without a doubt, Yourcenar came to Greece for stays of varying duration—perhaps even more frequently than she admits. For if the dates remain so vague, it's not solely on account of the witnesses' failing memories. Yourcenar was careful to establish imprecision regarding that time of her life and regarding her many moves from one place to another. In her reconstructed "Chronologie," which appeared in the Pléiade edition of her prose works and which is, thus, official, we find that at this or that time during the year 1937 or 1938 she was in Greece or in France. But in her correspondence dating from those years, there appears a letter from Belgium, which she claimed not to have visited between 1933—when she finished settling her mother's estate—and the fifties. Did she not want people to know exactly what she was doing with her life during those years? Or, at an even deeper level, was she herself refusing to remember, so much was that period still marked by her unfortunate passion for André Fraigneau? The end of her life would prove that she never forgot this man, nor her love for him, any more than she admitted a failure that, at all costs—and the costs were fearsome and pitiful—she had to efface.

7

Grace and Coup de Grâce

ALTHOUGH SHE WASN'T "settled" in France, Yourcenar was henceforth part of the Parisian literary milieu, or at least she was on its border, at once close by and distant—an "ironic" position she would always favor, in many domains. Though she didn't publish any books that year, she was very much present, by way of her texts, in the reviews. In 1937, notably, certain stories appeared that would be included in the collection *Oriental Tales*: "Notre-Dame-des-Hirondelles" ("Our-Lady-of-the-Swallows") in *La Revue Hebdomadaire* in January; "Le Lait de la Mort" ("The Milk of Death") in *Les Nouvelles Littéraires* in March; "L'Homme qui a aimé les Néréides" ("The Man Who Loved the Nereids") in *La Revue de France* in May; and "Le Prince Genghi" [Prince Genghi] in *La Revue de Paris* in August.[1] In February, she gave *La Revue Bleue* a rather lackluster text, "Mozart à Salzbourg" [Mozart in Salzburg], which she had the questionable idea of including in her collection of essays, *En pèlerin et en étranger*, published after her death.[2] It consists, from beginning to end, of a rather distressing collection of platitudes and commonplaces, which reveal nonetheless Yourcenar's incapacity to talk about music or to refrain in this domain from insipid impressionism or the conventional remarks about "the man and his work":

> The man who composed it [the *Jupiter Symphony*] was, however, drained by illness, plagued by poverty; he had his rivals and his detractors. Such is precisely the mystery of his art: this music of joy, balanced like a tightrope walker over the abyss that is every life, deep down, is not a flight away from the real; nor is it the equivalent of a beautiful dream; it does not, like Schubert's work, touch the most delicate and hidden fibers within us; it does not gently rock us, as Chopin's music does, the better to give comfort; it does not help us live, as does Beethoven's, by giving to us the courage that we did not have. It is quite simply music: the perfect construction of a universe of sound.

Such rhetorical fancywork and worldly observations might have been borrowed from Madame de Cambremer listening to Vinteuil in the salons of the hôtel de Guermantes.[3]

Besides André Fraigneau and Edmond Jaloux, she was friendly at the time with Emmanuel Boudot-Lamotte, a member of the reading committee at Editions NRF, whose sister, Madeleine, was Gaston Gallimard's secretary.[4] In 1936, Yourcenar met Paul Morand, who suggested she publish *Oriental Tales* at Gallimard, in the "Renaissance de la nouvelle" collection, which he had been in charge of since June of 1933. Testifying to this is a note written by Morand to Boudot-Lamotte dated 7 December 1936, stating: "I have an appointment at my place with Madame Marguerite Yourcenar next Thursday. Would you be so kind as to come by and bring the contract?"[5] Which must not have been done, since Yourcenar wrote to Morand on 25 January 1937: "I received the contract signed by Gallimard, but I am waiting to discuss it with you before sending it back to him."[6] And to Boudot-Lamotte on 13 February, she wrote: "I am leaving Friday for a few days in London and, if convenient, I would like to pass on to you the manuscript of *Kâli* [she refers to "Kali Beheaded," one of the short stories in *Oriental Tales*] and get the copies of the contract returned to you before my departure."[7]

THIS TIME we know the reason, or at least one of the reasons, for Yourcenar's trip to London: she had agreed to translate Virginia Woolf's *The Waves* for Editions Stock. Her financial situation was unstable—all she had was the money "saved from the disaster" at the beginning of the decade—and the limited sales of her books were surely not enough to live on. Thus, she had decided to visit the author in order to ask her a few questions, which, apparently, did not prevent the translation from being riddled with misrenderings. We already know, from her work with Constantine Dimaras on Cavafy, that Yourcenar took a slightly offhanded approach to translation—which was hardly a matter of concern to her: "I don't think the Virginia Woolf translation caused me any particular problems," she would write to one of her correspondents nearly forty years later: "it was merely a question of letting oneself drift along with the current, not always too clearly aware of where that current was taking one; but Virginia Woolf herself seems to have desired that impression of vagueness (no play on words intended).[8] In an attempt to be a conscientious translator, I went to see her at the time, to ask her certain questions about how she would prefer that I translate certain sentences containing allusions to themes or images from English poetry: literally, or by trying to achieve the same effects with similar themes familiar to French readers. But this problem was quite alien to her, as were problems of translation in general."[9]

Yourcenar alluded to this project and her visit in two texts, the first from 1937, originally published in *Les Nouvelles Littéraires* and since reprinted as a preface to *Les Vagues,*[10] the second, which appeared in the review *Adam International,* from 1972.[11] In the first, she sketches a brief, incisive portrait of the English novelist: "Only a few days ago, in the sitting room dimly lit by firelight where Mrs. Woolf had been so kind as to welcome me, I watched the profile emerge in the half-light of that young Fate's face, hardly aged, but delicately etched with signs of thought and lassitude, and I said to myself that the reproach of intellectualism is often directed at the most sensitive natures, those most ardently alive, those obliged by their frailty or excess of strength to constantly resort to the arduous disciplines of the mind." [12] In the second she pays a more direct tribute to the writer: "I translated *The Waves* into French, Virginia Woolf's next-to-last novel, and I am not sorry to have done so, since my recompense for ten months of work was a visit to Bloomsbury, and two short hours spent beside a woman at once sparkling and timid, who greeted me in a room taken over by twilight. We're always wrong about the writers of our time: we either overrate them or we run them down. I do not believe I am committing an error, however, when I put Virginia Woolf among the four or five great virtuosos of the English language and among the rare contemporary novelists whose work stands some chance of lasting more than ten years. And I even hope, despite so many signs to the contrary, that there will be a few minds aware enough in around the year 2500 to savor the subtleties of her art." [13]

Being overrated or run down—this was a premonitory diagnosis, not only where Woolf was concerned, but also where Yourcenar herself was concerned: between the "fetishists" of her work, ready to launch thoughtlessly into raptures, and those who consider her an academic, even pompous, writer for having read her hastily, she has not yet found her own place. And what will be the status, "in the year 2500," of her work?

In her *Journal,* Woolf made a brief reference to the visit of "the translator," but one that attests to her perspicacity: "Tuesday 23 February: That extraordinary scribble means, I suppose, the translator coming. Madame or Mlle Youniac(?) Not her name. And I had so much to write about Julian. . . . So I've no time or room to describe the translator, save that she wore some nice gold leaves on her black dress; is a woman I suppose with a past; amorous; intellectual; lives half the year in Athens; is in with Jaloux &c, red lipped, strenuous; a working Fchwoman [*sic*]; friend of the Margeries; matter of fact; intellectual; we went through The Waves. What does 'See here he comes?' mean & so on." [14]

WHEN SHE GOT BACK from London, at the Hôtel Wagram, Yourcenar had a decisive encounter, though she didn't know it at the time: she met Grace

Frick, an American academic of her own age. Frick was born on 12 January 1903 in Toledo, Ohio, and Yourcenar, of course, on 8 June of the same year. This would allow her to refer to Frick, with a delicious coquettishness, as "a friend older than myself."

There exist two somewhat different versions of their meeting: the story told by Yourcenar to Jerry Wilson, who copied it down in one of his personal journals, and the story told by Frick, back in 1937, to a fellow university student, Florence Codman, whose testimony is particularly precious. Codman, an editor, an intellectual, and a Francophile, who was Jane Bowles's friend, is one of the rare persons still alive who knew Grace at the university, and who subsequently maintained relations with Yourcenar and Frick until the latter's death.

Frick had been in France that particular year since the month of January. She had come to settle the estate of one of her cousins who, to the great displeasure of her family, had taken the veil in a French convent, where she had just died. On this February evening, Frick was alone at a table, in the bar of the Wagram. At the table next to hers, Yourcenar was conversing with Emmanuel Boudot-Lamotte. In Yourcenar's version, they were talking in a general way about traveling, and also about their respective travel plans. It was reportedly then that Frick intervened asking Yourcenar, in order to start up a conversation, if she would like to make a trip to the United States. "The next morning," Jerry Wilson goes on to say in his journal, "the young 'chasseur' [page boy] came to Mme. Y's room saying that the American lady sent a message that some lovely birds could be seen on a roof through her window, wouldn't she come up to see. She did and they became friends," concludes Wilson euphemistically.

Frick herself gave a different account of the scene in the bar to Florence Codman: "Grace called me on the telephone as soon as she got back to the United States, in 1937, to tell me the story of her meeting with Marguerite," Codman recalls.[15] "Grace was in fact alone in the bar and Marguerite was engaged in conversation with a man. They were talking about literature, about Coleridge in particular. 'They were saying things that were so inaccurate, indeed so stupid, that I intervened to tell them they had it all wrong,' Grace told me."

Of the two versions, and given everything we know about Frick and the peremptory way in which she would intervene without being solicited, the second version is certainly the more plausible. This is even more likely since the first one verges on stereotyped caricature, unless, perhaps, the two versions complement one another—and this is not unlikely: Grace irrupts into the literary conversation, there is talk of travel, a "why not the United

States," and, later, an invitation to gaze upon the birds soaring over the rooftops of Paris.

"She was immediately dazzled by Marguerite; it was a real case of love at first sight," Codman goes on to say. "I'm not sure if Grace had had other women in her life before Marguerite. Or even other love affairs. We had never talked about this." This is all well and good, but when one knows something about Yourcenar's appearance during that period, it is doubtful, barring an unimaginable innocence, that Frick's invitation was extended without some ulterior motive.

Having said this, we don't know very much about Frick's private life before that time. A young woman from a well-to-do family of the American South, she had been orphaned early on and raised, as was her brother Gage, by an uncle. She had studied at Wellesley, a chic East Coast college. It was there that she came to know Codman. She earned her Bachelor of Arts degree in 1925 and her Master's in English Literature in 1927. "I met Grace at Wellesley, early in the twenties," Codman relates. "She came from Kansas City. It was only much later that I learned that both her parents had died when she was still very young. We never talked about our families. No more than we talked about money. But it was clear that our families were well-off; otherwise we would not have been able either to attend that college or to take trips to Europe. Grace was a very brilliant student. She hoped to have a teaching career. I think she could have been a prominent university professor. She was rather on the tall side, and thin. Not without appeal. Nonetheless, she sometimes made a kind of haughty display when she would speak. We were not really close friends, Grace and I. We didn't live in the same building in college. We has classes together, and, even then, she loved to teach. This would remain one of her dominant character traits, throughout her life. I was the only person she knew in New York. In fact, it was after she had become involved with Marguerite that we became more like real friends. When I met Marguerite, I understood right away how one could fall in love with her head over heels. I was immediately impressed by her intelligence. She spoke perfect English, though it was barely intelligible because of her accent. I spoke French with her. It was truly a pleasure, just as it was a delight to hear her speak the language. Right away, I noticed how she carried herself, the way she was—very erect, with a natural majesty. I said to myself, 'When she gets out of bed, in a nightgown, she must walk like that even then.' Like a queen. As if doors should open in front of her. With a way of holding her head that everyone must always have envied her. It was hard to resist her charm and her authority. Furthermore, she was very stubborn and had very firm ideas. Regarding literature in particular;

but I was not subjected to her wrath, for we talked about French literature essentially—I don't believe American literature interested her really—and we usually agreed. Grace was crazy about Marguerite and I think she stayed that way. For Marguerite, over the years, it became a good marriage, I think. In any case, certainly a marriage."

Before her encounter with Yourcenar, Frick was not necessarily the "innocent young thing" her friends somewhat hastily imagined. It would indeed be perilous, however, to claim that they are absolutely wrong, given how silent she was about her feelings—as much so before her encounter with Yourcenar as afterward. It takes a good deal of effort to find, amid the unflagging chronological notelets devoted to Yourcenar, a hasty retrospective look at a few years of her own existence. She reports that in September 1927, just after receiving her Master of Arts degree, she left to teach at Stephens College in Columbia, Missouri. She would stay there until June 1930. In 1928, she took her first trip to Europe "to meet Phyllis Bartlett at Oxford, then go to Paris with her." We do not know the nature of Bartlett and Frick's relationship. From June 1930 until September 1931, Frick was in Kansas City, where her family resided. Then she lived in New Haven and took courses at Yale, until 1933. "In 1934," she writes in the notebook in which she jotted down these dates, "Paris via Italy and Switzerland. August in France, with Uncle George La Rue. I stay at the Hôtel Wagram. In September I go to Munich before returning to New York where I stay with Ruth Hall." Hall would remain a friend of Yourcenar and Frick's. So perhaps she was only a friend with whom Frick was sharing an apartment. In June 1936, Frick went to England to teach. It was from London that she would go to Paris—in January 1937, and again in February. And it was then that she met Marguerite Yourcenar.

FRICK HAD TO go back to London and spend the whole month of March there. Yourcenar continued to concern herself with her professional affairs. On 8 March she received a copy of her contract for *Oriental Tales*, "for your files," the letter from Gallimard indicated. She had suggested that Frick go with her to Greece. Thus she waited for her to return. Frick came back in April, and after going to Biarritz to see a certain Betty Lou Curtis, she got ready to follow Yourcenar. Frick, inaugurating what would turn into a habit that verged on obsession, noted down the stops made during their trip—in the third person: "Grace and Marguerite to Sicily via Genoa. Italy, Rome, Florence, Venice, the Dalmatian coast, Corfu, Greece, Athens, Delphi, Sounion. Back to Naples. Grace left again in August for New York City after a brief visit to Capri. Grace would once again be in New Haven at the end of the month of August and would stay there until the fall of 1939."

WE DON'T KNOW exactly what Yourcenar's feelings were toward Frick during that time, except from what she briefly conceded later on: "at first it was a passion." Certainly Yourcenar no longer desired a passion like the one she had experienced for Fraigneau—which was not yet in the past, as is indicated by a letter of 24 August 1937 mailed from the Hôtel Meurice in Lausanne, to which Yourcenar had just returned after leaving Grace: "I have not had any news from André for a long time," she asserts, "and the state of my health has not allowed me to spend much time in Athens this year." One thing that is certain is that she played the "lovers' journey" to the hilt with Grace: from Venice to Capri by way of Corfu and Delphi. There are no traces left of those first months spent side by side, except a photograph of Grace, in profile, in an unidentifiable place, and another one of Marguerite, probably taken by Frick, on the Piazza del Duomo in Florence. They are ordinary pictures that don't reveal a thing. The photographs of Frick allow for only one observation: she was not very pretty. Yourcenar always maintained—and would never stop doing so, until her final day—that beauty was of the utmost importance to her, where amorous emotions and sensual pleasure were concerned. Frick, it would appear, was an exception—a very long exception. The underlying reasons for this will perhaps emerge from the correspondence these two women exchanged—a correspondence sealed until 2037. Whatever the case may be, we can vouch here and now for the fact that Yourcenar was too intelligent to conform herself exclusively to any hackneyed formula, and that she always, as she used to say, "left everything open." Moreover, during that dark time, suffering much longer than she herself imagined from the wounds of her amorous defeat with Fraigneau, she had an immense need, in her own turn, to be madly loved. She had very quickly realized that Frick would afford her such unbridled devotion.

So it was that she made the decision to accept Frick's invitation and spend the winter in the United States, as Frick hoped she would. She embarked in September 1937, while her translation of Virginia Woolf's *The Waves* was coming out at Stock. And it was aboard ship, "on the rolling sea of the first hours of [her] Atlantic crossing,"[16] that she put the finishing touches on "Le Chef rouge" [The Red Head], a final text for *Oriental Tales*. The title was changed to "La Veuve Aphrodissia" ("Aphrodissia, the Widow") in the second edition. She spent the winter in New Haven—Frick was still at Yale University, where she hoped to begin a dissertation. She did a little traveling: in Virginia (Charlottesville), South Carolina, Georgia, and even made a short trip to the Canadian province of Quebec.

Yourcenar—who returned to Europe at the end of April 1938—never consented to speak about that winter, which must have been the most intense moment of her passion with Grace. She had made the firm decision, moreover—we don't know exactly when—to indulge herself in no disclosures regarding her intimate affairs, a resolution she would faithfully adhere to until the last years of her life, when she had grown weaker than she herself realized, and weaker than even her friends could detect. What traces remain of this visit show a Yourcenar turned much more toward Europe than avid to explore a new continent, or eager to find a place for herself there. Her primary concern was for her forthcoming book, *Oriental Tales,* whose corrected manuscript she returned, on 20 November, to Boudot-Lamotte, adding in an enclosed note that "Your solicitous attention to my book makes me feel as if I am not entirely absent from Paris."[17] Did she miss Paris all of a sudden? Far from her sybaritic Greek friends and her elegant French intellectual companions, was she finding out about provincial life, about the general tedium of a small American city with a convent-like university? Quite probably. But how could she have admitted as much, years later, after an entire life spent trying to convince everyone—beginning with herself—that she had "left things to chance" and succeeded at transforming chance into true freedom? That winter, "chance" seemed to be on the run from that young woman of thirty-four years, who couldn't resist slipping this into another letter to Boudot-Lamotte: "Tell André [Fraigneau, of course] that I think of him."[18]

Yourcenar was again drawn back toward Europe and its intellectuals by her correspondence with Charles Du Bos, beginning in November 1937. She got in touch with him—which proves, if any proof is still needed, her desire to be in contact with Europeans rather than Americans—by sending him a word of welcome to New York, in which she expressed her regret to be missing the lectures that the Catholic essayist was to give there: "I too was eager to extend to you this clumsy welcome of sorts and to express yet again my admiration (and my gratitude) for a writer whose views hearten me along the path—such a slow one, moreover, and one that in your eyes no doubt is still quite off the track—that my own views are imperceptibly taking."[19]

"As far as 'paths' and even paths 'off the track' are concerned, no one is in a better position than I, not only to understand, but also to be grateful for them," responded Du Bos to her letter.

If I told you that it was more than thirty years of reflection on the nature of genius—of genius in general and more specifically the genius of Keats, Giorgione, and Bach—that finally led me to be ready to receive the Truth (Truth with a capital T, Truth-the-Person and not simply the principle, the truth of Him who said: "I am the Way, the Truth, and the Life"), you would have every right to be surprised, and yet nothing is more literally accurate. Each one of us has *his or her way,* and the one that is the farthest off the track sometimes ends up nearest to the center. In a first letter it wouldn't be fitting to say more about this, and certainly we all prefer a simple, open exchange in person. But if you cannot come [to South Bend, Indiana, where he had accepted a position at the University of Notre Dame], and if you would like to pursue this discussion through the mail, do not hesitate to do so.[20]

Yourcenar did not hesitate; and at the end of the month of December she sent him a very long letter, an attempt to sort out the state of her reflections on the subject of religious feeling and, more specifically, Catholicism:

I realize that from now on something new is being added to the intelligent interest you have always so generously displayed toward me, increasing it endlessly: a Catholic's moving concern for all human souls; and I hesitate now for fear of responding to your urgent, friendly call with nothing more than reservations you cannot accept, and that it will perhaps be difficult for you to appreciate. . . . Perhaps reading your last book was what it took to make me recognize that, however close to your thought I may feel myself to be, I am nonetheless not situated on the same plane, and that the difference, no doubt much more essential yet in your eyes than my own, can be fully summed up in this one word: faith. Strictly speaking, the problem of religious anguish does not exist for me. Pathos and anxiety (from which none of us, happily or unhappily, is excluded) are situated elsewhere in my life. But along with hellenism, for which it provides all at once the complement and the corrective in my thought, Catholicism represents in my eyes one of the rare values that our epoch has not managed to shatter completely. More and more in the world's current (and perpetual) disorder, I have come to see the Catholic tradition as one of the most precious parts of our complex heritage, indeed one infinitely broader than the strict domain of belief, and the disappearance or the disintegration of these traditions in favor of a crude ideal of force, of race, or of the mob strikes me as one of the future's worst dangers. If Christianity does not seem divine to me (or divine only in the sense in which this adjective applies to the Parthenon, or to the sea on a lovely summer's day), at least I see in it, with an ever-increasing respect, the admirable sum of twenty centuries' experience, and one of the most beautiful of human dreams. . . .

Perhaps I shall one day revert to a more rigorous interpretation of church dogma, or rather arrive at such an interpretation for the first time (as the

Catholicism of my childhood years never got beyond the stage of an indolent childish acceptance). Perhaps, but such an evolution seems to me quite improbable at the date of this writing, and I am doubtless too far removed from the dogma to attach much importance to possible changes in my thought on this point. In order to wish one had faith, one must already believe in faith's vital worth. But in the midst of the troubles of our time, if it were a matter for me of taking sides, which I have so far avoided, and which I hope to continue to avoid (for, unfortunately, taking sides almost always obliges one to enroll oneself in one side or the other), the great Catholic tradition represents in my eyes one part of the ark that should above all be saved.[21]

During that period, Yourcenar was, as she often reiterated, "at [her] furthest remove from Christian thought and from religious concerns in general," and she was always grateful to Du Bos for "not having tried to convert [her]." In 1964, the Friends of Charles Du Bos Society requested her permission to publish some of her letters, prompting her to reread them. She was astonished to find a religious anxiety of which she had no recollection and pointed out: "The person that I was during those years before 1939 seems now very distant from myself; . . . I am especially struck to see that the religious problem—if you go by the attempt to sort things out after a fashion that one of those letters contains—was already a matter of much greater concern to me than one would suspect in reading the books I wrote during those years, greater even than I myself had retained any memory of (it is especially in such domains that one has the, often illusory, feeling of making an ever-new discovery)."[22]

At that particular time in her life, Yourcenar was above all in a state of uncertainty regarding her feelings, to which she would never admit. The only true advantage she saw in spending the winter of 1937–38 in the United States was, as she wrote to Du Bos from Canada, on the day before her departure, "the calm of my American retreat. It's curious, and quite contrary to the legend of the United States, that it should be precisely these opportunities for meditation, detachment, and peace that we have sought and found here."[23] "Detachment"? Is this yet another pious vow? As Yourcenar made her way toward Europe, during the last days of the month of April 1938, she did not know where she stood regarding her attachment to Fraigneau. The "affair" would only be partially resolved in the writing of *Coup de Grâce*, a symbolic settling of scores with him (which was intended to be cathartic). As for her attachment to Frick, it is quite difficult to hazard comments on this subject without falling into overinterpretation. But Yourcenar was certainly "in the grip" of two mad passions: the one she bore Fraigneau, as she had for some four years by now, from which she had finally decided to escape, and the one Frick bore her, to which she had not yet fully made up her mind to acquiesce.

AS SOON AS she reached Europe, at the beginning of May 1938, Yourcenar went to Capri where she had rented a small villa, La Casarella, before leaving for the United States. She was no longer in pain, almost desperate, as she had been before meeting Grace and, particularly, before publishing *Fires.* Nonetheless, she was still troubled, vaguely uncertain. There was, as always, one remaining means for her to try to see things clearly: writing. So it was that in one month, just barely, she wrote the initial version of a short novel—a hundred pages or so—that she would finish in Sorrento in August of the same year: *Coup de Grâce.* Even her fiercest detractors—or perhaps especially they—"rescue" this little text, a dry and violent one, from an *œuvre* they judge in the main to be "pompous" and "overdone."

Apart from questions of literary analysis and discussions of the comparative merits of *Coup de Grâce* and the postwar works—which earned their author her celebrity—the purely biographical aspects that came into play in the writing of this novel are as fascinating as what had led to the composition of *Fires,* explicitly referred to as "the product of a love crisis."

Against a background of Baltic wars and anti-Bolshevik fighting, Yourcenar presented three characters: Erick von Lhomond, who "[t]hough nearly forty, . . . seemed young, as if his kind of hard, youthful elegance would never change," and whose "narrow profile bespoke French ancestry, [though] his mother was Balt and his father Prussian, hence the pale blue eyes, the tall stature, the arrogant smile"; Conrad de Reval, for Erick more than a friend, "a fixed point" "[i]n my perpetually unsettled existence"; and Sophie, Conrad's sister, who had "real beauty, and [whom] the fashion for short hair became. . . ."[24] Erick does not like women; he likes only Conrad, unless he likes no one at all. "Away from Conrad I had lived as if on a journey," he says. "He was the ideal companion in war, just as he had been the ideal childhood friend. Friendship affords certitude above all, and that is what distinguishes it from love. It means respect, as well, and total acceptance of another being."[25] Sophie develops an impossible and mortal passion for Erick, who wonders "[w]hy [it is] that women fall in love with the very men who are destined otherwise, and who accordingly must repulse them, or else deny their own nature."[26]

"So I was bound to be mistaken about Sophie," he adds, "and all the more that her voice, now brusque, now tender, her cropped hair, short smocks and heavy shoes perpetually encrusted with mud made her seem to me but a brother to her brother. I was wrong, of course, then saw my error. . . . Meanwhile . . . my feeling for Sophie was just that sense of easy familiarity that a man has for boys who are of no special interest to him. . . . After a certain time it was she who led in the game, and she played all the more intently because her life was at stake. Besides, my attention was necessarily divided; not so, hers. For me there was Conrad and the war, and a few ambitions gone overboard since. Soon nothing counted for her but me alone, as if all human kind around us had been reduced to minor figures in the cast. . . . I was fated to lose, even if no joy were to ensue for her; I had need of all my powers of resistance against so ardent a being, for she gave herself utterly over to her one consuming thought."[27]

Sophie and Erick pursue and flee one another, then, caught in the twists and turns of political conflict, they are separated. When they meet up with one another again, Sophie has "gone over to the other side." She is a prisoner, condemned to death. It is she who demands that Erick execute her, give to her "the coup de grâce": "I fired, turning my head away. . . . At first I thought that in asking me to perform this duty she had intended to give me a final proof of her love, the most conclusive proof of all. But I understood afterwards that she only wished to take revenge, leaving me prey to remorse. She was right in that: I do feel remorse at times. One is always trapped, somehow, in dealings with women."[28] These are the last words of the story.

Yourcenar claimed, as she notes in the Pléiade's "Chronologie," that this novel "was inspired by an authentic event," an account of which she had taken down. Alix De Weck, the daughter of a Swiss friend of Yourcenar's, Jacques de Saussure (the son of the linguist Ferdinand de Saussure), confirms that her father "helped Marguerite during the time she was about to start *Coup de Grâce* by giving her information about the Baltic wars in 1918—19."[29] In *Coup de Grâce,* the "Chronologie" points out, "Erick von Lhomond . . . related an experience of love, of military camaraderie, and of violent death in a devastated country. The author returned, but with an acridity that was new, to the deliberately controlled tone and the almost abstract style of *Alexis.*"

So be it. All the same, it is felicitous that Yourcenar pointed out that her style had taken on "an acridity that was new" in this text, undoubtedly the most profoundly violent and the most autobiographical in her entire *œuvre.* After all, a woman madly in love with a man who loves only men—who wouldn't recognize Marguerite Yourcenar and André Fraigneau in this description? And if Fraigneau was only thirty years old whereas the novel's Erick was ten years older, he surely had his haughty good looks, his "narrow profile," and his "arrogant smile."

Even Fraigneau let himself go, during one of those Parisian parties where one can never be sufficiently on one's guard, if one is in the presence of people who keep personal journals, and made an allusion to that "old story." Matthieu Galey faithfully reports it in the second volume of his *Journal,* which came out after his death: "Regarding Marguerite Yourcenar, whom he gave a great deal of support to at Grasset, before the war, he [Fraigneau] claims as well that it was he and Boudot-Lamotte who served as the models for the two masculine characters in *Coup de Grâce,* Marguerite, of course, being the young girl in love . . . with him. If we follow him, she supposedly consoled herself with ladies, unable as she was to be a man who loves men, or the mistress of men who love men. Yeah. But it nonetheless appears that she frequented the Thé Colombin, where certain persons would meet."[30]

"Of course we were the heroes of *Coup de Grâce,* Boudot-Lamotte and I," Fraigneau confirms. "But there was nothing at all out of the ordinary, or abnormal about that. Such things happened with extreme frequency in our milieu back then. We would say to each other: 'Say, you're going to be in my next book.' There is nothing exceptional to look beneath the surface for here." Is this what he really believes, this man who paid so dearly for his resemblance to Erick in the novel, for exalting manly virtues and the new men, those, in short, who occupied France at the beginning of the forties? We're entitled to our doubts, but there is no point in dwelling on the matter. Fraigneau is an inflexible man. Indeed, that was what Yourcenar could never pardon him for.

In point of fact, *Coup de Grâce* can be read entirely as a methodical settling of scores, as a personal message. It is a message that Yourcenar addressed as much to herself as to Fraigneau—an exhortation to be "done with it." Everything in *Coup de Grâce* can be understood in two or three ways, beginning with the title. As Yourcenar was writing this novel, Fraigneau was publishing a collection of short stories entitled *La Grâce humaine* [Human Grace].[31] "It was by way of a reference to my book that she named hers *Coup de Grâce,*" he comments today. The "coup de grâce" refers also, of course, to the one she delivers to their disastrous affair. Lastly, she had just met up with Frick, which probably made possible, within herself, the real split with Fraigneau, and the writing of this book. The dedication she wrote to Frick attests to this: "To my very dear Grace. The dedication of every copy of this book should bear her name. In any case her first name is there. 'I always astound them in saying that I have known happiness, the real thing, the inalterable gold piece. . . . [S]uch happiness leaves one proof against vague philosophizing; it helps to simplify life, and life's opposite, as well.'"[32]

Within the novel, over the course of the narrative, we could add many more items to the list of traces from Yourcenar and Fraigneau's story—such as this one: "What was ludicrous in the whole affair was this: it was my coldness and unresponsiveness that had won her; if in our first encounters she had seen in my eyes what she now sought there in vain she would have repulsed me with horror." [33]

Indeed, Yourcenar emphasized the violence she would have preferred that Fraigneau at least grant her: since he was unable to love her, perhaps he could have hated her, even struck her, expressing thus something else besides friendly indifference. Erick von Lhomond, for his part, renders this paradoxical homage to Sophie, offering her that recognition, that painful existence: ". . . women are fools to fall for us, and I am right to mistrust them. With her shoulders showing bare in that blue dress, and her short hair tossed back (she had singed the ends trying to curl them on an iron), Sophie was presenting that bastard the most inviting, and most feigning, pair of lips that ever movie actress offered while keeping a weather eye on the camera. That was too much for me. I took her by the arm and slapped her. The shock, or the surprise, was so great that she staggered backward, stumbled against a chair and fell, so there was a nosebleed to add one more ridiculous touch to the scene." [34]

Sophie is so close to Yourcenar that, evoking the voice of her character, she describes her own voice exactly, the singular inflections that all her interlocutors would notice, the strange timbre, at once "husky and tender, like a cello's deep tones." [35]

Conrad, on the other hand, crystallizes the loathing Yourcenar felt toward a certain kind of weakness, a, notably masculine, "frailty": "Natures like Conrad's are frail. . . . [T]urned loose in the world of society or of business, lionized by women or a prey to easy success, they are subject to certain insidious dissolution, like the loathsome decay of iris; those sombre flowers, though nobly shaped like a lance, die miserably in their own sticky secretion, in marked contrast to the slow, heroic drying of the rose." [36] Even without lapsing into an immoderate psychoanalytic interpretation, one's mind can't help but wander in the face of the astonishing comparison with which this sentence closes.

It is in connection with Conrad that the figure of Rembrandt's *Polish Rider* appears, which Yourcenar had just seen for the first time at the Frick Gallery (no relation to Grace's family) in New York. It was to be an image that would stay with her all her life, resurfacing strangely in the latter years, when she would identify a stricken Jerry Wilson with the character in this painting, described in *Coup de Grâce:* "the impression it made upon me was that of a ghost who had acquired an accession number and a place in the catalogue: that youth, mounted on a pale horse, half turning in his saddle as he rides swiftly on, his face both sensitive and fierce, a desolate landscape where the nervous animal seems to sense disaster ahead, and Death and the Devil."[37]

By an extraordinary "coincidence," the hero of André Fraigneau's novel, *Les Étonnements de Guillaume Francoeur* [Guillaume Francoeur, Astonished], also mentions the same painting, noted during his visit to the "second-rate Trianon that houses the Frick collection. Its small-paned windows open onto the magnolias of Central Park. A millionaire (whose name predestined him!)[38] has assembled several masterpieces of exceptional quality there, among them Rembrandt's *Polish Rider* who, on his sleepwalking horse and beneath a fur bonnet, resembles Greta Garbo."[39]

Nearly twenty-five years after the publication of *Coup de Grâce,* in a letter addressed to a young student, Yourcenar would return to the question of her characters' exceptional nature:

> Regarding Erick in *Coup de Grâce,* one can surely speak of solitude, but of a very particular type of solitude, due in large part to the vagaries of history, by which I mean the collapse of a caste and a world. Erick remains almost belligerently faithful to codes of discipline rendered useless by a transformed human milieu, and this is his tragedy, much more so even than his dealings with Sophie or Conrad. Alone, but linked forever to those whom he chose to consider his own people, to Conrad, and in a sense to Sophie herself. What is hard about him, and almost irremediable, is a function of his desperate qualities. . . . Sophie is just about as important as Erick in this little book; she is at once Erick's *paradrome* and his opposite, as generously set to take anything on (and not only at the sexual level) as Erick is instinctively set to refuse to. Sophie is not a being for whom the problem of solitude poses itself.[40]

Regarding Erick, then, "this young Prussian who hates women, indicts Jews, exalts war, death, and manly virtues, what is it that Marguerite Yourcenar really thinks?" asked Jean-Denis Bredin in his induction speech at the Académie Française, on 17 May 1990, evoking this "fierce novel" that "sheds light on the other side of Marguerite Yourcenar: her violent aspects." "This coup de grâce casts a strange glance on what was to come," he concluded. Indeed. And depending on what one thinks of its author, one denounces her ambiguity or one praises her clairvoyance. The inevitable biographical reading of this narrative proves that people who view Yourcenar as overly lenient toward all the Erick von Lhomonds of the forties are pointing the finger of blame at her unjustly. They point it more unjustly still in thinking that, when she commented on *Coup de Grâce,* a long time afterward, she attempted to present herself as a "resister" before the fact, one of the rare souls to have perceived "the demons" before everyone else. For, if she rewrote her life endlessly, it was less to erect herself a statue—as people who don't recognize the act of literary creation believe—than to build herself a novel.

Besides which, exasperated by the analyses of this book, by the accusations of indulgence toward the ideology and moral code of "this young Prussian," knowing how little this text—so full of personal violence and love-hate ambivalence—owed to any type of political reflection, Yourcenar explained herself, one more time, in the conclusion of her preface rewritten in 1962:

"With regret for having to underline, in closing, what ought to be apparent, I should mention that Coup de Grâce *does not aim at exalting or discrediting any one group or class, any country or party. The very fact that I have deliberately given Erick von Lhomond a French name and French ancestors (perhaps in order to credit him with that sharp lucidity which is not a particularly German trait) precludes any interpretation of him as either an idealized portrait or a caricature of one type of German officer or aristocrat. It is for value as a human, not political, document (if it has value), that* Coup de Grâce *has been written and accordingly should be judged."*[41]

At the beginning of June 1938, after an entire month devoted to concluding an extremely violent personal affair, in the most radical manner she knew—by making it into a book—Yourcenar was exhausted. But she could neither stay in Italy nor set off for Greece. She had to go to Paris, where it seems she had a lot to do, judging from the note she sent to Charles Du Bos: "Dear Friend, I shall be in Paris tomorrow, and only for a few days. Would it be possible to meet with you one day next week, in Paris if possible? If need be, I shall go to Saint-Cloud to see you, but my time is very limited. With my warmest wishes." [42]

She was still in Paris in July, since she wrote again to Du Bos, from the Hôtel Wagram: "My stay in Paris this time, has been rich in *favorable turns of chance,* and I place my meeting with you among the best of these." [43] One would obviously like to know more about these "turns of chance," which she underlines in her letter, but in the total absence of any information, testimony, or documents, it would be reckless, certainly, to hazard any guesses. Did she finally have some peaceful encounters with Fraigneau? If so, it would be hard to describe them as having happened by chance. Did she make some new feminine conquests? If so, nothing came of them, and they would simply have been credited to the account of what Yourcenar called "good fortune." Besides which, it's hard to imagine why she would refer to them, even obliquely, in a note to Du Bos. None of this is very convincing. And this is precisely the problem: there is nothing that gives us a view of her, that lets us really understand her, during that summer of 1938. In August, she left for the house on Capri, where she hoped to complete her novel. She fell ill there and went to Sorrento, where she stayed at the Sirena Hotel. This was where she finished *Coup de Grâce*.

Did she go afterward to Greece, at the end of August and beginning of September, and could this have been when those infamous photographs were taken bearing the caption "Greece 1938, at Mr. Athanase Chrystomanos's"? Here again, there is nothing specific that would allow us to say so. She has only stated that at the end of September she was staying in Sierre, in the Swiss canton of Valais "where she spent the anxious 'days of Munich.'" We can hardly deduce from this thoroughly insufficient commentary what Yourcenar's reaction was to the Munich Pact, signed during the night of 29–30 September. She probably felt, as did most of the French, what she herself called afterward "a cowardly relief," a desire to believe, despite the obvious reality, that the war would not take place. Immediately after "Munich," she left for Paris where she stayed until December. While there, she concerned herself primarily with her literary future, and particularly with negotiating her contract for *Coup de Grâce* with Gallimard.

During all those months when they were separated, Yourcenar and Frick wrote to one another a great deal. Frick's letters have been lost; they were probably forgotten in one of those trunks that Yourcenar had a habit of leaving in one or another hotel where she would stay for several weeks each year, in Switzerland, in Austria, or somewhere else. Yourcenar's letters, devotedly preserved by Frick, are in a sealed file at Harvard. Yourcenar who, upon the arrival of fame, would say "the friend with whom I share my house" when the need to mention Frick arose, did not want to leave behind any explicit traces of their private life. At least not until she herself had become an "historical character," which is to say, fifty years after her death. But apart from the fact that we need only read Frick's daybooks— which are not sealed—in order to understand the incredible love she bore Yourcenar, we have also had the good luck to find a minuscule testament to the birth of her passion. Since one can never be too cautious, or perhaps since one is always dying to say what one claims to want to hide, Yourcenar "forgot," in one of the photograph albums still kept at Petite Plaisance— and accessible to the public, to which the house is now open for two months during the summer—a short letter from Frick, clumsy and touching, written in 1938 (the heading does not bear the exact date) after Yourcenar's return to Europe.

516 Orange St New Haven
So I love you, believe it or not.[44] I had dinner with Alice [probably Alice Parker] last night in a great storm. She received her copy of *Les Songes* [Dreams] and I love you because you didn't forget it. Why are you so nice?

Yesterday, I worked too long into the night and I went to bed, not think-ing that I was very tired, but I must have been because I wondered why I seemed to be making an effort to call for you. You weren't there during the entire evening. But this morning, the moment I awake, there you are with no effort and I'm ready for you.

And you can tear this up if you wish, right away, without fail.

Beloved.

Grace.

"*Les Songes*," to which Grace refers in this letter, is that curious book, *Les Songes et les sorts*, that Grasset had just published that year, 1938, and that Yourcenar, at the end of her life, was thinking of having republished, with some additions. In it she offers twenty-two, quite brief, accounts of dreams; they are preceded by a preface in which she explains what she retained of her intense oneiric activity for this volume. "There is the region of memory dreams, which is dominated by the figure of my dead father," she points out. "The cycle of ambition and pride, which I hardly ever tra-versed except during the nights of my twentieth year; the cycle of terror . . . into which I enter less often than in days gone by, for with time dread goes out of us as hope does, and we shall no doubt grow old reassured as are the poor, who have no reason to fear that their misfortune will be stolen." "I am carefully excluding from these pages the physiological dreams, too visibly caused by a malfunction of the stomach or the heart," she adds.[45] "I am also passing over in silence the purely sexual dreams, whose intensity is often surprising, but which are hardly more than a simple acknowledgment of desire on the part of a sleeping man or woman." "What matters to me here is the stamp of an individual destiny impressed upon the metal of a dream, the inimitable alloy that those same psychological or sensual elements con-stitute when a dreamer associates them according to the laws of a chemistry that is his alone, charging them with the meanings of a destiny that will only happen once. There are dreams, and there are destinies: my main in-terest is that moment when destinies express themselves by way of dreams." [46]

"*Les Songes et les sorts* is not simply a pretext for reflection, philosophy, or knowledge," Edmond Jaloux would write. "It reveals itself above all to the reader as a remarkable florilegium of prose poems. One thinks, in read-ing it, of those of Baudelaire, and sometimes those of Rilke." [47]

In his column, Jaloux also dealt with *Oriental Tales*—a collection of texts inspired by Yourcenar's reading and by her discovery of the Orient, which would hold a lasting fascination for her—which appeared at Gallimard in the course of the same year. "This form of narration," he pointed out notably, "does not aim . . . to amuse us with events, be they comical, realistic, or recounted in the usual way, but to make us dream by opening up before us long perspectives on the past, on the legends of the future, on philosophy in action; it aims to bring us back to a reflection on human destiny, to gather together disparate analogies in order to extract a teaching from them. . . . Its means is transfiguration; its goal, poetry." [48]

"It is their style that forms the magnificent continuity among the nine tales," François Nourissier would write on the occasion of a reedition of the volume, "whether it's a question of medieval China or Japan, of Balkan or Greek legends rethought and adopted by Marguerite Yourcenar. . . . One thinks frequently of painters in reading *Oriental Tales:* of Rembrandt, of Vermeer, of Dürer, who take over where the poets leave off." [49]

FRICK'S LOVE did not stop Yourcenar from carrying on with her love life in Europe. Thus did Lucy Kyriakos join her at the end of December in Kitzbühl, Austria, so they could spend New Year's together. Several photographs of Yourcenar and Kyriakos walking in the snow attest to this visit, and it is impossible to be mistaken about the relations between the two women. They are clearly a couple, in which, just as clearly, Yourcenar is the dominant figure. We don't know how long Kyriakos stayed, but Yourcenar, for her part, extended her Austrian visit into March. We know this from her correspondence with Emmanuel Boudot-Lamotte regarding the publication of *Coup de Grâce,* for which she had signed the contract, on 10 December, with Gallimard: "In the event that the proofs of *Coup de Grâce* are ready before 1 February," she explained to him in a letter dated 6 January, "could you have them sent to me?" And she gives two addresses: until 18 January, c/o Baronin Gutsmansthal in Kitzbühl; afterward, and until 30 January, at a Viennese boardinghouse. "I may take a brief trip to Poland," she adds, "and I would enjoy going over this book again more or less on site." [50]

WE DON'T KNOW what became of this Polish jaunt, but at the end of March, Yourcenar turned up in Athens, rather clandestinely. She has said that she set off on this trip right after having finished the translation of *What Maisie Knew* by Henry James (the book would not come out until 1947 at Editions Robert Laffont). Frick maintained, for her part, that the translation was done in 1937–1938. Yourcenar also claimed to have been working at this time with Constantine Dimaras on Cavafy, which, as we have seen, is quite probably not true. On the other hand, some photographs taken of Kyriakos during Easter in 1939—we don't know by whom—offer proof of the extent to which this trip was made for purely private reasons. Those pictures, which Yourcenar kept throughout her life, show how beautiful Kyriakos was. For Yourcenar, Kyriakos represented the kind of beauty that, in her eyes, only Greece could produce. "I myself have never been (or even dreamed of being) a young woman admired by all for her beauty and elegance, but my friend L.K. has," she would say to Matthieu Galey.[51] Something of a mournful beauty, perhaps. She was a married woman for whom the encounter with Yourcenar was doubtless only an "exotic" affair, such as women have always had between themselves, right under men's noses. On Kyriakos, Yourcenar exercised her almost irresistible powers of seduction, that mixture of an almost masculine look, her obvious sensuality and intense desire, along with a will to intellectual power.

Yourcenar supposedly remained in Greece until August, which is not true, inasmuch as, in June, she wrote a letter from Paris to Jean Ballard, the editor of the review *Les Cahiers du Sud,* about a text on Ariadne from which she would derive her play *To Each His Minotaur:* "I am sending you the requested 'Ariadne.' I had not promised it to you without certain qualms, not knowing if this text would strike me as good enough to be reasonably worth submitting to you. Had there been a need to, I believe I would have lied and claimed that I had mislaid the manuscript. . . . But is it only the poet's incorrigible pride that spares me this untruth? It seems to me that this little operatic libretto can still hold its own well enough. You be the judge."[52]

We have already seen that what would be the framework of *To Each His Minotaur* came out of a friendly literary game played by Yourcenar, Fraigneau, and Gaston Baissette in 1932, at a time when all three of them were living in the grip of an enthusiasm born of their recent trips, and of the reading and writing they had done about Greece. It was a passionate discussion on the subject of the Labyrinth that induced them to play this round of *"petits papiers,"* in which each one wrote a text without consulting with the others.[53] All three sketches were published together, with a preface by Fraigneau, in a special issue of *Cahiers du Sud,* in August of 1939.[54]

Similarly, in a letter dated 18 June, once again to Ballard, she states: "I have just come back from a short trip to Belgium," which invalidates what she always maintained, namely, a total absence from Belgium during those years. "I hope that André Fraigneau has reached an agreement with you regarding his 'Minotaur,'" she adds. "I plan on seeing him within a few days, and if there were a need to, I would put my eloquence to work to convince him. But knowing his affection for *Cahiers du Sud,* I imagine him already won over with regard to this project."[55] This detail confirms—at the same time it exposes—the ambiguity of Yourcenar's behavior toward Fraigneau: in her rare disclosures on this subject, she spoke of her intentional, resolute "estrangement" after writing *Fires,* which grew even more pronounced following the composition of *Coup de Grâce;* yet she could not pass through Paris without seeking out an encounter.

In May, *Coup de Grâce* had in fact appeared at Gallimard. "*Coup de Grâce* is not a 'diabolical' tale," wrote Jaloux;

> it has the horror of something true; which is always more dreadful than anything invented. But its simple, as if natural, horror is equal to the terror of almost all the most gripping tales I know. Sometimes it brings *El Verdugo* (*The Executioner*) to mind.[56] But one must admit that it is better written and better presented than the latter story. To be perfectly candid, I consider it one of the best short novels of the last several years, and I would be very much surprised if this did not become known one of these days. . . . I have said that *Coup de Grâce* must be a true story: I know nothing about it, but that's what I suppose. There is a form of terror that is born of the activity of men and not of their imaginations; and it is the most terrible of all. . . .
>
> In this tragedy with three characters, only two are entirely visible to us: it's as if the third is absent. If this is so, it will be argued, then this is proof that he should have remained at the level of a minor character. I don't believe this and I regret his being kept in the background; in my eyes, this is the book's only flaw. The role Conrad plays is too important for him to stay so far back in the wings. . . .
>
> Madame Marguerite Yourcenar is the only writer who has extracted the subject of an authentic tragedy from the muddled elements of contemporary history, as Racine did in *Bajazet.*[57]

In a much later article, Henri Hell, too, would make reference to the novel's Racinian vein: "This narrative, at once red-hot and ice-cold, has the cruelty, the conciseness, and the formal purity of a tragedy by Racine." "One has to marvel at the ease with which, like a true novelist, Marguerite Yourcenar slips into her character's skin," he notes further. "There seems to be a personal misogyny, if one might put it this way (which it would be interesting to study throughout all her work), that enables her to be in intimate harmony with a man like Erick von Lhomond. If she sketches a portrait, both proud and tough, of Sophie, one surely has the feeling that her sympathies go to Erick."[58]

"Misogyny?" Yourcenar would promptly reply. "Let's say that I am very sensitive to a certain side of most women that is narrow and limited, superficial and grossly material all at once. But I nonetheless attempted to describe . . . Marcella [in *A Coin in Nine Hands*] and Sophie from the angle of a noble passion, be it political or amorous. . . . The word misanthropy would seem to me more accurate, in the discouragement it implies with regard to human beings whatever their sex may be, oneself often among them. . . . Nevertheless, and in spite of exceptions that serve to prove the rule, it would strike me as difficult to present a woman in a work of fiction whose primary concern would be judging herself and judging the world around her with complete clairvoyance. Sophie would not have been capable of telling her story, which gives Erick an undeniable advantage, at least in literature." [59]

DID SHE go back to Greece in July? There's no way of telling. Whatever the case may be, she couldn't have spent more than a month there, for she was in Switzerland on 11 August, at Lausanne's Hôtel Meurice, where she wrote to Ballard, regarding, as before, the *Ariane* manuscript. This text would appear in the issue of *Cahiers du Sud* dated August-September. At the end of August, she was in Sierre, in the canton of Valais, a place she was fond of and where she made, as she put it, "a customary stopover" every year—or almost every year—at the same time. We do not, unfortunately, know whom she visited. She had made plans to leave Europe over the course of the month of September, for she had agreed, at Grace's request, to spend another winter with her in the United States. But while she was getting ready to return to Paris, to then embark on the Dutch ship the *Nieuw Amsterdam* bound for New York, war between France and Germany was declared, on 3 September. Alarm bells rang all day in the villages of Switzerland and France. She heard them as she made her way to Paris. "That time it was the bells of seven or eight cities or villages ringing all at once, the great bell of the Lausanne cathedral standing out among them. Alone as I was, free as I was, not attached really to any particular place, except by my choice, to any being, except by my choice, it seemed to me for a long moment that my own life was being erased, was nothing more than a crossroads into which surged those waves of sound. Very quickly those alarm bells ceased being the signal of a danger, and became instead a death knell, that of all those who were going to die in that adventure, I myself perhaps among them." [60] These remarks were put down in an unpublished and, unfortunately, incomplete text she kept at Petite Plaisance, no doubt in order to complete and correct it—it already bears handwritten corrections—to which she had given the title "Commentaires sur soi-même" [Self-Commentary].

IN PARIS, she learned that the *Nieuw Amsterdam* would not take to sea. She no longer quite knew what she wanted to do, except get away from Paris. After considering a return to Greece, she asked Gaston Gallimard to help her obtain permission to leave France for the United States. He did so most willingly, writing a letter attesting that Yourcenar, in connection with her work for Editions NRF, had to go to the United States, whence she would return six months or, at the latest, one year later.[61] There then remained the matter of finding a ship to set sail on. Without really knowing what was going to happen, or even what she truly wanted, Yourcenar went to Bordeaux, where several ships, she had been told, were bound for North America. To leave or to stay? Yet again, alone, she had to choose.

PART 3

Memory Recaptured

8
The Dark Years

SHE HAD NO MORE MONEY: the funds recovered in 1929, after the financial disaster, had performed their function well, to "afford [her] ten or twelve years of luxurious freedom"—the luxury here, of course, being the freedom itself—but now they were exhausted.[1] And leaving for another stay with Frick, in the context of a war that could well make a quick return hazardous, rendered her departure even more grave.

In Bordeaux, there was still time to reconsider her decision, to turn back, to stay in Europe. But what would be the point, and where would she go? Surely not to Paris, where she already suspected what stance to expect from the man she'd loved in vain and now wished to flee, unable to forget him. Nor could she go to Greece, where she would only find Lucy again and settle into an amorous seclusion that hardly would have suited her. During that month of October 1939, in a Europe that was mobilizing for war, no doubt it was already too late to contemplate a trip to Greece, where she had unsuccessfully tried to obtain a cultural mission. Moreover, since she had made the trip to Bordeaux, it seems quite clear that she had made up her mind.

This new conflict had come as a shock to her. At the age of thirty-six, for the second time in her life, she had just heard war declared: between her love affairs, the attempts she made to take her mind off them, and her work, she had hardly seen it coming. Premonitory signs had been detected of course, but, like so many others, she had hastily dismissed them, naively determined to believe at any price that peace would prevail. Later on, many of the members of her generation—she herself among them—would have reason to ask themselves why they had adopted this attitude. As in 1914 with her father, she had to leave. Together, they had taken to sea to reach England. This time it was the ocean, and America. And she was alone.

Was she running away? Certainly. But not solely, nor even primarily, from the prospect of danger, death, or battlefields, which she could only conceive of in connection with the "other war." For, as she notes in her "Commentaires sur soi-même," "however deeply into horror my imagination may have drawn me, I did not go so far as to conceive of the millions dead in concentration camps, the communal graves of the Ukraine and Stalingrad, the hundreds of thousands burned in Dresden and Hiroshima, the victims of the raids over England, . . . the resisters hung from Norway to Yugoslavia." And as she said, citing remarks made by Edmond Jaloux, who "bas[ed] his notions as one nearly always does on yesterday's dangers rather than foreseeing tomorrow's," she no doubt imagined "a war of position like the war of 1914, with armies immobilized for years behind Maginot Lines or Siegfried Lines, civilian life reduced to nothing."[2] Above all, she entrusted to the unexpected eruption of that war the task of placing the greatest possible distance, and a lengthy separation, between her and André Fraigneau, and releasing her, if release was possible, from that passion, which she had already tried to rid herself of by writing *Coup de Grâce.*

After all, this trip to the United States was on the program. So why change a plan that had already been made? Ever since childhood, Yourcenar had hated it when reality dared to come along and thwart the choices she had made. However, the war had just turned everything upside down, and she was no longer an eleven-year-old child setting off for England as if for an adventure, her father holding her by the hand. She was leaving; that much was inevitable. But when would she return? What was going to become of Europe? And what was she letting herself in for with that woman "with a young Sibyl's features" who seemed determined to proffer her, beyond even a frightening passion, what she sensed was an all-consuming love?[3]

So she reached New York on the ship she had taken in Bordeaux—in November, according to her, "in October," according to Frick, "via SS. Manhattan." It is difficult, amid the confusion of the precipitous departures of 1939, to precisely retrace the steps that Yourcenar took, to follow her repeated attempts to find a ship. Nonetheless, in consulting the maritime archives of the city of Bordeaux, one finds that between the beginning of September and the end of November, only two boats left the port, at Quay Carnot, for the United States: the *Saint-John,* a cargo and passenger vessel, on 14 October, and the *California,* normally reserved for the transport of goods, on 15 October. The latter vessel, exceptionally (as is recorded in red ink in the shipping registers of the time), took on some passengers for New York.

While on board, she wrote an undated note to Jean Ballard—which she would mail in New York—in which it appears, even at this early juncture, that she was taking leave of Europe for a long time: "After staying for a while in the gloomy, yet beautiful, Paris of wartime—where I joyfully reread, thanks to you, *Ariane*—I have just crossed the Atlantic, and, apparently, we are coming into port. All my thanks yet again, and my good wishes for the *Cahiers* [*du Sud*] in these difficult times."[4]

She moved into Frick's apartment, at 448 Riverside Drive: Frick was teaching that year at Barnard College, and they lived in one of the many residential buildings, owned by Columbia University, of this upper-westside Manhattan neighborhood next to Harlem. They stayed there throughout the academic year. From the buildings on Riverside Drive, there is a view of the Hudson River, one of the arms of the sea that encircle the island of Manhattan. On certain mornings, if you open the windows, you can get a whiff of sea air, right there in the middle of the city man has dominated most, vanquishing both nature and the lack of space. Yourcenar could not have been insensitive to this incongruity, one of many paradoxes that make up the inexplicable mystery and charm, in the most violent sense, of this city. Moreover, she took a certain pleasure in returning to New York. Nonetheless, it was not her kind of city: triumphant urbanization and expansion on a gigantic scale were hardly in harmony with her conception of urbanity. Besides which, cities, once the initial euphoria of discovery had worn off, were beginning to provoke in her a kind of unease that would grow more pronounced over the years. Her own madnesses and excesses were Mediterranean. Not that New York was a Nordic city, but it lacked the nonchalance that Yourcenar had so much enjoyed in Athens. And furthermore, there was nothing, deep down, that appealed to her in the mixture of puritanism and megalomania that typified this people without a civilization.

Nineteen forty was a year of "odd jobs," as we might say today: a few commercial translations, a few minor newspaper pieces, and a lecture tour. In January, she published the first translations—done in collaboration with Dimaras—of the Greek poet Constantine Cavafy in the review *Mesures,* consisting of a few texts preceded by a critical essay, whose central focus would be that, later on, of the preface to the final work. This would be virtually the only publication until 1944. "For more than eleven years, her literary output would be limited to a few contributions to periodicals," confirms the Pléide's "Chronologie."

Yourcenar fought against the difficulties she had accepting her "confinement" in the United States, for what she began to realize would be a long time. This is especially so since Frick—to say the least—surely did not urge her to make contact with the European intellectuals who had come to seek refuge in New York. Everything that might keep alive the enduring existence of Europe for her friend—even in the midst of her exile—threatened Frick. And the idea of a return seemed extremely dangerous to this young woman who was on the way to finally obtaining what she most categorically desired: having Marguerite for herself alone. Nonetheless, it was in the company of Bronislaw Malinowski, the ethnologist of Polish origin, in his New York apartment, that Yourcenar heard about the fall of Paris, in June of 1940. She burst into tears. They both grieved because the Europe they had known and loved seemed to them irretrievably gone. They weren't mistaken. Never again would the carefree spirit of the thirties return—though there were those, with Cocteau in the lead, who would relentlessly attempt to make it seem that the latter had survived—nor Yourcenar's Mediterranean idylls, interspersed with plunges into the Parisian literary scene. Yourcenar was barely thirty-seven years old; her youth had just died and, with it, a certain notion of insouciance and pleasure. German tanks entering Paris and what was to follow—the despicable conduct of a large number of the people of France, beginning with the intellectuals, the revelation of how deeply Pétainistic was the French mentality, the overt or latent collaboration with the Germans—all of this brought to an end for her forever the era of happy, lighthearted intellectuals. This was even more the case since she had reason to fear the worst from the writers and persons of culture she had liked before the war, of whose ambiguous thoughts she was already cognizant. On the subject of Jaloux, she had already noted in 1939: "His sympathies—which were those of a man who, out of good sense and by temperament, detested crowds—tended as always to the right; a few months earlier, he had spoken to me once without irony of 'a review that published Hitler's texts, which I have the honor of contributing to,' and I had been struck, at the time, by the fact that this man who did not travel and had not known Hitlerian Germany was falling into the usual error of seeing Hitler as a man of order, and not as a monstrous, crude adventurer." And even though she added that Jaloux, in September 1939, "seemed thoroughly recovered from his naive and ill-fated marvelings," she did not fail to observe, after recalling his remarks—"Hitler amused us, because he is essentially a kind of Wallenstein"[5]—that he was "displaying thus the same incurable superficiality from which so many Frenchmen suffer in the presence of political facts." And, from certain of her friends, she could only dread more dramatic aberrations. Imagining that Fraigneau would make fun of her crying, while he himself, beyond a doubt, saluted the dawn of a new era, must have been hard for her to bear. She tried to fix her attention on the notion that, in France, everything would be hurtful to her so as to suffer less from not being in Europe. Fraigneau would not forgive her for what he no doubt considers vagaries of temperament. Nearly fifty years afterward, he calmly continues to say that she lost part of her talent as a writer "because of her contact with all those leftists, over there in America."

In spite of everything, one still had to survive, without depending totally on Grace's work for subsistence. Thanks to the assistance of a friend, Alice Parker, Yourcenar did a lecture tour on French literature in September. She started out in Chicago, then went, notably, to Kentucky, Missouri, Ohio, and South Carolina. It was from this last state—from Charleston, to be precise—that she wrote a short card to Kyriakos, in English: "Very dear Lucy, Do you remember Agios Geórgios (best wishes to everyone), only a year ago? I am in this delicious little city for a few days, in the middle of the magnolia gardens. I did receive your letter and I'm going to answer it. But I've had so much work to do that I haven't had time to yet. When will we see each other again? It's an awfully sad time but life still has some rather nice moments even so. Love from Marguerite." [6] This is something of a careless card, which verges on handing that young woman in love her walking papers. Learning of her death, Yourcenar would never mail it. According to Constantine Dimaras, Kyriakos died at Easter time in 1940 in the bombardment of Janina, Turkey. On Kyriakos's card—which should be sealed, but can be freely consulted at Harvard—Yourcenar added a handwritten observation to the effect that the card was never sent because Lucy had died during a bombardment in Turkey during Easter week of 1941. In the Pléiade's "Chronologie," however, Yourcenar claims that Lucy was killed in 1942.

AT THE END of October, when she had completed her lecture tour, Yourcenar rejoined Frick in Hartford, Connecticut. Frick had moved to this rather uninteresting city, about a hundred miles north of New York, in September. She had just been appointed Academic Dean at Hartford Junior College[7] and had rented a small house at 549 Prospect Avenue in West Hartford. Yourcenar and she kept that apartment until April 1951, when they moved to Maine for good. They spent their first "married" years there—the years of their passion, and also the years of Yourcenar's difficult adjustment to her new life and to a new country that would never be truly her own.

Yourcenar did not have very much to say about those years. To hear her speak of them, one might even have thought they only had lasted a few months. Nonetheless, almost ten years of her life were spent in Hartford. She would maintain a lasting friendship with her seamstress from that time, Erika Vollger, and would warmly remember those she knew, as a letter of

1 August 1959 attests, to her neighbor Emma Trebbe. It concerns the death of Emma Evans, another neighbor: "It seems to me that in that Hartford house during those years of war, which were often such dismal ones, I experienced the best the United States had to offer in the kindness, the mutual trust, and the good will that reigned among neighbors. And among those neighbors, those two women held the very first place."[8] What Yourcenar would be eager above all to forget after the fact was the despondency that overcame her during the end of that year, 1940. Letters from Europe grew rare and offered little comfort, with the exception of one Dimaras sent her from Athens on 25 November: "Just a couple of words to convey to you greetings from the Greece that you love and that loves you," he wrote to her then.

> We are fighting a magnificent war, of infinite symbolic richness. And our people, whom you know to be intelligent, rich, and hardworking, are fully conscious of their mission, which is to liberate humanity from the barbarity that threatened it.
>
> You have friends over there; talk to them about us; tell them that all of us here are proud and happy to be fighting this war. But also tell them how much we need to know that they are with us, near us, how much their moral and material support would be precious to us. Try even to organize their good will—you could be useful to them through your knowledge of our country's people and concerns.

"I recently got news form André Gide," he went on, "who much admired your essay on Cavafy. I am proud on your behalf."

"Please write to me, so that I can be sure you did indeed get my letter; give me your address and tell me what you've done for us."[9]

Was it retrospective irritation with her despondency during that period, perhaps even with her indifferent response to current events, that motivated Yourcenar to write "a short article, included in an official publication of the French Consulate in New York" that "attacks a slim volume of Nazi propaganda by Anne Lindbergh, *The Wave of the Future,* widely read at that time in the United States"? According to the Pléiade's "Chronologie," it dated back to 1940. The article exists, no doubt about it, and it reappears in the collection *En pèlerin et en étranger.*[10] But it is mentioned in connection with 1944 by Yourcenar herself, in the "Carnets de notes, 1942–1948" [Notebooks, 1942–1948] that appeared in the review *La Table Ronde* in 1955. No trace of its publication has yet been found, which led the editor, a bit hastily, to call it an unpublished piece in the posthumous volume of essays of which it is a part. In any event, it is a rather mediocre article.

Nineteen forty-one and nineteen forty-two were certainly the darkest years. Yourcenar had no real literary project to work on. The simple fact was that she had to apply herself to the task of surviving from one day to the next. She who had known her father Michel's splendid plunges into ruin was finding out what a chronic lack of money, small-time poverty, and keeping track of every dollar were about. Christine de Crayencour, her father's widow, was living in France, where she remained, and she was destitute. Yourcenar felt obliged to send her money. But where would it come from?

Her correspondence with Jacques Kayaloff bears traces of the despair into which she was sinking. Kayaloff, whom Yourcenar had met during her first American visit, in 1937, had an important position in the firm of Louis Dreyfus. He was one of those cultivated businessmen, in love with art, particularly literature, who enjoy the company of writers. At the end of the war, he was the one whom Yourcenar asked to recover a trunk left in Lausanne, at the Hôtel Meurice. He found the trunk, dispatched it to the United States, and thus was at the origin of Yourcenar's return to writing *Memoirs of Hadrian*. In New York, Kayaloff spent time with André Breton, Niko Calas, and others, most of them European intellectuals who had fled the war. Moreover, Kayaloff hoped that Yourcenar could meet Breton, as he told her in a letter of 22 July 1941: "I recently saw André Breton who read his latest poem, *Fata morgana* (*Fata Morgana*), to me and told me about his latest book, *L'Humour noir* [Black Humor],[11] which was supposed to have been published in France but, given the circumstances, was not. I spoke with him about you, and the next time you visit, I would like you to meet him." [12]

Nothing indicates, however, that this meeting took place. We can even assume that it did not. In the Pléiade's "Chronologie," the names of numerous émigré writers are cited, but Yourcenar does not mention a meeting, in her correspondence. About Jules Romains, who also lived in New York at that time, Yourcenar would only say, later on, that he encouraged her during the war to get back to her work on Hadrian.[13] Today we know that such was not at all the case. "When I received *Memoirs of Hadrian*, I was not familiar with any of your work. Nor had I even heard very much about you," he wrote to her on 25 December 1951.[14] Confined to Hartford, subjected to the most extreme economic constraints, Yourcenar came to New York only rarely and spent too little time there to have been able to integrate herself into the milieu of European refugees.

Yourcenar carefully eliminated from her correspondence with Kayaloff preserved at Harvard anything that might give the impression of a state of disarray approaching depression. She did not wish to appear touching, in the eyes of history, because of what struck her as weaknesses. Or perhaps she was loath to see descriptions of her mediocre, everyday difficulties when, on the other side of the Atlantic, horror was spreading far and wide. She did not want posterity to see snatches of "the individual, always necessarily manifold," evoked at the beginning of her essay on Mishima. And yet, if those moments of fragility neither add anything to nor take anything away from her *œuvre*, they allow us to better understand the kind of victories over herself and over the temptation to give up of which the major works were born. As Vita Sackville-West writes in her introduction to the diary of Lady Anne Clifford: "We should ourselves be sorry to think that posterity should judge us by a patchwork of our letters, preserved by chance, independent of their context, written perhaps in a fit of despondency or irritation, divorced, above all, from the myriad little strands which colour and compose our peculiar existence, and which in their multiplicity, their variety and their triviality, are vivid to ourselves alone, uncommunicable even to those nearest to us, sharing our daily life. . . . Still, since within our limitations it is necessary to arrive at some conclusions, certain facts do emerge, which . . . enable us to build up a portrait of perhaps sufficient resemblance to the original." [15]

Luckily, though Yourcenar picked over their correspondence, Kayaloff, for his part, kept all her letters and, after his death, his wife Anya saved his papers as she found them. While always dignified, each of Yourcenar's letters to Kayaloff is nonetheless a cry for help. Yourcenar had no bank account. She felt, in all respects, deprived. "I am not a businesswoman," she wrote to him one day when she was asking for advice about how to go about converting war loans. She "forces herself to work" but her "discouragement is very great." [16] She asserts that she will come to New York on 15 September, to show a book to the French publishers at Rockefeller Center. We don't know if this appointment was kept. If so, nothing came of it. It is hard now to imagine a demoralized Marguerite Yourcenar. However, in that year of 1941, she felt there was nothing much left to hold on to: "the news that seeps out of Europe is so bad (destruction, destitution, dead friends) that I hardly dare to read the letters that find their way to me." Days went by, and she would not open the rare letters arriving from Europe, no more than she would those bearing American stamps, for everything seemed to her a portent of bad news. Kayaloff's letters were an exception. And he was the only one to whom she would respond without concealing any of her difficulties, whatever their nature, or the makeshift arrangements she would have to devise in order not to be totally cut off from her friends.

"Things are going poorly," she confided to him on 7 December 1941, "tutoring in French and art history never having enriched French refugee writers in anything other than a very meager way. This, too, is the sole but sufficient reason for my prolonged absence from New York. One of my neighbors, a hatter by profession, goes to New York from time to time to buy felt and I hope that one of these days you will see me arriving in his truck. . . . Nonetheless, if I had even as little as an hour to myself every evening, I know that I would plunge into a new novel, to try to set down as soon as possible my recollections of a time that is at once so close and already so irreparably far from us." [17] This image of Yourcenar clattering into New York in a hatter's truck and coming back to Hartford amid rolls of felt would be enough to make one laugh if this letter weren't the sign of a life so engulfed in everyday concerns that any prospect of creation was excluded from the realm of possibility.

Not being a person, however, who can tolerate intellectual inactivity for very long, she began giving courses, at the end of October 1941, for no pay, in French and art history at Hartford Junior College where Frick was Academic Dean—Frick held this position until 1943, when she started teaching at Connecticut College. Well aware that this occupation, while forcing her to get out of the house, could not provide a permanent cure for her melancholy, Yourcenar attempted to write. In January 1942, she composed a few poems, among them "Drapeau grec" ("Greek Flag"), and the distich "Epitaphe, *Temps de guerre*" ("Epitaph, *Wartime*") inspired by Kyriakos's death, which would later be included in the collection *The Alms of Alcippe*. "I am almost done the final copy of a volume of four short pieces (titled *L'Allégorie mystérieuse* [The Mysterious Allegory])," she noted on 20 January 1942 in a letter to Kayaloff. "Life goes on, knocking one more or less senseless. I have no news from France, no news from Greece, and my discouragement attains to the breadth and depth of the Atlantic Ocean." [18]

The finest moment of 1942 would be, beyond a doubt—as the future would prove—the discovery of Mount Desert Island, located off the northeast coast of the United States and part of Maine. [19] It was then that Frick and Yourcenar spent their first summer on the island, still wild at the time. They stayed at first in Seal Harbor, with the Minears, married friends of theirs who were Protestant theologians. Then they moved to Somesville for the end of their vacation, into the little house next to the cemetery where their ashes are now buried. The house, made out of wood, was very modest, rather uncomfortable, sparsely furnished, and, as Yourcenar related, their suitcases, only partly unpacked—some of them not even opened—took the place of closets. During this first summer, Frick picked up a habit she would maintain almost until her death: organizing parties for children. They would put on little plays at these affairs. As far as this first summer went, for Yourcenar, the result of these festivities was hardly entertaining. In addition to her uncertainty about playing host to groups of children, she picked up lice from her contact with them and had to have her head shaved.

All the same, she decided to begin some serious writing and composed *Le Mystère d'Alceste* [The Mystery Play of Alcestis], a short play, in one act, inspired by Euripides' tragedy. In a long preface, titled "Examen d'Alceste" [A Study of Alcestis], she explained that "the traditional themes of sacrifice and heroism are treated with neither avoidance nor objection" in this play. "My goal in composing [it] was to piously modernize an ancient legend, to render it, if possible, more immediately accessible."[20] But despite that almost happy summertime hiatus, she was not well. Her friends were concerned about her: "Write me a long letter full of your news," one of her correspondents from that period wrote to her again and again.[21]

When school reopened in September 1942, however, a first step was made toward resolving her financial dependence on Grace: Yourcenar obtained a part-time position at Sarah Lawrence, a university that was very progressive and very attentive to pedagogical research, located twenty miles or so north of New York. She taught mainly French there until June of 1950, at which time she took a leave of absence (she was then finishing *Memoirs of Hadrian*). She did return to fulfill her contract obligations during the 1952—53 academic year.

In spite of the difficulties, notably the length of her trip back and forth, which she had to make by train—Bronxville, where Sarah Lawrence is located, is about a hundred miles from Hartford—this teaching position finally afforded Yourcenar an anchoring point, a first step toward integration into the country. Nonetheless, even though the vice's grip was loosening a bit, she who had found a kind of haven here in 1938 now felt oppressed: for from now on she was more or less a captive, with Europe off limits, mute, and devastated.

All was not bleak in her life, however, at least not as bleak as the lack of personal, amorous confidences would lead us to assume. This was the decade of love shared with Grace Frick. The proofs of this are sealed: fifty pages of a personal diary that Yourcenar kept between 1935 and 1945, along with the letters—from New York, Hartford, or Maine—she sent to Frick in 1940, when their respective activities kept them apart. But there are still enough photographs and traces left for us to know that the time of their passion lasted longer than two years, contrary to what Yourcenar sometimes suggested at the end of her life. The photographs taken in the

Hartford house around 1943 are photographs of love, the sort of childish demonstrations of happiness one can't resist when in the thrall of a passion—Marguerite photographing Grace at the window of *their* (this is indeed the exact word used in the caption of the photo, written in English in Yourcenar's hand) bedroom, then Grace photographing Marguerite. They are laughing. These are women with a happy, tender, gentle air about them.

Yourcenar, as we have seen, liked contact sports. She loved seducing, and conquering, of course, but one would not likely imagine her inclined to be interested for very long in someone in whom she aroused feelings of veneration. Nonetheless, and partly perhaps due to the circumstances, she "consented"—and, for a certain period of time, responded—to the mad passion she had inspired in Frick. Courage, which Frick would demonstrate throughout her entire life, took the place of energy for Yourcenar, at a point in her existence when she felt close to giving up.

We know how much Yourcenar strove always to be in control. If she left those captioned photographs behind when she died, it was no doubt because, no matter what she may have said in this regard, she was not immune to the delights of passion's contradictory impulses: the wish that no one know what one was, whom one loved, and the deep desire that no one remain in the dark ... as if too much secrecy insidiously called into question, even in her own eyes, the reality of love. A short note she "overlooked" between two pages of a photograph album offers similar proof. It was scribbled, in not quite confident French, by Frick on a list of errands made out by Yourcenar: "You are sleeping; I am going out; if I don't come back before you leave (for 11:30 meeting), perhaps I'll see you again one day. 7:30: I am having breakfast in the garden, then post office and (quick) library."

Yourcenar left Europe, if not on the heels of a failure in love, at least on the heels of a refusal, which she was hardly inclined to tolerate. In the United States, where life was more difficult for her than it had ever been since her birth, she enjoyed the comfort of a love that surprised even her. Grace was prepared to do everything she could to make her life easier, to help her, to support her, and, if possible, to make her happy. She spared no effort in getting her a teaching position. And it was she who introduced Yourcenar to Mount Desert Island, which became their refuge.

In 1943, they spent their first full summer in Somesville. The setting might have been out of a storybook: a stream and lots of ducks, little wooden bridges, and a bit farther away, the cemetery-garden whose silence was hardly broken by the footsteps of people coming to visit "their" dead.

Frick's love for Yourcenar evinced itself in the attentions she lavished upon her at every moment. At that time, Yourcenar did not know that this would last "for a lifetime"—for Frick's lifetime at least, until she died. But Frick already knew that all she wanted was to live for Yourcenar, and that she would do anything to keep her at her side. And if this was still the time when Yourcenar was amazed by the gift being given her, if she didn't consider it her due, which would not always be the case, Frick, passion or no passion, already possessed a certain merit. Sharing your life with whoever it may be is not necessarily a series of uniformly idyllic moments. Sharing it with Marguerite Yourcenar surely did not make things easier. But living with Marguerite Yourcenar depressed . . . Yourcenar was one of those people who can be alone and serene no matter where they are as long as they have an intellectual project to work on. Working at her desk, she never felt lonely. But during those years of the early forties, between Hartford and Sarah Lawrence, her intellectual activity seemed hampered, reduced to stale repetition. Above all, for the first time in her life, she felt her literary ambition, the conviction of being a writer first and foremost, diminishing. This was the woman who, since the age of twenty, had kept those unfinished stories in her head, the story of Zeno from "D'Après Dürer," and the story of the emperor Hadrian—roughed out during the thirties but abandoned because it lacked the proper tone—along with the certainty that she would realize her destiny in realizing theirs. This was the woman who, deep down, had only one real desire and one real design: to make herself useful to the community of men and women by leaving a few written traces making it possible for them, as they had made it possible for her, to better conceive of their freedom. This woman who had gone through the thirties with a kind of loftiness that many people envied suddenly found herself caught up in the most fearsome chain of events, one that, between kindnesses accepted and desertions agreed to, leads to banality.

On that immense continent, in that land of real freedom, what she felt was confinement of the worst sort. Cut off from her language, her writer friends, her peers, she had doubts, as never before, about her future. She let a certain process begin, vaguely sensing that it could be mortal. From the idea that, for her, nothing could come to fruition here, she slipped into something like distaste for undertaking any major project. She felt like a writer lying fallow and, on the days of utter pessimism, she even asked herself what a writer was, exactly, without a publisher or readers: no longer quite a writer, no doubt.

Concerned, as she constantly was, with putting everything in its proper place, and conscious that, during the years of the Second World War, millions of people physically suffered or paid with their lives, Yourcenar, later, would evoke that period with her exquisite sense of euphemism. To describe it, she would never go beyond a smiling "those were not very pleasant years." In fact, she had touched what was for her the deepest depths of despair, the idea that she could cease to be a writer. Toward the end of 1942, when, thanks to her job as a professor at Sarah Lawrence, material concerns, though she was not well-off, preoccupied her less, her self-examination on the subject of the future became all the more urgent. Wasn't she about to get "stuck" in the very kind of professional life she had devoted all her energies to fleeing, for fear of reaching the point where she no longer had the time or freedom indispensable to her writing? Wasn't she going to be snatched, she who worshipped the French language and European civilization, by another language and another culture? Failing to resist the latter danger, she thought, would surely toll a literary death knell. Despite her exhaustion, she decided to fight and made a vow, to herself, never to let herself be contaminated by English.[22]

When, much later on, one discussed with her the singular quality of her language, preserved, it was assumed, because it had lived on only in writing and had not been subjected to the vagaries of daily use, she took great enjoyment in pointing out that such was not all the case, and that "we always spoke French at home, except with the local people who came to work."[23] Her nurse and her secretary claim, on the contrary, that Frick and she, at least during the end of their life together, spoke English to one another. But attestations such as these from persons who only spoke English must be taken with a grain of salt for, with unflagging courtesy, Yourcenar never allowed herself, with either Frick or other friends, to speak French in front of anyone who didn't know the language. On the other hand, all of her friends who could speak either English or French with equal ease affirm that they never heard her using English, which she spoke, for that matter, with a "surprising" accent, as Mr. Harold Taylor—president of Sarah Lawrence when Yourcenar taught there—describes it, with such a typically Anglo-Saxon flair for understatement. "I would even venture that most of the colleagues who conversed with her pretended to understand what she said, more than they really understood her," he states. This accent, which was indeed "surprising," would remain a mystery. Did pronouncing English without making the slightest effort to emulate its particular rhythms, or at least to place the tonic stress essential to making oneself understood on the proper syllables, constitute in her mind the ultimate means of protecting herself? Or was it simply a question of nonchalantly yielding to her clumsiness at reproducing foreign sounds, a clumsiness that had already exasperated her father when she was twelve years old? No doubt it was a somewhat muddled mixture of the two, which would end up becoming a habit: her own unique manner of speaking with the same voice in every language. Even her French was tinged with a leftover accent from the Nord, a strange modulation, something like an echo of the music of a cello.

If she had to protect herself so as not to entirely lose the hope of continuing to write, she also had to adapt so as to continue, first of all, to live. Whatever she may have claimed, or let people assume, later on especially, her adaptation was not effected painlessly. Yet Yourcenar had always given the impression of being able to maintain an inalienable identity in any place and under any circumstances, an identity founded on the acute consciousness of being Marguerite Yourcenar. She did not feel very well, and she started gaining excess weight, to the point of having to go on a diet. "Marguerite did reduce on doctor's order,"[24] Frick noted in the caption of a photograph—of which we do not know the exact date—where she congratulated herself that "Marguerite looks slimmer than she really is" and she herself "a bit less thin." There were more and more signs of depression, to the extent that in April 1943 when George La Rue, the uncle who had raised Grace, died and she had to go to Kansas City, she was so worried about leaving Yourcenar alone that she asked their friend Erika Vollger, the seamstress, to move in with her.

It is hard, at nearly forty years old, to adjust to the rhythm of earning a paycheck for the first time, to observe an imposed schedule. Yourcenar submitted herself to it with absolute punctuality and precision; but what for others—beginning with Frick—was no more than routine, for her was something painfully new.

Fortunately, the arrival of June brought the end of the academic year. Yourcenar's courses came to an end at Sarah Lawrence and Grace left Hartford Junior College. They set out immediately for Mount Desert Island, where they spent, as we have seen, their first full summer. The island's wildness, that of a northerly Corsica, and its silence, but also the feeling of tranquility it brought, which one still experiences now despite the development of tourism, restored a bit of Yourcenar's energy. She started writing again, and Frick, as scrupulously as ever, noted down in that year's daybook the different stages of her work, with a jubilation translated by the size of the words and the way they are underlined. "Marguerite is writing *Electre* (*Electra*)," another play.[25]

Since her arrival in the United States, Yourcenar had written nothing but short essays, poetry, and theater, which she herself considered rather like appendages to her real *œuvre*, and which did not really console her for the lack of a major literary project. Secondary though it may have been in her eyes, her taste for writing plays is quite surprising, all the more so since Yourcenar herself admitted that she was hardly endowed with a sense of staging or representation. Her interest in dialogue, on the other hand, dated way back: her first text, *Le Jardin des Chimères,* is a poem in dialogue, and the first version of *Hadrian,* composed during the thirties, was also in dialogue form. The appeal that mythological subjects held for her, moreover, need hardly, at this point, be further demonstrated. It was also in the air at the time. Jean Anouilh's *Eurydice (Eurydice)* was produced in 1942 at the Théâtre de l'Atelier. And Monelle Valentin, who played the role—two years later, at the Atelier once again—would score a veritable triumph (five hundred performances) in the role of *Antigone (Antigone).* In 1943, Charles Dullin mounted Jean-Paul Sartre's mythological drama *Les Mouches (The Flies).* Did Yourcenar hope her work would be speedily performed in France? Since contact, for the moment, was cut off, this seems rather doubtful. More likely, she anticipated first being staged in the United States, in Frick's translation. She did not disapprove of entrusting the play to an amateur trope—quite the contrary. As it turned out, *Electre ou La Chute des masques (Electra or The Fall of the Masks)* would be staged on Mount Desert Island in 1944, while its first performance in Paris would not take place, at the Théâtre des Mathurins, until 1954.

But above all, during that period of flagging morale and doubt, writing dialogue was therapeutic. Since it spared her from calling on an "I" she was no longer sure of, it was the form that best suited her uncertainty about herself, her indecisiveness regarding her capacity to speak, and the danger of literary aphasia that threatened her. What she said in old age about the second play composed during that summer of 1943, *La Petite Sirène (The Little Mermaid),* only confirms this hypothesis.

The Little Mermaid, which she dates back to 1942 in her 1970 preface, was a play composed on request. Her friend Everett Austin, director of Hartford's museum[26]—which today would be called a cultural center—had suggested that she write a short divertissement, which Frick would translate and he would direct, for his amateur theater company. Yourcenar's short piece was part of a show devoted to the four elements. "It fell to me to do water," wrote Yourcenar in her preface, "and I immediately thought of composing a little lyric drama based on the Danish storyteller's exquisite tale." But the melancholy charm of the tale is coupled with more dramatic tones beneath her pen. The little mermaid, in love with a prince, wants to join the world of human beings. The water witch grants her wish, but she will only be a young girl without a voice. Mute, and thus incapable of standing up for herself, she will have to witness, alongside the prince—who is marrying an ugly, rich princess—an exhibition of cowardice, shady compromise, and dirty political dealings. A long time afterward, speaking of that play with Jerry Wilson, her traveling companion, she told him (and he recorded in his journal) how close she had felt to that little mermaid. Here was a young girl incapable of talking and hurled, as the result of a defective feat of magic, into a world where she was fated to die of suffocation, just as Yourcenar, at the beginning of the forties, had been torn away from Europe and planted in a country whose values she did not understand and whose language she spoke only vaguely. "In rereading it [*The Little Mermaid*], I realized that I had put more than I thought into that little play," she also wrote in the 1970 preface.

> Our least works are like objects upon which we cannot fail to leave our fingerprints, however invisible. I now understand, somewhat belatedly, what that creature abruptly transported to another world, finding herself bereft of both identity and voice, must have meant to me, in some obscure way, at the time. But in addition, and above all, that oceanic reverie dates back to a time when history's true face, a hideous one, was revealing itself to millions of men, a great number of whom died for having beheld it; even at the distance where chance had placed me, I had seen what I had seen. It was during that time and by means of a discipline still practiced that, little by little, the ascendancy of landscapes bearing traces of the human past, once loved so intensely, came to be replaced for me by that of places, ever more rare, that are still little marked by the ghastly human adventure. . . . This shift from archeology to geology, from a meditation on man to a meditation on the earth, was and still is from time to time a process that affects me in a painful way, although it leads, in the end, to some inestimable gains.

Yourcenar's radical pessimism regarding the human creature's future—which had nothing to do with a distaste for life—dated from this epoch of fracture. It was the same kind of thinking that would make her an ecological activist, which, flying in the face of the sickly sentimental and simplistic images that would prevail when she became a public persona—the memory of which still persists—prohibits us from seeing her as a woman whose primary concerns were acclimating rare flowers in her garden and taking care, in the winter, to give plenty of food to the birds.

The reasons for her distress, and what helped Yourcenar bear it, are very soberly expressed in her notebooks from the forties, which were later published in *La Table Ronde:* "1943. It is too early to speak, to write, perhaps to think, and for a time our speech will resemble the stuttering of someone gravely wounded undergoing rehabilitation. Let us take advantage of this silence as if it were a mystical apprenticeship. . . . What helps you live, in times of helplessness or horror? The necessity of earning, or kneading, the bread that you eat, sleeping, loving, putting on clean clothes, rereading an old book, the smile of the Negress or the Polish tailor on the corner, the smell of ripe cranberries, and the memory of the Parthenon. All that was good during times of delight is exquisite in times of distress. People who convert at the moment of their deaths are admitting by this gesture that they did not live well."[27]

Thus, despite their scattered nature, one gets the sense from Yourcenar's various literary efforts, during the second half of 1943, of a life that is starting up again. She began translating Negro spirituals and Greek poems, of which she was fond. At the same time, in the review *Fontaine*, a fragment of her translation of Frederic Prokosch's novel, *The Seven Who Fled*, came out. The rest of the translation would be lost, as Prokosch explains in his volume of remembrances *Voices: A Memoir*, while getting ready to pay a visit to Colette: "I'd written to her already saying that I'd pay her a call, and just to be on the safe side I sent her *Sept Fugitifs*, which had been published by Gallimard in a beautiful new translation. Years ago Marguerite Yourcenar had translated *The Seven Who [Fled]*, but this translation had been lost when the Germans invaded Paris."[28] It had been by way of a letter dated 26 August 1939, sent from Sierre, Switzerland, that Yourcenar accepted the terms of the contract proposed by Gallimard: "Many thanks for your letter of 18/8 regarding your agreement with Frederic Prokosch," she wrote to Gaston Gallimard at the time. "I hereby confirm my acceptance of the contract you proposed in your letter of 11 July. I have already finished translating the first book of *The Seven Who Fled*, and I hope, as had been agreed, to forward the entire manuscript to you by the month of November."[29]

Prokosch had met Yourcenar, but it has proved impossible to date that encounter precisely. Perhaps it took place in New York, at 820 Fifth Avenue, in the apartment of Josephine Crane, which during the war years was "a refuge for poets and a mecca for artists." "People spoke of Propertius and Pico della Mirandola," and Hannah Arendt came there to give a lecture on the nineteenth century.[30]

They did not see one another often, nor did they meet again in old age—or at least they left no trace of such a meeting. But Prokosch had not forgotten Yourcenar, and did not remember her as a woman depressed—Yourcenar could be relied on to hold her head high in public. He even wrote in *Voices: A Memoir:* "The three most intelligent women I have met in my life were Gertrude Stein, Hannah Arendt, and Marguerite Yourcenar, and in all three the amazing thing was their love for ambiguity, which went hand-in-hand with a startling clairvoyance. In all three the gift for seeing the unexpected side of things was linked with an age-old faith in the smoldering powers of divination." [31] This remark is so apt that one is surprised to find Prokosch, further on, attributing to a specifically masculine intelligence, in particular that of Thomas Mann (one of the three most intelligent men he had met), "the search for a cool, impersonal truth, which was closely linked to an acceptance of the impossibility of seizing the truth." This description better suits what we know about Yourcenar than the points Prokosch then makes, when he takes a go at describing the various types of intelligence: "There was the sorcery-like wisdom of the Baroness Blixen and the sibyl-like muttering of Gertrude Stein and Marguerite Yourcenar." [32] No witness evokes any "sibyl-like muttering" in connection with Yourcenar, but the comment is an interesting one to call attention to because of the comparison with Gertrude Stein. It's hard to imagine, beyond a shared intellectual acuity, what might lead someone to link these two women who, had they met, would no doubt have wasted little kindness on each other. On the other hand, one sees only too well what could lead, in the memory of an old man, to their assimilation: the same taste for women, a certain massiveness of stature, and the fact that each one shared a lengthy part of her life with a long and very lean woman. Beyond the anecdotal, the fact remains that it is possible to see in this comparison, which is more intuitive than it is deductive, a sign of Prokosch's extreme perspicacity. For if Yourcenar did share something, deep down, with Stein, it was her way—to which Hemingway attests in Stein's case—of appearing to be dominant in love relationships, and sometimes allowing herself, in everyday life, to be furiously dominated.

Beginning in 1944, we have a daily record of Frick's power—one is tempted to say tyranny—over everyday life, thanks to the engagement calendars she methodically filled out until she died. Although during the last years her attention to detail sometimes gave way to haste, since by then, her state was so frail. The only missing volume is the one from the year 1976, which was mislaid. These calendars, which Yourcenar always referred to as "Grace Frick's calendars," were in fact common property. At any rate Yourcenar would write things down in them when Grace was not around. If Yourcenar possessed her own daily records at that time—which is doubtful—no trace of them remains. Among the sealed documents, there are only some of the calendars she kept after Grace's death, when she took over, as it were.

Early in 1944, Yourcenar was keeping the daybook. She did not in fact record much beyond a few appointments, indicating only that on 17 January Grace left Kansas City. She had gone out there, as she often did, to spend the Christmas holidays with her family, with her brothers nearby. Not once did Yourcenar go with her. As we know, she was not overly fond of family life. Besides which, her presence was not particularly expected, or desired, inasmuch as Frick's family was not overflowing with affinity for the couple she had formed with a penniless Frenchwoman, barely capable of meeting her own financial needs, and in any event incapable of getting by on her own. In Kansas City, great Flemish families gone bankrupt were not considered impressive. And as for the literary aura of a writer who hadn't made a name for herself, and who, for several years, hadn't written a book, it would probably only have provoked sarcastic comments had Frick not been the kind of person who knew how to impose silence.

Unlike Yourcenar, when Frick kept the calendar, she was precise to the point of maniacal obsession. She not only wrote down all their appointments and the various errands to be run, but she made comments on the days, sometimes described meals, kept accounts, made lists and inventories—such as that of all the silver left in Maine, at the Somesville house. On 27 February 1944, she noted: "wedding in New York"; and on 6 March: "M.Y. ill from oysters *mais jolie journée!* [but a nice day!] Lunch *devant la fontaine* [in front of the fountain] at the Plaza [the famous hotel on the corner of Fifth Avenue and Central Park]," before going to look around at Bonwit Teller.[33] Yourcenar, who read all Frick's daybooks after her death, appended an occasional qualifying statement or a comment. On 10 November, in the margin of "M.Y. learns to knit," she inserted a peremptory "no," and where Grace notes that "M.Y. buys an extravagant bed for dormitory room in Bronxville," the latter added "I have it still."[34] Banal though they are, these curious little dialogues, sustained beyond the final separation, offer something of an echo of what their daily conversations, tender or biting, might have been like.

The winter and spring of 1944 were very much like these notes, containing nothing momentous. It is possible, however, to make one observation: their financial situation, though not flourishing, must at least have stabilized, because Yourcenar and Frick went quite often to New York during this time. They had quite a full schedule of activities, going to museums, to the theater, to the opera, in addition to seeing friends and relatives such as Karl Loewith and the Schiffrins.

It seems as though Yourcenar, having partially emerged from her depression, was forcing herself to participate in a certain kind of social life in the hope of finding a publisher. Her "Mythologies" were now being published in *Les Lettres Françaises,* a review that was edited by Roger Caillois.[35] In her acceptance speech to the Académie Française, poised to take her place in Caillois's chair, Yourcenar recalled this episode in her life: "Around 1943, when both he and I were in voluntary exile, he beneath the Southern Cross and I on an island quite frequently illuminated by the aurora borealis, he was so kind as to accept a long essay of mine for *Les Lettres Françaises,* which, with the backing of the admirable patron of letters, Victoria Ocampo, he edited in Buenos Aires. At a time when the voice of France reached us only rarely, those slim periodicals gave us reassuring proof of the vitality of French culture—a culture come, to be sure, from another point on the globe, but proving all the more convincingly thus its universal character. What those several rather formless pages consisted of is of little importance; later on they would serve as rough drafts for certain parts of other books. I even have to admit that, rereading them in old issues of *Les Lettres Françaises,* I am surprised that such an unerringly rigorous mind would have accepted them. No doubt he sensed, in that somewhat hasty essay devoted to the influence of Greek tragedy on modern literatures, a bit of the same respect with which he himself regarded everything that touches on the transmission of myths, the changes that they undergo in the hands of successive generations, and the great truths about human nature that poets have enfolded within them. Whatever the case may be, at a time when we were hardly feeling certain about the survival of culture (are we today?) or, for that matter, about our own future, such a welcome, for a young writer still feeling displaced in the United States, was a favor granted and a service rendered."[36]

During the summer, in Somesville, the idea of buying a house on Mount Desert Island and setting up residence there dawned for the first time. Frick's notes in the daybook became highly sporadic. Among them, however, are numerous doctor's appointments, which would be one of the leitmotifs of their forty years of life together, for good reasons—Frick's illness beginning in 1958—or bad—Yourcenar's hypochondria. During those years, Yourcenar was young enough, at forty-one years old, for her propensity to believe herself perpetually ill to make us smile. Grace noted that one day she telephoned from Sarah Lawrence "to tell world she had a cold."[37]

Also appearing in that calendar from 1944, in August, is an announcement of the liberation of Paris. There is not a word of commentary. Nevertheless, this announcement represents the first sign of an essential question to which Yourcenar would have to respond: would she, or wouldn't she, return to Europe? Coming to the United States in 1939 had been no more than an incident in her life that was involuntarily prolonged due to an historical accident: a planned trip that, coinciding with the beginning of the war, had been transformed into a lengthy stay. In no way was it a life choice. In contrast, the question of staying put or leaving would determine her future, the entire second half of her existence. She knew this—as did Frick. Not even the faintest echo of their discussions regarding this decision remains. Frick, usually so partial to commenting on every subject, is virtually mute about this one in her notes. There is barely an occasional allusion to "Marguerite in tears and desolate."[38] What should we impute this to? Stormy quarrels? An anguished inability to make up her mind? By March 1945, even if exiled intellectuals—at least the French ones—had not yet packed their trunks, they were already, in their thoughts, back on the old continent. Word of a jubilant Paris, the "martyrized, but liberated, Paris" of General de Gaulle, had reached their ears. They wanted to take part in this return to peace; they wanted to get back to their jobs, their families, their friends. For the most part, people were waiting for them. Such was not the case for Yourcenar. As for the family, she was no longer interested in having one; nor did she have an occupation (and as for money left in Europe, there was nothing to speak of). As far as friends went—at any rate, those one might wish to remember—they were either dead or gone their separate ways, without a trace. But in Europe she had her publishers, her language, her culture, all the things that, until then, had mattered most. The scale was bound to tip in this direction. Surely she would leave. Yet she stayed.

How did she arrive at this decision? "I didn't decide anything, I let things be decided for me," she would say in 1979 to Jacques Chancel.[39] Europe meant the prospect of returning with barely a suitcase, and living one had no idea where. Staying meant choosing, not America, but Frick, and a certain daily comfort, but also a relentless control. In any event, Yourcenar was too deeply attached to European civilization not to have seriously hesitated. Frick, we can be sure, must have put all her energy into keeping Yourcenar from leaving. The atmosphere must have been tense, more than just once. Though these discussions had no witnesses, Yourcenar did upon occasion make some pertinent remarks, toward the end of her life, remarks that surprised her friends but that, in light of what we now know about those first years in America and the violent possessiveness of Frick's love, become fully understandable. "Grace Frick did not like my books," she declared one day in what was viewed as a manifestation of her acute sense of paradox. How could Frick not have liked those books, which she had read, reread, copied over in some cases, translated, corrected, and corrected again at the proof stage? The statement was almost indecent; there are limits to how far one should go in indulging one's taste for provocative jests. But the explanation that Yourcenar went on to provide, in the face of the stunned, reproving silence of her friends, rings absolutely true: "My books belonged to Europe. Grace always thought there was a danger that Europe might steal me away from her."

Did Yourcenar one day say "I'm staying"? Or did she simply let the summer of 1945 go by, as the "others" departed, and fall in with what she would have called "the course of things"? We don't know. If she had needed to be rooted more firmly in her radical pessimism regarding the future—which pushed her toward staying with Frick and shielding herself from the turmoil of the world—the atomic bomb dropped on Hiroshima in August 1945 could well have done the trick. It wasn't the "Scientific Revolution"[40] accompanying this latest massacre that aggrieved Yourcenar. She wrote in her journal: "1945. The atomic bomb does not bring us anything new, for nothing is more ancient than death. It is atrocious that these cosmic forces, barely mastered, should immediately be used for murder, but the first man who took it into his head to roll a boulder for the purpose of crushing his enemy used gravity to kill someone."[41] It was the repetition—geared up— of the ancestral gesture—slaughtering the enemy to put an end to the war—that reduced her to despair. Just as in 1939, coming back from Valais, she had heard alarm bells in the villages of Switzerland responding to French ones in Savoy, she heard the fishing boat sirens, on Mount Desert Island, greeting the end of the war in the Pacific. Something, obscurely, had come to a close with that whining signal of a jubilation intimately linked to atrocity, and it struck her as so profoundly final that, for 1945, it would be the only notation to appear in the account of her life in the Pléiade's "Chronologie."

From now on she would make the United States, not her refuge, nor her country, but her base, it would seem, and Frick, her life's companion. She was very anxious that no one ever take her for a "refugee." She made this clear to one of her Polish correspondents in a letter of 29 June 1954: "Nor was I in the United States as a French refugee, in the true sense of the term, for I went there of my own free will, for reasons pertaining to friendship and literary projects (lectures, trips), and if political events, my health, and certain other personal reasons kept me there longer than I had foreseen, I was in no way *forced* to stay because my country was not open to me. I am pointing this out in order to show that our situations are not parallel. Nonetheless, I do know what it's like to find yourself in a foreign country where there is always an element of distrust or uncertainty concerning us that subsists no matter what you do, and I've known upon occasion as well what it's like to be a foreigner and penniless."[42]

Staying, however, did not mean she was abandoning herself to a tranquil American life or—contrary to what Frick perhaps imagined—to the latter's omnipresent solicitude. It was rather an indication that she had regained a certain faith in her future career and that she wanted to provide herself all possible means, including comfort on a day-to-day basis, of finally realizing her ambitions. A liberated Europe, despite the atrocious discovery of the concentration camps, with their piles of corpses and their living dead, was evincing a prodigious appetite for coming back to life. Yourcenar, on the other side of the Atlantic, shared in this, which was what made it possible for her to stay where she was. Letters arrived, friends raised their heads, and in her responses, Yourcenar showed that she had regained her self-assurance, her taste for living and for words. A long letter to Jean Ballard sums up what was for her the postwar period:

> During the past six years, I have very often thought of you and *Cahiers du Sud,* and, especially every time the newspapers would report bombing raids in Marseilles, the state of siege in Marseilles . . . I remember with regret the apartment, which had such a beautiful view of the old city . . . But the continuation of *Cahiers du Sud* is proof that certain essential values continue to hold when all around so much is falling apart. During those years spent at a distance, in that Ark of sorts that the United States was, the most horrible thing was the feeling of floating in the middle of a world disappeared, submerged, henceforth devoid of terra firma. We were misled by this feeling: every letter like your own received these past few months from France, from Greece, from Italy, remains for me a veritable miracle, a message from a world at least momentarily saved from the flood. . . .
>
> I was going to put an end to this letter, when I noticed that yours contains a question, on the subject of the Mediterranean spirit, which in itself could easily supply enough material for a long essay. What might I say? . . . I am writing to you now from Mount Desert Island, in the northeastern part of the United States, where I have been spending a good part of the year during the past six years. It's something of a Corsica, or a Dalmatia, located in what is nearly a polar climate: for the Greeks, this was hyperborean country, for people of the Middle Ages, it was the region of icebergs and fog explored during Saint-Brendan's Navigation.[43] Well, I see no solution of continuity here, no *essential* difference from what I loved best in Greece or elsewhere. The forests that, for the Indians, were full of sacred mystery and terror not so different from what filled Dodona and Epirus; the hard work of the sailors on "the sterile sea"; the old people sitting on doorsteps, speaking hour after hour of the past; the little Protestant churches, in villages built out of wood,

as, in fact, were the oldest Greek temples, but adorned with pure Doric pediments, the fruit of architectural traditions bequeathed by thirteenth-century England to the colonies of yesteryear; everything, even the library, the village school, the word democracy written on a wall—all these are ordinary things, belonging to everyone, but they prove to us that what was indispensable has been passed on. . . .

I also notice that I have not answered certain questions about myself, which you were so very kind as to ask. I hope to see Europe again soon, but for a thousand reasons—financial reasons (I have been living here for four years now thanks to teaching appointments in a college outside of New York), as well as reasons of friendship and health—I doubt that this trip and the meetings with friends that I look forward to will take place before two or three years from now. We'll have to write to one another from time to time, that's all.[44]

Things are quite clear. Yourcenar was forty-three years old, and her future would be spent far away from the literary milieu that had welcomed her during the thirties. And that future, at least as far as her literary work was concerned, belonged entirely to her.

9
Banality's Temptation

STAYING IN THE UNITED STATES meant keeping Grace—or being kept by her—but it also meant submitting to the "humdrum of the daily round."[1] Every Monday, Yourcenar had to get up at four o'clock in the morning to go, by train (she never learned to drive, and, for that matter, she did not have the means, at the time, to own an automobile), from Hartford where she lived with Grace to Sarah Lawrence University in Bronxville, some one hundred miles away, north of New York City. She taught French and Italian there, from Monday morning until Wednesday evening, and left on Thursday, since she only had a part-time position. She had been hired in 1942 by Mr. Warren Constance, who presided over this college of about three hundred fifty young women, considered very liberal and practicing avant-garde teaching methods.

It wasn't until 1945 that a very young president, Mr. Harold Taylor, who had a passion for pedagogical experimentation, arrived at this already quite unorthodox college; he remembers Yourcenar very well. What he recollects is the image of someone who was very conscientious but who, unlike him, had little interest in teaching. "She had a rather strange appearance, but she was only one bizarre character among others on this atypical campus where all kinds of people have crossed paths, one after another. Mary McCarthy, for instance, taught at Sarah Lawrence for a year."[2] Yourcenar, on the other hand, claimed that she always felt like "something of an exceptional case" at Sarah Lawrence.[3] If you go by Taylor, "Marguerite Yourcenar was very courteous, but inflexible regarding her decisions. When she had finished with her classes, she wanted above all to devote herself to her personal work and her reading. She did not mix with her colleagues and held herself aloof from university life. No one really got to know her. But no one thought the worse of her for this since a great spirit of tolerance and mutual respect reigned at Sarah Lawrence. Physically, she imposed respect: she stood erect, wrapped in ample skirts and shawls. To me she was a very typically French woman, neither young nor old. I knew nothing about her life. I didn't know why she lived in Hartford. I imagined that she wanted to save money, New

York having been even then a very expensive city. I always thought she lived there alone and that she only headed home so quickly, without ever lingering at Sarah Lawrence, in order to work."

The students in her classes were beginners, though they had had at least one year of language study. She taught them French using theater texts and poetry, an audacious pedagogical choice to say the very least, posing as it did the risk of rather singular consequences as far as learning the syntactical structure of the language was concerned. She also taught French civilization, for more advanced students, by way of literature and the arts, and offered Italian classes at two levels; they, too, were based on poetry and theater. Over the years of her teaching, she also devoted a series of courses to the historical novel, then to the epic and satire in the French novel, and to the Surrealist period.

"It's remarkable," Taylor continues, "to think that that great mind was put to work teaching French to beginners. She always carried out her work with the highest degree of seriousness, but she always refused to talk with us about our pedagogical research and to follow our lead in that area. Her mind was somewhere else. On the campus, she was like an invisible presence. She used the library a lot. In the evening, she had dinner alone in her room while she worked. No one would have thought of disturbing her. Especially after she had gotten back to writing the book that would become *Memoirs of Hadrian.* Everyone had understood how much this work meant to her, how much it was, more than important—quite simply, vital. One time, though, she offered to give a lecture on the role of the detective in French literature. That struck us as a strange sign of unsuspected whimsicalness on her part."

Her former university president evokes only one unpleasant memory connected with her: the fact that she wrote to *Commentary*—a journal published by the American Jewish Committee—saying that at Sarah Lawrence they had set a quota of Jewish students that was not to be exceeded. "For us who had been at the forefront of the battle against quotas of all kinds," says Taylor, "that was a little hard to swallow." *Commentary* was a monthly publication edited by Ralph E. Samuel. Between 1945 and 1953, it became a forum for the thought of quite a few American and European intellectuals, such as Martin Buber, Jean-Paul Sartre, Hannah Arendt, Mary McCarthy, Marc Chagall . . . Taylor must have been all the more shocked by Yourcenar's accusation in that he held the journal in high esteem: in the January 1948 "Letters from Readers" section, there is a letter from the president of Sarah Lawrence declaring: "You have one of the best intellectual journals I have seen in a long time." In the journal's tables of contents, there appear no traces of an article by Yourcenar, which leaves us to assume, though with no formal proof, that her remarks had been at the most in the form of a letter to the editor. It's hard to imagine, however, what could have motivated her, since all evidence confirms Sarah Lawrence's "anti-quota" stance, unless it was the kind of exasperation with her life and her temporary profession that sometimes seized Yourcenar, to the point of making her unfair.

"Where everything else is concerned," states Taylor, "she was always irreproachable. She was not suspected of being conservative. If she hadn't been liberal, she wouldn't have survived in our college. During the McCarthy era, though, I have no recollection of running into her at any of the faculty assemblies. Even less of hearing her speak. But knowing her, I never doubted her opposition to McCarthyism, her reprobation. Every excess, everything that displayed intellectual mediocrity, intolerance, a will to exclude, or pettiness was foreign to her and revolting. The only thing was that, when we were all holding one general assembly after another to fight McCarthy, Marguerite Yourcenar was in the middle of the second century and it was very hard for her to come back and join us. And, oddly enough, I think we understood that impossibility, all of us.

"We had a good rapport, she and I, though a distant one. I think that she was closer to me than to the others. Probably because she had a sense of hierarchy. She preferred to speak with the president than with underlings."

Be it out of modesty, in an effort not to claim he had been singled out by her, or because he had remained too far removed from Yourcenar, Taylor has committed an error of evaluation here. To think that Yourcenar might have adapted her behavior to comply with some notion of hierarchy would be to underestimate the very high opinion she had of herself. She never tolerated having conversation partners imposed on her. She always willed herself sole mistress of her choices, from her publishers to her gardeners, from the president of the French Republic with whom she refused to dine— Valérie Giscard d'Estaing—to the one whose table she shared—François Mitterrand.

Moreover, she took a certain interest in Taylor's intellectual work, to the extent of translating into French the chapter he had written for a collective work entitled *L'Activité philosophique contemporaine en France et aux Etats-Unis* [Contemporary Philosophical Activity in France and the United States]. This two-volume work, which Marvin Faber, a professor in Buffalo, New York, had been appointed to edit, was published by Presses universitaires de France [University Presses of France] in 1950. The first volume addressed American philosophy; chapter 17, which was devoted to the philosophy of education in the United States, was Taylor's. Nowhere is it mentioned that the translation was Yourcenar's: one can well imagine that she did not appreciate that omission, which she would undoubtedly have qualified as "disagreeable."

President Taylor's account, which, all in all, gives a more or less neutral view of Yourcenar, notices nonetheless that in her classes, each of which consisted of between ten and fifteen students, "people were very impressed by her personality." We can contrast this account with the recollections of Yourcenar's old students. "You only had to run into her once on campus to remember it forever, Marguerite Yourcenar was so unforgettable," says one of them, Charlotte Pomerantz-Marzani, who today lives in New York.[4] For all those young women barely beyond adolescence, Yourcenar was a singular and exotic personage. She dressed in an eccentric but very attractive way, "always cloaked in capes, in shawls, wrapped up in her dresses . . . You saw very little of her skin or her body. She made you think of a monk. She liked browns, purples, black, she had a great sense of what colors went well together. There was something mysterious about her that made her exciting. And then there were all those rumors circulating that she lived with a woman. That added to the side of her character that seemed to come out of a novel."

"She was not at all an orthodox teacher. First she gave lectures, which was no longer done. Plus she never said one word of English in class—and very few outside of class. It seemed strange to me that one wouldn't be required to speak English properly in an American college, but when you had someone with such a presence, you could certainly make an exception." "Marguerite Yourcenar set the passing mark really high," her students recall, and one had to adapt to her particular requirements, preferably quickly, as she was not very patient. To be sure, she tended to take more of an interest in the shining lights, "not just the students who were fascinated by her, but the ones who had a passion and a talent to boot. Still, she was never mean or pointlessly hurtful with any of the students."

"The thing that made the biggest impression on the students was the unique way that Marguerite Yourcenar had of treating them like adults, 'like responsible beings.' Her constant attitude toward the class was: 'you came here to learn, I'm not going to bring myself down to your level.' She did her work with an absolute sense of duty, even if it was not the thing in life that she was most interested in. She was having a writing problem at the time, she wasn't satisfied with the literary work she was doing, which seemed minor to her compared to her ambitions, and I think that the last thing in the world she could have hoped to do was what she had to do at Sarah Lawrence: teach a few rich girls. I have a very bad memory, myself, but I know that some of my classmates still have a dazzling recollection of her classes," Pomerantz affirms.

In fact, after her election to the Académie Française in 1980, several of her students from the years 1942 to 1950 wrote to Yourcenar. One of them, Olga Harrington, now Mrs. Giannini, who took classes with her in 1946, emphasizes "the complete and vivid memory" she retains of Yourcenar's comments on *La Princesse de Clèves* (*The Princess of Cleves*).[5] For Pomerantz, "you could see, from the very first day, that Marguerite Yourcenar was not a professor like the others. Her way of teaching was not that of a classical teacher but of someone who is crazy about literature. She couldn't have cared less about grammar or exercises. She was the only professor that I wanted to have twice, whose course I took two years in a row, in 1948 and 1949. No doubt this is why I wrote to her, years later, and we started corresponding. She pretended to remember me, out of sympathy, but I knew it wasn't true. How could she have? Especially since hers was the first class of the day and, for someone like me who couldn't manage to wake up, it was torture. So I was quiet and no doubt a little slumped over, since in one of her reports on me she lamented my 'distressing way of carrying myself in class.'"

There was little chance that Pomerantz could have misunderstood the reservations with which Yourcenar viewed her intellectual pugnacity at the time, as the passage devoted to her in the student reports for French Civilization in December 1948 attests: "She appears ... to be quite apathetic in several important ways. As an example of physical apathy, her posture in class is indicative of either extreme general fatigue or complete drowsiness. This laxity physically is paralleled by a lack of moral firmness; for example, by her too easy dismissal of what she thinks does not concern her personally. Likewise, she seems willing to limit herself in order *not* to acquire wholly new ideas and *not* to try to probe her own thinking too deeply, for she submits nothing to serious inquiry and research."[6] The nature of this evaluation, which Pomerantz has had the kindness and elegance to evoke with a smile, is less important than the authentic picture it paints of how Yourcenar regarded her students.

"I thought certain things with regard to her," remembers Pomerantz, "that I would undoubtedly challenge today because feminism has thrown a different light on them and because I've thought about the situation of women. To me, she had a male authority. Not so much because of a masculine appearance, which she didn't have at the time, as because of the dominating form of intelligence she had, her natural imperiousness, her loftiness. I have to admit, though I have never been attracted to women, that she was seductive like a man. I couldn't imagine her tending to the tasks of everyday life, using a toaster or a hair dryer . . . I had the vague notion, when I was taking her courses, that she must use medieval instruments in her daily life. Of course she didn't say anything about her private life. However, it was evident to all of us that she couldn't be concerned with starting a family, with having children. Someone who is so preoccupied with death is not apt to set about building a family, now is she? I think she knew about the rumor circulating that she lived with a woman. Basically, she couldn't have cared less about people knowing this and saying that she was a lesbian. But she made no allusions, and no comment. She didn't want to be turned into a stereotype. She was profoundly repulsed by anything that might label her, categorize her. I never knew anything about Grace Frick, except that she was an extremely good horsewoman. I'm delighted to be finding out now that Marguerite Yourcenar was afraid of falling ill, that she was something of a hypochondriac. It makes her more human. The memory I had of her was of someone carved in granite; even her face gave me the sense of being like stone. She was one of those people that are outside time, who you're convinced will never die."

For Yourcenar Sarah Lawrence represented a constraint. But she submitted to it. "I never established myself, to the least extent, in the American university milieu," she acknowledged in a letter to Jean Lambert on 14 May 1956.[7] "The rare friends I have there come either from Grace or from *Hadrian.* The experience, however, was an interesting one. I am grateful to Sarah Lawrence for having provided me the means of staying in the United States, but I would not recommend this type of life to anyone, unless it's someone with a thoroughly unqualified taste for teaching and an extreme amount of curiosity about American life and the particular variety of cultural disorientation it involves."

In fact, it was not really teaching that she found unpleasant: demonstrating, clarifying, correcting, setting people straight, none of this was in any way a chore for her. Unless she had noted at the top of a letter she received "Do not respond; mediocre essay (or poems)," many were the correspondents who were favored by her advice, corrections, and reflections—occasionally formulated in a highly peremptory way—when they had submitted their manuscripts or university studies to her.[8] What ran counter to her entire life, and to her own educational approach, was a kind of teaching comprehensively imposed on a group, at the risk of being met with indifference, or with apathy, to which, as we have seen, she reacted as she might have to a personal attack.

When Yourcenar spoke of her years at Sarah Lawrence, it was as if she was evoking a hiatus, a very brief period. One always has to reckon with her peculiar perception of time. All the same, for eight years of her life, it took up more than half of her week, in addition to exhausting commutes. Following a break in 1950—during which she finished *Memoirs of Hadrian* and went back to Europe—she scrupulously returned to her classes to honor the final semester of her contract, in 1952—53.

NONETHELESS, while she was there, time must have seemed to pass awfully slowly, especially up until early 1949, before she had set to work again on an extensive literary project. She had experimented on this campus with her great aptitude for living autarchically. When classes were over, she would read almost constantly. The maniacal care that Frick devoted to list making did not, it seems, alas, go so far as to include noting down the titles of all the books that passed through Yourcenar's hands. As a general rule, Yourcenar did not keep track—or rarely—of when she read a given book. The only references that are at all precise appear in her prefaces and comments on her own works. In "Reflections on the Composition of *Memoirs of Hadrian*," for instance, she mentions the reading she did prior to painting the emperor's portrait: "That same night I re-opened two of the volumes which had also just been returned to me, remnants of a library in large part lost. One was Dio Cassius in Henri Estienne's beautiful printing, and the other a volume of an ordinary edition of *Historia Augusta*, the two principal sources for Hadrian's life, purchased at the time that I was intending to write this book."[9] Sometimes, in the daybook, she would mention the books she had reread; Thomas Mann's *Der Erwählte* (*The Holy Sinner*), which she considered a masterpiece, is one example. There are even books she would reread every year, such as Thomas Hardy's *Far from the Madding Crowd*. But if we lack precise details, we find numerous traces in her correspondence of the enormous breadth of her reading. Thus one is tempted to say she had read everything there was to read, in every domain. She, of course, to the contrary, emphasized her gaps, explaining at the end of her life that she had too little time left for contemporary authors, particularly French ones. Nothing could be further from the truth, as the evidence we have at our disposal repeatedly confirms. Though she did not read everything she received, she "looked at" everything, including all the books that her publisher, or authors who admired her, would send. She read very quickly and intensely, as do those who have refused to submit to the passivity and laziness of the image, for whom the only real means of communication is the written word. When she decided that a book was worth making the effort to read, once she had finished a preliminary reading, she reread it immediately. This was a form of self-discipline to which she never failed to adhere.

In fact, the kind of "blank" that Sarah Lawrence always was in Yourcenar's memory can be understood and gauged, not by the number of years spent at this college, but by what those years were in the context of Yourcenar's life: from 1943 to the end of the war, things were going too poorly in general for Sarah Lawrence to weigh on her any more heavily than anything else. She saw it as a means of financial survival and left it at that. With the end of the war, Sarah Lawrence would become something of an appendage to her life, a necessity consented to, but Yourcenar, little by little, was resuming her identity as a European writer. Despite distance, her continent and her language were, little by little, taking possession of her once again, and the word "future" was regaining its meaning.

IN SEPTEMBER 1946, she wrote to her publisher, Grasset, to lodge a complaint about not having received a statement of sales since 1939 with respect to her six works that had been published by this firm—an indubitable sign of vitality regained. When Yourcenar again started standing up for herself every inch of the way against her publishers, wanting to control every detail, carefully checking to be sure she was not being cheated (and this, less for the money than for the principle of the thing), these were all indications that, once again, in her own eyes, she was a writer, thus herself. She had to renew her demand a few months later, claiming this time not to have received "any statement of sales since 1938" and pointing out that her works were then impossible to locate in France, both in Paris and in the provinces. She also mentioned in that communication her work *Dramatis personae*, a collection of the plays written during the war. To be sure, she had sent it to Albert Camus in 1946, but Grasset "could just as well lay claim to it as Gallimard," since both publishers had "a leftover option." It was in November that she had addressed the last section of her manuscript to Camus.[10]

"Please find enclosed the preface to the volume *Dramatis personae*; the three plays making up this book are no doubt already in your hands. I apologize for sending you the manuscript this way, in two parts and in so much disorder, but the preface took on the proportions of a long essay, and the final revisions required a lot more of my time than I had thought they would at first." After several months had gone by, Gaston Gallimard's response arrived; it was negative:

> We thank you most kindly for giving us the chance to read your collection
> of plays entitled *Dramatis personae*, which Monsieur Albert Camus transmitted to us.

We sincerely regret that the difficulties we are presently experiencing in France make it impossible for us to undertake its distribution; thus we shall retain your manuscript, keeping it available for you in the event that you would like to reclaim it.[11]

She held this refusal against Gallimard, and she would bring it up again on the occasion of the conflict that pitted them against one another regarding *Memoirs of Hadrian.*

As soon as she received the infamous statements of sales, she immediately wrote to Jean Blanzat, at Grasset, to contest them. It cannot be denied, she was coming back to life.

With Frick, since Yourcenar had evidently consented to stay on American soil, everything was going well. In the fall of 1946, they went, as Americans traditionally do, to pick apples in the immense orchards of the East Coast, which are open on certain days to the public, thus making it possible to stock up on fruit at a reduced price. At the beginning of 1947, Frick was in California, then Vancouver, returning by way of Chicago. Yourcenar wrote down in the calendar, most often in English, a few appointments or minor projects to keep in mind. On 14 February, the day of Frick's return, and Saint Valentine's Day, she drew a huge sun, covering almost the whole page. Who could believe her, knowing this, when she was still bold enough to claim, as she often did, that by then they had already arrived at the stage, if not of passion's disappearance, at least of joyless habit?

She thus got back to her work and attempted to substantiate her European literary existence: in 1947, *Cahiers du Sud,* which was still directed by Jean Ballard, whom, as we have seen, she held in esteem, published an excerpt from *Le Mystère d'Alceste.* During the same period, her comments about the United States became less distant and more understanding, as if something irreversible had been accepted. On 14 February, she wrote, as it happens, to Ballard: "Your description of today's Marseilles interests and touches me. As for what you say about the United States, transformed by the French imagination into an Eldorado, into Islands of the Blessed, I am not surprised; the magazines and newspapers I receive from France all display this same tendency. How can one respond? 'Rocks are hard, no matter where you go,' and as a little American girl to whom I recited this proverb said to me, sand is warm and soft at the seashore, and morning air is delicious, no matter where you go. During the last catastrophe, this country enjoyed certain immunities; we were neither cold nor hungry; these are great gifts. On the other hand, certain pleasures of Mediterranean life, so familiar we are hardly aware of them—leisure time, strolling about, friendly conversation—do not exist, or if one manages to engage in them (and I do manage), one does so against the current of what is properly speaking American life. And yet, I have grown to like this country very much, or at least certain places and certain people." [12]

Eight days before writing this letter, on 6 February 1947, Yourcenar had taken a step that rendered her move to the United States virtually permanent. We can find scattered traces of those days—about which nothing was ever confided but which we can imagine were haunted by the anguish of choosing—in several passages of *Archives du Nord.* In them Yourcenar remembers Françoise Leroux, the forbear for whom she held a preference and a fondness, based on their resemblance, and a woman upon whom existence had imposed a way of life that very strangely foreshadowed the one that she herself would choose: "A need to simplify life, on the one hand, and chance circumstances, on the other, make me more like her than like any of my forbears decked out in frills and flounces. In the midst of the amenities and even the luxuries of a different era, I still perform tasks that she performed before me. I knead bread; I sweep the doorstep; after nights of strong wind, I pick up the dead branches. . . . We have the same swollen hands in the winter. And I am well aware that what for her was a necessity has been for me a choice, at least up to the point where any choice becomes irreversible. . . . What she thought and felt regarding her joys and her sorrows, her physical ills, old age, the coming of death, the ones she loved who were gone, matters neither more nor less than what I have thought and felt myself. No doubt her life was harder than mine; however, I suspect we could just as well split the difference. She's like the rest of us, caught in the inextricable and the ineluctable." [13]

"Simplifying life," consenting to an "irreversible" choice, meant heeding this summons received on 6 February 1947: "Please come fill our your final application for naturalization"—which Yourcenar immediately did, forgetting even to stop by the French Consulate to retain her nationality of origin. By the end of 1947, she would definitively be an American citizen, absolutely no longer a French one. For her there was not very much symbolism in the document preserved today at Harvard, certificate of American citizenship number 6773753, bearing the following particulars: "US district of Hartford, Connecticut; Marguerite Yourcenar, 5 feet, 4 inches; 12-12-1947." Yourcenar gained in the bargain a legal name, to take the place of a pseudonym; she consented to make the United States her base; and she gave to Grace Frick—she would perhaps have denied it, but her sentimental situation at the time makes it obvious—a gage of love—maybe even a promise of "marriage." A few words in a letter from 1974 to her friend and proofreader Madame Jeanne Carayon sum up the situation quite well: "The

United States? I had never given one minute of thought to this country before the age of 34. Greece had become my center and I imagined that it would continue to be. The extraordinary concatenations of chance and of choice decided things otherwise." [14]

The nationality question did not trouble Yourcenar's conscience excessively. The notion of a homeland was more or less foreign to her, and belonging to a human group did not strike her as being linked to a passport one shows upon going through customs; the only thing that mattered to her was the language in which one chose, not to express oneself constantly—either orally or in writing—but to write, to perform the act of writing literature. The loss of her French nationality did not preoccupy her. It was the French Academicians who obliged her to recall, some thirty-two years later, that she had given up that citizenship—since French persons only are eligible for the Académie Française, which cannot induct foreign members.

On the other hand, few people who've decided to live on a long-term basis in a country other than their native land wish to protect themselves, as strongly as Yourcenar did, from being invaded by that country's culture and way of life. She retained until her death, which is to say for forty-eight years, an unshakable will to keep her own language intact—a language that was not the one she had to speak when she walked out her door and that was like a second form of insularity within the primary insularity she had chosen by taking up residence on Mount Desert Island. Yourcenar, nomadic and cosmopolitan, indifferent to the color of her identity cards, was invincibly French by way of her language. The word patriotism was not in her vocabulary, but the notion that she did in fact possess some would surge to the fore whenever the matter of defending her linguistic patrimony arose. And it was from her language that the feeling of exile she discovered (rediscovered?) at the very end of her life would arise. At Petite Plaisance, after Jerry Wilson's death, she would be surrounded for the first time by people speaking nothing but English, and she would constantly complain to her Francophone friends about having to spend entire days without uttering a sentence in French.

The vacations of 1947, both in spring and in summer, were spent on Mount Desert Island. During that particular summer, Yourcenar displayed a certain ill humor, perhaps because of the heat. Nonetheless Jacques Kayaloff came back from Europe in the spring bearing good news. He had taken care of having the trunk shipped to the United States that Yourcenar had left in Lausanne, at the Hôtel Meurice, in 1939, and he had brought back from France two of her books, which he sent to her immediately. Moreover, the review *Le Milieu du Siècle* published *Electra or The Fall of the Masks* in its entirety in the year 1947; at Editions Robert Laffont the translation of Henry James's *What Maisie Knew,* done by Yourcenar before the war, came out. Finally, writes Frick in her daybook, Yourcenar was working on *To Each His Minotaur,* based on a draft from the thirties (as we have seen, the framework for this play came from the game in which Marguerite Yourcenar, André Fraigneau, and Gaston Baissette indulged themselves in 1932). Here, contradiction with Yourcenar's official declarations reaches its peak.[15]

Nineteen forty-eight was an uneventful year of no great interest, except for the various signs indicating that the couple formed by Yourcenar and Frick was taking shape. In the notes she took down in her desk diary, Frick no longer had the imperceptible hesitation, the restraint, the reticence that are born of uncertainty. From the time of passion, then that of a cohabitation that could still have been perceived as provisional, they were moving into a truly conjugal life, and settling into it for good. Yourcenar was an American. She, the quintessentially authoritarian and independent one, had pledged allegiance to a place. To be sure, she could "take power" again—which is what happened. But the boundaries were set. The home port would be American. Without this particular victory, Frick would never have had any peace of mind. She would have lived in constant fear of seeing Yourcenar go off again. It was a very cold winter, with, for both of them, its procession of colds and indispositions, all of them meticulously recorded by Frick. In April, they set off together to spend several days in Virginia. In June, they made a trip to Nova Scotia before returning to Mount Desert Island for the summer. In August and September, they started looking at houses on the island, having firmly decided to buy one. The initiative for this project, of course, came from Frick, she being for the moment the only one able to invest a little money in it.

Nineteen forty-eight was also the year in which the pet name *Grete* appeared in the daybook, in Frick's hand, referring to Yourcenar. It would appear quite frequently over the course of the year 1948, more rarely during the following year, and it disappeared totally as of 1950. From then on, Yourcenar would be consistently designated by her initials, M.Y. We can only theorize about this change of appellation, but rather than imputing it to any profound alteration in the relations between the two women, we can see in it, perhaps, a change in the status of the notebooks, now more consciously turned toward a posterity about which neither one had any doubt.

On 30 October 1948, one notes, in Grace's hand: "Evening Grete***":

these stars or other signs, like empty parentheses and braces or brackets surrounding no text, are the only real secrets disclosed, by default, in these notebooks. They indicate moments of joy, happiness in love, or sensual pleasure (we can't affront Yourcenar by using the word "sexual" in her regard, a word that so displeased her, giving off, to her way of thinking, an air of technicalness, and thus of boredom). Yourcenar would use those same signs until the end of her life, when, after Grace's death, she went on by herself to keep the daybooks. Those "diaries," without really being intimate, have a great deal to say about the last part of her life, though they are always elliptical and, except on rare occasion, written in a telegraphic style. Moreover, real travel diaries or private notes, made on loose sheets of paper, sometimes provide a useful complement to the information found in the daybooks.

Two November 1948 was a great day for Frick. Her companion was from then on, like her, an American, and she went to the polling place to participate in the presidential election. "Grete is voting for the first time," wrote Frick, "and not the same as Grace." Of course, she does not say for whom each of the two women voted. The opposing candidates were Harry Truman for the Democrats, the winner with 49.6% of the vote; Thomas Dewey, the Republican, who garnered 45.1%; and several "fringe candidates," as we might say nowadays, designating themselves as progressives and receiving a total of 2.4% of the ballots cast. "Though I was born in a Republican family, I am becoming more and more a Jeffersonian Democrat," Frick would write to their friend Natalie Barney—the one friends nicknamed the "Amazon" and who was among the most "Left Bank" of American women in Paris.[16] But that letter was not written until March of 1954. It is thus entirely possible that Frick voted Republican in 1948. As for Yourcenar—its being highly improbable that she would side with the conservatives, not for political reasons but because they were the heralds of "moral order"—her sense of power and of the state would tend to situate her on the side of the "useful" vote, which is to say, in this instance, the vote for Truman. But she was so profoundly disenchanted with politics, and her view of the present state of democracy was such a pessimistic one, that we cannot rule out the possibility that she chose, both out of idealism and out of disillusionment, one of the marginal candidates.

Yourcenar would finish the year 1948 alone, Frick having left for California at the end of November, leaving her an impressive set of practical recommendations in the calendar. They wrote to one another a lot, almost every day—Frick would not get back to Hartford until mid-January—but all those letters are sealed. Yourcenar jotted down a few inconsequential notes—appointments, errands to run—in English. She only noted in French, on 29-30-31 December, "glorious days." We don't know if she was talking about what the weather was like, about her calm good humor—or about a "glorious" presence that may have lit up those days. It is somewhat hard to imagine her consenting to an absolutely solitary year's end.

When, at the twelfth stroke of midnight, 31 December 1948 gave way to 1 January 1949, Yourcenar was entering into a decisive year, without knowing it yet, that of the reconquest of her literary ambitions: it was the end of a nearly ten-year deviation from her course, conceived and resolved upon since childhood, toward the full realization of self.

10

The Rediscovery of Hadrian

ONCE AGAIN, it was one of those "extraordinary concatenations of chance" she was fond of evoking that made 1949 one of the pivotal years in Marguerite Yourcenar's life. When, in old age, she reread the daybooks—and no doubt in order to be the one herself to lead her biographers, yet again, to what she judged essential—she took care to point out on the cover of the 1949 volume, in English: "note on the composition of *Memoirs of Hadrian*, which began in February 1949."

Yourcenar was in her forty-sixth year. On 12 January, Frick's birthday— she was forty-six years old—Yourcenar noted that her father, Michel, had died exactly twenty years before, on 12 January 1929. What could have been her assessment of those twenty years, of what had been accomplished—and of everything that hadn't? What would Michel have said about his daughter, become a woman stuck in the routine of daily life, who was ceaselessly postponing the literary *œuvre* so much discussed and dreamed of since her youth?

On 21 January, she went to see Laurence Olivier in *Hamlet* and, like so many others, she retained a very strong memory of the performance. But, overall, there was nothing beyond the very commonplace: a life woven of small, everyday pleasures and pains, and a few grand aesthetic emotions— due to the talent of others. It was three days later, on 24 January, that "the event" took place: the arrival—finally—of the lost trunk that Kayaloff had tracked down in the precise spot where Yourcenar must have left it in 1939, at the Hôtel Meurice in Lausanne. That arrival is noted in large letters in the calendar, underlined and reunderlined by Yourcenar herself, in the absence of Frick who, as was often the case early in the year, was still visiting her family. They would not get back together again until 12 February in Santa Fe, New Mexico. Why was it, yet again, one might well ask, that the arrival of the trunk was mentioned in the Pléiade's "Chronologie" as occurring "in November or December '48," whereas everything is noted, day by day, in the calendar of 1949? It is hard to imagine how Yourcenar could have made a mistake in this regard, but it is even more difficult to fathom why she would have lied on purpose. All her remarks tend to indicate that her discovery of the old fragments of one of the versions of *Hadrian*—this is how she always referred to the book that appeared under the title *Memoirs of Hadrian*—had a kind of trigger effect and that she got back to work immediately. With the beginning of the rewriting of *Hadrian* dated in February 1949, Yourcenar's explanation is coherent, if the trunk did indeed arrive at the end of January 1949. If it had arrived in November or December of 1948, there would have to have been a few misfirings before this "trigger" was properly pulled.

The trunk, as Yourcenar often explained, contained lots of family papers and old letters, correspondence accumulated by her, but also before her, that no longer called much of anything to mind. Thus she burned a number of documents. She very much enjoyed "getting rid of things" in the fire, as she also related in *With Open Eyes*: "[I]t was a real trunk, actually two or three trunks, with quite an assortment of things inside. Of course the things of value had somehow or other disappeared in transit, into someone's pocket, and what was left was what nobody wanted, useless junk. I had several days' fun throwing things away or tossing them into the fire. I should add that Grace was away at the time. Had she been here, she might have wanted to save some things, while I enjoy a good bonfire."[1] Still, she took a glance at those papers before casting them into the flames. "I sat down by the fire to work my way through the débris, as if to take some gloomy inventory after a death," she recounts in "Reflections on the Composition of *Memoirs of Hadrian*." "I passed several evenings alone at the task, undoing the separate packets and running through them before destroying that accumulation of correspondence with people whom I had forgotten, and who had forgotten me, some of them still alive, others dead. A few of the pages bore dates of a generation ago, and even the names had quite gone from my mind. As I unfolded and threw mechanically into the fire that exchange of dead thoughts between a Marie and a François or a Paul, long since disappeared, I came upon four or five typewritten sheets, the paper of which had turned yellow. The salutation told me nothing: 'My dear Mark ...' *Mark* ... What friend or love, what distant relative was this? I could not recall the name at all. It was several minutes before I remembered that *Mark* stood here for *Marcus Aurelius*, and that I had in hand a fragment of the lost manuscript. From that moment there was no question but that this book must be taken up again, whatever the cost."[2]

AS EARLY AS 1924, at twenty-one years of age, Yourcenar had begun working on Hadrian. This Roman emperor of the second century, she would

later point out to her friend, the writer Joseph Breitbach, "was a great indi-
vidualist, who, for that very reason, was a great legist and a great reformer;
a great sensualist and also (I do not say 'but also') a citizen, a lover obsessed
by his memories, variously bound to several beings, but at the same time,
and up until the end, one of the most controlled minds that have been." [3]

In about the year 1927, she had come again upon a sentence, in a volume
of Flaubert's correspondence, that, from then on, she never forgot: "Just
when the gods had ceased to be, and the Christ had not yet come, there
was a unique moment in history, between Cicero and Marcus Aurelius,
when man stood alone." "A great part of my life was going to be spent in
trying to define, and then to portray, that man existing alone and yet closely
bound with all being." [4] Between 1924 and 1929, she had written, either
entirely or in part, several versions of what would become *Memoirs of Hadrian,* one of which was in dialogue. She had even submitted one of them,
under the title *Antinoos,* in 1926 to the publisher Fasquelle, who received
the following letter:

> Villa Loretta
> Boulevard d'Italie
> Monte Carlo
>
> Dear Sir,
>   Bossuet, in his *Histoire universelle* (*Universal History*), tells us that Ha-
> drian "dishonored his reign with his love affairs . . ."
>   His imperial adventure, which begins like a novel by Petronius and ends
> in an apotheosis, serves as the theme of the text entitled *Antinoos* of which
> I send you the manuscript. I have attempted to interest the reader in the ut-
> terly realistic evolution of the emperor; an acceptance from your house
> would be the finest proof that I have succeeded at doing so.
>   With my sincerest good wishes,
>
> Marg Yourcenar
> 28 June 1926 [5]

It appears that Fasquelle turned down the offer. Not very satisfied with
the results, Yourcenar had done away with everything, returning to this
project only in 1934. After doing some serious research, she had undertaken new rewrites, on several occasions. But nothing worked, perhaps because she could not bring herself to part with the idea that the work should
consist of a series of dialogues; and also, according to her own statements,
because she was "too young." "There are books which one should not
attempt before having passed the age of forty. Earlier than that one may
well fail to recognize those great natural boundaries which from person to

person, and from century to century, separate the infinite variety of mankind; or, on the contrary, one may attach too much importance to mere administrative barriers, to the customs houses or the sentry boxes erected between man and man. It took me years to learn how to calculate exactly the distances between the emperor and myself."[6] "This book has a long history," she would write furthermore, to Breitbach in 1951. "I began it more than twenty years ago, at a stage of life when one is apt to be impudent thus, or full of such a sense of self-importance. . . . I began it again in 1936 in its present form, as the memoirs of a man reexamining his life from the perspective of his fast-approaching death. But I only wrote fifteen pages. I was not yet mature enough at the time for this overly vast project."[7]

In the final version, only one unchanged sentence remained of what she had just discovered in the trunk that had finally reached America: "I began to discern the profile of my death." "Like a painter who has chosen a landscape, but who constantly shifts his easel now right, now left, I had at last found a point from which to view the book," Yourcenar commented.[8] Added to this, but greatly reworked, were the visit to the physician and the passage on renunciation of bodily exercise, both written in 1937, at the time of Yourcenar's first visit to the United States, during which she had done a great deal of reading related to Hadrian at Yale University's library.

Though the arrival of the trunk made possible the discovery that was going to transform the course of Marguerite Yourcenar's life to an extent unsuspected by her, it also raised a more immediate problem at that moment, one that shows how precarious her financial situation still was. Because the trunk contained a few remnants of the family silver (Yourcenar would note in her daybook the joy she took from eating with the family's tableware), customs viewed it as containing almost nothing but silverware and thus imposed a relatively high import duty, amounting to twenty-five dollars. In order to reimburse this sum to Kayaloff, who had taken care of everything, Yourcenar was obliged to sell a little anthology of Peruvian literature from the pre-Columbian era to the library at Sarah Lawrence—a lovely object, to be sure, as she indicated to Kayaloff, but a rather useless one since she could not read it. She was offered eighteen dollars for it, which she sent to Kayaloff, along with another check for seven dollars. A few weeks later, she sold some other items, for twenty-six dollars and fifty cents. She also gave some away (Frick had still not returned), as if the memory of Europe, after the fracture of the war and her decision to remain across the Atlantic, were no more than a bother or empty nostalgia—excepting the family silver, the sign of deep connection to a lineage.

So on 10 February 1949, she took up *Hadrian* again at about the same place where it had been interrupted in 1937. She was on vacation from Sarah Lawrence and had to take the train to Chicago, then Santa Fe, New Mexico, where she joined Grace. During this long trip (two days), she wrote almost without stopping, in a nearly compulsive way. "[I took] with me the blank sheets for a fresh start on the book (the swimmer who plunges into the water with no assurance that he will reach the other shore). Closed inside my compartment as if in a cubicle of some Egyptian tomb, I worked late into the night between New York and Chicago; then all the next day, in the restaurant of a Chicago station where I awaited a train blocked by storms and snow; then again until dawn, alone in the observation car of a Santa Fé limited, surrounded by black spurs of the Colorado mountains, and by the eternal pattern of the stars. Thus were written at a single impulsion the passages on food, love, sleep, and the knowledge of men. I can hardly recall a day spent with more ardor, or more lucid nights."[9]

On 12 February, Yourcenar was on time for her meeting with Frick, at the De Vargas Hotel in Santa Fe. It was a very beautiful hotel, which would progressively deteriorate as time went by, but which still retained several years ago the memory of its former grandeur. It possessed a very singular charm due to its lustrous wood paneling and its faded tapestries and above all to its proprietor, an old intellectual, dreamy and quit of his illusions, who would not deign to look up at his clients unless they were capable of conversing a bit with him about literature, notably French. The thought that *Memoirs of Hadrian,* in the form that has made its way to us, was in some small part written in that hotel is a savory one. Despite the planned trip, which she did not abandon, and her visit to Taos (where D. H. Lawrence lived), not far from Santa Fe, and to Taos's ancient pueblo and its Indians, Yourcenar did not stop writing, "at least a little every day." One senses that, for the first time since 1939, she was completely happy. Frick took note of this renaissance day by day. But Yourcenar also wrote in the calendar. Once again, she had the long-lost feeling of success at keeping her attention focused and of undertaking a long-term project, the first "since *Electra* perhaps." As this "perhaps" indicates, all by itself, she well knew from then on that she was devoting herself to a work of an entirely different order.

On the train during the return trip, from 20 to 22 February, she kept on writing without letup: she was right in the middle of the description of Hadrian's first steps in politics, she notes, when she reached New York. She did indeed have to go back to Sarah Lawrence. But the train trips and the merest scraps of free time were devoted to Hadrian. She would type and reread her manuscript over the weekends. All the same, Yourcenar took the time to attend a performance of Giraudoux's *La Folle de Chaillot* (*The Madwoman of Chaillot*) with Frick. Neither woman had much of a taste for this piece, which they judged "poor and thin as well as shoddily sentimental," Frick comments.

A young American professor, Olga Peters, who hoped to undertake a study of her *œuvre,* had just written to Yourcenar, asking her to comment on each of her works that had already been published and to provide her information about the projects that were then in progress. Despite her intense activity, Yourcenar answered her with care and attention: they would keep up a warm correspondence, moreover, for several years, for Yourcenar felt an immediate sympathy for her interlocutor, whose Greek origins brought back many memories for her. Describing her work on Negro spirituals and on Constantine Cavafy's poems, only fragments of which had been published at that point, she confided to her correspondent that an undertaking wider in scope was preventing her, for the moment, from completing it: "I plan to get back to those two works as soon as I have finished a very long book (long at least for me, who up until now have hardly written anything but rather short narratives) conceived some twenty years ago, which I started working on again, with an intense passion, at the beginning of last year when the notes and a draft of the first chapter, lost during the war, were finally found in Paris [*sic*]. At present, I am working exclusively on this (setting aside, of course, the time devoted to my job as a professor). . . . I speak of this volume, which is three-quarters finished, because it represents at once a confirmation of what I cannot but call my previous '*œuvre,*' and, at the same time, a thoroughly unforeseen development and transformation, even for me." [10]

Real life, from then on, was Hadrian. This did not, however, prevent Yourcenar, even though she herself was living "in the thick of the second century," from giving a course on Proust's *Remembrance of Things Past,* followed by a more global lecture on his *œuvre.* She also gave a lecture, on 21 April, on Flaubert at Barnard College in New York. In that year's daybook, Yourcenar added much later on that the spring vacation from the university, from 27 March to 2 April, had provided the occasion for a trip to Nashville, Tennessee, and the surrounding region. It is as if she wanted to stress, as she always maintained, that she was not a "house-bound writer" and that every one of her books, be it written with "one foot in scholarship, the other in magic arts," was so completely hers that she could work on it—at least in the early stages—anywhere. "Most people, I think, have a mistaken impression about scholarship," she said to Matthieu Galey. "French readers especially conjure up the image of a writer immersing himself in books from morning till night, like the bookworms in Anatole France's novels. . . . But that's not the way it is. Anyone who loves life loves not only the present but also the past, for the simple reason that the past, as I can't remember which Greek poet once said, outweighs the present, especially the narrow individual present that each one of us knows. Thus it is only natural for a person who truly loves life to read a great deal. I used to read Greek literature . . . over long periods. . . . After a while I had reconstructed for myself Hadrian's cultural universe. . . . I never sat down and said to myself, You're going to write a book about Hadrian, so you've got to find out what he thought. If you start out that way, I don't think you'll ever succeed. The writer must soak up the subject completely, as a plant soaks up water, until the ideas are ready to sprout."[11]

Frick, for her part, kept meticulous track of the episodes that had been written, making a list of them and reading them as they were composed. This would be a constant practice, throughout their entire life together, except at the very end. It is perhaps a rather surprising practice: how could Yourcenar, often seeming so supremely conscious of her literary mastery, submit a "first draft" to someone whose knowledge of French was necessarily inferior to her own? How can we conceive of such an intimacy, at the very heart of her creation? There is a tendency to dismiss the question by appealing to a widespread habit common to all couples. In this particular case, that explanation falls rather short. Two hypotheses suggest themselves: nothing indicates that the fact of regularly giving Frick every newly written passage was based on the latter having any right to intervene or comment that went beyond an expression of admiring approval; in this case, Yourcenar's gesture would have had no other intention than to procure for herself the comforting certitude that her text existed, since, having been read, it had inscribed itself in someone's memory as an object of veneration and devotion, and Frick would have been no more than the pure mirror of a creation with regard to which her sole function was to bear witness to its continuation and its breadth. But it is just as plausible to imagine that Yourcenar's intellectual esteem for Frick was far superior to what people were subsequently led to believe, or that Frick's authority over Yourcenar was much stronger than is generally assumed. In any case, because of this behavior, Yourcenar ended up renouncing all privacy, even epistolary, as numerous instances reveal. Everything was subject to Frick's control, if not her approval.

Who did the imposing and who the giving in? In the final analysis, this question is very difficult to resolve. As all the witnesses say, the dominant figure in this couple, often presented as "a good marriage," was Yourcenar.

Why consent to what was, nonetheless, a dependency? Though their forty years of life together allow us to appraise the relationship between these two women and offer some keys to their behavior, we certainly will not be able to shed any light, before having read their correspondence, on the mystery of their absolute intimacy, so effectively did their respective "jamming" techniques (Frick never appearing and Yourcenar minimizing, after her death, the place she had held in her existence) preclude a clear reading of those two existences with their ambiguous relations of power. It is probable that the tie that bound them together was much less univocal—domination on the part of one, submission on the part of the other—than those who knew them would have us believe. In the face of the discomfort or incomprehension that a homosexual couple commonly gives rise to, there is a great temptation to superimpose the most traditional model upon it: "the man," lord and master, on the one hand—Yourcenar, of course—and, on the other, "the wife," a subjugated servant—obviously Frick. This is a singularly antiquated scheme of things, but this is precisely my point: everything proceeds as if it were a question of compensating for the "abnormality" of the situation with an excess of conventionality. This is exactly what has been said about another famous relationship, that of Gertrude Stein and Alice B. Toklas, which, nonetheless, Hemingway's testimony, in *A Moveable Feast*, shows to have been governed by reciprocal power relations, far more subtle and complex. Yourcenar, for that matter, warns the hasty exegete as well as the naive biographer in one of her notes in "Reflections on the Composition of *Memoirs of Hadrian*": "Keep in mind that everything recounted here is thrown out of perspective by what is left unsaid: these notes serve only to mark the lacunae. There is nothing, for example, of what I was doing during those difficult years, nor of the thinking, the work, the worries and anxieties, *or* the joys; nor of the tremendous repercussion of external events and the perpetual testing of oneself upon the touchstone of fact. And I pass also in silence over the experiences of illness, and over other, more profound experiences which they bring in their train; and over the perpetual search for, or presence of, love." [12]

DURING THOSE FIRST months of writing (on 10 June, a date that, on rereading, she would encircle and underline with crosses, she noted that the book had been begun four months before), she would write, as we have seen, anywhere, including on the train, on her knees, thus without consulting any sources—as if she were composing an entirely imaginary novel or an autobiographical narrative, in short, a story for which she needed no external references. She often explained how she "fell to making, and then remaking, this portrait of a man who was *almost* wise." [13] "Sometimes I would write Greek for an hour or two, before setting to work, to get closer to Hadrian," as she would confide, and as pages found covered with hurriedly written, partly illegible, Greek confirm. In "Reflections on the Composition of *Memoirs of Hadrian*," she provides some other information about her method: "I pass as rapidly as possible over three years of research, of interest to specialists alone, and over the development of a method akin to controlled delirium, of interest, probably, to none but madmen. And yet this term *delerium* smacks too much of romanticism; let us say, rather, a constant participation, as intensely aware as possible, in *that which has been*."[14] And in another passage she writes: "Everything turns out to be valuable that one does for one's self without thought of profit. During those years in an unfamiliar land I had kept on with the reading of authors from classical antiquity: the red or green cloth-bound volumes of Loeb-Heinemann editions had become a country of my own. Thus, since one of the best ways to reconstruct a man's thinking is to rebuild his library, I had actually been working for years, without knowing it, to refurnish the bookshelves at Tibur in advance. Now I had only to imagine the swollen hands of a sick man holding the half-rolled manuscripts";[15] or again: "This book is the condensation of a vast work composed for myself alone. I had taken the habit of writing each night, in almost automatic fashion, the result of those long, self-induced visions whereby I could place myself intimately within another period of time. The merest word, the slightest gesture, the least perceptible implications were noted down; scenes now summed up in a line or two, in the book as it is, passed before me in fullest detail, and as if in slow motion. Added all together, these accounts would have afforded material for a volume of several thousand pages, but each morning I would burn the work of the night before. In such fashion I wrote a great number of decidedly abstruse meditations, and several descriptions bordering on the obscene."[16] The "Carnets de notes" [Notebooks] she kept during the war bear the trace of these practices: "Try to find, for pleasure, the equivalent of musical notation, or of the language of Numbers. Or else, the most total obscenity, the simplest monosyllables, provided you address yourself to quite a pure ear, quite devoid of empty fears ... Or let what is inexpressible be peaceably accepted as such."[17]

On 22 June, eve of the departure for Mount Desert Island, Yourcenar had reached the point of Hadrian's first meeting with Venus. From here on, one can follow the progress that was made on the book step by step, chapter after chapter, including all deletions, revisions, and copies (the use of photocopiers, confined in that era to businesses, was not widespread, and one had to copy over one's work), by way of references to certain events of everyday life: the gathering of the first edible blueberries, during the week of 3 July; comments on existence or the poorness of sermons attended (Frick went to church on Sundays, quite regularly); or an allusion to the jaunt to the very near and very beautiful Sutton Island, on 19 July.

It would be tiresome to list here all the little stages of the composition of *Hadrian*. Every evening Frick would read what had been written, "to check it over," as she asserted. At the end of August, from the twenty-fifth to the thirty-first, they finished rereading the part entitled *"Tellus Stabilita"* together. Yourcenar spent the entire day on the twenty-seventh, says Frick, "correcting minor errors and making slight but nevertheless important reductions and expansions in [the] text." The next day, while Yourcenar finished this work and Frick was "slowly sweeping [the] living room," there arose a discussion on "the actual cause of [the] lack of clarity in a few sentences," which the latter imputes, "as nearly always in cases of obscurity in the statement, [to] a lack of certainty about one or more facts on which the statement should have been based." We may well assume that, if Frick noted down this discussion so precisely, it was because she was not averse to pointing out how important, for the very intelligibility of the text, was her research.

Indeed, while Yourcenar returned to Sarah Lawrence on 20 September and, once again, wrote on the train and between classes, Frick dedicated herself entirely to the book, providing a gauge of the extent to which she was the vital linchpin of the project that fall, even more so perhaps than where the books that would follow were concerned. When they went to the Yale library, on 4 October, Frick spent the whole day there (Yourcenar only stayed for the morning, as she had to go to Stamford). She surrounded Yourcenar with constant solicitude, willingly serving her dinner in bed after forcing her to lie down amid assertions that she was more tired than she thought. When Yourcenar began copying over everything she had written, on 11 November, introducing critical changes, Frick undertook a new copy of the revised text to be kept at the bank. It was probably she who took the initiative to place the text in safe deposit, since we know that Yourcenar, before meeting Frick, readily let texts and other objects slip through her fingers, as her leaving the *Hadrian* fragments behind in the trunk in Lausanne attests.

Frick's energy never slackened and she imposed her rhythm on Yourcenar, forcing her, on 27 November for example, to continue copying over her text "all day and almost all night."

The homage that Yourcenar renders to Grace in "Reflections on the Composition of *Memoirs of Hadrian*" bears the trace of that force and that constancy: "This book bears no dedication. It ought to have been dedicated to G. F. . . . , and would have been, were there not a kind of impropriety in putting a personal inscription at the opening of a work where, precisely, I was trying to efface the personal. But even the longest dedication is too short and too commonplace to honor a friendship so uncommon. When I try to define this asset which has been mine now for years, I tell myself that such a privilege, however rare it may be, is surely not unique; that in the whole adventure of bringing a book successfully to its conclusion, or even in the entire life of some fortunate writers, there must have been sometimes, in the background, perhaps, someone who will not let pass the weak or inaccurate sentence which we ourselves would retain, out of fatigue; some- one who would re-read with us for the twentieth time, if need be, a ques- tionable page; someone who takes down for us from the library shelves the heavy tomes in which we may find a helpful suggestion, and who persists in continuing to peruse them long after weariness has made us give up; someone who bolsters our courage and approves, or sometimes disputes, our ideas; who shares with us, and with equal fervor, the joys of art and of living, the endless work which both require, never easy but never dull; someone who is neither our shadow nor our reflection, nor even our com- plement, but simply himself; someone who leaves us ideally free, but who nevertheless obliges us to be fully what we are. *Hospes Comesque.*" [18]

This text is the sole explicit testimony in Marguerite Yourcenar's *œuvre,* even though it is a supplement to the work itself, to her union with Frick. But despite the expression of praise it represents and the gratitude that in- spired it, this passage places Frick irretrievably in the background. She ex- ists there less by way of what she brings to Yourcenar than by what she makes possible. Deep down, the remarks made by Yourcenar are but an acknowledgment of Frick's devotion and an indication that she, Yourcenar, does not underestimate her loyalty. We should not draw any overly hasty conclusions from this text regarding the moment when, as Yourcenar would later confide, they passed from "passion to habit," for we can never neglect how little inclined Yourcenar was to intimate disclosures. But, just the same, one can perceive to what an extent she was again in the grip of that exclusive priority that was a sense of herself.

THE YEAR that Frick and Yourcenar turned forty-seven years old, 1950, marked Yourcenar's return, if not to French literature, which she had never really abandoned, then at least to the status of being a French writer. Was it out of fear that Europe would reclaim from her the woman she loved, by way of *Memoirs of Hadrian,* that Frick suggested to Yourcenar that she ask the president of Sarah Lawrence to find a replacement for her for several months? Yourcenar, then, would once again be dependent, financially, on Grace. On 25 January, a few days before writing the scene of Antinous's death (on Sunday, the 28ᵗʰ), Yourcenar met with Harold Taylor. The president granted her request. She would leave Sarah Lawrence on 25 May, after giving a final lecture on Proust, one of her favorite subjects during the years she spent teaching. In a letter to Olga Peters, she described this work in detail but drew out of it a more general reflection concerning the intellectual influences that nourish the work of a writer that no doubt illustrates her own theory of the diffuse nature of cultural impregnation:

> I have just given a lecture on Proust's *œuvre*, about which, as it happens, I quite frequently have occasion to speak; the students I addressed are scarcely familiar with his works, and, as a consequence, I strived to situate him as best I could; I was even prepared, in order to assist my young auditors, to simplify things if possible. And yet, among the influences that buttress or nourish that *œuvre*, I had to cite ancient literatures, encountered directly, which is to say by way of translations done during Proust's time, or indirectly, by way of French literature; and also all the foreign literatures, especially English and Russian; Bergson, to be sure, but also Plato, and in general all the books by the philosophers, the men of science, and the psychologists who came before Proust, even when the latter had no direct knowledge of their works; all the art, that of Italy and Holland just as much as that of the Impressionists, all the music, in sum all the cultural materials available to a man living in France between the end of the nineteenth century and the beginning of the twentieth. And I am well aware that among these influences one can, to be sure, cite some that were stronger, or more visible than others. . . . But, for all that, it is still no less true that he was, like all of us, the sole legatee of an extremely complex culture. Shall I even go so far as to say that the fact of being able to isolate and follow a predominant influence on a writer, especially that of a popular philosophy or psychology, strikes me as immediately reducing the value of the former, and placing him in the class of the disciple, the propagandist, or the popularizer? Sartre would be greater if Heidegger's influence were not so ponderously evident in his *œuvre*, and the modern writers overly influenced by Freud will fatally go out of fashion, as the parts of Balzac's *œuvre* directly inspired either by Swedenborg or by Lavater went out of fashion, to the point of no longer having any value beyond that of historical documents on the philosophical or scientific speculations in vogue at the beginning of the nineteenth century." [19]

Her departure from Sarah Lawrence, on that 25 May 1950, is noted in large characters, across the entire page—which did not prevent her, in the Pléiade's "Chronologie," from placing it in 1949.

ALL THE SAME, Yourcenar would take the time, during her final months at Sarah Lawrence, to see two Verdi operas, one of them *Simon Boccanegra*. [20]

Frick does not mention the title of the other and says she was, like Yourcenar, "struck by the absurdity of [the] current depreciation of Verdi." Apart from this little "interlude," when they went out it was almost always to libraries.

On 22 April, Yourcenar received a telegram informing her of the alarming state of her stepmother Christine de Crayencour's health; she died in Pau on 24 April. There is no comment. Though she had taken care to send money to Christine during the war, when the latter was utterly destitute, Yourcenar had never very much liked that overly conventional woman, not exceedingly intelligent to her way of thinking. "I had no affection for Christine Hovelt," she wrote in 1980 to her half nephew, Georges de Crayencour; "her conventionalism, her ignorance, a certain English snobism bothered me. Likable, but not 'kind' in the way I understand kindness, she was nevertheless a very useful companion for an ailing 'Michel' who had grown old. It was I (at twenty-two years of age) who advised 'Michel' to marry her in October 1926 (2 years and three months before his death), when the idea suddenly came to him to do so 'because it would please her.'"[21]

On 10 June 1950, two days after Yourcenar's forty-seventh birthday, celebrated on Mount Desert Island, in Northeast Harbor, there arrived a first letter from Georges Poupet, one of publishing's éminences grises, on the letterhead of Librairie Plon. He was highly laudatory regarding the first one hundred twenty-four pages of the manuscript that Yourcenar had submitted several weeks earlier and proposed to take an option with a view to an eventual contract. Yourcenar responded on 13 June:

> I am happy that this book, which I have been working on for years, has struck such a responsive cord in you. About ten days from now, I shall send you the second part of the work, "*Tellus Stabilita*" and "*Saeculum Aureum*," one hundred seventy-five pages in all. In "*Tellus Stabilita*," the narration is interrupted for forty pages or so to make room for a kind of essay, presenting the reign's political and artistic legacy, which constitutes the center of the book; "*Saeculum Aureum*," on the contrary, contains its tragic element. Let us wait, before talking about a contract, to see if your interest and that of Librairie Plon are sustained after that reading.
>
> I agree with you regarding the possibility of detaching the first 34 pages of the Memoirs for *La Table Ronde*, on the condition that nothing be cut.

Immediately after that exchange of letters, Yourcenar—whose life, since getting back to writing *Hadrian*, had no longer been punctuated, in Frick's accounts at least, by colds, feelings of malaise, and other various maladies—felt ill. On 7 July, she was hospitalized in Bar Harbor for a week. The tests, whose nature Frick does not specify, demonstrated that "no operation [was] needed," she comments. "Intense relief."

Over the course of the summer, with the manuscript of *Hadrian* all but finished, Yourcenar and Frick allowed themselves a few diversions: the island's fair, a performance of *Macbeth,* and some long walks, which would turn, especially for Frick, into a methodical search for a house. And here and there in Frick's notes, we occasionally learn some amusing things. We find out, for example, that on 28 November "M.Y. [had a] permanent; Grace a $1/2$ perm." It's hard to tell whether or not we should lament the fact that no photographic documentation bears witness to this dubious "experiment."

In Paris meanwhile, at Plon, the manuscript of *Hadrian* was being examined with utmost attention, as is confirmed by the reader's reports of André Fraigneau (dated 28 November 1950) and Georges Poupet (undated, but written at about the same time, since the manuscript had been dispatched to him by Yourcenar in several installments, between May and the end of September). Those reader's reports were in the form of responses to a preestablished questionnaire, seeking notably comments on the composition, the literary value, and the degree of interest of the work, its commercial value, the possibility that it might "be placed in everyone's hands," the books to which it could be likened, and finally, in conclusion, an answer to the fateful question: "Is this manuscript worth publishing?"

Poupet's report is entirely favorable and comes down to: "Excellent composition, remarkable in its firmness and clarity. Great literary value. The work has great interest. Cannot be placed in everyone's hands. Writers or books to which the work or the author might be likened: the best; not at all comparable to *Quo Vadis* and *Fabiola.* Worth publishing. Commercial value: the subject is not for a mass public, but the quality is such that we can expect a real literary success."

Fraigneau's remarks, which are more reserved, are also more interesting when one takes into consideration that Fraigneau was Yourcenar's reader at Grasset and that their relations were, if not truly intimate, at least very personal. First, Fraigneau noted "the obvious influence of Walter Pater (*Marius the Epicurean*)." But, he continued, he "felt ill-chosen to speak about this book," having been "responsible for her [Marguerite Yourcenar] from the time of her first book at Grasset," explaining that: "She became my friend until her departure for America." And he added: "Finally, and this is more serious, the genre chosen by her for her new manuscript is precisely that of one of my recent works, *Le Roi fou et le solitaire* [The Crazy King and the Recluse] and of the one that followed it, *Julien l'Apostat* [Julian the Apostate].

Today, Fraigneau explains that he obviously did not mean to say that Yourcenar had plagiarized him, well aware that she had not read the two books he had written. He merely sees in the similarities between their works a sign that, despite the distance and the absence of communication between them for more than ten years, their centers of interest had remained close. The only reason for recalling his own works as he did in his report, says he, was to convey his discomfort in the face of a text that he necessarily had to compare to them. "We know Marguerite Yourcenar's strengths," he added in the same report: "a perfect style that is supple and mobile, in the service of an immense learnedness and a disabused, decorative philosophy. We also know her weakness: the absence of dramatic pitch, of a fictional progression, the absence of effects. . . . Her life of Hadrian shows the influence of Renan's books . . . ,[22] and of the overly gratuitous detachment of its author. Advancing through this scrupulous biography of the emperor known for his monuments and his hellenism, a biography containing no surprises, we knew full well that the enterprise's culminating interest would lie in the meeting with Antinous, Madame Yourcenar, despite her sex, being one of those authors most interested in homosexuality. . . . Having said this, fully conscious of my responsibilities as a reader, Marguerite Yourcenar's book and especially her career could never be a matter of indifference to a publisher of quality." As for the rest, Fraigneau noted: "Writers or books to which the work or the author can be likened: Walter Pater, Ernest Renan. Composition: harmonious. Style: perfect. Literary value: certain. Degree of interest of the work: moderate. Public: a cultivated elite. Cannot be placed in everyone's hands. Commercial value: weak. Is this manuscript worth publishing: yes; revised?"[23]

This reference to the voluminous philosophical novel of Walter Pater—whose refined modes of expression were unanimously approved—would reappear beneath the pen of several critics. Before consenting to its publication, in 1885, Pater had devoted more than six years to his imaginary portrait of a Roman patrician, living at the time of the Antonines, under the reign of Marcus Aurelius. For Pater, the tableau of the different intellectual, political, and religious currents of that era, given rise to by this imaginary witness, was a pretext for "the accomplishment of a kind of obligation"—that of "showing the necessity of religion" (at least this is the response he gave to everyone who asked him what intention had presided over Marius).[24] Charles Du Bos, for whom this work, "from one end to the other" was "essentially a kind of chamber music of inner life," devoted a long and very laudatory chapter of his *Approximations* to him in 1923.[25] But many years later, Yourcenar confessed to their common friend Jean

Mouton that she had never wanted to broach this subject with Du Bos, because she felt herself to be too far removed from Pater, and declared that she had nothing in common with him.

Surely we can't blame Fraigneau for not having predicted the commercial success of the book—it was so unforeseeable. On the other hand, it is surprising to find him taking *Memoirs of Hadrian* for a biography—and still more so to find him describing it as "scrupulous." Today we know that reconstructing the personage of the emperor across the centuries—that act of sympathy, in the true sense of the word—mattered more than anything to Yourcenar, even though it was at the cost of a few historical "distortions."

It might seem far too easy to criticize Fraigneau's point of view, now that we possess all the comments Yourcenar made over the years on the subject of Hadrian. Nonetheless, even on a first reading, it would be difficult to assimilate this monologue, necessarily tinged with self-justification, to a biography, which should "instruct both on the attack and on the defense." "I quickly realized," Yourcenar would later say to Matthieu Galey, "that in such a formal discourse, he could do no more than sketch the bare outlines of his life." [26] Similarly, to make the Antinous episode "the enterprise's culminating interest," one would have to read the book from the perspective of someone who had spent time with Yourcenar during the thirties. "[H]ad I written about Hadrian at that point," Yourcenar would point out on several occasions, "I would have concentrated mainly on the artist, the great admirer and patron of the arts, and doubtless also on Hadrian as lover, but I would have missed Hadrian the statesman." [27]

Galey shared the reading bias of Fraigneau. According to him, without Antinous, Hadrian would have been "an emperor like the rest." "Certainly not," came the response. "He would have been a great civil servant, a great man of letters, and a great prince. But it may well be that his posthumous cult of Antinous, which has been so widely decried right up to the present day, marvelously symbolized Hadrian's religious and emotional ideal. A touch of madness is, I think, almost always necessary for constructing a destiny." [28] At that moment, Yourcenar could not have known how very close she herself was going to come, at the end of her life, to what she had imagined or sensed about the relationship between Hadrian and Antinous.

In short, it was already clear that Yourcenar had not taken a biographer's distance from her subject. Upon numerous occasions, in letters written while she was working on *Hadrian* or in conversations with friends of that time, then in "Reflections on the Composition of *Memoirs of Hadrian*," she described those "three years of continuous work," of which she also spoke with Galey, "exclusively on this one book, during which time I lived in a symbiotic relationship with my character to such an extent that at times I understood that he was lying, and allowed him to get away with it. He arranged things, just as everyone does, wittingly or unwittingly. I think he lied quite a bit on the subject of his election, of his coming to power. He must have known a bit more about it than he told me. He wisely left the whole subject shrouded in uncertainty."[29] In reading these comments today, one is not hard pressed to confirm that Yourcenar knew whereof she spoke when it came to "shrouds of uncertainty."

11

Petite Plaisance

IT HAD ALREADY been several years since Yourcenar and Frick had come up with the plan to buy a house on Mount Desert Island. But at the end of the summer in 1950, Frick became possessed of a kind of feverishness, or at the very least a certain agitation, regarding the purchase of that house—was it the effect of *Hadrian*'s near completion and the inevitability of a return to Europe if the book was published there? The old inhabitants of the island still remember seeing her go by, on horseback or a bicycle, inquiring round and about, asking questions about properties for sale. Finding a house conforming both to their desires and to their financial possibilities was no easy feat. They clearly did not have the means to acquire one of those immense and magnificent villas that served as summer homes for wealthy families, such as the home of the Millikens, the textile manufacturers, or Mary Rockefeller's house, which are across the way from the cottage they finally decided on. Nor would they have had any taste for such an abode. Not owning an automobile and having no intention of buying one in the near future—they would never have one, for that matter, preferring, Yourcenar would say, "to rent one rather than own an additional object"—they hoped to find something not far from a village center. The post office, at least, had to be close by. Thus it was that after looking at some houses in nicer locations—high up, overlooking the sea, for example—they settled on a more ordinary site, that of Brooks Cottage, on Sea Shore Road in Northeast Harbor, one of their favorite villages on the island.

The cottage, the purchase of which was concluded on 29 September 1950, is located on the road that follows the ocean, but it is the villas across the way that have access—private access—to the oceanfront. Originally part of an old farm built in 1866, this little house, endowed with quite a bit of land, although uncultivated—two and a half unfenced acres surrounded by woods—suited Yourcenar and Frick because up until then it had been a hotel annex. Consisting solely of bedrooms, the place could be redesigned the way they wanted it. They would call it Petite Plaisance, for the pleasure of a French name, and in memory of Samuel Champlain who in 1604 discovered that great rocky island with its very rugged coastline wooded with fir trees, oaks, and maples. The island was initially inhabited by Indians. Renowned for its lobsters, it consists today of seven villages with about two thousand inhabitants each, most of them fishermen and artisans, who earn the bulk of their living during the tourist season. Champlain had never actually landed on the island. It was in leaving what is now Nova Scotia, where repair work on his ship's damaged keel had retained him, that he discovered that horizon of low mountains: "The tops of most of them," he would report, "are without trees, because they are nothing but rock. . . . I called it the Island of the Desert Mountains."[1]

"Later, when Louis XIV was king and the marquis de Cadillac was governor of the region, French colonists settled here," Yourcenar recounts.[2] "In the midnineteenth century the population consisted chiefly of farmers, almost all of Scottish origin, whose entire consumption of manufactured goods had to be brought in by boat from Boston. These farmers lived quietly on what their small, rocky farms produced, with the help of a few water mills. Then, around 1880, certain painters discovered the island and it became a fashionable resort. A fairly large number of fashionable Philadelphians and Bostonians built themselves horrid huge houses—it was a dreadful period for architecture—to which they came for periods of three to four months at a time with an entourage of twenty-five trunks and a dozen servants and horses in a splendid parade. . . . It was the beginning of the Gay Nineties, when people gave balls or went riding in rustic carts wearing city gowns, flounced dresses I suppose, and the men wore top hats. They had fine lace table linen imported from Italy and silver from England. White-gloved butlers served elegant picnic lunches by lakeside or on mountaintops, rather like eighteenth-century paintings. This was the world of the young Edith Wharton and the young Henry James. Unfortunately it's no longer anything but a memory."

"The island, in reality almost a peninsula," Yourcenar explained in 1955, "is about twelve hours by train from New York heading up toward the Canadian border."[3] One reaches it by way of a bridge. The trip by plane, out of New York, takes three hours nowadays, but, during Frick's lifetime, Yourcenar never flew, since she "hardly favored" traveling by air. "The climate resembles that of Norway," she explained in an interview. "The winters are very cold. The temperature goes down to 30° below zero, sometimes 40°. Beneath the piles of snow, the garden has been 'put to bed,' as they say in the region. Toward the end of April, the half-frozen soil becomes muddy, swampy. From not being able to go out, people catch what they call cabin fever. . . . What is very beautiful is the grand season of Indian summer, which lasts until 15 November. With its red maples, its oaks turned almost purple, and its birches of a very soft yellow."[4]

Some today are surprised when they arrive at Petite Plaisance, a modest house made all of wood and painted white, set back a few yards from the road. It is hard for them to believe that the Marguerite Yourcenar seen on French television, with her somewhat haughty air, that of a chatelaine, could have lived in a "house in the suburbs," and, in addition, one located on the wrong side of the street, since there is no view of the ocean. It cannot be denied that, with the (so very typically) French mania for always wanting to present people—notably writers—as it is believed the public imagines them, the entrance to Petite Plaisance has often been filmed in such a way as to make it appear that the house was situated at the end of a long path, "in the depths of a garden, and whatnot, to establish my reputation as a recluse," Yourcenar would say to make fun of such practices. She herself always emphasized the "modesty" of Petite Plaisance, "a very simple house, with a big garden and lots of books."[5]

It is easy to come up with a list of the defects and shortcomings of Petite Plaisance, taking it only at face value: It is a "misshapen" house, with very small rooms. And the furnishings are of no great interest: a few English commodes, an ordinary dining room with a not particularly handsome china cupboard, bookcases in all the rooms, the books arranged from west to east by centuries (fictional works of the twentieth century were thus located in her bedroom), and some very common cabinets, beds, and armchairs. Nor was there anything much on the walls to retain one's attention, except for a painting by the court artist Antoine Coypel in the entryway; some Piranesi engravings—purchased in New York in 1941—in the living room and the dining room; the portrait of one of Yourcenar's ancestors at the top of the short, very steep stairway with its disproportionate steps (Yourcenar referred to it as a "stairway for Puritans"); and two small portraits—of Yourcenar and Frick, by Marie Laurencin—in a guest room.

"A house's walls are almost a collection of mementos," she confided during another interview. "Documents on what one has done. I thought a lot about Rome with regard to Hadrian. I also took an interest in Piranesi. So here is Piranesi on the walls, and some 'unpublished' nudes of Michelangelo, which for me represent the whirlwind of natural forces in human terms. If everything burned and I had these walls to decorate over again, perhaps I would put up something different. A lovely Chinese painting, for example. But I am attached to these things, because they are moments of my work. . . . There are also objects that are not even particularly beautiful perhaps, but that one is attached to. In my bedroom, over my bed, I have a modern Chinese engraving that has been much too excessively reproduced, with the result that I've grown a little tired of it. It is a horse painted by an artist of the mid-twenties. A friend gave it to me around 1930. He had bought it on the banks of the Seine and has since died. So I think of him when I look at that engraving. And I've come up with quite an association of ideas: a stone horse, legendary in China, sets off every thousand years to take a little tour in the sky . . . If you find the moment when he's going to fly away, all you have to do is hang on to him, and away you fly with him. I like this story. One day, an Orientalist who was visiting my house said to me: 'But how can you keep that mediocre engraving?' He didn't know all that."[6]

If, on the other hand, there is a certain charm to be found at Petite Plaisance, it is that of a house kept by women. We can't be sure that Yourcenar would have found this characterization, which she would no doubt have judged too imprecise and too restrictive all at once, to her liking. Nevertheless, this closed, soft, and somewhat static place is indeed a house belonging only to women—to women who did not have much money and who, little by little, surrounded themselves with objects, which were no doubt inexpensive, but which both of them liked. It is a house more "literary" than practical. On the ground floor, the large kitchen is like an *image d'Epinal*[7] of the kitchen in a country house: a good-sized stove, cupboards and drawers in a light-colored wood, and a work surface over which hangs a long shelf bearing large glass jars on which Yourcenar painted "noodles," "flour," "semolina," "sugar," and so forth, in French. On another shelf, there are smaller jars containing spices; in the middle there is a little square table, quite high, on which, most often, a basket full of fruit was placed. Against the wall whose two windows face the street, there is a table for informal meals; above it is a shelf where, in a typically American way, there hangs a set of mugs, large cups used mostly for breakfast. The refrigerator is hidden in a large closet. The sink, a very small one despite the absence of a dishwasher, is located in a tiny scullery. The living room—which is next to the kitchen—is made up of odds and ends, organized around the fireplace, which two armchairs face and a little table; against the wall on the left, from which a door opens onto the garden, there is a bench seat and a bookcase. It was against the back wall that Frick's piano had stood. Leaning against the right side of the fireplace was the special bookcase where Yourcenar had gathered all her own books; this was the room's only singular element, along with two lamps with parchment shades, classical except for the ancient Greek inscriptions she had transcribed on them in calligraphy. In the office, there are two tables, attached to one another—Yourcenar and Frick worked face to face.

They had a passion—especially Yourcenar, out of nostalgia for her childhood—for the blue ceramic tiles from Delft. Anya and Jacques Kayaloff had made a habit, over the course of their travels, of seeking out these tiles and sending some to them. They decorate the dining room and the bathrooms. The bathrooms (one on the ground floor, looking out on the garden, and one upstairs, on the same side of the house) are of a pure white (like a memory of Greece) that is heightened—as well as by the tiles—by flacons and glasses of a deep blue. For the dining room, Yourcenar and Frick chose grey-blue stoneware dishes, which blend well with the tiles: "these hues of grey-blue have always struck me as calmly bespeaking the good life,"[8] Yourcenar wrote to the Kayaloffs; "at this rate, I shall soon have reconstructed the Delft stove in my childhood bedroom, with its checked animal or flower."[9]

All the bedrooms are upstairs. Of course the largest one, with a big bed, was Yourcenar's, Frick making do with a room of more modest dimensions. But nothing proves that they did not continue, on a regular or irregular basis, to share the same bedroom, as in Hartford, at least while Grace was not ill. The two other rooms are guest bedrooms: one is adorned, on either side of the commode, with the two Marie Laurencin paintings: "The two blue and pink portraits now hang in the guest room of the little house (the only one whose proportions and light were favorable to them—and no one but Narcissus wants his portrait constantly beneath his gaze in the room where he lives and works). The walls have been repainted to their liking," she wrote in 1953 to Natalie Barney.[10] To Georges de Crayencour, her half nephew, she confided much later on: "Marie Laurencin turned me into the very good (?) little girl into which she transformed all her models." The drawing, unfinished, executed by Han Harloff in 1954, of Yourcenar's face, hung in the other guest bedroom, is "by far the one that I prefer," she went on.[11]

Yourcenar reasserted constantly that she saw Petite Plaisance as "a country house such as I could have had anywhere in the world." "The best reason for having a little country house on this continent, at least where work and reflection are concerned, is precisely its value in solitude," she stated in 1959. "On this little island . . . , in sum, it is somewhat as if I were in the United States while not being there."[12] This confirms a letter to Jean Lambert, who, in 1956, found himself in the United States and shared with Yourcenar his homesickness: "Until such time as one has managed to create on this continent, as Grace and I have done, a domain, however small it may be, governed by fantasy or one's personal wishes, what the transplanted European finds here, in contrast to everything he expected, is quite simply a poorer, harsher Europe, devoid of all the refinements that make Europe what it is for us; (with regard to which we are mistaken; how very small it is, that Europe of refinements, and how much more it resembles America than people profess; I don't see much of a difference between the Boulevard de Sébastopol and Eighth Avenue). That there is also something else, of this we can be certain: small islands of public-spiritedness, which are submerged where we come from; a will to progress that is grotesque when expressed in terms of publicity, but that has remained sincere and effective in the case of certain beings; despite the scandalous squandering of resources, an extraordinarily beautiful natural environment, when one manages to uncover its secrets, which are not our own; and infinitely more of a past than is generally said: those great reservoirs of the past that are museums and libraries; the old houses of New England and the plantations of the South (which, I willingly admit, belong to a vanished world, but is this not also true of Versailles?), and finally, the admirable Indian country. My objective in going on here as I have is at once to commiserate with you in your depression and to cure it, by showing you that there still is much to see and appreciate here. Are you sure you are right to return so quickly to New York? Yes, New York is the gateway to Europe, as Marseilles is the gateway to the Orient.... I'm not saying that the experience of New York is not worth having, for a few weeks or even a few months, but if I were you, I would start by hitchhiking to San Antonio or San Francisco. It takes time to get to know this great country, at once so spread out and so secret."[13]

To everyone who, coming to visit, asked her the traditional question regarding her choice of America and that island, she tirelessly gave the same responses, pointing out straightaway that, throughout her life, she had always felt a strong attraction for islands and out-of-the-way places. "The fact, for example, of living in a very remote place, a village, provides a way of educating oneself that city dwellers do not have at their disposal. One ends up knowing all the area's inhabitants. I have always liked isolation. If I left here, I would set myself up in another village, of the same type, moreover.... I live here in the same way I would live in Brittany, or anywhere. My life's choice is not that of America against France. It translates a taste for a world stripped of all borders."[14] "Besides this place," she confided elsewhere, "I see almost nowhere beyond an area northeast of Göteborg, Sweden, Brittany, and southernmost Portugal in which I would consent to live."[15]

IN 1950, it took a certain courage for these two women whose appearance left little mystery regarding their sexuality to settle down in a little island village in Maine, in a country as puritanical as the United States. Unless it was a lack of consciousness, in their case something of a doubtful hypothesis, or else, as is more probable, the calm certainty that they could make others respect their freedom no matter where they were. In Northeast Harbor, certain people still remember feeling ill-at-ease when they would cross paths with the two of them, out for a stroll: Yourcenar, the shorter one, would put her arm around Frick's waist, while the latter had her arm around Marguerite's shoulders.

"Their get-up made an impression," remembers Anya Kayaloff, evoking her first visits to Maine. "Marguerite was wrapped up in shawls, and wore roomy pants. Grace donned vividly colored turbans. Like hippies, one might say, except that Marguerite and Grace were already wearing those outfits at the end of the forties. I think it was Grace who rather pushed for this kind of clothing. When my mother-in-law saw them appear, she said in Russian: 'here come the disguised ones . . .' When Marguerite Yourcenar came to New York, she would wear a sober black dress. But up there, it was incredible." "In the house, Grace did everything, and Marguerite 'reigned,'" Anya Kayaloff explains, perhaps forcing the trait a bit: "Certain individuals were allowed to come to tea. Marguerite held court. The atmosphere was very Victorian. Marguerite, a good cook, was supposedly the one who did the cooking. But Grace cleaned and peeled the vegetables, getting everything ready. Then Marguerite arrived, like a sovereign, and 'cooked.' In compensation, Grace controlled everything. She answered the telephone and decided whether or not to let Marguerite know that someone wished to speak with her. Afterward, Marguerite would sometimes claim she'd had no news of us, when we had called two or three times. Marguerite very much enjoyed talking with my husband, who was a cultured man. Grace would not stand even for that. She had her little 'wifely' schemes. One day she hurled at me: 'If Jacques thinks that what he tells Marguerite about Paris is of interest to her, he is mistaken.' Which shows you how jealous she was . . . They were a rather incredible couple."

Rumors spread around at a good clip, and children made fun of the "witches" of Petite Plaisance. Today, the only ones who talk about such things are those who stood up for the two women right from the start. The others have a standard speech, in which it would seem that all they retain is the memory of the—belated—respect they have conceived for "the great mind" that chose their village as a place of residence.

Durlin Lunt, husband of Jeannie, who would become Yourcenar's assistant after Frick's death, in 1979, was one of those children to whom Grace seemed "a little like a witch," which is that much easier to imagine as she was in the habit of wearing one of those long hooded capes, called "monk-capes," which must have lent a most disquieting aspect to her appearance.

"She was demanding, and rather caustic, with people in the shops, but she also had some very good qualities. A keen, extraordinary sense of humor. She would invite the children for tea and also to play in the big yard. Madame [this is what Yourcenar was always called in Northeast Harbor, which Frick probably initiated, she being the only one who really talked with the villagers—to the point where there were quite a few people who didn't know whether 'Madame' spoke English] herself did not go out, except for her walks. She was always a recluse. She worked. You never saw her in town; for years, no one knew who she was. Grace would go to church; she was part of the community, even if people considered her eccentric. Madame did not take part in community life." Grace had no compunction about intervening in people's lives, and she particularly enjoyed the role of teacher. Early in the morning, she would occasionally get into Dr. Wilson's car (she knew precisely what time he left the house) to ask him, when he got there, to drop her off at the post office. But the day she saw a bow and some arrows in the back of the car, she did not deny herself the opportunity to give him a lecture on the ill effects of hunting.

Indeed, Robert Wilson remembers one of their quarrels. The Wilsons had a dog that barked a lot, which bothered Frick. One evening, she came to see them by way of the little path linking the yards of their respective houses. The Wilsons were out, and there was a baby-sitter staying with their six children. Frick asserted thereupon, without blinking an eye, that the reason why the dog was barking so much must be that Dr. Wilson was practicing vivisection on him. "I called her up to say how angry I was, especially since she had repeated her accusations in front of the children," Robert Wilson recounts. "The next day she came over to tell me I owed her an apology. I refused. We weren't on very good terms with one another afterward, she and I . . . She was a curious mixture of kindness and inconsiderateness. She would go into people's houses in the middle of the night—no one locks their doors around here—and leave one of those famous loaves of bread she used to make on the kitchen table, wrapped up in a red ribbon, while the house was asleep . . .

"Right before Christmas, there are cookies and eggnog in all the village shops. Grace would always make the rounds. One year—this is a story that the people who live here are particularly fond of—she arrived just before closing at the hardware store, which also sold firearms and ammunition. She launched into a diatribe against hunters and fishermen, and the people there, listening to her all the while, kept filling her glass up with eggnog, which she immediately downed. As her speech grew more and more impassioned, Grace Frick's big hat became more and more precariously perched on her head. With each new glass and each new tirade, it swayed more and more from side to side. She went home pretty well drunk, but 'Madame' probably never heard anything about that episode."

"I was not on good terms with Grace either," Dee Dee Wilson adds, "not only because of what happened with my husband, but because I began to get exasperated with her way of sticking her nose into everything and constantly giving advice to people who simply weren't interested. She thought nothing of knocking on the window to tell you that the table was set wrong, that you hadn't put out the right wine glass. I don't think that Madame knew about these kinds of things, or the real relations between Grace Frick and the village: that she would hold forth in the shops, that she would go into people's houses and give her opinion on everything, in the same professorial tone. One day I found her in my garden, in the process of cutting my dahlias, needless to say, without ever having asked me if she could. All she said was: 'Don't forget, you should always bring a pail full of water when you go to the garden to cut flowers.' I was speechless. But ever since then, I have to admit that I've never gone out to cut flowers without bringing a pail along with me ... As for Madame, I didn't meet her until several years after we came here, the day of the big fire on Main Street, in 1966, I think [it was 15 December 1966, Frick wrote it down]. I only used to see her from a distance. The day of that fire, we were standing next to each other, watching what was going on. I didn't dare say anything to her, since I was convinced, as many people are here, that she didn't understand English. And suddenly I heard a strange voice say, with a curious accent: 'Is it serious?' It gave me a start, I was so surprised."

Elliott McGarr, a near neighbor, along with his wife Shirley, was their gardener for a long time and something of a jack-of-all-trades around the house. "I would fix electric outlets, and do other small repairs—in a house, especially if it's made of wood, there's always something that needs to be done—and I would get rid of the squirrels when I had to, when they had gotten into the attic and were on the verge of doing irreparable damage," he recounts. He watched them move in: a tall, thin one, "Miss Grace," and a short one, a bit too plump, "Madame." "They were rejected by the community, because people weren't certain they were only good friends," says

McGarr. "Besides they had a funny look about them. As for me, I never cared one way or the other. Talking with Madame was like opening up an encyclopedia. Unlike what people will tell you, she was always willing to talk. But rarely without having something to say. It was really a pleasure for Shirley and me to be invited to Petite Plaisance now and then. We always came to spend the evening with them on Halloween, because the kids, when they would knock on the door with their famous 'Trick or treat,' were apt to be aggressive toward them, and, especially when they were getting older, this would worry them a little." "Grace was a character, and sometimes she had quite a foul temper. But I was quite fond of her, and I was not the only one," Shirley McGarr goes on to add. "Besides, she kept up some touching traditions, like Easter eggs that she would paint to give to friends. Every year, when I got up on Easter morning, I would find a basket on my doorstep left by Grace. I always get up very early, around five in the morning. Still, I never got up before she'd been there, and I never caught her in the act. Even today, I still wonder what time it must have been when she came with those baskets."

Yourcenar and Frick's integration into the Northeast Harbor community was not, thus, an easy one. To hear the accounts of certain residents, especially knowing them to be some of the friendliest toward the two women, one can hardly find this surprising or impute to this small community any special capacity for ostracism. Frick's peremptory unceremoniousness, Yourcenar's haughty isolation, and the extravagance of both women could have given rise elsewhere to a rounder rejection, particularly in France. The fact remains that Frick was no doubt somewhat pained by this state of affairs, without letting on. Yourcenar, surely, was not: she did not want, above all, to fit in, because she wanted to speak English as little as possible. However, she was not averse to conversing with this one or that one: "It doesn't bother me to be interrupted in my work," she contended. "Writers shutting themselves up in cork-lined rooms,[16] this is not at all my style."[17] Chances to run into people and chat were not lacking in that house constantly in need of repairs requiring the regular assistance of carpenters. "We had several carpenters, one carpenter after another. The first one was something of a crazy old gentleman; he would tell stories that didn't make any sense and do preposterous things without realizing it. We had another one—he was also very old—who sang and swore all the time. He would sing hymns and stop to say, 'Ah! God damn! This gizmo isn't working,' then go back to his hymn. The last one, who is also a lobsterman, is a friend of ours, as he himself confirms. He brings us fruits and vegetables from his garden and tells us his troubles. When he lost his cat, he came over to our house and cried. Literally cried. When our dog was run over, we received his condolences the next day. That was the carpenter." [18]

WITH THE PURCHASE of Petite Plaisance, there came an end, not to her nomadism—Yourcenar would never lose her taste for traveling, one "as violent as carnal desire," according to her—but to a certain form of wandering: the era of trunks left behind in hotels, the era of destroying papers and selling objects prior to precipitous departures, the era of suitcases piled up, hardly unpacked, in what were known to be temporary lodgings. She had a house in which she could stack up her files and shelter the objects she loved. The wayfarer, who had no past beyond the memories she carried around with her, from now on had a port. During the months, and the years, when she would not be a nomad (though she did not know it yet), she would be an islander. For the moment, during the fifties, she simply considered Petite Plaisance a "base": "Regarding the United States? I've kept a small house there," she wrote a friend from Europe in 1954: "It's in a spot rather far away from everything, which I think of, not as America, but as the 'country,' a bit of country where one finds oneself, by chance, in the position of owning a cottage, which I plan to return to from time to time to work, if I can do so, but no sooner than a year from now in any case. All this to get things sorted out ahead of time regarding residences and addresses." [19] We are a long way here from the caricatured representation of Yourcenar—the writer who supposedly shut herself away on a godforsaken island near the northeastern coast of the United States.

Nonetheless, Yourcenar would little by little let herself be won over by Frick's passion for that little house and its garden—yet another proof that Grace's influence was much stronger than is generally believed. "I can remember when, behind the house, there stretched a sort of jungle, a tangle of wild grasses that were choking out what trees there were," McGarr recalls. "It's hard to imagine today the enormous job that Miss Grace did, sometimes with Madame's help, to make this nice garden out of that mess." "The garden, indeed the grounds all around, had been very much neglected," Yourcenar confirms. "It was like a wild meadow and beyond this, where the garden, the little paths, and the trees are now, there was some kind of undergrowth surrounding dead and fallen trees. The trunks were rolled down the slopes of the land, generally by kicking them along. And after a while, from all the rolling, the tree trunks carved the paths." [20]

Yourcenar would take a keen interest in this little corner of nature, especially during the time when she would have to "spend eight years almost without budging from this garden, to take care of a sick friend," as she would say by way of precluding requests for indiscreet details. During those years of forced sedentariness, she would keep her impatience in check by turning her attention to the house and the garden. At the time, she professed to be deliberately moving closer to nature, parallel to her interest in Oriental wisdom, but one could bring many a nuance to this oversimplified depiction of the situation, which seems like a justification after the fact, yet another way of masking the wounds and covering her tracks. In order to make her supposed desire to stay at home exist, she had, of course, to write it into being. For her, this was always less a process of self-convincing, a more or less conscious deviation from the truth, than the only means of founding a reality.

There remain some testimonials in her correspondence to what she called the charms of country life, notably in a letter from 1971 to a French friend on the theme of "works and days." "And as you know so well, I must add to this [her literary work] the daily task of the house, the garden, and even the orchard (we are proud to have an orchard; sixteen or seventeen fruit trees, and the apple trees are so beautiful now beneath their mantle of apples that we make do for compotes with gathering the ones the wind brings down). Outdoor domestic help this year was limited to a long-haired boy of seventeen resembling a Saint John sculpted in wood by a sixteenth-century German sculptor; he was an assiduous worker, but he hardly knew how to do anything else besides dig. He has now gone back to school, where it appears that he is not learning anything. An old forester replaced him, and continues to, who cuts the grass and takes the dead branches off the trees; but he is distracted, he forgets to come, and his tools are rarely sharpened as they should be. Inside, a few hours a week, during vacations, we have a little fifteen-year-old girl, of intermittent energy. She has now gone back to school. Her sister, who is eleven years old and very pretty (a little Scandinavian sprite), makes herself useful running errands in the village when we don't want to go ourselves, or are unable to; she's the one who will drop this letter in the mailbox. She likes to brush Valentine [the dog], who adores her, because she contents herself with passing the brush and the comb over her without undoing the 'snarls.' Happily, there is also the laundress, who comes every week with her basket. A very energetic housekeeper, also very highly placed in her profession, who has 'taken care of us' (*taken care* = a euphemism here for working) in the past, but who, in the summer, does nothing else but work for the Fords—they have a country house in the vicinity—promises that she will come to clean twice a week starting at the end of October. I enjoy telling you all this because, living in the country, you will understand. The people who are writing about me in Paris haven't the slightest idea about my way of life." [21]

There is no way to be sure that Yourcenar was overly fond of this "way of life," once an ailing Grace could no longer fill her assumed role, that of protecting Yourcenar from all material preoccupations. Did she consider moving back to France in her old age, taking up residence somewhere in the country where the climate would not be so harsh and the winters less long? To Jean Montalbetti, who had asked her this, even before Frick's death, she responded: "I like Brittany, Alsace. But Candide comes to mind: when one is at home in a place, one should stay there." [22] Nonetheless, Yourcenar did give some thought to going back to Europe, after Frick's death, and even more so after Jerry's, to live in England or in some corner of Brittany.

She would regularly bring up the possibility of a move, but without ever making up her mind to do it: "It would be too hard for me to give up this house." She was not interested in being uprooted again, everything having fallen apart, or been destroyed, behind her: the house where she was born on Avenue Louise, in Brussels; Mont-Noir; the Westende villa on the Belgian coast purchased by her father and bombed during the war of 1914; the Lausanne apartment; and even the Paris hotels she was fond of: the Wagram, her prewar residence, where she had met Frick, was ruined by a fire, and the Hôtel Saint James et d'Albany, where she stayed with Frick during the fifties and sixties, was changed, part of it having been sold for apartments in 1977.

It was at Petite Plaisance, in this place, which—it must be conceded to those who don't care for it—is extremely humid and a bit gloomy, that she wanted to end her existence. And no matter what her "official" discourse was, during the last years—"Why do journalists want me to talk about Grace Frick? My life was always very different from Grace Frick's"—her real fidelity to Grace was in that house they set up together, which she did not want to see disappear, even after her death. In her will, Yourcenar entrusted its management to a foundation—what Americans call "a board of trustees." If at all possible, the house must remain the way it was at her death and be open to the public during the summer months. If this arrangement were no longer viable, the will goes on to provide, the furnishings and objects found in the house should be sold in France, and the cottage itself would pass to an association for environmental and natural protection.

Despite—or perhaps because of—her attachment to the house in Northeast Harbor, it is clear that the cottage with the French name was nonetheless more Frick's house than Yourcenar's. And, although Yourcenar was always referred to as the dominant figure in the couple, if there exists a clear sign of the allegiance she accorded to Frick, its name is Petite Plaisance.

12
First Renown

ONE JANUARY 1951 was the first "New Year's Day" spent at Petite Plaisance. Inaugurated then was what would become a tradition: inviting the neighbors to celebrate the new year, according to custom, gathered 'round that egg drink called "eggnog" that Frick was so good at concocting, and which, as we have seen, gave such a "punch," if one might be so bold, to her ecological demonstrations. The next day, Yourcenar herself put the conclusion of her manuscript in the mail, on the way back from the library where she had spent three whole days checking sources one last time.

During the period that separated the beginning of this year from the departure for Europe, in May, to sign the publishing contract for *Memoirs of Hadrian*, accepted in its entirety, Frick did not record much of anything in her new daybook. There are a few scattered comments about daily life and mail received from France, and the refusal, arriving on 9 March, of the grant Yourcenar had applied for from the Bollinger Foundation.

It was not without anguish that Frick undertook the trip to Europe. Though she never admitted it, according to her old friends, she couldn't help but be worried. For more than eleven years now, the two of them had stayed on Frick's home turf. Was this not the principal reason, if not the only one, that she had been able to "keep" Marguerite? She remembered the young, masterful woman whose path she had crossed at the Hôtel Wagram, that day in 1937, who had captivated her. During the war, she had seen that same woman in tears, despairing of the world and of herself, allowing herself to be comforted gently and, firmly, "taken in hand." Did Yourcenar begrudge having laid herself bare in this way? Did she resent Frick for having witnessed her distress, and for having derived from it a certain power? It is difficult to say; who knows from what distant sources came Yourcenar's obscure resentment, very perceptible at the end of her life, toward Grace?

Whatever the case may be, Yourcenar resumed contact, interrupted or intermittent before, with her European friends. Frick, who was already reading the mail and filing it away, did not fail to notice this letter from Constantine Dimaras, dated 11 February 1951 from Athens, responding to a note from Yourcenar:

What a great pleasure, my very dear friend, to read your good news and your promises! We had the impression we had lost track of you, and, I don't know why, I felt almost guilty about this. Did you know you had already promised us a visit for last fall? In any case, you are well, and you have the only excuse that could please me: the completion of a long work. I never followed literary trends in France very closely; and I follow them now from an even greater distance. Nonetheless, I don't believe I am mistaken to put forth the opinion that America has held you for too long, and that it is absolutely necessary, from the point of view—how shall I put this?—of literary strategy, that you reappear on this side of the Ocean.[1]

Nor could she ignore the letter in which Yourcenar described for Joseph Breitbach her "personal life, very happy in some respects (which is already considerable), but often difficult in others." "I trust you understand," she continued, "that it is not without regrets that I have been at this remove from Europe for such a long time. But my personal and financial arrangements did not allow for anything else. I have often suffered here from a great intellectual solitude," all of this aggravated by "my fragile health, which does not bear up well to the hectic pace of life in New York, itself rather disappointing and hollow."[2]

Frick's good fortune, however, was having found a way, out of generosity more than out of amorous self-interest—though, quite often, the former is naught but the latter's alibi—to make herself more or less indispensable. She would make it her business to remain so, in Europe. For the moment, it behooved one to rejoice at the news that was arriving from that very continent. On 5 March, the letter received from Georges Poupet attested to "unqualified" admiration and announced that Gabriel Marcel and André Fraigneau were supporting the book, which, having negotiated the barrier of the "little committee," would be examined by the "full committee." During the week of 25 through 31 March, Yourcenar indicated that she considered *Hadrian* to be "finished"; Grace went over the bibliography, and Plon sent a contract. The only thing left to do was leave, after final readings of *Hadrian*'s supplementary texts.

But she also received some news that was not as pleasant. It was over the course of a day spent working at the library in Bangor, "rereading those Fathers of the Church who took something of an interest in Hadrian's politics and a great interest in his love affairs," that Yourcenar learned of André Gide's death, which had occurred in Paris on 19 February. She retained a great admiration, and a kind of reverence, for Gide, one of the first great writers to have held her in esteem, and one who had exercised real influence on the young woman that she was when she had just made up her mind to dedicate her existence to writing: "I thought about his *œuvre* and his life during the night, as if keeping some sort of death vigil," she would confide to Breitbach; "the more I reflected, the more that *œuvre* and that life seemed to me an enormous success, and with respect to the attunement, the balance, and the use of all the faculties, an exemplary success."[3]

On numerous occasions, Yourcenar would express her thoughts, in greater detail still, on the subject of the *œuvre* of this writer, whose work left such a mark, sometimes a considerable one, on her generation. In November 1969, she gave a lecture in Massachusetts, at Smith College, as part of Gide's centenary celebration.[4] Much earlier, in August 1956, she had made laudatory comments on her friend Jean Schlumberger's work, *Madeleine et André Gide* (*Madeleine and André Gide*),[5] and, in a 1962 letter, written to Schlumberger after rereading his book, she developed at length the reflection she had outlined on the occasion of their first exchange:

> Your notes led me thus, somewhat despite myself, to try to reevaluate what André Gide represented for us. I believe that first of all, perhaps above all else (which, I think, would have disconcerted him), he served for us as a very precious link between the literary chaos of our time and the classical tradition such as we encountered it in the great works of the past. In the midst of the disorder of the twenties, which for the men and women of my generation was that of youth, we rejoiced at discovering a writer who was tackling the problems that concerned us all in a language as pure and as precise as that of Racine. Then, during the time when *Fruits of the Earth* and *L'Immoraliste* (*The Immoralist*) were reaching us, he was the finest example of a certain kind of mystical fervor with regard to beings, sensations, and things, the first, already vertiginous, level in a series of steps aloft that, for that matter, can lead in directions that Gide himself did not take. Finally, though here the gift is already a more questionable one, the Gide of the *Caves* (*Lafcadio's Adventures*) and of *Paludes* (*Marshlands*) (it was thus, at twenty-two, that I first came in contact with his work) showed us that the edifice we thought to be so solid, sometimes so oppressive, could be demolished (or appear to be) by an impertinent flick of the finger. I think that what caused certain readers, first off, to turn their backs on him was perceiving to what an extent he had remained almost exclusively a man of letters. . . . In spite of Gide's constant assertions, which, for that matter, you do not contest, it is hard for me to believe that he wrote the majority of his work in relation to his wife. (Why would he have, for that matter? And what merit would there have been in that?) More important still, I have a vague suspicion that there

is something made-up about that great love. And yet, it is in fact curious that something quite obviously disappears from his *œuvre* at the moment when an *avowed* fissure opens up between them. I am willing to grant you that *Corydon* (*Corydon*) and *Les Faux-Monnayeurs* (*The Counterfeiters*), written apart from her and against her, are, as you say, franker, more straightforward works (but are they really?). All the same, it seems that a certain kind of fluency or warmth is missing from then on, and that more and more the artist, and the man, solves his problems by evading certain of their fundamental facets. One would not wish, and for many reasons, that those two volumes had not been written, and they do of course set forth the image of himself that Gide wished to leave behind. But the desiccation had even then begun . . . And this itself reopens the debate: did the impoverishment begin the day Gide decidedly broke away from Madeleine in his mind, or, on the contrary, does the impoverishment I believe I detect not come from his failure to re-claim all freedom of expression with regard to her until so late?

This is not a dissertation: I simply wanted to show you how attentively I've read your work. Dare I add that as we see diminishing, not Gide's glory, certainly so well-deserved, but the clamor of public attention to his *œuvre*, it seems to me we hear more clearly the voice of certain writers of his generation (I have you in mind specifically) who stayed in the background, it would appear, almost voluntarily. Only with some hesitation do I venture this overly personal comment.[6]

The influence of the "couple" on creation . . . Is it going too far (Your-cenar's letter was written in 1962) to hear echoes in this letter of something beyond a judicious—but relatively abstract—literary analysis, with particular regard to the "impoverishment" of a Gide separated from Madeleine, an impoverishment, as Yourcenar speculates, that may have come above all from a separation too long delayed?

On 12 April, Yourcenar and Frick left Petite Plaisance for Boston, where they went to the library, once again, to check some sources in connection with *Hadrian.* From 15 to 29 April they were in Hartford for the final departure from their old apartment. Having brought back to Maine the few possessions they were attached to that were still there, they took the train for New York on 10 May. On the eighteenth, a Friday, they embarked, aboard the *Mauritania,* "on the trip that would bring Marguerite back to Europe after twelve years of absence," Frick noted (the Pléiade's "Chronologie" situates this trip in May 1950). They would stay there until August 1952.

One week later, they were in Paris. Constantine Dimaras, who had counted the days that brought Yourcenar nearer the old continent, wrote to her on 28 May from Athens: "So here you are, finally, dear friend, on the right side, on our side of the Ocean. It is not yet entirely what I would have hoped for, but we're getting there." If Yourcenar knew better than anyone else the dark days that her years in America had cost her, she was far from eager for those years to be viewed as nothing but the empty parenthesis of a life in exile, and even less as an ill-considered amorous foible; she set things straight in responding to Dimaras in July, with a hint of coldness: "I was extremely short of money during my last stay in Greece and could not determine how to face the future. My teaching position in the United States and the friendship of Grace Frick made it possible for me to live. By the workings of chance, it was the United States that gave me the peace and the security I needed to write."[7]

According to her friends, Yourcenar spoke little of her emotion, though it was evident, at seeing her native continent again. "Paris is still very beautiful, even more so than I remembered," she merely wrote in a short note she left at the Hôtel de Crillon, where the Kayaloffs were staying and where she "stopped in passing." "As for the people, they haven't changed, neither for the better, nor for the worse."[8] On 29 May, she visited the offices of Plon and, on 7 June, the contract was definitively signed. Plon's "literary agreement" is very "classical," with no surprises. Yourcenar stipulated simply that, "for any edition accompanied by photographic documentation, the author reserves the right to approve or to select the latter," adding that "for any translation into English, the author retains as well the right to select or to approve her translator."

The next day—although the aforementioned contract fixed her birth on 7 June—Yourcenar celebrated her forty-seventh birthday and, with Frick, left the Hôtel Loti for the Saint James et d'Albany, on the Rue de Rivoli where they had met, now more than fourteen years ago. The rest of the month of June was taken up, says Frick, by "a bit of society life." They hosted Gabriel Marcel, visited Marie Laurencin—who undertook a portrait of each of the two women—and on several occasions, saw Jean Schlumberger. They attended, at the Théâtre Antoine, a performance of Sartre's play, *Le Diable et le Bon Dieu* (*The Devil and the Good Lord*), with Pierre Brasseur—an entertainment about which they made no written comment. But one year later, at the end of May, Yourcenar would take pleasure in conversing with Brasseur, whom she considered an exceptional actor. The most important encounter of this trip, however, from which a long correspondence would ensue, took place at Laurencin's, on 28 June. It was that of Natalie Clifford Barney, the "Amazon." There is yet again with respect to that encounter a certain imprecision regarding the dates since, years later, Yourcenar told George Wicks, who was doing research on Barney, that the encounter took place in 1952, at the end of a lecture given by her, Marguerite Yourcenar.

Together, Yourcenar and Barney recalled Edmond Jaloux, who died in 1949, and André Germain, whose memoirs had just appeared under the title *La Bourgeoisie qui brûle* [The Burning Bourgeoisie]. In them, Germain views Yourcenar, "along with Colette, as one of our two great feminine writers."[9] On 3 July, Yourcenar and Frick attended a reception at Barney's, on Rue Jacob, and, on 5 July, Yourcenar wrote to Barney the first letter of a correspondence that would extend over nearly twenty years. While it is surely a traditional "bread-and-butter letter," it is one that, for those of us familiar with the cold civility of which Yourcenar was capable, provides a glimpse, at even this early stage, of the interest and esteem she bore Barney, which she never abandoned.

> Hôtel St James & d'Albany
> 20, rue St Honoré 202, rue de Rivoli
>
> Dear Miss Barney,
>
> You were so kind to my friend Grace Frick and myself, and we are in Paris for such a short time, that I am immediately making this attempt to see you again. Could we steal you away from your lovely setting on the Rue Jacob for one night and induce you to spend an evening being a tourist in your own neighborhood, as if you were only staying briefly in Paris? Grace and I are planning for tomorrow, Friday, to go to dinner around seven thirty at Chez Georges, 34 Rue de Mazarine, and then to attend the concert being given at nine o'clock in the courtyard of the *Institut.*[10] Would it tempt you to join us, either for the entire evening, or else only for the concert—which I make no promises about—or else only for dinner? The role of mistress of the house presupposes in a sense an admirable self-effacement and generosity: we would like to see you freed for a moment from your duties as a hostess (I like this graceful American word), and it is for this reason that we propose to transport you to the terrace of the smallest café in Paris.
>
> With best wishes,
> Marguerite Yourcenar[11]

On 22 July, Frick and Yourcenar arrived in Switzerland where they would stay for nearly two months and where Yourcenar, yet again, would be "ill"—any cold, discomfort, or vague feeling of malaise being placed by her in the category of "illness." They first went to the château of Vuflens-sur-Morges, the home of Jacques de Saussure: "My father and Marguerite Yourcenar had known each other during the thirties, by way of Edmond

Jaloux, who lived in Switzerland," relates Alix De Weck, Jacques de Saussure's daughter. "Upon her return to Europe, at the beginning of the fifties, when she was beginning to correct the proofs of *Memoirs of Hadrian,* my father invited her to the family's château, with her friend Grace. They went over *Hadrian* together. Marguerite Yourcenar was always very faithful to my father, until his death, in 1969. She was a woman who was never inattentive or forgetful."

On 20 August, Yourcenar and Frick went to Evolena, to a weaver's shop, run—long before crafts were back in vogue—by a certain Marie Métrailler, whose strange personality appealed to them. They would go back there numerous times. We find a trace of that encounter in a volume of conversations between Métrailler and one of her friends, for which Yourcenar allowed some letters from her to appear by way of a preface: "I hope that, as in Buddhist phraseology, we shall meet each other one day at the edge of the same waterfall or beneath the shade of the same tree," she wrote regarding Métrailler. And further on: "I consider this Valaisian, whom I met perhaps half a dozen times, as having been one of my *gurus.* She taught me a great deal, not only about the traditions of her country, but also about life, by which I mean her way of facing life and of living it. The further along I go, the more I observe that there are beings such as this about whom hardly anyone will ever hear a thing, or who are sometimes even prey, as your letter indicates, to irony or mockery, and who are quite simply great, or pure. It seemed to me right off that Marie Métrailler was one of these beings." [12]

On 27 August, Yourcenar wrote a letter from the Hôtel Bellevue, in Sierre, to Jenny de Margerie to discuss the philosopher Rudolph Kassner, whom she had greatly wanted to meet during this stay in Switzerland.

"You need no longer go to the trouble of sending me Kassner's address," she wrote. "Determined to find him whatever the cost, I went to Sierre, intending to go on from there to Montana to look for him, because you indicated he was there a month or so ago. But after several fruitless telephone calls, I learned that he too was in Sierre, in the same Hôtel Bellevue where I so often stayed in days gone by, and where he has resided for five years. Thus, the meeting, so precious for me, did end up taking place; thank you for at least having shown me what direction to take.

"You are right: Kassner's courage and his absorption in his *œuvre* are indeed a fine thing to behold. The look in his eyes is ageless. And, as you were saying of Europe itself (and with all the more reason), we must hasten to enjoy it." [13]

While Yourcenar was renewing ties with Switzerland and with the memory of her father's last years, the review *La Table Ronde* was publishing, in its July, August, and September issues, excerpts from *Memoirs of Hadrian,* which was to appear at Plon. This was the beginning of what Yourcenar and Frick would refer to as the "*Hadrian* affair," which shows the obstinacy and combativeness that Yourcenar would always display toward her publishers, or any other interlocutor, in order to defend what she judged to be— or at least had defined as—her lawful rights, be they slightly at odds with "the" law. For it turned out that Yourcenar was still under contract, since before the war, with Gallimard and Grasset. As early as April 1951, she had informed Joseph Breitbach of her negotiations with Plon in these terms: "I have no energy for toting *Hadrian* from publisher to publisher. As for Gallimard, they have done so little for my books up until now that I don't think they are capable of attending to this one, which matters a lot more to me than the others. . . . I put a lot more of myself in this book. . . . I made more of an attempt at absolute sincerity."[14] Breitbach, it seems, had not alerted anyone at Gallimard, despite the connections he had there, with Schlumberger most notably.

It all began, thus, with a note from Jean Paulhan to Claude Gallimard, bearing as a heading simply "Saturday." But we can date it at the end of July or the beginning of August, since the first documents bearing witness to the conflict are dated in August: "Marguerite Yourcenar is publishing a novel, *Memoirs of Hadrian,* in *La Table Ronde* that strikes me as custom-made for all the world's Prix Femina.[15] Moreover, it's not silly or awkward in the least. If I were you, I'd ask her for it."[16] At Gallimard, it very quickly came to light that the contract signed by Yourcenar in 1938 for *Coup de Grâce* provided for "a right of first option on her subsequent works"—a clause that obliges the author to give priority regarding any new manuscript to her previous publisher. On 5 September 1951, Gaston Gallimard thus informed Maurice Bourdel, the director at Plon, of his intention to publish *Hadrian.*[17] Now, at Plon, the book was already in proof—Yourcenar would put the last proofs, examined on 18 September, in the mail from Switzerland—and they had every intention of bringing out the book, which they were banking on, before the fall prizes. An "arm-wrestling match" got under way immediately, less between Plon—who feigned ignorance of the whole affair in the beginning—and Gallimard then between Marguerite Yourcenar and Gaston Gallimard. Both the former and the latter detested being opposed, and, letter by letter, the tone grew more bitter. Even petty jabs, so well suited to increasing the exasperation level, were not forgone: Gaston Gallimard, who knew full well that Yourcenar wished to be called "Madame," despite not being married, and who had never failed to observe this rule, sent her both a letter and a telegram, each one addressed to "Mademoiselle Yourcenar."[18]

The nature of the conflict was as simple as the conflict was difficult to resolve, especially since two equally stubborn individuals were mixed up in it. Yourcenar acknowledged—both in a letter to Roger Martin du Gard and in another to Schlumberger—that she had acted imprudently. To Martin du Gard she wrote:

"The fact that a volume of mine had been rejected in 1947 [it was *Dramatis personae*, the collection of short plays whose manuscript had been examined by Camus] by this house without the slightest allusion to any ulterior exercise of option rights with regard to my future works; the lack of any plan to reissue *Coup de Grâce*—as the contract obliges them to— which has been impossible to find and out of print for years, or to buy back the rights to the works published elsewhere that have gone out of print (like *Alexis*), a transaction that Gallimard had nonetheless reserved exclusively for themselves; the difficulty of obtaining statements of my account; everything, in other words, had persuaded me that this house had lost interest in me definitively, and that our outdated contract was in point of fact invalidated. An imprudent opinion, I admit, and one that puts me in the wrong where the letter of the thing is concerned—whereas, regarding the spirit, I am only too sure of being right. It goes without saying that, in the present circumstances, I consider myself to be under obligation to Plon; it also goes without saying that I shall not return anywhere under constraint. For me the entire question consists of immediately obtaining a rescission of the contract." [19]

Martin du Gard conveyed this letter to Gaston Gallimard, on 24 September, accompanying it with a handwritten note:

My Dear Gaston,
     I have already told you that the people who keep pestering me so that I might in turn pester you are legion—and you are very lucky that I have a discreet and not very altruistic nature . . . However, here is a letter I cannot put aside, as, with *Marguerite Yourcenar,* I have a very great literary sympathy and a friendship (by way of correspondence) dating back twenty-five years. I am simply sending it to you *without appending the slightest request.* You two work it out together . . . At first glance, it seems to me that, legally, Gallimard's position is justifiable. In fact, errors must have been made on both sides. And what is absolutely sure is that the utter integrity of Marguerite Yourcenar precludes any suspicion of bad faith. Was she "manipulated" by Plon? In any case, whether wrongly or rightly, having given her word, she feels obligated to Plon and, if I know her as well as I believe I do, she will let herself be ruined by a lawsuit rather than dissociate herself from Plon. [20]

On the same day, Schlumberger sent to Gallimard a letter he had received from Yourcenar, also with a handwritten note. In this letter she acknowledged "that an arrangement with Gallimard should be reached if possible before the book is brought out." But, according to her, that "arrangement" could only pertain to future works. She continued to take it for granted that *Memoirs of Hadrian* would appear at Plon.[21] Her stubbornness, the way she reiterated her grievances against Gallimard, in each letter—together with a note from Maurice Bourdel announcing, on 21 September, that "the book is presently in press and will be on the market in a few days"[22]—must have rooted Gaston Gallimard in his will to make her yield.

A legal official served notice at Plon—on the infamous day of 24 September—of "a formal injunction against pursuing the publication of the work."[23] At the same time, Gaston Gallimard submitted to the publishers union a request to confront Bourdel and assured Yourcenar of his desire to take "care of all expenses and consequences of the contract signed by you and Plon."[24] Faced with Yourcenar's refusal, Gaston Gallimard sent her letters as full of argument and detail as her own, leaving none of her objections unanswered. Simultaneously, he had his legal staff make various notes on the "Yourcenar cases"[25] and proposed to Bourdel an out-of-court settlement that the latter did not accept.[26] On 22 October, he wrote to Yourcenar in Switzerland—although she had been back in Paris since the fourteenth—to convey to her his intention to take the case to court: "I shall thus be obliged to place the case in the hands of Maître Maurice Garçon, our lawyer, for though I have done everything I could to avoid taking legal action, I am nonetheless determined to request of the court that any possible measure be taken, provided there be no overstepping the limits of our agreements, freely entered into by both sides, with notice being served to the parties concerned in a sufficiently timely manner."[27]

Not in the least impressed by the war thus declared on her by the most prestigious French publisher, Yourcenar sent a message, on 27 October, from her Parisian hotel, that, while masquerading as a wish to work things out, did not display a very active will to make concessions:

"The day before yesterday I received your letter of 22 October (sent back here from Switzerland) and I telephoned you yesterday at your office on Rue Sébastien-Bottin to set up a meeting, judging, as you yourself do I think, that the affair with which we are concerned stands only to gain from a friendly conversation between us. Monsieur Claude Gallimard, with whom I spoke, proposed a meeting for yesterday at six o'clock, which I was unable to agree to. I came back from Switzerland with a bad case of the flu and am going out as little as possible. Would it be possible for you to stop by my hotel next Monday, Tuesday, or Wednesday, between four and six o'clock, to discuss this problem with me before the situation worsens on both sides, to everyone's detriment?"[28]

One must undoubtedly feel the weight of generations of Cleenewercks de Crayencour behind one to summon Gaston Gallimard in this way. As for those ancestors, Mademoiselle de Crayencour—having rejected their name to forge one for herself that was very much her own—was fully able to recall their existence opportunely, tapping thus a source of thoroughly aristocratic haughtiness, when confronted with bourgeois social climbers, be they now publishers of the greatest writers of the century.

So the battle went on. Yourcenar even offered her work to Grasset, a house that also, she judged, retained preemptive rights—which Gaston Gallimard challenged.[29] Finally, Gallimard wrote to Bourdel, on 20 November, after one last meeting with him: "Our conversation made me see that we were men of the same species, the same tastes, the same education. This is worth something to me and I want you to forget this incident, as I shall. In giving up *Memoirs of Hadrian,* I am doing it solely for you."

Yourcenar had won, which did not fail to encourage her, throughout the entire remainder of her literary career, to prove inflexible. For the time being, a courtesy born of the armistice was the order of the day: "Thank you for your note, which puts an end to our current difficulties and allows us to anticipate complete harmony in the future," she wrote on 23 November to Claude Gallimard. "Thank you also for having enclosed it so gracefully in roses."[30] The affair would be crowned by a handwritten letter from Gaston Gallimard thanking her for having sent him an inscribed copy of *Memoirs of Hadrian,* stressing his hope that he soon would be able "once again to work for you and regain your confidence," and noting nonetheless that "it is not without a slight degree of bitterness and many regrets that I see your book on my table, without the NRF monogram."[31]

Memoirs of Hadrian had gone on sale on 5 December. We know how much Yourcenar was attached to this text, written in the euphoria of returning to the grand literary projects of her early youth. On 7 April of that year, 1951, she discussed her intentions and her misgivings with Joseph Breitbach at some length:

> As was the case with you and Gide, it was important not to lapse into hagiography; I was also anxious to show the—very narrow—limits within which individuality, no matter how superlatively rich, is necessarily confined, the subtle miscalculations, the imperceptible errors (who among us is without imperfections?), and the final agony, about which we do not know whether it is a pure and simple case of collapse, the inevitable result of wear

and tear, or a new and stranger development that shatters the old arrangement of things. . . . The more I progressed, the more I was seized of an immense respect for the facts and for the unique individuality of the personage to whom I was trying to draw nearer. It sometimes seemed less difficult to me to bring that man of the II^d century back to life without too many inaccuracies than to evoke, for example, a man of fifty years ago, whose experiences, emotions, and ideas would be too different from our own; one thing I was even concerned about was not to underline too crudely the similarities with our time. They are only striking provided they are barely indicated.[32]

At the time of the prepublication in *La Table Ronde,* her friends, among them Constantine Dimaras, conveyed to her, with neither obsequious flattery nor indulgence, their expressions of admiration along with their reservations regarding certain details. Yourcenar paid heed to some of these comments, notably that of Dimaras pointing out the impossibility of "balancing gleaming stacks" of Roman coins as Yourcenar claimed to, owing to their shape during the era of Trajan.[33] To the same Dimaras, whom she readily called Didy, as she had, before the war, during the time they worked together on Cavafy, she explained at length the part played by *Memoirs of Hadrian* in her personal evolution, representing a "victory over anguish, or at the very least an intelligent means of controlling the latter," and how she had wanted to guard against any post-Christian view of the world, in which the notion of sin subsists, more obsessive than ever: "The further I go," she added, "the closer I come on the contrary to a calmer, more even picture of man with neither highlights nor areas of shadow. Above all I strive to keep the flaws in my own vision from causing my models to grimace; I have little taste for mirrors that distort."[34]

As soon as it was published, the "success of *Hadrian,*" noted Yourcenar at the end of 1951, "surpassed all expectations." Jean Ballard, for whom "Hadrian is less the subject of a book than a quest theme, a search for self in balance and assuagement," was the first, in *Cahiers du Sud,* to devote a long and very laudatory article to it: "This assessment of a conscience exercised its appeal on an exigent writer. And, for us, the result is a great book. . . . The quality of the prose goes hand in hand with the quality of the thought. An admirable firmness of language and a skillful handling of effects collaborate to imbue the narration, which does not flinch at difficult admissions, nor crack at prideful moments, with a great sense of nobility."[35] The reviews were unanimously positive, and other writers' reactions flattering. Jules Romains, on 25 December 1951, after having admitted to knowing nothing of her work and being "a querulous reader . . . incapable of prevailing over boredom (which I take for a very revealing sign)," confesses his admiration: "Well, I've read *Memoirs of Hadrian* from the first page to the last. . . . I've gone back to certain passages. I've reread them. . . . At this point I would need several pages to tell you how remarkable your book strikes me as being. I see in it such a variety of qualities: astonishingly lofty and vigorous thought; a superlatively keen psychological sense; a style of nearly constant perfection and felicity."[36]

Besides Martin du Gard, who was also very laudatory, Thomas Mann displayed a genuine enthusiasm for *Memoirs of Hadrian* several years later. In a letter to Charles Kerenyi, dated 19 January 1954, he wrote: "I am at this moment (belatedly) under the influence of *Memoirs of Hadrian* by Marguerite Yourcenar, a poetic work full of erudition that has enchanted me as no reading had done for a long time."[37]

Just one month after the appearance of the book, Emile Henriot, member of the Académie Française, devoted his column in *Le Monde,* entitled "Literary Life," to her. "I very much admire Mme Marguerite Yourcenar for having so fully succeeded in her undertaking," he wrote. "In addition to her scholarly merit, she possesses a remarkable feminine intuition regarding the psychology of a man, capable of penetrating and explaining even the mysteries of his amorous life and his wild passion for the young Greek Antinous. . . . Hadrian eventually comes to see love as an invasion of the flesh by the spirit, but here, it is Mme Yourcenar who is speaking, from her feminine point of view: a man would say the opposite, it seems to me, for masculine eroticism is nothing other than the invasion of the spirit by the constant demands and constant thought of the flesh."[38]

Henriot, who wrote without ulterior motives, did not involve himself in the concert—which would become a hackneyed refrain—on "the virility of the thought" and the "male style" of Yourcenar, orchestrated notably this time by Denise Bourdet, in the *Revue de Paris.* In *Les Nouvelles Littéraires,* Jeanine Delpech would speak of "the virile force of her style"; Aloys-J. Bataillard would remind readers on the pages of *La Gazette de Lausanne* that Yourcenar wrote books that were "hardly feminine in their choice of subject matter."[39]

This stupidity would hound Yourcenar throughout her life. And more violently than ever at the time of her election to the Académie Française. It was then that the dark underside, and the exclusionary will borne by such comments, which wound while claiming to be laudatory, was revealed. If a man, instead of *Memoirs of Hadrian,* had written a magnificent first-person portrait of a woman, who would have thought of evoking "the delicious femininity of his style"?

Yourcenar was always exasperated by people who tried to get her to say, after the fashion of Flaubert's famous "Madame Bovary is my own self," "Hadrian is my own self." She stressed, on the contrary, how fascinating it was for a writer to make characters exist who are "not as 'poor' as we are, lacking our little weaknesses," "having acted on the fate of the world, on peace and war." "[A]ll things considered," she would have preferred to say, "I am Hadrian." For, she confided, "by way of the method akin to controlled delirium that I experimented with, I attempted to become, at times, that emperor struggling with himself, to the point, where certain interpretations are concerned, of preferring what I felt to be his version of the facts to the exact truth."

"You will read here and there and everywhere that: Hadrian is my own self," she related to the novelist and critic Jacques Folch-Ribas. "This is thoroughly witless, and negligent. I was only able to write the version of the book that you read, the final one, after many years spent entering Hadrian's domain. They should be saying rather that *I became Hadrian*. The nuance may seem delicate, but it is capital. You understood this and I thank you for doing so."[40]

Nonetheless, she always admitted to putting "a great deal of [her]self" in this text. A meticulous reading of *Hadrian,* which is the province of literary critics, might yield more proof of this assertion. But one only has to cite, side by side, one of Hadrian's remarks about age and one of Yourcenar's responses to Matthieu Galey, to grasp the workings of this mechanism, on the order of a subtle form of osmosis. It is not very easy to tell, in the end, if the current always flows from writer to character, or if it is not, on occasion, conveyed from the emperor to a Marguerite Yourcenar fascinated by what she discovered about Hadrian's approach to life.

"I was in my fortieth year," observes Hadrian. "If I were to die at that time, nothing more of me would survive than a name in a series of high functionaries, and an inscription in Greek in honor of an archon of Athens. Ever since that anxious period, each time that I have witnessed the disappearance of a man just at middle age, whose successes and reverses the public thinks it can judge exactly, I have recalled that at the same age I still figured only in my own eyes, and in those of a few friends, who must sometimes have doubted my abilities as I doubted them myself."[41]

"It's a serious matter for a writer to die at forty," Yourcenar responded to one of Galey's questions. "It would have been a disaster for Tolstoy, for Ibsen, even for Victor Hugo. Had Hugo died at forty, we would have had the Hugo of the Paris years under Louis-Philippe but not the Hugo of exile. A great deal of time is necessary. If you stop Hugo before *Les Misérables* (*Les Miserables*) and before *La Légende des siècles* (*The Legend of the Centu-*

ries), you have a very good poet but not yet the unique visionary that he is in the history of poetry. I would be loath to give up the early Hugo, including the poet of *Odes et ballades* [Odes and Ballads]. That was a necessary stage, even if, as I believe, it reveals nothing of the great Hugo."

In this particular case, it was one of Yourcenar's reflections that was transmitted to Hadrian, for she adds, in her conversation with Galey: "You know, I'm so strongly aware of the need for time that I have Hadrian refer to it." [42]

Numerous critics, like Jacques Brenner later on in his *Histoire de la littéra-ture française* [History of French Literature], would make "the emperor's love for Antinous" "the center of the book": "No one, for a long while, has spoken so well about love," Brenner judges. [43]

"The reviews were enthusiastic and emphasized the portrait of Antinous, as doubtless I had done myself," Yourcenar commented during her discussions with Galey. "But people weren't particularly eager to look at Hadrian's life as a whole. They wanted above all to see a success, an extraordinary triumph. . . . There are many things in the book that strike me as quite interesting but that the public has not been very quick to discern. One such is Lucius, the would-be heir, an elegant man who almost becomes a great prince but who dies instead without leaving a trace. To me the characters who 'almost exist' are also fascinating. It is curious, too, to watch Hadrian as he grows old. Each of us ages differently; as the years accumulate, each person follows his own path. Hadrian's lucidity grows with age to the point where in the end it becomes mistrust." [44]

Unlike André Fraigneau in his reader's report, people have rarely seen *Hadrian* as a biography. On the other hand, it has frequently been read as an historical novel. More accurate is the comment of Robert Kanters, who notes: "Madame Marguerite Yourcenar's domain is history, or rather meditation on the past. . . . But meditation on the past would be of little consequence if it were restricted to teaching us how we are going to perish: it must also help us live, even if it is in a world condemned." [45] Attacks, nonetheless, were not lacking, which is yet another sign of the interest generated by the book. In 1954, Yourcenar, on several occasions, lamented the criticism of a French archeologist, which she deemed rude: "A less pleasant distraction, which has fallen in my lap these last few days, is the necessity of responding to an extremely insulting and deceitful notice in the *Revue Archéologique,* which attacks me (I believe I know why and I shall tell you: it's like being in a Molière play) with respect to certain archeological details in *Hadrian* and to works mentioned in my bibliography, which they accuse me of not having read; the author also complains that there are not enough 'visual images of Antinous' in my book (!). But the specious tone, the dishonesty, and the ingeniously truncated quotations oblige me to refute him, on principle; which is simple, but tedious to do."[46] She was also irritated by a very hostile article by the Italian Evaristo Breccia, who complained because he did not appear in the bibliography.

IN 1951, *Memoirs of Hadrian* was only the beginning of a long career of still-enduring success, but the conflict with Gaston Gallimard had prevented the book from being considered in the competition for the major fall prizes. The Prix Femina, for which Jean Paulhan had recommended *Hadrian* to Gaston Gallimard, had fallen to Anne de Tourville, for her novel *Jabadao*, published at Stock, while the 1951 Prix Goncourt went to Julien Gracq—who refused it—for *Le Rivage des Syrtes* (*The Opposing Shore*), from the Librairie José Corti. It is curious to note this coincidence today, as the same critics who neglected, or even scorned, Yourcenar cannot stop praising Gracq, celebrating his publication by the Pléiade in 1989 with some fanfare. Anyone willing to reread *The Opposing Shore* and *Hadrian* with a truly critical eye would no doubt acknowledge that favoring one over the other is a matter of taste rather than of literary "hierarchy." And while we're on the subject, for that matter, of literary hierarchy, it would be fitting to remember that in that same year of 1951 Samuel Beckett's *Molloy* (*Molloy*) and *Malone meurt* (*Malone Dies*) also appeared.

Memoirs of Hadrian, which in June 1952 received the Prix Femina Vacaresco, has enjoyed numerous republications over the years continuing into the present, each of them examined by Yourcenar.[47] With the coming of age, and over the period of forced sedentariness during the final stage of Frick's illness, examples of her propensity for meticulousness, if not maniacal attention to detail, would grow more and more numerous. But even during the fifties, every new printing of *Hadrian* provided an occasion for one of those fastidiously thorough and contentious reviews to which Yourcenar submitted any text she had been asked to pass for press. With regard to the forty-third printing, she sent to Plon the list of proofreader's suggestions she approved and the list, "a much more serious subject," of modifications she challenged, justifying herself in this way:

"In general, I believe it is extremely important that an author, while still conforming as often as possible to standard usage, maintain the freedom to deviate from it deliberately in those instances where he believes it is indispensable to do so. It is on these grounds that I insist on retaining the unaccustomed conditional form *would recumb*. For reasons that are also too long to go into, I wish to keep the feminine form of *afternoon;* the expression *at his side* sometimes in the plural and sometimes in the singular; to keep the old spelling of *payement, lilie, to mingle, to endeavor;* to not necessarily place an exclamation point after *Ah;* to retain certain alternative spellings that are still allowed, such as *spoonsful;* to allow myself some leeway with regard to the agreement of past participles followed by infinitives, a freedom defended by the grammarians of the XVIIth century and XVIIIth century and one that makes it possible to maintain certain nuances that are otherwise well on their way to disappearing; finally, in spite of the famous *amours, délices, et orgues,*[48] I wish to retain *nos amours vivants* [our living loves] in this sentence in which loves is not used, moreover, in its usual abstract sense in the plural (*cherished loves . . . she inspired great loves*) but in a sense that comes closer to the English *his amours,* which are essentially love objects. . . . All of this is highly serious, because one of the reasons for writers to exist is to fight against a certain superficial conformity of langage [*sic*], which, accepted as an article of faith, runs counter to the more subtle or more complex laws and tends in the end, on the pretext of standardization, to impoverish the French language."[49]

Between 1951 and 1958, Plon would print, in various editions, 96,500 copies of *Memoirs of Hadrian.* At Gallimard, where Yourcenar's titles have since been gathered in their entirety, the overall printing (in the Collection Blanche, a bound edition, and Folio) amounted in 1989 to 821,870 copies. For someone who maintained: "I didn't expect more than ten people to read the book. I never expect anyone to read my books, for the simple reason that I don't think that the things that concern me are of interest to most people," this was quite a nice surprise, and one that attracted very early on the attention of the American publisher Farrar, Straus and Giroux.[50] Roger Straus, moreover, would remain Yourcenar's American publisher. She had a respect and an esteem with which she generally did not tend to be lavish for his talent, his generosity of spirit, and his enlightened aristocratic ways.

Until February 1952, Yourcenar would very obediently go about fulfilling the thousand and one obligations created for an author by the promotion of his or her book, consenting to book signings in various bookstores, granting interviews (for which she always used the older French term *entrevues,* rather than the more recent, anglicized *interviews*), thanking critics for their praise, appearing at receptions. It was during one of the latter that she ran into André Fraigneau. "We spoke to one another like old friends," he recalls. Yourcenar, on the other hand, confided to Dee Dee: "I saw the man I had loved before the war at a party that was given when *Hadrian* came out. I ignored him." She wrote the same thing to Gabriel Marcel: "Since 1939, I have only caught sight of him once, at a reception given by

Plon; he came up to say a few words to me, but I did not wish to resume a dialogue that had formerly been intimate and that I no longer think would be sincere."[51] Who is right?[52] She was happy to see Martin du Gard again, as well as her first publisher René Hilsum, with whom she would maintain ties until her death; she went to Sylvia Beach's bookstore, Shakespeare and Company, and submitted, without displeasure, to a bit of society life—to the point of attending, with Frick, Pierre Balmain's presentation of high-fashion clothing. This is a detail that will only surprise those who, disapproving the nonconformity of Yourcenar's clothing and her taste for certain eccentric costumes, never noticed what care she devoted to choosing her wardrobe, to the quality of its fabrics, and to the harmony of its colors.

In mid-February, however, Yourcenar and Frick, weary of this overly long stay in Paris, left on a trip. They traveled to Italy via Pau (to see to Christine de Crayencour's estate), Nîmes, Aigues-Mortes, Saintes-Maries-de-la-Mer, Marseilles, Cannes, and Vence. They stayed for nearly a month in Rome beginning on 27 February before heading down to Naples, following in their own footsteps—those, that is, of the trips they took during a time of budding passion. They crossed over to Spain, where they would stay for a month, by way of Gibraltar, exploring Cadix, Seville, Granada, and yielding to their readily whimsical nature by inviting "two American sailors to lunch" one day in Algeciras, as Frick noted on 7 May. The return trip to Paris, which they reached on 22 May, would be serious (the Prix Femina Vacaresco), societal, amicable (numerous visits to Natalie Barney), professional (an interview with Janet Flanner, the famous columnist for the *New Yorker*), and literary (a dinner at Madame Conrad Schlumberger's with Ernst Jünger and a meeting with Colette).[53]

In the entry for 7 July, the daybook that Frick was keeping bears visible traces of tears, and one finds written there, in English, this sentence: "M.Y. [which, of course, one can read "My"] firmly declares hatred of Grace."

Resistant, as we know, to making any comment whatsoever pertaining to herself, Frick said no more about the matter, regarding either her feelings or the causes of this outburst. It is even surprising that she noted the incident itself. It must have been a very fierce quarrel, and she must have wanted to be sure that she would never forget that day: in English as in French, "declare" is the word that is used in reference to starting a war. It appears that in Paris, a sought-after, celebrated Yourcenar was rediscovering her taste for the solitary imperiousness that had been hers in the thirties and no doubt a desire for a kind of independence that was compromised by Frick's continual presence at her side. Having noticed this—the daybook notation seems to echo the climax of an argument in which the

exasperation of the one must have grown in proportion to the tearful re-
crimination of the other—Frick likely was not uninvolved with Yourcenar's
absence from Paris between 1956 and 1968. After the incident on 7 July
1952, and until their departure a month later, Frick would decline several
invitations, leaving Yourcenar to go alone to some receptions, or even to
meals at the homes of friends they had in common, such as Natalie Barney.

When Yourcenar left France, on 6 August 1952—she had to return in
September to her courses at Sarah Lawrence, at least for a semester—she
knew that her "American period" of doubts and of material and spiritual
difficulties was definitively over. As before the war, she was once again a
French writer. And a successful one besides.

Nevertheless, it was without enthusiasm that she arrived in New York,
on 11 August, then returned to Petite Plaisance, where there was much to
be done after being gone for more than a year. She had no great desire to
cross the Atlantic again, as a letter to Jean Ballard proves: "I confess that
this change of continent represents a difficult transplantation, and I hope to
be back in France by the end of next spring."[54] Though we know little about
what happened between Frick and her after the violent argument of 7 July,
it is possible to observe that, in Frick's calendars, the entries grew more and
more factual and terse, that the signs (crosses and suns) marking happiness,
tenderness, love, and the joy of being together disappeared almost totally,
and forever, as though, after the love story, there came what their friends
from the fifties and sixties described as a "marriage of convenience."

At Sarah Lawrence, a rather unpleasant surprise awaited Yourcenar: she
could not obtain a room on campus for the coming academic year. Not
that she had any particular taste, as we have seen, for the very particular
"conviviality" of American universities, but the obligation to commute
would take up time that she was hoping, now, to devote to her own projects.
So she rented a small apartment in Scarsdale (north of New York, halfway
between Bronxville and White Plains), and, at the same time, announced
to the president of the college that she did not wish to renew her contract.
"My thoughts on the level of studies in the United States this year might
amuse you," she wrote to Barney, "but would undoubtedly irritate your
sister, in view of which I abstain. In any case, I have informed the administration at Sarah Lawrence that I am freeing myself for next year; my use-
fulness there is too limited for me to oblige myself to stay, and the necessity
of spending the winter on the outskirts of New York devours the financial
advantages of the situation, and in the end cancels them out."[55] In the same
letter, Yourcenar explained to Barney that Frick "is working on *Hadrian*
[the translation], admirably but slowly." She would return to the subject

several months later: "the translation of *Hadrian* advances slowly, partly because of Grace, who is very scrupulous and cannot work quickly, partly (and especially for the last few months) because of the very bad influence exerted by the English publisher's reader . . . who involves himself in very obscure corrections of the fragments we send him."[56]

For the first time, Yourcenar and Frick were confronted with a project—the translation of *Memoirs of Hadrian*—of which Frick was the architect and in which Yourcenar, in a way, played the role of an accessory resource. It was hard for Yourcenar to hide her irritation at Frick's slowness. After the latter's death, she would sometimes allude to it, in a not-very-generous way, that of longstanding anger contained.

Yourcenar had extraordinary powers of concentration. She read with uncommon rapidity and could write for whole hours at a time, almost without deletions, with nothing capable of distracting her. She was often less energetic, less tenacious than Frick, who, she confided, "forced [her] to stay awake late into the night if the work planned for the next day, putting final touches on a chapter or correcting proofs for example, were not finished." But she loathed the intellectual slowness and uncertainty, the hemming and hawing pushed nearly to the point of incapacity that seized Frick in the face of her translation work. Of course, Frick was incapable of speeding up her rhythm, and Yourcenar's reaction was not out of the ordinary: people who, like her, have a prodigious capacity for intellectual work are always exasperated by those who can't keep up with them. But this common situation was coupled here with singular psychological factors: it was now Yourcenar who, in the evening, reread the day's work, and it's hard to imagine her taking over the role of admiring acquiescence that must so often, in another time, have belonged to Frick. It is easy to imagine the latter's constant anxiety: without a doubt Yourcenar would explain to her that such and such a word was not well chosen, and would contrive, as was well within her way of being, to prove that, of the two, it was obviously she who possessed a better knowledge of the English forms and words capable of conveying the subtleties of *Hadrian*.

DURING THAT YEAR, 1952, Yourcenar proceeded from recognition on the part of her peers, which had already been acquired before the war, to a degree of renown. She was more affected by this than she wished to admit, and no doubt less astonished than she said she was: "So I was naturally quite surprised," she related to Matthieu Galey. "I received some very moving letters, some that brought me pleasure and even a few that overwhelmed me. . . . I wasted a great deal of time answering those letters and doing all the other things that one does when one enjoys great success for the first time."[57] Throughout her life, she would claim that she "wasted time answering" the mail, but this did not prevent her from writing an enormous volume of correspondence, of which she tirelessly made duplicate copies.

For the moment—whether sincerely or out of feigned modesty—she had not yet reached the point of claiming herself overwhelmed by letters from admirers. She was savoring the sweetness that came from returning to the country where her language was spoken, of being read and celebrated there, and she wished once again to belong to that country, even at a distance. Before the year ended, she became a member of the *Société des gens de lettres*;[58] learned that *Memoirs of Hadrian* had been purchased by the *Club du meilleur livre* [Best-Book Club], which would provide her another type of distribution; and, in early December, accepted the contract proposed to her by Gallimard for a second edition of *Coup de Grâce*. The year came to an end at Petite Plaisance, where Yourcenar wrote her New Year's cards and letters—more numerous than in other years—in particular a warm letter to Natalie Barney in which she asserted: "I do not wish to spend another winter on the outskirts of New York. Let it be either Europe, or this *cella del conoscimento da se* in Maine." And as is frequently the case, the message ends with a sentence that pertains as much to her as to the missive's addressee: "I often dream of the beautiful account, clear and unimpeachable, of your life that I would like to see you write. But perhaps you are better served by half-silences."[59]

13
Balance

WAS YOURCENAR fully aware, on board the ship that brought her back to the United States, in August 1952, that "the extraordinary concatenations of chance" that had presided over her life with Frick were rendering her choice "irreversible"? Probably so. But she had been far too pleased by the sudden reversals of chance to be fully satisfied with the conventional routine of the "irreversible." And no doubt she was often subject, too, as she had Hadrian say, to the "mania for avoiding exclusive dependence on any one being."[1] No sooner thus had she stepped foot on American soil than she made known her intention to leave again quite shortly, as soon as her semester at Sarah Lawrence University was over. In the spring of 1953 she wrote to Natalie Barney announcing her imminent arrival in Europe and added: "Springtime in New York was very beautiful (even though it is such a harsh city), and in many ways. Here I now have been for two weeks in the island house, a most pleasurable grand exile of sorts; I enjoy reading Greek beneath the blossoming apple trees."[2] Exile is a word that Yourcenar, during the American years that went from 1939 to 1951, did not use. Perhaps it would have been too painful. After having renewed ties with Europe, after the end of her actual exile, the one imposed by external circumstances and that may or may not have had an end, it was easier for her to speak of it, as something of a metaphor for a state consented to, not endured. This implied, of course, the possibility of debate regarding a return trip.

The discussions between Yourcenar and Frick on this subject have remained secret. As in the case of the years when they were ceaselessly together, there exists no correspondence—even sealed—and it seems quite likely that this must remain one of the tenebrous parts of their life. It was only once the question had become moot that one finds, in one of Yourcenar's confidences to Barney, a trace of the difficulty involved in maintaining the decision of that American "exile": "The further we go along, the more we note the wisdom of the resolution that *brought us back* here, and this despite regret at not seeing our friends from France at greater length or more frequently."[3] There is the proof, for those who might have doubts about the subject, that debate had indeed existed. But relocating in Europe would have been unacceptable for Frick. Where else but in an English-speaking country would she have found the one compensation for her self-effacement, the indispensable feeling of being absolutely necessary to Yourcenar's survival? Yourcenar, despite her acquired nationality, would never be totally autonomous in the United States because she feared being part of a community in which she risked losing her mastery of what was so essential to her work, the French language. The balance of their couple came by way of keeping Petite Plaisance.

But their "modus vivendi" could only be shaped around travel, accepted by Frick, required by Yourcenar, who could not imagine a return to the sedentariness of the past decade. The compromise had perhaps been imparted to Frick couched in one of those apparently innocuous sentences that Yourcenar was so good at devising. The deceptive insignificance of those sentences was contradicted by a tone that revealed long-nurtured decisions, admitting not the slightest discussion: "We're returning to Petite Plaisance, but we'll travel." She was liable to make these little pronouncements, of which all those who dealt with her remember having been the beneficiary—or the victim—at any time, while heating up water for tea, closing a door, or right in the middle of a conversation. Those who didn't manage to absorb them always had reason to regret it.

Regarding what made travel a vital, almost ethical, necessity, Hadrian served, indirectly, as interpreter: "Few men enjoy prolonged travel; it disrupts all habit and endlessly jolts each prejudice. But I was striving to have no prejudice and few habits."[4]

It was at the end of January 1953 that a letter arrived from Victoria Ocampo. Their meeting in December 1951, on the occasion of a Parisian dinner in the company of Max-Pol Fouchet, had only confirmed the esteem that Yourcenar had borne her since the Argentinian period of *Les Lettres Françaises,* at the end of the war, and they had stayed in touch with one another. Alas, we don't know the precise content of the remarks to which Ocampo was responding: thus far Yourcenar's letter—if it hasn't been destroyed—has not been rediscovered. Its subject, at least, was clear since Ocampo comments: "Like you, I believe that sexuality is of great importance (and especially what derives from it). But I dislike the interpretation of RS [?] for many reasons; we shall speak of this again. It so happens that I am in the process of writing my memoirs and I find *investigating* difficult."[5] There is all the more reason to regret not having Yourcenar's letter since, though she always thought and claimed that sexuality—which she generally preferred to call sensuality—held a large place in every existence, she varied greatly over the course of her life regarding the necessity of making pronouncements on this subject, especially when it came to remarks of a private nature: "Where one's personal life is concerned, one must either firmly tell all leaving no room for misunderstanding, or, on the contrary, say nothing at all," she wrote in 1973 to one of her friends.[6]

For her part, she always shrank back somewhat, was even slightly repulsed, in the face of public debate regarding what she referred to as "sensual choices." In 1954, the year it was founded, the magazine *Arcadie,* a precursor of the fight for homosexual rights, had made contact with personalities whose sexual preferences it suspected. Marcel Jouhandeau had made public his very violent objection to this initiative, which garnered him this note from Yourcenar, on 6 May 1954: "May I tell you that I am surprised to see you taking this badly written magazine, *Arcadie,* to task so publicly? I received the same letter from the editor and I confined myself to expressing objections that were more or less (not entirely) similar to yours by return mail. But wouldn't it be better to give lessons in good taste, if not 'good behavior,' with less bitterness and less of a racket?"[7] Yourcenar's silence on her taste for women, which has often been imputed to a jitteriness that would hardly have been like her, resulted rather from a clear conviction that the freedom, legitimately claimed, to stop hiding how one lived went hand in hand with the freedom, one just as legitimate, to say nothing about the matter. Yourcenar never believed she was obliged to provide anyone with explanations on this point, or to plead for acceptance of her preferences and choices. She did not hope to be tolerated, nor seek to be granted a freedom she had, quite simply, taken. She always acknowledged herself to be a woman of privilege, who, by reason of her birth, her education, and happenstance, had been able to escape, to a certain extent, the pressures of society. She never scorned homosexuals who were fighting to make their way out of a stifling clandestine existence, quite the contrary. But, for her, one gained freedom less by way of making demands than by quietly affirming oneself.

Ocampo's remarks seem nonetheless to show that in the early fifties Yourcenar took an interest in the discourse on sexuality—which does not mean she was inclined to make intimate disclosures regarding *her* sexuality. Unless, of course, the contents of the vanished letter sent to Ocampo had not at all been a matter of abstract intellectual speculation. To stay prudently on the level of ideas, we can understand this interest in a person who had just published *Memoirs of Hadrian* and heard herself praised for being able to talk about love and the senses better than anyone else.

It was in fact because of the emperor's love for Antinous that *Memoirs of Hadrian* saw its first adaptation. *Le Ballet d'Antinoüs* [The Antinous Ballet] was staged by the company of the Marquis de Cuevas, whom Yourcenar had met during her last stay in Paris. A student of Nijinsky, who maintained with an inimitable accent that, for him, "style" was more important than anything else, he was a colorful figure, well known at that time by Parisian audiences of the Empire, the Champs-Elysées, and the Sarah-Bernhardt theaters. A descendant of the conquistadors, the Marquis had married Margaret Strong Rockefeller, the billionaire's granddaughter. In 1947, he had taken over as director of the "Grand Ballet de Monte Carlo"—a troop of fifty or so male and female dancers whom he engaged on a yearly basis.

It was a Greek musician, Louis Nicolaou—whom Yourcenar had found highly sympathetic and whom she had encouraged and recommended to Natalie Barney—who composed the music for the *Ballet d'Antinoüs,* based on Yourcenar's libretto. The preview performance took place on 14 May 1953, without the author, who was beginning to chafe at the bit four thousand miles away.[8] Besides teaching at Sarah Lawrence, a burden rendered even more onerous for her by its imminent end, and the McCarthyism atmosphere of—intellectual and "communist"—"witchhunts," the stupidity of which overwhelmed her, Yourcenar's daily life was cluttered with practical details that got on her nerves: the dentist, tax questions—taken charge of, happily, by Frick—and renting their house while they would be away, with respect to which they were in contact with Mrs. Nelson Rockefeller.

But above all it was Europe that occupied Yourcenar. She worked on her essay on Cavafy from her collaboration with Constantine Dimaras in the thirties, and for which she made use of the articles she had given to the reviews *Mesures* (in 1940) and *Fontaine* (in 1944). Then she hatched the plan of taking Frick to her favorite spots on the map of her own personal Europe. After England—where they were to arrive on 28 July—and the professional trips—to Scandinavia for lectures, and Paris—Yourcenar hoped to spend the winter in Italy and Greece: the letters from Dimaras had made her nostalgic for Athens as never before. This trip would not take place, however, and Yourcenar would only return to Greece for a brief stay, thirty years later, in 1983. It was as if choosing Grace had ruled out the country that Yourcenar had made her symbolic homeland, in another life.

In Paris, Marcel Herrand—become the sole director of the Théâtre des Mathurins since Jean Marchat's return to the Comédie-Française, in June 1952—was to stage *Electra* and had scheduled an opening for the beginning of the new theater season that September. But his death, in June, brought everything back to square one. At the Théâtre des Mathurins, it was Madame Harry Baur, the great actor's widow, who took over as interim director until Marchat could return. Yourcenar left the United States not knowing if the project had been retained. Before leaving—they would not come back until twenty-two months later—Yourcenar wrote to Gaston Gallimard to ask him for a few copies of *Coup de Grâce*, of which a new edition had just appeared, and which the press had greeted with enthusiasm.

FRICK AND YOURCENAR landed in Liverpool on 28 July: for more than two months they would travel the length and breadth of the England of their memories (especially those of Yourcenar's childhood), their youth, and their wistful reminiscences, finishing up with a stay, from 8 to 15 October, in London—a city Yourcenar found soothing, as people who don't really like cities often do.

From London, they embarked on 16 October for Denmark. In Copenhagen on 20 October, Yourcenar had to begin a series of lectures in the Scandinavian countries. Her first subject would be "the novelist and history." During this era, she accepted this kind of invitation out of necessity, in order to finance the long trips for two. But Yourcenar would retain this habit almost until the end of her life, and if death had not come along to interrupt what she would have called "the desirable course of things," she would have "closed the circle" by giving a lecture on Borges, on 9 December 1987, in none other than Copenhagen. Her enemies, and even some of her close friends, viewed her eager acceptance of such paid appearances as the sign of a certain avarice. She herself did not hide the fact that she was loath to spend her money, even when her age and the assurance of comfortable royalties made it pointless to economize: she had always lived believing that one "must make what one had last" in order, above all, not to be obliged to go back to working for a salary.

Besides the fact that in 1953 the "threat" of working for a salary had not yet been eliminated and that such invitations constituted a windfall, Yourcenar derived more pleasure than is generally conceded—than she herself wanted to admit—in giving these lectures. She liked to speak, and until the end she did so in a manner that equaled the strength of her writing. She never stumbled, did not hesitate, allowed herself no abruptly broken-off sentences taken up again somewhere else with no concern for coherence, even in conversation. When she would interrupt a long, well-tempered sentence, thinking better of a word, it was in the same way one corrects a text, with a light pencil stroke, to zero in on her thought as close as possible, to introduce a more exact term, to offer her interlocutor the homage of the most precise word. She had a taste for convincing, for being heard, and possessed, denying it all the while, something resembling a universal peda-gogical drive. Besides, she liked to listen to herself talk—not in the stupidly vain way that is commonly ascribed to this expression, but for the pleasure of handling her language, with infinite dexterity. On those occasions when, as all of us do, she would utter banalities, her phrasing itself would suffice to keep her listener from judging them as such.

YOURCENAR had announced her arrival to Parisian friends, for November, then for early December, "the tour having been extended." Finally, after Stockholm, Uppsala, Oslo, Helsinki, then Stockholm again, from 25 No-vember to 17 December because she was ill there, she went back to Copen-hagen on 18 December, staying there nearly ten days, and did not reach Paris—the Hôtel Saint-James et d'Albany once more—until 28 December. She saw Natalie Barney, who was waiting impatiently for her, the very first thing. "We did not arrive in Paris until yesterday," she wrote to her. ". . . So I am writing to tell you that, on our arrival, I found your charming letter, which fills me with remorse toward you, and with regrets for having taken so long to return to Paris. Excuse me for having so poorly foreseen that everything, the lectures, my literary work, the trips, and life itself, always demands more time than one anticipated."[9]

Like the first months of 1952, the winter of 1954 was shaping up to be societal, amicable, and entertaining. Yourcenar saw much of Barney; Frick saw her less frequently, often declining invitations to lunch. Between the continuation of her work on Cavafy, meetings with Marchat about *Electra,* seeing Jean Schlumberger, Gabriel Marcel, and Pierre Gaxotte, and lectur-ing on Hadrian (on 6 February), Yourcenar still found the time, yet again, to be ill as well as to sign, alongside Elena Craveri-Croce, Carlo Levi, Han Harloff, and others, a petition appealing to the Italian authorities to put an end to the depredation of the Appian Way.

Yourcenar and Frick went occasionally to the Opéra's ballet perfor-mances, and more frequently to the theater, going from Madame Simone's play *En attendant l'aurore* [Waiting for Dawn] to *Amédée ou Comment s'en débarrasser (Amedee)* by Ionesco, with a detour through *La Machine infer-nale (The Infernal Machine)* by Cocteau—which Yourcenar liked very much—with the well-known actor Jean Marais.[10] Frick noted everything down in her yearbook, but without comment, which allows us to assume, knowing the virulence of her criticism the moment a performance disap-pointed her—or them—that they rather liked these plays, or at the very least that they had not been incensed by them.

During the month of March, an astounding thing happened: Yourcenar, who had filed a request for a passport renewal at the American consulate, received notice—instead of the expected two-year extension—that her passport would expire on 24 May. Were they planning to contest her American citizenship? After several unsuccessful attempts at explanation, long letters from Yourcenar and from Frick to the "authorities in charge," along with the intervention of Marguerite Barratin (the administration's representative in France from Sarah Lawrence College) it was, in the end, Natalie Barney's energetic protestations over the telephone that unblocked the situation. Though relieved, Frick was quite simply scandalized that it had been necessary to call on the renown of their friend to resolve an affair in which Yourcenar had been perfectly within the rules, and she showed her indignation in her thank-you letter to Barney:

"Believe me, I am greatly distressed that such a clear-cut, run-of-the-mill case could not be resolved without pressure being brought to bear from on high. What happens to the hundreds of people who don't have a Natalie Barney battling for them on the telephone—and on a Monday morning at dawn, no less? . . . Though I was born in a Republican family, I am becoming more and more a Jeffersonian Democrat. It is simply intolerable that everyone does not enjoy the same vigilant attention at the embassy, and I am delighted with the way you put those bureaucrats in their place by saying: 'If it's easy for me, why isn't it for everyone?'"[11]

Without lapsing into overinterpretation, how can one not notice that it was Frick, and not Yourcenar, who wrote this thank-you letter to Barney? Of course there can be no doubt regarding the authentic indignation of this citizen of a free and democratic America, outraged by this mixture of obtuse bureaucracy and latent ostracism. All the same: what would have happened if, by reason of her lengthy stays abroad, they had forbidden Yourcenar from going back to the country of which she had nonetheless become a citizen?

But there had been more apprehension than there was damage done: Yourcenar remained an American and, in May 1954, both women left for Germany—a trip, including lectures, of course, that lasted four months. Yourcenar plied her author's trade with application, giving interviews on the radio and television. After Heidelberg, Tübingen, Stuttgart, Frankfurt, Cologne, and Würzburg, they arrived in Munich on 6 July. They would stay there more than two months on account of "a rather lengthy indisposition of Marguerite's," according to Frick. Also considered was the proximity of the library of the Archeological Institute, where Yourcenar worked on a short essay on the third-century Greek poet Oppian. That text had been solicited by her friend, the princess Hélène Schakhowskoy,[12] as a preface to the new, deluxe edition of Oppian's *Quatre livres de la vénerie* [Four Books of Venery], originally translated by Florent Chrestien in 1575. (This new edition was published by the Société des Cent-Une.)[13] Yourcenar had moved into Munich's Grand Hotel Continental. To her correspondent, then vacationing in Abano, Italy, she sent several letters abounding in details and recommendations that attest yet again to the particular care she took with each piece of her writing.

> The essay is finished, and tomorrow I begin copying over its 160 lines. If it is too long for the preface, as you would like to have it, all you'll have to do is remove the central expository passage, on hunting, keeping only the parts on either end. But I am opposed to dropping a sentence here and there, because the ideas would not be coherent.
>
> Oppian was a pleasure to write. I composed the poem during a bad night brought on by a serious hepatic attack, complicated by fatigue, that I have been suffering from for over a month and that forces me to rest. Rhyming was the most charming of distractions. . . . You will see that I left a blank on the last page, at the end of a sentence referring to the first edition of Florent Chrestien's translation, of which you did not give me the date. The same thing applies regarding the format of the book. Since you have had this volume in hand, perhaps you yourselves could complete this, and put something like "the octavo edition of 1599" (or 1601, or whatever the correct date ends up being) or "the little sextodecimo edition of 1595" or any other suitable phrase. If you are not sure about the format, simply put "the volume" or "the small volume" of (whatever date). Let me know what you have done in this regard, as well as with the cuts.
>
> In any event, even if it were only for the sake of the proper nouns, I shall have to correct the proofs. . . . The city's fine libraries are a great help to me, and Grace is taking advantage of them for checking over the proofs of her translation of Hadrian, and for going back to the Latin texts themselves when she prefers to.
>
> I still hope to spend a few days in Switzerland in order to take a real vacation in the country finally. We do not plan on going back to Paris before 15 September.[14]

In fact, by the end of August Yourcenar was rather tired of Germany. She wanted to return to Paris, and still dreamed of a Mediterranean winter—which she would have, but it would be spent in the south of France and not the south of Europe. She was impressed by the powerful vitality of Germany rebuilding itself, but professed to be worried somewhat about the Germanic sense of discipline, which to her seemed conducive to obliquities and tragedies like those whose traces Germany was desperately trying to obliterate. One scene affected her deeply: the demolition of a newly built house, which probably did not conform to the established norms or to the land-use plans. Not only did the people around her watch that demolition without uttering a word—at a time when everything needed rebuilding—but the same workmen who were building yesterday were destroying today, in the same spirit of obedience to orders. She would not go back to Germany and would do no more than cross it in order to reach Austria or Switzerland on subsequent trips. But she had been planning a brief stopover there at the end of 1987 or early in 1988, during the trip that was precluded by the stroke she suffered on the eve of her departure. She did not reach the point of sharing with Germany either, unsurprisingly, the intimacy that tied her to Italy, or even the particular variety of tenderness and benevolence she bore England, where men and earth seemed to her to have sealed a profound and ancestral alliance.

UPON HER RETURN to Paris, on 22 September, just after finishing the article "Le Temps, ce grand sculpteur" ("That Mighty Sculptor, Time") for *La Revue des Voyages*,[15] the "*Electra* affair" began. Yourcenar attended rehearsals of the play, which was finally to be staged after a year's delay. Forthwith, she contested the distribution of roles: she would not have Jany Holt in the part of Electra and expressed reservations regarding Laurent Terzieff as Orestes. Rather unfriendly discussions with Marchat followed. They became all the more unfriendly when Yourcenar, having attended a performance of Strindberg's *Miss Julie* on 27 September, became thoroughly captivated by the interpretation of Eléonore Hirt. She invited her to visit and spoke with her about Electra, but Marchat objected to this choice. As she was composing the "Carnets de notes d'*Electre*" [Reflections on the Composition of *Electra*], she continued to see Hirt, with whom she dined on 24 October. Relations between the author of *Electra* and the producer grew more bitter.

For Yourcenar, the crux of the matter resided in the failure to respect her right to a "tryout clause," which Marchat had promised her. On account of her absence from Paris, Marchat had in fact proposed to her that he himself audition and choose the play's actors, allowing her in return the option of evaluating, over the course of five rehearsals, his assignment of roles and, if necessary, making changes. On returning to France, Yourcenar noticed that the much-touted clause was not mentioned in the contracts. In total disagreement with the choice of the two lead actors, she obtained a written statement from Marchat agreeing to replace them. New auditions began, but after a few days Yourcenar received a letter from Madame Baur informing her that when the existing contracts expired, she would have no right to a tryout clause. According to Baur, it was only possible to invoke such a clause in the event that renowned actors were engaged. She pointed out, furthermore, that the expenses for those five days of auditioning would be charged to her, as would the amounts due the actors by way of compensation. Marchat, for his part, disavowed his prior agreement. From registered letters to acknowledgments of receipt, the tone grew more strident and the affair took on a pettifogging aspect. By 1 October, the split was definitive, as the short article appearing in *Le Figaro* on 1 November attests:

"Last night we learned that Madame Marguerite Yourcenar, upon the first performance of her play *Electra,* at the Théâtre des Mathurins, had expressed formal opposition on the subject of certain role assignments and that the management of the theater had believed it had to carry on regardless of the author's wishes. Madame Yourcenar declares on this subject: 'Given the serious disagreement between me and the Théâtre des Mathurins, I have not lent my assistance to preparing the rehearsals of *Electra,* and I have no comment to make on the conditions in which my work is being performed at this time. It will be up to the public to judge.'"

In *Le Monde,* dated 11 November, the first review of the play appeared: it was by Robert Kemp and did not contradict the reservations, soon to be followed by the outright hostility, of Yourcenar. "Over the past few days," he wrote,

> the rumor has been spreading that quite a bit of sniggering went on at the gala of *Electra or The Fall of the Masks,* and I was still hearing some fatuous laughter yesterday evening . . . What may have disoriented the spectators— let's find some excuses for them—was the abominable presentation of the play. . . . Of course I set Madame Jany Holt apart. She is not in her element here. It can be said that Electra is not necessarily a she-bear, a she-wolf, a large beast; and that one can imagine her as a "minute serpent . . ." Nonetheless, this little Electra is nervous; her nimble fingers, tinkling away at the air, are not the fingers of a strangler. . . . A strained smile on this delicate face does not suffice as a frightful expression. . . . Her voice is forced and is never the voice of a Nemesis. . . . No, Jany Holt, who has some very lovely moments of fever and alarm, is not the woman for the role. . . . Nevertheless, it is hers. We follow her movements like those of a weasel in a cage. We listen to her. But the others! Those young men with neither physical nor vocal nobility, those apprentices. . . . Where do they come from? They are hurled upon the stage. Once there, they know not how to speak. To transport us to the height of vexation, they are decked out in brown jerseys on which white lines represent a set of muscles or vague breastplates. They look like gingerbread men, decorated with sugar, for Saint Orestes Day. They are unbeliev-

ably bad. Orestes is the worst. He howls and one can hardly understand him. . . . All in all, an absolute mess![16]

This attack was all the more unbearable for Yourcenar since Kemp seemed, with certain minor reservations, to have appreciated her text: "This first act, radiating intelligence, drags on a bit and is tiring. But the second has such beauty!"

After a second article, every bit as fierce, that appeared in *Combat,* Yourcenar appealed to her lawyer Maître Mirat, asking him to file suit against Marchat in the matter of *Electra.*

WE DON'T KNOW Frick's opinion on this dispute, any more than we know the state of her relations with Yourcenar that fall. We can only observe, since she notes it herself in her daybook, that she refused to accompany Yourcenar to certain dinners, particularly at Anne Quellennec's. On 30 November, a Tuesday, Yourcenar went alone to a meeting that Marie Laurencin had arranged with her, on the Place Saint-Sulpice.

Yourcenar and Frick spent several days in Belgium, in Ghent, for a lecture, then in Ostend and in Brussels where Yourcenar saw her "Aunt Loulou" again, Louise de Borchgrave, her "half sister-in-law."[17] Oddly enough, Yourcenar used the informal *tu* instead of *vous* with Louise de Borchgrave—an intelligent, cultivated woman, musically inclined (she played the violin)—with whom she would maintain ties until the former's death, in 1986, at the age of one hundred.

From Belgium where she was born, Yourcenar quite naturally went on to Lille, where she had spent part of her childhood, then to the south of France, as if to revive the tradition of her first Mediterranean winters with her father. All her life she liked to combine the pleasures of discovering new landscapes with the vaguely nostalgic emotion of returning to places remembered. This time, after Scandinavia and Germany, it would be the Midi of Michel de Crayencour. Much later, in 1982, after the belated realization of an ancient desire—a trip to Egypt—it would be Venice, no doubt in a crazy attempt to believe she was returning to the loves of her youth.

So Yourcenar and Frick would spend the entire winter of 1954–55 in Fayence, in the département of Var, in a house owned by one of their American friends from Hartford, Everett Austin, for whose amateur theater company, in 1942, Yourcenar had composed *The Little Mermaid.* Several years later, when Yourcenar received the Prix Combat, in 1963, Ghislain de Diesbach—a cousin of Yourcenar's by marriage—shared the impressions he had retained from his visit to Fayence, where he met Yourcenar for the first time: "The residence put at her disposal by one of her friends was a rather attractive house in the old city, but I was struck by the barrenness of the rooms, and by the way Marguerite Yourcenar put up with that almost complete absence of furniture. . . . Of Marguerite Yourcenar herself, I retain only an imprecise vision. . . . I remember a dress of a cut gone out of style, with some sort of white collarette, hair cut short and plastered down on her ears, an aquiline nose, very beautiful blue eyes, and something in her appearance or her bearing that made her resemble one of those portraits of women from the Renaissance."[18]

In Fayence, they received a few friends, among them Natalie Barney and Romaine Brooks, the publisher Charles Orengo—with whom Yourcenar kept up regular relations and a continuous correspondence—and certain members of Yourcenar's family, to whom she began posing questions of genealogy.[19] They also took some short trips in the region, notably to Nice where Yourcenar gave a lecture on Antinous and lent herself to a few society engagements. She spoke at length to Jerry Wilson, over the course of their travels during the eighties, of that winter in the Var.[20] Those discussions with Wilson provide an occasion to observe that Yourcenar's meager taste for village socializing was not due solely to her determination to escape "linguistic pollution" at Petite Plaisance. Frick, who was nonetheless the "foreigner" this time, had, as was her custom, successfully fit in to the community and was organizing her immutable little festivals for the children of the village. Yourcenar remained stubbornly standoffish. She was working on her article on Thomas Mann, which she completed on 17 February, the very day she received a highly laudatory letter from this writer. Diesbach recollected Yourcenar reading it to him: "One day I heard Marguerite Yourcenar read a letter from Thomas Mann who congratulated her warmly on her play *Electra of The Fall of the Masks,* and waxed indignant that this play was not generally ranked among the finest of her productions: 'People say that with "Hadrian" you have realized your destiny, written the book of your life, and that afterward, there will be nothing else . . . What idiots! When one has written such a book, it proves on the contrary that one has capacities from which even better things can be expected, and along came your "Electra"!'

"I must admit," Diesbach added, "that, for my part, I judged *Memoirs of Hadrian* superior to *Electra,* and I modestly placed myself in the category of those idiots that Thomas Mann was stigmatizing."[21]

If Frick had become a good adoptive citizen of Fayence, she began to have a hard time putting up with Yourcenar's guests, especially those who in her judgment stayed too long after dinner. With Pierre Monteret, the painter friend of Elie Grekoff, who had designed the costumes for *Electra* and with whom Yourcenar kept up a correspondence until her death, Frick went so far as to be barely polite, getting huffy over a harmless remark concerning the lack of a housekeeper, and astonishing the guest with a sententious "we believe that cooking is a good alternative to literary work." This would be nothing more than a slightly ridiculous tale, were it not the first sign of a stiffening on Frick's part that would get worse and worse as the years went by and would unnecessarily complicate relations between Yourcenar and her visitors, at Petite Plaisance.

The second half of March in 1955 was taken up by travel within France: Bordeaux, Poitiers, for a lecture, Tours, Blois, then Paris, to review the "*Electra* affair" with the lawyer and attend a performance of Montherlant's *Port Royal* [Port Royal], before returning to Fayence on 3 April, taking the long way around, via Avignon, Vaison, Saint-Rémy, Les Baux, and Arles. Finally, they set off again for Scandinavia; from there they embarked for the United States on 1 June.

ON 12 JUNE, they were back at Petite Plaisance, after being away for nearly two years. It seems that a certain rhythm of life had again been attained, alternating peregrinations all over the world with long periods of work and rest in Maine.

During the last months of 1955, Yourcenar decided to work on a new version of *La Mort conduit l'attelage,* which had appeared at Grasset in 1934. She turned first to the story entitled "D'après Dürer": thus began what would become not another short story, but her major work, *The Abyss.* If Frick had no trouble contenting herself with enjoying their yard, working in the garden, inviting neighbors to tea, going to dinner at their houses, and attending the Congregational Church every Sunday, Yourcenar, having settled in again at Petite Plaisance scarcely six months before, could not even then stop herself from framing plans for faraway journeys: "I hope to be in Damascus and Beirut in February or March," she wrote to one of her friends.

It was at the same time that Yourcenar began systematizing a practice that was to become a veritable mania: she would write to various French and Belgian booksellers to order copies of her own books: "As you might imagine," she explained, perhaps anticipating a slight degree of perplexity on the part of those receiving her requests, "this order represents an attempt on my part to verify what editions of my books are currently in circulation, certain editions having turned out to be extremely faulty." As we have already seen—and as we shall see even more clearly with regard to the "Plon affair," which went so far as to be taken to court—one needed a certain amount of courage to be Marguerite Yourcenar's publisher.

From Christmas Eve until Easter, the winter of 1955–56 in Northeast Harbor was one of "uninterrupted ice and snow," Yourcenar noted in her daybook. Even though she maintained that this "weather is highly favorable to reflection and work," she sank into a cocoon-like spell of low spirits, with a few sieges of physical discomfort, as the increase in the number of her allergies attests. Frick, for her part, liked the snow. Their friend Florence Codman visited them for a few days, from 13 to 17 January.

"On returning to New York," Codman remembers, "I sent them a recording made by Colette, for we had talked about her a great deal, Marguerite and I. More than anything else I liked talking about French literature with her. Everything she said was always very astute, very pertinent, very convincing. I do not remember us ever disagreeing. To get back to the recording, they were obliged to go listen to it at the village library: they did not even possess what we called, at the time, a record player. And yet Grace, who played the piano, loved music. But they led, deliberately, and due I think especially to Grace's influence, a very thrifty, very frugal existence. Nonetheless, Marguerite went to listen to the record, despite that winter's cold and her reluctance to confront it. And that earned me a very lovely letter."

"Thank you for *Gigi Chéri* [Gigi Darling], which we listened to this morning," wrote Yourcenar on 16 February. "One can follow her entire life by way of the contours of her voice: the rich and fulsome tones of Burgundy, the street-urchin element from Willy, the literary element, and also, if I might be so bold, the concierge-and-fortuneteller-adored-by-the-little-local-ladies element. For she was all of this. She was incredibly representative of a certain France between 1900 and 1946, with her spicy, vernacular flavor, her affectations (for there are some), her own personal notion of the good life, and her whole code of what is proper and improper, as complicated as ancient China. A France that, deep down, I am not very sure that I like."[22]

A Burgundy accent, affectations, a street-urchin element, a vernacular flavor, concierge- and fortunetellerlike—savory though it may be, this "vocal portrait" of Colette betrays a kind of distance that, though it does not rule out literary esteem, tinges her with a vague, bemused condescension. Decidedly, with Yourcenar, the vial of vitriol is never very far from the teapot.

IN MARCH 1956 judgment was rendered in the case against Jean Marchat and the Théâtre des Mathurins concerning *Electra*. Yourcenar won and found herself allocated five hundred thousand francs in damages "as a result of Marchat's not having kept his promise, in contradiction with the letter he had sent to me regarding this matter, to change Jany Holt," she wrote to Natalie Barney. "As you can well imagine, I am thrilled with this judgment, which marks a significant date with regard to the question, such an important one, of the author's right to oversee and protect his *œuvre*."[23]

At Petite Plaisance, they would have to wait until the month of June to be able finally to sit out in the garden. Firmly determined not to spend the winter of 1956—57 in Maine, but rather, once again, in the south of France, Yourcenar, who had some lectures to give in Belgium from 20 October to 6 November, reserved a house in Beaulieu. She planned on arriving there—from Paris where she would just have spent about a month—around 15 December.

Disembarking at Rotterdam on 3 October, in the company of Frick, she went to Arnhem, to Amsterdam, then on to Belgium where she delivered several lectures. Yourcenar decided to make a stop—which she described as "touristic"—in Namur, to visit the Suarlée cemetery—where her mother, Fernande, her Aunt Jeanne, and two of her uncles, Octave and Théobald, were buried. It was this first visit to the family plot that she described in the first chapter of *Dear Departed:*

"Despite all my efforts, I did not succeed in establishing a rapport between those people lying there and myself. I had known personally only three of them, the two uncles and the aunt, and I had lost touch even with them before my tenth year. I had traversed Fernande; I had nourished myself for several months on her substance, but the facts I had gleaned were cold knowledge to me, as if they had come from a textbook. Her grave affected me no more than that of an unknown woman whose death someone might describe to me briefly and in passing."[24]

It was on arriving in Mons, on 30 October, that she discovered her small volume *The Alms of Alcippe* on sale. It was published by the poet Alexis Curvers—who edited a little quarterly magazine in Liège, *La Flûte Enchantée*—and whose acquaintance she had made in 1954. In July 1956, following an exchange of correspondence over the course of which Yourcenar had sent him several poems, Curvers had suggested he publish them in a limited edition, to be printed by hand. Yourcenar had given her permission, which was backed by no official document granting consent, given the friendly nature of their relations.

The way certain poems were divided disconcerted her, as did the drawing by Aristide Maillol chosen for the frontispiece: Curvers, pressed for time, had imprudently anticipated the wishes of his correspondent. She wrote him right away to inform him, courteously, of her reservations. But when she arrived in Liège to see to sending out review copies, Curvers displayed a certain hostility toward her, which transformed itself into outright animosity when he observed that, on every copy she was inscribing, she was making several corrections, by hand, of the titles or the typography. The situation grew more acrimonious when she learned that Curvers, contrary to his original agreement, had taken back the forty or so copies that she was to have at her disposal. When she got back to Northeast Harbor, she attempted a final reconciliation by registered letter, to which Curvers responded by way of his lawyer. Between complications and sudden new developments, the affair—yet another—which Yourcenar placed in the hands of Maître Jean Mirat, in December 1956, would last more than nine years, at the close of which Yourcenar would win the case.

BUT, quibblingly litigious though she was, Yourcenar did not have her eye fixed merely on typographical misprints, and there were, during the end of that year, 1956, more substantial subjects of distress than this unfortunate story of an imperfect publication.

IT WAS in Holland, then in Belgium—where the irony of history would have it that she was delivering a lecture on "Europe and Humanism"—that the disastrous news of the Suez Crisis and that of Budapest reached her:

> In the Hague the newspapers were full of the kidnapping of Ben Bella, the latest sensational turn of plot in the North African melodrama. A few days later, announced with great fanfare by the radio and the press after clumsily covert preparations, the unfortunate Suez episode began. In a large city in Flemish Belgium, I witnessed the chauvinistic euphoria of a group of official-looking Frenchmen as they toasted the victory—over whom it was no longer very clear. Some English industrialists, glimpsed a day or two later, echoed this bellicosity with a British accent. There was already talk of a black market, and Belgian housewives were hoarding kilos of sugar. The shrewdest people bought lead foil to cover their windows, as protection against atomic radiation. Meanwhile, the Soviets were able to fortify their buffer zones, taking advantage of the fact that the West had turned its attention elsewhere. I arrived in Brussels as the news erupted that Russian tanks were surrounding Budapest. Further darkening the picture—which was, to be sure, already fairly gloomy—our jovial taxi driver exclaimed: "The Russians are tossing phosphorous bombs there! Those things really burn! What a show!" ... Brutality, greed, indifference to the sufferings of others, madness, and folly held sway over the world more than ever, exacerbated by the proliferation of mankind and supplied for the first time with the instruments of ultimate destruction. Even if the current crisis resolved itself after destroying only a limited number of people, other crises would come, each aggravated by the after-

effects of the ones preceding. The inevitable had already begun. The museum guards who came to announce closing time, pacing the halls with their military tread, seemed to herald the shutting down of everything.[25]

Can we attribute this to distress about the European situation, in those "cold war" times when any conflict seemed to carry the seeds of an impending apocalypse? Was it anguish in the face of a world so crazy that one's sole remaining refuge was to bury oneself away in the snow of Mount Desert Island? Whatever the case may be, Yourcenar and Frick were back in the United States on 27 November, after staying ten days or so in Paris, a city to which Yourcenar would not return until 1968. We know that the trip was meant to continue, and we don't know what part Frick played in the decision to cut it short. Yourcenar would have only this to say, in a letter to a friend a few months later: "I had at first planned to go relax for a few months in the south of France . . . which would have served as the point of departure for a trip to Greece and the Near East. But the atmosphere in November hardly seemed favorable to plans that included Damascus, Aleppo, Alexandria, and perhaps Israel. . . . I must also confess that the state of the world has thrown me into a fit of despair from which I have yet to emerge and which is insane, for how could we expect anything better?"[26]

What is equally certain is that Frick wanted Yourcenar to work. She had been irritated by the refusal of an article on Chenonceaux that Yourcenar had offered to a review whose name she does not mention. It was a mediocre text, for that matter, which Yourcenar would nonetheless have published—with, admittedly, a few modifications—in December 1961 in *Le Figaro* under the title of "Celle qui aima Henry III" [She Who Loved Henry III].[27]

Thus, as soon as she returned to Petite Plaisance, Yourcenar was summoned to get back to her desk. She was tackling the revision of *Fires* while the several copies of *The Alms of Alcippe* signed in Liège were reaching her friends and acquaintances.

Yourcenar was very attached to her poetry, "in the manner of those who are not poets," observed André Fraigneau, not without reason. For we have little choice but to acknowledge that this was not a genre in which she excelled. And Jean Cocteau's thank-you note, light-hearted and courtly, accompanied by a drawing, does nothing to change this observation, all the less so since he is very careful not to appreciate anything beyond her intention: "My Dear Marguerite. There exists no homage from the heart that approaches the gift of a poem. I thank you for this book that enters through the window, flies across the room, and finally alights on my table."[28]

Numerous, however, were Yourcenar's correspondents who sent her their own collections, soliciting her approval or her advice, with which, for that matter, she was most willingly lavish, sometimes in a singularly doctrinal tone. Attesting to this is a note that was attached to her translation of Hortense Flexner's poems and addressed to one of her friends:

"A few pieces of advice regarding poetry (to the extent that it is possible to give advice):

"Poetry too is a translation; we translate our intimate emotions into a language that the reader can understand. It is therefore a question of being faithful (transmitting accurately): I mean that words and sounds should be used that best render our impressions, however inexpressible they may be. Beware of catch-all words and words corrupted by use (ravishing, charming, beautiful, etc.). You can use them, but then you must clean them off and renew their value by combining them with other words that are very strong and very pure.

"Always take the simplest expression (you very often do this, which is good), but remember that the simplest expression is never the most ordinary one, on the contrary: it is the one that comes directly from things without being influenced by any convention.

"Have no complacency toward your own emotions (the reader won't have any). Judge your work when reading it over as if you were reading it for the first time. Are you convinced? Are you moved? Have the courage always to follow your thought through to the end. Poetry is made to be heard. Give great importance to rhythm. Every living creature has a rhythm."[29]

All of this, one must admit, has more to do with begging the question than with an original analysis of poetic experience or singularity.

More interesting are the reflections on poetry—and contemporary poetry in particular—that she confided to the poet and essayist Dominique Le Buhan:

> I do not believe in the death of poetry, any more than I believe in the death of *life's breath*, or indeed in the oft-heard "What's the point?" What's the point of trying to fill our lungs with fresh air and attempting to conduct ourselves in such a way that the air around us stays pure or becomes pure again?
> I wonder if the real tragedy, for you and for so many other young poets (for tragedy there is, and your word "grievous" admits as much) does not consist of an incapacity to react in the presence of what is a more and more vile kind of conformity. The very fact that the word "marginal" has been invented in our time to refer to what does not belong to the rabble of the mind—and also that other obscene word "elitism," which cuts any desire to do better right off at the root—attests to this conformity, which is worse than

the categorical imperatives of yesteryear because it was easier to rebel against them. But however odious this aspect of our era may be (and all eras have had their odious aspects, albeit that our own is particularly rich in them), you are too much of a philosopher not to be aware that time and place are nothing more than concepts one can push aside to discover underneath them a biological time and a cosmic place, both of them real. Nothing prevents you from being a poet "of another time," and/or of all times.

All the young poets who write to me seem tragically stricken with *autism:* ill at ease before that supreme mode of expression that is poetry, they confuse it with an individual cry or mumble, without making the effort of moving, with open arms, toward others (others-readers), or of quite simply setting free a vibration that will sustain itself through others (or over their heads, it makes no difference), and that, coming from them, *is* more than they are. . . .

It was on account of having lacked this sense of what is natural and this sense of what is sacred (it's the same thing) that the Surrealists failed so lamentably.

Incidentally, but for reasons resulting from the assertions that precede, I believe (I have tried to explain myself on this point in the preface to *La Couronne et la lyre,* which I am presently finishing) in modulated, metrical verse. I do not think that French verse has exhausted its potentialities: it is we who for the moment are incapable of taking advantage of them. . . .

Of course, there is always the danger that constraints turn into routines, but their absence causes the poet to lapse right back into prose: here a prose of exclamations and ejaculations, a disjointed prose, which goes the way of the syntactical dislocation that you deplore, there, and this is worse still perhaps, a prose of the "information-processing" variety, with neither lymph nor blood. . . .

On the one hand, there is prose, infinitely richer in crypto-rhythms than is generally imagined, and, on the other hand, verse, sustained by repetitions and sequences of sound that are very much its own. Between the two, it appears to me that the modern poet no longer knows how to choose.[30]

Yourcenar always affirmed her taste for set forms of poetry, saying that she placed the expression of emotion ahead of that of abstraction and intellectualization. Her preferences were for Villon, Racine, and Hugo. "In our era I see hardly anyone beyond Valéry, Apollinaire, and the Cocteau of certain poems, such as 'Plain-Chant' [Plainsong], that bears mentioning," she conceded to the poets of her century.[31] Indeed, she granted very little credit to works written outside the strictest rules of versification. "Contemporary poetry tires me for several reasons," she said during an interview. "Free verse itself, new in 1880, also became a routine. Moreover, the destruction of the forms has drawn poetry further and further away from the musical plane and has at the same time put off the masses, for whom rhythm is breath. Which results in poetry very often being a slightly more obscure, more dissociated prose. There is great beauty in the skillful devices of ancient poetry." And if one evoked the texts of André Breton, Renée Char, or Yves Bonnefoy, she did not equivocate: "Those devices are of an intellectual order much more than they are rhythmic or emotional. This is what brings about their real obscurity for many readers. Laboratory experiments."[32]

Her own poems are prosodically perfect—only barely did she allow herself the hiatus "Ami, Ombre" [Friend, Shadow] in "Intimation," and this was late, very late, in 1963—but of such mediocre quality, to put it mildly, and so conventional, with their "fragile bronzes," "pensive lakes," and "supple-tendrilled vines," that they do not even emanate that somewhat old-fashioned charm that might compensate for their anachronism. It is a fact that there are no "laboratory experiments" here, but, I fear, no poetic experimentation either: Yourcenar's poems are more akin to exercises in versified composition than to an investigation in poetry. No one dared to tell her this candidly, except for her enemies, and she took little notice of them. And so it was that in 1984, Gallimard would let its hand be forced by "its Academician" and publish a new edition of *The Alms of Alcippe*. These works in verse, most of which date from the twenties and thirties (some of them moreover had appeared in various reviews during those years), retain nothing more than biographical interest today. This is particularly the case with "seven poems for a dead woman," dedicated to Jeanne de Vietinghoff,[33] which was published in 1931 in *Le Manuscrit Autographe* under the title "Sept poèmes pour Isolde morte" [Seven Poems for a Mortal Isolde], and, with the poems "Greek Flag" and "Epitaph, *Wartime*," written in 1942 in memory of Lucy.

"I have staked my career as a writer on prose," Yourcenar herself admitted, "with the result that poetry is only a by-product now; but the long allegorical piece that lends its name to this little volume (*The Alms of Alcippe*) was already, haltingly, expressing thoughts in 1929 that more recent works have confirmed. It is strange that the young woman I was at twenty-six perceived this so strongly through the mists of youth."[34] It is less strange, and highly fortunate, that the same young woman chose to make that confirmation in prose.

FOR THE WHOLE MONTH of December the revision of *Fires* hardly left Yourcenar time to give in to the low spirits that can nonetheless be detected in her Christmas cards and greetings. To friends she would have liked to see in Paris she confided: "'we'll make it another time' is particularly melancholy when friends live separated by 6000 kilometers."

Nineteen fifty-seven was a year without travel, if we except a few days spent in Montreal, where Yourcenar had been invited by Jean Mouton, then a cultural consultant in Ottawa, for a series of lectures on "the novel and history." That first meeting between Yourcenar and Mouton was a warm one. They only knew one another by way of a few letters exchanged on the subject of Charles Du Bos, and Yourcenar would offer Mouton the correspondence she exchanged with Du Bos, during the two years preceding his death in 1939. In Montreal, Mouton took the organization of the program of lectures entirely upon himself, but he also had to take care of hospitalizing Yourcenar, who was suddenly stricken with phlebitis. Rapidly and effectively treated, Yourcenar made a visit, on 19 November, to Wellesley College near Boston, where Frick had once been a student; the subject of her talk there was "Greek poets and their influence on French poetry."

Thus began a long period favorable to work. In addition to *Fires,* Yourcenar began writing what would be *The Abyss,* as is shown in a letter of 10 March 1957 to Louise de Borchgrave where she indicates: "At this moment I am somewhere between Innsbruck and Ratisbon, in 1551."[35] Was she already aware that, out of what was only supposed to be a touching-up of "D'après Dürer," a new work was emerging? And was it a new work? Several months earlier, Yourcenar had said she was working on revising *La Mort conduit l'attelage.* At least this is how she responded to Gaston Gallimard, who had asked her, in September 1956, for more information concerning the work "on the Renaissance" that she was in the process of writing.[36]

Later on, after finishing the book, she would explain that she had written "La Conversation à Innsbruck" ("A Conversation in Innsbruck") in 1956 and 1957, then the main part of the volume between 1962 and 1965 (the book would not appear until 1968 because of difficulties with Plon and lengthy legal proceedings, at the close of which Yourcenar would, yet again, win her case).[37] As she would restate on several occasions, it was in that experience of writing, or rather rewriting, that she discovered her "will to exist not *for oneself,* but *through oneself* and to let oneself be guided solely by the requirements of one's own development." In writing that "expansion" of "D'après Dürer," she observed that she considered her different books as various parts of a single, never-finished work that she would return to, improve, and little by little do her best "to enrich or to simplify." They were the avatars of a unique object, a kind of literary parthenogenesis in which she, as its origin, played only a limited part: "I have tried to encumber my works as little as possible with my own persona," she notes in her daybook. "This is far from being understood. Biographical interpretations are, of course, false, and above all naive."

FOR YOURCENAR, several months at Petite Plaisance was, of necessity, a particularly propitious time for correspondence. In a general way, she wrote lots of letters. Sometimes one can use them to follow variations in her thought, in her moods, as if they were substitutes for a personal diary. Rarely—to refrain from saying never—does one find confidences, except when they are made indirectly. Thus, upon learning of the death of the mother of one her relatives, she wrote to her: "Wasn't it rather your stepmother? I tend more to remember your father's face. . . . I hope that the readjustments inevitable in such cases will be made in your own without too much difficulty."[38] Yourcenar was, unavoidably, "Daddy's girl." But it was not her own mother's absence that founded her lack of interest in maternal figures. Whatever she may occasionally have said about the subject, when delivering speeches in the "off-the-thought-rack" mode on "women" in general—creatures close to nature and the "stuff of life"—everything she saw that had to do with mothers, beginning with her grandmother Noémi, rendered her absolutely hostile to this particular function. And this refusal played at least as important a part in her sterility wish as her "official" explanation regarding the terrible overpopulation of the planet. She had a genuine distaste for procreation, one common to many homosexuals of her generation—of both sexes—which Diane de Margerie, whose mother, Jenny, Yourcenar had known for a long time, had an opportunity to observe in Rome, in 1952. Yourcenar had come to dinner at Monsieur Randol-Coate's. At the table, she had a rather long and very pleasant conversation with Diane. "At the end of the meal," recounts Diane de Margerie, "when we all got up and Marguerite Yourcenar noticed that I was pregnant, I caught her looking at me, full of disgust. She became, in a flash, as cold as ice. And we did not converse together again." Though she was less attentive to children than Frick, Yourcenar was neither annoyed nor revolted by them. At the end of her life, she would even spend some long and agreeable moments with Jeremy, the son of her secretary Jeannie. Thus it was foursquare on maternity and mothers—or mothers-to-be—that her hostility concentrated itself.[39]

Yourcenar's epistolary activity would grow more and more intense, beginning at the end of the fifties, as her journeys abroad were spaced further and further apart, and it would once again diminish when, in 1980, Yourcenar began traveling again. Not only did she keep up a regular correspondence with several friends, but she also responded, abundantly explaining all the while how much this put her out, to a great many letters from admirers and people seeking advice of various kinds. She read the manuscripts that were sent to her, and made comments on them, occasionally going so far as to excuse herself for being "too lengthy." "In my estimation, a writer should not answer his letters," she was in the habit of saying, "but if he does so, he must do it completely." By following the thread of her diverse correspondence, one can gauge Yourcenar's immense intellectual curiosity, and the variety and extent of her culture. Not one of the letters that arrived escaped Frick's (critical) perusal—no more than did the outgoing mail in its entirety: often, Yourcenar would read her letters to her, in the evening by the fire, and would then add a postscript generally beginning with: "Grace has brought to my attention that . . ."

It was during this period as well that she began receiving questionnaires on literature, to which, at that time, she was happy to respond. It was not until later, when media attention was intense, that people started telephoning her to ask for her opinion on anything and everything: then, her responses would be terse, coldly and minimally polite. In 1957, she responded in great detail to a questionnaire from the journal *Prétexte*, having to do with autobiography and fiction in the modern novel from Gide onward. With regard to the lack of imagination generally invoked to characterize the work of contemporary novelists, she responded:

"I believe that one can hardly deny the existence of a form of imagination (perhaps more poetic than strictly fictional) in certain novelists or writers of today. André Breton (I am thinking of *Nadja* [*Nadja*]), Gracq (*Le Château d'Argol* [*The Castle of Argol*]), Cocteau (*Les Enfants terribles* [*The Holy Terrors*]), even Genet (for example the description of the old hard-labor prison in *Querelle de Brest* [*Querelle*]). Moreover, one might well ask if certain novels classified no doubt as being 'realist,' such as Montherlant's admirable *Célibataires* (*The Bachelors*), would not presuppose in their authors a type of psychological imagination just as essential to the novel as the fictional imagination itself. One does not go far in apprehending the inner reality of a character without sympathy, in the true sense of the word, and there is no sympathy without an exercise of the imagination."

Next came the very classical questions—which she was often asked, and to which she almost always gave the same response—concerning the presence of autobiographical elements in her *œuvre*, a presence that she declared "nil and very great; everywhere diffuse and nowhere direct. A novelist, worthy of the name, devotes his substance, his temperament, and his memories to the service of characters who are not he." To the question on the importance she ascribed to fiction, she responded:

Fiction and reality tend, at least where I am concerned, to form in a novel a combination so homogeneous that it rapidly becomes impossible for the author to separate them one from the other, so solid that it is no more possible for the novelist to alter a fictional fact than a real fact without distorting it or without destroying its authenticity. It would certainly be possible for me, in *Memoirs of Hadrian*, to distinguish the part played by fiction from the part played by reality, but that's because Hadrian is not, strictly speaking, a novel, but a meditation or a narrative situated on the limit of history . . . There too, moreover, the question of the limits of the relations between fiction and reality would be more complex than one might think at first glance. Let me add that the elements of which a novel is composed are not, as your survey seems, by omission, to indicate, autobiography on the one hand and fiction on the other. Between the two, there is the impersonal observation of reality.

I am working presently on recasting an old novel: its characters, created by me years ago, manifest themselves now vis-à-vis myself as would real beings that I might have known, forgotten, then met up with again. I can push the analysis further, bring out certain episodes in their lives that in the past I had neglected to explore or preferred to leave in the dark, shed more light on certain of their actions. I cannot, without destroying them, change them.[40]

A not inconsiderable part of her correspondence was reserved for her relations with her lawyer (her litigious side, already in evidence at the time of the probate of her father's estate, had gotten worse since she had been living with Frick, who possessed this very American characteristic to the highest degree) and for her endless quarrels with her publishers. It was to the point where Bernard Grasset saw "the hand of Plon" behind her incessant complaints, and accused the director, Maurice Bourdel, of this: "Madame Yourcenar is looking to haggle with me. I feel that you're behind it. Now I did a favor both for her and for you [at the time of the *Hadrian* affair]. I don't understand."[41] But Yourcenar did not need to be "pushed" by anyone, not only to request "her" accounts from whoever was publishing her, but to contest them, argue, demand specifics, explanations, proof. She had always done so. Exasperated, Bernard Grasset saw to it she was sent a report on the status of her sales, as of early 1956, for all the titles published by his house: *La Nouvelle Eurydice* (1931): 5000 printed, 2667 sold; *Pindare* (1932): 4000 printed, 2032 sold; *A Coin in Nine Hands* (1934): 4000 printed, 2500 sold; *La Mort conduit l'attelage* (1935): 4000 printed, 2024 sold; *Fires* (1936): 3000 printed, 1786 sold; *Les Songes et les sorts* (1938): 3000 printed, 1044 sold.[42] These sales figures—over some twenty years—are liable to convince any writers who have not yet found their public, or possibly a publisher, that certain other commercial successes have been a long time coming.

DURING THE SUMMER of 1957, *Coup de Grâce,* translated by Frick, appeared in the United States at Farrar, Straus and Giroux, where all of Yourcenar's work was published. She agreed to do a book signing in Bar Harbor, the largest town on the island. Several weeks later, she told Natalie Barney that the book "has, contrary to all expectations, earned a place for itself on this week's best-seller list, which doesn't prove a thing, least of all the reader's intelligent comprehension, but which is nice, like learning one has just won a prize in the lottery." [43]

Everything, decidedly, was happily calm at year's end in 1957: on 30 and 31 December, for Frick who had just returned from a month-long stay with her family in Kansas City, the only thing worthy of lengthy commentary was the illness of their dog, a black cocker who accompanied them on all their trips and whom they named, with questionable humor, "Monsieur."

PART 4

Forks in the Road

14
Confinement Consented To

ON 12 JANUARY 1958, Frick celebrated her fifty-fifth birthday. Yourcenar would do so on 8 June of the same year. They had known each other for twenty-one years and had lived together for nineteen of them. On a copy of the new edition of *Memoirs of Hadrian*, Yourcenar wrote: "For G. F. this (the first) volume whose printed page bears the expression of an affection and a gratitude that have filled my life for twenty years. Marguerite. 16 November 1958. Mount Desert Island." It was during this year that the fifth edition of *Memoirs of Hadrian* appeared at Plon, really the first standard edition, in which "Reflections on the Composition of *Memoirs of Hadrian*" was included with the fragment dedicated to Frick. Through the inevitable compromises of a life lived together, Frick's moments of impatience, even anger, Yourcenar's haughty ways and her occasionally abrupt remarks, they seem to have found a rhythm that suited them: alternating travel with the studious life of Petite Plaisance.

Nineteen fifty-eight was shaping up to be a good year, since Yourcenar would be spared part of Maine's winter and would spend nearly four months in her cherished Italy. They set sail from New York on 19 February and arrived in Algeciras on the twenty-fifth. Their stay in Rome would above all be societal—"very social," noted Frick with a certain displeasure. Their stops in Turin, Milan, Florence, Siena, and Perugia would, however, be more intimate, more soothing. In Sorrento, where Yourcenar had written *Coup de Grâce*, in 1938, after the first winter spent in the United States with Grace, they corrected the final proofs of the translation and critical introduction of Cavafy's poems together. Yourcenar had developed this "critical introduction" on the basis of a critical essay published in the review *Mesures*, in January 1940. Following it are the translations done during the thirties with Constantine Dimaras. The reflection on Cavafy elaborated in that essay is often very close to the ideas and preoccupations of Yourcenar in her own regard, which plays something of a part in the interest she bore this poet, even if, for her, "from a solely literary viewpoint, there remain nonetheless in Cavafy some poems of an insipidness and, thus, an indecency that are not acceptable":

> Cavafy said over and over again that his *œuvre* has its origin in his life; from now on, the latter lies entirely within the former. . . . Any notion of sin is totally foreign to Cavafy's work; on the other hand, and solely at the social level, it is clear that the risk of scandal or blame mattered to him, that, in a way, he was haunted by it. At first glance, it is true, all traces of anguish seem to have been eliminated from this sober *œuvre:* this is because anguish, where sensual matters are concerned, is almost always a phenomenon of youth; either it destroys a being, or it diminishes progressively as a result of experience, of a more accurate knowledge of the world, and, more simply, of habit. . . .
>
> His point of departure seems to have been what might readily be called the romantic view of homosexuality, the idea of an abnormal, unhealthy experience, overstepping the limits of the ordinary and the permitted, but by virtue of this very fact remunerative in secret joys and knowledge, the prerogative of rather ardent natures or natures free enough to venture beyond the licit and the known. . . . From this point of view conditioned precisely by social repression, he proceeded to a more classical, if one might be so bold, and less conventional view of the problem. The notions of happiness, of plenitude, of the validity of pleasure gained the upper hand; he ended up making his sensuality the mainspring of his *œuvre*. . . . We are so accustomed to viewing wisdom as a residue of passions spent that it is difficult for us to recognize it as the hardest and most condensed form of ardor, the bit of gold born of the fire, and not the ashes.[1]

For Yourcenar, the only obstacles to the affirmation of one's freedom, to pleasure, to inventing one's life were those that one imagined or created for oneself. She repeated this constantly, without ever wanting to explain why she herself had imposed no small obstacle to the exercise of her own freedom: Grace Frick. Part of the explanation is perhaps in what she wrote about Cavafy: "he ended up making his sensuality the mainspring of his *œuvre*."

The work on Cavafy—which would be revised and supplemented with the translations of some unpublished poems twenty years later—came out at the end of the first half of 1958, at Gallimard. For the moment, Yourcenar and Frick would take a boat home, from Genoa. While they were returning to Petite Plaisance (they landed on 10 June in the port of Halifax, Nova Scotia), France became involved in events that would lead to the Algerian War, which at that time no one wished to refer to as anything more than "the events in Algeria." General de Gaulle was dragged out of retirement in Colombey-les-Deux-Eglises and, on 1 June, the National Assembly invested him, as he had requested, with "full powers." The Left was roused by this "power play." Among the very first opponents to this seizure of power there was a deputy, already a former cabinet minister and one destined for a more brilliant future: François Mitterrand. Yourcenar, who as yet did not know him, was not far from sharing his point of view: "I join you in your wishes for the recovery of France," she wrote to Natalie Barney, "but I very much fear that the present solution will not magically cure all our ills (does dictatorship ever do so?). It seems to me that it is from every Frenchman that the salvation of France will come—and not from a savior, even if that savior is very genuinely a great man—and even then only at the cost of a stern self-criticism of which no signs can yet be seen."[2]

But Yourcenar, whose pessimism regarding the state of the world was growing progressively worse, wanted first of all to abandon herself, in that month of June 1958, to the summer that was beginning. "Your letter reached me the day before yesterday," she wrote to Barney on Saint John's Day, which for me is still the most beautiful and magical day of the year (the mystery of the beginning of summer: every year, on 24 June, I celebrate within myself a holiday as solemn as Christmas or Easter, but much more secret)."[3] She did not yet know that Frick would be the source of an ordeal, to be shared, that would constrain her to change her way of life. Neither did she know that what she would go through as a result, sometimes not without unjust exasperation, was an imposed acceleration of her own aging.

On 24 July, when Frick came out of the hospital where she had just spent several weeks following an operation, she made no comment in her daybook. She is as verbose about Yourcenar's headaches and other trifling signs of fatigue as she is laconic on the subject of herself. Nonetheless, she had just been subjected to the removal of a breast, and her doctors had prescribed radiation treatments in an attempt to contain the progression of the cancer. She would fight this illness without respite for twenty-one years, amid a succession of remissions and relapses, then an unremitting decline over the course of the seventies, until her death in 1979. Frick's determination and the manner in which she faced up to her illness, in an era when the word cancer was, more than today, synonymous with imminent death, compel respect. And Yourcenar was not one to abandon herself to public whining about life and its reverses. The traces of this shock, in the daybooks as well as in the correspondence, have a great dignity. One can observe, however, in photographs, that this was a time when Yourcenar's face grew

somber, losing its look of mischievous irony as well as the sensual, passionate mouth that would return in her old age, with "a certain acceptance of
life as it comes, and a way of taking people as they are," as she used to like
to say.

The end of the year 1958 was rather gray, marked no doubt by a diffuse
fear that neither Yourcenar nor Frick wished to voice. Yourcenar was working on *A Coin in Nine Hands*. That rewriting—"this is the only one of my
books that has really been rewritten," she was in the habit of saying—would
remain "one of [her] great experiences as a writer. I learned a tremendous
amount and (this is even more important) I unlearned a tremendous
amount."[4] Though the novel's set of themes, its characters, and the organization of the chapters were not modified, this second version underwent
some considerable changes with respect to the novel of 1934. Certain expressions deemed infelicitous were carefully eliminated, such as this sentence of Sandro's to his wife Marcella: "You still have ten years ahead of
you before the final thickening"; or else, about Mother Dida who sold
flowers: "She had been false like the root that writhes underground, hard
like water, hot like the sex of flowers." In the second *A Coin in Nine Hands*,
the political subject mater—an assassination attempt in the fascist Rome of
1933—superseded the ensemble of themes. The character of the protagonists and their intentions were more fully developed, the space within which
they evolve was better defined, and the setting was better described. Yourcenar explained herself with respect to the extent of this revision in her
afterword.

> In some places, I tried to enlarge the role of realism; elsewhere, that of
> poetry—in the long run, these are, or should be, the same thing. . . . I had
> already used the stylistic devices of direct and indirect narration, dramatic
> dialogue, and sometimes even lyrical passages resembling arias; I added now,
> on rare occasions, the device of interior monologue—not, as almost always
> in contemporary novels, to show a mind-mirror passively reflecting the flood
> of images and impressions flowing past, but reduced here to the basic ele-
> ments of personage, or almost to the simple alternation of yes and no.[5]

And she concludes: "The opportunity of expressing ideas and emotions
that were still mine, with improved craftsmanship and through the insights
gleaned from a longer human experience, seemed to me too precious not
to be accepted with joy and humility."[6]

The press would give more coverage to the fifth edition of *A Coin in
Nine Hands*, which appeared at Gallimard in 1971, than to the profoundly
reworked version of 1959. Nevertheless, on 19 August, in the weekly publi-

cation *Arts,* there appeared a long article by Guy Dupré. While laudably evoking Yourcenar's literary career, Dupré proved to be particularly critical of this new version of the 1934 novel:

> This is the first novel of Marguerite Yourcenar's we have read in which the reign of the voice is sacrificed to a novelistic arbitrariness of times gone by. . . . Like every tapestrywork, this one turns into allegory. Added to this is a subtle deterioration of the relations between the author and her characters—in which strings are substituted for ties—which makes of this novel published in 1934 a stylistic exercise heralding *L'Ere du soupçon* (*The Age of Suspicion*). . . . *A Coin in Nine Hands* bears no resemblance to a novel of conviction; the political theme and that of individualism rebelling against the established order have a value that is merely somehow musical, on a par with the theme of illness or that of old age. The author plays with these themes in an abusively classical manner—sometimes giving the impression she is trying to please a panel of conservatory judges. . . . Perhaps in *A Coin in Nine Hands* the moralist's gift works to the disadvantage of the novelist by destroying the mirage; its classical stamp bestows an unpleasant authority upon the cliché. . . . Far from Paris, untempted by the lure of a legend that she could have taken it entirely upon herself to construct, perhaps she has suffered on account of her withdrawal and her discretion; in the process she has gained one of those brilliant reputations owed only to the exercise of talent. Let us dare to name the malediction peculiar to her, a more singular one than hatred of the other sex or the drama of a certain solitude: the need for perfection. It often pays; sometimes it betrays.[7]

Remarks such as these clearly did not delight the author of *A Coin in Nine Hands,* both because her work was judged so harshly and because of the public allusion to "hatred of the other sex." And Yourcenar would remember them, in the midst of the suit that was filed against Plon—the publisher for whom Dupré worked—when expressing her resentment, at some length, in a letter to her friend Natalie Barney: "A final word on the subject of Guy Dupré," she wrote to her at the time:

> [It was] in 1959, right after the appearance of one of my books that I'd rewritten (I don't have to add, with immense care and effort) on the theme of a work published in 1934 whose title had been bought back by Plon (though the firm never managed to see the difference between the rough version of 1934 and the work as it was finally developed and recomposed); so in 1959 Dupré published in *Arts,* I think, an extremely vile article whose tone might well be compared to that of a blackmail tabloid. Slipping on spit is a slight occupational hazard; still one has the right to feel a healthy mistrust when the spit comes from a man who started out by showering you with obsequious praise and who, it seems, holds an important position in the firm where

the book he is doing all he can to insult was published. You will no doubt tell me this is how things are in Paris: that's precisely why I don't live there.[8]

In his article, Dupré had taken note of the fact that, in its new edition, *A Coin in Nine Hands* was "stripped, one knows not why, of its dedication to Edmond Jaloux."[9] Yourcenar would offer an explanation of this retraction, in a letter to Jean Lambert whom she was thanking for having dedicated one of his short stories to her: "I myself very rarely dedicate my works," she confided,

> and the few names that had appeared in certain of my early books were removed when reprintings were done after I had reached maturity. The reasons for this abstention are complex. . . . A very important one to my eyes is nonetheless worthy of mention: it is the fact that there is rarely complete harmony between the personality of the one to whom one dedicates something and the work with which one pays him homage. I have grown very sensitive to this kind of dissonance.
>
> Thus had I dedicated the original version of *A Coin in Nine Hands* to Jaloux, a very dear friend. Even leaving aside the inferiority of this first draft, it was absurd to offer *A Coin in Nine Hands* to a man who refused as completely as Jaloux did to understand the thought of the Left or to accord to it a place in the wider scheme of things.[10]

Frick, throughout this time, was keeping quiet, noting few events in her calendar. According to her friends, she valiantly overcame the blow that had been dealt her, firmly determined to fight and not to let the illness get in the way of her life—or rather their life. For Frick was obsessed by one idea: that Yourcenar should be recognized and celebrated, in France, as one of the very great writers of this century. For this, Yourcenar needed her. She needed to be freed from material concerns, and she needed to be protected from intruders and herself, from her pessimism, her fits of weariness. Frick was persuaded that she alone was in a position to carry all this out— and she may not have been mistaken. She could not falter. And she would not falter. She would only miss out on the crowning of her achievement: she died four months before Yourcenar's election to the Académie Française.

From now on, in the daybooks (where one would previously find, sometimes with a touch of humor, reports of Yourcenar's maladies), there would alternate regular mentions of the care received by Frick and the illnesses— real ones mixed from now on with imaginary ones—of Yourcenar. Observing daily life at Petite Plaisance at the end of the fifties and during the sixties, particularly at the time when *The Abyss* was being written, one gains a better understanding of the underlying meaning—once the period of passionate love had passed—of the "arrangement" between Yourcenar and Frick. One can also better appreciate the confinement consented to by Yourcenar in order to concentrate on her occupation as a writer without giving way to her "demons": her alternating passions and the depressions that ensued, romantic dissipation, a taste for nomadism pushed to the point of temptation to roam, a taste for turning in upon oneself pushed nearly to the point of silence and ineffectiveness. As with Louis Aragon and his wife Elsa (provided the comparison remains restricted to the question of lifestyle, Yourcenar's *œuvre* never having claimed to rival the extent or the power of Aragon's), Yourcenar agreed—thus chose—to "marry," to spend her life with someone whose mission it was to keep her under "control"—and to encourage her. She could have made this line that Aragon dedicated to Elsa her own: "You whose arms found a way to block the dreadful path to my dementia." Frick knew exactly what she wanted, and her energy never seemed to falter. Subtle, cultivated, with a passion for literature, she knew the measure of the creator's incalculable good fortune, however much the latter might suffer. And she would not have tolerated watching the woman she loved give way to weakness or squander her efforts. Yourcenar knew all this and acknowledged it, as some of her dedications to Frick reveal: in the no. 2 limited edition of the reworked *A Coin in Nine Hands* she wrote: "To G.F., whose critical judgment has never failed me and who has frequently lent me her courage. M.Y. Mount Desert Island 1959"; and in another copy of *A Coin in Nine Hands,* in the Club des éditeurs edition, which came out the same year: "To G. without whom I would often have lost heart. M. 27 July 1959."

Of course Frick was too intelligent not to be aware that Yourcenar had written before she came along, could write without her, and even despite her, as was the case during the critical phase of Frick's illness. A writer always finds a way to escape from everyone and everything in order to accomplish what is indispensable for him or her, that which justifies living. But Yourcenar also knew that, in the perilous gesture that leads one to leave behind a trace of oneself believing that it is and will be useful, the creator needs witnesses, intimates who have faith in him or her, who are the first to attest to the absolute necessity of the creator's work. Yourcenar having severed her ties to the literary milieu that, during the thirties, provided that certitude for her, Frick had become her unique, and constant, witness. What is more, she had long since come to understand that in relieving the other of every concern of daily life, of every "administrative" detail, one renders the other dependent, however domineering she may be. It was in this fragile combination of love, of calculated self-interest (on both parts), of devotion (on Frick's part), and of a certain submission (on Yourcenar's) that their couple became indestructible. From now on, it could only be dismantled by death.

After Frick died, Yourcenar would return to the penchants of her youth, taking one trip after another. She put off writing the last volume of her family trilogy, *Quoi? L'Eternité,* so long that she left it unfinished. In returning thus to life as it had been before Frick, she was almost trying, in a manner sometimes shocking for anyone observing her or hearing certain caustic remarks that she let slip, to nullify the life they had shared. It was as if she was taking her revenge, with a kind of fury, for their last years of life spent together.

But in 1959, the discovery of Frick's cancer—due to her strength of character—had not yet really disrupted their existence. One merely has the sense, from the daybooks (there were two of them that year), of a certain abstention on Frick's part, a sort of conservation of energy. She who as a rule had been so "talkative" no longer gave details concerning daily life, as if she were mobilizing strength in view of something essential—"holding on" and letting no one glimpse the threats that blocked her future. She noted, rather, "signs of life," concisely, but with an acute awareness of a permanence accruing to beings and to things that, for herself, would be from now on of limited duration: the birds, which she watched and delighted in, the lilacs in bloom, the first of June.

Bereft of any plans to travel, Yourcenar gave herself over, in addition to her literary work, to her correspondence. For her friends, she intermixed news of Frick's health and more general reflections on literature—"how is it that our French wisdom falls so often somewhat short, that it's even, I daresay, somewhat lifeless, or rather that it dwells too comfortably within itself? Even if you compare Montaigne to Marcus Aurelius, it seems that with us the safety catch is always flicked on a bit too quickly"—and on the state of the world and of "the same poor, sometimes touching, and always discouraging humanity."[11]

Though Yourcenar had had for years, and especially since the success of *Memoirs of Hadrian,* alongside her strictly literary work, an intense epistolary activity, meticulously itemized by Frick, the latter could not have been unaware that all this could never justify, in the eyes of her companion, staying put for an extended period of time. (We don't know, moreover, who was responsible for that epistolary cataloguing: it is not certain that it was Yourcenar, who had, in spurts at least, a clear-cut taste for destruction.)

Frick knew that Yourcenar still wished just as much as ever to travel, and inasmuch as she herself did not want to give in to her illness, she planned a new departure for Europe that would take place on 12 December 1959 in New York aboard the SS *Olympia Greek Line*. Yourcenar was ill aboard ship and also after arriving in Lisbon, where she spent the end of the year and the beginning of 1960. After a short trip to Spain, from 29 January until 3 February, she came back to Portugal and gave a lecture on 12 February in Lisbon on "the responsibilities of the novelist." Between excursions, notably to Coimbra and Oporto, she worked on two of the essays that would become part of the collection *Sous bénéfice d'inventaire* (*The Dark Brain of Piranesi*): "*Les Tragiques* d'Agrippa d'Aubigné" ("Agrippa d'Aubigné and *Les Tragiques*"), which she would finish in Cintra in March, and "Le Cerveau noir de Piranèse" ("The Dark Brain of Piranesi"), which she would not complete until the following year at Petite Plaisance. In Oporto she met the poet Eugénio de Andrade, who retained a vivid memory of that "woman with such an extraordinary presence." "At that time, she had not yet become the sizable woman she later would be, who resembled a Greek goddess, not at all; she wasn't thin; but she was imposing," he remembers.

> She was traveling with an American friend. We went to a restaurant. It was a very official dinner, with certain notables and important personalities. Her friend Grace was across from me, with a very cute little dog, and Marguerite was at the other end of the table. Grace was very nice. Older than Marguerite; much older. She spoke French very well. While I was conversing with her, Marguerite Yourcenar really broke the rules of etiquette. She said to her neighbor, "Excuse me, sir, I'm going to change places with my friend, because I want to talk with Monsieur Andrade." She told me she was very interested in a certain legend of an unhappy love affair, that of Prince Don Pedro and Ines de Castro, whom King Alfonso had had assassinated for political reasons. It was on the basis of that legend that Montherlant wrote *La Reine morte* (*Queen after Death*). As we were speaking, I said to myself: "It's funny, this woman, like nearly everyone else for that matter, even in Portugal, doesn't know that that man who had such a violent passion for a woman also liked boys." And since I had seen in *Memoirs of Hadrian* that this was something that interested her a great deal, I told her so. She was absolutely . . . speechless. She was fascinated. That conversation, which was a bit on the taboo side, was very frank. We continued, in a somewhat more intimate mode. We left the dinner, I accompanied her back to her hotel, and we stayed in the bar talking until two o'clock in the morning. And the next day, at nine o'clock, we were together again, to walk around Oporto, and we spent the entire day with one another, until her departure.[12]

It was also during this trip to Portugal that Yourcenar met Alain Oulman, the heir to Editions Calmann-Lévy, with whom she would maintain ties. Yourcenar also meet Oulman's mother whose sense of hospitality and taste for life she greatly appreciated, as she confided on numerous occasions in various letters to friends. Several years afterward, she would evoke that meeting for Jeanne Carayon, her proofreader become also a friend, and the impression that her stay in Portugal had made on her:

> I rather regret that an "attachment" prevented you from experiencing Portugal before the war. At that time it must have been even more beautiful than when I saw and loved it in the sixties. . . . I know of no country, except perhaps for certain places in England, where poetry is more alive and breathing in the merest patch of countryside, the merest wood, endowed with the infinite sweetness of the Portuguese poets of the Middle Ages. . . . Even right near Lisbon, on the hillsides of Cintra, the ancient hermitages carved into the rock, among the immense cork-oaks, leave one with a unique impression. William Beckford, a good observer, may well tell us that the hermits of the eighteenth century were by then nothing more than merry rascals, there still remains a strange green twilight, and an ineffable reflection of a pre-Christian, perhaps Celtic, world that has vanished . . .
>
> Did you know that living in Lisbon, in a beautiful eighteenth-century house, is an elderly lady, Madame Oulman, who was the daughter of one of the Calmann-Lévys (but which one?) from the great era of that publishing house, and who still recalls the celebrities grouped around the family table? . Her son, Alain Oulman, runs the firm today, I am told, at least in part. He is a great connoisseur of Spanish and Portuguese music.[13]

It was probably during this trip that she discovered Pessoa's poems, a selection of which had appeared in a slim Portuguese volume, well before he became known in France. His poetry struck her as "extraordinary," as she would write to her friend the writer Jacques Masui, who at that time was in charge of the collection "Documents spirituels" at Librairie Fayard.[14]

During the last week of March, Yourcenar and Frick were in Madrid, where they undertook a systematic visit of the Prado. They spent several hours a day there for a week. Yourcenar had always been particularly interested in painting and in all forms of graphic art. She herself drew very well, even though she only rarely put this talent to use. Of music, on the other hand, she had almost no knowledge. She listened assiduously to what Frick played on the piano or wanted her to hear. She could speak, not without subtlety, of the kinds of music with which she was familiar, but this was more an effect of her intelligence and sensitivity than of any specialized knowledge or true passion. She was not very sensitive to the nuances of musical interpretation: when she selected a piece, for a radio or television program, it was "never in its finest version," the specialists say. Curiously, she did not care for soprano voices. Sometimes she would receive records from friends that they thought she might like. One of her friends sent her a version of Bellini's *Norma.* He received a comment from her that must have left him in a quandary: "Despite the excellence of the record, my unbearable physical antipathy for soprano voices remains total."[15] Nonetheless, she went to concerts and the opera regularly with Frick. (They had just attended, on 8 January of that year, 1960, in Lisbon, a performance of Wagner's *Lohengrin.*)

In the realm of the plastic arts, on the other hand, her judgments were always more fully worked out, her tastes on a much sounder footing, and her enjoyment obvious. She had quite a marked taste for the Dutch and Flemish schools. She felt a certain affinity with these artistic styles to which she often referred, as in a letter to her friend Niko Calas, on the subject of Hieronymus Bosch: "I have the impression somehow of being linked to him; and especially perhaps to Breughel, by my Flemish connections, and by a certain peculiar sensitivity that only found its full expression between the North Sea and the Meuse over the course of the sixteenth century, of which there still remain some traces today (I have in mind, for example, the Temptation of Saint Anthony side of Rimbaud's *œuvre*). And above all, more and more, I see in these two painters (without wishing to line them up with one another more than is warranted) a disturbing sort of prefiguration of the world around us, a radioscopy of the human world such as we can no longer fail to recognize it nor suffer because of it."[16] Several years later, she would also take an interest in the Belgian Symbolists and Surrealists. "I have in fact noted in myself certain affinities with some of those painters," she would comment for the benefit of one of her correspondents, "perhaps especially with Ensor, or else with those aspects of Knopff and Deville that are not marked by a kind of fin-de-siècle hysteria. Does there really exist a 'sensibility of the Low Countries,' both Belgian and Dutch as well as French (the borders, all in all, being only very recent), a kind of visionary realism that I feel also dwells in me? It's possible, even though one would have a hard time, if such is the case, explaining Matisse, a man of the Nord whose temperament was so purely French."[17] Later still, solicited by the *Nouvel Observateur* for "Le Musée égoïste" [One's Private Museum], she would choose a canvas by Ruysdael, one of her father's favorite painters, evoking his parallels with Rembrandt: "Ruysdael's predilection for pollard or pruned trees and for the remains of buildings in ruin (the tower of Egmont Castle, which he often painted, resembles a dead tree trunk still standing straight up) makes one think of Rembrandt's predilection for sturdy and solemn old men. Something of the same feeling of strangeness, of the old Talmudic or cabalistic dream, which gathers sometimes in Rembrandt's interiors, also floats upon this *campo santo* of another people."[18]

Rembrandt's browns were a source of lasting emotion for her (about his painting titled *Two Negroes,* among the holdings of the Mauritshuis museum in The Hague, she wrote one of her last texts, which is reprinted in the posthumous collection of essays *En pèlerin et en étranger*.[19] To Nicolas Poussin, in whose work "all of French thought, all of the French sensibility . . . finds its pendants and its signs," she had devoted a short text in 1940, on the occasion of a Poussin exhibit in New York. It had gone unpublished until its happy inclusion in *En pèlerin et en étranger*. "As does Walt Whitman's 'The Sleepers,' as does 'La Bénédiction du soir' [Evening Benediction] in Victor Hugo's *Contemplations (Contemplations)*," she wrote in concluding, "this crepuscular masterpiece [*Echo and Narcissus* by Poussin], which puts our flat definitions of classical and romantic to shame, situates itself on the edge of the ineffable: between sleep and dream, between life and death, between the falling day and the wakening night. All that afterward remains is to explore the night itself."[20] As for her fascination with Velázquez' *Las Meninas (Maids of Honor)*, which she shared with numerous contemporary creators, from Michel Foucault to Picasso of course (who painted a series whose interpretation has yet to be exhausted), it was something that never left Yourcenar.[21] Surely it is true that "the place of the artist in the painting," in all its symbolic ramifications, was a question with which she had played too many tricks for it' not to have been constantly on her mind.

FROM MADRID, Frick and Yourcenar went to Seville for the processions of the *Semana Santa* (Holy Week). "It was the first time that I'd seen, in Seville, the *Semana Santa* ceremonies," she wrote to a friend. "It's an extraordinary bit of the past winding its way along the tortuous Sierpes; a strange superimposition of the *Mater Dolorosa* or of Christ breathing his last upon the street lamps and neon signs of our age. I said to myself that, for once, we were seeing externalized and exalted right there in the street the tragic reality that everything in our time conspires to keep hidden from us: pain, solitude, death, sacrifice, the condemnation of the Just."[22] Toledo, Compostela, and Segovia made "an admirable impression" on her, in spite of the brief stays she made in each of these cities. But she was particularly moved by her visit to the spot on the hills of Granada where Federico Garcìa Lorca "fell."[23] She wrote to Isabelle, the poet's sister, the day before she set sail for the United States:

> What I especially would like to write to you is that in leaving the place that had been pointed out to us (and these reflections are valid even if it was only approximately accurate), I turned back around to look at that bare

mountain, that arid soil, those few young pine trees vigorously growing in the solitude, those great perpendicular folds of the ravine through which the torrents of prehistory must in the past have flowed, the Sierra Nevadas unfurled on the horizon in all their majesty, and I said to myself that such a place puts the marble and granite rubbish of our cemeteries to shame, and that one envies your brother for beginning his death in this landscape of eternity. Please understand that in making these remarks I am not striving to diminish the horror of that premature death, nor the particular anguish that consists (or that at least would consist for me) of trying to reconstruct the scene that took place here at one instant in time, and about which we shall never know all of the details. But it is certain that one could not imagine for a poet a more beautiful grave.[24]

The rest of the year 1960 was spent at Petite Plaisance: months devoted to work, barely interrupted by occasional visits from friends—among them Charles Orengo at the end of May—and by the usual correspondence— including an exchange that, unexpectedly, had begun with François Augiéras. As he had in the case of Gide and several other French novelists, this singular young man, a painter and a writer, had sent to Yourcenar *Le Vieillard et l'enfant* [The Old Man and the Child], an autobiographical text— lyrically fictionalized—from 1950, and revised several times under the pseudonym of Abdallah Chaamba. In fact it was the 1953 version, published by Editions de Minuit, that Augiéras sent to Yourcenar. He was twenty-seven years old at the time.

She had answered him for the first time on 16 May 1953. She told him of her interest in what she had read, but, she added, "what disturbs me more (even though I was deeply touched by certain passages) is the tone of excitement and unhealthy pride that reigns in your book. Having discovered, in a bed or elsewhere, one of the rhythms of the world is in itself a very rare *joy* but one that's good for nothing if you are not capable of rediscovering that same rhythm each day and in all things and of devoting to that pursuit all the humility and courage you have."[25]

In a second letter to Augiéras, the same year, she remains as attentive to him as before but puts him on his guard against standing still, against the risk of becoming "a bird that always emits the same cry."[26] He spoke to her at length, she says (Augiéras's letter has not been found), about the prostitution in which he was engaging. Anxious to prevent him from seeing this as an exceptional experience, no doubt in order to turn him away from it, she pointed out that "as soon as one consents to ply any trade, it is always a form of prostitution," against which Frick revolted, in the margin of the copy of the letter, with a burst of exclamation points.

After a few years' interruption, at least in the documents such as they have made their way to us, we find several letters to, as well as from, Augiéras between 1960 and 1964, at which date the correspondence seems to have come to a close, on Yourcenar's initiative. When she responded to receiving a reworked version of Augiéras's book *Le Vieillard et l'enfant*, it was with that singular mixture of clarity and hardness she reserved for those whom she bore a real interest:

> I found in that new, revised edition a gift, on which I had already congratulated you, for painting objects and landscapes with a kind of clear intensity, and for portraying with convincing acuity a maniacal, senile—and very particular—character who is nonetheless ordinary enough to seem human. It is not for me, who am fond of revising and often recasting certain of my books, in order to improve or enrich them if I can, to blame you for offering a new version of your work, which is tighter, it seems, than the previous ones, and closer to being quite simply a poem.
>
> One forgives anything of poets, even the rather naive arrogance of your preface (but if these are your thoughts, it is better to express them); still, your perpetual confinement, not only within the same theme, but, more seriously, within a single experience, ends up giving the impression of claustrophobia in the open air. It is less for your work than for you that one wishes you would undertake something else as well, and try to be yourself in another way.[27]

The manner in which Augiéras replied says a great deal about the ambiguity of their exchanges:

> It would have been unfortunate if we had not been in touch with one another, if there had not been a more or less sustained correspondence between us, slightly hesitant though it may be, on account of an unfailing mutual incomprehension, like a dialogue of the deaf. . . .
>
> Someone other than you would have trembled with joy at the discovery of a "barbaric" kind of writing, slowly, tragically unearthed on the borders of the empire. . . . Thus, when you acknowledge my "gift for painting objects and landscapes with a kind of clear intensity," I can only be saddened by your blindness; you have always had a way of minimizing my efforts that distresses me.[28]

And despite the response she issued to him after receiving *L'Apprenti sorcier* [Sorcerer's Apprentice], a provocative one this time—"There is still, deep down, an impasse, and it seems that it is inside that impasse that you have elected to live"[29]—Augiéras was insistent: "Direct contact between us would dispel all our misunderstandings at once. . . . I would be very happy to have your opinions, your advice. But above all I would like to see you, to talk with you."[30]

More than for the literary debate, this example is a useful one for revealing the strange relationships that Yourcenar would establish with young writers, made up at once, for them, of fascination and exasperation in the face of the peremptory character of her judgments.

THERE WERE more letters: a few days after her return from Spain, Yourcenar received an autobiographical collection, *Souvenirs indiscrets* [Indiscreet Memories], from her friend Natalie Barney, and she communicated her initial reflections at once: "Without having read it all yet, I already have the impression that you have carried the day and set your legend straight, without destroying it in the process. In these indiscreet memories—which hardly are, deep down—I admired the tact, the light touch, which is nonetheless firm, the imperceptible humor, and even your perspicacity with regard to the beings whom you loved. One is especially grateful that you have remained so jauntily yourself, without ever letting the vogues that have successively arisen between 1900 and our time rub their colors off on you; neither the philosophy of Bergson thinned down for persons of the world, nor neo-Thomistic conversion, nor Freudianism, nor psychological or sociological jargon, nor one-size-fits-all existentialism (I shall skip over some, and some of the worst ones): and what results is that these almost light-hearted remembrances of more than half a century ago are the least old-fashioned ones of all.

"My thoroughly personal testimony perhaps has all the more weight in that, if truth be told, the 'Belle Epoque' holds little charm for me."[31]

Indeed it was a thoroughly personal testimony, and less for the way she inveighs against "fashions" than for the homage paid to someone who had found a way to "set [her] legend straight, without destroying it in the process."

In the correspondence from that time, one notes a rather dry letter to Jean Ballard, a blunt refusal, almost a final split, with a man upon whom for a long time, since before the war, she had bestowed if not friendship at least cordiality: Ballard had been the first, we should recall, in December 1951, to review *Memoirs of Hadrian* at length and with subtlety, in *Cahiers du Sud.* If Yourcenar's remarks are neither unjust nor unfounded, they nonetheless attest to an unmistakable rigidification, almost a harshness, of which numerous signs would come to light during the sixties:

> Your letter dated in the month of August contained a request for a "good text." Dare I say that even if I had a text available, which is not the case at

present, I would hesitate to send it to you, because the review has, very steadfastly, and for nearly eight years now, passed my works over in silence, despite the fact that I have contributed to it more than once during that time. I can understand that you might not have announced the reissue of *Alexis* (1953), nor that of *Coup de grâce* (1953), or *Fires* (1957), although others did so; I find more surprising that neither the poems published in 1957, *The Alms of Alcippe,* nor the *Présentation critique de Constantin Cavafy,* in 1958, attracted the attention of a review concerning itself particularly with poetry, and with what is rightly or wrongly called Mediterranean thought. This silence continued when *A Coin in Nine Hands* came out last year, despite a publisher's release and a preface indicating that the novel, rewritten as is customary for me on the basis of an old version, was at once the newest and one of the most thoughtful of my books. I am not in the habit of soliciting articles in reviews, even friendly ones, and nothing surprises me less as a rule than silence, but in the case of *Cahiers du Sud,* it is impossible for me not to see in that abstention a proof of meager interest in my work in general, perfectly legitimate in itself, but hardly apt to encourage me to publish in the review.[32]

As for her literary activity, Yourcenar continued to work on her Piranesi essay, modified the preface of *Alexis,* for a new edition to be published by Plon, and conceived a strange project, which would never see the light of day: to compose a novel on the basis of certain characters from *A Coin in Nine Hands,* whom writer and reader would link up with again in 1945 and whose existence would be followed until the end of the fifties, no longer in Italy, but primarily in Paris and Germany. The idea, which was not necessarily a good one, is, however, yet another proof of the astonishing, autarchical conduct of Yourcenar, who always sought to inflect, prolong, or amplify what had already been partially accomplished, rather than forging ahead, effacing all traces of her passage, or "leaping into the void" in order to invent something totally new. Needless to say, she was often asked why she had rewritten most of her books. She would invariably answer that she saw rewriting as a means of redoing what had been ill-conceived, or of setting things right in those instances where she had fallen short: "I have something of a horror of things that are poorly expressed. One lapses into emotions one cannot authenticate. . . . I do, in fact, abandon myself with great humility to my characters, to that slow process of creation into which the author puts something of himself and a great many other things. In Tibet, every monk is advised to create the image of his guardian saint piece by piece. Then he is told: 'Go back into the world and see if he follows you. If he does, destroy him, for it's you who have constructed him.'"[33] "Every time the problem of rewriting comes up—for me such an important one—

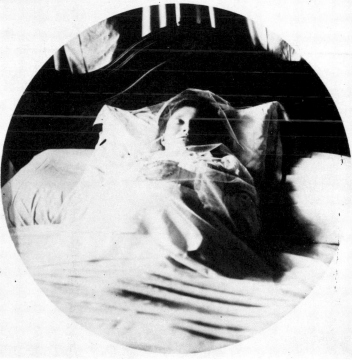

1. Marguerite, several
months old.

1

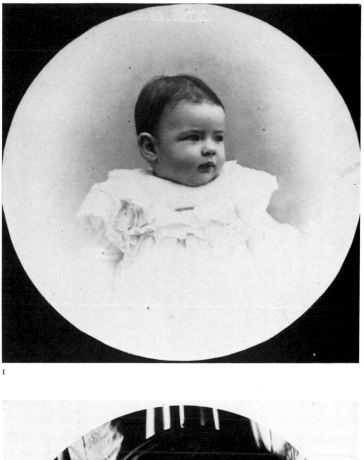

2. Fernande on her deathbed.

2

3.

4

5

3. Marguerite at Scheveningen in 1905 with Egon de Vietinghoff, having her hand kissed for the first time.

4. Circa 1906: "I admire the loyalty of that good, if somewhat fierce, little woman to her clown."

5. Jeanne de Vietinghoff: "I would no doubt be very different from what I am, if Jeanne, from a distance, had not molded me."

6. Michel René de Crayencour, Marguerite's father.

7

8

9

10

7. Handwritten sonnet for Camille
Debocq, Christmas 1915.

8. Marguerite about age thirteen:
"Though my face betrays my awkward
age, the eyes are determined and brave."

9. Mont-Noir. Marguerite, about age
seven, with her governess Barbara.

10. In the south of France, around 1919.

11. The only existing photograph of
Marguerite Yourcenar in glasses. She
would say somewhat coquettishly, "I
have always been nearsighted, but I
wouldn't care to wear glasses."

11

Recevez avec mes remerciements réitérés
l'expression de mes sentiments très
distingués.

Marguerite de Crayencour

P.-S. J'ai pris comme pseudonyme
Marg Yourcenar, qui est, comme
vous le voyez, l'anagramme de
mon vrai nom. —

Villa Loretta
Boulevard d'Italie
Monte – Carlo

— Je crois qu'il est d'usage de
payer la moitié des prix
d'avance — Pour faire un chiffre
rond, je vous envoie un chèque
de sept mille francs à valoir —

12. Letter sent to Editions Perrin on
4 October 1920: The game played by
father and daughter was pushed to the
point of mixing up their signatures.

13

13. André Embiricos.

14. André Fraigneau. "Two men who
[were] dear to me."

14

15

15. Marguerite around 1936.

16

16. Grace about the same time.

17

17. In Greece. From left to right:
Nelly Liambey, Marguerite, Lucy
Kyriakos's sister, and Lucy.

18. Lucy and Marguerite in
Austria, early 1939.

19. Marguerite in Bordeaux,
October 1939, just before her
departure for the United States.

18

20

21

20. Marguerite and . . .

21. . . . Grace, at the window of
their room in Hartford.

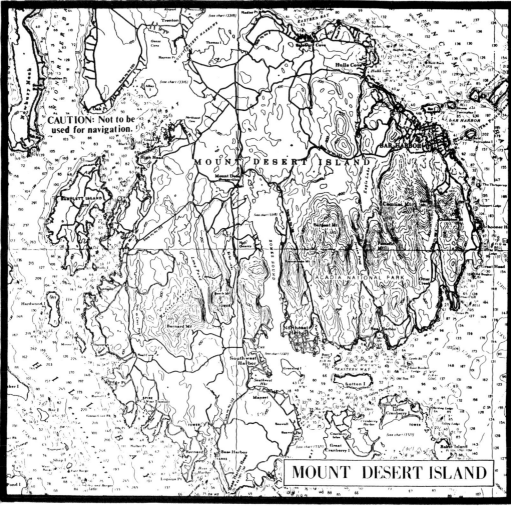

2. Map of Mount Desert Island.

23. In Somesville, their first house on Mount Desert Island.

24. One summer on the island.

23

24

25

26

25. Marguerite: "Grace and I at the harbor as we were setting off to sell our bread at the island [Little Cranberry] fair. We both have on blue cotton peasant blouses over thick pullovers." Grace: "Correction! We *gave* our bread away at the fair (and at four or five other local fairs). We got ourselves a handful of customers this way who bought bread from us all summer! It was hard, but fun."

26. Grace: "We both liked these photographs very much. Marguerite, because she looks slimmer than she really is, and I, because I look a bit less thin than I am! But Marguerite did reduce on doctor's orders."

27

28

29

27. Petite Plaisance in winter, seen from the backyard.

28. Petite Plaisance in summer.

29. Marguerite at the time of *Hadrian.*

30. Marguerite Yourcenar and Grace Frick's ex-libris, designed by Elie Grekoff.

30

J'ai cru longTemps avoir peu de souvenirs
d'enfance; j'entends par là ceux d'avant la septième
année. Mais je me Trompais: j'imagine plutôt ne leur
avoir guère jusqu'ici laissé l'occasion de remonter
jusqu'à moi. En réexaminant mes dernières années
au Mont-Noir, certains au moins redeviennent peu à
peu visibles, comme le font les objets d'une chambre
aux volets clos dans laquelle on ne s'est pas aventuré depuis
longTemps.

Je revois surtout des plantes et des bêtes, plus
secondairement des jouets, des jeux et des rites ayant
cours autour de moi, plus vaguement et comme à
l'arrière-plan des personnes. Je grimpe à Travers les
hautes herbes la pente abrupte qui mène à la Terrasse
du Mont-Noir. On n'a pas encore fauché. Des bluets,
des coquelicots, des marguerites y foisonnent, rappelant
à mes bonnes le chapeau Tricolore, ce qui me déplait,
car je voudrais que mes fleurs soient seulement des
fleurs. Nous ignorions, bien entendu, que cinq ou six
ans plus Tard, ces "pavots des monts de Flandre"
allaient se parer d'une gloire funèbre, pavots en
vérité, sacrés au sommeil de quelques milliers
de jeunes anglais tués sur cette Terre, et dont
des reproductions en papier de soie écarlate sont
encore vendues de notre Temps pour certaines
31   œuvres de charité anglo-saxonne. La pente de

32

33

34

31. Manuscript page of *Quoi?*
L'Eternité.

32. Marguerite with Hortense
Flexner, whose poems she
translated into French.

33. Grace, a good rider, shares
her passion with Marguerite.

34. Marguerite Yourcenar, in her
mature years as a writer, seated
in front of her own bust.

35. She never stopped thinking.

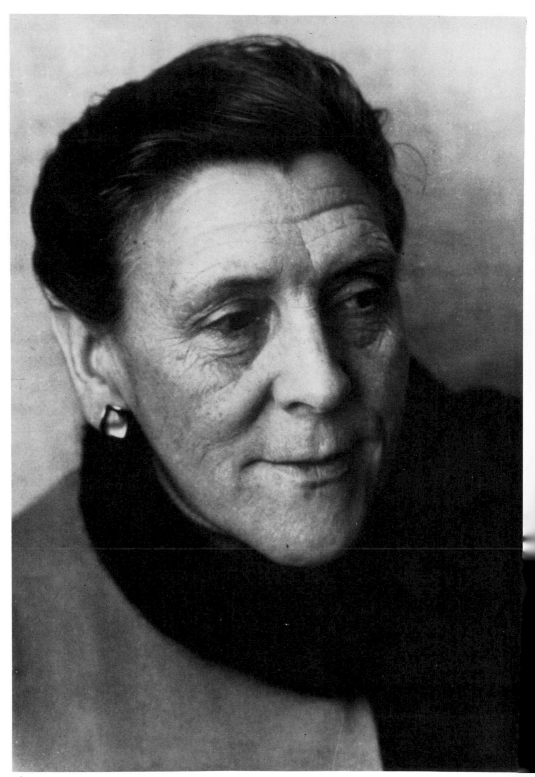

37

36. 1971: "The last good photograph of Grace."

37. 1980: Returning to her childhood: Marguerite in Saint-Jans-Cappel outside the wall surrounding Mont-Noir.

38. With Jerry Wilson and Marion Williams.

38

39

40

39. Petite Plaisance: Marguerite
Yourcenar at her desk.

40. In the living room at Petite
Plaisance.

41

42

43

41. Marguerite Yourcenar about to enter the Académie Française.

42. The new Academician as depicted by Wiaz.

43. 1984: In Kenya with her nurse Monicah; Marguerite's first outing after the accident in Nairobi.

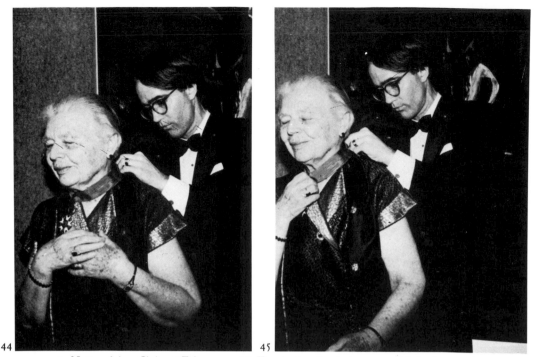

44 45

44, 45, 46. National Arts Club, 26 February 1986: The tired smile gives way to a kind of renewed energy, to a certain satisfaction with being there, with being honored and recognized, in a word, with single-handedly triumphing over herself.

46 47

47. With Walter Kaiser.

48

48. At the ocean near her home on Mount Desert Island.

49. Well before her death Marguerite Yourcenar had seen to it that her gravestone, similar to Grace's, was in place. It bears the French text of a line spoken by Zeno in *The Abyss:* "May it please the One who perchance is to expand the human heart to life's full measure."

49

50

50. 1987, her last summer: "I began to discern the profile of my death."

I am tempted to cite yet again the Irish poet Yeats's admirable phrase: 'It is myself that I correct in correcting my work.' This phrase describes my own point of view completely," she said to Patrick de Rosbo.[34] "When a book seems to me to be as good as I can make it, I do not rewrite it, I am very careful not to touch it, unless it contains a serious error, if I've been mistaken about a date or something along those lines," she went on to explain in another interview. "Most writers go about it differently: they do another book on the same themes but with different characters. Having botched a novel set in Touraine, they plunge into writing another that is set in Provence more or less on the same subject, only Marie's name is Josephine. This is their way of rewriting. Since I am loyal to my characters, since they exist for me, I prefer to use them as the basis for rewriting a book. It is more or less the same as with love. One can ask oneself whether it is more useful to meet someone new every week or to deepen the relationships one has. I am for deepening the relationships one has."[35]

This reiterative gesture sometimes led her into unsuspected places. She certainly did not imagine, in setting out to recast her short story "D'après Dürer" in *La Mort conduit l'attelage*, that out of that revision, that process of refinement, an important novel would emerge: *The Abyss*. It was one that (along with the definitive version of "An Obscure Man" no doubt) would mean the most to her.

For the moment, *The Abyss*—which was commonly referred to by Frick, while it was being written, as "Zeno"—was still in its very early stages. Nineteen sixty-one, though it was a totally American and very studious year, saw no progress on the composition of "Zeno." Yourcenar wrote *Rendre à César* (*Render unto Caesar*), a theatrical adaptation of *A Coin in Nine Hands*, which was supposed to have been staged in Paris. She gave an account of the circumstances that led to the theatricalization of her novel in the preface of the play, written in 1970:

> In 1961, less than two years after the highly discreet publication of the definitive version of *A Coin in Nine Hands*, a theater director invited me to dramatize one of my books. This text, still hot off the burner, struck me as lending itself to such an attempt. . . . By the time I sent the finished play to the friendly director, as one might perhaps have been able to anticipate, he was devoid of both a company and funds. But no matter: it is to him that I owe the particular experience that consists of proceeding for a given subject from the novelistic form, in which an author grants his characters the prize of a monologue or dialogue only here and there, to a form in which the same characters occupy the entire stage and relegate the author, put back where he belongs, to the prompter's box.[36]

As for the subject of "Marguerite Yourcenar versus her contemporaries," the year 1961 began in a rather uncongenial manner: on 4 January she wrote to Jacques Kayaloff[37] informing him that she had returned, without a word, a book by Roger Vailland, *La Loi* (*The Law*), which he had sent to her.[38] She detested this novel, which, in her eyes, gave off a stench of rottenness, of mold: "no, not mold," she concluded, "rather an odor of bad breath."

Since Yourcenar had once again agreed to do some lectures, she and Frick would travel for two months, from 22 February to 22 April, in the southern states of Virginia, West Virginia, Kentucky, Louisiana, Tennessee, and Mississippi. They went down and then back up the Mississippi between Cincinnati and New Orleans. Everything was ready that year for a grand tour of Egypt, but they had to cancel it at the last minute, because of Grace's health—she would have to undergo another operation on 26 April. Yourcenar took advantage of this trip to the South to gather the materials that would be used for her translations of Negro spirituals, having decided to devote a book to this subject. Both women were fascinated by what was brewing in the South—the great battles of the black community during the sixties. They became more and more active in associations promoting civil rights, which interested them more than traditional political life. Nonetheless, they voted for Kennedy, sickened as they were by the sectarianism of the anti-Catholic campaign of which he was the victim. But it was the battle alongside the minorities, blacks in particular, that was a constant preoccupation for them both and for which they took a stand whenever necessary. On their island, where there were no blacks, except in the summer when wealthy families would come with their servants, rampant racism was not even challenged by the slightest form of protest: yet again, their commitment, and the visits of their black friends, would single them out.

During their trip through the South, Frick paid a visit, by herself as always, to her family in Kansas City. This seems to confirm accounts attesting that the reticence of Frick's family with regard to Yourcenar never waned.

In the summer of 1961, after a trip to Northampton, Massachusetts, to receive her doctorate *honoris causa* from Smith College, Yourcenar often saw Hortense King, who wrote poems under the name of Hortense Flexner, on the neighboring island of Sutton where she lived. Yourcenar subsequently translated a selection of Flexner's poems, which were published by Gallimard in 1969, accompanied by a "critical introduction."

Nineteen sixty-one was also, curiously, a "sporting" year: Yourcenar had, "rather late in life," as she would say, "developed a taste for horseback riding," and had agreed, in order to keep up with Frick who was a good horsewoman, to take riding lessons. Frick recovered well from her second operation: she went riding, she accepted the intrusions at Petite Plaisance— Gabriel Marcel was invited to spend the night there on 17 November. But also, and most valuably perhaps, there reappeared in her daybooks the superbly disjointed daily notations one could use to construct some of those marvelous "exquisite corpses"[39] dear to the Surrealists: from the dog's birthday—"Monsieur's Birthday party"—on 23 July, to "M.Y. and G. went to see the sunrise on Mount Cadillac and then went to buy a vacuum cleaner"—on 15 September, by way of "Visit to Sutton Island. Monsieur delighted"—on 14 July.

"Monsieur," in fact, broke one of his paws during April 1962, which took up an enormous amount of Frick's time. Yourcenar, meanwhile, was finishing up what would be *The Dark Brain of Piranesi,* a collection of essays scheduled for the end of the year.

During this same month of April, Yourcenar wrote to an archeologist friend asking her for information regarding the existence of a certain fresco in Syracuse, with a view, yet again, to rewriting her essay *Pindare:* "I am currently working on revising, or rather rewriting, a work I had the naiveté and audacity to undertake at the age of twenty or twenty-two on Pindar's poetry, which the French publisher, as well as the foreign publisher, wants to reissue. Since I clearly cannot let it be reissued as is, which is to say full of gaps that are only too obvious to me now, I am deeply involved in an enormous reconstruction job."[40] But, whether out of weariness, or out of clearheadedness, that "reconstruction" would never see the light of day.

AT THE BEGINNING of 1962, Yourcenar was saddened to learn that Alice Parker, one of her oldest friends in the country of which she had become a citizen, had passed away; and she sketched for the friend who conveyed to her this news a moving portrait of that witness of her first years in America:

> As it happens, Alice Parker was one of my first American friends. . . . It sometimes seems that, through her, I encountered the enlightened and rational world of the eighteenth century, with her generous optimism regarding human nature and at the same time her courageous lack of prejudices. Even in her religious faith, even in her contacts with the invisible and the unknown (contacts so essential for her), I see something of the turn of mind of the great Puritan mystics of that age she knew so well and with which she had such deep affinities, it seems to me. Through her one could touch the great America of old, which does not mean that she was not thoroughly and admirably concerned with contemporary problems. When I came back to the United States during the war, and as little by little events kept me here, she

was one of the very rare persons whom I implicitly knew one could turn to both for moral support and, if circumstances dictated, material support in times of danger.⁴¹

From the United States, where "little by little events [had] kept" her, according to a phrase about which one wonders how much can be attributed to discreet euphemism and how much—already—to denial, Yourcenar prepared herself to depart on a trip with many destinations: Iceland, Norway, Sweden, Finland, the Soviet Union—for only three days in Leningrad—Denmark, Germany, and the Netherlands. Frick and she left the United States on 11 June and disembarked on the seventeenth in Reykjavik. Yourcenar paid particular attention to the discovery of Iceland and her short visit to Leningrad, the rest being only on the order of happily revisiting places one enjoys. After returning to the United States, on 16 July, she wrote—in English—to one of her hosts in Iceland to thank him for his hospitality. She told him that she was in the process of reading, in a French translation, *The Grettis Saga,* and that her too-brief glimpse of Iceland was nonetheless helping her to better understand these ancient texts. "As for the short (3 days) visit to Russia, it was full of impressions rather unexpected— as [*sic*] least by us, who were trying to be completely open-minded and to ignore all anti-Russian propaganda. But the final, and also immediate, impression was that of dismay and of impatience at the eternal police-state."⁴²

These remarks herald a long letter that Yourcenar would send to her Italian translator, Lidia Storoni, at Christmastime in 1962: "That experience, which was such a brief one," she said about her three days in Leningrad,

> had an effect on me (and also on Grace) that I had not anticipated; all in all, as far as I'm concerned, it was one of immense discouragement. What had I hoped to find? I certainly had not expected to glimpse some Eldorado. But, reacting no doubt against America's stupid anticommunist propaganda, with its infantile clichés, no doubt I believed I would at least encounter a newer world, perhaps a more "vital" one, even if that world were hostile or foreign to us. What I found—from that moment at dawn on the first day when we caught sight of the Russian officials boarding the boat in the fog, until the sleepless night of the third day during which, for a long time and very close up, we went around the fortress of Kronstadt rising up from the sea, with its closed-down-church dome and with the ships of the Baltic fleet surrounding it—was quite simply the Russia of Custine, that eternal mixture of bureaucratic routine, suspiciousness of strangers, an already-Oriental nonchalance, and cautious mistrust; and that inert and almost suffocating sadness that so

often appears in Russian novels, which I did not expect to find there still . . . ; then there are the crowds come from the provinces, filing through the immense Hermitage Museum in their organized groups, looking vaguely at those works of art from centuries and countries situated so far away from them; and the peasant who, standing before a Christ painted by Rembrandt, looked as if he was praying; . . . and on the stairway of honor, done in a monumental Italian baroque style, but from an unfortunate period, that is, dating back to Alexander I rather than Catherine, beneath the feet of the crowds going up and down those marble steps (excuse the hideous pettiness of this detail, which neither proves nor signifies anything, but which became a kind of symbol for me, in spite of myself) was the humble and scandalous fragment of a feminine toiletry item having belonged to some traveler too tired to take notice of her loss, a scrap of bloody linen that no one took the trouble of shoving toward some darker corner with the end of his shoe, much less of bending down to throw it in the trash.[43]

In spite of Storoni's repeated requests, Yourcenar refused to let this letter be published in a review. In her view, fragments of a writer's correspondence had no place being cited while their author was alive, unless they were gathered in an anthology of correspondence "assembled and published so late in a writer's life that it is nearly posthumous."

THROUGHOUT the last three months of the year, months marked in the United States by the blockade of Cuba—Frick recorded their anxiety regarding these events—Yourcenar worked assiduously on "Zeno" and went over the proofs of *The Dark Brain of Piranesi.* The collection was published by Gallimard at the end of 1962 and in February 1963 received the Prix Combat, which was awarded that year for the fourth time. The previous winners had been René de Obaldia, Cioran, and Roger Caillois. Along with Yourcenar, the jury also honored André Pieyre de Mandiargues, for the whole of his life's work.

The book, even before the prize, had been very well received by the critics: "Marguerite Yourcenar will never disappoint her readers: her penetrating views as well as the classical grace of her style will never cease to make her books works of high quality," judged Adrien Jans on the pages of *Le Soir.*[44] "The cultivated reader—who is wearied by novels and finds relaxation in intelligent writing—will discover in this collection of essays by Marguerite Yourcenar the most refined and nourishing of feasts," affirmed Jacqueline Piatier in *Le Monde.*[45] Only Pierre de Boisdeffre, in *Les Nouvelles Littéraires,* voiced certain reservations: "a collection of historical, aesthetic, and critical commentaries of uneven quality, some of which, however, are captivating. . . . Upon closing the book, though it is not always equally compelling, one has learned a great deal."[46]

Nineteen sixty-three was the year in which *Le Mystère d'Alceste,* the play written during the summer of 1942, was finally published, in France—it would be the last of Yourcenar's titles to appear at Plon; also appearing was a new edition of *Oriental Tales,* at Gallimard.[47] In her correspondence Yourcenar often commented on the works that friends, editors, or authors would send her from France. Thus did she write to Roger Caillois to thank him for an essay on dreams,[48] which she had "deciphered by way of [a] German translation." "I don't want to miss this opportunity," she continued, "to tell you how much *Méduse et Cie* (*The Mask of Medusa*)—one of the richest books I've read in a long time—*L'Esthétique généralisée* [Generalized Aesthetics], and your *Pilate* (*Pontius Pilate*), which goes such a long way in its meditation on the possible, have meant to me."[49]

At Petite Plaisance winter was too cold and summer too hot. During the summer of 1963, Yourcenar received a copy of the tribute paid to the Amazon, her friend Natalie Barney (it was from the review *Adam International*), and wrote her a magnificent letter. She begins by explaining why she had not wanted to participate in that tribute, despite entreaties from the editor of the review: "Incapable as I am of the short view, of the brief and telling remembrance for which you, on the contrary, are gifted, if I had accepted this gentleman's proposition, I would rapidly have found myself stopped dead in my tracks, or on the contrary I would have foundered in drawers full of notes, beneath reams of paper and torrents of ink, indeed everything one would need to write the *Memoirs of Natalie* or *The Dark Brain of Natalie,* which I am not, however, qualified to do." But a bit further along, in spite of what precedes, she draws *her* portrait of Natalie Barney:

> I am very capable of foreseeing your future legend, having first been acquainted with the one that your contemporaries devised for you.
>
> But despite the information in the volume of "*tributes*" (the genealogies in particular are fascinating), how very much is left unexplained. For example, the perfect "naturalization" of the foreigner you were, who managed to make herself at home in Paris without ever entirely losing her extraterritorial privileges. . . . Finally, one especially admires, without really being able to say why, the calm enduringness of that true tour de force: a life of freedom.
>
> I have given some thought to all of this: I have said to myself that you had had the good fortune to live in an era when the notion of pleasure was still a civilizing notion (which it no longer is today); I have been particularly grateful to you for having escaped the intellectual viruses of this half-century, for having been neither psychoanalyzed, nor an existentialist, nor busy performing gratuitous acts, but for having remained faithful on the contrary to

what your mind, your senses, and indeed your good sense told you. I cannot stop myself from comparing your existence with my own, which will not, in the end, have been a work of art, but rather so much more subjected to happenstance events, rapid or slow, complicated or simple, or at the very least simplified, changing and formless . . . How quickly the rhythms change, from one generation to another, and also the goals.[50]

A "simple, or at the very least simplified," existence was what Frick afforded her. We can't be certain that it absolutely suited her, and the remarks she made in a letter to Suzanne Lilar, who had sent her a copy of her essay on the *Couple* (*Aspects of Love in Western Society*), are not perhaps mere generalizations. Frick knew what was in all of her letters, and one can wonder if Yourcenar may not, also, have been sending some sort of indirect message to her companion:

> With regard to love, I am not sure that glorifying the "couple" as such is the best way to unburden ourselves of our errors and transgressions; so much aggressivity, so much egoism shared by two, so much exclusion of the rest of the world, so much insistence on exclusive property rights to another being all go into this notion: perhaps we need to purify it before we make it sacred again . . . It is all flesh, moreover, that we should hold sacred, were it only in order to bring the flesh nearer to its sister the spirit, and such an attitude would perhaps end up diminishing improper uses and abuses. There are times when, sociologically speaking, and without paradox, I find it regrettable that prostitution ceased to be sacred more than two thousand years ago. Maidservants in the temples had their privileges and their virtues, which we have taken away from the registered prostitute.[51]

In 1963, the beginning of the winter left all the world reeling from the shock of President Kennedy's assassination in Dallas, then that of the assumed murderer Lee Harvey Oswald by Jack Ruby. Once again, it was in Barney that Yourcenar confided:

> Your two charming letters (which must have crossed my brief message) arrived here on Friday morning, 22 November. Just when I was going to sit down at my desk to thank you right away, a neighbor called us with the dreadful news of the shooting that cost President Kennedy his life, and, like the rest of the world, we spent the three days that followed near the television set or the radio, full of horror for this stupid act of violence and pity for that man cut off in mid-career, who seemed to be on his way to becoming a great statesman. But I could not fail to think of what I had Hadrian say about "interrupted careers" and about his compassion toward any man of politics killed in his fortieth year, before having developed all the possibilities within himself. . . . Moreover, we are stupified by the "tough-guy," crime-thriller

aspect of the murder of the man accused of the crime, and by this "good-guy" dance hall manager taking into his own hands the vengeance of a chief of state (and eliminating forever, deliberately or not, the possibility of learning more about the authors of the murder and the causes). Just as Proust marveled that Rasputin's death was such a "Russian" crime, we cannot get over the fact that the details of the tragedy in Dallas are so "American."[52]

Yourcenar and Frick were sixty years old, and both of them were growing increasingly pessimistic. To combat that sinister year's end, they indulged themselves in the little rituals they were fond of, as Frick notes, on 13 December, for example: "Snow is falling. Delicious cardamom cakes prepared and served by M.Y. with coffee, by candlelight amid the shadows of the fading day, as in Sweden. A custom strictly observed since our stay there in 1954–55."

Snow, twilight, their little rituals . . . At Petite Plaisance life was slowing down, and stagnating.

15

The Abyss *and*
Its Attendant *Clashes*

THE BEGINNING OF 1964 was hardly an improvement on the end of the previous year. No account of it remains from Frick, her calender having been lost. But we do know, notably by way of Yourcenar's correspondence, that the month of January was marked by "intense cold." She would have liked to escape it and had planned a trip to the Near East—Lebanon, Egypt, Israel—(the one that the Suez Canal affair had dissuaded her from taking in 1956). It must have been canceled, Frick's illness obliging her to begin a new round of treatment. "My last letter told you how much I was hoping, if not perhaps to see you, at least to talk with you on the telephone on 7 January next, when we would have passed through Marseilles," she wrote to Natalie Barney. "Unfortunately, we have had to put the trip off for the time being, an entirely routine medical examination undergone by Grace before our departure having informed us that she was suffering from a recurrence of the illness she had five years ago, of which we had believed her to be perfectly cured. She must undergo a series of X-ray treatments, like the ones that went so well for her in 1958 (I believe I told you about them at the time), and these treatments will keep us here at least until the end of January. Grace is interrupting me to ask me to tell you that she feels "disgustingly healthy" and that she is not for the moment languishing on a couch, which strikes me as hardly needing to be mentioned, since you know her."[1]

Despite Frick's apparent resistance to the disease, Yourcenar, who had believed her to be cured, remained persistently worried, to the point of confiding in Barney: "Grace is feeling well, and still has her extraordinary energy (she is away at the moment on a trip to the Midwest) but there was considerable cause for alarm this winter. . . . The treatments checked the spread of the disease, but the doctor and I remain worried. All we can do is live from day to day with ardor and with wisdom (such wisdom as we have) and tell ourselves that days placed end to end make up months and weeks, and hope that they make years. Why do I have such inexcusable selfishness as to sadden you with all of this? Out of friendship, and because I talk to you as if I were talking to myself. Keep on providing us, dear Friend, your fine example of endurance and serenity, and trust that I'm affectionately yours."[2]

In January Yourcenar wrote to Gaston Gallimard that she was sending him *Fleuve profond, sombre rivière* [Deep River, Dark River], "which consists of a study of the popular poetry and the mysticism of American blacks, along with the historical backdrop against which this mysticism and poetry developed, as well as a translation of approximately two hundred Negro spirituals, many of them unknown in France."[3] In that same letter she broached a topic preoccupying her, which eventually gave rise to very lengthy legal proceedings between her and Librairie Plon. She did not wish to publish with that firm the work that was supposed to have been a recasting of *La Mort conduit l'attelage;* it was shaping up to be an important novel whose first part, "La Vie errante" ("The Wanderings"), she was in the process of completing. "This novel . . . has become for me a project of the *Memoirs of Hadrian* variety," she wrote to Gaston Gallimard, "though its technique and its plot are entirely different, which, of course, does not by any means prove that I can expect such a wide reception for it. I believed I was writing *Memoirs of Hadrian* for ten people, and I was mistaken. Right now I believe I shall complete *The Abyss* for ten people, and it is highly possible that I am not mistaken. In its present state, this manuscript, of some two hundred fifty typewritten pages, 'corresponds' as a 'new version' to the seventy printed pages of a short story from 1934 entitled 'D'après Dürer' in *La Mort conduit l'attelage.*"[4]

She "remembered" that Gaston Gallimard, for several years, had hoped to publish one of her novels. The extent of the work required by *The Abyss* did not allow her to contemplate fulfilling this hope for a long time, but it was already distinctly clear to her that *The Abyss* would correspond perfectly with the literary tradition of Editions Gallimard. "I shall go further: *The Abyss,* a novel whose technique is very complex, whose intentions are rather abstruse and sometimes bold (it is a question of the turbulent, but also meditative, life of a man who makes a totally clean sweep of the ideas and prejudices of his century in order to see where his thought would then freely lead him), strikes me, in its spirit, as being much more appropriate to Gallimard, and, frankly, hardly suited to a house that seems to experiment less and less with difficult literature. It is in no way a question—this I could not overemphasize—of trying to disadvantage Plon in favor of Gallimard, but of establishing as judicious a program as possible, in view of the content of the manuscripts I have to offer, such as they turn out in their final form."[5]

The end of that letter asserted her confidence in Gaston Gallimard's judgment; still hesitant, without a doubt conscious of the coming difficulties with Plon, Yourcenar seemed to be leaving the matter entirely in his hands and implicitly asking him to support her in her choice. He did not fail to do so by return mail, even though the promised manuscript of *Fleuve profond, sombre rivière* had not yet reached him.

FRICK'S HEALTH having improved, Yourcenar nonetheless abandoned this important project—or at least let it lie dormant—to leave for Europe. This would be their last trip outside the United States until 1968. They went, in April and May 1964 (and not in March as the Pléiade's "Chronologie" maintains, several letters from Yourcenar to friends testifying to this), to Poland, Czechoslovakia, Austria, and northern Italy, always with the same plan: seeing other things, other people, somewhere else. "You tell me that publishers don't wander through Maine," she wrote to Jacques Kayaloff from Vienna; "and that is why I've chosen to live there. It could have been the High Pyrenees . . . , any patch of quiet landscape where one might work in peace. I have the same point of view when I travel: seeing monuments and sites, entering into contact with human beings, and preferably choosing those who are not involved with literature. Otherwise I would go to Paris, rather than Vienna or Cracow."[6]

It was in Salzburg, during "musical May," that Yourcenar began writing the second part of *The Abyss*, "La Vie immobile" ("Immobility"). When she returned to Northeast Harbor, at the beginning of the summer, she decided to devote herself entirely to this book, which she would finish in August 1965.

In Paris, in the fall of 1964, Gallimard published *Fleuve profond, sombre rivière:* "it is the first of my books—and perhaps it will be the only one, who knows?—devoted to an 'American' subject," Yourcenar would comment.[7] It was, of course, a book that could not compete with *Hadrian* or other novels for the conquest of a wide public, but one that earned her several highly pertinent reviews, notably that of Yves Berger in *Le Monde*. He concludes quite simply by comparing, with reference to the same original text, Yourcenar's translation and the one done by Sim Copans, during the same period.[8] The latter writes:

> *I'll no longer be sold at an auction,*
> *Never again, never again.*
> *I'll no longer be sold at an auction.*
> *Thousands have gone*

> *I'll no longer live on a bushel of corn*
> *(the master's corn)*

And Yourcenar:

> *No mo' auction block fo' me!*
> *Oh, never again!*
> *No mo' lashings o' the whip on my back!*
> *Oh, never again!*
> *(By the thousands, men have gone.)*
> *No, no mo' corn rations fo' me!*
> *Oh, never again!*[9]

"The difference speaks for itself," concludes Berger.[10]

From 1965 until 1968, time passed in the "immobility" mode at Petite Plaisance, as Yourcenar confided to Barney, who was the one friend of hers in France to whom she seemed to grant a genuine trust based on Barney's constant generosity and her spirit. She was as disinclined to pettiness as to a taste for gossip, two "very Parisian" faults in Yourcenar's eyes. Over the course of those years, Barney's letters were occasionally accompanied by checks, a gesture that profoundly moved Yourcenar: "I see proof in them of that entity so rare," she wrote to her,

> a genuine friendship capable of being troubled by a period of silence and obsessed by a desire to be useful. . . . I accept this gift with gratitude as I have accepted the previous ones, not because I am in need of material assistance at this time (I swear to you that I am not short of money), but because this check is a symbol equivalent to an unalterable piece of gold. . . . I have just done something that perhaps you will dislike: from that five hundred dollars, I've deducted a tithe. You know how much I am interested in the conservation of the earth: every year, I send a small gift to the Nature Conservancy Association, which three years ago bought a 152-acre island in Bar Harbor bay, Turtle Island, to save it from the developers and the wood merchants who would quickly have transformed those lovely trees into paper pulp for the "comics" and useless illustrated magazines . . . ("Halt, woodcutter . . .") This year, I have just sent them fifty dollars to help them pay off what is still left unpaid from that purchase, telling them that, this time, the present came from you; it pleases me to think that a few mossy hollows, a few rocks, and a few seabird nests thus owe their security to you. I thank you for them.[11]

At the very beginning of 1965, it was extremely cold in Northeast Harbor. Yourcenar admitted to her friend the painter and illustrator Elie Grekoff (the creator of the decor and costumes for *Electra* and the designer of their ex-libris—"from the library of Marguerite Yourcenar, Grace Frick"—Yourcenar had already pasted on more than 3000): "Grace and Monsieur love the snow, but I hate it." [12] Once past the brief moment of childlike wonder in the wake of the first snow, Yourcenar associated snow with winter. And she detested them equally. The more years that passed, the more she found Maine winters interminable, "biting" into April, sometimes spilling over into May. She was going to be sixty-two years old in June, but it was hardly her age she was thinking about. It was in her sedentariness that she felt life's vitality waning. How many years would she now have to spend without budging from this corner of America, doomed to "almost endless" winters? She who had always described Petite Plaisance as a "country house"—and she might well have said a summer house—found herself cloistered there. During this month of January 1965 she had had an attack of phlebitis, an affliction that, this time, owed nothing to her habitual hypochondria. Grace was visibly irritated by her wintertime despondency. The voluntarism with which she herself faced life prevented her from understanding that one could be affected by the weather—to say nothing of accepting it. There were days when the atmosphere was heavy.

Yourcenar, happily, could "vacate the premises" whenever she wished—in broad daylight or in the middle of the night, as she was fond of doing, having always had a taste for long spells of nocturnal writing, penning page after page without holding back, even if only to destroy them at dawn. Surrounded by the silence of Petite Plaisance, whether Frick was in bed or across from her reading or working, Yourcenar would "get away," rejoining Zeno. It would be a mistake to take her subsequent remarks about the one she said she loved "like a brother" as a pose. The boundary separating reality from fiction was, for her, more than hazy; it was almost nonexistent. She wasn't lying when she confided that she had turned to Zeno more than once to seek advice. The date of his birthday, 23 February, appeared in Yourcenar's personal notebook, alongside the birthdays of her friends and relatives that she didn't want to forget. The day she wrote the final page of the manuscript of *The Abyss,* she proceeded to lie down in the hammock she was fond of "to say Zeno three hundred times," as she related on several occasions. This was a final tribute to the man who, for her, existed as a living being and who had just died, in his prison in Bruges.

As she had previously written to Louise de Borchgrave (the member of her family whom, without a doubt, she liked the best), "At this moment I am somewhere between Innsbruck and Ratisbon, in 1551." [13] And she was, during those first months of 1965, in Bruges, where Zeno, now using the name Sebastian Theus, practiced his medical profession and helped Jean-Louis de Berlaimont, the Prior of the Cordeliers, who had begun his mortal agony. Maine's icy, crusted snow gave way to the mists and soft humidity of Bruges. The Prior of the Cordeliers, after ordering Zeno to depart, knowing that after his death Zeno would be in danger, let him once again take up his place at his bedside, for the final night:

> The time for verbal communication, even the briefest, had passed; the Prior limited himself to requests by signs for a little water, or for the urinal hung on a corner of the bed. It seemed to Zeno that within this world in ruins, like a treasure beneath a heap of rubble, a spirit subsisted still, with which it was perhaps possible to remain in contact above and beyond the use of words. He continued to hold the invalid's wrist, and even so feeble a connection appeared to suffice for passing on some slight strength to him, and for receiving in return some degree of serenity. From time to time, thinking of the tradition that would have it that the soul of a man who is dying floats over him like a flame wrapped round in mist, the physician peered into the surrounding shadow, but what he saw was probably only the reflection, in the windowpane, of a lighted candle.[14]

In spite of everything, one eventually did have to come back to the American reality of 1965. In Vietnam, where the United States was getting bogged down as the French had several years earlier, disturbing things were happening. Meetings opposing the American engagement in what had been Indo-China were held even on Mount Desert Island. Yourcenar and Frick attended them assiduously, since for them this was one of the most serious questions of the time. "It is extremely hard to have suffered the errors committed in the past by France in Asia, and now to see America taking over where France left off, previous experience having counted for nothing. Fortunately, a large number of voices are being raised against these errors (especially in deeply religious milieus, and in scientific circles well aware of the dangers), and we are doing what we can to keep up their courage," she wrote to Barney.[15]

The Abyss was not merely Yourcenar's dream, her way of surviving the status quo and blizzards. It was a nearly finished novel and one that was going to be published. From May 1964 until June 1965, prior to the novel's publication, Yourcenar gave five of its chapters or fragments therefrom to different reviews, two of them to the *Nouvelle Revue Française:* "A Conversation in Innsbruck" and "La Mort à Münster" ("Death in Münster").[16] Although Frick mailed several chapters of the book to Plon in March 1965, for Yourcenar, "my heart isn't in it anymore." Plon's evolution toward works that seemed to her "very remote" from literature inspired in her no confidence at all, and she feared that her own books would be poorly defended, this one in particular, to which she specifically attached a great deal of importance, as much as to *Memoirs of Hadrian,* if not more. She would have liked to assert a kind of "conscience clause": one cannot continue to publish with a firm whose production has lost all connection to what one writes. But such a clause was not used in the publishing world, as her lawyer, Maître Marc Brossollet, pointed out to her.[17]

Yourcenar stepped up her expressions of impatience with her publisher, as evidenced by this threatening telegram she sent in May to Georges Roditi:

> Reprint *Alexis* demanded since 1961—Promised since 1962—Passed for press February—Please publish without delay.
>
> Yourcenar[18]

She received the response that *Alexis* would appear in July. But the new edition came out in the hardcover collection of the "Nouvelle Bibliothèque Française" [New French Library] and not in standard softback—a choice Yourcenar would immediately disapprove, and one that would constitute for her an additional grievance in what quickly turned into the "Plon affair."

Rejecting what she considered the "spinelessness" of authors with regard to their publishers and making light of the first-option rights that linked her to Plon, Yourcenar entered into legal proceedings that would last for some two years and would substantially delay the publication of *The Abyss:* "I only know that I have some very good reasons to complain about the treatment I've received from Plon, and to wish to divest them of a book that, in any case, is not right for what Plon has become. I also know that there is a distinct need for someone to rebel against the negligence, against a certain insolent carelessness on the part of publishers, for which, it is true, most authors, by virtue of their spinelessness, are responsible. I don't blame anyone; most authors are obliged, in the usual conditions of their lives in Paris, and in their desire to obtain success such as they define it at any price, to go a very long way in compromising themselves. My situation is different, and I am perhaps one of the few who can usefully protest."[19]

At Plon, meanwhile, people were worried, and an attempt was made, in a letter, to "set the record straight"—there would be no question of side-stepping a contract: "I impatiently await the full text of *The Abyss,* which must be very near completion," Roditi wrote to her, at the beginning of August.

> If I receive it this summer, we shall be able to publish the book in January.
>
> I have not been pleased to learn that emissaries from a rival publishing house have been arriving on your island one after another! This worries me, not for the sake of this book, which is most securely under contract with

Plon and cannot be taken away from us, but for that of books *yet to come.* I hope you are not signing anything. When we see each other, I shall submit to you a proposal for a contract that no other publishing house could offer you.[20]

In fact, on 3 September 1965, Yourcenar wrote to Maître Brossollet to explain the situation to him: she had no desire to publish *The Abyss* at Plon. She suggested that her lawyer meet with Charles Orengo and Bernard de Fallois, both of them at that time in executive positions at Hachette, whom she, out of friendship, had entrusted to preserve all the documents relative to the numerous conflicts between her and Plon since 1962. She listed her grievances (works not reissued or not reprinted in the standard softback format; slippage in the "literary" objectives of the house . . .) and declared her wish to recover the rights to *The Abyss*, along with those to *La Mort conduit l'attelage*, of which the first text, "D'après Dürer," constituted the embryo of *The Abyss*. Finally, she asked that those texts out of print in the standard softback editions be taken back (*Memoirs of Hadrian* and *Alexis*— also those out of print entirely—*Electra* and *Fires*—as well as *Le Mystère d'Alceste*, of which the supply of available copies was "nearly exhausted"). She hoped for an out-of-court settlement with Plon, but Maître Brossollet warned her that the situation did not appear favorable, taking into account the commercial value and the prestige her work represented for the publisher. "I had never met Marguerite Yourcenar," remembers Maître Brossollet. "She sent Charles Orengo to my office to discuss the matter. My remarks must have convinced him. A few days after that, Marguerite Yourcenar informed me that she wished for me to 'see that matter through with her to the end.' I was touched by the confidence she was placing in a young lawyer whom she did not know. I was also, very quickly, astonished by her determination. She had in her possession a finished manuscript, or one that was close to being finished. She knew that this was her most important work since *Memoirs of Hadrian*. She attached perhaps even more importance to it. Yet she was determined not to publish rather than publish at Plon. Her relations with Georges Roditi deteriorated. Both of them dug in their heels. But as Gallimard had had to with *Hadrian*, Plon finally had to give in. For it was quite clear that she would not yield. Nonetheless, the proceedings took a long time. I still have an enormous dossier with many, very detailed, letters in it from Marguerite Yourcenar, who followed the most trivial developments about which I kept her informed with almost maniacal attention. Fortunately, we were able to reach an agreement before the matter went to trial. Otherwise, between verdicts and appeals, I wonder when *The Abyss* would have finally appeared."[21]

In fact, after several months of conciliation attempts, hemming and haw-ing, and summonses unanswered by Plon, the conflict took a judicial turn in mid-July 1966. But the docket of the third chamber of the Tribunal, where matters of literary and industrial property are settled, was very con-gested, and the hearing could not be scheduled before the month of January 1968. Meanwhile, new negotiations commenced, and amid both complica-tions and concessions, the parties would finally agree to put an end to this voluminous dossier, an agreement signed by Marcel Jullian, the new presi-dent of Librairie Plon as of July 1967.

DAILY LIFE did not cease for all this, no more than did Yourcenar's avidity for any form of intellectual exchange. She annotated and, in her correspon-dence, carefully commented upon the books that were sent to her from Europe. Thus began, in mid-August 1964, an epistolary exchange with the essayist and academic Gabriel Germain (an exchange of reflections per-taining to the spiritual realm, which would be kept up on a regular basis until the latter's death, in October 1978). "I read *Homère* (*Homer*), which you so kindly sent me, with very great interest," she wrote to him in one of her first letters. "As in *Epictète* [Epictetus], I admire your wisdom, which keeps you from believing that everything is resolved, or is going to be, and also from falling headlong into the trap of the more or less seductive hypotheses that be." [22] During that same period, from Italy, the essayist Ele-mire Zolla sent his article on *The Turn of the Screw* by Henry James, which she particularly liked:

> It made me reread this novel, which struck me yet again as a masterpiece and which interests me all the more because, having translated Henry James's *What Maisie Knew* into French quite some time ago, it prompted me to reflect on that other tale of childhood voyeurism, in which this time it is not with specters, but with adults who are very much alive that the little girl forges strange bonds of complicitous knowledge. *The Turn of the Screw* goes much further than this nonetheless extraordinary novel, because it is not, this time, only the problem of childhood innocence and perversity that preoccu-pies James, but that of our dealings with evil. James goes beyond the psycho-logical, at once consciously and unconsciously, to enter into the theological and metaphysical as well as the occult. How right you are to eliminate dis-dainfully Wilson's hypothesis reducing everything to hysterical fantasies on the part of the governess. A fine example of the flat and rudimentary aspect that spiritual problems take on in the minds of certain of our contemporaries. In reality, sexual obsession fills *The Turn of the Screw* by virtue of the very fact that it is in the form of contacts with fornicators that James (typically a man of the nineteenth century) treats this problem of connivance with evil,

and the first chapter, so offhandedly worldly, strikes me as proving *a contrario* that he knew how dangerous from all points of view was the terrain upon which he was advancing.[23]

Frick, for her part, during the last months of 1965—from August to December—was occupied essentially with the illness of the little black cocker spaniel, the famous "Monsieur." Day by day she noted his crises, his convulsions, between two lines on the problems of *The Abyss* and the telephone calls from Paris that went with them, three lines on Yourcenar's illnesses, and a few rapid references to friends coming for tea. "Monsieur" died on 6 December 1965, Saint Nicholas's day. He was buried, as were the dogs that succeeded him, in a corner of the garden, "beneath the birches and among the ferns," wrote Yourcenar in one of her notebooks. Each grave is marked by a little tombstone bearing an inscription: "And still my spaniel sleeps" (John Manston), for "Monsieur," and "Yet a kind heart within a little body" (Ronsard) for the other cocker, a reddish-brown one this time, who would arrive at Petite Plaisance on 14 February 1966, Saint Valentine's day (and would die on 2 December 1971). The young dog was called Valentine—apropos of which, we might observe that Frick and Yourcenar always remained faithful to the American custom of sending a card on Valentine's day to one's true love. Even at the worst moments of their life together, during the final years, as if the ritual, testifying to what once was, continued to give it an existence in the present.

DURING THAT year's end, on 28 December to be precise, Yourcenar wrote a very long letter to a Canadian student who had initiated an exchange of letters with her in 1963. This text is a new example of the "pedagogical" variety of correspondence, at once warm and a shade sanctimonious, that Yourcenar carried on with young people more or less unknown. She is responding to the complaints, regarding his own fate, that her young correspondent had expressed:

> In this unfortunate era during which every instant that we live is marked by horrible warrior "exploits," during which the money that we so badly need to restore the earth is spent by the States to the benefit of no one, under the cover of supposedly scientific projects that poorly mask the goal of building up their military strength and powers of future destruction, during which we are polluting the air and the water and destroying the innocent animal world (and, more insidiously, ourselves) . . . , in this sad end of the year of grace 1965, do we really have the right to suffer for ourselves alone and on account of ourselves alone? Think about it.
>
> I am perfectly aware that adolescence is an age that has its privileges: one

of the most sacred of these consists of having the right to think of oneself first, to think about educating oneself, about serving one's apprenticeship in matters intellectual, material, and sensual, finally about developing oneself in a harmonious way before confronting that struggle that the whole of life will be. But you are no longer an adolescent, Jean-Louis, and you will never be a man if you don't make more of an effort to be one. Don't think that your complaints, poured forth at length in your ten-page letters, will cure you or facilitate your accession to a better life. . . . If I understand correctly, you are still a student, which means that yours is the good fortune of having a family that furnishes you the means to be one. Are you really doing everything you can to take advantage of that good fortune? To go away and profit from this change of scenery . . . [a]s a member of some beatnik peace corp [*sic*] or a sailor on a cargo ship, you will have no other resources for making a living or establishing yourself in any milieu than the knowledge you have acquired and the qualities you have developed on Daly Street in Ottawa.

You complain of being intellectually, sentimentally, and sensually alone. Ask yourself if you are not partially responsible for that solitude. Are you making an attempt to be one of those people who bring sympathy or enrichment to others, or on the contrary, without knowing it or wanting to, do you bring them a heavy weight to bear? For you who love literature, allow me to remind you of the passage from Valery Larbaud: ". . . MYSELF. The Most Serene Republic in its entirety. A lone being in the face of life as I shall also be one day in the face of death." On the day when you have partially realized this project (which one must not confuse with that of the egoist) and recognized solitude for the good mistress it is, you will have earned your colors, like a knight from medieval legends, and acquired friends with whom to be alone.[24]

Nineteen sixty-six and nineteen sixty-seven were two completely "immobile" years, which at the time struck Yourcenar as nearly insurmountable. She did not yet know that an entire decade, or just about—from 1971 to 1980—would be spent in this way. At Petite Plaisance, life was cadenced by the progress of the Plon affair in Paris, by letters to friends, by their rare visits—still, Florence Codman came and Erika Vollger, the seamstress from Hartford, during the summer of 1966—and by illnesses. Although her legendary hypochondria tends to make us minimize them, Yourcenar's illnesses this time were very real. In 1966, her doctor subjected her to quite a number of tests, fearing that she herself might also have cancer. This did not turn out to be the case at all, but she was overcome by attacks of sciatica and by more and more bothersome allergies, which succeeded one another throughout 1967.

In the literary realm, Yourcenar took an unmistakable pleasure in getting back to her translations of Greek poets (in point of fact, more free adaptations than real translations), which would appear at Gallimard more than ten years later, in 1979, under the title *La Couronne et la lyre*. A fragment of this text was published in the *Nouvelle Revue Française*.[25] It was also during this time that one of her half nephews, Georges de Crayencour, began corresponding with her. This correspondence, initiated toward the end of 1964 by way of Louise de Borchgrave, "Aunt Loulou," would really begin on 12 May 1966, and would continue sporadically until November 1987. And it was to the "indefatigable obligingness" of Georges, who had a passion for genealogy, that Yourcenar would appeal, beginning on 1 April 1973. She asked for his help in the initial research for what would become *Archives du Nord*.

But plans for a family trilogy were still far from being laid; and the intensity of the moments spent writing Zeno's story had disappeared. Indeed, this text, which she was beginning to believe might never be published during her lifetime, was preventing her from launching another long-term enterprise. Everything was coming together in a way that created a confusion, a dreary tangle that she could not accept—she who had built her life, for some twenty years now, on a constant wish to clarify, to simplify, she who had continually tried to substitute self-discipline and an experience of freedom and firmness of purpose for the half-truths of falsely complicated existences. She reminded herself, as she did every time she felt herself wavering, what Edmond Jaloux had said to her when, at thirty years of age, she had complained of having gone six months without writing and without any desire to write: "Why don't you accept that the mind also undergoes its periods of hibernation?"[26] But she could not resign herself to this.

Even out of consideration for Frick, she could not manage to keep completely quiet about what was weighing upon her beyond the effable. "We have not left Mount Desert since our return from Poland, Austria, and Italy in 1964," she wrote to Elie Grekoff in December 1966—in a letter, of course, that Grace read and put away in the files.[27] "I don't know when this misfortune will cease. For it is always a misfortune to be immobilized against one's wishes." She did not mention, during that period, the reasons for her immobility, for that double reclusion way up there in the northeasternmost corner of the United States: insularity and illness. But one perceives, running through all the letters in which this question comes up, that, even at this early stage, she no longer considered herself to be responsible for a choice in which she nonetheless had shared. She all but pointed out the "guilty party." Only barely did she concede to Frick, upon whose initiative they had purchased and moved into Petite Plaisance, a few—nuanced—comments on the beauty of the island—"Mount Desert is still very beautiful, but it has changed since I saw it for the first time in 1942. Overuse of the tourist routes and certain 'improvements,' which are not ugly in themselves, have transformed what was still something of an 'enchanted isle' into a kind of scenic park, along the lines of the Forest of Fontainebleau or Compiègne; though, it is true that the sea and the rocks are still the same."²⁸ A few remarks regarding choices made for the sake of frugality, which, common to them both, still justified a "we," were reduced to rather modest dimensions. Thus they made their decision not to own an automobile—the most impractical, however, of all possible things on an island, American or not, that is most of the time without any means of public transportation: "We have no car. This is not for reasons of economy. We could afford such an appliance, but a car is yet another burdensome possession."²⁹

To add the final strokes of grayness to the picture, if there were any need to, Frick and Yourcenar were arriving at the age when, inevitably, if one survives, one loses family members and friends. The older ones go first, and soon one's contemporaries. On 15 June 1966, Frick noted the death of their old friend Malvina Hoffman (the *New York Times* would not address it until 11 July), who in 1962 had sculpted a bust of Yourcenar. Eighty-one years of age, Hoffman had been a student of Rodin and had been acquainted with Brancusi. Yourcenar and Frick still remembered the parties she had given in her New York studio on 35ᵗʰ Street, which they had enjoyed, during the era of their long-ago life in the city and the socializing that went with it.

On 24 June, in Brussels, Yourcenar's half brother, Michel-Joseph, the son of Berthe, died of a stroke. Yourcenar's correspondence on this subject shows no hint of emotion. As she would report some years later in a chapter of *Archives du Nord,* her dealings with this half brother, eighteen years her senior, had never been easy.³⁰

In 1961, Yourcenar had resumed her correspondence with the maid who had watched over her adolescence, Camille Debocq-Letot, to whom she had explained her final split with Michel-Joseph: "As for my brother and his family, I have had no contact with them for years, never having forgiven Michel for his poor conduct toward his father and toward me. You know him, so this will not surprise you, but what you don't know perhaps is that he left it up to me, with Christine, to handle all the responsibilities and all the expenses of my father's lengthy illness; that he lost, without a word of apology, in his own speculations, the major share of my wealth, which, on the advice of my stepmother, I had entrusted to him (this, moreover, having been very stupid on my part); and that I then had to make my way in life, unprepared to do so, and in the most difficult conditions. I did not speak of this at the time, because it was important to Christine to maintain an appearance of family harmony, but as soon as there was no longer her opinion to consider, I ceased all commerce with Michel and his family.[31]

She rehashes the same grievances in another letter to Debocq-Letot: "My long estrangement from my brother will not surprise you, who surely remember 'Monsieur Michel' and his so very violent character. I still remember with gratitude that you often intervened to defend me, when I was a little girl of ten or eleven. . . . I have not seen him again since our departure from England in 1915, except during a period between 1929 and 1933, when my stepmother Christine had settled in Belgium, and that renewed contact was not felicitous, for I let 'Monsieur Michel' look after some properties I had inherited from my mother in Hainaut and near Namur, and he quickly lost almost everything. Between 1915 and 1929, he never saw his father (who died in Switzerland in 1929), and he never did anything to help him during his final illness either. It appears that he was very hard on his children, but they treated him better than he had treated his father, for he was well cared for by them until the end."[32]

Decidedly, Yourcenar was not one to let go of a grudge. Moreover, nothing prevents us from doubting her good faith. Whatever might have been the reasons for Michel-Joseph's attitude at the time of his father's death, it is curious that Yourcenar, both in her correspondence and in *Archives du Nord*, insists on the fact that she had not seen her brother again between her departure from England and the years when her stepmother Christine settled temporarily in Belgium. Debocq-Letot herself may have been surprised by this since it was to her that Yourcenar had sent, from Switzerland, a postcard dated 25 August 1928, on which happens to be mentioned a visit from Michel-Joseph, five months before his father's death: "My father is feeling much better; we have been in Glion for two months and we are staying until the end of September. I am having a very gay summer. I have many friends in Switzerland and I am taking lots of little trips. . . . Michel and Solange came to see us for two weeks or so."[33]

AND THE MEMORIES continued to pour in when Yourcenar received, in June 1966, a long letter from a professor at Harvard who had undertaken research on Lucien Maury. She conveyed to Yourcenar the comments made by Maury in letters to the Swedish writer Ahlenius, in 1951: "Soon there will be no one but women keeping the fictional imagination alive in France," Maury wrote notably. "I believe that you have received that other feminine work, written with a pen of bronze by a talent that strikes one as virile: *Memoirs of Hadrian* by my admirable friend Yourcenar. Our male novelists are suffocating themselves in emptiness and subtlety; the women (certain ones) have not severed the umbilical cord that attaches them to life, to the eternal."[34] "I feel as if it is to Lucien Maury that I owe my knowledge of Sweden," confided Yourcenar to her American correspondent.

> Not only by way of contacts with living writers that go back to an introduction made by him, but above all because it is thanks to his translations from the Swedish that I acceded even as a child to Swedish legend and reality. My immense admiration for Selma Lagerlöf in particular, which has never diminished, dates back to the first French translations of her tales and short stories, by Lucien Maury (around 1910), which I read, or which were read to me during my childhood. I believe that if I have continued to serve upon occasion as a translator throughout my life, Maury's example had something to do with it: he is one of those people who taught me the beauty, and even the greatness, of devoting oneself to a foreign work that one endeavors to present to those who don't have access to it.
>
> As for my personal relations with Lucien Maury, they were quite frequent, and quite regular, between 1930 and 1939, which corresponds more or less to the time he headed up the *Revue Bleue,* during which I occasionally contributed to it. . . . As a review editor, M. Lucien Maury gave a great deal of encouragement to the young writer I still was during the thirties. In fact, his review published certain of my works from that period that I am the most attached to, in particular the long prose poem entitled *Sixtine* ("Sistine"), which has not reappeared in France since that time.[35]

In February 1967, Yourcenar responded to a letter from her friend Roger Lacombe—who, as it happens, had been director of the French Institute of Stockholm at the time of Yourcenar's first visit to Sweden in 1953. Lacombe informed her of the work he had begun on a critical edition of a text by the Marquis de Sade, an excerpt from *Les Crimes de l'amour* (*The Crimes of Love*).

"I must confide that I do not like Sade," Yourcenar responded,

> whose lack of realism vexes me. He seems to me to be the most striking example of a certain deficiency that is very French, or one at least that has affected a very large part of French literature since the seventeenth century, by which I mean the use and abuse of purely intellectual concepts accompanied by a total incapacity to apprehend the facts. There is nothing less physiological than this man who believes himself concerned with sexuality. One catches no whiff of blood in this bloody author's work, nor any other odor of human excretion or secretion. Sade strikes me as being the equivalent in the realm of pleasure of those strategists (who are much more sadistic than he) who talk about wars of attrition and targets picked out in advance while thousands of beings are burning alive. It is possible to say anything, even do

anything (Sade, however, seems to have imagined more than he did), when one lives in a mental laboratory from which life itself is excluded.

I am well aware of how terribly prophetic he was, but the very fact that today there is a swarm of humanity that resembles him would appear to divest him of much of the excitement value he might have had a century ago. Compared to the hydrogen bomb, little artificial volcanos erupting in the gardens of eighteenth-century seigneurs are a modest diversion indeed.

And yet I understand your interest in him and your taste for what one is indeed obliged to call his rigor. Like Spinoza—and I await your essays on him with even more interest—he is a great systematizer. And then, doesn't the amused curiosity of those French gentlemen who used to make the rounds of the bookstores in old Stockholm asking "Habesne libros eroticos?" enter into it somewhat? I am glad that *Ernestine* has brought you back intellectually to Sweden, a country you speak about better than anyone else.[36]

These remarks are quite characteristic of Yourcenar's bent where literary judgment is concerned: a mixture of intuition—regarding the conceptual rigor of Sade's work—and what one can only call platitudes, or worse still, utter misinterpretations of what was at stake in the work.

The year 1967 was taken up entirely by *The Abyss,* but in a less agreeable way than when Yourcenar was writing it, excepting only the brief interlude when she would go over the final manuscript and Frick would start working on the translation, around 20 August. "I am sure you can imagine that I do not plunge into this business lightheartedly," she wrote to Natalie Barney evoking the conflict with Plon. "It is a very weighty decision for me not to see a volume published (perhaps *never* to see it published) that has cost me years of reflection and work." "The change in the publisher's moral personality," she said elsewhere in the same letter,

> on account of a series of financial arrangements that have nothing to do with literature, also counts for something. On this point, the important thing, not only for me but for everyone, would be "to set a precedent." The old law regarding literary contracts did not anticipate a disastrous state of affairs due to groupings and regroupings that often transform a house from one day to the next, and that place the writer in a difficult and false position. Sooner or later, a law will indeed have to come into effect, to protect the author who has signed with a certain house, and who finds himself, under the same name, in the presence of something entirely different. I don't know yet if this argument will be used or not (I hope it will be), but, even if the case is not decided in my favor, I shall at least have made an effort in what I believe to be the right direction.[37]

The case against Plon took its normal course, but Yourcenar worried about it constantly. Even her friends were mobilized for this affair and did not fail to convey to her anything that might validate her thesis. Jacques Kayaloff sent her an article from *Le Monde*, "Sven Nielsen, un vendeur avant tout" [Sven Nielsen, Above All a Salesman].[38] In this article, it was notably reported that, "a salesman before becoming a publisher" (with a turnover equivalent to one-fifth that of all general literary and young people's publishing in France), Nielsen had acquired the business interests of Plon and Julliard "along with everything that went along with them." As a result of this publishing concentration, "Plon's enormous stock of unsold books was shipped off to be pulped, and booksellers could no longer fulfill their occasional requests for titles." Finally, in addition to the announcement of the creation of Editions Christian Bourgois, specializing in literature—"an orchid in Monsieur Nielsen's buttonhole?" asked the author of the article—the publisher's mass-market strategy was revealed, a strategy in complete contradiction with the methods of the "Hachette-Gallimard duo." "We would have no reason to regret the passing of these potentates if, out of their calamity were to flood the light that publishing needs more than ever," the article continued, concluding: "But there is a risk that many quality houses that up until now have remained independent will be trampled underfoot in the battle by the giants."[39] This, let it be noted, was in 1967.

Yourcenar must have shed her concern that year about not being published, a profound one since the beginning of open conflict with Plon. For there was no shortage of candidates to publish her, quite the contrary. Besides Gallimard, her other publisher, with whom she had long been discussing the subject of *The Abyss*, Grasset, all of a sudden, came forth. People there remembered having long ago published her first books, and house strategists had decided they would be well advised to attempt to get her back. In April 1967, the literary editor, Yves Berger, came to lunch at Petite Plaisance. On 27 July, Bernard Privat, Grasset's C.E.O., expressed in a letter to Yourcenar his regret at having let her go. "Grasset, who also knew that yours was one of his house's most glorious names, bore that loss bitterly. I still can hear him reading aloud to me, which he seldom did, passages from *Memoirs of Hadrian*. Therefore, it will not surprise you, dear lady, if I say how proud I would be if your next novel could be published with us.

"When a writer holds the place in a country's literature that you hold in France, it is difficult and almost indiscreet to speak to him of the admiration one feels for his work. Let me simply tell you—this will suffice—that I know what that place is and that I appreciate at its true worth what an honor it is for a publisher to contribute to its further glory."[40]

Privat proposed that she make only one commitment to Grasset, for *The Abyss* ("then you could judge us by the way we do this work"). And he offered her an advance of "ten million old francs" ("new francs," of course, had been in use for years, but he judged, with good reason, that the sum would be more eloquent thus for a woman of mature years). He also proposed an author's royalty of 15 percent, a first printing of 20,000 copies, a book launching and a campaign of advertising and promotion "that I could come discuss with you before the publication of the book, if you felt this to be necessary." Without any doubt, this comforted Yourcenar, compensated her for her rigor toward Plon and for the risks she had taken. Besides, she didn't mind feeling she was wanted (who would, really?). Privat did not content himself with that letter. As had Gaston Gallimard sixteen years earlier, with *Memoirs of Hadrian,* he had internal notes written up on the "Yourcenar affair" to be entirely certain that he had all the elements of the case in hand. According to a conversation that Berger had with Yourcenar, she supposedly hesitated—this was at the beginning of August—between Grasset and Gallimard. Privat asked Charles Orengo, who had taken over as director of Fayard several months earlier, to help him. Orengo had enjoyed good relations with Yourcenar since the beginning of the fifties. She always took his advice, and, as we have seen, he was her Parisian emissary to the office of Maître Brossollet in connection with the conflict between her and Plon. His opinion, thus, judged Privat, would carry "great weight." It was a matter of explaining to her that she would find "more enthusiasm and efficiency in her defense" at Grasset than at Gallimard. "I believe that in taking such action we would, both of us, be making an important contribution to the life of the group," wrote Privat to Orengo. "All the more so in that we are dealing with a writer of the greatest literary importance, whose career is of the utmost eminence."[41] But Yourcenar's concern was, from now on, to have all her works gathered together at the same publishing house. This tipped the scales toward Gallimard, where, over a period of nearly ten years, the following works had already appeared: her translation of Cavafy's poems, *The Dark Brain of Piranesi,* the new edition of *Oriental Tales,* and *Fleuve profond, sombre rivière.* Thérèse de Saint-Phalle—who worked for the Presses de la Cité group, to which Plon belonged, and was striving to reconcile the two opposing parties—attempted to set up a meeting at Petite Plaisance, by way of Roger Straus, Yourcenar's American publisher. She did not succeed. But this did not prevent other publishers from coming forth. Orengo, who must indeed have been the center of much flattering attention in Paris during that time, conveyed a proposal to Yourcenar from Paul Flamand: Editions du Seuil also wanted to publish *The Abyss.*

It was in the midst of this stir that Yourcenar and Frick learned, on 10 October 1967, through a call from their lawyer Maître Brossollet, that an agreement had been reached, that *The Abyss* was free, and that Yourcenar could publish this book where she wished. They celebrated the event with champagne, a drink to which Yourcenar had long been partial. With no small amount of pride Yourcenar had, yet again, won her case; she had stood up one more time, and alone, to an important publisher. And it surely did not bother her to find herself at the center of a little joust among Parisian publishers. But her choice was probably already made.

Gaston Gallimard's stubbornness had finally triumphed. This querulous woman, with whom he'd had words in times past, who had been so casually audacious as to summon him to her hotel, and whom he had called "Mademoiselle Yourcenar," knowing she was far from fond of this, was going to pack up and move to his firm. Gallimard would take over all her books. *The Abyss* would be added to the house's successes, and the name of Marguerite Yourcenar to the list of writers in the Gallimard "stable."

16
Public Recognition

A SIXTY-FIVE-YEAR-OLD writer achieving an important success and a kind of "literary consecration" for a serious novel on the Renaissance published in France on the eve of "May '68": this could well serve as a composition assignment on "the height of paradox."[1] However, this is what did happen to Yourcenar with *The Abyss*. And her hero, Zeno, even if he didn't accompany the students—too preoccupied then, and rightly so, by their own society—was nonetheless a prototypical protester. "If by 'protest[er]' you mean anti-institutional, then, yes, certainly," Yourcenar responded to one of Matthieu Galey's questions on the anti-establishment nature of the hero of *The Abyss*.

> Because Zeno is against everything: the universities, when he is young; the family, in whose eyes he is a bastard and whose vulgar riches he disdains; Don Blas de Vela's Spanish monastery, which he hates so much that he abandons the old Marrano who is being pursued by its monks, to his later regret; the professors at Montpellier, where he studies anatomy and medicine; the authorities; princes; and so forth. He rejects the ideology and intellectual endeavor of his age as nothing but a magma of words. Though he has experienced various forms of carnal pleasure, in the end he even rejects sensuality, up to a point. He naturally rejects Christian thought, though he gets on best with certain ecclesiastics, like the Prior of the Cordeliers. He looks on, disdainfully, at the collapse of Protestantism's left wing and finds scandalous the counterreformation alliance of the Church with monarchy. As the world crumbles around him, he realizes that it is the human condition itself that is at issue. . . . Consequently, for me *The Abyss* became a kind of mirror, which concentrated the human condition itself in the series of events that we call history.[2]

When Yourcenar received, at Petite Plaisance, on 6 February 1968, the very favorable contract that Gallimard offered her for *The Abyss* (its conditions were more or less the same as Grasset's),[3] she saw it only as the sign of a bond now happily broken—her tie to Plon. The contract was no more than a formality, for the book was already in production. She only sent it back on 20 February, but before the document even arrived in Paris, the first proofs of the novel reached her, on 24 February. She worked assiduously on correcting them, with Frick of course. They had decided to go to Paris for the appearance of the book, scheduled for the end of April, and had informed certain friends of their arrival, among them Jean Mouton, with whom they hoped to dine on 2 May. "I write to you in the wake of Martin Luther King's death," explained Yourcenar. "The murder of this great pacifist adds a new link to the chain of violent acts of which there is no end in sight."[4]

So they left for France—the boat went to Cherbourg—on 17 April. Earlier, on the seventh, Yourcenar had gone to her lawyer's office to sign a new will (up until the time of her death, she would make out several successive wills, with incessant modifications).

On 22 April, Frick and Yourcenar took rooms, as was their custom, though they had not come back to France for twelve years, at the Hôtel Saint-James et d'Albany. Very soon after the visits of their friends, come to bid their traditional welcome—Charles Orengo having been the very first— there arrived a succession of journalists, on whom, for the most part, *The Abyss* had made a strong impression. Received on 3 May were Jean Chalon, for an interview to appear in *Le Figaro Littéraire*, and Michel Polac for television. However, the event of the day, early in this particular month of May, was not exactly the appearance of *The Abyss*, "but rather the uprisings of young people, which shook the whole world," Yourcenar admitted a long time afterward, with the smile of one who remembers without disgruntlement. She and Frick, no doubt unlike quite a number of the people at whose homes they dined on certain evenings, looked on the unrest with no particular anxiety, watched what was happening with interest, day after day, and trekked about the city, given back to the pedestrians. "Left Bank Manifestations [Demonstrations]," noted Frick on 11 May—then, "more and more strikes"; "General strike. Walked in Tuileries." Finally, on 24 May, the day after Ascension Day, she wrote: "worst day of [the] insurrection after De Gaulle's long-awaited but empty speech on television. Barricades built and charged by police."

On Friday, 17 May, Natalie Barney gave a reception in Yourcenar's honor. She and Frick determined that the simplest way, during that period of demonstrations, to get from the Rue de Rivoli to the Rue Jacob was to walk. Jean Chalon, who attended the party, remembers their arrival. To the great astonishment of some of the guests, they recounted how they had crossed the Seine by way of the Passerelle des Arts,[5] then had reached the Rue Jacob, occasionally passing by "hedges" of C.R.S. agents.[6] And they spoke with a placidity that was hardly fitting, according to certain persons present. Yourcenar took issue in an amicable way with a few of Chalon's recollections of that day, recorded in his *Portrait of a Seductress:* "[t]hen the large white lace jabot of Marguerite Yourcenar appeared, together with the white foxes of her translator, Grace Friks [*sic*]," he wrote notably.[7] Yourcenar rectified matters: "Grace has pointed out to me that she has never worn white foxes, which for that matter would have been superfluous on a stormy day in June [*sic*]. M.Y.'s large white lace jabot was a white-nylon jabot of modest dimensions; I have it still. In any case, nothing serious."[8] Nothing serious indeed, to say the least, and nothing marking any great disturbance in the face of what were soon called, for lack of a more adequate word, "the events" of May 1968.

Frick would recount later on: "The last reception at Natalie Barney's that Marguerite Yourcenar attended had been organized by the former in her honor in May '68 at the time of the student uprisings. The Rue Jacob was right in the midst of a 'hot zone,' and it was not easy to find a way to get there. But Natalie Barney behaved as if there were nothing going on. She was not a woman to pay any attention to what was going on in the street."

Yourcenar, for her part, could not *not* pay attention to what was taking place in the streets of Paris—or rather to what it revealed. A great part of her life had been spent rejecting that which the students of Paris and other Western capitals were revolting against: the civilization of "Take-the-subway-Work-all-day-and-Hit-the-hay,"[9] of "the station wagon and the washing machine," of equating possessions with success. "Both of them were hippies before the fact," says their friend Anya Kayaloff today, "as much in their manner of dressing as in the way they rejected certain consumer goods, from the automobile to the television, in their habit of not eating meat, of making their bread, and in their pacifistic and ecological activism." Yourcenar explained years later: "Zeno, I think, is rather closer to some of the lost youth of our time, though few that I've known have his passion. Most suffer from a rather feeble brand of nihilism, comprehensible enough in an age even more chaotic than Zeno's was. They want to escape what they see as complacency, but their escape becomes in turn complacency of another kind."[10]

On 3 May 1968, during an interview, Chalon asked this question: "Do you think that an experience like your own—that is to say a woman who devotes herself to her *œuvre*, lives on what she earns, and only publishes texts of her choosing—is still possible in the present day? Do you believe that there could be a twenty-year-old Marguerite Yourcenar today?"[11] It provided an occasion for her to express what she sensed to be the confusion of a very great portion of the young: "I am sure of it. We carry the fatalism of our era too far. There are, of course, fateful economic circumstances, I grant you this. If a young man or a young woman hope to succeed according to the technocrats' formulas, automobile-television-washing machine, then they will be trapped like slaves. Trapped as much as Zeno would have been had he consented to becoming a canon." "At the age of twenty," she said about Zeno, "he had thought himself freed of those routines and prejudices which paralyze our actions and put blinders on our understanding; but his life had been passed thereafter in acquiring bit by bit that very liberty of which he had supposed himself promptly possessed in its entirety."[12]

Perhaps the young people of 1968 were a bit too much like Zeno at the age of twenty, believing that their words, their imagination, their diffusion —which had had a kind of unveiling effect and had caused a government fossilized around an old man to falter—gave them liberty, by way of a viaticum. Nonetheless, Yourcenar was no doubt closer to them than to many of her contemporaries. She was closer, also, to those young people than she would be today to their children, those who at the age of twenty already have stock portfolios and make the "enterprising spirit" a substitute for reflection—and definitely closer to Daniel Cohn-Bendit than to Bernard Tapie.[13]

She was fond of evoking the slogans from May '68, especially the ones that emphasized the powers of the imaginary: the famous "What's underneath the paving stones? The beach," of course; along with "Power to the imagination" and "Be realistic, demand the impossible." In her home, at Petite Plaisance, she always kept on the bookshelves in one of the guest rooms *Les Murs ont la parole, Sorbonne, Mai 68* [The Writing on the Walls, Sorbonne, May '68], the red volume published by Editions Tchou that assembled those slogans, those inscriptions, in short all the "little phrases" from May '68 in Paris.[14] She had underlined many of them—from "we are all German Jews" to "get out of my sight, object," "merchandise, let's burn it," and "I chew society's ass but it pays me back in good shape," by way of Artaud's phrase, "These days, it isn't man, it's the world that's not normal," or Valéry's line, "the wind is rising, we must try to live," to the very ecological "the forest came before man, the desert will come after." "I am always annoyed by the obligations that people create for themselves," she would also say to Jacqueline Piatier in an interview published in *Le Monde* on 25 May 1968, in the midst of the turmoil. "They believe they need certain forms of success: to earn money, to join the management ranks, to belong to certain groups. One cannot always do what one wants to, but there are innumerable instances where it is possible to choose what one prefers."

Several months later, in a long interview published by *L'Express,* she would clearly give her position on certain political questions. "What worries me most in France, for example, is what the Americans call paternalism. The fact that people say to themselves: here we are, we have someone very good, he's in power, we consider him a kind of father who makes decisions for us. Now, even if this figure were supreme in his genius or honesty, even if he were superhuman, this would still be bad because of what it represents."

When asked what she had made of the student demonstrations, she responded: "Perhaps it is a question of age. I didn't feel I had the energy to go for kilometers on foot. But it was fascinating. We took part, just the same. We were well aware of the errors committed, but we supported the students' hopes. Reforms could be brought about, the world could change, in part." [15]

It is strange that, in spite of this, many have persisted, and still persist, in taking Yourcenar for a woman "of the Right"—whether they be highly pleased about it, or whether it be cause for lament. Would this not seem to indicate a deplorable slippage, or a dangerous amalgamation—on both sides—between literature and the conduct of one's life? Do a knowledge of the past, the imperfect subjunctive, and an aptitude—one that's in the process of vanishing—for wielding subordinate clauses somehow cause one ineluctably to tend to the right; whereas casual language and loose writing are deep signs of leftist thought, in the manner of a test in the *Nouvel Observateur*—which, granted, only claimed to be a summertime diversion—giving lovers of Brie right-wing tastes and lovers of cream cheese a few points for leaning left? André Fraigneau, we might recall, tends to see in Yourcenar's postwar works, which he judges boring and ponderously moralizing, the nefarious influence "of all those leftists she met in America." "In the milieu she frequented in France before the war, everyone was right-wing, and that did not bother her," he insists, probably correctly. The only things he is forgetting are that Yourcenar always wanted to be free and many-sided, and that her Greek friends, beginning with André Embiricos, were very committed to the Left. Among the little group of intellectuals that she was part of back then, in Greece, several men fought alongside the Republicans during the Spanish civil war, and were killed.

"If she was not a 'leftist,' Marguerite was absolutely not a woman of the Right," asserts her friend Anya Kayaloff. "She was very anti-Nixon, very anti-Reagan. Like all of us, she voted for Kennedy. That was the last election, for that matter, in which we voted 'for' someone. Since then, we have voted 'against.' Marguerite was 'liberal,' as people here say. Absolutely. Only in France have I heard people say anything to the contrary. No doubt because she spent time with some very right-wing people before the war." Georges de Crayencour confirms: "My aunt told me, 'Georges, my ideas are of the Left.'" But to distinguish herself from her family, Yourcenar was capable of "left-twisting" everything, including her political opinions. She proved to be more of a centrist in responding to a Québecois journalist: "Rightist? No. Nor leftist. The word 'Right' is less dear to me than the word uprightness." What she most deplored in leftist thought was its "incurable optimism." [16]

On the other hand, she would turn out to be very harsh on the subject of the Vietnam War: "The Catholics in Vietnam put anyone who has been or is a Catholic to shame," she responded in November 1969 to Jacques Kayaloff, whose opinion on the matter—too favorable in her eyes to the American governmental "line"—she did not share. "I fear I am and have always been one of those 'inflamed minds,' perhaps also one of the members of that vast group of 'intellectual snobs' to which you allude." [17] Shortly thereafter, on the question of the conflict between the individual and the state, she wrote to Gabriel Germain: "But what you are failing to observe, it seems to me, is the fact that in any conflict between an individual conscience and the State, it is the personage being called 'aberrant' by the powers that be who most often represents the silent collective conscience, which never expresses itself except by way of the intermediary of those few rare individuals who have the courage to say no. It was in the concentration camps, with the few rare Germans who had protested against Hitler, that the collective conscience of the country of Angelus Silesius, Goethe, and Schopenhauer resided, reduced by fear to silence everywhere else or drunk on propaganda. It is in the young men and young women burning draft cards and protesting against napalm that the collective (and Christian) conscience of the United States resides, elsewhere besotted by government rhetoric." [18]

WHATEVER the case may be, whether she viewed the unrest of May '68 with a benevolent eye, as she did, or condemned it, *The Abyss,* on account of the "events," should have suffered serious neglect. But, from the moment it appeared, on 8 May, the book started selling, less no doubt than it would have in a calmer spring—but selling just the same. "I realize how much the events of May were prejudicial to your enterprise," she wrote in September to Baron Etienne Coche de la Ferté—who had organized an exhibit entitled "Israël through the Ages." "They were only a very small hindrance to me, personally, with regard to the publication of my latest book, and I was amply repaid for the few difficulties I had by the extraordinary spectacle of Paris during that troubled month."[19]

The initial printing was 25,000 copies, and 15,000 more came out as early as July. The critics, with an occasional exception, spoke of a masterpiece: "Critics do not have at their disposal a fine enough homage for Marguerite Yourcenar," André Billy would even go so far as to say.[20] Patrick de Rosbo evoked a "prophetic rigor" with regard to the "image at once beyond time and, paradoxically, close to us" incarnated by Zeno: "It seems that Marguerite Yourcenar's novel is above all, in the vehemence of its tone and its writing, in the sometimes unbearable harshness of its dialogues, a book of combat, of provocation, counter to all the partisan beliefs behind which hide most often the bloodiest of fanaticisms."[21]

But once again, and this time even more so than before, the author's "virile" style, sometimes marked with praise, sometimes with vexation, provided fodder for many an article's conclusion. For Robert Kanters, *The Abyss* is "without doubt the virile masterpiece of our feminine literature," and "belongs to the very small number of books that can become for the attentive reader the vessel of an inner alchemy, at once sentimental and intellectual."[22] At the end of long, rather favorable, analyses, Henri Clouard, in *La Revue des Deux Mondes,* and José Cabanis, in *Le Monde,* concur with one another in saying that "despite its power" the book "lacks warmth" and grace.[23] This is an observation that Edith Thomas reiterated in *La Quinzaine Littéraire:*

> Marguerite Yourcenar writes well, with perfect classical form; people no longer write this way today, in an era that prefers the wail. She knows how to paint portraits, set a scene with the precision of the old Flemish masters, and at the same time paint what is essential with broad strokes. . . . Why is it that so many qualities do not entirely satisfy us? What is missing? Behind this distinction and detachment, no doubt one would also like to find more warmth.[24]

The greatest reservations were expressed in *Paris Presse-L'Intransigeant* beneath the pen of Kléber Haedens, who evoked "the long sullen life of the lugubrious Zeno."

> It does not go by quickly. One must plod painfully along unto death. It has many times been said that Marguerite Yourcenar was the most intelligent of all our women novelists, that she was endowed with a very fine style, and that she seemed to have a culture of singular depth for a woman of our time. None of all this is exaggerated. . . . Yes, no doubt, but it must be firmly stated

that all this is not sufficient. . . . *The Abyss* is a book in which one is not often given the occasion to dance. The narrative is wooly, scattered, a bit confused; it smells of magic formulas and old libraries, has almost nothing to draw us in. . . . Zeno himself is hardly a sympathetic character. . . . He roams gloomily around in this story, rudely occupied by matters that cause us not the least emotion.

Marguerite Yourcenar has some very great merits. There is reason to fear that she has not been touched by grace.[25]

Jacques Brenner, for his part, took exactly the opposite view of those for whom emotion and intelligence are contrary virtues, but he did not escape the stereotype of "virile literature":

There might be reason to fear that Zeno, a composite character, lacks life and that the book as a whole has a certain pedantic coldness. Such is not at all the case. . . . His humanism does not consist in preserving a kind of wisdom: it is "directed toward the unexplained." Likewise, Marguerite Yourcenar's classicism is always subversive by way of her reinterpretation of human thought and conduct. . . . Emotion is never absent, but always held in check. There is no giving way to the nerves, the cries, or the lewd vocabulary that betray disordered sensibilities. We are much surprised to rediscover a virile literature: and it's a woman who offers it to us.[26]

One might be irritated by this simplistic partition of warmth, emotionalism, and grace taken as an index of the "feminine" style whereas intelligence, rigor, and the absence of effusion are presumed to be specifically masculine literary attributes. Nor was it absolutely necessary for women to invent, as they did at the time, the dubious "concept" of "feminine writing."

THE ABYSS was read on the radio on 3 June, the day before Yourcenar and Frick departed for the United States, via Ireland. They were in Dublin when they heard the news of Robert Kennedy's assassination, and attended the religious service held in his memory. They landed in New York on 11 June and went immediately to Mount Desert Island. It was there that Yourcenar received a copy of the second printing of her novel. She wrote to Charles Orengo on this subject on 1 August, once again giving an example of her almost maniacal attention to everything having to do with her books. For this time it was not a question of typographical mistakes or errors altering the meaning of the text, but of a simple peculiarity, which seemed to irritate her almost as much: "I also received the day before yesterday from Gallimard an advance copy of the second printing, decked out in its jacket, which is very good-looking. I was a bit surprised that the last page bears the mention 'Print run completed on 20 July 1968' and a new copyright registration for the first quarter of the year, since this is only a simple re-printing. Granted, the second printing of *The Dark Brain of Piranesi,* which came out three months after the first one, had a new print-run date, but it retained the same copyright registration, which seems natural to me."[27]

Summer and early fall were spent in the tranquility of the island while in Paris, as soon as September's famous "literary season" commenced, marking the beginning of the race for all the prizes, people started hearing Yourcenar's name. It seems that she had ardent support on the Femina panel particularly, beginning with the most senior member of the jury, Madame Simone, who was then ninety-one years old. Yourcenar had to leave the United States on 10 November and give a few lectures in Belgium before arriving in Paris on 24 or 25 November. The Femina, as it happens, was to be awarded on 25 November. The people at Gallimard would have been well pleased if Yourcenar did not take too long getting there. "I am leaving Northeast Harbor on 7 November," she wrote on 26 October to Orengo. "A letter from Madame Léone Nora [Gallimard's press attaché] asks me to move that date up a little because of the prize, but you know my views on that topic."[28] Clearly she would not make any changes in her plans, and would leave on the day she had set, not without stopping by the office of her American lawyer, Mr. Fenton, yet again with regard to a "new" will.

Yourcenar finally reached Paris on the day the women on the Femina panel awarded her the prize, on the first ballot and unanimously, which happened for the first time since the creation of the prize in 1904. The day before, several members of the jury, the Duchesse de La Rochefoucauld, Agnès de La Gorce, and Zoé Oldenbourg, had voiced opposition to award-ing the prize to Yourcenar, arguing that the Femina-Vacaresco had been conferred on *Memoirs of Hadrian,* in 1952, sixteen years earlier. But finally, Madame Simone had succeeded at rallying her troops and extracting a unanimous vote from them. "I have feelings of gratitude and wonder, for it is very rare to see women agree to this extent about a book," Yourcenar would comment. On that day she met Elie Wiesel, who had just received the Prix Médicis—awarded on the same day as the Femina—for *Le Men-diant de Jérusalem (A Beggar in Jerusalem).*[29] She would remember this in writing to him a few years later, in 1972, after reading *Célébration hassidique (Souls on Fire: Portraits and Legends of Hasidic Masters),* which she found particularly moving: "I shall never forget that chance caused us to meet in Paris at the prize bazaar in 1968. Your presence sustained me in two or three of those moments that are supposed to represent one of the summits of success for a writer, but during which it seems to me that we were, both of us, suffocating. I felt right away that, for you, there was another reality." [30]

The Abyss, before the Femina, was already a success; Gallimard had issued more than sixty thousand copies of the novel, which, when one recalls the book's length and subject matter, and its—at least apparent—dryness, came as a surprise to more than one observer.

At the end of the day, on 25 November 1968, Editions Gallimard organized a cocktail party, as custom would have it, for their laureate. It was there that Dominique Rolin, the novelist who succeeded to Yourcenar's place in the Académie Royale of Belgium, saw the latter for the first time. She gave a highly pertinent account of her observations in her reception speech to that institution, delivered in April 1989: "I had confined myself to observing her from afar," remembers Rolin, "though I still noticed an interesting detail: instead of acting like a star, she held back from the crowd, in the manner of someone disturbed in the midst of contemplation. The massiveness of her stature, her benevolent but distracted face, the sea-blue light and shadow of her eyes taking cover under heavy brows made a strong impression on me. Draped in dark clothing, she reminded me curiously of Auguste Rodin's imposing Balzac. For the muted sobriety of her attitude was only there to mask an inflexible pride." [31] Did Yourcenar even give any thought to masking her pride, which she was far from considering a sin? Had it not led her to the success that they were celebrating that day at Gallimard, without making a single concession to the norms of the Parisian literary milieu? When it had weakened, by spells, during the war years, she had teetered on the brink of the abyss. For her it was not a synonym of arrogance, presumption, and self-importance, as certain dictionaries define it. It had been, it still was, and it would be until the last day of her existence the instrument of her survival. What would she have done without that pride, which was in fact inflexible, to keep herself from "losing hold," some four thousand miles from the place where her merits as a writer could be judged and acknowledged? Where would she have found the strength to think the thoughts she attributed to Zeno, for herself, and still go on living: "His sedentary life weighed on him like a sentence of imprisonment which, as a precaution, he might have imposed upon himself. But the sentence was revocable. . . . And nevertheless, his destiny moved on: though he did not know it, a gradual change was at work within him. Like a man swimming against the current, and in the dark of night, he had no landmark whereby to calculate exactly how far or in what direction he was being carried." [32]

For whoever doesn't tend to believe, as did Yourcenar after the fashion of Shakespeare, that life is a "chaos of shapeless and violent episodes in which can be discerned, it is true, certain general laws, but laws which almost always remain invisible to protagonists and to witnesses," it is certainly in *The Abyss* that "keys" for drawing up her intellectual, political, and moral portrait are found.[33] "Biographical interpretations, of course, are false and naive," she repeated time and again. And surely this is true, with regard to any crudely referential aspects of the latter. But Yourcenar herself knew full well how to weave subtle connections between the state of the world, the state of her reflections, and her fictions.

"It was during the war that, on the basis of an already very old preoccupation, I began *Memoirs of Hadrian*," she would recall for Claude Mettra, on the occasion of an interview, "a book that no doubt would never have seen the light of day if there had not been Europe's fight against Hitlerism, if there had not been that combat of the light against the darkness."[34]

To a student who had sent her his comparative study on Hadrian and Zeno, she would explain:

> Hadrian, written between 1949 and 1951, reflects the idea, which abided in me during that time, that a certain number of fair-minded individuals could still organize a livable world. . . . *The Abyss* on the contrary expresses the torments that are ours today. The book, obviously, owes nothing to the events of May since, having come out on the thirteenth [*sic*] of the same month, it had been written in its final form between 1960 and 1965; after that it had only been subject to a few revisions of detail and a few additions (several pages of the chapter called "The Abyss" among others). The fact is that I was overwhelmed by the "protests" of last May, because they taught me something I had not suspected, at least where France is concerned (for there had long been several signs of this in the United States): that countless members of the young generation, whom one would have thought immunized by force of habit against any skeptical reaction or revolt with regard to a world in which they had grown up, *refused* it on the contrary as Zeno refuses his own. Even if their revolt breaks down too often into acts of violence, which have no other consequences than to aggravate the situation, at least momentarily, it proves that one cannot manipulate the human spirit as easily as people believe and that, just as Christianity during the sixteenth century, and even much earlier, had its atheists, cautious though they surely were, but equally virulent (whatever certain modern historians desirous of denying the fact may say), the society of consumption and destruction is also beginning to have its own heretics.
>
> You are very right in saying that Hadrian in our time would be a conscientious minister (along the lines of a Dag Hammarskjöld or a U-Thant freer to act and impose himself) and Zeno a protester. What should be emphasized perhaps is that besides their passion for understanding (Hadrian's supreme

luxury, the bread of life for Zeno), those two men of such different situations and temperaments are bound to one another by what Hadrian calls "the determination to be of service." "There is still much to be done" the old emperor says, and, similarly, it is to his medical activities and services that Zeno steadfastly devotes himself until the end, in a world of destruction and change. There is a kind of discipline that would be worth calling attention to, for I believe that nothing solid is built, not even freedom, without it.[35]

Yourcenar would often return to the subject of what linked or separated Hadrian—"an Aquarius, the sign of abundance and giftedness"—and Zeno—"A Pisces, the secret, cold sign; passage through the abyss"—(she had had their two astrological charts prepared).[36] They are "two beings profoundly different from one another," she wrote in the "Carnets de notes de *L'Œuvre au noir*,"

> one of them reconstructed on the basis of fragments of reality, the other imaginary, but nourished by a pabulum of reality. The two lines of force, one of them starting from within the real and climbing toward the imaginary, the other starting from within the imaginary and plunging into the real, intersect. The central point is precisely a sense of the BEING. . . . Hadrian believes in the possibility of rational communication from man to man, in language that *translates* thought (and this is why one can almost oratorically cause him to recount his life); Zeno knows that every conversation has its misunderstandings and its untruths, even with the friendly Prior of the Cordeliers.[37]

"There is also," she would say elsewhere, "the difference that the perspective adopted by Hadrian is intellectual, and ceases to be so only at very rare moments, and never completely. With Zeno, there is on the contrary the dimension of the visionary."[38]

In a letter to the Belgian critic Michel Aubrion, she hypothesized

> that a Hadrian fallen into the power of his enemies would die like Zeno, and with eyes equally open, so much so that the thoughts and visions that would haunt his mortal agony would remain different. The dying Hadrian looks back upon the joys, the games, and the intellectual advantages of man's condition; Zeno concentrates his attention on the rasping of opening doors. . . . I certainly do not deny the profound difference between the two books, one that resides as you state in that darkest of epochs depicted in *The Abyss*, and also in the fact that Hadrian is more or less all-powerful and Zeno obscure and persecuted, but I have a profound sense of its being a question of two stages of the same journey, and this is no doubt what explains that I could have dreamed of writing these two books at the same time around the age of twenty, without, of course, managing to do so. I was already, and was to remain, committed to the one and to the other.[39]

However much these two works were in fact those to which she was most "committed," Yourcenar would lay a great deal of stress, in interviews and in her correspondence, on distinguishing herself from her heroes:

> There is a kind of difference here between the substance and the person. As far as the substance goes, yes; the person, no. There is Zeno the person, Zeno the individual, who is not myself for all the world, no more than I am Hadrian. . . . Except when I imagine Hadrian ill or tired, or facing a decision that needs to be made . . . The same goes for Zeno: I base myself in part on what I know about a Renaissance man of science and in part on what I do in more or less similar circumstances. When a tired Zeno offers himself a somewhat better dinner, I would have done the same thing that day. I attach an enormous amount of importance to that nonintellectual base—I don't want to say nonmental, I don't want to say not linked to the spirit, but one that does not proceed from our intellectual formulas, that is our body, our physiology, our general way of being, everything one tends a bit too much to forget when one is intelligent.[40]

"When I speak of having put all of myself into my books," she would point out, "I am a long way from believing that I could ever identify myself with one or another of my characters. I find this process of identification, which has become an obsession of contemporary psychology, profoundly repugnant."[41]

"Speaking for myself," she asserted in a very long response to a questionnaire, "I have constantly, but not always consciously, been concerned with making the main characters by means of whom 'I have expressed myself' differ from me on many points—first off in their appearance, their temperament, their physiology—or with having them inherit only a very small fraction of my own characteristics. . . . I am more and more persuaded that we are never more fruitful than when we consent to being grafted onto beings very different from ourselves."[42]

It was not identification with her characters, but their credibility and coherence that Yourcenar laid claim to: "As long as a being is not as important to us as ourselves, he is nothing," she asserted, once again in the "Carnets de notes de *L'Œuvre au noir*":

> During the winter of 1954–1955, in Fayence, I stayed up often in the company of Zeno on the edge of the great hearth in the kitchen of that early-sixteenth-century house, where the fire seemed to leap freely between the two stone pilasters protruding into the room. Later on, beginning in 1956–1957, ever so many times were spent in front of the fireplace at "Petite Plaisance."
> Moreover, I left him wherever I wanted to. Leaving Salzburg in 1964, I

had made up my mind to leave him on the stone bench of the old bakery. He waited, as sure that I would come back to him, that I would go get him, as our living friends are sure.

If I were writing this for the public, in some well-crafted essay, I would have to indicate—but how?—that this is not a matter of hallucinations. So far, I have never had one. I often said to myself in composing Hadrian: "What good is it to conjure up a ghost, when the spirit itself is always present at one's bidding?" ...

When Grace, translating, asks me to explain why a certain character makes a certain gesture at a certain moment, I hesitate and look for a reason. I *saw* him make that gesture.

Ever so many times, at night, when I'm unable to sleep, I've had the impression of *holding out my hand* to Zeno taking a rest from existence, lying on the same bed. ... This *physical* gesture of holding out my hand to that invented man I have done more than once. Let me hasten to add for the imbeciles who might read this note that, if I have often been in the position of watching my characters make love (and sometimes with a certain carnal pleasure on my part), I have never imagined myself coupling with them. One does not go to bed with a part of oneself.[43]

And if one believes the "I loved Zeno like a brother" so often repeated by Yourcenar—and one would be mistaken not to believe it—one can only see in Zeno the expression of her life ethic, whether practiced or ideal. It is curious, moreover, to observe that people have always preferred to identify Yourcenar with Hadrian rather than Zeno, an infinitely more disturbing, marginal, and transgressive character. This of course went hand in hand with her partisans' constant concern with drawing her toward the norm, toward a conformity that was nothing more than the echo of their own conformism—and from which arose her constant reminders, more numerous at the end of her life, on the subject of the misunderstandings still surrounding her *œuvre*, on the subject of those books that were "much read, certainly, but often poorly understood." It was one thing for her to be able to say that, like Zeno, she did not like "digesting death's agony" and that she refrained from eating meat. But how could one tolerate the thought that she might see herself in this portrait of Zeno:

In Basel he had merely shrugged when the cowardly burghers there had finally refused him a chair at the University; they were frightened by rumors that reported him to be a sodomite and a sorcerer. (He had been each of these things at one time or another, but names bear no relation to facts; they stand only for what the herd imagines.) ...

It was the same for the complicated domain of sensual pleasures. Those which he had preferred were the most secret and most dangerous, in Christian lands, at least, and at the time when he happened to have been born. Possibly he had sought them out only because they were prohibited, and thus had necessarily to be concealed, making for violent sundering of custom, and a plunge into that seething realm which lies beneath the visible and licit world. Or perhaps this inclination was attributable to tastes as simple but as inexplicable as those which we have for one fruit rather than for another: it mattered little to him what the reason was. The essential was that his excesses, like his ambitions, had, in sum, been rare and brief, as if it had been his nature to exhaust rapidly whatever the passions could teach or give.

This strange magma which preachers define by the not ill-chosen name of lust (since it would seem to be a matter of the luxuriance of the flesh expending its force) defies examination because of the variety of substances which compose it, and which in their turn break down into other components, themselves complex. . . .

. . . Such consuming passions had seemed to him then an inalienable part of his liberty as a man, but now it was wholly without them that he felt himself free.[44]

It was easier for certain people who liked Yourcenar for her "classicism" to speak of her reflection on power with Hadrian or on intolerance with Zeno, than to consider that the senses, the body, and the experiences induced by them had been and would be until the end her most constant preoccupation. When she had written this in *Fires,* hardly anyone had paid attention. Even when she said it clearly, reiterating time and again her aversion for sentimentality, people would refuse just as flatly to hear her.

DESPITE the misunderstandings, which are inevitable, and possibly desirable and salutary, between a writer and his or her readers—in order that a work not become rigidly set in a meaning wrought out for all eternity, whether "in conformance with the author's intentions" or not; in order, on the contrary, that it might retain its living force as a statement—*The Abyss* having been read, admired, and celebrated, something had most definitely shifted in Marguerite Yourcenar's destiny. What she had dreamed of in her now distant youth had, in part, been realized: not only the desire expressed in those few words she had put in the mouth of Alexis—"As a child, I yearned for glory"—but the determination to be useful, to leave a trace, a proof that one has not lived in vain. From then on she believed that there would always be—even in this world that she feared would return to darkness, to a technology-induced illiteracy, out of irresolution and intellectual laziness— men and women "mad enough and wise enough" to understand Zeno's message. There would always be people seeking to free themselves, wherever they might be, from their constraints, without pleading for tolerance or approbation, knowing all the while that they would have to wear "the livery of [their] time, whether willing or no" and would allow "the world in which [they] moved to incline [their] faculty of judgment in certain directions."[45]

THUS SHE COULD have calmly returned to Petite Plaisance. But she had no desire to, not before springtime at least. She preferred to go along with the literary laureates' inevitable tour of the provinces and, perhaps, make a foray into Spain. During that entire period, Frick, in her daybook, did not say a word in her own name. Less than ever before. She confined herself to recording facts: 1 December, death of Erika Vollger (their old seamstress friend); 5 December, Natalie Barney; 8 December, Anne Quellennec ... Frick had wanted this triumph for Yourcenar too much not to have felt an unquestionable pride. But, as happened every time she was no longer in complete control of things, not even the appointments, which Gallimard's press relations department was arranging, she grew rigid. She shut herself off, was often absent, even making a rather spectacular show of her withdrawal, as several people noticed that year at Gallimard. While Yourcenar was signing her books on the long table in the library, Frick was sitting on the floor next to the radiator, writing on her knees. This was certainly not solely because she was cold.

On 15 December 1968, before leaving Paris for Saumur, then Avignon, where they would spend Christmas, Yourcenar and Frick received a few friends in their apartment at the Hôtel Saint-James. Frick had prepared the traditional eggnog. Jean Chalon had been invited. He remembers finding himself alone in the middle of a group of women—if other men had come, they were not present at the same time he was. "It's a bit far off," he says, "but I remember having met Pauline Carton there, who stayed at the Saint-James on a yearly basis, and Germaine Beaumont, one of the members of the Femina jury at the time. I believe I headed straight for Germaine Beaumont, one of the only guests I was acquainted with. But Grace Frick soon came and separated us, insisting that people should meet one another, and not stay in a corner with those they already knew. She led me to another group. She resembled one of the characters in that old comic strip *L'Espiègle Lili* [Mischievous Lili]." In this comic strip created by the Frenchmen Vale and Vallet, in 1909, Lili was a saucy little blonde. Physically, Frick was more like Lili's cousin, Julia, but it would be stretching matters to push the identification with this character any further. She was a veritable menace: envious, bitter, and small-minded. "As for Marguerite Yourcenar," Chalon also recalls, "she was sitting in an armchair and did not budge, whereas Grace bustled about incessantly. When one got a chance to speak with her for a few minutes, one was taken, as always, by the charm of her conversation. But it would not be long before Grace interrupted the exchange to bring someone else over to speak with Marguerite and let you know you should go elsewhere."

Until March of 1969, Yourcenar and Frick would traverse the south of France, going both to the east (Aix, Marseille, where they attended concerts and the theater a great deal) and to the west (Perpignan, Toulouse). Their time was much taken up by interviews and signings in various bookstores, which Yourcenar submitted to with no real displeasure despite their repetitive nature: she still had a curiosity for those brief encounters, into which upon occasion enters something of the complicity and fleeting closeness that sharing a universe, however provisionally, affords both a reader and an author.

In January Yourcenar wrote a tribute for the *Nouvelle Revue Française* to Jean Schlumberger, one of the founders of the review, who had died at the age of ninety-one, on 26 October 1968. "It was around 1930," she recalls, "in a Parisian salon that I met for the first time this quick, dry man with a courtesy that no longer exists." But it was twenty years later, in Paris, when *Memoirs of Hadrian* had just been published that "communications were definitively established." In that apparently too cautious *œuvre*, laid out like "French gardens," Yourcenar nonetheless saw an "almost tragic poetry," and concludes: "It appears that the characteristically cautious bearing of Jean Schlumberger was more useful than harmful to his true freedom: his puritan rigor, which, according to him, was mitigated rather late in life but never rejected, for many years gave him a sort of gluttonous desire to live as a discreet presence in his books—a quality which stands in contrast to Gide's more hectic avidity. . . . If you listen to him carefully, it sometimes seems that this man, who almost voluntarily withdrew from our generation and even from his own, nevertheless advanced bolder propositions than many of his contemporaries who were thought to be more adventurous than he."[46]

YOURCENAR put her few moments of solitude to equally good use for the purpose of answering the large volume of mail that *The Abyss* had brought her way. Thus did she respond, for example, to a letter from Montherlant received at the end of December, in which he told her how enthused he was about the book and confided having cast his vote for *The Abyss* for the novel prize awarded by the Académie Française. "Receiving your letter, as

I did this morning, has been for me like finding the charm in my piece of Twelfth-night cake."[47]

> I am infinitely touched that you took the time and the trouble to write to me. One of the principal virtues of your letter is that it gives me an opportunity to express my admiration to you better than I could in a few dedications. I would have already written—perhaps at too much length—to tell you how much certain of your books have meant to me, if I did not know you to be one of those people who are quick to be put out by intrusions. I shall confine myself to saying that *Le Chaos et la nuit (Chaos and Night)* strikes me as being one of the greatest books it has ever been granted me to read, and that the moment in *La Rose de sable (Desert Love)* when two men see death coming in a medina is quite simply unforgettable. The only play that I went to see during my rather empty, rather heavy-laden stay in Paris was *La Ville dont le prince est un enfant (The Fire That Consumes)*, and I was happy to observe that, contrary to my fears, the theater did it no disservice. . . .
>
> I was, in my turn, amused by your questions revolving around Zeno, and shall answer them . . . Though they don't call for a response. Zeno, at the outset, wants to be a god; he ends up like a saint set off on non-Christian pathways. Is he an angel or archangel? No more than the rest of us, and I tried to leave him his human physiology right up until the end. That he might, rather, feel his Genius (with a capital G) or his god (small g) within himself. *Sequere deum,* Casanova said in this sense; no doubt he was a charlatan, but he was bolder than those who think his only audacity was lifting up skirts believe he was.[48]

Just the same, there was still some spare time, in this early part of 1969, for Yourcenar, and Frick, to do a bit of sightseeing. Without regret they abandoned the idea of going to Spain, where a state of emergency had been declared, but instead they visited the cloisters of Saint-Michel-de-Cuxa, Saint-Guilhem-du-Désert, and went, on 17 March, to Monségur,[49] where Yourcenar remembered that "exactly 725 years earlier that same meadow was blackened and covered with still-glowing embers."[50] They also took advantage of this trip to see Joseph Delteil and his American wife in their farmhouse, at the Tuilerie de Massane, near Montpellier, and the home of Jeanne Galzy, one of the members of the Femina jury, whom Yourcenar telephoned at Natalie Barney's suggestion. They saw each other numerous times. Galzy, who had something of a taste for women, was quite captivated by Yourcenar and would keep up a correspondence with her. She would even complain about her silence occasionally: "so write a little more just the same, to either Natalie or me. I have long been friends with Natalie and I admire the courage with which she dared to be herself in a time and milieu that were so conventional."[51] Yourcenar, who never ceased to enjoy charming others, liked "the vigor" and "the simplicity" of Galzy, "a native of Auvergne, and indestructible like the granite of her region."

During her stay in Hérault, Yourcenar heard of an event in the news that had occurred in Orange; it made a lasting impression on her, as is shown in a letter to Elizabeth Barbier, another member of the Femina jury whom she had seen again briefly in Avignon:

> I only know about [this news item] from a few lines in *La Dépêche du Midi*, which, ever since, have haunted me. A certain Marc Morel, a sixteen-year-old lycée student, who was circulating petitions against the war in Vietnam and the slaughter of the seals, and was collecting donations for Biafra, committed suicide (by fire) on the hill of Sainte-Europe. And it was not a sudden decision, as they found this note where he lived (or did he tell someone?): "one day I shall surely have to find the courage to die." This image of a young being (and there are many others) who does not accept the world in which he is forced to live has not left me since. I thought about composing an article on the subject, but I realized I knew too little about it to base any kind of writing on his case, even were it committed in the best sense of the word. If I had been there, I would have made a discreet attempt to find out more about it. Perhaps this boy in distress was one of the teenagers whose path I crossed in the streets of Orange without thinking of looking at them, when I stopped there last March with Grace Frick coming back from Pont-Saint-Esprit where I had gone to retrace the steps of my Zeno.[52]

Here again we find exemplified the real concern she had for understanding young people of an entirely different generation, to which the long letters exchanged with this or that young writer or this or that budding researcher, had already testified, even if the tone of those letters was sometimes a bit sententious.

On 20 March 1969 Yourcenar and Frick boarded ship in Le Havre and reached New York six days later. Yourcenar gave a lecture at Columbia University on "the historical novel, authenticity and topicality," and on the thirty-first they were back at Petite Plaisance. It was a very quiet spring, summer, and fall made up of visits from friends, especially the McGarrs; champagne on 8 June for Yourcenar's birthday, in the rediscovered intimacy of days gone by; picture taking—on 2 August—with Hortense King (Flexner) for the translation and critical introduction by Yourcenar to Flexner's poems, which would come out at Gallimard at the end of October.

And, as ever, there was a more and more consuming correspondence, which took up part of Yourcenar's days at Petite Plaisance. It was during this time that a brief exchange of letters commenced between her and Patrick de Rosbo, a French journalist who hoped to come to Mount Desert to tape some interviews. Their acquaintanceship, which ended in a violent quarrel, after the radio interviews and their publication as a book, began beneath the sign of a genuine courtesy.[53] Yourcenar responded most willingly to Rosbo's preliminary questions, notably in a letter of 26 April 1969. She mentioned the times when she was absent from France, from 1939 to 1951 and from 1956 to 1968, but pointed out that before 1939 she had spent part of the year in Paris. Asked about her friends, she was very evasive, as she nearly always was, never having thought that confidential disclosure was a mode of public communication. "I have both many friends and very few," she wrote. "Many correspondents unknown to me become friends, through my tendency to settle rather quickly into friendship as soon as an initial, sympathetic contact has been established." Nevertheless, she had few close friends left "because of my long absences from Paris and numerous trips from one spot on the map to another (sporadic meetings do not favor intimate friendships)." Perhaps also because of "a certain independence or singularity of thought that is responsible for my never having belonged to any group and having quickly left those I had happened to frequent."[54] But it was also, though she does not say so, because of Frick's jealousy, which would have complicated her life. By staying with Frick, Yourcenar had admitted that, in order to avoid that particular complication, she would have to renounce pursuing any friendship to a deeper level. Frick, in effect, would not tolerate Yourcenar having friendships from which she was excluded. By definition, no one is the "intimate friend" of two people making up a couple. The only true space of intimacy that Frick left Yourcenar was her dreams and her literature. And it was precisely in Yourcenar's books that everything that troubled Frick revealed itself. She had read too much of Yourcenar's work, line by line, word by word, and had observed her too closely not to know that the only thing that interested her was a sensual approach to the universe, that she was curious about others, enjoyed the notion of seducing, and was happy now to be admired and courted, to be fascinating young men and women, she who had never ceased to be a lover of physical beauty and youth. As Frick's illness grew worse, her rigidity and habit of "controlling" Yourcenar turned into nervous agitation, then obsession. This explains Yourcenar's growing resentment over the course of the seventies, which she would never have let herself express in front of Frick, heroic as she was in the face of her illness. And it explains in part what happened during the eighties: Grace's memory and that of their life together were put on the Index.[55]

The decade that was coming to an end in the fall of 1969 closed thirty years of Frick's mad love—in the full sense of this adjective—for Yourcenar, thirty years of the existence of a couple who, through their moments of grand passion and their little rituals, their odd ways, their kindnesses, and their exclusions, managed not only to survive but to live. The seventies would be the years of illness, of the slow contamination of old age. But, as always, this slide did not reveal itself flagrantly until after the fact.

At the end of 1969, Yourcenar was off to war again against Editions Plon, which had just published the fifth edition of *Alexis* and the fourth edition of *A Coin in Nine Hands,* both of them riddled with errors: a "mess (for I can find no other word)," Yourcenar would write to her friends Hélène Schakhowskoy and Anne Quellennec. "A hundred sentences or parts of sentences are missing and senseless transitions abound . . . which is why I am no longer corresponding with those people except by way of a lawyer or some other legal official."[56] One more time, Yourcenar would win her case: the faulty editions were no longer sold, and the affair led to the signing of a contract with Gallimard, on 3 September 1970, establishing—among other things—the transfer of rights for these two works.

Apparently, this was a period of "above average" activity in the American life of Yourcenar and Frick, including dinner with someone who proposed to make *Hadrian* into a movie (Yourcenar refused); a book order from Yourcenar to a French bookseller, as always, "to check if the faulty editions are still in circulation"; a lecture at Smith College for the one hundredth anniversary of Gide's birth; a visit and lectures at the French Library in Boston; sending the manuscript of *Render unto Caesar*—the play based on *A Coin in Nine Hands*—and a text on Oppian followed by the translation of a few verses to *La Revue de Paris;* and a demonstration in Bar Harbor, on 13 December, for "Peace Now" in Vietnam. It was one of those very American demonstrations where one transforms oneself into a sandwich man or woman and spends the entire day on a section of sidewalk, "to testify." "It was an experience of the pillory," Yourcenar would say. To Bernard Pivot, whose astonishment at seeing "Marguerite Yourcenar going to the sit-in" amused her greatly, she explained how much that all seemed normal to her, like belonging to forty-odd societies "of defense, of protection, of conservation . . ." If Yourcenar was in any way American, it was surely thus: in this form of public-spiritedness that brings one to write or send telegrams to senators or governors protesting against such and such a project. "And don't think it's not effective," she emphasized to a somewhat incredulous Pivot. "All those letters and telegrams are carefully checked off. It is very important in electoral terms."

With her election to Belgium's Académie Royale and the operation she had to undergo on 27 August (once again it was feared that she, too, had breast cancer), the two dominant axes of Yourcenar's life over the course of that decade took shape. On the one hand, she received steadily accumulating expressions of literary recognition, and on the other, she faced growing old and illness. Frick, no doubt unable to ignore the pull of death, despite her fierce will to live, gives the impression through her notes, which grew progressively scarcer, that everyone around her was on the verge of mortal agony—and she was not always wrong. In 1970 the daybook speaks of nothing but visits to doctors, biopsies and other tests, Yourcenar's stay in the hospital, Charles Orengo's last visit to Petite Plaisance—he would fall ill the following year and die of cancer in 1974—and the codicil to Yourcenar's will, which she signed at her lawyer's office on 25 August 1970, two days before her operation.

Barely a week after that operation, on 2 September, Rosbo arrived in Northeast Harbor to tape his radio interviews. He planned to stay until the tenth. The date was clearly not very well chosen, and everything transpired in such a way as to exasperate Frick, beginning with the telephone call he made at nine o'clock on the evening he arrived. He was at the airport in Bangor, on the mainland, and had no American currency with which to pay a taxi to take him to Mount Desert Island. Grace gave him the name of a hotel, where money would be waiting for him at the reception desk. Regarding that visit all that remains, from Frick, is a few furious sentences in her daybook: 6 September, Rosbo to dinner. Stays late; 8 September, M.Y. exhausted. Rosbo camping out here; 10 September, Rosbo finally leaves. The quality or mediocrity of an interview always revealing more about the interviewer than the interviewee, it is easy to see—since today we can read over those published conversations at our leisure—that Rosbo was not at all in control of the situation, and that, clearly, no current of sympathy flowed between him and Yourcenar.[57] Was this due to Yourcenar's fatigue? To the pressure and tension generated by Frick's mute reprobation? This is probably so to a certain extent, but not solely. The questions are too long, and badly formulated; they discourage one from responding. However, Yourcenar already possessed that "gift of speaking of herself with an eloquence as calm as it was veiled" described by Dominique Rolin, and Rosbo at least deserves credit for having been the first one to try to make her do so at length.[58]

ABOUT THE PHOTOGRAPH of Frick set atop a low bookcase in the living room, it was Yourcenar's custom to say: "That's the last good photograph of Grace." That is, it was the one from before the irreparable disaster of her cancer getting worse. The photograph was taken in 1971, in Belgium. Grace was sixty-eight. It is one of the most becoming pictures of her that still exist. She has lost the severity of her youth, beneath wrinkles etched by time and physical suffering. On her face mingle a certain weariness, as if from some furtive deterioration, and an unwavering energy. Her look conveys what will never be said about her often enough—one tends to be so easily distracted and annoyed by her bad side, her maniacal, authoritarian ways: it speaks of her intelligence, her delicacy, her humor.

Nineteen seventy-one, which began in the midst of a blizzard, would in fact be a year of ultimate torment, especially for Frick. She would make her final trip to Europe to accompany Yourcenar to the Académie Royale of Belgium. Yourcenar was inducted on 27 March by Carlo Bronne, and she delivered a formal address in praise of the professor and essayist Benjamin Mather Woodbridge.[59] Beforehand, having left the United States on 7 March aboard an oceanliner headed for Algeciras, they had crossed through Spain again, where they had left behind so many pleasant memories, of Holy Week in Seville and the week they spent almost entirely at the Prado museum, in 1960. Yourcenar delighted in retracing her steps—as in her books. She would return in order to take total possession of the sites, to appropriate unto herself what was unique about them and changeable, to enjoy them alone, without a guide, following a purely internal itinerary. This was one of the constants of her behavior, a form of autarchy remarked upon time and again, that probably goes back to her peculiar childhood. The silent homage she rendered to Frick after her death—despite statements attempting to refute this—was her relentless return, alongside her discovery of new lands, in the Orient especially, to the sites that they had savored together.

In Madrid, of course, they went back to the Prado. Once again Yourcenar had a chance to marvel at Velázquez's *Las Meninas*—and ponder over them. Would she ever come up with her own answer to the question of the place of the painter in the painting? She who was becoming aware that her hidden persona—distant, insular, and nomadic—was intriguing, fascinating, irritating sometimes, but in any event attracting more and more numerous readers, concluded that she was going to have to confront the question of her own "visibility" in the art work. She would either have to meet it head on or sidestep the issue, cover her tracks a little better still, an activity in which she excelled.

In Brussels, the members of the de Crayencour family, seeing Yourcenar honored by their country's Académie Royale, suddenly became aware that she existed and was related to them, despite having renounced their patronymic. This renouncement was no source of annoyance for some, who held writers in very low esteem, especially when they took it upon themselves to treat themes still licentious in their eyes, notably sexual relations having nothing to do with procreation and the perpetuation of the sacrosanct family. Yourcenar met with them, or rather crossed their path. Her attitude would vary between chilly politeness and outright hostility, deeming as she did these belated attempts at rapprochement to be in rather bad taste. The only one she took pleasure in seeing was one of her half nephews, Georges de Crayencour, with whom she'd been in touch for several years, since 1966 to be exact, thanks to Louise de Borchgrave, of whom Yourcenar had always been very fond. Yourcenar appreciated Georges's enthusiasm—which he did not shrink from expressing, although in his milieu and his family he had no doubt been enjoined to hold everything back at all times. This also included his taste for drawing and literature, and, it would seem, his interest in her. As mentioned earlier, Georges de Crayencour would be a great help to her while she was writing the second volume of her family trilogy, *Archives du Nord.* During that time, they would carry on a lengthy, precise, and fascinating correspondence.[60]

After Brussels, Yourcenar and Frick traveled in Belgium and Holland for a month and a half, happily staying for a time in Bruges. Yourcenar went for walks and dreamed of Zeno. Together the two women saw some old friends again, like Monsieur and Madame Jean Eeckhout, whom they had met during the fifties in rather comical circumstances. Yourcenar, in fact, had to give a lecture, and one of the organizers, Jean Eeckhout, had come to pick her up at her hotel. She wanted to wear a dress with a long zipper in the back but could not manage to zip it up by herself, and Frick, indisposed by an attack of lumbago, couldn't budge. Thus, no sooner were the introductions out of the way than Eeckhout found himself transformed into a lady in waiting. After the lecture he noted that "there is the matter of a zipper that needs to be unzipped": Yourcenar accepted this second assist with an utterly aristocratic informality.

The two weeks in Paris, from 16 May to 30 May 1971, would be uneventful ones, with the usual allotment of visits with friends, meetings at Gallimard—to take care of some minor problems since they were there—and interviews with journalists. It was thus that Yourcenar saw Jean Chalon, whom she looked on as a friend. That particular interview, published in *Le Figaro,* would garner its author one of those letters of rectification for which Yourcenar seemed to have a singular penchant: "I surely did not utter this sentence, which is unthinkable for me: 'my anthology of Greek poets is lying dormant for the time being . . . Who still cares about Empedocles in our era?' as if that indifference were my reason for not going on and publishing this book. This, dear Jean Chalon, contradicts every aspect of my personal orientation: when did I care to know if people cared or not?"[61] On this last point she was right, and Chalon readily acknowledged as much in the response he made to her on 1 August: in her work as in her life, Marguerite Yourcenar did not seek primarily to please . . . anyone other than herself.

The ten days or so spent in Rouen and the surrounding region, before boarding ship at Le Havre on 13 June, would leave Yourcenar and Frick with a soothing remembrance of the gentle beauty of Normandy. From Le Havre they took a Soviet ship that was to land in Montreal: the route heading down to Mount Desert from Montreal seemed more appealing to them, especially at that time of year, than the one coming up from New York—through its most sinister sections—to Maine, even though, after Boston, and after Portland especially, Route 1, which follows the ocean, retained the charm of days gone by. But, as if Chance were attempting to tell Grace that she was on the threshold of a cruel time, just as soon as the boat left port she took a serious fall. She dislocated her knee and had to make the entire journey immobilized in her cabin, with one leg in a cast. She who loved nothing as much as the sea had her final transatlantic crossing ruined by this accident. Upon reaching Montreal, she was, needless to say, not in any shape to drive—she even had to use crutches to walk for several weeks—and since Yourcenar had always refused to learn to drive, they would return to Petite Plaisance with a chauffeur. It was the end of June, the weather was springlike, and the garden was colorful and pleasant. Yourcenar did not yet know that her "country house" was going to be the sole location, for more than nine years, in which her life would unfold.

July brought Frick back to the hospital in Bar Harbor where the results of her X-rays and mammography tests gave scant cause for optimism: the cancer was gaining ground. Florence Codman's visit brightened up the month of August. They also took pleasure in talking with her, in hearing her elegant French, which she spoke with the jubilation of one who loves the language. She was cultured, subtle, astute. She was exactly the same age as Frick, since they had been in college together. Seeing how much younger and more alert Codman seemed, Yourcenar suddenly could measure the ravages already wrought by Frick's illness, which daily contact had concealed from her.

During that same month she wrote to the Nabisco company one of those letters of protest she had evoked in her conversation with Bernard Pivot.

It's too bad that she hadn't had it with her and read it—or rather translated it—for her interlocutor. He could not have failed to find it toothsome:

> Having long been a faithful consumer of Nabisco wafers, I cannot protest vigorously enough against the production of commercialized horror toys by your new subsidiary, Aurora Plastic. This incredible, repugnant brutality illustrates to what abysmal depths has sunk what we continue to call this Christian civilization. It heaps opprobrium on the very word America.
>
> Obviously, I shall no longer be buying any products whatsoever from your firm until you officially announce that these revolting toys have been taken out of circulation, and I also have the firm intention of doing everything I can to dissuade anyone else I come in contact with from buying your products, for the same reasons.[62]

Nineteen seventy-one was also the year that Gallimard published the two volumes of *Théâtre* [Plays], variously judged by the critics, more than one of whom observed that the pieces were more "to be read than mounted": "The three Greek dramas that I tried to write are all allegories, in one way or another," Yourcenar explained, "which is to say that the characters count less for themselves than as signs, or as components of a certain experience. (This is almost the opposite of my technique in *Hadrian,* and in *The Abyss*). There is almost no attempt at hellenistic realism."[63]

WHEN, in the month of September, Editions Seghers brought out the first long study devoted to her, signed by Jean Blot, Yourcenar wrote to her friend Jeanne Carayon that this work "came very close to plunging me into the darkest despondency, though the author apparently imagines he is praising me."[64] It was not until the eve of the study's publication that Blot told Yourcenar about his book: "Your work, its treatment of time, its acceptance and rejection of myth, its warm eroticism, have inspired me to write an essay. . . . Being a critic yourself—and an admirable one—you will not be surprised that I did not seek to contact you before finishing my essay. Nothing so inhibits a free approach to literary work as knowing its author."[65] Yourcenar, who noted at the top of Blot's letter "not answered," and who later indicated—and on numerous occasions—with regard to its author that "I didn't even know that he existed," wrote to him on 1 September:

> I had read in various newspapers that a work by you, on me, was going to come out at Seghers. I shall read it, as you can well imagine, with very great interest, just as I read not long ago the article you published, on the subject, I believe, of *The Abyss,* in the *Nouvelle Revue Française.* As for your desire not to meet the author you are writing about while you are doing

your work, I understand it very well. For my own part, ardently desirous as I am to penetrate a being's complex individuality as much as one can, I think that I would very much have liked to meet Cavafy or Mann if I had been able to, but perhaps such encounters would have been singularly disconcerting. And I would have had to step back quite a ways, afterward, in order to amalgamate what those encounters had taught me with what I had learned from the books themselves . . . But I also accept the freedom of the painter for whom what counts is to recreate the model in his particular fashion and with methods all his own.[66]

"I shall never understand such an attitude," she would nonetheless write some time later, to one of her correspondents, "I who would have given so much to know Cavafy, or to have had a different experience of Mann than that of simply exchanging letters."[67] "I who would have given a year of my life to meet Hadrian," she would often say, "how can I subscribe to Jean Blot's attitude?"

But the truth is that what Yourcenar blamed Blot for above all was having focused his analysis on the works published before the war, and neglecting what was much more important to her, *Memoirs of Hadrian* and *The Abyss.* "I wrote somewhere, on the subject of critical biography, that one always built the monument in one's own fashion, but that working with authentic stones was, in itself, a step in the right direction," she would respond to Marcel Lobet, the author of a review favorable to Blot in *La Revue Générale.* "But the stones used by Blot, by which I mean the books taken out of their chronological context, cease to be authentic, and as if by chance, all the cornerstones are missing."[68] The updated essay reissued in 1980 seemed to her "certainly preferable"—a just barely courteous assessment, accompanied by many reservations.

With the arrival of fall, Yourcenar and Frick took advantage of the pleasures that the garden had to offer, particularly those lavished upon them by the "orchard"—pleasures that Yourcenar expanded on at length for her friend Carayon.[69] "I enjoy telling you all this," she wrote, "because, living in the country, you will understand. The people who are writing about me in Paris haven't the slightest idea about my way of life."[70] The main objective of that long letter, a very friendly one, was in fact a scrupulous rectification of the proof corrections of certain works about to be reissued. First of all, Yourcenar paid tribute to the work Frick had done on the revisions in question: "Grace Frick has also been a great help to me, checking the corrections one by one after the fact (a job that takes hours), and most often writing them herself in the margins, as she has finer penmanship than mine. At those moments when my head was literally spinning, her acuity and attention took over where my own left off. But naturally I always have qualms about time stolen this way (and many other ways) from her translation work."[71] Yourcenar—who was particularly demanding in this domain—judged this work, "half of it" done in France by Carayon, "admirable": "Every time I finished reading a batch of proofs," she wrote to her, "I wanted to write you a long letter discussing the corrections in detail, thanking you for the suggestions I used, and explaining why I had set others aside." She did not fail to do so.

But this particular letter, which Yourcenar finished the following day, 3 October, was lengthened on account of bad news—the dog Valentine's death:

> 3 October, half past two in the afternoon.
> I had just barely finished this letter when we suffered a very great loss. I had gone out to pick some flowers, with the little dog. Valentine joyously bounded across the street, which is very quiet at this time of year, to go run around in the neighbors' very large yard. I crossed over with her, always having made it a point not to be on the opposite side of the street from her, but she had already jumped out in front of an oncoming car, which, for that matter, was moving at a very moderate speed, and just a second later I saw her lying in the road, with her neck broken. She did not suffer at all. With the help of our excellent neighbor, the gardener, and his wife, we buried her nearby her predecessor, Monsieur, laid out on armfuls of ferns turned yellow by autumn. A little atom of joy in the world.

Frick, who finished typing this letter, was upset by the sobriety and apparent lack of emotion in this account written "right after the fact"—to the point of adding this note in her own hand:

> Dear friends, I am beginning to understand why her less subtle readers consider M. Yourcenar to be a "cold" writer. Only someone who has lost a being or a creature so brutally can know the state of anguish in which she wrote this postscript, on the same afternoon. As you know, Valentine was always with her. She lived literally at her feet, in the office, in the garden, on trips. . . . Sadly, G. F.

We might well wonder what somber reflections were aroused in Frick by observing, in Yourcenar, a grief so masterfully contained in the face of losing a precious creature.

In point of fact, as Yourcenar would admit a long time afterward, recounting this accident orally, she had been so "shocked" that she fell to the ground, saying over and over in French, "they killed the dog, they killed the dog . . . ," in front of a woman who didn't understand a word of it and could only offer money to replace her. "As during several such hours of my life, I felt all the oppressiveness of time," she would also say. A few years later she would write in her "Carnets de notes de *L'Œuvre au noir*": "In 1971, I retraced each one of Zeno's comings and goings in the streets of Bruges. . . . Morning walks, all one month of April, sometimes in the sun, more often in fog or in drizzle. And with me there was Valentine the beautiful, the gentle, the blonde, she who barked full-throatedly at horses (and I would stop her), she who ran around joyfully in the courtyard of the Gruuthuse mansion, she who jumped among the jonquils in the garden of the *Béguinage*—and now (six months later, on 3 October 1971) as dead as Idelette, as Zeno, as Hilzonda. And no one will understand me if I say that I shall never get over it, no more than I would a human death."[72]

IT WAS IN October that a crew arrived from the Office of French Radio and Television accompanied by Matthieu Galey. "A somewhat oppressive prospect," she commented in a letter to Carayon. "But I'm glad they're coming during 'Indian summer' when the trees start taking on their beautiful alchemical colors."[73] Matthieu Galey: the beginning of a long friendship that would end rather badly, after the publication of his book of interviews, *With Open Eyes*, in 1981. It is as if writing a book on Marguerite Yourcenar were already, whatever its nature, committing a kind of offense, indeed a sin, an inadmissible captation, the assertion of an unacceptable autonomy. This amounts to stating the obvious when one knows Yourcenar's relationship to the written word, a relationship of total appropriation, in which her megalomania nearly led her to deny the other his own way of expressing himself: "I speak for myself, I know what I'm saying, I'm the one who says."

So in 1971 French television made the trip to Northeast Harbor, marking the beginning of Yourcenar's portrayal in the popular media; that crew would not be the last. Petite Plaisance's gardener, the friendly, obliging, faithful neighbor Elliott McGarr was interviewed alongside her. Such would *never* be the case for Frick. Perhaps to anticipate Yourcenar's wishes, and surely out of pride, she abstained. Frick would always be an intaglio image, the exemplary figure of effacement.

A sign of where the real power was . . . perhaps; a mark of elegance and intelligence, without a doubt.

17
Yourcenar, Marguerite

WHILE MARGUERITE YOURCENAR, now enthroned as "a great French writer" by virtue of *The Abyss*, was on the road to glory, with the recognition of her peers, and even that of a public well beyond the already vast circle of her readers, Grace Frick was on the road to pain and death: the relations between them could only grow strained and deteriorate.

Yourcenar, nonetheless, remained totally faithful to her commitments. Just as Frick had been her rampart, from 1939 to 1945, against a gradual slide into depression whose outcome no one could foresee, she would from now on be Frick's mooring. But there was one big difference: this time, no one could fail to foresee either the outcome or its imminence. It was not so much a battle as a death watch.

Frick wanted Yourcenar to stay with her and refused to entertain any thoughts of travel. According to certain friends, Yourcenar's nurse Deirdre Wilson in particular, Yourcenar, without Frick, would have been incapable of traveling on her own. But Yourcenar's abstinence from travel cannot be entirely explained by such a simplification. All the correspondence pertaining to previous travel arrangements is proof that she did her share of making hotel reservations and taking care of other formalities: a practical, organizational sense was not totally foreign to her. Besides, it would have been easy for Yourcenar then to find other people to deal with her "administrative" problems—her publisher, for instance, would have liked nothing better than for her to be right there in Paris promoting her books. As always with these two women and the strange life they shared, things were more subtle, more violent, and no doubt more perverse as well. It was as if from the compulsory quarantine of the one and the accepted but detested quarantine of the other could be born an ultimate emotion, and perhaps a form of ultimate pleasure.

"It was her wish that I stay with her and that was quite natural. I also loved those springs and summers, falls and winters in my garden," Yourcenar would later confide. But this consentment to a sedentary life, which had already proven unbearable for her on more than one occasion in the past, was not as easily accomplished as she tried to make out, caught as she was in the role of a woman advancing in years having reached a state of serenity, having supposedly made her way through all the storms steady on.

Proof of this can be found in the letters that Yourcenar wrote, in early 1972, when she was awarded the Prince-Pierre-de-Monaco literary prize, in the amount of fifty thousand francs. She told Louise de Borchgrave that she had every intention of going to Monaco, as is customary, to receive her prize: "I think that my father would have been amused and pleased by this Monaco prize," she wrote. "I almost feel as if I'm getting back some of those gold louis he so loved to wager."[1] Yourcenar did not, however, go to Monte Carlo: Frick had to be hospitalized for a few days in April, and things were no better in December, at the time of the presentation ceremony.

In her daybook, Frick hardly wrote down anything now besides doctor's appointments, stays in the hospital, and the comings and goings of workers taking care of maintaining the house: for the first time in thirty years, she failed to give a faithful account, in her calendar, of Yourcenar's work, though she was nearing the end of writing *Dear Departed.* It had always been at the moment a manuscript was nearing completion that Frick ordinarily, went into high gear, rendering a scrupulous account of her activities in the daybooks. From rereadings to photocopies, "The Book" that Yourcenar had written, whatever it was, occupied her totally. It seems that she did not take part at all in *Dear Departed,* as if she had withdrawn at that point from the sphere in which the literary *œuvre* was produced. Perhaps it was because Yourcenar had gone off in search of her own family, to regions of memory in which she played no part. Between the quest for a past that repudiated her and a literary future from which she was barred by her illness, she could only feel excluded, had no choice but to absent herself—at least with respect to that personage called "Yourcenar," for she would write down "Marguerite's" daily doings, her friend's headaches and colds, right up until her dying day. Nonetheless, this lack of interest can only be seen as a first sign of the end. Yourcenar and Frick were growing distant from each other because, from then on, face to face without reprieve, they were condemned to one another, confined to the house and the yard—like an old couple. And yet neither one of them would have imagined that this was the way things would end.

Grace could not bear the idea that Marguerite would outlive her. The predominant feeling she had, a constant trait of her character, was less a fear of death than an extraordinary desire to live—which would even lead her to begin a new treatment, still at the experimental stage, a few weeks before her death. It was on account of that very energy that Frick had always considered herself the "survivor." The court clerk, then, would end up being the judge as well as the indispensable witness. Her admiration and her love for Marguerite no doubt prevented her from recognizing this clearly, but those daybooks, and her habit of writing "everything" down, were a way of both possessing her friend and concealing her from others at the same time. Whether Frick used them after Yourcenar's death or they were left to bear witness after her own—which was the case—they would, of course, tell the tale, day by day, of the existence of Marguerite Yourcenar. But one would more likely find in those records the maladies suffered than the books that were read, the mention of a stroll in the garden than the conversation that was held there.

Yourcenar was well aware of this, in rereading them, and she attached a card written in English to the last calendar, the one from 1979, indicating: "For Houghton Library (or if that library isn't interested, for the Grace Frick collection at Wellesley). Grace Frick's daybooks. Travel diaries or records of visitors to Petite Plaisance, or else—previously—stays in Hartford and Kansas City. Very few (relatively) mentions of M.Y." Reading this short text for the first time is confusing. It is perfectly clear that the daybooks concern no one but Marguerite Yourcenar, or nearly. However, the picture they paint is much more that of a sickly, plaintive woman, one who likes to travel though she's often tired, or even depressed, than of a writer borne by the desire to establish an *œuvre*. Thus, although she arranged for her own texts to be preserved at Harvard, Yourcenar foresaw—or hoped for—the possible exclusion of Frick's daybooks: the gesture—and what it symbolized—is positively chilling.

Once she knew there was no hope, the final power Frick retained was that of retracing Yourcenar's life during the seventies, by means of her lacunary daybooks, and as her own life was shrinking. Frick knew, however, that nothing could be done against the books—which would remain—that nothing could be done to keep a writer from meeting her public; that nothing could be done to fend off recognition and fame. She knew all this, and her way of excising her companion's literary *œuvre* from their daily life, the nearer she drew to her death, seems like the desperate attempt of someone who knew, indeed had always known, that living in the shadow of a creator means being nothing on one's own: nothing at the time since, instead of accomplishing one's own goals in life, one dedicates oneself to the other, and nothing later on since the creative act is the only guarantee of a possible posterity.

Frick was the one by whose "grace" everything had been possible—

Yourcenar, in French, always wrote her first name thus: *Grâce.*[2] But she had reached the point where she wondered sometimes if she had been something else besides, a "tool" used by Yourcenar, whose egocentricity and narcissism often went well beyond all bounds. But her devotion to Yourcenar's "genius" and the gratitude she felt toward her for agreeing to live with her, for letting herself be loved by her to the point of becoming a shut-in, prohibited her from probing any further on this point. Even had she tried to do so, she would only have come up with a snarl of contradictions, as everyone else is doing today. Even by observing what transpired after her death, it is anything but easy to evaluate the singular story of Grace Frick and Marguerite Yourcenar.

After Frick's death, Yourcenar, swept up in a new passion, reclaimed by the "madness" and demons of her youth, would try to make out that the life they had shared was nothing more than a not always peaceful coexistence. But forty years spent so totally together cannot be reduced to this banal description. Everything she thought or said about this subject in her final years was no less than the ultimate metamorphosis of a love that had withstood all assaults, and not only on account of Frick and her supposed submission. "For years I thought that Madame, who was always so sweet, and so calm, was Grace's prisoner, imprisoned by her authority, her energy, and her bad temper," Dee Dee Wilson has related more than once. "When I came to Petite Plaisance to look after Grace, I realized that I had been mistaken: she was the one who was the prisoner." If this remark is profoundly revealing, it is less for what Dee Dee believed to be the truth about the dependency relationship between these two women than for the very state of indecision in which those who knew that strange couple still find themselves. Which one of those two women imposed her priorities, her choices in life, her values—and according to what subtle system of division? Whatever the answer to this question may be, the fact remains that, in 1972, Frick had indeed become the prisoner, even though in a prison that she herself had built: she was a sick woman, completely at the mercy of the fate of the woman she loved, and that woman had now become completely preoccupied with no one but herself. The worst years, which began in 1972, provide a better look at the complexity of this couple, which was not simply, as most of their American friends tend to say, "a good marriage."

Like many couples—but even more so because Yourcenar was a writer—Grace and Marguerite lived out a fiction: the creation of a singular entity that was known, to the outside—to the public in its broadest sense—as Marguerite Yourcenar, but that was in fact made up of two individuals. We have seen—by way of her correspondence especially—how, as the years wore on, after moving to Petite Plaisance, Yourcenar completely abandoned the notion of a "private life" with regard to Frick, who saw everything that came into and went out of the house (letters, literary works, and so on), and who controlled all the telephone calls, making up her own mind whether or not to hand over the receiver to Yourcenar.

Yourcenar had no personal sphere except that of reverie and reading, where it was up to her to share her thoughts with Grace . . . or keep quiet about them. But unlike those who, having consented to such a state of utter dependency, no longer have any way out, Yourcenar could always escape for she possessed a place of absolute privacy: she could write. And it was in her own language—not the language of the other, even if she spoke it. Alone in an Anglophone universe, on an island much more symbolic of that universe than a large cosmopolitan city would have been, she was wielding a nearly lost language, French in its most classical form. She was building an *œuvre* in the language she loved, her native French, while immersed in a language impoverished by people who had not learned it well and had turned it into little more than a tool, a language whose degraded form was on its way to invading the planet: English. She was erecting an exceptional *œuvre,* one that shunned current research, whether on language or narrative structure, and one that would only touch those readers, or so she believed, who could grasp the singularity of her undertaking. And this is why she always imagined the members of her public to be few; when they grew more numerous, she complained, not without reason, that they didn't understand—might it be to build one's own fortress that one accepts being confined?

Frick would start to hate their unalterable intimacy, and the utter self-possession that Yourcenar the writer would put on display. Over the course of the year 1972, which marked a turning point in her life and in her relationship with Marguerite—Grace, who would never admit it, vaguely realized that she would probably die before Marguerite did. Frick became highly concerned with her companion's health and very little concerned with her work. Not a word was said about the work in progress; there was hardly a mention on 3 June of the doctorate *honoris causa* that Yourcenar received from Colby College in Waterville, Maine, not too far from Mount Desert Island. On the other hand, she wrote down everything about the variations in Yourcenar's blood pressure, and her allergies, which kicked up in October, after two days spent with a television crew—thus confirming Frick's opinion that visits were very bad for Yourcenar's health.

Toward the end of October, Yourcenar fell ill. For five weeks she suffered high temperatures of unknown cause, dizzy spells, intense fatigue. She was finally hospitalized in Bar Harbor from 31 December 1972 through 11 January 1973. When released, "after twelve days of hospitalization and painful tests," wrote Frick, "she [was] very weak and seriously undernourished." Her doctors, of course, had uncovered no illness. Yourcenar's hypochondria was at its zenith—and would become more and more shocking as Frick's physical suffering grew more intolerable. Yourcenar decided to keep a "health journal": "after two months and two weeks of undiagnosed illness, now let me try to get better and keep track of the temperature curve," she wrote at the beginning of this notebook. She would keep it until shortly before Frick's death (the journal ends in March 1979 and Frick died at the end of November).

Yourcenar might have asked herself what had caused her to stop at that particular time. Perhaps she did; there is no way of knowing. We do know, in any case, that she hardly asked herself, in 1973, the year she turned seventy, what the true causes were of her maladies, which were very real even if they had been "overrated" by the yardstick of her hypochondria. Was it impossible for her to accept that Frick was "the" sick one? Was it a way of transforming her unbearable sedentary state into a necessity? "I'm sick too, so there's no way we can go anywhere." Since traveling was now out of the question, one had to fall back on observing oneself.

Needless to say, the term "psychosomatic" never appears in Yourcenar's health journal. She wanted "real, very scientific names" to be given to her ailments, as the physician Robert Wilson attests. Being Dee Dee's husband, Dr. Wilson would be very close to her in the last years. "As she got older, of course, this tendency got worse and worse," he explains. "I ended up giving some high-falutin names to what were really minor problems. I think it made her feel better." No doubt about it: when one only believes in the power of words, as was the case with her, one must be able to give something a name. Her "case," in this domain, was an utterly ordinary one. One might have expected a person of her intelligence and perspicacity to distance herself somewhat, to raise herself a bit above the situation, which would have enabled her to reach this conclusion herself: nowhere in her health journal is there the least indication that she did so.

Instead she lost herself in systematically contesting what all the doctors said and did, without the slightest attempt at self-criticism. Thus in 1973: "no examination of the asthma and other problems though they seriously limit my activities. Cf. the prohibition to take the metro since 1968 because of serious attacks." Later on, in 1978, when she had noticed an "eye problem"—"I see flies flitting by and sparks"—she indicated half-resentfully "but no glaucoma, no cataracts, no detachment of the retina"—Molière is not far away.[3] Nor did she shy away, moreover, from quoting *Le Malade imaginaire* (*The Hypochondriac*) herself, in all seriousness: "Though there are certain exceptions, most of the doctors I know are doing their best. But, all in all, Béralde in *The Hypochondriac* is still right: 'they know how to name, define, and distinguish diseases: they know nothing about curing them.' Or so little."[4]

She was already complaining, to Jeanne Carayon, in August 1972 about how tired she was, even before undertaking the meticulous inventory of her ailments:

> If I do not begin my letters to my friends early in the morning, before my actual literary work, I am often too tired to get to them in the evening with the kind of energy that's needed.
>
> Fatigue . . . You are the only person whose friendly eye noticed this word in the preface to the *Entretiens radiophoniques* [Radio Interviews with Patrick de Rosbo]:[5] yes, in fact, I am tired. I'm even ill, for in early August a slight attack of angina pectoris, a disease whose symptoms I have been acquainted with for more than twenty years (which allowed me to describe them in *Hadrian*), attracted my doctors' attention. . . . Since then I have been rather heavily medicated, which is also tiring. I am much better, without being perfectly well. But the truth is that I have not been perfectly well now for years. I don't think that doctors, even when they're very good, as it appears that my own are, have any idea of the tremendous mental fatigue that is due to the fact of living in the world in which we find ourselves, and to the kind of impersonal anguish that weighs on so many of us.[6]

She would comment on the effectiveness of the medications she had been given ("Parabid: quite a good effect on the spasms and on waking up with a start"), making a list of the medications that had been prescribed for her, the ones she had heard about, and the ones she kept in stock without using, like Valium: "supposedly a very good sedative. I have some but haven't tried it yet." Often enough she would prescribe herself a cognac, as a pick-me-up. It was a habit she had had for a long time, which probably went back to her father, and she never gave it up.

The most unpleasant thing about this journal, and the hardest one to accept, is not so much the extreme interest that Yourcenar took in herself—many women, and no doubt some men, keep scrupulous track of fluctuations in their weight the same way she kept track of her blood pressure and her temperature—but the part played by an ailing Frick in monitoring her friend's health, notably in January 1973, when Yourcenar had just come back from the hospital. Several times each night Yourcenar was waking up with a start, drenched in sweat: Frick wrote these incidents down every time, specifying whether she did to did not have to dry her hair with her electric dryer. She noted them as well in her own daybook, though she never said anything there about what she herself was going through, and though Yourcenar, in her health notebook, ignored Frick, except for mentioning her blood pressure when they both had theirs taken together. Frick even made a few comments, which means that she took part in every minor episode. Just as she scrupulously followed the temperature curve, which occasioned some remarks whose comical side one would have a hard time imagining that she was not cognizant of: "after the evening meal Marguerite at 99.3°," she wrote one day. "Then her temperature went down to 98.1°; this is not enough." Or else: "good evening at 98.6°!" (which Yourcenar noted in the same terms). A person would have to be totally wrapped up in illness, in old age, in mad and morbid fascination with the other, as Frick no doubt was, to write this all down in utter seriousness. We have come a long way from her "Marguerite called to tell world she had a cold" of the forties.

The most interesting thing about this notebook is, in Yourcenar's own reference to herself, the same lack of any distaste for the body—even when that body is sick, even when it falls prey to afflictions universally considered repugnant—that one finds throughout her work: she describes the various episodes of bleeding, sweating, itching, as well as the spasms and other ailments she experienced, with a complacency bordering on pleasure.

Thus, in early 1973, it was as if the life that Frick and Yourcenar shared had been deprived of oxygen. No doubt far from realizing this were the people in Paris where, with the publication of *Dear Departed*, in 1974, they were talking more and more about Marguerite Yourcenar. Unless one had access, as we do today, to the various notes and exchanges of letters, it would have been quite difficult to understand the extent to which not being able to travel weighed on her life, in an everyday way. On the other hand, when one follows step by step the stages of a confinement that was no longer chosen but endured, it is easier to account for the impression she had of rediscovering her youth when she set off again, after Frick's death.

WHEN THE FIRST PROOFS of *Dear Departed* arrived, in February 1973, Frick resumed her usual activities in such situations: making copies of the set of proofs to make it easier to go over them together, mailing the corrected chapters as they went along, and so forth. Over the course of that empty winter, overcome by aging and illness, Yourcenar had seemingly settled into silence. Thus when there appeared in the magazine *Gulliver* an article by Patrick de Rosbo extremely insulting to Frick, it caused quite a stir, in that universe of chamomile tea. It cannot be denied that Rosbo's remarks are more than unpleasant.

This journalist, it will be recalled, had gone to Mount Desert in September 1970. The long account entitled "Huit jours de purgatoire avec Marguerite Yourcenar" [Eight Days in Purgatory with Marguerite Yourcenar] relates the numerous instances of misunderstanding and frustration he believed he had been subject to during his visit. In Rosbo's portrait, Frick emerges as an evil, fierce keeper of the gate, of indeterminate sex: "I caught sight of a little, bony face. A shrunken head? The mummy of Ramses II? Her gray hair, sparse and messy, reminded me right away of a little old man, very thin with emaciated features, of some much older sister of Nathalie Sarraute's, of some woman artist from the twenties, also in a way of André Gide's little wife. I wasn't sure which sex." Or else: "Miss F . . . leapt out of her car, an English schoolmarm, Bismarck's sister; her blue eyes, protruding and pale, would take one by surprise, with their vigilence utterly devoid of any hint of kindness; an hermaphrodite skeleton, Cocteau in a skirt, the medieval facies Pasolini invented, on the verge of burning some heretic . . ." Frick—concerned that Yourcenar might become overtired—had given very strict orders regarding the length of the interviews, which exasperated Rosbo: "At exactly five o'clock, there suddenly appeared from the kitchen the bony silhouette of the one I might be tempted, perhaps, to call the Confidante, this expression being justified by the frequent, even nearly constant, presence of Miss F . . . during those hours when I was given access to the novelist." As the interview was not yet over, "Grace would leave, a rather surly expression on her face, without a smile, whispering some things in an inimitable English—grayness fading back into grayness." During another session, he spoke up about how much it bothered him that Yourcenar would not cease to look questioningly at Frick: "I simply cannot keep myself from looking into Grace's eyes," she supposedly answered. "Far from becoming more relaxed, our exchanges, which took place under the constant, efficacious fire of that angular goddess of Discord, were growing more and more stilted before my very eyes. There was a striking contrast between the rare moments when it was granted us to be alone—moments of near abandon in which I could finally hope to be heard without anyone making a scene—and those, alas more frequent, when, with the Confidante back on the scene, arrows whizzing, bullets flying, rigidity and mistrust were once again the order of the day."[7]

Yourcenar, who always loathed boorishness and who was violently shocked, as one can well imagine, by this accusatory portrait, dictated a letter to Orengo for Pierre Belfond, the publisher of *Gulliver.* Besides the fact that the portrait of Frick was absolutely ignoble, she explained, all of Rosbo's statements were erroneous, whether they concerned the rented car, the anti-Catholic pamphlet she was supposedly working on, the objects he described. In short, the remarks of Monsieur de Rosbo, she concluded, contained "neither accuracy, nor truthfulness, nor decency, nor propriety." "Indeed his article contained an extraordinary mixture of vileness and lunacy," she commented in the letter she sent to one of her friends. "The conversations published in *Gulliver* are every one of them invented from whole cloth. It's an extraordinary case of an imagination running wild." "It's not a very interesting story," she explained:

> In 1969 . . . I asked Gallimard (who didn't have anyone else to propose) to let him do some writing, less than a hundred pages, on me for a collection on "contemporary writers." The plans Rosbo submitted during the following year should have been rejected; they were as crazy as his description of Northeast Harbor, but in an adulatory way, and it was in vain that I corresponded with him in an attempt to clarify or simplify. . . . A few months before the death of this project, he announced his impending visit (an unsolicited one) to Northeast Harbor to tape a series of radio interviews. This stay, which he had planned on lasting two weeks, but which I managed with some effort to reduce to eight days, came at a very bad time for my work. It was no fault of Rosbo's if, in the wake of some bruises sustained in a fall, they made me have emergency biopsies done on both breasts . . . ; but it was his fault that, having learned upon arriving (we had not been able to alert him beforehand) that I had only returned from the clinic two days earlier, still rather weak as a result of the operation, he nonetheless persisted in imposing himself on me. This explains the animosity of Grace Frick, who was doing her best to defend me, knowing I did not have the strength to do so myself, and was trying to shorten those interminable daily visits a little. Poor Grace, of whom the charming old Dutch translator of my books so aptly said "that he thought he had seen in her the very visage of fidelity" . . .

Thus was notice duly taken of "poor Grace." After which Yourcenar got back to the essential, which is to say her *œuvre:*

> I still think that *Entretiens radiophoniques* is a useful book for people, if people there be who want to go a bit deeper into my works. I revised the proofs a good deal and added a lot to them. I had tried my best to make my interlocutor change the wording of certain questions, which were so vague that it was difficult to answer them at all clearly; and many others hardly seemed to me to be worth bothering with (but this is often the case). Just the same, it gave me an opportunity to say certain things about my work that I surely would not have said otherwise.[8]

A year later, Rosbo was back on the attack, this time unloading his bitterness on Yourcenar:

> I have already written, in other circumstances, that this stay in Northeast Harbor was a kind of Purgatory for me, and I do not take it back. . . . I do not set off again today in the direction of the State of Maine (at least in my mind: it's less dangerous) without apprehension. It is not without good reason that I have compared this writer to a Frankish fortress, for the massive and arrogant way she has of ignoring you, but also for the many imperceptible fissures crisscrossing the walls. . . . Yourcenar the haughty, her beret, half-Scottish, half-paratrooperlike, partly hiding her war-goddess profile, her nostrils combative, her ample cape flying in the sea wind. . . . I have said elsewhere that Marguerite Yourcenar wants to be both off-limits and recognized, discovered by the intellect and inaccessible to the soul. Let those who seek her out experience her culture, interrogate her thought and the meditation that amplifies it, and she will not object; she will even be pleased. But the drawbridges go up very quickly the second one presumes to interfere with the inner workings of this Port-Royal,[9] this Montségur.[10] One then gets the distinct impression that the violence, or scorn, kept under control until that moment needs no more than a snap of the fingers to erupt on that vigilant face. . . . It is a matter of grabbing hold of everything. Keeping everything under control. Never being put in the wrong or found lacking: What kind of freedom can you expect, in such conditions, for what by rights should be a spontaneous dialogue? . . . The radiance of an exemplary *œuvre* does not prevent one from sometimes judging pointless, or monotonous, the prideful serenity of her victory bulletins.[11]

During that period, and until 1979, it was most often in the letters to Jeanne Carayon that Yourcenar voiced her reflections—on what she was reading, on growing old, on the authors they mutually liked. Such was the case, in particular, for Montherlant, whom she evoked on numerous occasions. In 1973, commenting on a text by Gabriel Matzneff, who had scattered Montherlant's ashes in Rome, at the Forum, she declared: "even if this personage [she is talking about Jean-Claude Barat, Montherlant's heir and the executor of his will] sincerely believes himself (does one ever really know?) to be the writer's son, it is not up to him to attempt to make it known, as long as Montherlant himself did not do so."[12] She took Montherlant to task for "caricaturing ancient funeral rites, the effect of which was not even that of a bad film but of a bad cartoon," and for "his compulsive need" to talk about his private life, coupled with a "terror of saying too much about it." "Where one's private life is concerned," she asserted, "one must either firmly tell all leaving no room for misunderstanding, or, on the contrary, say nothing at all."[13] Obviously, this did not in any way alter the admiration she felt for part of Montherlant's *œuvre,* no more than it altered her judgment of those texts that were in her eyes "odious": "I am only too sensitive to the obtuse and crudely brutal spots in this great writer's work; it's as if on occasion some sublieutenant takes his place who would have us believe in his offhandedness, and, unfortunately, he finds this substitute enchanting. It is extraordinary that a man who so loudly and so justly protested against the ignominities of our era should not have noticed he was laying himself open to those same ignominities."[14] "It is hard for me to countenance that Montherlant was so inferior to his own greatness."[15]

In another letter she remarked on the amorous vitality of certain figures, even in old age; she cited "Hugo, Pindar, Goethe, Ninon [de Lenclos]," and reflected on what she called "the amorous octogenarians." "Just the same, the older—sometimes very old—people, of both sexes, whom I have seen contriving to obtain yet a few more of love's pleasures, or ceaselessly rehashing their memories, have always struck me as having forgotten that there is a time for everything." One is always mistaken to be so categorical, as she herself constantly reminded us: the day she stooped, caught off guard, to that rather hackneyed pronouncement, that totally conventional idea, she did not know that what she was describing was exactly what would happen to her. It was Jeanne Galzy who brought this to her attention, one day when she had been "accused" of being too passionate: "Why be surprised by so much passion? . . . it seems to me that the power to love, if it grows more tender, does not dim."[16] Yourcenar herself had been more perceptive in her youth, when she spoke of the erotic desires of an elderly Pindar.

She had not yet taken the measure of all this when she wrote to Jean Chalon about his *Portrait of a Seductress,* a book retracing the fortunes of Natalie Barney.[17] She said she disagreed with him regarding "the 'love' (in the precise, restricted meaning of the word)," between Natalie, then in her eighties, and Gisèle, the "Amazon's" last love, thirty years or so her junior: "In the last years of her life, passionate love and the pleasures of passion had become for our friend the kind of obsessive, legendary, and, dare I say, somewhat excessively dwelled-upon themes that they also can be for certain elderly gentlemen. Even during her lifetime, this was what I liked least about Natalie; she had so many qualities and virtues of a different order. There is a time for everything, as Ecclesiastes says, and once that time has passed, certain importunities become disturbing."[18]

A TIME to write, a time to read. In 1975, despite her reservation about Montherlant, she read and reread—"I always reread a book that's worth the effort from beginning to end, immediately after my first reading"—his posthumous, previously unpublished works. With regard to the *Fichier parisien* [Parisian Notes], she observed "how much Hugo and Montherlant resemble one another in their ability to limn the here and now." In *Tous Feux éteints* [All Fires Quenched], she was irritated by the "needless repetitions": "Was it forgetfulness or fatigue on the part of an aging, sickly writer? Or the ineptness of the heirs who retained repetitions, perhaps without noticing them, that the writer would have eliminated? In any event, what we have on those pages is a regrettable instance of negligence." [19] In editing the text of Yourcenar's principal posthumous work, *Quoi? L'Eternité*, Yvon Bernier could have profited from reading and heeding that sentence. Instead he published, devoutly, a first edition of this text about which qualified researchers will have to decide whether it too is not "a regrettable instance of negligence."

Indeed, she was already thinking about *Quoi? L'Eternité*, even before the appearance of *Dear Departed*, just as she would mention, again in her correspondence with Carayon, certain elements of *Archives du Nord*, which she was in the process of framing. For her this ascent into the realm of familial memory was but a single gesture, an identical way of inventing by way of remembrance; it constituted a whole that had to be divided only for the sake of literary expedience. Struggling with the figure of Jeanne de Vietinghoff, Yourcenar confided to her correspondent: "I still can picture Jeanne de V. in 1924. By then she was already nothing more than a shade . . . she never was really quite a writer. Too many things got in the way . . . the reticence and little niceties proper to a ladylike society woman." [20] "*L'Autre Devoir* [The Other Duty], by Jeanne de V., is a long novel that seemed to me to have no merit, even when I read it at twenty-five years of age," Yourcenar wrote later on to the same correspondent. "The only detail that struck me is that Jeanne describes her first encounter with a man who from all indications is my father, among the cypresses and ruins of the Villa Adriana." [21] Now this first encounter, as we know, took place at the marriage of Fernande and Monsieur de Crayencour. "But this imaginary setting draws it curiously near to my own constellation," Yourcenar concluded. Where her emotional ties were concerned, curious "magnetic fields"—like those "objective chance" occurrences dear to André Breton—often surrounded the protagonists in her mind. [22] Yourcenar's sense of literary pleasure could be counted on to perpetuate them. Thus it is possible to imagine that this detail prompted her to invent the episode in *Quoi? L'Eternité* where Jeanne believes she catches sight of Michel de Crayencour at the Villa Adriana. [23] Naturally, this is only an hypothesis, but we can't forget that she constantly referred to *Quoi? L'Eternité*, while she was writing it, as a "novel," pointing out in advance, where this work was concerned, the role already played by fiction in the first two volumes of the trilogy, which she had not seen fit to emphasize.

In *Dear Departed,* published early in 1974, when Frick had to undergo a new operation (on 18 January at the Bar Harbor hospital), where we find a few leads concerning her childhood and how she got on without a mother, Yourcenar had not yet completely mastered her technique of reconstructing the past. Though the book is fascinating when read from a biographical perspective, it is slower going, on a first reading, than *Archives du Nord,* and sometimes almost tedious. Certain ancestors' portraits are too long, and less precise than in *Archives du Nord.* Nonetheless, in the figure of Octave Pirmez, a poet and a writer and Yourcenar's maternal great-uncle, Jean Chalon believed he detected a self-portrait of Yourcenar. He wrote this in an article published in *Elle,* which earned him this little rectification: "Granted, *unum sum et multi in me,*" Yourcenar wrote to him;[24] "but the *multi* here evoked are not the same thing as our little self. And this book contains neither 'confessions,' nor 'admissions,' least of all involuntary ones." "Perhaps I shall one day write a volume (only one) about my own life, or rather about the people I have known and the events I have witnessed," she had already informed him.[25] "If I do so (Deo volente), I know in advance that I shall only play a very minor role therein."

Nonetheless, in general, as she confided on numerous occasions, the reviews of this book were in her view "intelligent and reassuringly warm." She particularly singled out Dominique Aury's, "as lovely as a poem," which appeared in the *Nouvelle Revue Française* in July of 1974. Part way through the commentary, which is in fact a sensitive and pertinent one, Aury asserts: "In addition to the evocative strength, to the serene nobility of thought that make Marguerite Yourcenar's book so powerful, to the restrained and constant compassion that renders it so moving, one must also note a singular characteristic, so singular that it is absolutely peculiar to her and her alone: she destroys, without ever appearing to touch them, the barriers that separate the kingdoms, by which I mean the vegetable, the animal, and the human. We are all of the same blood (or the same clay). She alone never forgets this."[26]

Frick, after returning from the hospital on 25 January 1974, didn't make a single entry in her daybook for months. She had a hard time getting back on her feet, and one gets no sense that her life was returning to normal, however haltingly, before the beginning of summer, at which time she reported, once again, a concert she attended with Yourcenar on 23 July, as she did a theater performance in Somesville on 1 August. It seems that

Yourcenar, for her part, was living first and foremost through her work and her correspondence, particularly her very regular exchange with Carayon. After having read Claude Lévi-Strauss's reception speech to the Académie Française (he took Montherlant's place and was invested by Roger Caillois), she commented on it in a letter to her. She liked the beginning of the speech, his comparison between induction into the Académie and an initiation into a secret society, "of some tribe or other, but he carries on too long about this idea," said she; and the part about Montherlant was "awfully poor." As for Caillois, "his severe critique of the social sciences, with their uncertain and peremptory aspects," pleased her greatly. Where the Académie itself was concerned, "one hesitates," she wrote, "between the beauty of an institution that has lasted three centuries, even if it uses uniforms Napoleonic prefects wore," and "the scheming and the bowing and scraping that every election represents, the art of pointless speechifying practiced both by the one who inducts and the one who is inducted. What you are struck by, mostly, is a certain uselessness."27

BEGINNING IN the summer of 1974, media attention to Yourcenar intensified again; it would increase progressively until her death. This phenomenon was all the more striking since one was now obliged to go to her. She was no longer traveling. Thus did Radio Canada, in late August, and Belgian television, from 7 to 14 September, follow one upon the other. From 26 through 30 September, Gisèle Freund came to photograph Yourcenar. It is understandable that Frick, still unwell even though she kept it to herself, did not take kindly to these intrusions. They were like an invasion of what had always been her territory, the site of her possession—to the extent that Yourcenar ever really belonged to her. If Yourcenar got away from her here, Frick would lose her completely. Thus she could only look upon such visits unfavorably. She must have taken just as little pleasure in the warm relations that Yourcenar maintained with certain Parisian journalists, notably Matthieu Galey from *L'Express*—who had made the trip to Petite Plaisance in the fall of 1971. With him, on occasion, she was almost little-girlish: "we had a good crop of apples. So apples for dessert three days out of four until New Year's. It's a little monotonous but we are very proud of them."28

As if by chance, after the publication of *Dear Departed*, which was extremely well received, after being awarded the Grand Prix national de la culture, after all those visits, signs of growing interest on the part of the entire Francophone world, Yourcenar wrote to her friend Jacques Kayaloff on 17 December: "I'm feeling much better than last year," which she immediately emended with "but my strength is growing decidedly more limited and is only still entirely reliable when I'm at my work table." [29] She was seventy-one years old: knowing how, at eighty-four, she was traipsing all over the planet, one can gauge what such remarks owed to her psychological state.

Charles Orengo, sick with cancer, did not survive the year 1974. With his death, at the age of sixty-one, "it is a friendship of 23 years, from *Hadrian* to *Dear Departed,* that is coming to a close." A strange friendship it was. Orengo's friend Anne Quellennec—the sole survivor, at ninety-four years of age, of those who had met Yourcenar even before the publication of *Alexis*—still speaks today of the great admiration he bore Yourcenar, whom he considered to be "one of the great minds of this century." He kept up a regular correspondence, for more than twenty years, with the writer. He always supported her, helped her, advised her in her dealings with her publishers, without regard to the ups and downs of his own publishing career. And yet, in the thick file kept at Harvard containing both his letters and Yourcenar's, what one finds is much more the trace of a professional and utilitarian relationship than of a genuine friendship. Might Yourcenar have extracted from that correspondence what she judged incompatible with the image she wanted to leave of herself, as she had in the case of her letters to Jacques Kayaloff? This is entirely possible. The fact remains, however, that in every letter to Kayaloff, even the most insignificant, one feels a warmth that is never perceptible in her exchanges with Orengo. Perhaps because, since Kayaloff had known her and helped her during her "dark years," he remained evermore a different kind of friend.

With Orengo, Yourcenar did not have the freedom of expression, the pleasure of talking about unimportant things, the reassuring everyday banality she had with Jeanne Carayon, with her Italian translator Lidia Storoni, and a few others—all of them women, one cannot help but notice. It is as if there existed some ancestral tradition of conversation among women, rooted in the gynaeceum and the harem, that one never entirely escapes. Yourcenar, who resisted this form of "enclosure," who thought she could extend unto infinity the sphere of her liberty, would have detested hearing anyone make this observation. And yet . . .

It was always with women—perhaps also because the latter confided in her, which is a sign of the same tradition—that she would talk, for instance, about growing old: "Dare I ask you not to give too much thought to old age?" she wrote to Carayon. "I have never believed that age was a criterion. I did not feel particularly 'young' fifty years ago (when I was twenty or so, I very much enjoyed the company of old people) and I don't feel 'old' today. My age changes (and has always changed) from one hour to the next.

When I'm tired, I feel like I'm ten centuries old; when I'm working, I feel forty; in the garden with the dog, it seems as if I'm four years old."[30]

Throughout 1975, Yourcenar worked on *Archives du Nord*—which was then still called *Le Labyrinthe du monde,* a title that Yourcenar would eventually give to the entire family trilogy—and drew up plans for what became *Quoi? L'Eternité.* Attesting to this are the research requests she made to Carayon, and the correspondence with her half nephew Georges de Crayencour. But Frick had nothing to say about any of this. At the end of September, they received a visit, for a few days, from Madame Denise Lelarge, a friend of Georges de Crayencour who had helped him put together the documentation for *Archives du Nord.* Here again, Frick did not make a single comment related to Yourcenar's literary work.

These years were also a time when friends, fellow witnesses of an era or privileged intellectual interlocutors, were disappearing. In February 1972, it was to be Natalie Barney, the "Amazon" denizen of Rue Jacob, first met in the Paris of the fifties: "Even then I had the impression of a shade, charming and ethereal, lingering among us. Now she has entered her realm once and for all, and her legend has already begun," Yourcenar wrote to Chalon.[31] After Orengo's death, came that of the philosopher and publisher Jacques Masui, in November 1975 (he was the director of the review *Hermès,* among others), with whom Yourcenar had kept up a regular correspondence, especially since the beginning of that decade, at which time he had directed a collection called "Documents Spirituels" at Fayard.[32] "Masui's death was a great loss for me," she wrote to their mutual friend Gabriel Germain. "We were friends, he and I; he had even spent a few days here that I look back on with great fondness. I did not know his wife, but her final gesture moves me [she committed suicide the day after her husband's death]. It's not only for ourselves that his passing away leaves a gap that will never be filled, but also for the intellectual work that we are doing. The appalling diminishment of culture frightens me. He was an admirable exception."[33] Germain, whose *Le Regard intérieur* [The Inward Eye] Yourcenar had particularly liked, would die three years later, in October 1978.

When she heard about the death of André Embiricos, in September 1975, by way of their mutual friend Nico Calas (who died in January 1989 in New York), Yourcenar, at seventy-two years old, knew she had embarked, irrefutably, upon that stage of life in which one becomes the "survivor." The only news arriving then about one's oldest friends, sometimes almost forgotten, is the ultimate news of their death, bringing with it the resurgence of a past that at the very same moment becomes The Past, since its protagonists and witnesses are gone. Embiricos "takes with him much of the life we once lived: he is inseparable from it," she wrote to Calas.[34] "I liked him very much, even though I had not seen him since 1939, and even though, since then, he seems to have refused all contact, immersed as he was in his own writings and dreams. . . . I have no real desire to see Athens again. In all those places one has loved, one rather has the impression on returning of paying a last visit to a friend struck down by an incurable illness. (With respect to those places that one has not seen and would have liked to see, occasionally one thinks that it may not be too late [India, Japan, Egypt])."

THIS ADMISSION of interest in those countries that one "would have liked to see" and about which "occasionally one thinks that it may not be too late" bears within it the terrible confession that she was waiting—waiting for Frick to die. Yourcenar could no longer conceal that her " 'immobility' [was] much like that of Zeno in Bruges, churning in place; and there are moments when, like him, I no longer am able to calculate exactly how far or in what direction I am being carried."[35] Deep down, nothing could cause her to abandon her desire to live. She knew that "what the astrologers refer to as 'the end of it all' [was] near" and "that there is ultimately something that says 'I've had enough.' But despite the immense sadness of the world . . . this miracle of sensitivity and lucidity that is life seems to demand that we live it right up until the end without discouragement, and with a kind of trust. We slip so easily between a wise and serene acquiescence to whatever might happen, or what one day or another inevitably will, and giving in too easily."[36]

Frick's daybook for 1976, it seems, has been lost. And, curiously, it was during this time that Yourcenar's correspondence, notably with Carayon, came more and more to resemble a journal. The letters are long, numerous, closely spaced in time, and they have more and more to say about life from day to day, including the thoughts one forms, to oneself, about such and such a subject, or the views one forms, day by day, regarding such and such an incident or event. It grows more and more clear that they were a stand-in for the personal journal that Yourcenar did not keep. She even says so, for that matter, since it was she who directed that the "[p]ersonal journals in the form of letters" addressed to Carayon dating from the years 1979 and 1980 be sealed for a period of fifty years. She wrote in them the things she needed to express, things that, no doubt more than ever, she did not wish to keep to herself at a time when Frick was no longer "responding." More generally, though, one might well ask whether all of Yourcenar's correspondence, so carefully preserved, is not the equivalent, read chronologically, of a journal. Since she always kept a copy of her letters, the record left behind after her death is identical to that of a journal, and the letters bear a similar relationship to posterity. It would also be possible to publish them, were it not for the hindrance of myriad legal precautions. But a certain jubilation on Yourcenar's part at the thought of complications created after her death, by that mass of correspondence, is certainly not to be dismissed.

Thus do we witness the appearance, over the course of the year 1976, from one letter to the next, of the person that Marguerite Yourcenar would be in the final decade of her life. It is one who took part in the village Christmas and New Year's rites: "an exchange of little homemade presents, cookies, rolls, and jams. At this time of year I practice my mediocre talents as a baker, making rolls with raisins, cardamom seeds, etc., and Twelfth Night cake." [37] And it is one who supported Ralph Nader's battle for consumer protection; who belonged to a women's group fighting against "adulterated foodstuffs," among other things; and who joined in protesting the consumer society along with many young people, all over the world, who had done so since the mid-sixties. Yourcenar complained about "those lugubrious supermarkets with their enamel-painted walls," as well as their "almost total absence of employees, which eliminates human contact, and the mechanical music that flows like poor-quality syrup. And the products that are everywhere the same, the trusts, the monopolies, and the stifling of competition that end up giving capitalist grocery stores the same lugubrious uniformity one finds in stores in socialist states." [38]

One gets the sense she was retreating into insignificant gestures, trying to protect herself from what was happening at Petite Plaisance, from the deteriorating state of Frick's health and from the degeneration of their relations with one another—which would little by little reach the limits of the tolerable. Yourcenar at once turned in upon herself and sought to maintain and increase, by way of her correspondence, her contact with the outside world. Still, perhaps we are deluding ourselves; perhaps we would do well here to remember, and ponder, Henri Michaux's statement in *Ecuador* (*Ecuador*): "When I think that there are two or three clucks who imagine that they have reconstructed Rimbaud's life from his correspondence." [39]

In her "immobility," Yourcenar read and reread Montherlant, still, with a highly critical eye, as if she saw in him a privileged adversary. "From time to time he skirts what is essential," she observed, and went on: "It's becoming more and more of a preoccupation for me to attempt to evaluate a writer's *œuvre* while taking all his behaviors into consideration, as I attempted to do for Cavafy, Mann, and Selma Lagerlöf. I am thinking about undertaking the same kind of work on Mishima, but despite extensive reading I don't feel I have reached the point of even being able to begin."[40] She would nonetheless write this piece, which would not be an essay in a collection but a small book that appeared in 1981, *Mishima: A Vision of the Void.* Her interest in Mishima also led her to study Japanese and to translate *Cinq Nô modernes* [Five Modern Nō Plays] in 1984. More generally, the Japanese literary tradition "seemed [in her view] to be one of the greatest," as she put it in a literary questionnaire: "whether it be a question of great novels like those of Murasaki, poetic reflections like those of Sei Shonagon, great Haiku poets, such as Bashô and so many others, or Nō dramas, which I place alongside Greek drama in our human heritage."[41] "Whenever I'm asked what woman novelist I admire most," she pointed out to Matthieu Galey, "the name Murasaki Shikibu comes immediately to mind. I have extraordinary respect, indeed reverence, for her work. She was truly the great writer, the great novelist, of eleventh-century Japan, which is to say, of the period when Japanese civilization was at its height. In a word, she was the Marcel Proust of medieval Japan: a woman of genius with a feeling for social gradations, love, the human drama, and the way in which people will hurl themselves against the wall of impossibility. Nothing better has ever been written in any language."[42] In *Le Tour de la prison,* a collection of essays and stories, Yourcenar devoted several texts to the Japanese dramatic forms, particularly the Nō plays, which she indicates she discovered very early on. Their influence is evident in the one-act play of 1930, *Le Dialogue dans le marécage*:[43] "Let us hasten to repeat (it will never be said often enough) that the Nō plays constitute one of the two or three triumphs of universal theater. . . . As for me, I have thought more than once that my sensitivity would have been different if happenstance had not seen to it that I became acquainted with *Atsumori* and *Sumidagawa*[44] at the same time as *Antigone*."[45]

SHE ALSO reread Céline, a little; she did not like him "with the exception of a slim technical volume published under his family name."[46] This detail is an unwittingly savory one: Yourcenar's reference, back in 1976, to a publication by Céline "under his family name" seems to indicate that what she had in mind was *La Quinine en thérapeutique* [Quinine in Therapeutic Treatment], which would thus be the only work to find favor in the eyes of this unrepentant hypochondriac. In English, she returned, as she did every year, to Thomas Hardy's *Far from the Madding Crowd.* "I very much like to read and also to reread," she would confide once again to Galey, "much as music lovers like to play the same piece again and again or listen to the same record over and over. Of writers from the generation preceding my own,

I've reread a great deal of Hardy, Conrad, Ibsen, Tolstoy . . . some Chekhov, some Thomas Mann . . . And the book that has been reread, if not most often then at least with the most beneficial effects, is Gandhi's *Autobiography*."[47]

SPIRITUAL, indeed religious, concerns, long absent from her mental universe, drew her increasingly toward Oriental wisdom. She had already read and reread the basic texts, but she recurred to them ceaselessly. Yourcenar, for whom "[i]t is always dangerous to claim exclusive possession of a truth or a God or an absence of God," had never wished to belong to any particular denomination.[48] Having said this, her intellectual curiosity, the desire to "make some kind of contact with all the human adventures" led her to a reflection on the monk, as her long and rich correspondence with the publisher Jacques Masui and the hellenist Gabriel Germain attests. She also pointed out to the critic Michel Aubrion, who devoted a very long study to her in the Belgian *Revue Générale,* at the beginning of the seventies:

> In everything I write I am highly conscious of a pervasive preoccupation, and I would almost go so far as to say a religious fervor, that goes unnoticed so often only because it strays from the molds in which religious preoccupation and fervor are most often cast by those around us, and because it is linked to a certain radicalism of thought that religion ordinarily is not a party to.[49]

In a letter addressed to a young woman who had undertaken a thesis on *The Abyss,* she retrospectively outlined the course of her investigations:

> You are perfectly right to say that I am neither a Cartesian (rightly or wrongly, I have no taste for Descartes) nor a stoic in the popular sense of the word . . . ; the bases or the harmonics of my thought have been from the beginning Greek philosophy (Plato in my adolescence, soon left behind in favor of the neoplatonists, who in their turn were replaced by the presocratics), the Upanishad and sutra meditations, and the Taoist axioms. If I have alluded in my books only very discreetly to this ground on which the latter are erected, it is because this kind of research is too little practiced, especially in France, not to occasion yet another misunderstanding. The hellenist Gabriel Germain, author of the very remarkable *Regard intérieur* (from Le Seuil), immediately noticed that a goodly number of Zeno's meditations in "The Abyss" were Buddhist meditation exercises (on water, fire, bones, this last one shamanistic more than anything else). . . . It is not my intent, moreover, to reject or deny the influence of my Christian, particularly Catholic, origins. . . . I feel instinctively less at ease in the Protestant religion, even though I've had occasion to observe its grandeur (otherwise I would not

have been able to write *Fleuve profond, sombre rivière.* I also feel the grandeur of Islam. What bothers me, however, in all of the religions referred to as Abrahamic, or those comprising, rather redoubtably, "the People of the Book," is the intransigence and dogmatism, which is much more extensive than in other religions, and a literalistic tendency that has ceaselessly caused them to invent heretics for themselves and shunt their mystics to the margins, when it is not to the other side of the ditch. The Tantric disciple is not un-aware that the gods whom he visualizes ever more clearly every day in his cell can also be dissipated, by a contrary effort of will, as the wind dissipates the clouds in the sky. In the European mind, or the Mediterranean one if you prefer, the Real, with a capital R, has always been opposed to the Imaginary, and the imaginary has never constituted a powerful part of the real, which one nonetheless perceives as soon as one devotes oneself to a comparative study of religions, of the evolution of ideas, and even of political opinions. . . . It is less this or that dogma that shocks me with regard to Christianity (for the idea of a divinity partially engaged in human suffering seems to me to hold within it a truth, or, if you wish, an admirable metaphor) than, if I may put it this way, the dogmatism with which the dogmas are treated.

As for Jewish thought . . . I did not come into contact with it until I was much older, and only when I realized that it had acted (admittedly in its dissident forms) as a ferment for a very large number of thinkers in the West. . . . Personally, I found some sublime flashes of insight in the Cabala, but also a great deal of muddleheadedness, a numerological superstitious-ness that is carried even further than in other religions (we can call it an obsession if the word superstition is overly distasteful), a turning inward and an involutedness that strike me as often having characterized Jewish thought, no doubt on account of Judaism's circumstances during the Middle Ages.[50]

In her interviews and in her correspondence, Yourcenar also many times emphasized her marked affinity for religious rites, as well as her hostility toward intolerance and dogmatism: "I find it enormously difficult to counte-nance that religion such as it has been taught to us has distorted and petri-fied God to such an extent," she wrote to Carayon.[51] This is a subject of scrutiny that she returned to and developed in a letter—expressing, in addi-tion, at some length her regret with regard to the "modernization" of the Church—addressed to Father Yves de Gibon in 1976:

Dare I speak of a sclerosis of dogma, which communicates less and less with the powers of the imagination, and of what one cannot but call the human soul? I fear that the answer is yes. Of all the great religions, Christian-ity, and Catholicism in particular, seems to me to be the one that is densest with dogmas. (Islam has defended its own with equal inflexibility, but its dogmatism is much simpler.) A Buddhist can meditate *ad infinitum* on *Buddhahood.* . . . Catholicism, on the contrary, has put more and more emphasis on the literalness of its dogmas. One could say that there is a Catholic fundamentalism as there is a Protestant fundamentalism. . . . Moreover, I am always very struck by the fact that a Frenchman who stops being a Catholic becomes, ninety-five times out of a hundred, an "atheist" or a "materialist" in the most simplistic sense of the term. It is the rigidity and narrow-mindedness of religious teaching that turn people into the likes of Homais. Not only is the notion of religion eliminated once and for all by people who think this way, but what subsists is a very marked hostility toward the Church, and in the event that discussion or dispute is resumed, it is at the very lowest level.[52]

In contrast to such "compartmentalizations" and "rigidities," it was Buddhism that garnered Yourcenar's favor, "for it is the only religion that has constituted for itself a truly profound psychology. With a sense of being and a sense of the opposite of being; a sense of passage,[53] a sense of the evil in the universe, and the suffering, a sense of the particles that make up the human personality. It goes a long way without reposing on a dogma. A very rare feat."[54] Finally, because she judged "that perfecting oneself is life's principle purpose,"[55] she awaited no ultimate solution or consolation, and it was once again Buddhism that best corresponded with this vision of things, as she explained to Germain:

> I understand and I share your desire that nothing be lost from the reli-gious domain, be it Occidental or Oriental, which we later civilizations, liv-ing in the twentieth century, are the first to have been able to explore on both sides. But it seems to me that it is still within ourselves alone, and almost secretly, that we can foster an admixture of Christian charity and Buddhist compassion, a stable sense of the divine and the numinous as expressed by Shintoism, the orthodox churches, and Catholicism, with the dynamic ge-nius of India and the double notion, such a Greek one, of the dignity of man and the limits of man. . . . Very far be it for me to deny the value of the extraordinary joy or tranquility, ecstasy, enstasy, or satori, that practicing the religious life can radiate within us, at least for an eternal instant. It does not prevent an enormous sea of troubles from surrounding us, nor keep us—who are the freest of all—from still being nine-tenths submerged in that sea. . . . Whether we are happy or not is, in the end, of no importance, and Bud-dhism's immense victory is having sensed that liberation itself is of no impor-tance either, and that having none is perhaps its secret condition for being. The only palpable benefit bestowed upon us seems to me to be the admirable wording of the last of the Four Vows: "However innumerable are the living beings suffering throughout all of the Three Worlds . . . ," which, moreover, brings us face to face with our immense weakness. But this is still the best the human soul has come up with.[56]

These reflections, and the abundant correspondence they entailed, clearly did not stop Yourcenar from pursuing her specifically literary work, which is without a doubt what kept her so alert. She decided, during the summer of 1976, to bring *Archives du Nord* to a close, for the book was already "very full" and went "as far [in its depiction of her father's side of the family] as the tragic picaresque of Michel's life." She was already thinking about the third volume: "the story of Monique [Jeanne de Vietinghoff], which I would very much like to write, my own personal awakening, and the spectacle of a man growing old."[57] In addition to working on this new volume and firming up her plans, she continued to reread the new editions of her works with maniacal attention, in the paperback collection for example, making changes in an attempt to come as close as she could to exactly what she wanted to say.[58]

It was also during the summer of 1976 that Frick's last project appeared: *The Abyss,* her translation of *L'Œuvre au noir.* It took her ten years to translate this text, and Roger Straus, Yourcenar's American publisher, remembers begging the author on several occasions to get a new translator, so that the novel could finally appear in the United States. She always refused, judging such an act unworthy of the past they had shared and insulting to Frick, who wanted to believe, if not in her recovery, at least in her survival— just as Yourcenar never allowed anyone, while Frick was still alive, to undertake translating into English even the most minor of her other texts.

"The summer was more congested than I could possibly say," she wrote to Georges de Crayencour excusing her delay in corresponding with her half nephew. "The relatively low prices offered by the airlines to people coming over for the American 'Bicentennial' brought a whole series of visitors here, most of whom had invited themselves—but we still had to attend to them, more or less. This would be minor were it not for other problems and worries looming in the background, the chief worry being brought on by Grace's health; she has suffered quite a few complications."[59]

THAT SAME YEAR in Paris, *Balade américaine* [American Jaunt] came out at Stock, a book by Elvire de Brissac, who had also stopped by Petite Plaisance for a conversation with Yourcenar. Like Patrick de Rosbo's recent article in *Gulliver,* this book contained a distorted portrait of Frick. On the date of Brissac's visit, 1 July 1972, Yourcenar wrote down on the calendar after the fact: "her vileness rivals that of Rosbo, and she doesn't even have the excuse of being delerious (as Rosbo did) or having had a critical essay on me rejected by Gallimard." Jean Chalon, who wrote a mostly favorable review of the book for *Le Figaro*—without, of course, referring to the parts concerning Frick—was sharply rebuked in a letter. With the elegance and humor he is known for, he did not seek to conceal what will endure as a perfect example of Yourcenar's art of settling the score: "The truth is," she wrote,

> that the snickering caricature of Grace Frick, of which most of it consists, calls to mind the gleeful chortling of guttersnipes flinging to the ground and trampling underfoot some nameless passerby—with this one difference, entirely to the credit of the guttersnipes, that the latter, to begin with, had not sought an invitation to their victim's home. Besides which, guttersnipes run certain risks, and Mademoiselle de Brissac does not think she's running any.
>
> The atmosphere in Paris must certainly be toxic since it keeps you from seeing how ignoble it is to insult a woman publicly who has always stayed out of the limelight, whom the French reader does not know, since he naturally is not familiar with her admirable work as a translator, and whose only fault is having welcomed a visitor, who supposedly wanted to see me, with her usual cordiality.... Your having sung the praises of a volume like this one obviously places our relations, which I thought were friendly, on a new footing. I have put off writing to you, because I did not want it to appear I was doing so under the influence of a passing irritation. Moreover, I sense that this letter will be useless if you do not realize that I would have been just as disgusted (unfortunately, this is the only suitable word) if I had watched you acclaim a book grossly insulting a stranger.

Yourcenar ended the letter with this "complimentary" close: "With changed regards, Marguerite Yourcenar."[60] But her "changed regards," happily, would take on a friendlier tone before too long. That is, until Chalon, with his customary sincerity, said what he thought of *Anna, soror...*, reissued by Gallimard, calling it a "pompous" text. Yourcenar did not forgive him for this, which is not to be counted in her favor.

All these letters, these "distractions," did not keep the feeling of confinement, nor lucidity, at bay. Thus did Yourcenar write to one of her old Parisian friends, Max Heilbronn, a Russian translator and interpreter, in addition to being the manager of Galeries Lafayette: "Grace had a recurrence of her illness, from which she has suffered without interruption since 1972, which explains my absence from Europe. She keeps on fighting with astonishing energy, but the specialists no longer hold out any hope."[61] A cruel lucidity, when one thinks that Frick was still filing away *all* the correspondence. One can also observe the veiled animosity that was growing between the two women in such trivial, almost childish, comments as this one, about a photograph of Yourcenar and the dog Valentine, taken at the time of the publication of *The Abyss* in France: "Grace doesn't like it because she thinks I'm holding Valentine like a doll. I like it myself."

But must we really see rancor and intolerable bad taste in such comments, as certain people have in the last volume of Simone de Beauvoir's memoirs, *La Cérémonie des adieux* (*Adieux: A Farewell to Sartre*), in which she so straightforwardly talks about Sartre's physical and intellectual decrepitude, about his incontinence as well as his "absences"? Perhaps not— or perhaps not only. Perhaps what we should see, rather, is the final proof, an ambiguous and wrenching one, of a love, the absolute refusal to make the other an appendage of oneself, to confiscate her destiny from her by trying to disguise her state. Yourcenar and Beauvoir, five years her junior, did not know one another. Nonetheless, in their self-willed lucidity, in their fierce determination not to sugarcoat reality in order to hide from its harshness, they were of the same mettle. And it is not at all by chance that both of them were subject to identical reproach from certain quarters. Their paths had crossed one day, Yourcenar remembered, in an embassy. They had not read each other's works, or very little. Remote in space and in time, seeking out the raw materials of her *œuvre* as far from the present day as possible, Yourcenar was not likely to attract the attention of Beauvoir, whose approach to matters intellectual and literary she claimed she did not comprehend. She surely did not see to what an extent Beauvoir had been an irreplaceable chronicler—still not recognized at her true worth—of a certain group of intellectuals, although the latter held, admittedly, little interest for Yourcenar.

Yourcenar had nonetheless read *Le Deuxième Sexe* (*The Second Sex*), not being one who could ignore the importance of such a theoretical reflection. She did not really comment specifically on this text, but a letter to Suzanne Lilar about one of her essays, *Le Malentendu du deuxième sexe* [The Errancy of the Second Sex], gives a few indications: I should have written to you regarding *Le Malentendu* immediately after I read it, when I had just registered each thrust in your battle with Simone de Beauvoir. It seemed to me occasionally that both of you were hitting home. As a matter of principle, I am passionately in favor of everything that heightens human dignity, hence that of women. As a matter of practice, there's no such thing, in my view, as fighting too hard to obtain the de facto equality that, as you very well show with regard to salaries, has not yet been attained."[62]

AT PETITE PLAISANCE, the year 1977 would represent Grace's final burst of life, even though she had to be hospitalized once again from 6 through 14 February. In her almost unreasonable determination, no longer just to keep on surviving, but to come back to life, she undertook a new chemotherapy treatment, which was exhausting. When she came back, on Saint Valentine's Day, she found a card in her room, a token of love, in keeping with tradition—a tradition much stronger in the United States than in Europe, which Yourcenar in spite of everything, did not fail to honor.

Although she was forced to return to the hospital from 13 through 21 April, as soon as she was released she decided to go to a wedding to which she had been invited, and then take a trip to Alaska. The plans she had made would admit of no discussion. Yourcenar and she left Petite Plaisance on 30 May and came back on 15 June. They were in Montreal on 31 May, in Vancouver on 4 June. However reserved she may have been regarding Frick during the last years of her own life, Yourcenar liked to tell the story of this trip, not only because the beauty of the countryside had overwhelmed her, but because the trip constituted, in and of itself, without anyone needing to say so, a tribute to the courage of Grace Frick. "We spent four days and four nights in the train on the way out, and as many on the way back," she confided. "Even broken up by two stops at two different places in the Rockies, it was draining. Then we had an eight-day cruise, to the heart of the beauty of those immense, still-inviolate landscapes."

"In sailing up and down that archipelago of islands and promontories overhung by glaciers, where most often the forest comes right down to the edge of the water," Yourcenar wrote to Carayon in July 1977, "I often said to myself that it was literally indescribable and that only the visions of the poets offered an equivalent here and there. Rimbaud: 'I have seen sidereal archipelagos! and islands'; Vigny: 'free as the sea on the shore of somber islands' . . . the great silent lands. The entire end of Baudelaire's *Voyage* (*The Voyage*), minus the last line, which always irritates me; and Hugo, in whose case it is less a question of any particular line or poem than of a sense of the sea throughout his *œuvre*. These men have seen, even the ones who haven't seen with their eyes of flesh and blood. . . . It was not yet quite the midnight sun that I so loved in the Scandinavian north. To the point of giving it to Zeno for his last vision and as a symbol of immortality. . . . An enormous moose was swimming in a very wide river." Finally, she closed saying she would never forget "the great primeval sound, unlike any other, of glaciers calving their icebergs."[63]

Frick and Yourcenar would defend Alaska publicly, alongside American environmentalists with whom they had long been involved, providing them both moral and financial support. They belonged, moreover, to numerous societies for the protection of nature all over the world. Yourcenar had probably been much more influenced in this domain by Frick—"a hippie and an environmentalist before the fact" according to her friends—than she admitted. But her battle against the irreparable damages done to the planet went hand in hand with her growing pessimism regarding the activities of men, their vague relation to the notions of present and future, their incapacity to think of themselves as links in a long chain whose preservation had to be assured. Yourcenar's thinking on ecology was not fairly represented by pictures of a complacent old woman looking out the window at the resident squirrels or going out to fill the bird feeders, in the yard, with her dog. "I suffer to see the polluted cities, the coast inundated with oil, fewer and fewer species of animals," she said to Matthieu Galey. "When the Italy of the Romantics, the Italy whose image people still cherished thirty years ago, is nothing but a myth, when they replace trees with pylons, one is looking at a world that is dying. So I try to fight by all sorts of legal means, helping out the people who are attempting to protest. Political and humanitarian organizations play a very considerable role in my life. I belong to countless societies both in America and in France. I write, I send telegrams. . . . [64] But I don't believe I am at all cut out for direct action. It is not simply by asserting his opinions, but in showing a certain angle of vision, a certain image of the world, that a writer can express himself. . . . We must stay close to nature, indeed to everything that binds man to his planetary destiny." [65]

AFTER RETURNING from Alaska—that land for which she was prepared to mobilize all of the strength she had left—Frick, "was really little more than her own ghost, even though she did everything she could to hide it right up to the end," Yourcenar much later confided. From then on, it was as if Yourcenar herself was divided between two universes she no longer could unite: the universe of Petite Plaisance, illness, and all her own various troubles, and the universe of Paris where preparations were already under way to admit her, the first woman, to an institution that had previously shunned those of her sex, the Académie Française. Indeed, the Académie awarded her, in 1977, the Grand Prix de littérature, crowning her *œuvre* as a whole. Frick, who had practically stopped writing in her notorious daybooks (inadequate in former days, despite her fine, close handwriting, to the many details she had wanted to record there) noted nonetheless on 30 October 1977: "visit of Dr. and Madame Dausset from the Académie des Sciences . . . urging M.Y. to consider three months annual residency in France to become a member [of the Académie Française] but M.Y. refused these terms."

With the appearance of *Archives du Nord* came another consecration.

Critics—with an occasional exception—were particularly enthusiastic—nay, dithyrambic—about "this rich, exuberant, youthful, and passionate book":[66] "It is dense, round and subtle, sonorous and noble, with now and then a rare word, cruel and admirably chosen among all the possible words, that plunges to the heart like a blade," wrote François Nourissier with jubilation in *Le Point*. "Of all our writers, her French is among the most beautiful, less ductile than Aragon's, less deliberate than Montherlant's, juicier than Gracq's or Mandiargues's. She possesses a sense both of grandeur and of the trivial, the familiar. It is hard to imagine who, today, could rival with Marguerite Yourcenar on this terrain. . . . She has a sense of violence, of crowds, of frozen countrysides as Breughel, Bosch, or Patinir did. Her pen aflame, her eye cold and keen, she relates the births, the vanities, the agonies, the madness of men. This is what a writer is: not someone or other *plus* some books, but a person whose life and words, whose books and Time seem consubstantial."[67] "Thus she creates a new genre wherein her writer's talent magnificently executes the assumption of genealogy unto literature," opined Jacqueline Piatier in *Le Monde*. "Marguerite Yourcenar has written her own intimate, personal *Légende des siècles* (*Legend of the Centuries*)."[68] In *L'Humanité*, André Wurmser stressed that "the aristocracy of her phrasing, the rhythm of her narrative are grounded in a philosophy of stoicism and skepticism that concerns itself little with proselytizing," concluding that, "The question has been raised of extending the equality of the sexes to that secular institution that ignored Madame de Sévigné, George Sand, Marceline, and even that Anna who was nonetheless Countess of Noailles, and the great Colette. The Académie would prefer, rumor has it, Marguerite Yourcenar to some minister. What a delight this would be."[69] Dominique Fernandez, for his part, expressed reservations: "From a writer of her stature, there was reason to expect something else besides this superficial stroll through the past. The minute the father comes on stage, the chosen mode of narration, little anecdotal probings, reveals its insufficiency." The difficult thing to accept, in his view, was the distance at which Yourcenar placed herself vis-à-vis Michel de Crayencour: "It's one thing in the case of the grandfather, who attended his first ball sixty years before her own birth. But in the father's case, no. Treating him like a stranger, like some anonymous member of the numberless *gens,* like a particle of dust that fell by chance from among the family papers, like a grain of sand picked up in the archives of the Nord amounts to willfully denuding her narrative of all the emotional tension, Electrean or otherwise (I am no fan of complexes), that existed in reality. It also amounts, and this has much more serious consequences for a writer, to making her style banal as she chats by the fire, in vain."[70] However much Fernandez may deny being a "fan of complexes," his remarks "speak for themselves," if one might be so bold: how dare a woman fail to render homage to her father, a homage laden with "all the emotional tension" that a daughter, in reality, should possess?

YOURCENAR, highly satisfied with these reviews, showed herself to be just as delighted by "Claude Gallimard's marvelous letter on the subject of *Archives*, which was full of the warm understanding one never dares anticipate."[71] "At first I was tempted in writing you this letter to highlight everything that struck me, but in the end there are so many facts, so many details, so many razor-sharp remarks, that I had the impression above all of penetrating to the heart of a truth expressed with lucidity and freedom," her publisher wrote to her. "Your writing is crisp, direct, marked by an imperturbable good humor. I am convinced that we have here an extraordinary work, whose prestigious labyrinth one is able to confront thanks to forceful writing that is every bit as modest as it is superb in its nobility. I wanted to express to you my admiration sincerely, but with delicacy; instead, I haven't been able to contain my enthusiasm, it being so rare to encounter such a work."[72] Yourcenar answered him right away, attempting to explain precisely what she had set out to accomplish. "I had said to myself that I would indeed have to try once to evoke the past of a family, or rather a group, without a tear in the corner of my eye, without hiding the occasional eruptions of vanity on the part of the families behind an amused condescension, without recriminations, embarrassment, or, for that matter, exasperation. Using only what we know, and with the courage to put question marks where there is something we don't know. I have no idea whether such a book can or cannot be a 'literary' success, but it was a fascinating human experiment to attempt. That you should have perceived this so quickly and so well reassures me with regard to this work's fate, and quite simply fills me with joy."[73]

WITH YOURCENAR reaching the point where she found virtues in a publisher—and literary ones, no less—Frick had every reason to fear she might return to Europe. In fact, she was more in France, in her mind, than at her friend's side, all the while she and her book were being talked about so much. More than ever, she was sending thank-you notes to literary critics, whose errors she corrected, with more humor, for once, than persnickety bitterness. She pointed out, notably, to Georges Frameries, who published an article very favorable to *Archives du Nord* in *L'Unité:* "I am not 80 years old, but 74. Six years is nothing, and it's all the world! And one must always

live as if one were going to die in ten minutes or go on forever." She affirmed
that if six years were granted her, she would be able to write *Quoi? L'Eter-*
nité, make a little progress in studying Sanscrit and Japanese, travel in the
Far East, see a few corners of Europe that she loved once again . . . and
"continue to fight on behalf of the protection of nature, and consequently
man."[74]

IN EARLY 1977, Yourcenar had to confront what was for her a new and
unexpected experience: the first cinematic adaptation of one of her books,
namely *Coup de Grâce*, produced by the young German director Volker
Schlöndorff. On 1 January 1977, there was a private showing of the film at
the Maine Coast Mall cinema, in Ellsworth. The next day, Yourcenar began
a long letter to Schlöndorff, which she would not complete until a week
later, and which constitutes something of an indictment of his reading of
the novel. Expressing all the while her respect for his creative freedom,
for his specifically cinematic undertaking, she voices what are more than
reservations regarding his interpretations, and particularly his treatment of
the characters. Nonetheless, when she points out what she calls Erick's "re-
pressed homosexuality," one can hardly blame Schlöndorff for not noticing
it in the text: does one not have to know, to understand this remark, that
the model for Erick was André Fraigneau, with whom Yourcenar had been
so much in love, and know how ill-disposed she was—as the future would
prove—to acknowledge her rejection by him? She would find herself on
more solid ground when, years later, she discussed the adaptation of *The*
Abyss with André Delvaux.

But she had surely not made much of an attempt to see, at the time, just
what it was about her novel that had captured the attention of Schlöndorff,
about whom she knew nothing. As she wrote to her friend Joseph Breitbach: "I was not aware in signing that contract that Schlöndorff was, as you
say, 'involved with the German Far Left.' I don't feel I am particularly right-
wing; I would rather be, as Jean Schlumberger so happily phrased it, 'right
in the middle.' But one does not write history with *Epinal* images of hate."
She urged Breitbach, however, to keep her remarks to himself: "Schlöndorff
made his film as he believed he had to; I don't wish to do him any harm."
She added, furthermore, in a postscript that she had thanked Jean-Louis
Bory for his article in the *Nouvel Observateur* "and his talk on the radio,
both very favorable to the film. His enthusiasm proves that there are specta-
tors who, in spite of everything, can find something of what I attempted to
put into the book in that film."[75]

News reached her in April 1977 of the closing of the Hôtel Saint-James et d'Albany in Paris. Although this was not a central locus of her past, it added nonetheless to the curious list of places "destroyed" behind Yourcenar, from the houses of her childhood to the Hôtel Wagram. The Saint-James building, on the national preservation list, would not be destroyed, but would be sold one apartment at a time.[76]

As was her habit, Yourcenar had left a trunk there containing original editions of her works from before 1939, some other books, and some papers and reviews. She lost them all, making only this quick comment on the subject: "I have lost things left behind this way so often in my life (be it on account of wars, sudden departures, longer absences than had been foreseen, because of illness or whatever else) that I have reached the point of accepting this sort of misfortune philosophically."[77]

IN FRANCE the press's interest in Yourcenar was growing, as was the public's desire to get to know her, attracted as people were by her reputation of "living on an island she never left"—it wasn't known then that her reclusion was not at all voluntary. "I am aware of the fact that a legend has grown up around my presumed solitude," she would note in one of the chapters of *With Open Eyes,* appropriately titled "La Solitude pour être utile" ("Solitude, to Be Useful"), "partly because of the name of this island but partly, too, because throughout my life, even when I was young, wherever relations with other human beings who really mattered were concerned, whether lasting or brief, intermittent or continuous, I've always tried to keep them in the shadows that conform so well to the important things in life. As a result, when people began to take an interest in me, a legend developed, or several legends. I've seen excited visitors arrive here thinking that Mount Desert Island was a sort of Capri. Others have cast inquisitive glances at the bottles in my kitchen, thinking they detect an odor of alchemy or magic. And I could tell you many other stories of the same sort. But such myth makers have their value: they teach the poet-historians to be wary of historical gossip."[78]

Yourcenar continued to put up some resistance to a behavior—talking publicly about oneself—she disapproved of sincerely and profoundly. She finally gave in, but not without a grudge against those, such as Matthieu Galey, who had witnessed her doing so. In October 1977, she refused permission to the singer Hélène Martin to do a show inspired by her and explained: "I detest what seems to be some kind of pathological excitement on the part of the public about pouncing on a writer's life, as if he or she were not a man or a woman like everyone else. A writer shows his worth by way of his books. And that's where one must look for him—or rather, for it is not a matter of looking for him—one must look for the ideas he has to offer."[79] Two days later, nonetheless, Jean Montalbetti and André Matthieu were there to do a radio interview. Yourcenar, as well as Frick, who said so in her notebook, appreciated "their intelligence, their kindness, and their sensitivity." In November, it would be a French television crew, come from Washington D.C. Yourcenar well knew that she needed that expression of warmth, that expression of interest, the recognition of her country, she who would soon find herself alone on a continent she had only "adopted" for Grace Frick. But of this she spoke as little as possible, for therein would lie the real affront to her sick friend, much more than in daring to tell her correspondents that Frick's case was from now on beyond hope. To all the journalists who asked her when she intended to return to Paris, she responded evasively, just as she did to those who urged her to come for a visit in the spring of 1978.

18

The Silent Piano

THE YEARS 1978 AND 1979 would be even more unbearable and "schizophrenic" than the five painful years tête-à-tête that had just passed. Grace Frick's illness was now little more than a drawn-out mortal agony, and Marguerite Yourcenar was reaping the harvest of a writerly career: glory. On 23 January 1978, Claude Gallimard telephoned: all around him people were insisting he convince Yourcenar to submit her candidacy for the Académie Française. She explained her position, from which she would not deviate. Under no circumstances would she propose herself as a candidate. Having said that, if they elected her she would not be so rude as to refuse. "Those gentlemen" could do as they saw fit. But by no means should anyone request that she submit herself of her own initiative to their approval.

Whether Grace lived or not—and she knew better than to think that she would—Yourcenar was slipping away from her for good. What Frick had feared so much, and for such a long time, was happening: Europe was taking back the woman she revered. Surely we cannot affirm without the slightest reservation that Frick looked favorably upon the Académie affair. Of course attending Yourcenar's induction would have been like seeing her life's work crowned, justifying her devotion, her abnegation, her blind faith in Yourcenar's greatness. And in the final months, convinced as she was that Yourcenar's election was near, she could not bear the idea of missing the ceremony. Still, for Yourcenar, becoming "immortal" was such an absolute way of belonging to France, thus of moving away from her, that she could not possibly have derived from it an unqualified joy. And to this was added constant physical pain, growing worse all the time—a fact that no one, in France, could have been fully aware of at the time, so much did Yourcenar, in interviews, on film, appear serene, amused by what was happening to her, ironic, sometimes haughty, but never defeated.

The atmosphere at Petite Plaisance was becoming oppressive. Or rather, it would have, if feelings of reciprocal exasperation, sometimes verging on hate, had not been counterbalanced by a love of forty years. On both sides.

With all the ambiguities, the compromises, the things never said and, for that matter, impossible to say that such a number of years spent together presupposes. One cannot assert that that love was simply transformed into resentment, even if resentment far outstepped everything else in the last two years, showing up in petty conflicts, in stubborn refusals. Thus, for months, Frick had absolutely forbidden access to the big closet in her room. When it was opened, after her death, Yourcenar confided, papers were found there pertaining to problems that should have been taken care of. And there were bills, unpaid taxes.

The rare notations Frick made in her daybook are the writings of someone who has given up. "Things are only limping along here," Yourcenar conceded in several letters. But above all she stressed Frick's energy and courage, which compelled her respect. Her admiration was such that she erupted in anger when some French people told her that it was unfitting to use the word "cancer" in the presence of a person who is ill (later on she would reproach Frick for preferring "toward the end, if not perhaps to ignore her illness, at least to stop calling it by name"). "Dare I say that keeping silent does not at all seem to me to be the best policy?" she wrote.[1] "I believe one shows a lack of respect by doing anything other than speaking the truth. I also think that a sick person who supposedly does not know, but of course suspects the danger he is in, suffers much more in his uncertainty than one who knows. Besides which, I don't see how a sick person can collaborate intelligently with his doctor . . . if he is not fully informed. Finally, with any person who has religious sentiments or philosophical opinions, it seems to me that one has a duty to let him prepare for death in his own way." Summing up Frick's illness, she concludes: "we thought we had lost her last year . . . but since then, while she's still very much in danger, she is holding on and making the best use of what strength she has. I am sure these good results would not have been obtained if we had kept her in the dark." Yourcenar would always lash out against this "very French" attitude of silence, "this rather odious way of depriving people of their destiny." Her vehemence, when she spoke in private on this subject, was no doubt one of her ways of paying posthumous homage to her companion.

In reality, "things" were not going at all well, even if Frick did decide in July to go spend two days in Boston visiting a Pompeii exhibit with Yourcenar. This would be her last "pleasure" trip. They would make it by car, and Frick obviously drove—it takes six hours or so to get to Boston—since she was the only one of the two who knew how to drive. In the daybook, Yourcenar put XXX on the dates of 7 and 8 July 1978, those signs of rapture they had been in the habit of using during the time of their passion, signs that would soon reappear in the daybooks Yourcenar kept alone, on the occasion of her trips with Jerry Wilson.

Frick, who on top of everything else had fallen down and fractured her shoulder in May 1978 while attempting to put a screen in the kitchen window, was undergoing one treatment after another. But it was with only relative effectiveness. They were not succeeding at curbing the spread of the metastases. Her left arm swelled up excessively. She had to bandage it to keep the swelling down and, even so, in a photograph taken by chance when she was turning around, it looks like a monstrous protuberance, no longer even attached to her body. Her torso also swelled up, and, once this began, there was no respite from the pain. Her frenetic will to control everything was now focused also on herself, and she refused to give up in the face of the illness invading her. On 3 January 1979, she set off alone, by car, to Buffalo, New York, to undergo an experimental treatment. Two weeks later, still alone, still at the wheel, she returned.

Even though she sincerely admired Frick's strength and dignity, Yourcenar could not accept making that illness, that death foretold, the center of her existence. "My immobility dates back almost ten years (1978)," she wrote in what would become the "Carnets de notes de *L'Œuvre au noir.*" "In certain ways, it is rather 'imprisonment' than 'immobility' since it is no longer up to me to walk out the open door." She continues with no other commentary: "Obsession with illness observed in another."[2]

She began working "in [her] mind," she told Louise de Borchgrave, "on the third and final panel of the triptych, in which 'Michel' will grow old. But I shall have to grant myself some time to reflect before I write it."[3] She kept on with her literary work and corresponded with her friends: "things are not going very well here," she repeated in December 1978 to Anne Quellennec. "I'm writing a lot, I'm finishing my collection of translations from ancient Greek, *La Couronne et la lyre,* but although Grace is still active and courageous (too active, too courageous), there are health problems that will have to be dealt with, no doubt by way of dangerous medications. As for me, I am well, sometimes more so, sometimes less, depending on the day."[4]

DETERMINING PRECISELY what Yourcenar was privately thinking that year is not easy, unless one wants to substitute for the evidence we have at hand—and for the conclusions that can reasonably be drawn from it—interpretations bordering on fiction. What really went on during those first visits of Jerry Wilson, the young man who was part of a French television crew and would become her traveling companion? Did their actual "encounter" really happen the first time he came? One thing we can observe is that, "after the fact," as the different inks attest, after Frick's death—and perhaps even after the death of Wilson—when Yourcenar reread the daybooks, she folded the pages for the week of 1 May 1978 and noted on that date: "Maurice, Jerry." Frick for her part, had only mentioned on 3 May: "television crew; six people," and on the sixth: "M.Y. going around with them." Likewise Yourcenar folded and annotated the page for the week of 1 November of the same year, which Frick had filled with mundane details. 1 November: "Maurice Dumay arrives with his friend Jerry Wilson to make an addition to the last film." 3 November: "An entire day of work with the television people. Marguerite has to read some excerpts from *Archives du Nord* but she loses her voice coming down Mount Cadillac." 4 November: "Departure of the television director and his photographer friend Jerry Wilson." Yourcenar would often say, later, how much Grace had liked Jerry and felt close to him because they were both from the American South—which there is no reason to cast doubt on a priori. But the sole comment written by Frick about Wilson indicates only that she thought him a "nice boy," which should not be taken lightly, knowing how unfriendly she could prove to be.

Yourcenar herself did not fail to write to several of her friends to say how stupid she found *Le Pays d'où je viens* [The Country I Come From], the program that brought about the visit of Dumay and Wilson. But curiously, and contrary to all her usual habits, in a letter to her nephew, she minimized the responsibility of the crew that had come to Petite Plaisance. Since this couldn't possibly indicate a sudden indulgence on her part, it must be the sign of an already great liking. "I hope you haven't seen the television program, *Le Pays d'où je viens*, for which they came to interview me here," she said in a first letter. "The rest of the program was incredibly vulgar, which I didn't know until later. It seems there was a platinum blonde, with a mike in her hand, representing the Countess of Flanders, founder of the Countess Home, which has just been turned into a museum."[5] "The person in charge of this program," she resumed a week later,

a likable boy named Maurice Dumay, who came here to interview me, may not have known what kind of cabaret-type deal he was getting himself into. The first time he met his two rather mediocre collaborators from Lille was in New York, a few hours before arriving here. They came with him to Northeast Harbor and they didn't say a word about what their studio was cooking up in Lille. Still, Dumay *should have* had a rough idea of what the regional crews were going to produce, and I am angry with myself for having served as a decoy for this music-hall performance whose vulgarity, alas, is confirmed by some newspaper photographs I've seen. The various friends of mine whose names Dumay had asked me for in order to inform them, politely, that this fine program would be shown on TV are unanimously of the same opinion as you. One of my good friends, a painter [Elie Grekoff], writes to me from his farm near Saumur: "An ocean of whipped cream."[6]

WE ARE ENTERING into a period of Yourcenar's existence in which it becomes even more difficult than usual to distinguish what, precisely and actually, was lived from what was rewritten, or imagined, in the aftermath. This is an utterly rhetorical question for her who, from the figure of Hadrian to that of Jeanne de Vietinghoff, from the character of Zeno to that of her father, had "lived" everything she had imagined, and had imagined much of what she had lived. But it is not so trifling a question for a biographer, doomed to confusion or to drawing rash conclusions. Nonetheless, the uncertainty may not even be lifted in 2037, the year they will open the sealed documents—there is no reason why the boundary between the real and the imaginary should be any clearer there than in all the bits of "pseudo-information" left behind by Yourcenar.

If there is one thing that cannot be contradicted, however, it is certainly the horror, the madness, the hell of the year 1979, a prefiguration of another abominable year, 1985. No longer was there any room for doubt: Frick was dying; equally certain: Yourcenar was at the height of her glory. It was clear by now that a battle was under way to make her the first woman to sit beneath the dome at Quai Conti.[7] Paradox of parodoxes, she was the writer in vogue, the one who was selling, who even managed to get an imposing number of readers to buy her "translations" of ancient Greek poems, collected in the volume *La Couronne et la lyre,* a hefty tome of 480 pages that came out in November 1979. One would still be taking quite a risk to call these texts translations. According to the specialists, beginning with Constantine Dimaras—who knew Yourcenar's "art of translating,"[8] having practiced it with her on the Cavafy poems—they are more adaptations than translations in any strict sense of the term, French poems loosely inspired by fragments of Greek texts. They were texts that Yourcenar, of course, understood: no one would take it into his head to suggest that they are faulty translations. But as Dimaras very perceptively explains, Yourcenar had no sense of what a translation should be. She quite readily and consciously amended the texts, imposing her will with a sentence that admitted of no possible response: "It's better this way."

That anthology of some one hundred ten poets—from the seventh century before Christ to the reign of Justinian, around A.D. 520—was assembled, for the most part, during the time Yourcenar was writing *Memoirs of Hadrian*, between 1948 and 1951. "The translations of ancient Greek poems that the reader will find in this volume were in large part composed for my own enjoyment, in the strictest sense of the word, which is to say without any thought being given to publishing them," Yourcenar stresses in her long introduction.[9] She also explains the variety of her selections and discusses her preferences in the matter of translation: "Granted, there is no good translation that is not a faithful one, but the same thing is true for translations as for women: fidelity, without other virtues, is not enough to make them bearable. Except for interlinear translations, perhaps the most useful ones, which immediately let us see the structural differences between two languages, no good prose translation is ever literal: word order, grammar, syntax, to say nothing of the translator's individual touch, all work against a literal rendition. . . . He among us nowadays who translates into verse takes the risk of being seen as old-fashioned or eccentric," she warns further on. Yet, this is the choice that she made and one she justified at length—just as she would once again explain the necessity, when questioned by Matthieu Galey, of resorting to versification (alexandrine verses in particular) in order to better transpose the verbal charms and rhythms of those ancient compositions.[10]

Otherwise, Yourcenar continued to make progress writing "An Obscure Man." Since she had survived her now long-past plunge into despair, during the forties, nothing could keep her from writing. Journalists, nonetheless, were coming to Petite Plaisance one after another: Matthieu Galey, Jacques Chancel, Bernard Pivot, Jean-Paul Kauffmann, to mention only the best known among them. Frick continued to keep an eye on everything, to do the things that have to be done for one's guests, and to protect Yourcenar from "bouts of weariness" brought on by her interviews, which was more than enough, after all, to have to do. Whether she proved to be polite or rather disagreeable, those she dealt with must have seen nothing in her behavior beyond the particularities of her character and not what she was playing at that moment in time: in a way, a hero's role.

Why did Yourcenar consent to this procession at Frick's worst moment? Was it purely an effect of her egocentricity? Doubtless no. She wanted to avoid being permanently face to face with Frick, with Frick's death, a source of deep anguish for her, though she would say this as little as possible, and as if inadvertantly. For example, there is the time of Jacques Kayaloff's death in 1984, when she urged his widow Anya to take very good care of herself: "Right now you're holding on, but you'll see, it is afterward that things will be difficult," she told her during a telephone conversation. "I went through that with Grace. At the time, it was almost like a deliverance, but it's afterward . . ."

She needed to be reassured regarding what awaited her after Frick's death, to feel the interest, even the warmth people felt toward her in France. This would tend to indicate that Jerry Wilson did not really exist for her at the time in any way that might have given her comfort. She was on the verge of panic—which she never would admit, though she did speak one day of her "burden of fears." "I am taking advantage of Grace's absence— she is seeing her doctor—to write to you. I have the feeling I am in a long and very dark tunnel," she admitted in that letter, a letter she immediately filed away herself (the notes appearing on the top are in her handwriting) to keep Frick from seeing it.[11]

Simply reading Frick's daybook for the last year of her life leaves one with the impression those two women gave way to a madness of sorts, neither one of them now entirely in control of reality, a madness very much along the lines of their first encounter—even though it was a tragedy that brought the madness on. It was the final madness they would share, at seventy-six years of age, and one that sometimes bordered on the ghastly. Frick wrote down with one stroke of her pen: "the Pivot project appears on the scene. The pain never goes away now." Or on 15 July, four months before her death: "Marguerite's health is worrying me. She lost her bridge." On 15 May, she copied over by hand, as she always had, a card from Marguerite to a friend bearing these words: "As for Grace's health, it's not outstanding right now, and most of all, she is suffering a great deal."[12]

However, when Frick writes down the visits of this one and that one, she makes it seem, once again, that nothing else matters besides Yourcenar, her health, her comfort. Galey came from 12 through 18 February 1979 to do the interviews that provided the material for his book, *With Open Eyes.* This visit sowed the seeds of all the conflicts that erupted between Yourcenar and him at the time the book was published. She was in fact extremely tired. She doubtless truly needed to talk. And there she was with an intelligent, attentive interlocutor who knew her work very well, with whom she had the feeling of speaking in confidence. Later on she would have the impression of having said too much, of having "taken off [her] clothes." This is the expression she used according to Galey, who noted it in 1981 in his *Journal,* adding: "When I put up something of a protest, 'It's far from a strip tease,' she replied, 'I have an awfully low-cut neckline.' What bothered her, got her worked up, was that circumstances took her by surprise, so she had let her guard down without realizing it."[13]

Between Frick and Galey relations were not overly warm, unless she confined her complaints to her notebook: "he comes every afternoon from two o'clock to six, or even two to seven. On 16 February M.Y. has to stop. She's too tired. She has pains in her chest and has to be taken to the hospital. On 17 February, Galey stops by the hospital to say goodby. He brings a plant. An azalea. He comes back to the house with me, and stays, and stays . . . On 18 February Galey comes back and insists on going on with the interview, at the hospital, so he would have a conclusion. I call Marguerite, adamant, to ask her to see him this morning and send him back to Paris. He stays with her for an hour and ten minutes before she makes up her mind to send him packing for good."

With Kauffmann, everything went wrong, and his article bears witness to the fact.[14] "I had to throw him out, after five hours," says Frick. Regardless, he had no success at getting Yourcenar to talk, and she would answer in writing, in a rather disagreeable way, the supplementary questions he sent since she refused to see him again. One finds in her responses some examples of the stony anger that sometimes came over her—which certainly had less to do with Kauffmann than with her own state at the time—making her abrupt, and even pointlessly cutting: "Let us be careful not to use the word 'secret' for any form of knowledge or culture in which, out of laziness or inertia, we refuse to participate." "What is the point of crossing the ocean to ask me things about Samuel Champlain that can be found in a dictionary? What is the point of crossing the ocean to ask me how many rooms there are in the house where I live? Allow me to add that personality worship is a form of idle curiosity that has existed in every age but that may never have been as widespread as it is today. By what measure do you judge that a person you don't know is not being totally forthcoming with you? My personality, like my house, is open to whoever walks in . . . only fools believe in secrets, only show-offs claim to have any"[15]—words singularly similar to some she had Hadrian pen: "the observation of our fellowmen, who usually arrange to hide their secrets from us, or to make us believe that they have secrets where none exist." She had already struck this particular note on another occasion a few years earlier, in an exchange of letters with Georges Wicks who was working on Natalie Barney. Wicks having submitted his text to her, Yourcenar had corrected it and pointed out to him without excessive courtesy: "I have deleted the passages concerning me. First of all, because it's pointless to go on about me, second, because those lines irrefutably prove that you know nothing about anything that has to do with me and have not read my books, which, of course, is not a crime, but why then presume to define someone? Who, pray tell, are 'the Roman emperors' (in the plural) I have 'frequented in my literary life'? What's more, why this description of a library when you don't know what books it has in it? Let's drop this, shall we?"[16]

Chancel, on the other hand, found favor with Frick: "his entire crew, for the two days they were here, 12 and 13 May, was charming and highly efficient." And Yourcenar commented: "constantly assuring me that we could stop whenever I wanted, Chancel got ten hours worth of discussion out of me altogether, and I don't seem to feel the worse for it. I'm only tired of so many words that seem futile somehow." Here, manifestly, Yourcenar gives way to striking something of a pose; she was not at all reluctant to talk—this is very clear in the *Radioscopies*, as it would be some months later with Pivot on the special *Apostrophes* program devoted to her.[17]

"Two weeks ago we had three days of radio presided over by Jacques Chancel, a likable man, and the technicians, who were very nice, as always. . . . Why is it that the media force a writer to expound on every subject under the sun, when his job is to write about a few things specifically? But I got a sense that it's important to my publisher for publicity reasons, even though he was kind enough not to force me to do it. One can hardly cut off all communication, especially living abroad. . . . Frankly, I don't know if it's worth listening to or not."[18]

With those interviews, Chancel inaugurated a new format for his show. After being approached on this topic by several newspapers, he related his stay, which made a decidedly more positive impression on him than Rosbo had taken away:

> So we had taped more than six hours. Stopping now and then. . . . She answered my questions just as she works . . . with great care, great seriousness, almost severity. With a kind of authority, a superiority, that she unconsciously knows she possesses. Never a hint of familiarity, but we sensed something much more, much better than familiarity in her way of greeting us or suggesting when our work was done that we walk over to the sea, to the ocean one sees out the window. We left happy and I don't think she felt too "put out" either. . . . Mrs. Grace, for her part, saw to it that things went as well as they possibly could, calling us at the hotel in the evening to ask if there was anything we needed, with that kindly solicitude so characteristic of her. Certain people have described her as annoying; this is not so. She protects Yourcenar, who needs her, completely. That's all there is to it. And her devotion is magnificent.[19]

When Chancel questioned her about Frick, Yourcenar, for the first and only time, in public, could not contain her emotion: "I wish I could tell you how remarkable that woman is," Chancel asserted. "She welcomed us, she took care of us . . . But I believe I know what she must represent for you . . ."

"Probably loyalty; a great passion for devotion."

Then on to this question: "If she were to go away one day, would you find yourself alone?" It was in a voice choked with emotion that Marguerite Yourcenar replied, "Yes, I would find myself alone," before regaining control of herself very quickly when Chancel pressed on: "She's your family."

"She's my family for the moment . . . Things go on for as long as they can."

When it was broadcast in France, from 11 through 15 June, the press gave a great deal of coverage to this new manner of "Radioscopie," all the more so since people had not often heard Yourcenar's voice. In *Les Nouvelles Littéraires,* Jérôme Garcin marveled: "We were expecting a muted and discreet conversation, timid and restrained; what we heard, in fact, was nothing of the kind: alert, lively, quick, Marguerite Yourcenar caught every question on the fly . . . readily evoking her personal memories. . . . In short, the time is ripe to put an end to the established myth of this woman in exile, cloistered like a nun on the coast of the United States, rejecting the confessional."[20]

Even more surprising was the special edition of *Apostrophes* devoted to her by Pivot, with whom she engaged in a kind of ironic complicity while they were on the air. She enjoyed herself, visibly, with this highly enthusiastic journalist, who had read her work but found it surprising that the reincarnation of Hadrian should be a lively, amusing woman who protested in the street against the war in Vietnam, or made fun of French sentimentality where amorous matters were concerned.[21] In the press commentary, picking up on this complicity and the obvious pleasure that Yourcenar derived from that on-air conversation, there is no dearth of sexist cliché, as we have so often seen: "a seventy-six-year-old, corpulent woman, with a mischievous glint in her eye, who flawlessly manipulates tenses and moods and sweeps away in three sentences the old feminist ashes they don't fail to dump on her doorstep. . . . The secret of the strength of this woman who smiles and cultivates her garden is without a doubt this virile pessimism."[22] Bertrand Poirot-Delpech, for his part, was not of course completely satisfied, but he enjoyed the performance, and he said so in *Le Monde:* "Mischief-maker that she is, as she herself admits, Yourcenar had warned us: in a parlor game like this one, it is always the commonplace that triumphs. . . . There remains the guided tour of a very great *œuvre.* Pivot excels in this domain. . . . A miracle of intelligence and sensuality combined, Marguerite Yourcenar's face helps us understand how sensual it is for this writer to use the subjunctive—oh! that *'bien que je pensasse'*!—so exquisitely natural—or to search for just the right term."[23]

In the letter to her half nephew relating the visit of Chancel's crew, Yourcenar imparted a little information about Frick's tragic situation, not without sealing off these confidences with a comment on her own physical ailments: "Things are rather out of kilter here. The state of Grace's health has gotten worse on the whole since the beginning of the year, and sometimes she's in quite a lot of pain. But her energy never completely gives out. On Saturday and Sunday she spent part of the night making a big loaf of bread worthy of the finest baker. As for me, I am slowly getting over my lengthy bout with bronchitis, with little help from the humid, cold spring we are having."[24]

BETWEEN HER ASSESSMENTS of Yourcenar's visitors and occasional admissions, without any further comment, of the pain she suffered, Frick continued to note down, as always, details of derisory importance: "the Chancel crew bestowed on us the magnificent gift of a radiocassette"; "on 8 June, for Marguerite's birthday [the last one they were destined to celebrate together] we ate strawberry cake and that's all." These queer habits Frick had, which brought indulgent smiles to people's faces, these minuscule comments devoid of any interest, except for what they say about the person who made them, suddenly become almost pathetic when one knows, as we do today, thanks to Dee Dee Wilson's testimony, the other side of the story that year. Wilson relates:

> Miss Frick lived in horrible and constant pain. Her entire chest had been burned by an overdose of radiation, which left her skin raw. She was in such a bad state that more than one person was needed to treat her. That's why her nurse, Ruth, talked to me about her. I was not on particularly good terms with Miss Frick, not only because she'd had words with my husband, but because I was annoyed with the way she was always sticking her nose into everything and overwhelming people with advice they simply did not want. Still, since Ruth was in a bind, I said that if Miss Frick agreed I would take over part of her care. When I went to Petite Plaisance, the first day, I was feeling a little awkward. "Hello, Miss Frick," I said, a little uncomfortably. All she had to say was, "My name is Grace." As the days went by, I admired her courage more and more. She was an exemplary patient. The dressings I put on did not relieve her pain, and they even made it worse momentarily. I never once heard her complain. That woman's dignity moves me, even today. With Madame, on the other hand, she was extremely severe. But I have to admit that Madame, though she wasn't unwilling to help, didn't do anything right. To begin with, she was not used to being in charge of what had to be

done around the house, to say nothing of taking care of Grace. She would try to do things to amuse her, to get her to eat, but she never got anywhere. The only thing that kept Grace going was her fierceness and some kind of unspoken resentment. Madame never failed to enter the sick woman's bedroom at the worst moment—out of absent-mindedness, or perhaps out of anguish. Grace would yell, "Get out of my room right this minute. I've already told you that you aren't allowed to come in, especially when I have the nurse here."

When I went back downstairs, I would find Madame prostrate in the living room. Distraught. In moments like these there was no more Marguerite Yourcenar, no more writer revered by the woman who had chosen to do everything within her power to promote her greater glory. Only two old women in a battle with suffering and death.

Whatever the price might be in pain, Grace wanted to survive. Everything she did was for this. Right up until the end. She would have even gone beyond the humanly tolerable, if we hadn't talked her out of it. A few weeks before her death, she still wanted to go somewhere, I don't know where, by car, to try a new experimental treatment. I was alarmed by this, because it was completely absurd, and I told her doctor about it. He decided it was time to have a talk with her, and make her understand that the process was irreversible at that point.

All three of us went to see the doctor together, Madame, Grace, and I. I'm not positive, but I think it was exactly a week before she died. The doctor took Madame aside to tell her that the end was very near. To Grace, he attempted to say that she shouldn't try any more treatments, that there were no other possible treatments besides the one she was getting, but that everything would be all right, that she wouldn't suffer.

On the way home in the car, which I was driving, Grace didn't open her mouth once. She had this look on her face . . . She looked more furious than desperate. That night at Petite Plaisance there was quite an unpleasant scene, but one so symbolic of who that woman was, that I think I should tell you about it, as a tribute to her strength of character. Grace summoned us, Madame and me, to her room. She was sitting on her bed, propped up against her pillows and she screamed at us, in English of course, since Grace and Madame never spoke French in front of me:

"So that's all there is to it! I'm dying."

"I know," Madame said softly, which made Grace even angrier.

"How do you know?"

"The doctor told me."

"And you didn't tell me right away? How dare you? It's disgraceful . . ."

Grace was poisoning herself with her own anger. Madame let the storm pass, but the blow had struck home. I decided it was time for me to step in. I felt I had the right to speak up, in my professional capacity as a nurse, as a "technician." For the first time since I'd started taking care of her, I spoke to Grace quite harshly.

"Listen," I said, "you don't feel any different today than you did yesterday, or two days ago. And you won't feel any different tomorrow. So will you please stop screaming and carrying on like this? Besides, you've always wanted to take charge of everything, and control everything; let's see how you take charge of *this.*"

I was surprised at myself. But I couldn't stand the way she lashed out that way all of a sudden in such a rage. She was usually so admirable. It was thoroughly obvious to everyone that she was going to die soon; you'd think she would have been resigned to it, at seventy-six years of age. From that day on, not a word was said about the fact that Grace was dying. Things got worse day by day. We gave her medication for the pain. There was nothing else we could do.

On the eleventh of November, Grace started needing oxygen to breathe. Around the fifteenth, she wasn't conscious anymore, but since she was moaning, in her semicomatose state, we kept giving her painkillers. Madame was quiet but very much present. On the eighteenth of November I told her that the end was near.

It was then, in the afternoon, that Yourcenar played the little music box at Frick's bedside that she talked about in her interviews with Matthieu Galey: "the modest little Swiss music box that plays pianissimo an arietta of Haydn, which I started playing at Grace's bedside one hour before her death, when she ceased to respond to word or touch." [25]

Dee Dee goes on to say:

> You felt an infinite gentleness and caring throughout it all, one woman caring for another whom she'd had at her side for forty years, performing the ritual act that millions of women before her had performed: accompanying someone to their death. Grace died peacefully, almost imperceptibly. It was nine o'clock at night, exactly. Madame looked at me as if she couldn't believe it.
>
> "Is it over?"
> "Yes."
> "Are you sure?"
> "Yes."
>
> Then she went to the window, and opened it wide, saying something like: "I don't know . . . but they say you have to let the spirit slip away freely" . . .
>
> At that very moment the telephone rang. Madame went to answer it and came back panic-stricken. It was Grace's brother calling to see how Grace was doing. I told her to say that she was on the verge of dying and that we would call him back right away. That night, Marguerite Yourcenar was not at all the famous writer that people in France had just been introduced to on

the radio and on television, so sure of her choices and her life. Nor was she the woman she became in old age, too demanding sometimes and often quarrelsome. She was simply pitiful to see.

That very evening, Yourcenar took over the tradition of writing notes in Frick's daybook, which then became her own.

18 November: at nine o'clock in the evening, death of G.F. XXX A beautiful sunny day. Ruth, Dee Dee, and I got her ready to be cremated. Around eleven thirty at night, they took her away on a litter. I went with her to the hearse by the marvelous light of the stars.

19–20 November: arrangements, visits, telephone calls.

21 November: cremation in Bangor.

22 November: Thanksgiving dinner with a few good friends.

23 November: Ruth, Dee Dee, and I at the cemetery.

There follows an account of laying Frick's ashes in the ground, but Yourcenar's handwriting is as illegible here as it became in the last weeks of her own life. "With his shovel, Toni dug the square hole, similar to one that might be used to plant a tree. I poured the contents of a big vase full of dried leaves, and dried roses in the bottom, and a little lavender. Then poured (and touched) the ashes into a highly gilded old Indian basket lined by me with two brown silk scarves [illegible passage]. I wrapped all of this up in her brown wool scarf. Dee Dee and Ruth put in a few sprigs of cut flowers. Then the hole was filled in properly with earth and the stone put in place."

On Monday, 26 November, a religious service in memory of Frick was held at Northeast Harbor's Union Church. Yourcenar's service, more than eight years later, would be a mirror image of it. The same texts would be read.

"That funeral service really impressed me," Dee Dee Wilson remembers. "Everyone in town was there. This showed all of us—Madame first and foremost—how much Grace was valued in the community, despite her strange and difficult ways. Of course, we did still say sometimes, if we interrupted someone's conversation, 'watch out, Grace is back . . .' But deep down there was a tremendous amount of affection for her, eccentric though she was. What a character! We all liked her, and everyone admired her courage in dealing with her illness and her physical pain.

"Over the next few days, Madame was heart-stricken. Grace had protected her too well."

Jeannie Lunt, whom Frick had hired to help her out with various jobs during the summer of 1978, and who would stay on as secretary to Yourcenar until her death—she is also the executrix of her will—remembers the "lessons" Frick recited to her daily, exhorting her to be absolutely quiet:

"'Madame is working,' 'Madame is working' was a constant refrain. She made it seem as if you had to walk on tiptoe to keep from disturbing her . . . When I think that later on I found out that when 'Madame was working,' she had such incredible powers of concentration that you could have exploded a bomb next to her without even making her jump! . . ."

Yourcenar later confided that she didn't even know the telephone number of the market they called to have their groceries delivered, that she had never called a merchant, or a restaurant to make a reservation, that she had even gotten out of the habit of taking the phone off the hook to answer it, because "Grace took care of these things."

According to Wilson, "she was distraught, but not only for practical reasons. To me, she seemed to be in shock, a bit frantic. However, I heard afterward that she hadn't let any of this show when she was in France." Not much, in point of fact. There was hardly anyone in whom Yourcenar confided in her darkest hours besides Georges de Crayencour. In early September, she disclosed the situation to him, and the full extent of its gravity:

> Yes, it is the ultimate redoubtable ordeal to watch as a human being is slowly destroyed by a terrible sickness—even putting aside the ties of affection, gratitude, and esteem one has for a person. Since 1972 (date of my last stay in Europe), Petite Plaisance has not seen one single day without afflictions and worries of all kinds. Grace's illness, for a time, had been only very painful, except for the very serious heart trouble she had in 1977 caused by the ill-effects of chemotherapy (it was in the wake of that attack, as if defiantly, that she insisted on going to Alaska for a month, a wondrous journey, but a torturous one). Last January, though, her sickness became a genuine torment, for a generalized cancer of the lymphatic system attacks the body almost everywhere. . . . There are some very good people helping me out at the moment: the nurse for this area lives 500 yards away; she is an excellent, highly capable woman who comes here twice, and sometimes three times a day. . . . Finally, there are quite a few people—a number of ladies from the village, the old fisherman, Dick, the gardeners, Harry and Elliot—who come by with things for us: one might bring a dinner dish she's made or some sweets, another some vegetables from his garden, and someone else an offer to run errands in her car. . . . Such are the blessings, in the darkest times, of living in a small town. . . . Grace is too much of an Anglo-Saxon to share her thoughts with me, whether concerning her health or concerning her future, in this world and beyond. The only thing she seems to be sustained by is her courage, which, of course, falters sometimes when her attacks are too severe.

Moreover, she gets up for part of the day, and is determined to "look nice" for our guests or for the radio and television envoys, such as Jacques Chancel in May, or Bernard Pivot just recently. Last week, unsteady on her feet and out of breath, she insisted on serving a crew of ten photographers![26]

"And now the news, so sad and so expected," she wrote to him three months later.

Expected by everyone but Grace, who kept fighting up until the next-to-last day. For nearly eight years, she had been suffering atrociously, with a few weeks, sometimes even one or two months of remission, naturally, but since the beginning of the year it had been almost constant torture. So, when she stopped breathing, so imperceptibly that the nurse and I were not even sure right away that she had, during a soporific sleep brought on by a powerful injection (of a morphine derivative), we couldn't really regret it for her sake. But this plunge into the void after the work and the existence we shared for so many years . . . It's a kind of new rhythm to acquire. Let me say right away, to get everything said that has to do with me, that I have good people around to help me out, on an everyday basis and as far as the house is concerned: a good housekeeper, a nice secretary who is keeping her head above water in the sea of papers left behind by Grace, who had for several weeks been unable to tend to her affairs, and kindly neighbors . . .

There are so many things that could be said . . . Georges, if by chance, this summer, you have a sudden urge to take a vacation in the U.S.A., I would gladly invite you to Petite Plaisance for a week. You should think about it.[27]

Matthieu Galey drily recorded in his journal one of Yourcenar's statements regarding the way things were rearranged in the house after Grace's death: "Did I take down this comment of Yourcenar's a few weeks ago? 'It was too painful for me to look at Grace's piano. I sold it and I've already had a bookcase built in its place.'"[28] Certainly, one can see in this an incipient attempt at the posthumous "expulsion" of Grace, which did indeed occur. But the unbearable presence of this piano, which there now would be no one to play, is no less plausible a reason for getting rid of it. Yourcenar's grief does not necessarily deserve to be put into question, as Galey seems to do. We find an echo of the feeling that might have been hers in an autobiographical work published in the fall of 1989 by Vassilis Alexakis, a Greek writer living in France: "the sight of a closed piano always saddens me a little. . . . Is this because of its funereal appearance? It seems to me that no other musical instrument at rest produces quite as much silence as a closed piano."[29] Galey would also mention later, on the occasion of a meet-

ing in 1981—though his relations with Yourcenar were by then indisputably bad: "Toward the end, a few minutes of emotion over Grace's death.
The way monuments express emotion. A little mist, dry in no time."[30]

The most solemnly moving account is undoubtedly one that Yourcenar
gave, in an interview with Claude Servan-Schreiber, of laying Frick's ashes
in the ground, to illustrate her fascination with rites and her belief in their
cathartic power.

> I had brought a basket with me, one of those Indian baskets made of
> sweetgrass that never lose their sweet smell: all it takes is a few drops of water
> to revive it. I poured the ashes, which, in reality, were more like little bits of
> gravel, into the basket. I put all of this in a wool scarf the person had fre-
> quently worn, that she was fond of. We filled in the hole after having put
> some greenery in and the sturdy clump of sod was put back in its place. You
> couldn't see a thing anymore. We all three left, the two nurses and I, like the
> women who, for all eternity, have seen to taking care of the sick and burying
> the dead. It was a rite. . . . So you see, we avoided the urn in fake bronze, the
> velvet-draped bier, and the casket filled with satin, artificial of course. We got
> out of all that. One can reinvent a rite at any moment in life.[31]

Of course, she would subsequently say that even before Frick's death
she had already turned toward her future, toward that perfectly bilingual
young American of thirty, Jerry Wilson, Maurice Dumay's friend, who offered to become her traveling companion. But we shall see, through the
contradictions in her statements and attitudes over the course of the eighties, how cautiously we now must scrutinize what she has to say. It is true
that Wilson had come shortly before Frick's death. On 19 August all she
had indicated was: "Jerry Wilson to come after 22 August." It was later on
that Yourcenar checked off the week beginning 16 September and jotted
down some rather muddled notes: "18 September: Jerry. 19 September:
Jerry and M.Y. to the Rockefeller Garden. 20 September: visit from Jerry.
Jerry leaves." Yourcenar always maintained that Frick had "recommended"
this young man to her. Perhaps she had. In the Pléiade's "Chronologie,"
under February-March 1979, one reads: "In a sudden burst of energy,
Grace Frick wrote a series of brief notes, sometimes leaving them unfinished, to her Parisian friends, recommending that they see a show, Gospel
Caravan, conceived and devised by a young American, Jerry Wilson. This
project, which brought her back to the time she was collating Negro spirituals for Marguerite Yourcenar, is the last one she would have the strength to
take an interest in." None of this, however, can take the place of absolute
certainty. Whatever the reality was Yourcenar believed so deeply in all rites
of transmission, she so fervently wanted the "baton" to have been passed

from Frick, who had constituted "the matrix" of her life—as she confided one day—to Jerry, who to a certain extent was taking over for her, that it would have been impossible for her not to say this sort of thing.

On top of this there was her almost uncontrollable desire to be on the move, to set off again, to travel, and her repudiation of old age, which she had been immersed in for nearly eight years. All the things she had lived and written and thought compelled her not to stay at Petite Plaisance. And rather than too hastily conclude that she was thus betraying Frick's memory, we must first observe that, in addition to the new countries she was determined to discover—with Wilson, attempting, once again in Zeno's footsteps, not to die without having made "the round of this, [her] prison"[32]—nearly every year, she retraced one of Frick's favorite journeys, in a country that had always enchanted her, England. She evoked these "unforgettable moments" in *Quoi? L'Eternité:* "In my mind's eye I see a young woman, with a young Sibyl's features, sitting on one of the gates that separate the fields from the pastures over there; we're at the foot of Hadrian's Wall; her hair is waving in the wind from the mountaintops; she seems to embody that expanse of air and sky. I see the same woman in the canopy bed of an old run-down house, in Ludlow, talking about Shakespeare, imagining him rehearsing with his actors, or rather talking to him as if she were there."[33]

Clearly, Grace Frick was too essential to the life of Marguerite Yourcenar the person who existed in private, and to Marguerite Yourcenar the writer, for Yourcenar not to have attempted, if not to forget her, then at least to blot out this memory. But her anger when journalists would try to make her talk about Frick—she who had long since banished excess from her speech—and her outright refusal to do so, then the things she would immediately say to her friends about it afterward, at once annoyed and distraught, were surely not signs of indifference. Having followed the course of their passion and observed their chaotic life together in the final years at Petite Plaisance, how can we believe in the infamous sentence that Yourcenar granted to her friends, who would sit in uncomfortable silence as she railed against "those people who insist on making me talk about Grace Frick when my life was always very different from hers": "essentially, it's very simple: first it was a passion, then it was a habit, then just one woman looking after another who was ill."

Who could believe this? Only someone who hadn't seen the look on her face when she would point out, on a shelf in the living room, the photograph of Frick taken in Belgium in 1971, saying softly "that's the last good photograph of Grace." Only someone who hadn't been oddly moved upon discovering the terse lines written in a calendar found among Yourcenar's papers at Petite Plaisance after her death. She had circled the dates of 18, 23, and 26 November 1979 and simply written: "18 November: (Sunday), the death, nine o'clock in the evening, beneath a beautiful starry sky. 23 November: the ashes are returned to the earth on a beautiful misty, sunny morning. 26 November: the memorial service." But with this calendar there was also a letter, received from Paris on 6 December 1979. Yourcenar had saved the envelope, writing down on it these simple words: "the last letter that came addressed to both names."

PART 5

The Nomadic Academician

19

Turning Back Time

NINETEEN EIGHTY was the first New Year's spent without Grace in at least thirty years, except for the times in the forties when she sometimes traveled to her family home in Kansas City for the holidays. Yourcenar could not help but think of the solitary life that lay— for how long?—ahead of her. But foremost on her mind was the trip that she wanted to embark on, she who had hardly left her house in nine years. It will never be sufficiently acknowledged how much Marguerite's absolute fidelity to Grace was revealed in her accepting a particularly painful constraint, the worst one of all in her eyes: immobility. No doubt Yourcenar exaggerated the joy she felt, in subsequent written and oral comments, when Jerry Wilson and Maurice Dumay arrived at Petite Plaisance in December 1979. They stayed at the nearby hotel, not in the house, and were not yet considered to be intimates. Nonetheless, she already saw Jerry as the sign of her forthcoming departure. And there cannot be any doubt that this was an intense source of happiness for her.

With the assistance of Wilson and Dumay, she made her plans for this trip, which would include a Caribbean cruise—precisely at the moment the Académie Française had chosen to elect someone to Roger Caillois's chair. We cannot rule out the possibility of Yourcenar's intention to assert that, whatever the results of that election, she would be radically "somewhere else." Dumay and Wilson left Mount Desert Island on 5 January. Wilson was to come back, by himself this time, around 20 February, and they would leave, heading first for Florida, around the twenty-fifth.

Just as soon as Wilson left, Yourcenar returned to her usual medical obsessions, compiling meticulous records in her various notebooks: blood pressure, "attacks of stomach cramps," and so forth. In addition there were memories ("12 January: the two anniversaries, G.F.'s birth and Michel's death in 1929") and legal matters ("25 January, went to see Fenton about the will and setting up a trust"). And there was the usual correspondence— in which she talked about her father, among other things, and in the process about what she herself wanted once again to become at the dawn of that new decade, recalling a "'man with the wind at his heels,' at home every-where and nowhere, his taste for life and his way of almost never looking back on the past, and finally a supreme and *instinctive* disdain of ambient opinions and biases."[1] Almost never looking back on the past was no doubt what she was aiming for, after the horrendous years of Frick's slow death. Did she know she was incapable of this, or that forgetting was a word with no content, for someone who ceaselessly remade, relived, reconstructed her past? She had not yet turned into the woman we saw traipsing all over the world during the eighties, bodily recapturing her youth. "She didn't complain, she did what there was to be done," her friends and neighbors say. "Though she wasn't in shock anymore, as she was on the night of Grace's death, you could sense that she was still distraught," her nurse Dee Dee Wilson asserts. "Like many women when they are widowed, after the long illness of a spouse they've had to watch over and stand by, she was heart-stricken; but she also had come out of a long tunnel almost relieved to have found a kind of freedom, and not knowing yet what to do with it."

WHILE YOURCENAR was trying to get used to a life without Frick and an existence where forty years had just collapsed all at once into an irrecover-able past, in France she was the topic of many a conversation. She was even a topic of debate. At the root of this "Battle of the Académie Française" was Jean d'Ormesson.[2] He had decided to present Yourcenar's candidacy and was firmly set on getting her elected. In the eyes of the Academicians, she clearly had one incontrovertible defect: she was a woman. The "illustrious assembly" had never admitted a woman. For certain members, she nonethe-less had the advantage of that famous "male talent" people had for so long ascribed to her. For others, a more numerous group, her supposed "virility" was a major obstacle: in point of fact, she was "not woman enough" they subtly managed to convey in delicate allusions to what people assumed about her sexual preferences. Finally, those with no distaste for dubious humor put the two arguments together to arrive at the conclusion that she was "a good compromise candidate."

These events, spawned perhaps by a determination to "wake up" an apathetic institution, the Académie, also deserve credit for "waking up" women—who were somewhat demobilized following the battles of the sev-enties—by making them brutally aware once again of the perennial dis-course of men regarding those of their gender. The dubious jokes about Yourcenar, and the peremptory judgments of her work did not in any way differ from the insults hurled some forty years earlier at Simone de Beauvoir when *The Second Sex* came out, then in 1954 when *Les Mandarins* (*The*

Mandarins) was published. Beauvoir had been accused of "loose writing" and "army-barracks language," and called the "giant ant of existentialism."[3] In Yourcenar's case, reference was made to "the pompous and pretentious style" of a "woman who takes herself for a monument." Some even went so far as to say, as Albert Cohen had done on Jacques Chancel's radio show, that being "so fat and so ugly" she could not possibly be a great writer.[4]

As for her sexuality, it should suffice to reiterate a comment she was fond of making, with regard to this subject and many others: "we'd be giving too much credit to those who talked about it were we to repeat what they had to say." What they did say brought to light only one interesting thing: in everyday life, homosexuality in women is much less ridiculed and condemned than in men. There is something about it that seems an extension of boarding-school naughtiness, attesting to a charming but incurable puerility that prompts men to a certain indulgence. But as soon as such women are in line to accede to an important social position, their sexual preference becomes a much more serious handicap. The mere fact of being a woman, in the eyes of many men, becomes unseemly the minute it appears one might acquire a status heretofore reserved for them. Being a woman who loves women represents an unseemliness—and a negation—of absolute proportions.

As if all this were not sufficient, or sufficiently dissuasive, there were some here and there who brought up, more or less publicly—in "hallways," at "dinners in town"—the rumors and the accusations of anti-Semitism sometimes hurled at Yourcenar in the context of a literary commentary. This was an unlikely argument, applied as it was to an institution already too little inclined—and one that would become even less so—to ask its male members to account for their pasts. This comfortable amnesia having cleared the way for the election of Félicien Marceau[5]—who met with certain difficulties on France's liberation from German occupation—there had even transpired, in 1976, a reputedly impossible event at the Académie: a resignation, that of poet Pierre Emmanuel. At the time Yourcenar had written to Emmanuel expressing her support and admiration. This does not, however, represent an adequate way to put an end to the debate on Yourcenar's presumed anti-Semitism.

"Accusing Marguerite of anti-Semitism is so stupid that it makes me laugh," says her American publisher Roger Straus calmly, "and I know whereof I speak. During one of my visits to Petite Plaisance—it might even have been the last one—we had some conversations on this subject, because I had picked up on the anti-Semitic attitude, a very visible one, that the managers of the hotel where I was staying had toward me. Up there in

Maine, there is something of a 'pocket' of anti-Semitism. That kind of brutal, irrational rejection, which anti-Semitism is, is completely the opposite of the attitude, the philosophy, and the life ethic of Marguerite Yourcenar. It's quite simply absurd."[6] Straus is right. Accusing the woman he knew and spent time with of anti-Semitism seems rather ignoble. But as Yourcenar herself pointed out, in this domain things are never simple. Had she not, at the age of eighteen, heard her father, a confirmed Dreyfusard, call the wife of Doctor Hirsch, the physician that Michel de Crayencour considered responsible for the death of his first wife Berthe and her sister Gabrielle, a "dirty Jewess?" "I can still hear the cries: 'Assassin's wife! Murderer! Thief!' and, as if bubbles of noxious air were suddenly escaping from the underground foundations of a rotting house: 'Dirty Jewess!'"[7]

"I was not unaware that Michel who, like myself, did not like the Old Testament, a book comforting for some, odious or off-putting for others, had, on the contrary, an instinctive sympathy for the Jews of the Diaspora, a misunderstood and persecuted people; this favorable bias extended both to the rich and to the poor, to the bankers and the simple tailors of that race endowed with genius and nearly always with human warmth. But, beside himself with anger, he adopted as his own the insults of an Edouard Drumont or of the anti-Dreyfusards whom he had abhorred in his youth."[8]

It is difficult for the writer of this work, who shares Straus's point of view, not to render herself suspect of trying to defend Yourcenar "at any cost." However, this is not what I am doing. I am thoroughly willing to admit that Yourcenar carried within her, as her father had, the "biases" inherited from a social class and a family immersed in the old Catholic tradition of anti-Semitism. And that she used and she abused certain stereotypes in her work, such as that of the Jewish prostitute incarnated by Saraï in "An Obscure Man." On the other hand, it is only in bad faith, as we have seen, that her use of the word "race"—a word she used constantly, as did nearly all members of her generation, in place of the word "people"—can be attributed to anti-Semitism: she referred to "the French race" or "the Dutch race" every bit as often as she did "the Jewish race."

She herself did not attempt to flee this issue and was not at all shocked when people enjoined her to explain herself, as Matthieu Galey did at length. It was thus that she refuted point by point the accusatory references to "anti-Semitic allusions" in her *œuvre*, insisting that an "author would be a poor novelist indeed" if his characters spoke in his name.[9]

The subject had also been raised in her interviews with Patrick de Rosbo, regarding *Memoirs of Hadrian*. Yourcenar pointed out Hadrian's incapacity to understand the Jews' refusal of "the benefits of Greco-Roman

civilization" "(and here, one is compelled to admit, he shows a certain naiveté and blindness)."[10] Such explanations, according to Thomas Gergely,
the author of an article on "La Mémoire suspecte d'Hadrien" [Hadrian's
Questionable Memory], "hardly divest certain passages of *Memoirs of Hadrian* of their dubious character."[11] Highlighting certain obvious errors or
inaccuracies in *Memoirs of Hadrian* pertaining to the Jewish tradition, he
asserts that the novel's emperor has "more [to say] about hidden aspects of
the inner world of Marguerite Yourcenar than about the mental and physical universe of her creature." Gergely is not necessarily convincing, since
he too is not one to shy away from simplifications and hasty deductions;
here is one example: "As a cultivated Roman, Hadrian would certainly take
care not to confuse '*enlightened Jews*' with '*fanatics.*' . . . Here the speech
imputed to Caesar hardly dates back any further than the men of the Age
of the Enlightenment, who enjoyed contrasting 'fanatical' Jews, where religion and behavior were concerned, to 'enlightened ones.' From Holbach to
Voltaire and Rousseau, the entirety of French philosophical literature attests
to this. . . . The idea of 'hatred for the human race' attributed to Jews and
Christians is a common one in Latin literature (see, for example, Tacitus's
Annals, book XV, 44), but combined with the notion of 'unsatisfied ambitions,' it takes on a different coloration, one also found in the *Protocols of
the Learned Elders of Zion,* that famous lie of the nineteenth-century czarist
police, fated to spread far and wide the fable of a Jewish plot aimed at taking
over the world."[12] One can hardly refrain from observing that taking it upon
oneself to leap from Tacitus to the *Protocols of the Learned Elders of Zion* by
way of one lone reference to "unsatisfied ambitions" is at best somewhat
dubious.

   In this matter as in others, Yourcenar did not have any sense whatsoever
of "forbidden speech": it did not seem to her that there was any need to
banish the word "Jew" from the language, from her language, as many
have done, often with a vaguely guilty conscience. Perhaps this indicates
she wasn't much inclined to suffer from a guilty conscience, but we cannot
infer from her use of the word "Jew" that she was thoughtless, let alone see
it as proof of anti-Semitism. Nonetheless, there were occasions in her personal life when she had to answer for comments deemed "suspect." Meeting
Madame Oulman, heir to Editions Calmann-Lévy, in Portugal in the sixties,
Yourcenar, who had appreciated this woman's graciousness, her company,
and her culture, had spoken to some friends about the "very Jewish sense
of hospitality that Madame Oulman possessed." She was sharply rebuked
for that sentence. Thus she explained herself in her correspondence and
sometimes brought up this memory, not to make a show of irritation or

annoyance, but in an effort "to see the situation clearly," as she would say. "I understand that after what happened in the last war people are hunting down anti-Semitism everywhere, including the kind that is referred to as unconscious. Prejudice and racism of all types are forms of madness that won't die. But perhaps we should cease to see an anti-Semite in every person who attributes to a Jew some particular quality. Quite clearly, the belief is that the person in question also attributes particular faults to them as well. And, in fact, that danger does always exist. What I myself had simply wanted to say was that any community that had been compelled to move around a great deal, that had been condemned to multiple migrations, was necessarily more open to the unfamiliar, more welcoming than groups that have stayed in one place. Which I believe. I was not understood." True, this was during the sixties and seventies, when, in many circles, the slightest reticence regarding the policies of the State of Israel was considered a patent indication of anti-Semitism. Today most people seem to acknowledge that one can disapprove of the parties of the Israeli Right without being an anti-Semite. "Jewish fanaticism is no more respectable than any other," said Yourcenar to Galey.[13] Is this an anti-Semitic remark? It could be. Everything depends on what one knows, or thinks one knows, about the person who made it. No definitive answer to this question will be provided here, for Yourcenar is not in need of being "justified." In an area like this one, one can only leave the issue open: each individual, looking at this woman's life and at her books, will forge his or her own "private conviction."

Thus, during the first few months of 1980, Yourcenar, without realizing it, had become the stake in a game that went beyond a simple election to the Académie Française. All the discussions and the bad plays on words could not mask the truth: Marguerite Yourcenar was a woman, whether one liked it or not. And if she crossed over the Académie's threshold, there would be no turning back: from then on women *in the plural* would be entering that still-"protected" place. It did not displease the president of France, Monsieur Valéry Giscard-d'Estaing, to finish out his seven-year term—which would end in May 1981—on the symbolic note of a woman joining the Académie Française. "It has even been said that I was 'activated' by the president of the Republic, which is utterly untrue," relates Jean d'Ormesson.[14] If d'Ormesson's account of that entire affair is now a savory one, the conversations that took place at the time were not always replete with the courtesy and loftiness of purpose one might consider fitting among Academicians, and the "victory" of Yourcenar's partisans was acquired at the price of some dubious bargaining.

"The affair was basically quite simple," says d'Ormesson, with the mischievous glint in his eye of someone who has mounted quite a "coup." "I was very close to Roger Caillois. We used to work together at UNESCO, where he edited the review *Diogène*. I was his assistant. Caillois had been elected to the Académie in 1970, to the third chair, previously occupied most notably by Georges Clemenceau and Jérôme Carcopino.[15] I myself entered the Académie three years later. I had often talked with Caillois about Marguerite Yourcenar, whom he had known since the war years." Caillois and Yourcenar had indeed admired and respected one another, as Yourcenar's correspondence with her friend Jacques Kayaloff, who was also close to Caillois, attests. Upon several occasions, she spoke to him of "Caillois's extraordinary intelligence," adding: "to all appearances, without making the least attempt to shine."[16] When she received Caillois's book *Méduse et Cie* (*The Mask of Medusa*) from Jacques Kayaloff, she responded: "It is one of the finest books I've read in a long time. Superior even to *L'Incertitude qui vient des rêves* [The Uncertainty That Comes from Dreams], which is nonetheless a remarkable book. It's encouraging to think that, in this age of nearly total dissociation, a pooling of minds seems to be happening somehow all the same unbeknownst to us, which one day perhaps will lead to a more complete knowledge of things."[17] After his election to the Académie Caillois had written to Kayaloff about the ritual "sword committee"[18]—which assembles friends of the new Academician to present him with his sword—pointing out that "the innovation this time will consist of bringing in foreigners [appearing on the committee were Kawabata, Asturias, and Borges among others] and women.[19] I have thought of two. Victoria Ocampo and our friend Marguerite Yourcenar, whom I've mentioned in the newspapers and on the radio as a choice victim, perfectly cut out for the Académie. I don't have her address. But I am under the impression that you can get in touch with her easily. Would you do so and get her to agree?"[20]

"When Caillois died, I admit that I indulged myself somewhat in the 'grieving widow's' ploy, telling myself that we had to find a successor worthy of him, because Caillois was concerned about this," d'Ormesson relates. "He would often say, 'There's something annoying about the Académie; you never know who's going to take your place.' Three names came to mind: Raymond Aron, Aragon, and Marguerite Yourcenar.[21] I didn't think I was going to 'advance the cause of women' in deciding to get Marguerite Yourcenar elected to Caillois's chair. I just thought that she was the perfect person to succeed him. Nor was my intention to abandon the other two candidates I had thought of. But I was so exhausted by the battle to elect Marguerite Yourcenar that, in the end, I gave up pushing my other two candidates."

Had d'Ormesson perhaps underestimated the sexist biases of his fellow members? Most certainly. He had foreseen their objections on "technical" issues, and their questions—the first and foremost being "Is Marguerite Yourcenar a candidate?" Yourcenar was not really a candidate, but she had decided to accept in the event she was elected. She had said and written on several occasions that she would neither formally declare her candidacy nor make any visits to members, but that if the Académie paid her the honor of electing her, she would not refuse. On the other hand, she had always said that she would under no circumstances oblige herself to spend several months a year in Paris in order to be present at the Académie.[22]

Thus she did not wish to make the traditional visits to Academicians. Another obstacle? Not at all, d'Ormesson pointed out. She was right. Article 15 of the Académie's regulations stipulates that "visits are forbidden." Custom alone dictated otherwise. But what d'Ormesson had not imagined was the radical hostility of some against "the" woman. "For me, she was first of all a great writer," he comments, "and as such she would be an honor to the Académie, much more so than certain men who would have been elected with no trouble. I had the traditionalists against me. And a few leftists, like André Chamson, who thought she was right-wing, which wasn't true. And Claude Lévi-Strauss, who was ardently opposed to her candidacy, 'because you don't change the rules of the tribe.' All that squabbling was quite amusing really." And the comments that were made back and forth are worth recording, if only as historical footnotes.[23] D'Ormesson can conjure up a store of deliciously choice passages from memory.

"The Académie Française is like the Eiffel Tower, it's only held together by the paint. If we scratch it, everything will collapse." "The Académie is founded on a series of rites. One of the rituals is that we are all equal, the only order being that of seniority. An immutable order. So what would we do with a woman? Would we stand back and let Madame Yourcenar come in or go out ahead of us? Clothing is another important element of the ritual. What uniform would Madame Yourcenar wear?" "In the Académie we grow old with one another. How would we be able to stand watching a woman grow old?" Between specious arguments and verbal side-slips, the fighting became, to use d'Ormesson's term, "insane": "An article in *L'Express* claimed that blows had been exchanged. Another publication, a newspaper, specified that I had been slapped in the face, which isn't true. But it is true that André Chamson called me a 'street urchin,' adding: 'our young fellow member, who has so many talents, is doing this because he likes television so much.' I got up and left, followed by Félicien Marceau, Maurice Rheims, and five or six friends who were in favor of Marguerite Yourcenar. Later on we received some semblance of an apology."

Fast upon the discussion of regulations and "tribal honor" there succeeded that of nationality. First the word was spread around that Yourcenar was Belgian. This wasn't true. But people then became aware that she was American and that she had neglected—as we saw in 1947—to retain her French citizenship. "That needn't matter," declared Alain Peyrefitte, then minister of justice and, within the Académie, a fervent partisan of the Yourcenar candidacy, "she will renew her French citizenship. In fact, this has already been taken care of. The French consul in Boston went to see her. She's now French once again." "The fact of the matter is that we put the Academicians in a position where they were obliged to vote for her for fear of seeming ridiculously fixated on the past and notoriously hostile toward women," d'Ormesson explains gaily. "Right up until Marguerite Yourcenar's death, I don't think they forgave me for it. They always had the impression that I had forced their hand. They didn't want her among them. That's very clear. We mollified them by saying she would never be there. Then they had the nerve to say that she had "snubbed" the Académie. First of all, she did the right thing. You should have seen the way she was received. Besides, what right did they have to complain about her not coming when they had absolutely no desire to see her?" Regarding her absence from the Académie, Yourcenar always had the same thing to say: "I warned them." If one pointed out that, when passing through Paris, she might perhaps honor the Quai Conti with a visit, she responded invariably: "I went there once. They're a bunch of aging little boys who get together on Thursdays to have fun. I don't see much of anything a woman could do there." As early as 1976, she had written on this subject to Jeanne Carayon: "I've been thinking about what Françoise Giroud says about the politicians' clubs or societies that, like sporting groups, don't care for the idea of admitting a woman who would keep them from slipping their jackets off. Not that one is in the habit of appearing at Quai Conti in shirt-sleeves, but, psychologically, it's the same thing."[24]

The Academicians made her pay for all this in a particularly crude way: there was no one representing the Académie Française at the funeral service held in her memory on 16 January 1988 on Mount Desert Island.

D'Ormesson, who condemns the boorishness displayed toward Yourcenar, is, however, less at ease when one alludes to the way he is said to have achieved the victory of her election. On 6 March 1980 there was a double election. Those elected were Yourcenar and Michel Droit.[25] Since neither of them—especially the latter—was apt to win a majority, it became apparent right away that a maneuver had occurred. When Yourcenar learned of this and, having made inquiries, judged that the "other party" in the deal was not at all to her liking, she wrote to d'Ormesson who responded assuring her that there had been no "exchange" of any sort. "Please note, particularly, that I engaged in absolutely no 'bargaining' in which your name might have played a part . . . in no strategies, in no maneuvers. . . . In presenting your name with your authorization, the only thing I did was to resist some pressure, which was admittedly rather strong. That is utterly everything."[26] Ten years later, he will only say: "If there was a deal, I can assure you that I wasn't in on it." Others claim that Maurice Druon, who was quite friendly with Droit, campaigned on the theme: "You at least have to give Michel Droit a 'tip of the hat' on the first ballot, so his defeat won't be too cruel." Of course, he was elected on the first ballot, as was Yourcenar. Two very strange elections, for an "armchair," both of them won sitting down.

DURING THOSE frenzied weeks, Yourcenar, for her part, had fallen prey to a feverish urge to depart. Jerry Wilson arrived on 23 February and they left by car two days later, heading for the South: they traveled to Florida where they were to set sail on 6 March—the day of the election at the Académie— for their cruise of the Caribbean, which would take them to Jamaica. For Yourcenar this trip was like coming back to life: every day she put more miles between her and Petite Plaisance, every night there were suitcases and a hotel—things she had always considered indispensable, things that had been lacking for so many years. Add to this the company of a young man of thirty-one, who was awestruck by the energy of this woman going on seventy-seven. "I must say," Wilson observed in a notebook, "tiring as [this day] was Mme. Y never lost her humor and laughed a lot."[27] For, as Wilson goes on to say, "she was talking to someone who had everything to learn, which hadn't happened for a long time."[28] Thus she told him about how "she wrote *Alexis* at twenty-four—just after coming back from Portugal (she confided that the book was almost placed in Portugal, but decided to situate it somewhere else—Austria finally being chosen)." She spoke to him of Gide and of Zeno as if each one had actually lived. And Wilson took notes, in the evening, like a child astonished: "She told [her audience] three things: 1) Gide was Protestant, 2) at one time a member of the Communist party, and 3) preferred living with young men more than his wife." "We also talked about makeup, and the fact that she gave it up very young."[29]

Or else: "She has the most beautiful of smiles and something in her eyes is younger still."[30] He was surprised there were so many things she didn't know about everyday American life: "It's true she doesn't listen to the radio and doesn't watch television."[31] Yourcenar confided to him about the "difficult time" of "these last years with Miss Frick" and "all the problems caused by this illness and the sheer length of it. The psychological aspect being quite confusing and she readily admits not being 'out of the woods' as we say at home. This has been such a trial for her. I only hope that this trip will start to help bring her out of it." And she went on about Cocteau "whom she liked a lot 'et qui a toujours dit des choses intelligentes' [and who always said intelligent things]. She remarked that the outside mondainety [show of urbanity] covered a great sensitivity and some of the most beautiful modern poetry was written by him. His plays always had some parts very good even if he put in elements for the public. Cocteau liked G.F., who, as always, was insisting that he should eat more, smoke less, etc."

Listening to Yourcenar, Wilson discovered a world unknown to him, in which one crossed paths with the great writers of the century, in which one proceeded from discussing Murasaki and Japanese literature to the story of a Grecian tour during the thirties, "on a cargo ship . . . with just a friend, the captain, and his wife," then on to "Italy and Sienna [*sic*] where she and Miss Frick and a third person had parked and the car rolled backward into an outdoor cafe terrace filled with opera singers in costume on their way to sing Dido (*Didon*).[32] They all laughed, made friends, and went to hear the opera. She really doesn't like a lot of opera."

As one can easily imagine, the young man was utterly captivated. Though this is no doubt harder to imagine, she was too.

On 6 March in Miami, at the very moment when the boat was to set sail for the islands, came the news of Yourcenar's election to the Académie. Wilson observed, in the laconic, "flat" style that Yourcenar would comment on, rereading his notebooks after his death: ". . . relaying this [the news of her election to the Académie Française] to her didn't provoke much of a reaction. . . . The photographer, Mademoiselle Pelletier, that we had feared would be there, was. . . . [T]he captain . . . had champagne waiting [and hoisted the national colors, as a photograph showing him with Marguerite Yourcenar in front of the French flag attests]. . . . The 'great discretion' of the compagnie Paquet [Paquet line]' was beginning to look doubtful. . . . The telegrams kept coming (she asked who was Raymond Barre?)[33] but we managed to have the telephone calls refused. . . . We talked and talked, laughing mostly about various things having to do with L'Académie—the designs for costumes—one academiciens [*sic;* Jean Dutourd] remark that she had read too much to be a good writer etc."

"I now believe she had everything planned," says Dee Dee Wilson today, half-mocking, half-admiring. "That departure for the islands precisely at the moment the election was announced, the hoisting of the colors . . . she loved that. And you have to admit, it had a certain style." On 7 March a letter arrived on board from an American friend, Katherine Gatch, which Yourcenar carefully saved. After the customary congratulations, Gatch lamented that "Grace was cheated by so short a time of the final triumph"; "not the least of your achievements," she added, "is what you did for her life."[34]

The rest of March was taken up by the cruise and the return trip, made by car as the trip south had been. This time, though, they went by way of New York (where Jerry had some friends, in particular Stanley Crantson who, after 1986, would travel with Yourcenar) and New Jersey. They reached Northeast Harbor on 29 March. Yourcenar found a "veritable mountain of mail" that had arrived since her election to the Académie. Wilson from now on would sleep at Petite Plaisance. He had been "chosen," definitively, and wrote down in his daybook: "She showed me the upstairs— I'd never been—and my room. . . ." That room was Frick's bedroom—although there are two others on the same floor.

Over the next few days—until Wilson's departure on 8 April for New York and then Arkansas, his family home—Yourcenar made several trips to the cemetery in Somesville, where Frick's ashes are buried. She also began sorting out her voluminous mail, throwing much of it away, keeping certain letters that she marked "do not answer," and answering others, many of them. In addition to her friends, the letters were from strangers who admired her and from organizations, generally for the protection of nature, to which she belonged. These letters were carefully filed, even though Frick wasn't there anymore to carry out this task previously reserved for her, and they now reside at Harvard's Houghton Library. Among them is a congratulatory letter from the A.V.S. (Association for Voluntary Sterilization), of which Yourcenar was a member.[35] Thus, despite her moments of tenderness toward the children of people close to her—from Jeannie Lunt's little son Jeremy to Jerry Wilson's nephew, whom she gently holds in her arms in a photograph—her repulsion for procreation, which we have already had occasion to observe, was pushed to this radical extent. She explains herself on this point in a little notebook discovered by accident in January 1990 in her office, behind a box of crayons, by Jean-Denis Bredin, who had come to Petite Plaisance to prepare his acceptance speech to the Académie Française, where he would take Yourcenar's chair. On a list of wishes for the world in which she would have liked to live, after "A world without artificial, useless noises. A world without speed," one finds brutally: "A world in which it would be shameful and illegal to have more than two children (sterilization after the third child)[36] [Yourcenar indicated next to this sentence '1980']. A world in which every unwed mother would be more or less in the position of a divorced woman today (which is practically the case now), and would receive financial support from the state, but she would be sterilized after the birth of a *second* child. A world in which contraceptives judged to be free of harmful side effects would be freely sold (this is almost achieved in certain countries)."[37]

It cannot be denied that these statements are enough to send a shiver down one's spine: with time—and advancing age—some of Yourcenar's obsessions (overpopulation being one) took on fearsomely neurotic proportions.

WHEN WILSON returned, on 1 June, they left for Boston, where a reception was planned at the French Library in honor of Yourcenar, who had just received a promotion in the Order of the Legion of Honor (she was becoming an officer). It was there that she first met Yvon Bernier, a teacher from Quebec who had a passion for her work and had been writing to her for several years. They struck up a friendship. It was he who would compile the bibliography for the Pléiade edition of her works and help her go over the proofs. Bernier is one of four trustees whom she appointed in her will. After Yourcenar's death, he worked on two of her posthumous manuscripts, *Quoi? L'Eternité* and *En pèlerin et en étranger*, for which he composed the annotated bibliography.

Having returned to Petite Plaisance, on 11 June, Yourcenar began writing her essay on Mishima, which would appear at Gallimard in January, at the time of her induction into the Académie. Jerry Wilson left Mount Desert on 14 June for New Caledonia. He did not come back until a month later, only to leave again immediately. So Yourcenar had good stretches of time to devote to her manuscript, interspersed with visits from her publisher, Claude Gallimard, and his wife Colette, and from her friend, André Desjardins, a priest from Quebec. She rediscovered, intact, her incredible powers of concentration: *Mishima ou La Vision du vide* (*Mishima: A Vision of the Void*) had to be finished, or near completion, by 23 September, the date Wilson would return and they would prepare for a long trip to Europe, and probably North Africa.

They were to board the *Queen Elizabeth*, for England, in New York on

28 September. On the twenty-fifth, Yourcenar and Wilson traveled, via Salem, to Boston, where they saw Walter Kaiser, a professor at Harvard, a friend of Yourcenar's for several years, and one of her translators since Frick's death. Yourcenar retained, until the end of her life, a very strong feeling of friendship toward Kaiser. He, whom she referred to as "a true friend, and so much more desirable than any other translator," was alongside Dee Dee Wilson and Jeannie Lunt when Yourcenar's ashes were returned to the earth. It was Kaiser, at Union Church in Northeast Harbor, who delivered her funeral oration."[38]

After an uneventful crossing, Yourcenar disembarked on 3 October 1980 in Southampton, eager to show England—a country that had meant such a great deal to her since childhood—to her young traveling companion. For the first time in years, she was really happy. It is not to be overlooked that she reported no illnesses or indispositions of any kind during that period. It is true, though, that she no longer kept her daybooks with her former meticulousness, and that Frick wasn't there anymore to take down the slightest variations in her temperature. Furthermore, her correspondence grew more limited and brief. From now on she had "better things to do." She taught Wilson to recognize the different birds. With him, she was considerate, attentive. Where he was concerned, however intensely she may have felt an amorous passion—whether real, or fantasized, or reinvented—she always displayed the kind of absolute indulgence only mothers possess: she would admire his "handsome sleeping face"; she would always find the photographs he took throughout their journeys "magnificent"; she would forgive all his sins, all his acts of violence in her regard.

In England, however, Frick could not have been entirely absent. Yourcenar was thinking of her, in a Dorsetshire abbey: "I tried to imagine her, a very young woman whom I did not know, with a knapsack on her back, crossing England." As for Wilson, there was no need to imagine him. He was there, she looked at him, and she was moved. "A young man wearing a white sweater with a white hood climbs sure-footedly down a *Tor,* one of those pyramids of pointed rocks, older than history, in the Forest of Dartmoor," she wrote in *Quoi? L'Eternité.* "The clothing he has on is ageless. It's a cold fall day; the shriveled body of a dead sheep, which fell from the same height a few days earlier, is lying on the ground. The same one again, dressed the same way, visiting a swan preserve with me. The same one, on the narrow landing of an English country inn, barefoot in his grey cotton kimono, our arms joined together in a tight embrace that nothing seems capable of breaking; it was broken, however."[39]

Maurice Dumay, Jerry's "friend" at the moment, came to join them.

They made a strange trio. Since the spring, Dumay, most often over the phone, had been expressing his jealousy—whether real or affected—with regard to Yourcenar, thus grounding the old woman in the notion that she and Wilson formed a couple capable of giving rise to jealousy and resentment. As a consequence, the trip to New Caledonia that Dumay and Wilson had planned—which Wilson had declared he would renounce—gave rise to something of a drama in which accusations of promises scorned alternated with feigned magnanimity. Yourcenar was thus "taken in hand" and was entering, unbeknownst to her, upon a rather chaotic period of her existence. She would reconstruct it after the fact, as was her habit, not attempting to show herself in a flattering light but claiming she had always been thoroughly aware of everything that was going on. Nonetheless, it's not entirely clear that she was not insidiously manipulated. All the same, she did concede one day: "I didn't realize what a complex human 'web' I was getting entangled in."

It was over the course of this trip that Yourcenar decided to begin her account of the around-the-world voyage she intended to attempt, before devoting herself to the third volume of her family trilogy. She hoped finally to make the trip to Egypt she had had to renounce in 1964 when Frick had had a relapse. She wanted to see India and Japan for the first time, countries that had increasingly whetted her interest during the "years of immobility." She had even, on her own, learned some basic Japanese. This book of her world voyage, which she would call *Le Tour de la prison*—in memory of Zeno's famous query, "Who would be so besotted as to die without having made at least the round of this, his prison?"—deviated greatly from her initial plans. In fact, certain exceptions notwithstanding, it turned out to be much less an account of her travels than a collection of stories and essays—most of them devoted to Japan. At the time of Yourcenar's death, this volume was still largely unfinished. She left some three hundred pages of manuscript, both typed and handwritten, and numerous preparatory notes, all in scattered fragments and essentially unusable, except as biographical documents in the case of personal remarks written alongside marginal commentary on the countryside she was presently traveling. The biographical value of these papers holds especially true for the travels of 1982. For the latter part of 1980, there is only an occasional notation, such as this one: "27 October. Outing [with Wilson and Dumay]. Our talk moving and satisfying. One of the very fine days of my life. Looked at the little figure of Mercury with Maurice. The sensuality of all those Greco-Roman sculptures. Even when it's a bas-relief like this one, you feel as if you could take it in your arms."

She who was so fond of retracing her steps took one of her favorite trips again with Wilson: Copenhagen, Hamburg, the island of Texel, and Amsterdam. At the Mauritshuis museum in The Hague, she saw Rembrandt's *Two Negroes,* about which she would write a beautiful text for the museum's reopening after renovations.[40] In Brussels she saw Louise de Borchgrave, her "Aunt Loulou," who was "still very beautiful in the farthest reaches of old age" [she was ninety-four years old]. In Bruges, where she showed Wilson the traces left of Zeno, she agreed to do a signing at a bookstore. "What a nightmare," noted Wilson in his journal. "I think that'll be the last of that." A curious remark. Was he discovering, as Frick had thirty years earlier, how objectionable it was that Yourcenar did not belong to him? On 15 December Yourcenar was welcomed with all possible honors in Bailleul and at Mont-Noir, where she had spent her childhood. All the pictures taken that day show a surprisingly young and smiling woman. She has often related how truly happy she was when, seeing an old woman coming toward her saying "Marguerite," her eyes brimming with emotion, she recognized "Marie Joye," the caretakers' daughter she had played with as a child. "In those two old women looking at each other we alone saw two laughing children," she confided. "Nearly eighty years had passed." Jerry Wilson suddenly took in the full extent of Yourcenar's celebrity and realized what a public persona, what a "star," she had become since her election, such a highly symbolic one, to the Académie Française. Yourcenar, for her part, was naively, and violently, bowled over by Wilson. For her, time had been abolished.

They arrived in Paris (staying then with Dumay, in the Marais)[41] on 17 December, the day of Yourcenar's appointment with Yves Saint Laurent, who designed the attire she would wear as an Academician: a long velvet dress of a sobriety and elegance that only Saint Laurent can achieve, and a large shawl in white silk, which she would wear on her head upon crossing the threshold underneath the dome at Quai Conti, and which she would let slip onto her shoulders to deliver her speech. This shawl is now wrapped around the Indian basket containing her ashes.

Just as she had rejected the Napoleonic uniform, Yourcenar also wanted nothing to do with the Academician's sword. Having guessed this, d'Ormesson wrote to her amusingly: "I have taken it upon myself to dispense with the idea of the sword. But would you like a brooch, a necklace, a tiara, a live elephant, a porphyry swimming pool . . . ?" "I would very much have liked to have an object of which I possess a rustic version made out of wood," Yourcenar was fond of recounting. "It's a 'dagger for killing the self.'[42] But I feared those gentlemen would not be apt to understand . . ." In the end they gave her a Hadrian coin, which today is the property of one of her dearest friends from the decade of the eighties, Jean-Pierre Corteggiani, an Egyptologist, and the librarian of the French Institute of Cairo.

On 22 December, after making the traditional visit of the new Academicians—Marguerite Yourcenar and Michel Droit, accompanied by the Duc de Castries[43]—to the president of France (protector of the Académie Française), Yourcenar attended a dinner at the home of Colette and Claude Gallimard with, notably, Bernard Pivot, Jacqueline Piatier, Pierre Nora, and Maurice Rheims.[44] Wilson didn't like the things that went on in Paris any more than Frick had—at least not all those "official" events, where he remained necessarily in the background, and where Yourcenar, moreover, made no effort to make him feel welcome.

Wilson was probably not unaware of the falling-out between Yourcenar and Matthieu Galey, whose book of interviews with her, *With Open Eyes,* had just come out. Regarding that affair, everything—and its opposite—has already been said. After Galey's death, Yourcenar even denied that there had been a falling-out, stating: "If I had known that Matthieu Galey was ill, I would, naturally, have gone to visit him." There was indeed a quarrel, however, at the end of which Yourcenar, with a certain lack of elegance, refused to have Galey present with her on the set of "Apostrophes," on 16 January 1981: only d'Ormesson, who six days later would welcome her at Quai Conti, was there.[45]

Today, with the passing of time, it is possible to say that between Yourcenar and Galey the misdeeds were more or less equally divided. *With Open Eyes* is a fascinating book, even though Yourcenar maintained: "Matthieu Galey asked me questions on the subjects that interested *him.* Not on my real preoccupations." Without a doubt, she felt that she had, on the contrary, revealed too much about herself. On the other hand, she had good reason to protest regarding the cover of the book. On the spine all it says is "Marguerite Yourcenar, *With Open Eyes,*" and on the cover, up high and in very large letters, "Marguerite Yourcenar, of the Académie Française, *With Open Eyes.*" Then in small letters, at the bottom, underneath a photograph of Yourcenar, "interviews with Matthieu Galey." "People have the deplorable habit of adding this title to the list of my works," she complained. "I am not the author of this book." Who could disagree with her on this? That maneuver, no doubt linked to marketing considerations, was hardly more delicate than her own gesture, of barring the author of *With Open Eyes* from joining her on "Apostrophes." As far as lacking delicacy goes, however, the prize goes to Galey himself, in his *Journal.* It's true that one is under no obligation to be delicate in one's most private thoughts. But the minute one puts them on paper, a threshold is crossed, revealing a will to express one's resentment, and to make it last. All the more so in that, behind this *Journal*, there surely must have been, early on, an ultimate intention to publish. It was over the course of 1980 that Galey's animosity toward Yourcenar grew.

"In the Yourcenar manuscript I'm typing—and correcting," he wrote, "she declares that she is not opposed to what, in French, she calls '*abortion*' instead of *avortement*, an Anglicism possibly excusable after a stay of forty years in the U.S.A., although in the case of an Academician . . . But what am I to think of her invented '*propensité*'? To say nothing, of course, of the bandy-legged, muddled-up sentences I'm trying to set back on their feet. I wonder if Grace Frick didn't perform this little task while she was alive . . . She'll be greatly missed."[46]

Even granting that his anger had the upper hand, Galey never should have gone so far as to insinuate that Grace Frick rewrote Marguerite Yourcenar, which is simply absurd. There is no doubt she did the diligent labor of a worker ant, performing tasks that were difficult, substantial, and indispensable. Yourcenar never concealed this, as numerous documents testify, from "Reflections on the Composition of *Memoirs of Hadrian*" to the dedications she wrote to Frick by way of their personal correspondence.

The level of exasperation was mounting: with no fear of being called mercenary, which perhaps is a proof of his candor, Galey also reported one of his telephone conversations with Yourcenar:

6 April
Tonight, I call Yourcenar. Serene, barely pleasant, hardened by glory, it would seem, into stainless steel; she informs me very calmly that I shall not have the twenty pages I'm waiting for for several months, that she has not even opened the package of proofs, and that if her fame is really not going to last beyond the summer, then it would hardly seem worth bothering with. What can I say? I gnaw on the vulcanite of my telephone, thinking that Rosbo, all alone on the market, is calmly sweeping up all the sales. It would be one thing if she were giving me a text that would last for all eternity. But no, just pompous platitudes, which will end up striking everyone as tedious. Will people buy this book, even in the midst of her induction? For once I had luck by the tail, and look what happens; its enough to make you gnash some teeth.[47]

Yourcenar probably detected his unvoiced hostility. In such cases, she was hardly inclined to indulgence. Indeed she tended, rather, toward inflexibility.

We would surely be remiss to leave out Galey's description—an example of his talent, but one from which emanates a fearsome abhorrence for women—of Yourcenar's reception underneath the dome at Quai Conti. That event took place on Thursday, 22 January 1981, in the presence of the president of France, which was utterly exceptional.[48]

> Naturally, it takes me a week to get around to recording the only historic event I ever attended. For her reception truly was a show, entirely out of the ordinary. Not at all an academic reception: along the lines of a *Tastevin* installation ceremony,[49] or Queen Victoria's jubilee. In her ample, black-velvet greatcoat, with a white collar, and a shawl, also white, on her head, Marguerite's entrance was quite stunning.
>
> A consecration, to the sound of a drum. A Franciscan tertiary, followed by a priest (the Reverend Father Carré), or an old empress being judged in the High Court by all these strange magistrates with green tails.[50] With their insectlike appearance, one also got the impression of some mysterious confrairy; it was as if a large termite, inseminated by her insects, which were buzzing excitedly around her, were going to lay some eggs, beneath the gaze of the presidential couple, impassively perched on their Louis XV chairs.
>
> After which the heavy bundle, wrapped in velvet, propelled itself to a little table, underneath the platform of the director's office, and started to read a fine speech—but a long one—on Caillois, in which it was a question of diamonds, but this must have been unintentional . . . At the end, the entire room rose to its feet to applaud. Except the Giscards, who take themselves for hereditary monarchs.[51]

This "fine speech"—as Galey concedes—began, very ironically, with a tribute to the women whose ghosts perhaps accompanied the one of their number to whom, finally, the men had "officially offered a chair":

> You have welcomed me, as I was saying. This uncertain, floating self, this entity whose existence I myself have contested, which I only feel to be truly delimited by the several works that I have happened to write, here it is, such as it is, surrounded and accompanied by an invisible troop of women who should, perhaps, have received this honor much earlier, to the point where I am tempted to step back to let their shadows pass.
>
> Nonetheless, let us not forget that it was only a little bit more or a little bit less than a century ago that the question of the presence of women in this assembly could have arisen. In other words, it was toward the middle of the nineteenth century that literature became in France for certain women both a vocation and a profession, and that state of affairs was perhaps still too new to attract the attention of a society such as yours. Madame de Staël would no doubt have been ineligible by virtue of her Swiss ancestry and her Swedish marriage: she contented herself with being one of the best minds of the century. George Sand would have caused a scandal because of her turbulent life, because of the very generosity of her emotions, which made her such an

admirably womanly woman; the person even more so than the writer was ahead of her time. Colette herself thought that it was not for a woman to go calling on men soliciting their votes, and I can only agree, not having done so myself.[52]

Certain of the "gentlemen" to whom Yourcenar was expected to express her gratitude must have been a bit miffed by this. All the more so in that, during the evening, she saw fit to go celebrate her admission among the "immortals" with Jerry Wilson, Maurice Dumay, and a few friends, rather than with her new fellows.

As tradition would have it for any new member, Yourcenar had taken part in a work session on the Académie's dictionary.[53] "Each new Academician must comment on the word in the dictionary at which we have arrived at the time," Jean d'Ormesson explains. "It was Marguerite Yourcenar's lot to draw 'madwoman.' This made us rather uncomfortable. So we cheated and gave her 'madly.'"

Unaware of the subterfuge, she who was already "madly" in love with Jerry saw this as a favorable sign from Chance. According to a rumor, which still hasn't died more than ten years later, she should have gotten the word "pod," used in slang for "lesbian." Typically masculine humor . . .

At the height of her glory though she was, Yourcenar still found the time—this is one of her habitual paradoxes—to be driven to an old people's home near Chartres where Sherban Sidéry, a long-standing acquaintance, had retired. Sidéry had been friendly with Marie-Laure de Noailles and had written a dramatic adaptation of an anonymous English novel that Yourcenar was particularly fond of, *Madame Solario*.

AS FOR her lavish reception at the Académie, Yourcenar considered it, profoundly, her due. She was not displeased to be the woman who had "forced the door open," nor to have gone, in the course of several months, from being thoroughly removed from the world and her time to being thoroughly immersed in the "show-business society" she had always condemned. She was no doubt more surprised, on the other hand, to suddenly find herself bearing the standard of a "women's issue" that she ill understood, never having been subjected, even during her childhood, to the constraints that ordinarily befall those of her sex.

MANY OF the things she had to say about feminism do in fact betray a certain incomprehension of the problems faced by women subject to the rule of their social milieu and the constraints of their professional environment.

They nonetheless display a great lucidity regarding the traps into which "liberated women" can fall. If "liberation" means acquiescing to the "values" of masculine society, engaging in that all-out competition of which war is the crowning example, then where exactly is the liberty? Where is the potentially new, the experience of a world that is finally mixed? "If the issue is one of fighting to insure that women with qualifications equal to men receive the same pay, then I am involved in the struggle," she said to Galey.

> If it is to defend a woman's right to use contraceptives, then I am an active supporter of several organizations that do just that. Even if the issue is abortion, if the man or the woman involved was for some reason unable to take appropriate steps in time, or ignorant of what those steps might be, then I am for abortion, and I am a member of a number of groups that aid women in trouble, though I should add that abortion, in my view, is always a very serious matter.[54]

Contrary to what certain men—only too happy to think that such a famous woman was speaking out against women—have said, Yourcenar did not think feminism was tantamount to some kind of racism or, more accurately, sexism. As we have seen, on specific points—contraception and abortion first and foremost—she supported women in their battle. If she had been as hostile to their fight as some have said, she certainly would not have been so frequently visited, at the time of her induction into the Académie as well as during other stays in Paris, by Gisèle Halimi, one of the eminent figures of French feminism.

The Académie was probably for Yourcenar the first site of confrontation with men. For the first, perhaps the only, time in her life, she felt their—irrational—reprobation. It was a reprobation founded uniquely on her belonging to the other sex. Their hostility toward her was, and remains, greater still than the hostility borne women who fight for women's rights. For Yourcenar didn't even *clash* with men socially. She ignored them. And this they could never tolerate. Even today, young men make no bones about judging her in a hasty and peremptory manner. In 1989, for example, François Sureau—still a young author, but a member of the Council of State[55] and the second in command at a large firm—calmly spoke, with d'Ormesson, of the "religious and almost totalitarian conception of literature" that Yourcenar supposedly had, before concluding: "My distaste is very superficial. That attitude she has—the great writer polishing her statue (just look at her biography in the Pléiade)—with her solitude on one side, her opinions about everything on the other, the high-flown airs she puts on . . .

perhaps this all makes me unfair. Her style is cold, heavy, and provincial, her philosophy is ponderous, but there are some fine things, *Coup de Grâce*."[56] As to the matter of having "opinions about everything," some might prefer the "opinion" of Mishima, declaring shortly before his death in the *Figaro* that *Memoirs of Hadrian* was one of his favorite French novels. Or one might prefer that of the young Austrian writer Christoph Ransmayr who, he says, would never have written his novel *Die letzte Welt* (*The Last World*)—resurrecting the Latin poet Ovid—if *Memoirs of Hadrian* hadn't existed.[57] Or, yet again, there is William Styron explaining how much Yourcenar's narrative force in *Memoirs of Hadrian* helped him with the difficult process of writing his novel *Confessions of Nat Turner*.[58]

THE OLD WOMAN who had just, while still alive, become a legend, seeing this as nothing more than the accurate measure of her destiny, was prey to a young girl's desires. Barely a week after her reception, she left, with Wilson, on a long trip. She showed France to her young companion, as in the past she had shown it to Frick: La Rochelle, Saintes, Royan, Toulouse, Le Thoronet's abbey. In Albi, on 12 February, she visited the Toulouse-Lautrec museum and noted: "The only ones I really like are the women from the bordellos in their thick, divine [illegible] of feminine detail, women, no doubt, hardly more vulgar than the clients' wives and probably more adept. Their total absence of beauty takes away any hint of attempted seduction. A girl in black stockings, an artistic cliché of the period, attracts by way of something somehow more sensuous than in the other sketches. I find nothing here that quite equals the painting I saw somewhere—but where?—of the two feminine lovers, rumpled and tired."

After an excursion in the Camargue,[59] Yourcenar and Wilson went to Saint-Paul-de-Vence to visit James Baldwin, whom Yourcenar would see again on several occasions. In 1982 she translated into French his play *The Amen Corner*, which came out the following year. She enjoyed the company of that "warm and subtle" man who, she observed, had "hands of an astonishing sensitivity, feminine and very masculine at the same time." On 21 February, Yourcenar and Wilson embarked, from Marseille, for Algeria. They then spent three weeks—"very happy ones," Yourcenar confided— in Morocco, before going on to Spain, where on 22 March they celebrated Wilson's thirty-second birthday. At the beginning of April, in Portugal, Amalia Rodriguez and Alain Oulman—who has written many of her songs— treated them to an evening described as "delicious." But the way the two of them traveled suddenly took on a strangely excessive aspect, as if they had speeded up blindly. They returned to Paris on 14 April, to leave again for Bruges on the twenty-sixth. On the twenty-ninth they were in England, and headed back from there to the United States. In New York, on 8 May, they visited the Frick collection, where Yourcenar showed Wilson Rembrandt's famous *Polish Rider,* one of the paintings of her life. It was a strangely haunting image for her, as it is for the narrator of the Philippe Sollers novel *Femmes* (*Women*): "There he is, rising up oblique and fierce out of the yellowish-brown landscape . . . Fur cap, bow and arrows . . . Apocalypse on the alert."[60]

Wilson would only stay on Mount Desert until 17 June, at which time he returned to Paris for the summer, accompanied by Dumay, who had arrived on 12 June. Yourcenar spent a studious summer, broken up by a few visits, notably that of Colette and Claude Gallimard. In addition to the proofs of the first volume of her works in the Bibliothèque de la Pléiade, which she went over in early August with Yvon Bernier, she worked on "An Obscure Man." She finished writing this text—one of her favorite works—which she dedicated to Wilson, on 7 September. He had come back to Petite Plaisance on 26 August. On 9 October, they left together for Europe, after stopping by the cemetery in Somesville, a visit Yourcenar obliged herself to make before leaving the island. They landed, as they had the year before, in England and returned to the spots Yourcenar had introduced Wilson to, which—by chance?—were those loved by Frick above all else.

As of the end of October, Yourcenar was in Paris, leaving for a few days at the beginning of December for a quick trip to Amsterdam and Bruges. She often went, on Sunday, to the Russian church on Rue Daru, as she had done in times past with her father. Up until the end of her life, she would continue to observe this rite. She made an appearance at the Académie—the only time she would do so after her induction—at the moment of the vote for the Grand Prix in the novel category. Her preference went to Michel del Castillo, who did not receive the prize. This sort of thing was not likely to improve relations between Yourcenar, who hated to lose, and her fellow members. She saw Galey who, of course, commented on her visit in his *Journal:*

> Saw Yourcenar again for the first time since the falling-out. At her hotel, on Rue de l'Université. Unchanged, if not for her hair, now neatly trimmed at the nape of her neck, à la Gertrude Stein, and her usual bizarre get-up: a shapeless pair of slacks, a very chichi blouse with ruffles, and a vest that a valet might wear, with grey and black stripes, all of this topped off with a little black cape from the Maison Saint Laurent . . . We have a very "worldly" tea, without going into anything in any depth: the last prizes given out by

the Académie (she favored Castillo, for his "modern" qualities), England where she has just spent a few weeks, in Salisbury, Stonehenge, Tintagel (?), Amsterdam, the Frisian Islands and the bird sanctuaries there, Morocco's oases, Northeastharbour [sic] chitchat, and of course her work. Overwhelmed, she said, by her work: correcting the Pléiade. . . . Besides the plans for her next trip to Japan, where she intends to spend six months. As for *Quoi? L'Eternité,* the third volume of her Memoirs, she has only written the beginning, but she'd rather let it lie. "It is so hard to talk about oneself, when one is somehow, it seems, a special case."

Why recompose those ancient worlds instead of inventing other ones? "Because my characters never leave me. I am content to watch them live in different circumstances, enriching them with my present experience."

Regarding *With Open Eyes,* she told him: "in Holland, on television, they made me read the final pages, about death: I was very embarrassed." "But she read them nonetheless," he comments.[61]

Dumay was ill—he would die of cancer some months later. His relations with Wilson became difficult, angry. "At the end of that year, on Rue Pavée," recalled Yourcenar, "you could have cut the tension with a knife." Was she still sure she had been right to tell a friend in October, before leaving the United States, that Frick and Wilson were "one of the most beautiful alliances" of her life? She thought then that "if Grace knew and if she were still the Grace she had been before becoming too enfeebled and confused by her illness, she would say 'thank you' to Jerry." Having "taken such sweet pleasure in tasting the savor of living for a year and a half," as she confided, had she not allowed herself unwisely to get mixed up in the petty intrigues of a group of male friends who, no doubt, reminded her of her youth, but who were far from having the panache and the talents of her companions of yesteryear? And, though she did not wish to be reminded of the fact, on 8 June 1981 she turned seventy-eight years old. She wasn't any longer the young woman, nomadic and free, who embarked on a cruise with André Embiricos to write *Fires* and to quell her painful passion for André Fraigneau. If she wanted to keep traveling, in time—her own time—as in space, she had to submit, to a certain extent, to Jerry Wilson.

20

The Slipups and the "Tale of Horror"

THE TRIPS THAT Wilson made possible for Yourcenar were, as she herself said, "unanticipated" for a woman her age. But, beginning in January 1982, nearly two years after their first departure from Petite Plaisance for Florida, their cohabitation occasionally became difficult, if only because neither one of them was what might properly be called "good-natured."

A posteriori, after having matched up the various accounts of those who saw how they lived during that period and shared in certain confidences, it seems that Yourcenar's affectivity and her strong sensuality, both having too long lain dormant, suddenly reemerged in an unbounded, almost obsessive way. Did she try to get from Jerry Wilson what André Fraigneau had refused her, to avenge that rejection she had never acknowledged? Did she get what she was after, as she sometimes insinuated at the very end of her life, or as certain of Wilson's close friends maintain?[1] Or did she fantasize, believing in a dream that was stronger than reality, as we know she was capable of doing? But is it really necessary to settle this point once and for all, to try to "get to the bottom of it," to banish this uncertainty? The uncertainty is probably definitive, regardless of the letters sealed away, and whatever the contradictory assertions of this one or that one may be. we have already seen on numerous occasions how difficult it is, and always will be, to separate what Yourcenar really "lived" from what she "reconstructed." Whatever the case may be, as we well know, it was probably the things she reconstructed that she lived most intensely.

What is certain—even though Fraigneau, astonished by what he's being told, interjects: "Oh come on, she hadn't seen me for thirty years!"—is that, for Yourcenar, more and more over the course of the eighties, the images of Fraigneau and Wilson became superimposed on one another. In just the same way, an identification would form in her mind between Antinous and Hadrian, on the one hand, and Wilson and her, on the other. After nearly forty years "away" from the emotions of the heart and the flesh, this woman was once again living a passion. In 1985, when she had her serious heart operation, Yourcenar, waking up in a haze, talked on and on to Wilson calling him "André" all the while. "Confusion gets the best of you at a time like that," says Dee Dee Wilson. "The blurring of the differences between those two men, which no doubt had often happened when she was awake, surged forth then without anything to hold it back. When I heard her say the name 'André,' I immediately thought of the man she had told me about, the man she had loved before the war. She was not at all sorry to have left him, she said, since he had taken sides with the enemy."

No less certain than the affective fusion of Wilson and Fraigneau was Yourcenar's desire that Jerry and she appear to be a couple. We have seen what this desire may have owed to the possible jealousy of people close to Wilson. Be that as it may, in January 1981 Yourcenar decided to wear a gold necklace that Wilson had given her, never to take it off again. She did take it off in 1983 "after a particularly unpleasant scene," but put it back around her neck two days later. Wilson, of course, took advantage of the passion he aroused. Nonetheless, he felt a strange bond with his elderly companion. There is no reason to doubt that he too brought his share of sincerity to this strange relationship. And as with Frick, it is very hard to say which of the two, Yourcenar or Wilson, was more the other's prisoner.

BEFORE MAKING the trip to Egypt that she had awaited for nearly twenty years—it would be a one-month cruise, from 12 January to 13 February 1982, from Venice to Venice—Yourcenar wanted to pass through Verona, the city she had liked so much during the twenties. While there, she saw "the bronze-plated doors of the San Zeno church, and the Pisanellos"— among them the magnificent, unforgettable wife of the famous Saint George striking down the dragon.

The first stop on the journey was Alexandria, which goes unmentioned in Yourcenar's shipboard notebook;[2] but we know that she enjoyed herself seeking out traces of Constantine Cavafy. Then, heading up the Nile, the boat put in at Cairo. Yourcenar and Wilson stayed at the Hotel Meridien: "The pipes, which were six years old, were already in bad shape," she remembered. "I became practically a personal friend of the plumber, whom I had to call constantly. To effect his 'repairs,' he would wind bands of cotton around the leaky pipes. I liked watching him work. When he left, he would kiss my hand. Or my shoulder."

Yourcenar, who more than ever seemed to be roaming the world to find out if reality resembled what she had imagined, noted that "the Sphinx is as beautiful as it is in photographs," adding: "strange absence of emotion, however." She was not particularly moved by the pyramids either: "From behind, since they've cleared the site there, the pyramids are more beautiful. But those grandiose, four-sided triangles strike me as nothing more than what they are: great funerary monuments, and admirable ones, of a race that still believed it would endure. . . . The enormous disproportion between the technical feat and the effect obtained is the same in the end as in our cathedrals and industrial complexes. . . . But the cathedrals, erected to unite man with God, were no more successful in fulfilling their purpose, to exalt God by sanctifying man, and the industrial complexes supposedly created to bring man prosperity will turn out to be his perdition. . . . It seems that from time immemorial the human ant has wanted to create real or mental constructions that crush him in the end." The "sultan's mosque," on the other hand, struck her as "overwhelmingly beautiful": "sometimes it seems as if I saw it in a dream."

Visiting the Cairo museum, Yourcenar was guided by Jean-Pierre Corteggiani, librarian of the French Institute. He offered to take her to the site of Antinoöpolis; she and Wilson could then catch up with their cruise boat upriver as it continued on its way. She joyfully accepted. She would be in Antinoöpolis on 22 January 1982, the first anniversary of her induction into the Académie Française. "When we arrived in Antinoöpolis, it was as if she was coming back to a familiar place," relates Corteggiani, "as if she was remembering what Hadrian had seen, what she had made Hadrian see and had seen through his eyes. It was fascinating to watch. I had long admired her as a writer. But during that time we spent together, which I did not know then was the beginning of a friendship that was infinitely precious to me, I was dazzled by that woman. By her knowledge. By her incredible capacity for attention and concentration, by her intellectual curiosity, which was still so keen at age seventy-eight—and I found out how extensive it was when we visited the Cairo museum. I was also surprised by the way she had of being 'at home everywhere and nowhere,' as she used to say about her father. As for Jerry Wilson, he was not a person I particularly liked. He kept very quiet and you wondered whether or not this was a sign of hostility."[3] Wilson definitely did not like to see Yourcenar enjoy herself too much in someone else's company, and even less to see her strike up a friendship. And learned conversations, perforce, left him out. We shall never know if that silence of his was imposed on him or not. In Europe, Yourcenar's friends—those who were not also Wilson's friends—always knew him to be silent in her presence, and as if standing back, giving way to the woman whom, with deference, he called "Madame"; when she was not there, on the other hand, it had come to be a habit for him calmly to speak in her name. Those who knew how they lived on Mount Desert, Dee Dee

Wilson and Jeannie Lunt in particular, were extremely surprised to learn of this reserve: at Petite Plaisance, from late 1981 on, Wilson had reigned supreme.

IN ANTINOÖPOLIS, Yourcenar endlessly "thought about [her] description of Hadrian, 'sustained by a clearsighted frenzy.'" "I also thought about the marble stairways I had envisioned, linking the city to the river. Finally I thought throughout all this of the scene of lamentation and mourning of the first day of the month of Athyr."

"We took a small boat," adds Jean-Pierre Corteggiani, "and, about ten yards from shore, at the spot where, perhaps, Antinous had drowned, Marguerite Yourcenar, symbolically, threw a little purse full of coins." In her travel notes, Yourcenar attributes this gesture to Wilson. And she adds:

> I would like to have visited the place, on the other shore, where Hadrian brought his friend to the embalmers. But besides my not wanting to overlay Antinoöpolis with any other visits, it was time for our friends to get back on the road for the return trip to Cairo. We did well, for that matter, to leave when we did since once we got back on the boat we witnessed an unforgettable scene. . . . I was in my cabin. Jerry was on deck. Jerry came rushing in to get me. He had seen a policeman go after a woman who was dashing toward the river and then lead her away. She was wailing. Some other women came, and they were wailing too, with that long, Oriental shriek that is the cry of mourning. They all were waving their shawls in a repeated, rhythmic movement, thrusting the long black folds of cloth in front of them like wings. A thirty-year-old man had just drowned, his felucca having drifted back to shore. . . . The woman wailing was his wife. An older woman, the mother, perhaps, went down to the river without anyone stopping her and rubbed her hair and her face with mud before rejoining the chorus. Throughout all of this, the men of the village, who were present as well, looked on, in silence. One man wiped his hair with his loose-fitting gown. A bit later, he would go sit down on the stone embankment, his head on his knees, a mute image of grief, very dignified and infinitely moving (perhaps Hadrian also dried his eyes discreetly with his toga, perhaps he sat down resting his head on his knees, between his arms). The men prayed. The beauty of those prayers whose earnestness is palpable. Yes, I am enough of a creature of the immemorial world to believe that bridges irritate great rivers. I ponder the strange coincidence that caused us to witness that scene of mourning for a drowned man on the very same day we visited Antinoöpolis. Corteggiani told us that Hadrian is called "the soul of the Nile," he who deified his friend. His brow must have furrowed ironically when he heard that epithet applied to him.

In the constant company of Hadrian, she carried on her visit to Egypt: "They told us, when we were on our way to Luxor, that on 24 January 131

Hadrian celebrated his birthday there," she noted. "If this fact, which I don't recall ever seeing mentioned, is true, what might that fifty-five-year-old man have been thinking on that day?" She liked to tell the story of an incident that probably played a part in intensifying the assimilation she imagined between Antinous and Wilson. One evening, he dove off the boat into the Nile. He had underestimated the current and had some difficulty getting back on board. Rather frightened, "dripping ice-cold water," he apparently took refuge in Yourcenar's arms, like a child, and said: "I should have drowned myself like Antinous." At a distance, this episode strikes one as somewhat distasteful, tempting one to think Wilson might be guilty of crudely manipulating his companion. But is the story true or, yet again, fantasy? And supposing it were true, how could those days, those places, those conversations inhabited and haunted by a dead Antinous with whom Yourcenar enjoined Wilson to identify himself not have been anything but a tremendous burden for the young man to bear?

On 28 January, Yourcenar began feeling tired. She often let Wilson go exploring on his own. From the boat, at its berth, she watched the pier and wrote down what she saw: "an old viola player [who] perpetually repeats a sad, rather grating melody, haunting and thin," or else: "[i]n the almost absolute solitude between batches [of tourists] the daily life of this wretched little wharf, [where] unhappy, shackled donkeys lie down in the dust to roll around in it and then strain to get up, or else go, with their muzzles low down near the ground, seeking out some improbable grass in the sand." Back in Cairo on 5 February, she announced that she wouldn't be leaving her room for three days. The boat left again on the eighth. Wilson was falling prey, it seems, to fits of bad temper. No doubt being with a woman who was constantly tired weighed on him sometimes. She noted, elliptically: "it's hard, finding out that one lacks vigor." Before returning to Venice, the boat put in at Piraeus. Yourcenar did not wish to go ashore. Was she afraid of seeing Athens again, after forty-three years of absence? Her publisher Jeannette Hadzinicoli, who wanted to see her, visited her on board. Yourcenar promised to come back to Greece. And she did.

In Venice, where the boat docked on 13 February at seven o'clock in the morning, Yourcenar began taking her travel notes in Italian. Was this a way of feeling more in harmony with the city where she was, or an attempt to hide from her companion—who didn't read Italian—what she was writing down? "I am stringing all these days together, 13—14—15 February, without distinguishing them from one another because they have dissolved, for anyone capable of seeing and living and breathing, into some kind of strange dream." Carnival time had taken Venice by storm. Yourcenar settled in every day on the Piazza San Marco, at the Caffè Florian, for quite a while.

She watched "the flood of masks" go by. She had always liked theatrical or holiday disguises, and the "mysterious beauty" of people wearing masks. However, she noticed a man dressed up as an SS agent, "a solitary Nazi who gave me something of a fright." On the eighteenth, she expected to spend a pleasant evening, dining with Paolo Zacchera, an Italian friend who shared her ecological concerns and with whom she maintained ties throughout the eighties. They dined on the Zattere. Wilson suggested they go back to the hotel on foot. Yourcenar didn't dare to say no. Halfway there, she felt dizzy. When they finally got back to their hotel, Wilson "flew into a white rage," she noted later on, "blaming me for having embarrassed our guests with my dizzy spell. I couldn't manage to slip in between his rude remarks the simple fact that I was expecting to take a boat back from the Zattere." According to her, Wilson's fury was nourished "by the fright I caused him and the underlying exasperation one has for those one lives with, even when one loves them." From verbal violence, Wilson proceeded to physical abuse, which Yourcenar did not seem to find shocking. With astonishing placidity she observed: "I think back on it at night and I'm surprised by the unconscious choice that has caused me several times to attach myself to beings of an intransigence and violence that suddenly tear through the fabric of a peaceful life together. I tell myself that I owe J. two years of happiness and perhaps life, which is something unheard of in the circumstances I was in and at that stage of my existence. One accepts people such as they are. When we greeted one another the next day, it was on the same tender note of friendliness we were accustomed to." Was she thinking to herself, better this mark of interest, of passion perhaps, than the calm indifference manifested in times past by the likes of an André Fraigneau? Wasn't it better to have this acknowledgment of her physical self, even though it was a violent one, than unawareness that her body existed? Sophie in *Coup de Grâce* saw things no differently. Did she so much as ask herself, on occasion, where she got her talent for pushing the people with whom she was passionately involved to the limit of their patience?

When they arrived in Paris, at the beginning of March, Maurice Dumay was very ill. He died on 24 March. Yourcenar entered at that time into a strange period of her existence. She had two lives, hermetically sealed off, as it were, one from the other: her work life and the pleasure of getting back to Paris, which she liked a lot more than she let on, as she observes in a notebook. "Seeing Paris again, as *arresting* every time as returning to Rome or to Athens. More arresting even, because I feel I'm more connected, more attuned to these surroundings. . . . What would be left of Paris if they razed the areas between Saint-Germain-l'Auxerrois and the Etoile and from the

Sainte-Chapelle to the Madeleine and the Opéra and built office blocks there? What would be left of a certain French spirit?"[4] During those months of March and April 1982, she reread the Pléiade's "Chronologie," translated some blues, which would appear on an album in 1984, and began writing *Quoi? L'Eternité*. She was a celebrity and a celebrated one. People sought an audience with her. She was taken care of, as was her family.[5]

For the past year she had been seeing new people, like Gisèle Halimi and some others, who were drawn by the symbol of her election to the Académie. She would have "dinner in town" (as she had in Frick's time) for instance on 21 March with Robert Kanters—"who is adorable to me and a warm, enthusiastic critic, though I don't quite feel that we are friends." None of these people suspected what kinds of things were going on between Wilson and her. Wilson seemed to them to be the prototypical young companion of an elderly person who is rich or famous—or both at once. Their coexistence remained the fruit of an "arrangement" out of which both protagonists got something they wanted. Thus did Wilson decide, without a very clear plan, to "mount a show." Yourcenar felt it was her duty to help him. So Patrice Chéreau and Antoine Vitez dropped by to see them. Nothing came of it though.

Yourcenar and Frick's old friends, such as Anne Quellennec, on the other hand, were more perplexed to find her suddenly under someone's "influence," and abandoning them for a young man "we knew nothing about, beyond the fact that he went out a lot at night," remembers Quellennec. "He enjoyed indulging in life's pleasures, and I don't think Marguerite was the sort of woman to condemn that particular bent." She had even retained from her youth a secret attraction to sensual excess, she who had had Hadrian say at the close of a beautiful meditation on pleasure and love: "One would end by preferring the plain truths of debauchery to the outworn stratagems of seduction if there, too, lies did not prevail."[6] What most worried those who once had been her good friends was that Yourcenar did not seem to feel as well as she tried to make people believe. Indeed she wrote down in a notebook: "1 April. I am decidedly unwell, both intellectually and physically. Shaken to the core of my being." "All the relationships of my life—or rather, let's say, of life such as I have lived it—have been strangely askew, and all the more intense as a result."

Yourcenar had just barely returned to the United States with Wilson— who, for his part, was headed back to Paris for the summer—when *Comme l'eau qui coule (Two Lives and a Dream)* came out at Gallimard, in May. It consisted of three texts: "Anna, Soror . . . ," "An Obscure Man," and "A Lovely Morning." When *Anna, soror . . .* was published for the first time in

1981, it received very mixed reviews. Angelo Rinaldi, highly irritated by the volume's "copious" postface, objected at length to the exhumation of this early work. "Montherlant, for instance, specialized in revamping old texts, patching them up with multidinous prefaces, postfaces, and variants: we're lucky if he spares us his dry-cleaning bills. Madame Yourcenar follows in his self-centered footsteps. . . . She has the same taste for the highly wrought story, the same starchy formality when it comes to the expression of feelings. And were one a disagreeable person, one would add the same knack for sculpting noble bas-reliefs in unctuous Marseilles soap, with a chisel borrowed from some nineteenth-century Grand Prix de Rome awardee. . . . It's almost enough to make you wish that, resurrection for resurrection, Madame Yourcenar had chosen to bring out her Pindar biography again."[7]

Yourcenar's fictional "account of an obscurely incestuous episode between a brother and a sister, in late-sixteenth-century Naples," inspired no more clemency in Jean Chalon, who concluded his article this way: "But what demon made Yourcenar publish this volume foretelling her induction at the Quai Conti, since its atmosphere is already that of what Cocteau so rightly called 'the deadly boredom of immortality'?"[8] "We now must pray to the heavens, beseech Gallimard, go down on our knees to Yourcenar, to prevent a third edition of *Anna, soror . . .* from being published," he wrote when *Comme l'eau qui coule* came out. He too was annoyed that the texts were accompanied by too much discussion of their genesis, in which Yourcenar herself expressed surprise at how precocious her original drafts were. "The regal Marguerite never pretended to be a shrinking violet but, up until now, she has waited for her praises to be sung, without penning them herself in advance. . . . As for praises, she will get some above all for *Un Homme obscur. . . .* In *Un Homme obscur* Yourcenar is not the pompous painter of *Anna, soror . . .* anymore, she shows herself to be an incomparable painter of seascapes, a new Horace Vernet of storms in which words replace colors."[9]

AS WOULD BECOME her custom, she spent the summer at Petite Plaisance. She was preparing a collection of essays, *That Mighty Sculptor, Time,* and translating James Baldwin's play *The Amen Corner*. She was quite satisfied with her work but waited somewhat impatiently for Jerry to return so they could leave for the Orient. One of her oldest dreams was finally about to be realized. Wilson arrived at Petite Plaisance on 4 September 1982, and, two days later, the two of them were on their way to Japan by way of Canada, California, and Hawaii. Yourcenar finished her translation of *The Amen Cor-*

ner and wrote her preface at sea. She was fond of saying, long afterward—
was it by way of convincing herself?—how intensely happy she had been
in Hawaii and on that late-September ocean voyage, en route to Yokohama.
The notes she took during her trip to Japan—descriptions of places, sculptures, people she saw briefly, such as Mrs. Yukio Mishima—are rather confusing and quite difficult to read. Regarding those three or so months, we
know the regions she passed through or visited (they are listed in the Pléiade's "Chronologie") and certain details that she liked to recollect. For example, there were the traditional Japanese hotels where she would stay and
where Wilson shared her room: "They would unroll little mattresses for us,
right on the floor. Then, at an hour that was not ours to choose, they would
wake us, and fold the mattresses back up without the slightest consultation
with us. And it was time to make one's toilet."

YOURCENAR was in Japan—where, with Jun Shiragi, she began the translation of *Cinq Nô modernes* by Mishima (which appeared in early 1984)—
when the first volume of the Pléiade edition of her works was published.
After Saint-John Perse and André Malraux, and just ahead of René Char,
Yourcenar was one of the rare authors to be granted admission to this Pantheon of French literature during her lifetime. And that admission was variously commented on in the press. In François Weyergans's *Le Matin* review,
which struck a particularly scornful note hardly suited to a so-called analysis, the publication of *Œuvres romanesques* [Prose Works] gave rise to the
dubious amusement of plucking sentences here and there from different
texts, with the intention of provoking the "reconsideration of an *œuvre* that
is no doubt overrated": "I have just read one thousand pages. Half of them
are pointless," he wrote. "Ten or fifteen adjectives per page could be crossed
out. Yourcenar gives her readers the illusory impression they are reading
deep texts written in very good French, in the same way that Viollet-le-
Duc made people think he understood Gothic architecture. . . . Yourcenar
oscillates between seventeenth-century preciosity and the artistic style of
writing so favored in the nineteenth century. She is a *précieuse*. I'm not
making any of this up: she talks about it herself. I'm merely adding the
adjective 'ridiculous.'"[10] In lieu of this florilegium of passages taken out of
context and mistakes (one can happily indulge oneself in this little game
with any writer), it could have been noted that this was a "false Pléiade,"
since it contains no critical apparatus. Yourcenar had insisted on this, and
her publisher was hardly in a position to refuse anything, no matter what it
was, to the first woman Academician in history. Nonetheless, in the case of
this writer who spent her life revising her work, it would be fascinating to

study the variants. But in that act of forbidding any critical apparatus we can easily recognize a will that we have seen at work a hundred times in Marguerite Yourcenar: to be in control of everything, to keep others from judging her work, her revisions, and sometimes her hesitancy.

Nineteen eighty-three began for Yourcenar and Wilson in Thailand, prior to their one-month stay in India, from 14 January to 19 February. "I've misplaced many of my notebooks," she said, "but I remember some curious incidents. One night during a dinner in Bangkok, a man collapsed silently behind the chair where I was sitting. Just as silently, some people came over and revived him. Jerry told me what had happened after it was over. I was afraid that an end might be near, felt that such a misadventure could have happened to me." We have a few scattered notes about the time spent in India, but they're not really usable by anyone other than Yourcenar.[11] They were taken as she went along, wherever she happened to be, and probably intended for use in *Le Tour de la prison*. Here is an example that, despite a certain awkwardness, is still understandable: "added onto Japan, India has been one of the great experiences of my life—or more accurately of life itself. What can one say that doesn't ring hollow? Japan, such a secret place, so different from almost everything people say about it, is an isolated human experience, one pushed to the limit for centuries in a corner of the world that up until 1570 (1670?)—and, much more than is generally thought, even up until the present time—drew everything, in that mental realm that goes beyond concrete facts, from within itself, with the exception of the great enrichment brought by the presence of Chinese art and thought, which came to Japan gradually, and peacefully, without conquest and most often thanks to Nipponese who courageously immersed themselves in the color yellow." Still, these fragments are in too crude a state to be looked on even as a "first attempt."

As she had promised Jeannette Hadzinicoli she would, Yourcenar did go back to Greece. While there, she was ill. Was it a long bout with the flu, as she called it, or was it depression, and psychosomatic complications linked to the power of her past? Hadzinicoli speaks of asthma attacks and spells of difficulty breathing, which seems to plead more in favor of the second hypothesis. Nonetheless, she went back to see Nauplia, Mycenae, and Epidaurus again. One gets the feeling from following her geographical progress in the Pléiade's "Chronologie," or in her own notes, that she had fallen prey once again to a certain sense of urgency; it seems she had to be in a different place every night, or nearly. What was she seeking to escape? Her commentaries dwindled down to practically nothing: "Rome, attack in the street; the hell of Pisa; nice in Portofino with Paolo [Zacchera]; Marseilles and the Defferres; Carpentras; Lyons, M.Y. with a bad case of the flu goes back to Paris in an ambulance; six weeks of work and confusion in Paris."

"15 May, sweet pleasure of returning to Petite Plaisance. Over the next few days, getting things put away, garden, sweet pleasure of life." She was settling back into the studious rhythm of her summers, or so she thought. She read an essay, "in a state of wonderment," that Walter Kaiser had written on her, she reread Thomas Mann's *The Holy Sinner* and observed once again "what a masterpiece it is." But she wrote: "27 May: sweet pleasure just the same, but tinged with sadness; 28 May: one of the worst bouts of depression and its consequences." What kind of consequences could she be referring to? Violent ones? "She was afraid," remembers her secretary, Jeannie. "Jerry was drinking a lot. He wasn't the nice guy we'd known anymore. One night, Madame called me very late. She was very frightened. I offered to come over and get her. She said no. I told her: 'If Jerry is drunk, don't speak to him, stay in your room and pretend you're asleep. I'm sure he'll stop hollering. If he doesn't, call me back.' It wasn't until quite a while later that I realized she was probably afraid that he would hit her. Fortunately, he left to go down South." For the first time in her life, Yourcenar had become a pathetic character.

Nevertheless, she went to work in earnest on *Le Tour de la prison* and continued to translate the Blues and Gospels, describing her state this way: "A great deal of courage, but my body is all too clearly suffering the ill-effects. Allergies. Aphonia. Cold sweats. Extreme nervous tension. A storm that doesn't break and seems to gather inside, above and beyond the organs themselves; but wear and tear, assuredly." One is hardly tempted anymore to make fun of her hypochondria. The life she led was very trying. She distracted herself with "lots of visitors who came for a few days," such as Yvon Bernier and Silvia Baron Supervielle—"a good translator endowed with a sense of the poetic"—who translated her work into Spanish. "Alone without Jerry, partly happy, partly sad, I attempted with all the strength I had to live," she observed as if trying to convince herself, "in order to keep from being one of those people who depend on someone else, suffer when that person's not around, and strangle him with affection as swimmers sometimes do their savior. I tried to work a great deal (proofs, ... *Le Tour de la prison*, of which some seventy-five pages are done), to go out a lot, to lead a good, full life, to take advantage of the garden's delights ('every herb in the garden is a piece of myself'). And to trust in the life force that carries us along. And not to project any worries onto the future. Marvelously assisted by Jeannie (and the child), by Georgia [the housekeeper and cook], and Zoé [the dog]." Jeannie Lunt, in fact, tried to dissuade Yourcenar from going off on another trip with Wilson. Dee Dee Wilson and she doubted that he would give up his abuse of alcohol. But Yourcenar, as she would from now on every year, awaited his return with a certain feverishness: he was the sign of her departure.

IN FRANCE, *That Mighty Sculptor, Time* came out, a collection of essays and articles of varying degrees of interest, all previously published in several different periodicals. Probably the best text in the volume is the title piece, which opens: "On the day when a statue is finished, its life, in a certain sense, begins."[12] "Escaping from chaos by way of the artist's conception and his chisel, the stone returns to chaos little by little by way of the violence of nature and of men: yes, time has reclaimed its rights," Danièle Sallenave would comment.

> The work of art would thus appear to be a brief interlude between two eterni-ties of insignificance. . . . But the way time acts upon the work of art is some-thing else again: in submitting itself to time's power, the work of art does not immediately return to the shadowy realm it had provisionally left. Time does not restrict itself to relentlessly undoing what the artist has done: it completes the artist's work, not as his enemy but as his rival.[13]

As soon as Wilson got back, the bags were packed for Europe. The first stop would be Amsterdam, where Yourcenar was to receive the Erasmus Prize. In the Pléiade's "Chronologie," she gives a date of 5 October for that ceremony. In her notebooks and Wilson's things are entirely different. Jerry comes back on 15 October, happy with the work he's just finished on *Satur-day Night Blues,* a film on the South and the blacks.[14]

On 18 October, they were in New York, and they flew from there to Amsterdam on the twentieth. Yourcenar, who had flown very little, suffered a great deal from jet lag. She recovered quickly, as she always did when she had to make a public appearance. No matter what she may have said on this subject, she was quite fond of official tributes and distinctions. Besides which, she was pleased to see her Dutch publisher, Johan Polak, again, whose company she particularly enjoyed, and she was pleased to be getting together with her friends and translators: The American Kaiser—who de-livered a speech about her when the prize was awarded—and the Greek Hadzinicoli. Most important, she had invited her childhood friend Baron Egon de Vietinghoff, "Alexis's son," she would say to Kaiser. To speed her progress on *Quoi? L'Eternité,* Yourcenar wanted to know more about Egon's father Conrad, who, as we have seen, served as the model for Alexis. "But," she lamented, "Egon said something vague about 'my parents.' The figure of Conrad remains uncertain. No doubt Egon did not know him completely either. I told him I had seen his mother [Jeanne] again three years before she died. I said nothing about the visit to the doctor, or about the circle she was part of in Geneva and Bern, or about my visit to Zurich. I mentioned, as if in passing, that she was buried near Lausanne, but did not speak of my visits to her grave." Yourcenar wanted to save the confession of her secret "worship" of Jeanne for her book. "Certain details make one dream," she wrote in what were intended to serve as preliminary notes for *Quoi? L'Eternité.*[15] "I say I saw Jeanne for the last time by chance, in Cap Ferrat. Egon tells me she had bought a villa in Roquebrune. Michel lived near Roquebrune and Jeanne knew that. Egon says his mother's life was rather unhappy. Did she want to get away from Conrad? None of this seems to make much of a ripple in Egon's awareness. I realize that the most important thing that's lacking for *Quoi? L'Eternité* is information about the dealings between Conrad and Michel. There is something magical somehow in that whole story that I have hesitated up until now to share with the reader or with anyone at all." "When I consider my life, I am appalled to find it a shapeless mass," she wrote, borrowing a sentence from *Memoirs of Hadrian,*[16] "but is Egon's any less so?"

The only aspects of the official ceremony for the Erasmus Prize that she commented on were Kaiser's speech, which was "moving and beautiful," and her own, about which she observed with a thoroughly typical hauteur: "My allocution well received. Understood perhaps by one or two people."

In a passage touching for its coquettishness, she also made note of this gesture: "Prince Bernhard, handing me the ritual spray of flowers, after the address, said to me 'no one would guess how old you are.' Despite myself, I felt a little burst of joy for reasons supposedly too shameful to admit."

During the day she liked to spend her time, as she always had, visiting her favorite museums. In the evening she would have dinner with Wilson and some friends—"discussions about life," she noted on one unspecified evening. "Marriage or freedom? In the end it amounts to the same thing." Less prosaic were her nighttime strolls in what she called, probably translating from English, "the red-light district." She was not at all reluctant to talk about those nights in 1983, along with other nights, in other countries, avowing: "I have a tender affection for those women on display." Perhaps she would have discussed them in *Le Tour de la prison.* In her notes about India she had described "the prostitute district in Bombay at night. The girls in saris, looking used. There was only one very beautiful one, in a silver sari. Much less sensual than in Amsterdam or Hamburg. Serene passivity . . . One girl very nearly got herself run over. The almost indefinable

beauty of all those scenes." "As for the Geishas," she said, "are they prosti-
tutes? Not in the crude sense this word had for American boys getting off
warships and clamoring for geishas." The account she wrote in Amsterdam
in 1983 is more specific: "We went out once again in the red-light district.
That explicit, naive poster with the different love-making postures was still
there, and the shadow plays, and the sex shops with their enormous phal-
luses. A young woman said in French 'Would you ladies and gentlemen
perhaps care for a little fantasy?' But the group was looking for a taxi because it was starting to rain. J. hadn't heard her, he was watching a good-
looking Spanish boy and his puppets. We never see or hear the same things
together. Alone with J. or even with Jeannette, I believe I would have given
the fantasy a try, would have wanted to see where it went. With four people,
this would have been impossible. With five, intolerable. I have looked back
on that stranger several times since then, offering the sweetest part of herself
to the first men and women to happen along. Then the image took on
something of a spectral quality, a funereal eros [written in Greek]. But I try
to let all that mythology drop away: there was nothing but a young woman,
somewhat disillusioned, a little timid, offering herself to a group of strangers
in the rain."

After a short stay in Bruges at the beginning of November and two weeks
or so spent in Paris, for the usual professional activities—publisher-related
and social (notably a visit from Minister of Culture Jack Lang)—Yourcenar
and Wilson left for Kenya. They planned to visit animal reserves. "Jerry
wanted to take some photographs there," Yourcenar would point out. Wilson, whom Yourcenar tended to take for a better photographer than he
actually was, left lots of photographs, when he died, of the countryside they
had traveled through together and the animals they saw. Testifying to this
today is a small book that Yourcenar had explicitly intended as a tribute to
her companion, *La Voix des choses* [The Voice of Things], a collection of
texts chosen by Yourcenar (quotations copied down from books she had
read, which had accompanied her throughout her life) and of Wilson's
photographs.[17]

During the evening of 14 December, after a lecture at the French Institute of Nairobi, Wilson and Yourcenar were victims in a traffic accident that
immobilized them in Kenya for the winter. Yourcenar would tell this story,
as she almost always did with regard to serious things, with a mixture of
humor and serenity: "The newspapers said that I had been run over by a
minibus. According to others, it was a full-sized bus. So why not a tank? It
was simply an automobile. We had decided, Jerry and I, to walk back to
our hotel, which was not very far from the French Institute. A car went off

the road and hit us while we were on the sidewalk. It hardly touched Jerry, but I was thrown several yards down the road. The driver got scared and took off—later on I found out it was a policeman and, since he had been drunk that night, he was afraid he would be in big trouble. I was on the ground, unconscious and covered with blood—the arch of one of my eyebrows had split open, which always makes one bleed a lot. Jerry was trying to stop some cars to get someone to help us. In vain. It's quite common in Nairobi for people to fake accidents as a way of attacking unsuspecting motorists. Finally someone did stop, the providential 'Monsieur Siméon,' whom I shall never sufficiently thank. According to him, there was no point in trying to call an ambulance. It would cost us too much time. He and Jerry thus loaded me into the car as best they could, worrying all the while, since they didn't really know what kinds of injuries I had and thought they might be making them worse. Finally we got to the hospital. Actually, I was not seriously injured. A few contusions, and several of my ribs and one of my legs had been hurt. I had to testify for Monsieur Siméon. They refused to clean his car until he had proven that the blood stains all over the seats were not 'suspect.' I was in the Nairobi hospital, where I received very good care, for five weeks, and we stayed in Kenya, Jerry and I, until the end of the winter." [18]

In March 1984, on the very day that spring began, the two of them arrived in Marseilles. They would stay for some time. While there, Yourcenar saw Gaston Defferre and Edmonde Charles-Roux, whose company she enjoyed. After a short stay in London, they departed at the end of April for Boston, and were back at Petite Plaisance in early May, where Yourcenar had ahead of her the usual summer devoted to literary work. Jerry left on 7 June, before Colette and Claude Gallimard arrived for their traditional summer visit. When he came back at the end of the summer, Wilson filmed a documentary on Mount Desert Island, *L'Île heureuse* [The Happy Island], in which Yourcenar participated. Only Yourcenar's indulgence where Jerry was concerned and the Yourcenar fetishism beginning to assert itself in France made this film possible. An "event," it was broadcast at the end of the year on French television. A private showing of the film had been organized in Paris, in November, for a select few, first and foremost among whom was Jack Lang, the minister of culture. Nonetheless, it is hard to imagine a flatter, more naively "illustrative" film. No sooner does Yourcenar utter the word "flower" than we have a close-up of a flower. And it's all like this. Yourcenar herself is very badly filmed, in clothes that are simply not appropriate. As for what she has to say, there is no way of getting around the fact that it's pathetically prosaic. The only thing that lingers from this film one would sooner forget is the memory of her voice—a melody, at least for some viewers, that "carried" the text and the images.

On 15 November, the day after the showing, Yourcenar had agreed to do an interview for *Le Monde,* which I had requested and arranged, and which was published on 7 December.[19] It was that interview, in essence, that gave rise to this book—not that the idea chanced to be conceived on that day, over the course of our conversation, but because that interview was not the last one of its kind, and because our professional relationship transformed itself, as happens rarely, into a personal one.

On that particular afternoon, as she would afterward every time we met, Yourcenar, for more than two hours, exercised her powers of seduction, her irony, her humor, which often was fierce: appearing before someone who was conquered in advance, but who still had a feel for the game, was clearly a pleasure for her. After the customary civilities, she let me ask the first questions, observing me closely, no doubt rather pleased to see that I was tense, impressed. I knew what she wanted to find out: had I read her books? Once she was convinced that I had, the interview took on a different cast, as if I had just been "admitted," just left the group of "those who come wanting to talk to you about everything under the sun when they've never read your books," as she said wryly. We took leave of one another by way of one of those startlingly coquettish repartees she sometimes indulged in: when I confessed that our interview had allowed me to tie the exercise of my profession to the desire I had had, for years, to meet her, she commented: "Well? You weren't too disappointed, were you?"

Yourcenar was not destined to return to Paris until 1986. We saw each other again several times, both that year and the next. Most of these meetings were the work of Yannick Guillou, who had by then become her primary contact at Gallimard, as well as one of her close friends.[20]

Having heard over dinner one night in March 1987, in Paris, that I came to the United States quite often, Yourcenar tossed out: "If you should find yourself in the area of Mount Desert Island . . . feel free to come stay at my house." I knew that she had banished from her lexicon all those pat phrases one says without thinking, purely out of social habit and indifference to others—"we'll get together soon"; "let's keep in touch"—and that for her any remark was as good as a commitment.

Thus it was that in early June 1987 Yourcenar opened the door for me, literally speaking, to Petite Plaisance, where she was visiting with Guillou who had come to spend a few days with her. In her own home, in that house she liked sharing with others, she delighted, even more so than in Paris, in exercising her singular charm. Probably in an effort to prove to herself—and to see in others' eyes—that she was alive. It made her infinitely touching. Every morning when she would come down from her room for breakfast, after Dee Dee Wilson had been by to help her bathe, she would be wearing a silk dressing gown, always a different color from the one she'd had on the night before. Like an eternally coquettish young woman, she would change her clothes and jewelry several times during the day. If one neglected to comment, she would suddenly embark on the story of the family brooch clasping her blouse, or of the garnet necklace purchased in India. She was an expert in an art that's almost lost, the art of conversation, passing with the same simplicity, the same sense of just the right phrase, from describing an Indian temple to describing a flower in the garden, where she was trying to acclimate certain rare species, then on to memories light-hearted or serious: many of the remarks reported in this book come from such moments. She liked to talk, she liked to feel listened to, and she liked having someone admire the way she spoke. She was attentive to the people with whom she spoke. She had lost neither her curiosity about others nor her desire to seduce them.

Driving around the island with Yourcenar as your guide; going with her to the Somesville cemetery, or to the mainland . . . This could only be a dream, at least for her who once had been an adolescent of the sixties reading *The Abyss* and *Hadrian* in a dreary provincial lycée, imagining—and wanting to know more about—this singular woman said to live on an island in the middle of nowhere, who was supposedly a "recluse," sharing a house with her translator, and whose eyes and mouth had so much to say about her appetite for life.

During what would prove to be the final period of her existence, there were, between us, a few letters and lots of "telephonage," to use the word she favored. We were to meet on 9 December in Copenhagen, where she had arranged to give a lecture on Borges. But she did not come, having crossed the threshold of her mortal agony a full month earlier.

"There is no better stroke of fortune," as one of her expressions would have it, than having been able to travel back in time with her, having had the chance to recapture her as a child, then as a young woman, having loved her, then grown tired of her, having happily discovered her faults, her obsessions—everything that made her more exasperating than one had anticipated, and more moving as well. Than being able to affirm, having gone with her as far as one can into the depths of her mystery, that twenty-five years ago, in that provincial lycée, one was right to have harbored that immense curiosity about Marguerite Yourcenar and to have felt, even then, an instinctive sympathy.

NONE OF THIS would probably have happened had it not been for the events that took place "just after our first meeting," wrote Yourcenar in a letter dated 27 March 1986, one month prior to her return to Europe: "The entire year 1985—along with the two months that preceded and followed it—was a long, dark tale of horror with very few bright spots."[21]

Wilson had just met a young man named Daniel, and he insisted that Daniel accompany them to India, where they would be going once again in early January. Yourcenar agreed to this arrangement. "I spent a terrible Christmas in Amsterdam with them," she said simply, giving an account of what she called "the horrible year" (November 1984–February 1986). In her notebook there appears, written in her own hand for the first time, the single word "cry." She knew that never again would she find solace for having reached "the age in which the night is meant for sleep."[22]

"On seeing the handsome Daniel, one of my Dutch friends said premonitorily, 'he's the angel of death,'" she related. "Even before we reached India, that trip was shaping up to be an utter catastrophe." No sooner had she arrived in Bombay, on 2 January, than Yourcenar began to feel ill. She greeted the effects of "physical decline bitterly," as she noted. She had bouts of nausea, and other psychosomatic disorders. She couldn't bear this relationship between Wilson and Daniel, from which she was excluded. But she did not lose her sharp eye, her taste for observing human bodies. After a more or less official dinner attended by Rudolf Nureyev, she commented: "Body grown a bit heavy, more Roman than Greek, but admirably controlled. Very handsome in his own way." She sketched a portrait of Daniel, doing her best to keep it neutral: "Discreet, considerate, still there is something vaguely offhand and careless about him that seems to stem from indolence. But one senses that he comes from somewhere else, a somewhere else impossible to pinpoint: totally illiterate of course, but with very refined tastes." All ties were loosening, whether ties with the past or with the present; on hearing of the death, on Mount Desert, of her dog Zoé, she noted: "she didn't travel much. But it's the breaking of a tie. Zoé belonged to Grace."[23]

At the end of January, Wilson repeatedly complained of not feeling well, having fallen prey to sudden bouts of high fever. On 5 February, when they were in Jaipur, he was growing more and more seriously ill. They thought it was malarial fevers at first, but very quickly Yourcenar, like Wilson himself, suspected AIDS. "As soon as that disease came to light, knowing it was transmitted sexually, we talked about it, Jerry and I," she confided. "He made it clear that he did not want to make any changes in his habits, whatever the risks he was running might be. I didn't share this view, but all the same I wasn't about to start moralizing."

Yourcenar found herself grappling on the one hand with Wilson, whose state grew progressively worse from mid-February on, and on the other hand with Daniel, who was constantly in need of money. Yet again, much later on, she related the incidents this situation gave rise to with a singular placidity, something almost akin to indifference: "Suddenly Jerry and Daniel would ask me how much money I had in my bag. And Daniel would take all the bills." One day the young man was arrested and Yourcenar herself had to go to the police station to get him out of jail. She was inspired by this episode in *Quoi? L'Eternité,* transposing it into the story of Jeanne de Vietinghoff, her husband, and her husband's friend Franz, when the latter is "charged with possessing and trafficking drugs." "The white powder, and the vials and syringes that went along with it, and the hemp resembling ground up tobacco disappeared amid sounds of toilet flushing; they also threw away some aphrodisiac tablets, which Jeanne had never allowed him to use for her. Not a word of blame passed her lips; she knew simply that one of the things she had feared had come to pass, and could just as easily have done so in Paris as in Rome. But Egon's anguish tortured her."[24] When she told Dee Dee Wilson the story of this terrible Indian winter, speaking, as always, as if all of it were thoroughly normal, Dee Dee reacted with "What saves you in the end is that you use it all as material for your books." And Yourcenar emitted her sole and definitive commentary: "Why of course."

IN INDIA, moreoever, in order to escape from a frequently sordid reality, she would write. "In the midst of the confusion of the final days," she explained, "I set to work fervently on *Quoi? L'Eternité,* which I now seem to have under control. For the moment I am setting aside *Le Tour de la prison;* I have reached the final pages on Japan and I cannot continue it in India; some distance is needed from what is right here in front of my eyes and from this slightly different exoticism. Michel and Jeanne, on the other hand, are in my bones."

Jerry was no longer fit to go on with the journey that would have taken them to Nepal. He returned to the United States on 17 March and was immediately hospitalized. The doctors confirmed his suspicions regarding his illness. Jerry knew that he was going to die. Twenty-two March would be his thirty-sixth and final birthday. He spent it in the Bar Harbor hospital, the same one in which Yourcenar would later die. As had been the case with Frick not so long before, the strange relationship that Jerry Wilson had for five years carried on with Marguerite Yourcenar gave way to what she described as "a growing animosity toward me."

From early May, at which time Wilson left the island for New York, until his death in February, Yourcenar lived through some months that had little rhyme or reason, especially for a woman her age: she was eighty-two years old on 8 June 1985. When people in town found out the truth about Wilson's illness, the housekeeper who had worked for years at Petite Plaisance refused to go back there. And no one could be found to replace her. Dee Dee Wilson, whom Yourcenar dubbed at that time "the Indispensable," remembers how she "tried to reason with all those women. But there was a kind of hysteria surrounding that illness and how contagious it was that ruled out the possibility of rational argument."

There were days when Jerry Wilson, who was hospitalized in New York, then in Arkansas where his family lived, fell prey to fits of rage. At other times he was simply a lost child. He would telephone Yourcenar, sometimes crying, and make her read long passages from *Suicide mode d'emploi* [Suicide, a User's Manual]. "It was trying, but I understood his desire not to endure that illness, whose outcome he knew, any longer" she confided. "I understand people trying to die a good death." "His mind entirely healthy, handsome in spite of how tragically thin he had become, dying from an illness rooted in the passions he had always indulged himself in ardently, Jerry died, essentially, the way he had lived. I shall never forget the end of one of our last conversations on the telephone. He said to me: 'Don't think of it as a great misfortune, think of it as a great experience.'"

Happily, Yourcenar received a few visitors, among them Colette and Claude Gallimard, at the end of June. In order "to keep from foundering," she tried to carry on writing *Quoi? L'Eternité.* But she made very little progress. And the book remained unfinished when she herself died, despite her unremitting work after Wilson's death.

Wilson came back to Petite Plaisance from 5 through 9 September, before leaving for Paris, where he would undergo a new treatment. Jean-Pierre Corteggiani, who was visiting Yourcenar at the time, moved to a room in the nearest hotel. "She was nervous and worried," he remembers. "She was afraid of seeing this young man again who was dying, afraid of how he often got exasperated with her, afraid of the sudden fits of rage he might have. But she retained her incredible capacity to face up to anything, to accept all the ups and downs of life." Barely ten days later, on 18 September, she had a heart attack. "I think I was drained," she said, "by that very difficult year." From the Bar Harbor hospital, where she had been rushed by ambulence, she was transferred to Bangor, on the mainland, then to Boston where she underwent quintuple coronary bypass surgery on 9 October. As soon as Jerry Wilson found out she was ill, he came to be with her, on 30 September—though he knew that he himself was doomed. And this should prompt one to abstain from any hasty conclusions regarding their complex relationship. "I don't think I would have made it without that friendly presence." Yourcenar wrote to her half nephew.[25] In her preface to *La Voix des choses,* she related an incident from one of Wilson's first visits to the hospital, which provides an explanation for the title of this collection dedicated to his memory: "Jerry Wilson, who had arrived two or three days earlier from Paris to look after me, though he himself was ill, placed in my hands the handsome piece of malachite that I had haggled over on several occasions, in 1983 and 1985, in New Delhi in hopes of giving it to him as a gift. I had finally given it to him on the previous 22 March, for his birthday, when he himself was hospitalized in Maine. He hadn't been without it since. But no doubt my hands were weak, or I myself was dozing off a little, for I felt something slip: a slight noise, fatal and irreparable, woke me from my sleep.... The sound it made meeting its end was itself a lovely one ... 'Yes,' he said, 'the voice of things.'"[26]

AFTER YOURCENAR was taken on 19 October to the hospital on Mount Desert Island, Wilson returned to Paris, on the twentieth. Yourcenar and he would not see one another again. On 28 October Yourcenar was able to come home from the hospital, though in a very weakened state. She could not get up the stairs, so a bed was installed in one of the downstairs rooms. She convalesced to the rhythm of Jerry Wilson's worsening condition, in Paris, of questions concerning apartments for rent, security deposits needing to be forwarded to landlords, a variety of money problems. All the while she was trying to work on the manuscript of *Quoi? L'Eternité,* the only proof in her eyes that she was not merely a sick old woman.[27]

Jerry Wilson died on 8 February 1986 in Paris, at the Laënnec hospital. Like Hadrian with whom, as we have seen, she sometimes identified herself, seeing Wilson, in a way, as Antinous, she had been abandoned by her young companion. During the time she had left to live, time devoted to a lengthy journey, a strange pilgrimage to the sites she and Wilson had visited together, no doubt she would not fail to reflect on this observation, made by Hadrian after the death of Antinous: "Even my remorse has gradually become a form of possession, though bitter, and a way of assuring myself that, to the end, I have been the sorry master of his destiny."[28]

21

The Final Journey

WITH JERRY GONE, Marguerite Yourcenar felt old and infinitely tired.[1] Despite her indifference now regarding the "time [she] had left," she remained the woman nonetheless who, finding a thought jotted down haphazardly in a notebook—"I believe that I have finally succeeded at totally destroying the *avidity* within myself"—had written in the margin: "1980. No."[2] Thus she wrote, at the end of March: "Since I am, little by little, regaining my strength, I plan to be in Europe as of 20 April."[3] She arrived in Amsterdam as planned on 20 April accompanied by Stanley Crantson, a longtime friend of Jerry Wilson's, and Monicah, the Kenyan nurse she had liked so much during her hospitalization in 1983.

Before going to Bruges for a few days she made a detour through Brussels, wanting to meet with the filmmaker André Delvaux who, for several years, had hoped to make a film based on *The Abyss,* and who by that time was quite far along in his plans. Yourcenar, who wasn't familiar with Delvaux's films, was "very favorably impressed" by "that refined and cultured man, possessed of a great feeling for literature." She wanted him to be the one to film *The Abyss.* She would never see the film, whose chiaroscuro effects and mixture of violence and delicacy she would have liked, but she closely followed all the stages of its progress, through the end of her life.[4]

Delvaux remembers how gratified he was "to see how that woman, so remote from the world of the cinema, had understood perfectly the problems involved in transposing the written word to the screen, how she sensed what was and was not possible, where it was appropriate to stick as close as possible to the text, and where it was necessary to reinterpret." "We had reached a perfect agreement, persuaded as we both were that the film could only deal with the end of Zeno's life, with, of course, a few flashbacks. As we were talking about the beginning of the film, she came up, spontaneously, with the idea I was going to propose, of starting with Zeno's return to Bruges, in a carriage, with the Prior of the Cordeliers. It was a pleasure to meet with her or write to her, for she truly paid attention. She would give herself over entirely to what one had to say."[5] Yourcenar had approved the choice of Gian Maria Volonte, who was a feverish, fiery Zeno, but with that "mute being of the depths" quality she had spoken of in a letter to Delvaux. In that letter she had sketched a portrait of Zeno, citing lines of poetry from Empedocles that she had translated in *La Couronne et la lyre.* "Over the course of the Ages, I have been the boy and the girl / the tree, the winged bird, and the mute being of the depths."[6] The "mute being of the depths" is the fish (she had made Zeno come into the world under the sign of Pisces), silent even when, out of its element, it dies.[7]

In Paris, where she arrived on 3 May, she decided, after much hesitation, to stay at the Ritz. About that hotel she would say with a twinkle in her eye: "for old people, still convalescing, like myself, it can take the place of a rest home. It's a bit expensive, of course. But what quiet, right in the middle of the city! And they'll serve you soft-boiled eggs—or whatever you want—at all hours." It was not so much, however, for these amenities that she had chosen the Ritz as it was to retrace the footsteps of Jerry, who had twice attempted suicide while staying there. "There was something morbid about that trip," remembers Crantson. "Madame wanted to follow Jerry's tracks right down to every last detail. To see everything. To fix the places firmly in her memory." This had always been indispensable to her in order "to recover the story." Thus, after seeing the room at the Ritz in which Wilson stayed, on several occasions, Yourcenar had wanted to visit the room at the Laënnec Hospital where he died, and then the Père-Lachaise crematorium where his remains were incinerated.

She spoke of none of this, nor of her fatigue, in her "official" life, which found her having lunch on 13 May at Claude Gallimard's with François Mitterrand, president of France, whom she respected less for his talents as a politician (about which she was not really very well informed) than because he had read her books.[8] As she often did after this type of "ceremonial meal," in her phrase, she made sharp, ferocious comments about the guests and what they had to say, and about their attempts—carried "to the point of stupidity"—to attract the attention of the French president, who, she said, "surely can't be taken in."

Why did she then go to Austria? To see cities again from far-off times in her memory, such as Salzburg and Innsbruck? To join Zeno and Grace Frick, to seek out their traces, as several weeks earlier in Bruges she had persistently searched for the street where she had walked the dog Valentine in days gone by? First of all, without a doubt, she went to "be somewhere else." She had a specific reason for going to Italy: she wanted to see her friend Paolo Zacchera again. And in Geneva, Switzerland, she was going to visit Jorge Luis Borges, at the hotel where he was staying before moving into a new apartment. She came back from this visit very moved. "I found him pale, tired [he died on 14 June 1986], but so present, so attentive," she confided on returning to Paris at the beginning of June. "I went to see his new apartment, so I could describe it to him [Borges was blind]. It could have come out of one of his books. A curious place. With mirrors. I didn't describe to him the things I disliked about the decor. Then we talked. I asked him when he would get out of this labyrinth, and he answered: 'when everyone gets out.' After such all too brief moments with people one admires, one always regrets the things one has not had time, or the presence of mind, to ask. How I wish I had asked him to comment on a sentence of his that I cannot get out of my head: 'a writer thinks he's talking about many things, but what he leaves behind, if he's lucky, is an image of himself.'"

Back at Petite Plaisance, in mid-June, she did not believe she would make it through the summer. "With Jerry, I had grown used to the delight of speaking my own language all day long," she would say, "and suddenly I had to wait for friends to drop by in order to do so." She was so genuinely tired that her hypochondria had gone away. Rather, if she didn't feel well, she tried to ignore it. She felt very much alone. Utterly alone. But her profound will to live, which had allowed her to overcome all of the discouragements, and which stemmed from her desire to keep writing, was stronger than anything else. She went back to writing *Quoi? L'Eternité*, which she decided to extend as far as 1939, rather than stopping in 1937, in order to be able to include her meeting with Frick and talk about the immediate prewar period. "After that, I don't know," she would invariably respond. "If I am granted the time to, perhaps I shall continue, in another volume."

How could she get back to Europe? Stanley Crantson was no longer free, nor Monicah. Nonetheless, she had to find a way, "for as of now spending a winter here is unthinkable," Yourcenar asserted with some urgency. She asked Janet Hartlief, a young Dutch nurse she corresponded with, if she would care to accompany her. Hartlief accepted. They met up with one another on 11 November in Amsterdam, where Yourcenar had traveled in the company of Dee Dee Wilson. After a stay of ten days or so, during which she saw her publisher, Johan Polak, again, as she did "each time with the very same pleasure," Yourcenar went with Hartlief to Zurich, where she saw Egon de Vietinghoff again one last time. Seeking material, as always, for *Quoi? L'Eternité*, she noted, as she did every time they met, that his memory was "very sketchy."

The month of December, a studious one, was spent in Paris. Yourcenar worked with Yannick Guillou, to whom she had submitted the first half of *Quoi? L'Eternité* and with whom she was working on what would be the last volume published during her lifetime, *La Voix des choses*. She left Paris on 27 December for Morocco, where she spent two full months, one of them in the south with Jean-Marie Grénier, an old friend of Jerry Wilson's who was now a friend of hers: they traveled together, notably, to Ouarzazate, Zagora, Agdz, and Aït-Benhaddou. "In January in Fez," remembers Christian Lahache, another friend of Grénier's, who with Hartlief had gone on part of this Moroccan tour, "an incident occurred that frightened us all, except for the victim herself, Marguerite Yourcenar. She was absolutely determined to go to the medina, as she was looking for a particular kind of candle she and Jerry had liked very much. She wanted to burn some on the anniversary of Jerry's death.[9] She hadn't noticed that the streets where she was walking, in the medina, were sloped, because she was going downhill. Nor had Janet and I paid any attention to this. Since she had a very hard time finding the place where the candles were sold, she covered a lot more terrain than she should have. When it came time to go back, that is, to climb uphill, she was having difficulty walking. Suddenly she stopped. She was short of breath and couldn't take another step. Her lips were purple, her face white, her nostrils pinched. Curiously, she didn't show any concern whatsoever. We, on the other hand, had no idea what to do. Finally, a man who was headed in the same direction with his cart offered to help us get out of the medina. We heaved Marguerite Yourcenar, half-unconscious, into the cart, which attempted to plough its way through while some curious children, drawn to the spectacle, followed behind shouting 'old mama is sick, old mama is sick.' We took her back to the hotel, and put her to bed. She recovered quite quickly. During that trip, she never complained."[10] She even laughed telling the story of how she almost died "while [she] was sleeping": "One night, I was dropping off into a very sweet sleep, when I was wakened with a start by Janet shaking me, and by cold air coming in from outside. Janet had thrown open the window. Coming into the room, she had discovered that the stove was giving off carbon dioxide and that I was in the process of suffocating."

IN MOROCCO as in Paris, where she spent a month beginning on 8 March, Yourcenar worked with a certain feverishness on *Quoi? L'Eternité*, but also on the lecture she was to give at Harvard on Borges in May.[11]

This neither prevented her from seeing friends nor from receiving Delvaux once again to talk about his film. When she left Paris for England, in early April, she felt much better than she had the year before. She who had left the city in June 1986 telling herself she wouldn't be back intended to return in the fall. But she would not see Paris again, and she was also seeing London for the last time. In the company of Carlos Freire, a Brazilian photographer living in Paris and one of her new friends, she attended the changing of the guard, as she had with her father in another time. Freire's photographs on that day show an old woman overwhelmed for a moment, before whose eyes seventy-three years of memories are passing by. Then she pulls herself together again and her face regains its serenity.

At Petite Plaisance, where she arrived in late April, everything had been arranged by Dee Dee Wilson and Jeannie Lunt so that daily life would be as easy as possible for her. "Everything is perfect," said Yourcenar, "a whole team of women are looking after me, taking care of the housework and the errands, and staying here so I don't have to spend the night alone in the house. Sometimes, though, I don't even know who is going to be here at night. All the same, it's a little trying. And then we don't have much to say to one another." As for talking about what she was writing or had written, she had to confine herself to Dee Dee Wilson's visit, in the morning; as for speaking French, which became more and more an incessant obsession for Yourcenar, she had to wait for telephone calls from Paris or Cairo, or visits, which in her view were always too short—while most of her visitors cut their stays short for fear of imposing. "My calendar is hopelessly devoid of engagements," she confided over the telephone. After Yannick Guillou's visit in June there was nonetheless that of Carlos Freire and his wife Héloïsa, and several others, Jean-Marie Grénier's and Jean-Pierre Corteggiani's among them. Corteggiani recalls how intensely she was working on *Quoi? L'Eternité* every day: "When she was in the garden, you could watch her from a distance. Such powers of concentration as she displayed are extremely rare. She could sit down anywhere, and write on her knees. Sometimes she would throw some pages away, but she hardly ever crossed anything out. She could interrupt what she was doing to say a few words to whoever might be in the vicinity. Then she went back to her work, spiriting herself away."

As of the end of September, Yourcenar thought life would be less dismal, as she had managed to organize her winter trip. She would not content herself this time with returning to countrysides traversed with Wilson or Frick. She would go to Nepal to see the January flowers in bloom. Her itinerary was almost entirely laid out in advance: Amsterdam, Copenhagen, Belgium, Paris, then Zurich and the flight to India on 22 December. She spent the last days of September in Quebec, as she had promised Yvon Bernier she would. He came by car to pick her up at Petite Plaisance. Dee

Dee Wilson went with them. "For the first time, I was really worried," she says. "You could see on Madame's face how tired she was. Not only was she exhausted from the long hours we spent on the road, without stopping, but the official side of her visit to Quebec also put a heavy burden on her. I was saying to myself: 'This old woman is sick and no one seems to realize it. They're making her talk too much, treating her as if she were fit as a fiddle, when, in fact, her resistance has been pushed to the limit.' She herself felt they weren't taking her age into account, that, since she was there, they felt compelled to 'make the most' of the situation. She was worn out by the time she got back to Petite Plaisance." Nonetheless at Harvard on 14 October, she enjoyed finally giving her lecture on Borges, "which went marvelously well," and she was happy to be leaving once again.

The bags were packed one more time. An 11 November departure was arranged, and her friends were informed that, beginning on the twelfth, they could call her at the Hôtel de l'Europe in Amsterdam. On the calendar that Yourcenar was going to take with her on this trip, she had written down all her plans through the end of the year. The entries made between the eleventh and the fifteenth were crossed out, Crantson having postponed their departure for a few days due to his mother's ill health. Afterward, one finds: "6–9 December, Copenhagen: Yannick, Josyane"—she was also scheduled to deliver her lecture on Borges again there. Then "19 December [in English]: leaving Paris for Zurich." "22 December [still in English]: leaving for India."

Since the middle of October and her lecture at Harvard, Yourcenar had been complaining of pain in her back. She had even written "back trouble" down on 16–17 October. She also said, during almost every telephone conversation, that she was suffering from persistent headaches. This time no one was attributing these symptoms to hypochondria, and everyone, beginning with Dee Dee Wilson, was urging her to see a doctor. But, like a good hypochondriac, she made almost no distinction between minor ills, which she amplified, and more serious afflictions, which she overcame "with an uncommon force of character," as all the people who had never heard her talk about her colds were wont to say.

Still, on 7 November Wilson, arriving for the morning bath, found Yourcenar extremely fatigued. "It seemed to me that she was having a little trouble keeping her balance. And she was talking about not having slept well the night before, like someone who wasn't quite awake. This confusion worried me. I had noticed it certain mornings, but Madame would pull herself together so quickly that no one I talked to, except Jeannie, would believe that her age had finally caught up with her. And reading her last book, written up until her last night, it's still hard to believe, as I well know. But the facts are there." So on this Saturday the seventh, Wilson doggedly insisted on taking Yourcenar to the doctor. Her argument that it was a good idea to "check everything out before leaving for Europe" ended up carrying the day.

"That day, she gave me yet another example," remembers Wilson with emotion, "of her strength of character, her stubbornness, her dignity, everything that made me believe, as all her friends did, that she was indestructible, even though, from where I stood, I could see better than anyone else the progressive, irremediable impairments and ravages brought on by old age." "The doctor very quickly suspected that if there was any one threat that she faced, it was a stroke. I had informed him of the equilibrium problem and the slight mental confusion. He asked Madame to walk. I saw her stand up, straighten her back as she always did, assume the dominating, ceremonious posture that we all were so familiar with but that never failed to impress us, and proceed, very erect, to the back of the room. When she got to the wall, all she said, with just a hint of provocation, was 'and now, would you like me to turn around?' The doctor then began an interrogation of sorts, to test her memory. She sidestepped his questions constantly, with a kind of arrogance, malice, and irony you couldn't help admiring. For example, when he asked, 'Madame Yourcenar, can you tell me your date of birth?' she answered, 'And you, can you give the emperor Hadrian's date of birth? I, for my part, can.' Having said this, she gave no date at all."

The doctor insisted that she stay in the hospital for observation, and spend at least one night there. She refused. "Her decision was final," Wilson states. "Sick at heart, I brought her back to Petite Plaisance. Her attitude seemed irrational to me. But no one could have made her change her mind."

The next morning, Sunday, 8 November, when Wilson entered Petite Plaisance shortly after seven o'clock, as she did every day, Yourcenar could not conceal her exhaustion. She hadn't slept a wink all night. "I suggested that she stay put. She agreed to let me wash her in bed. Then she went to sleep. I didn't want to go back home until she had woken up. I came in, at regular intervals, every ten minutes at the most, to see how she was doing. On my third or fourth visit, I saw that she had just had a stroke. The ambulance came very quickly, but, just the same, if she had spent the night at the hospital as we had urged her to, we wouldn't have lost as much time." On 8 November 1987, eighty-seven years to the day after the marriage of Michel de Crayencour and Fernande de Cartier de Marchienne, their daughter, Marguerite de Crayencour, born on 8 June 1903, had begun to surrender her life. But over the long course of that life, she had become Marguerite Yourcenar, an admired, then a celebrated, writer. And over the last several years, she had survived so many incidents, accidents, illnesses, and tragedies that no one was willing to look at that stroke as the beginning of the end.

At the hospital, when she regained consciousness, she was alternately lucid and confused, "which is not very surprising in a case like this," Doctor Robert Wilson confirms. "But when a patient remains in this state for more than forty-eight hours, there is reason to fear that the lesions are irremediable." "*I* believed at one point that we had won the battle," Dee Dee Wilson relates. As I was trying to explain to her, for at least the tenth time without her seeming to understand, that she had been unwell and was in the hospital, she sat up, irritated, and hurled at me abruptly: 'That's the third time you've told me this, which seems sufficient to me.' I thought she was back to her normal self. I was wrong."

On 11 November, then over the following days, Dee Dee Wilson talked with Yannick Guillou, in Paris, every morning and tried to be reassuring. But she who only left "Madame's" bedside to go home to sleep already knew that "Marguerite Yourcenar" had "died." That enormous intellect, without yet foundering completely, had come apart. She who "talked like an open book," as the gardener, Elliot, would say, she whom one could listen to for hours, for she imparted such a singular expression and tonality even to trivial things, had only one battle left to fight: that of dying with dignity, and, as she always had wanted to, with open eyes.

She had forgotten, by this time, the sentence from *Dear Departed* where her end had nonetheless been foretold. She was simply in the process of living it: "The child [she herself, at birth], who does not yet know (or who no longer knows) what a human face is, sees, bending over her, great indistinct orbs that move about and produce sounds. In the same way, many years later, she will perhaps see bending over her the faces of the doctor and nurses, blurred this time by the confusion of her death agony."[12]

For the first two weeks, Dee Dee Wilson attempted to pacify Yourcenar's French friends, while at the same time gently but firmly dissuading them from coming to Mount Desert Island. "She alternates between spells of lucidity and confusion. But physically, she is on the mend. She gets up, she walks to the end of the corridor. Just wait awhile and you'll be able to visit her again. But if you came now, she would never forgive you for seeing her in such an extremely feeble state, not entirely lucid and helpless." In fact, the spells of lucidity were dreadful, with Yourcenar summoning the doctors and demanding that "they get this over with, that they put an end to this state of affairs, which made no sense, immediately," and her spells of mental confusion were often moments of violence and anger.

In Paris, it had been decided that nothing would be said about what was happening on Mount Desert. Guillou, canceling all of Yourcenar's appointments, said only that her departure had been put off because she was feeling a bit unwell. After the disgraceful photograph of Salvador Dali—bedridden, emaciated, loaded down with catheters and tubes—that had just been on the cover of *Le Figaro Magazine,* there was every reason to fear the small-time "scoop" mongers' rapaciousness and morbidity. But at the Bar Harbor hospital, Dee Dee and Jeannie were keeping watch. In spite of this, an Academician—Maurice Schumann—who, for family reasons, knew someone on Mount Desert, got wind of what was going on. He informed his colleagues, as is customary. In keeping with the exquisite delicacy of which it had shown itself capable with Yourcenar, the Académie began spreading the rumor that she had a "terminal" illness. She was "already in a coma," they knowingly asserted.

There was no coma, however. On the contrary, after two weeks of being ill, "Madame was, physically, as well as a person could be after suffering that kind of attack," Dee Dee Wilson relates. But she was also in a state of total mental confusion, which, in her case, was more dreadful still. "She no longer recognized us. But she calmed down, finally, and even when she was delerious, she was fascinating. She would tell stories from her travels, sometimes in English, sometimes in French; she would imagine herself at the theater and comment on the play, approving, applauding. Yet again, she was unique, unlike any other woman, even out of her head. She still spoke as beautifully as before, and what she said was coherent. It simply wasn't in touch with reality anymore." Yourcenar was no longer the creator she had been; she was a character now: all distance was abolished.

This strange madness that everyone got swept up in, which was linked to the power of her speech, blocked out the "discourse of reason" that all, at the outset, had agreed on: "If she is no longer Marguerite Yourcenar, perhaps it would be better for 'things' not to go on for very long." Once again, literature won. Looked at today, from a distance, those two weeks of "peaceful delerium," in Dee Dee Wilson's way of putting it, seem unreal. Yourcenar, as usual, had imposed herself on those around her. For Dee Dee Wilson and all of us who spoke with her, the conversations we had back then are now almost beyond belief. After giving us news about the patient's physical health, Dee Dee Wilson would tell us Yourcenar's stories, without anyone finding this incongruous: "Today she was in Japan . . . she had gotten lost in the city with Jerry. No one wanted to help them find their way."

"She was attending a theatrical performance, Mishima's *Madame de Sade;* she applauded a great deal." When *La Voix des choses* arrived at the hospital—ironically, a little collection containing the quotations she had carried with her like talismans throughout her life—she began translating the texts for the nurses, who would look at the book when they came in to check on her.

"When she saw the book," remembers Dee Dee, "she identified it perfectly. She held it close, brought it to her lips. She was happy, she smiled that magnificent smile we knew so well. And yet, she was still incapable of putting my name together with my face and continued to say to me: 'You can ask Dee Dee . . .' When I would protest 'But I *am* Dee Dee,' she invariably answered 'I know, but I'm talking about the other Dee Dee.' Needless to say, there was no other Dee Dee."

For all of the people who had spent any time with Marguerite Yourcenar during the last years, one thing was obvious. Lucid or not, if she was going to die soon, she needed to hear someone speaking French. After four weeks of hospitalization, her physical condition was stable, and quite good. But there was no way to tell what might happen. Still, they were thinking about letting her out of the hospital and were waiting for a room to open up in a nursing home. There they would be able to bring her things from Petite Plaisance in the hope that an irruption of objects from her personal universe would, if not bring her back to reality, which seemed by now beyond the realm of possibility, at least draw her closer to it, and, most of all, comfort her.

Yourcenar's Parisian friends were of differing views. Some thought that Yannick Guillou, who had been closest to her in the last months, should be the one to make his way to her bedside as quickly as possible. As soon as Dee Dee Wilson stopped dissuading him from coming, he left Paris—on Monday 14 December. But instead of taking the most direct route, he made a detour through Quebec, giving in to the pleas of Yvon Bernier. Though Guillou did not know Bernier very well, he had been in regular contact with him since Yourcenar's hospitalization, and he agreed to the suggestion that he "come pick him up" in Quebec. This idea, in the middle of a North American winter, was a singular one. And it was all the more inopportune in that Bernier had decided to travel to Mount Desert Island by car. Was he afraid of going there alone? Perhaps. For, as Yourcenar was fond of repeating—and we all have seen proof in our own lives—social evolution has had almost no effect on one ancestral sentiment: watching over the sick and the dying is "a matter for women." In the face of illness or death, men are nearly always, if not helpless, at least prey to a curious discomfort.

Arriving in Quebec, Guillou was told that Yourcenar's secretary had asked them not to set out immediately, but to wait a day. Which they did. When they finally did leave Quebec, they were caught in a snowstorm and unable to make it to the island until Wednesday night.

In the meantime, the situation had worsened considerably. Two days earlier, Yourcenar had developed an "absolutely monstrous" case of facial edema, according to Dee Dee Wilson, probably resulting from a certain medication. "In thirty-five years of nursing, I had never seen such a thing. Since I was alone at her bedside, of course I was the one the doctors asked to make a decision: do we give her morphine, with all its well-known effects, or do we wait? I just did not know what to do and was feeling overwhelmed by this responsibility. When Madame said suddenly: 'I shall not tolerate this excruciating pain in my throat.' So we started giving her morphine. As the dying often do, she had regained her lucidity and she had made the decision to get it over with as quickly as possible, refusing everything we tried to get her to drink."

When Guillou and Bernier arrived at the Bar Harbor hospital, on Thursday morning, 17 December, everyone there knew that Marguerite Yourcenar had one or two days, at the very most, left to live. "As soon as I saw her, midway through the morning, I knew that I was in the presence of a dying woman," remembers Guillou.[13] "When she recognized me, she smiled that smile of hers, always such a youthful one, and, at that precise moment, it was breathtaking. As soon as I began to speak, in French of course, I saw an expression as if of relief spread over her face, almost a look of happiness."

Contrary to what she had expected, especially over the last three days, since she had begun to feel herself succumbing, she was hearing someone speak her language, before death came to take her—the language that had made her a writer, the language that assured her a posterity; the only thing, deep down, that she had loved without a moment of doubt. Her language had allowed her to escape from everything and everyone, to survive whatever came her way, to live until the end the same human life that she had once maintained "was not necessarily a stroke of good luck." She who would say that, at her birth, she had just missed having "the luck not to exist"[14] had been enduringly saved, not by the doctor who, no doubt, at Fernande's bedside had chosen the child over the mother, but by her absolute love for a language whose legacy she wanted to pass on and perpetuate, by the certainty, forged in adolescence, that she would earn a place in the lineage of great "crafters" of that language, by her fascination with understanding and experiencing everything, in the process of putting it into words. She had thereby escaped the temptation that for a long time had haunted her, one that represented, in her eyes, the supreme expression of human liberty: the act of taking back, by one's own will, a life that has been given one by chance.

She had given that liberty to Zeno, who decided to kill himself in his Bruges prison cell, and it was as if she had taken it herself:

> And nevertheless his decision had been taken: he recognized it less in indications of lofty courage and sacrifice than in some indefinable, blind refusal which seemed to close him off like a block from outside influences, and almost from sensation itself. Thus installed in his own ending he was already Zeno *in aeternum.*
>
> On the other hand, and placed, so to speak, in reserve behind the resolution to die, there was another, more secret resolve which he had carefully concealed from the Canon, that of dying by his own hand.[15]

Unlike Zeno, however, she had resolved to write "until the moment the pen falls from my hands. Time will tell."[16] She said this in *Archives du Nord,* where she gives a brief sketch of her life:

> The child who just arrived at Mont-Noir is a socially privileged being; she will continue to be. She has not experienced cold or hunger, at least she has not done so up until now, as I sit writing these lines. . . . [S]he will not, except over the course of seven or eight years at the very most, "earn her living" in the monotonous, everyday sense of this expression; she has not, like millions of beings in her time, been subjected to forced labor in a concentration camp, nor, like other millions of beings, who believe they are free, has she been pressed into the service of machines that spew forth strings of objects either useless or harmful, be they gadgets or armaments. She will scarcely be hindered, as so many women still are today, by the fact of being a woman, perhaps because it didn't occur to her that this should have been a hindrance. . . . She will fall down and get up again on her skinned knees; she will learn, not without something of an effort, to use her own eyes, then to keep them open wide, as divers do. . . . Her personal life, to the extent that this expression means anything, will go on as best it can in the midst of all this. The events of that life interest me above all as means of access whereby certain experiences came to affect it. It is for this reason, and for this reason alone, that I shall write them down perhaps one day, if I am granted the time, and if I feel the urge to do so.[17]

She did feel the urge and she was in the process of "writing down," in *Quoi? L'Eternité,* a few of the "events" of that existence—perhaps more than she had meant to at the outset—when illness, her last one, knocked the pen out of her hand. Submitting part of the manuscript, a few months earlier, to

Yannick Guillou, she had said to him in her uniquely euphemistic way: "From now on, even if I am 'obstructed,' you'll be able to go ahead and publish." Thus he alone was capable of assuring her a peaceful death, of making her see that, whatever her faith or her doubts, she had a future. On that morning of 17 December 1987, she no doubt understood only confusedly the things he said to her, and he did not understand even one of her words, which were already muffled and blurred by death. But each of them knew that everything was as it should be.

In the afternoon, when Guillou came back for a second visit, there was nothing left of Marguerite Yourcenar except the moribund shell of a being. She was beyond anyone's reach. The only thing left for anyone to do was pray, provided one knew how, then leave. Dee Dee Wilson went back to his hotel with him, but decided that she would return then to the hospital.

"Nothing had changed since our last visit," she says. "Madame was breathing softly, peacefully, not at all like a dying person. It looked as if she might go on this way through the night. Maybe even longer than that. Still, I wanted to stay with her. It was a strange feeling watching over that woman whom so many people loved without ever having seen her, whose death the whole world would soon be hearing about and commenting on, and who lay before my eyes, as if asleep, in little room 114 of the simple Bar Harbor hospital—simple like the little house she hadn't wanted to give up, on our island. I was not at her side merely because it's a nurse's job to be there at the final moment, if by some chance there should be no one else there. I was there because I loved her. I thought about the curious thing she had said when she had understood that she was going to die: 'There *must* be a paradise somewhere.' Was she praying to that God whose existence she questioned, 'whoever it is that he is,' as she would always say? I saw myself again at Grace's bedside, eight years earlier, with the delicate sound of the little music box in the silence of the house. But this time, Madame was not keeping watch alongside me. She was the one who was dying and I refused to accept it. Two days earlier I had said to one of her friends from Paris who wanted to know if 'it was over': 'for anyone else besides her I would say yes, but with her, you never know.'"

"Professionally, I was well aware, as the night wore on, that it was only a matter of a few hours. But I didn't want to hear what my experience was telling me. I looked at her, so calm. There was no noise, no death rattle."

"Suddenly Madame drew in a great breath of air. It was nine thirty at night when Marguerite Yourcenar opened her eyes for the last time, and kept them open. Still just as blue, and just as clear. I would be the last person to see them. I was also the one who had to close them, and perform a final gesture, in memory of her, in memory of what we had gone through together on the eighteenth of November 1979, eight years and one month earlier, minus a day, at nine o'clock at night." As Marguerite Yourcenar had done for Grace Frick, Dee Dee Wilson opened the window, waited for a moment—the air outside was freezing—and closed it again.

Mademoiselle de Crayencour, at eighty-four years of age, had just brought to a close the life of a singular fictional character, one who was going to survive her, by a long time perhaps: Marguerite Yourcenar.

Marguerite Yourcenar, for her part, was merging with the title of the book she would not get to finish: eternity—or nothingness, which, as she would have said, is perhaps the same thing. Dee Dee Wilson, like everyone else, didn't know yet that she had left behind, as this book's final sentence, an allusion whose irony she would have liked: "The telegram that he had sent the night before arrived after he did."

Appendixes

APPENDIX 1

Sonnet

This sonnet, referred to in chapter 3, was written by Marguerite Yourcenar for her governess, Camille Debocq, at Christmas 1915. Letot Collection, Gallimard Archives.

In the silver goblet or in the urn of clay
The eternal fragrance of the tenderest bloom
Remains ever the same enervating and frail
Conserving its strength it retains its sweet perfume

The indispensable urn will not retain its liquor
If the goblet is cracked it trickles meekly away
To find in another vase a comfortable jail
Retaining as of old its strange savor

What, my admiration, which I've said to be immortal,
Should have shattered the ideal, the sap of life maternal
For having shattered some dream long void of substance?

If I take this or that amphora and into it pour
My whole divine dream, or if I tip it o'er
Another goblet hosts the glorious fragrance!

European Diagnosis

This text, referred to in chapter 4, "I, the Undersigned, Marguerite Yourcenar," was published in June 1929 (when Marguerite Yourcenar was twenty-six years old) in issue 68 of the *Bibliothèque Universelle et Revue de Genève,* pp. 745–52. Following the text appear the handwritten comments that Marguerite Yourcenar wrote on the first page of the article, quite probably sometime after the seventies.

The threat of locomotor ataxia hangs over modern Europe.

He who would characterize faith should address himself to the Semites; mysticism has taken on its most perfect form among Indian sages benumbed by ecstasy; and moral doctrine in all of its guises, from military honor to worldly ceremonial, has never been codified better than in yellow Asia, in the Japan of the Samurais steeled by its warrior heroism. The only place intelligence in its pure state exists, if indeed it exists at all, is between the Baltic states and the Aegean Sea. Acclimated somewhere else, it still bears the mark of its origin. Whoever acquires it becomes Europeanized. Between the immense heart of Asia and the inexhaustible African womb, Europe has the function of a brain.

It is something other than science: a science, empirical it's true, can exist if need be without objective intelligence. It is something other than art, which has willingly gone without it. It is something other than piety, kindness, virtue, and all that is commonly referred to as wisdom. It is something more and better even than thought: logical thought. As other races say: Buddha, Confucius, Jesus, we say: Aristotle, Galileo, Bacon, Descartes, Spinoza, Claude Bernard. Today European reason is in danger of dying.

It has been ailing now for quite a while.

The truth is it has never had more than a precarious existence. Even in the best times—especially during the best times—it was still exceptional. The immense store of animal material, treated with more and more highly perfected processes, yielded only a comparatively small residue of intelligence. But that intelligence was sure of itself. The European mind could adopt an attitude of absolute skepticism with regard to things: such universal defiance merely confirmed it in its role as the unique and stable measure against which all else was gauged. From Socrates to Voltaire, intelligence did not doubt itself; it was faith that doubted. Everyone recalls how Pascal doubted. Today, European intelligence is beginning to doubt itself.

One could almost assign a date to the first signs of malaise. After the magnificent intellectual effort of the Renaissance, after the era of relative equilibrium that the seventeenth century was, occurred the admirable surge of free intellectualism that preceded and brought on the Revolution. It was around this time that the human mind, overtaxed, gave way.

Just as the French Revolution was only a prologue to future revolutions, just as the Napoleonic Wars were only the first act of a greater war of which the war of 1914 was perhaps only one episode, to the spectator placed at a distance of several centuries, modern writers would look like a strain of the Romantics. From Jean-Jacques [Rousseau] to Gide, from Chateaubriand to Claudel, the nuances that differentiate individuals would lose their importance—and an observer located far enough away to see only the whole would recognize in these dissectors of the suffering Ego the same predominance of feeling over reason, the same diffuse mysticism, the same preoccupation with moral doctrine or immoralism, and the same preponderance given to woman, or at least to the feminine. Jean-Jacques's thesis asserting that science and the arts do not contribute to man's happiness would lead Ruskin and Tolstoy to their final gospel of simplism. Half-conscious states in which feelings are confused with instincts would be ever more deeply probed from Balzac to Proust; the mechanism of instantaneous reactions, accelerated from Stendhal to Dostoyevsky, ended up reversing the order of its functioning, and, instead of transforming sensation into thought, it transformed thought into sensation. From Chateaubriand to Barrès, there is an ever-increasing refusal of culture. The ideal is no longer knowledge, it is hyperesthesia. Ideas and facts are only accepted to the degree they are in keeping with instinctive affinities. Loti claimed he never read; Barrès, visiting Greece, pretended to be less interested in Lacedaemonia than in the Frankish fortresses that reminded him of his race; Gide, an evangelical disparager of intelligence, looks to the heart's humility for the secret of the beatitudes. Whether nonbelievers or believers, anarchists or nationalists, they are what they are for reasons of sentiment in which reason plays no part. The years preceding 1914, date of the international warrior exhibition, saw that subjective fever exacerbate. It is reaching its paroxysm in the disorder of the present peace, which is no more than an unfinished war.

There is a kind of tragic beauty in this individualism, that of a world on the verge of dying. The old Romantic world-weariness is suffocating this great invalid, which only makes him become all the more desperately attached to life as it ebbs away. The traditional economy was not the only thing to disappear in the financial disaster; the entirety of civilization perceived that it was ceasing to be. What a strange spectacle it is, this machine whose gearwheels, warped by the catastrophe, have ground to a halt, or, disengaged, keep on spinning in the void. The popular expression is more accurate: spinning out of control.

Goethe's mind and Da Vinci's were firm while at the same time being nimble: the European mind by contrast is no longer firm, only nimble. There is a lack of solid ground beneath these builders of smoke, these analysts of fog. Intelligence has lost its capacity to discriminate and weigh: scales tipped, it has been thrown upon the scrap heap. We are witnessing a stupendous inflation of every fiduciary value: having sought to render the unconscious conscious, we have ended up granting to the unconscious a justified preponderance, but one acclaimed by our fatigue.

And the latter is immense. Ill-prepared minds are weighed down by the diversity of knowledge that there is to be acquired; our cultural frameworks, progressively expanded, have snapped. The strict Aristotelian and Catholic education of the past has molded more than one free thinker; its quality made up for what was lacking; by means of a few venerated texts, always the same ones, at least a method was imparted. All it took to make Descartes and Spinoza was Latin and mathematics. Today's prodigious vulgarizing effort—always hasty, often clumsy—made in books and in newspapers affords a vast, inexperienced majority the illusion of universal knowledge. Forgetting that the discipline of research, for cultivating the mind, is just as important as the results one obtains and sometimes more so, the masses stampeding into this laboratory open to all take a blind leap over methods, heading straight for the formulas. Unfortunately, when the latter are brutally pressed into service, turned into simple assertions, transplanted from the world of pure thought into that of circumstantial applications, they become warped. One thinks of delicate instruments of physics put to use in everyday life. Finance, politics, history, the literature of every age, of every race: the European brain, in the twentieth century, is as congested as our traffic intersections.

Certain minds assimilate this overwhelming abundance of material; most transform themselves into recording devices; others—and these are not the least healthy—regurgitate it. Never has the intellect, confronted with the brute facts, displayed so much weary passivity. While the spirit, given over to capricious sensations, ceases even to coordinate them, the mind, desperately seeking an ethic, reaches only to the level of mental gymnastics. In both instances, by way of reaction, it is the body that triumphs. All of them, each one in its turn, resort to mystical opiates. One wonders what the steadfast Christianity of the past would have thought of this mysticism. Paradise: but an artificial one. The body, and the spirit too: between the body and the innermost spirit, between instinct and the unconscious, reason is dying.

The futile efforts of an improvised moral code . . . Every philosophical conception of life is a legacy slowly accumulated by history. Every race, every century has one, and only one, that is its own: an attempt made by a group of men to adapt and resist. In our time, these legacies from different eras, the objects of interminable controversy, are overwhelming in their multiplicity. On this continent of Europe, which is painfully organizing itself into a unitary State, the past is an immense, disputed inheritance. Theories, those eternal antagonists, are performing for an audience of consciences a drama whose conclusion is skepticism. Whether they be traditionalists or open to persuasion, the combatants are wielding their beliefs as if they were clubs: living beings battering one another to death with dead bodies. All they are lacking, once the battle is won, is the capacity to resuscitate them.

And they would like to, frantically. Or rather, they would like to want to.

The less one believes, the more positive assertions one makes: this is a way of resigning oneself to not believing. On all sides, the artisans of thought are doing their best to take the rust off old formulas or forge new ones; all of them equally intransigent concepts, which end up resembling one another in the realm of the absurd. Nationalism, internationalism, Bolchevism, fascism, pacifism, the Asiatic dream of nonresistance to force, which is no more than an admission of being powerless to appropriate that force, a brutal materialism that glorifies might substituted for right, and is no more than an admission of being powerless to determine what is right. These concepts wend their way in the world, where they are distorted with a singular rapidity: the most contrary doctrines, in a moment of lucidity, end up finding themselves identical.

And so appears a long line of dabblers in the absurd, playing with the leftover fragments of a world. Every age of decadence can call itself an era of sophists and prophets. In Rome from Antoninus Pius to Romulus Augustulus, with its countryside emptied of people, its hypertrophied bureaucracy, and its ailing currency, while the authorities attempted to lower the high cost of living by means of ineffectual edicts, while dictators, clever or committed, haphazardly installed for no fathomable reason, obstructed an historical movement out of either stubbornness or arrogance, while people's associations, subversive entities, the original versions of the church and the commune, grew, as have today's unions or political cells, from underneath the vast legal organizations they would one day replace, while hordes in Asia could be heard slowly beginning to stir, though no one was paying much attention as yet, the scene was littered with Sophists and Prophets. It is an age of sophists, of paradoxical apologetics, of erotic biographies, of coterie poetry, of psychological novels for which all that is needed is subtlety, of adventure novels whereby the boredom of an overly calm existence is conveniently compensated for. It is an age of prophets: an age of public professions of faith and public confessions. From Russia to Spain, from Hungary to Norway, above the frightening brouhaha of the cities, never has a more unexpected concert of voices been raised to celebrate deprivation, inner peace, humility, God. Romain Rolland, biographer of Ghandi, Gide, translator of Rabindranath Tagore, Henri Barbusse, evangelist of Christ: the summits of an overwrought Europe are dimly lit by an Asian dawn.

Style, too, has been distorted in attempting to expand. Following the style of the brothers Goncourt, perpetually trembling like the flame of a gas lamp, came a dry writing seemingly electrified. Nietzsche, that admirable mirror of intelligence broken by madness, and Rimbaud, that smashed-in tavern window whose glittering splinters shine like diamonds in the night, bequeathed to their successors, in the first case, the secret of his insanity, minus that of his grandeur, and in the second, the secret of his anguish, minus that of his energy. An increasingly dissociated style is but one aspect of dissociated thinking, the brain's incapacity to reestablish a logical order of images. They ignite and fly out in fits and starts, like sparks from a broken-down motor that's on the verge of giving out completely. The loss that art suffers is above all that of composition. The style of Proust subdivided in the extreme, confusing by dint of its abundance, ceaselessly foundering in thoughts that are submitted to rather than directed, and the style of Breton, spasmodic and dry, full of thrusts and tensions, alternate like nervous prostration and excitement—a dynamism unique in Western literary history. It seems for us that life, perhaps because it slips through our fingers, perhaps because we are beginning to have doubts about it, contains in and of itself its own justification, its own confirmation: he who formerly watched others act is now learning to watch others live. The interest attached to children, whom classical art almost ignored, is a gauge of the ever-increasing role we are according to the unconscious and the unformed. Modern man, suddenly discovering how restricted is the field of consciousness, even organic consciousness, has set out to uncover the internal mechansim. Unfortunately, our consciousness, with its thoroughly utilitarian origins, still remains purely superficial, and deep introspection will seem abnormal and dangerous for a long while yet. The novel, which won't settle anymore for a ready-made humanity, oscillates between abulia and split-personality syndrome.

And round we go. Cinematographers have taught us about breaking down movement: novelists are imitating them; life, filmed by this one in slow motion, speeds up in the hands of a different cameraman. Foreign languages, a kind of knowledge that does nothing more than juxtapose and interchange words, end up eroding the distinctive value of every idea. The mind is adjusting its rhythm to that of a more and more agitated life; it works at speeds of a thousandth of a second. Art, once a slow creator, specializes now in the instantaneous. One might say that, in the last years of the nineteenth century, the European mind acquired the sensitivity of photographic film.

The poets, those guardians of thought's hereditary disciplines, are also breaking free, and their liberation has the appearance of a decline. An admirable instrument, crafted and tuned by the centuries, to which each generation has added its enhancements, is breaking in convulsive hands. Symbols of an intelligence accustomed to obeying itself, meter and rhythmics disindividualized the idea they enclosed in a neat, rigid, durable form, accessible to everyone's memory and consistent enough to resist any imprecise language. Modern aesthetics of thought, like those prevailing in the linear arts, whether out of a disdain for virtuosity or, perhaps, on account of fatigue, are lapsing back, as liberation follows liberation, into the troubling conventions of dying civilizations: sharply delineated colors, clumsy drawing, summary forms—fashion's bias confers upon feminine beauty the anemic, angular, rigid look of the Ravenna mosaics, to which the abdicating art of a century committed the image of the last patricians. The turbulence of life, exotic travels, the shocks transmitted to the brain by jolting sequences of cinematic images, and sensual obsessions or financial worries are fraying to shreds the nerves of an elite that no longer trusts in the future. From the laziness of employees to literary Hamletism, one finds the same agitated lassitude, using "agitated" in its medical sense, the same *anguish.* It is not so much pleasure that the modern novel depicts as the pursuit of pleasure. It is not so much suffering as the fear of suffering.

It is not so much sensuality—and this may be more striking still—as neurosis. And, punctuating the clamorous, fitful expressions of this amazing mortal agony, Afro-American music, a sudden burst of passion, is transporting to a barbaric world a world that is itself becoming barbaric again.

It is possible to deny the seriousness of the symptoms. But the only illness that a civilization eventually dies of is its duration. And ours is an old one. Several are the features that it shares with other old civilizations: a disparate appearance, as if it had been mended with patches of history; the weighty materialism of the many set off against the wild idealism of the few; a bloody-crisis humanitarianism; and wear-and-tear-embellishing refinements—in short, all that is pathetic about what cannot be salvaged. The danger of periods of decadence is that they make one view the classical eras as having been dull. And if I have said so much about our age being sick, it is only to reserve myself the chance to say at the end that it is beautiful.

That our successors will pay a price for our nervous expenditures is certain. So will we, perhaps. We are already paying. But a duly settled account gives us the right to enjoy such a diverse spectacle. It's not just anyone who wants to that gets the chance to witness the spectacle of a cultural consummation. Consummated, finished—the word contains at once the notion of perfection and that of an end. Rilke, Pirandello, Gide, all represent rather well the point of culmination we have reached. The age that follows ours, a disciplined, recuperative one, will surely be dismally boring. Let us not be too quick to assert that it will be better; this word has no place in a vocabulary that strives for precision, and we know that history swings back and forth between centuries of saving and years of spending. If every time of disorganization engenders a new discipline, every long-suffered discipline is a promise of anarchy to come. While we wait for other spendthrifts, several centuries after we are gone, to dissipate the riches accumulated by our successors, let us appreciate this chance to be the squanderers of a race. Ernest Renan said that being pope in an age of total corruption was one of the best numbers a person could draw in the lottery of the world. Perhaps there is one that's even better: being simply a witness. Let's enjoy this show that only gets billed two or three times a millennium—or rather, resigned in advance to the darkness that will follow, and grateful for our good fortune, let's go watch the fireworks finale of a world.

Handwritten Comments

Essay published in 1929 (*Revue de Genève*), written in 1928.

Like almost all glances cast upon the future, and even on the present, this one was wrong. The [description] of the writers of the time, for instance, Gide, is [wrong]. Had I even so much as read *Numquid et tu . . . ?* ("*Numquid et tu . . . ?*")?[1]

The predictions were wrong because I imagined that an era of discipline was coming next: on the contrary, it was a much more total chaos that proved true, one that made 1928 look like it was still a period of near stability. I had not been able to imagine: the ecological tragedy, appearing in the fifties, which would eclipse all the others. The monstrous political crimes and the genocides perpetrated by all countries; the breaking into pieces of cultures considered central; the horrifying wave of ineducation caused by the media and reinforced by a sense of "what's the point?" "there's no use."

APPENDIX 3

"Which affords one certain fleeting glimpses"

Unpublished excerpts from the handwritten text found in a notebook titled "Notes on 'Michel' to be used for *Quoi? L'Eternité,* parts of which have already been used for *Archives du Nord"* by Marguerite Yourcenar. Gallimard Archives. This text was referred to in chapter 4, "I, the Undersigned, Marguerite Yourcenar."

Walking around one day together in Antibes, in the old city, we were talking about something, I've forgotten what. We sat down on a bench, in front of a very old house in the Provençal style of the seventeenth or even the sixteenth century. Nostradamus's house in Salon is somewhat along the same lines. Michel was absorbed in his reflections. "Yes," he said dreamily, "one can imagine someone spending his whole life in a small town, alone, immersed in magic."

Another time, on the subject of how one might use one's last hours of life: "If I were on a boat run aground, which could not be set afloat again, and which was certain to sink within the hour, supposing there weren't any women on board, I would take a youth, a ship's boy."

I write these comments down only because I don't believe I ever saw Michel show the slightest interest in magic, nor, as far as he was concerned, in what is called homosexuality. It is true that, though he scorned adult inverts, he did not scorn pederasts. Nevertheless, the sentence that precedes is something that only a sensual man who passionately loves women would say. The boy would be a substitute, a last resort. This makes it no less a testimony to the extraordinary plasticity of desire, in a so-called "normal" man.

Another remark, made while watching me read one fine day: "If you died, I would take your books, your clothes, whatever is yours, and fill up a dinghy with everything; then I'd tow that dinghy out behind another boat and sink it all on the open sea." I was eighteen years old. My imagination was struck by that violent image, that Viking's sacrifice. But his thoughts were already somewhere else.

These glimpses bear all the signs of coming from unknown, unused parts of the being itself, perhaps from an ancestor, or perhaps from the obscure effluvium of some past life. Bearing no perceptible relation to the rest of the man.

During the years when I knew him, between the ages of fifty-five and seventy-five, he would faint, or nearly, at the sight of blood. (Two examples.)

During those years, in the event of an accident, an automobile collision, or a dog getting run over, he would make the involuntary gesture, for an instant, which is also my own in such cases, of plugging his ears, as if he were expecting a cry that he knew in advance he would not be able to bear.

The second movement—which one constrains oneself to—is to offer help.

Toward the end of his life, for the last four or five years, though he loved all animals passionately, Michel was afraid of big dogs. One day, a neighbor's German shepherd affectionately jumped up on his chest. I watched as his face grew pale, his legs wobbly. I in my turn have become the same way, at about the same age. Such are the effects of having a heart you can't count on anymore.

During the years, once again, when I knew him, I never heard him "speak ill" of anyone. He would occasionally comment on a human being scornfully, and relate a wrongful deed, or a scandalous act, impersonally, for its potential factual or psychological interest. But he would never malign anyone, never insinuate, and, in most cases, never judge. Whether because some poor wretch was involved, like the obscene old beggar who hung around the house, or because the case struck him as too complicated to be justly assessed.

What he did judge with extreme harshness were the errors not of individuals but of groups; those of the bourgeoisie, for example, which he had observed with indignation all his life.

Any form of eroticism that was at all exaggerated, artificially "whipped up," if one might be so bold, was instinctively distasteful to him. (I don't want to force the point and say: disgusted him.) He simply deemed this sort of thing unacceptable.

I never heard him use a hackneyed phrase, or let his speech fall prey to the contagion of the moment. During the war of 1914, he never used the terms "Kraut" or "William."[1] (Proust makes the same comment with regard to Saint-Loup.)

I never saw him try to obtain anything. I never heard him be impolite, quarrelsome, or cutting in private, with anyone.

His violent fits of anger with his son (reciprocal ones) were something else again.

His language could be extraordinarily obscene.

His character was naturally cheerful, and his spirit naturally somber.

His sense of diction was exquisite.

I never knew him to be one for showing forced admiration or respect. He would wax enthusiastic or criticize in total freedom—no one admired Shakespeare or Racine more than he, nor was anyone more sensitive to these two authors' failings.

APPENDIX 4

"Self-Commentary"

This is an incomplete text, of five typewritten pages, bearing numerous hand-written corrections (additions or deletions). The indecipherable handwritten passages are indicated thus: [. . .]. These pages are referred to in the chapters titled "Grace and *Coup de Grâce*" (chapter 7) and "The Dark Years" (chapter 8).

In Greece, I was working on a translation of Constantine Cavafy; I had booked passage on the *Nieuw Amsterdam,* whose maiden voyage was to take place in September, planning to spend several months visiting an American friend. Having returned to Europe, as people in Greece were in the habit of saying when they were leaving for the West, I encountered the war almost immediately. The war that we had been expecting for years from one day to the next, as we continue to today, the reality or the prediction of which will not [. . .]. The *Nieuw Amsterdam* did not set sail. I was informed of the opening of hostilities that morning by the radio in a Sierre café, describing the incursion of Hitler's troops into Poland. On the same day, crossing Lake Leman in a ship that was more or less empty, I heard the tocsin sound, from the Savoy side as well as from the Swiss side, announcing the war. The great waves of sound arrived one after another, enveloping the ship; I was caught in the middle of this sonorous net, inevitably remembering the Belgian alarm I had heard sounded during my childhood, along a road in the dunes, during a holiday on the Belgian coast. This time it was the bells of seven or eight cities or villages ringing all at once, the great bell of the Lausanne cathedral standing out among them. Alone as I was, free as I was, not attached really to any particular place, except by my choice, to any being, except by my choice, it seemed to me for a long moment that my own life was being erased, was nothing more than a crossroads into which surged those waves of sound. Very quickly those alarm bells ceased being the signal of a danger, and became instead a death knell, that of all those who were going to die in that adventure, I myself perhaps among them; and however deeply into horror my imagination may have drawn me, I did not go so far as to conceive of the millions dead in concentration camps, the communal graves of the Ukraine and Stalingrad, the hundreds of thousands burned in Dresden and Hiroshima, the victims of the raids over England, of the long marches in the Burmese jungle or the fighting in Cyrenaica, or in the forests of Finland, the resisters hung from Norway to Yugoslavia. That *Requiem,* or at least that *Dies Irae,* was none the less spoken for them.

In the lounge of a Lausanne hotel, shattered faces all around me, I heard France's belated declaration of war, after England's more rapid one. Shortly thereafter came the news that the *Athenia* had been torpedoed and had sunk off the coast of Ireland. The *Nieuw Amsterdam* announced it had postponed its crossing indefinitely, shunning the dangers of the high seas in favor of the safety of its Rotterdam port, which, for that matter, was completely destroyed in a bombardment some months later. For most people, caught up in the responsibilities of a job, a household, or a career, the war ushered in an element of danger, but did not require that any immediate choices be made; for me, on the contrary, it became an occasion for rethinking the future. I have always tried to interpret a certain type of occurrence of this type, a boat weighing anchor, or those [. . .] alongside the quay, as an omen. Should I abandon my plan to spend a few months in the United States, where all that awaited me was a friendship, but a unique one, and consider returning to Greece? I could not imagine being able, at that time, to live away from there for long. I talked about this with a Greek friend who had lived in voluntary exile in Lausanne for years and who rather enjoyed playing sibyl: "If I were you," she said, revealing the penchant for fantastic and sensational things that was part of her nature, "I would arrange to do some reporting, and I would choose the most extraordinary events: be in Paris the day it burns and in Berlin the day Hitler gives himself up." I only half-listened to these facile remarks: I knew that this was not my way of making contact with events; my commitment was to slower methods and less showy results.

Edmond Jaloux, with whom as usual I had several meals in the taverns of Lausanne or the gardens at Ouchy, was somber. Basing his notions as one nearly always does on yesterday's dangers rather than foreseeing tomorrow's, he imagined a war of position like the war of 1914, with armies immobilized for years behind Maginot Lines or Siegfried Lines, civilian life reduced to nothing, and revolution setting in at the rear. His sympathies—which were those of a man who, out of good sense and by temperament, detested crowds—tended as always to the right; a few months earlier, he had spoken to me once without irony of 'a review that published Hitler's texts, which I have the honor of contributing to,' and I had been struck, at the time, by the fact that this man who did not travel and had not known Hitlerian Germany was falling into the usual error of seeing Hitler as a man of order, and not as a monstrous, crude adventurer. Whatever the case may have been, in September 1939 Jaloux seemed thoroughly recovered from his naive and ill-fated marvelings. "Hitler amused us, because he is essentially a kind of Wallenstein," he said displaying thus the same incurable superficiality from which so many Frenchmen suffer in the presence of political facts, "but the current situation carries things too far. This man is dangerous, and he will destroy us, and God knows by means of what kind of death." Sitting at that table with a plate of little cakes in front of him, he dreamed on lugubriously. I shall not add, as one might be tempted to, that there was no reason to worry as far as he was concerned, his death, all in all a peaceful one, having occurred some years later when his heart suddenly stopped, as he sat having tea. I knew him too well not to realize that this man given over to the powers of the imagination had died a hundred times and would do so yet again, less out of sympathy and pity, virtues he more or less refused himself for fear of suffering too much as a result, than because of an almost excessive capacity to bestow upon what he imagined, upon the images he created for himself, the proportions of the real. [. . .]

Despite my horror of bureaucratic offices, I had gone in September to visit the Ministry of Information, which was headed up by Giraudoux: having come back from Greece a few weeks earlier, I imagined, not without a certain naiveté, that I could render myself useful to the French cause in that country I knew well and had just left; and more naively still, I imagined that the Ministry of Information might offer me a job there. I have always lacked powers of persuasion, and I quickly perceived that the answer was no. Later on, André Morize, who knew that I had taken quite a long trip to the United States the previous year, advised me to go there instead to propagandize for France, at my expense. This last interview moreover was shortened somewhat by an alert that brought together in the corridor of the Opéra metro station secretaries from the ministry, which was then right nearby, and the kitchen boys from the Café de la Paix: no bomb fell however; in that phony war there were phony alerts such as that one, whose primary [purpose] seemed to be to convince the Parisians of the seriousness of the moment. [Handwritten variant: that we were in fact at war.] For a while longer still, I stayed on in Paris. It was a Paris in which one went roaming, in the night without lights and on little-traveled streets, from the Place de la Madeleine to the Place de la Concorde, and from the Place de la Concorde to Place Vendôme, as if one were part of some Roman scene engraved by Piranesi, not without apprehending, with a pang of anguish, the ruins to come, which moreover did not materialize that time. Uncertainty about the future enlivened the few friendly encounters that took place in the city, which most people I knew had left (many would come back before long only to leave again during the exodus of June 1940); more or less at random, I remember seeing Cocteau in the bar at the Ritz, as always more concerned with charming and bedazzling than with the things that were happening, which had not yet affected him; Dadelsen, light-hearted, going back to his regiment; Marianne Oswald dreaming of starting up a nightclub in New York, exclusively for women, a plan, I'm quite sure, that was never carried out; Julien Gracq in uniform, glimpsed in an English friend's salon, peopled with Chirico paintings, as deserted as nighttime Paris also was, where I heard a woman sing a song one evening in Gaelic whose name I don't remember but whose rhythm later found its way into *The Little Mermaid;* and, here and there, unsure like everyone else, some Germans of the Jewish race, wondering if they should stay in Paris or obtain a passport to go to Portugal. The atmosphere was that of the beginning of a storm, when birds are restless, flying low in the sky. One night, after a little reception on the Rue du Bac, which was livened up by a pointless alert, and a descent into the basement animated by the remarks of the concierge, who talked to all of us about [. . .], I fell, in the total darkness of the street, into a hole dug by a public works crew and lost my shoes in the mud. The next [day] I went back to retrieve them.

APPENDIX 5

The Memorial Service for Marguerite Yourcenar

On 16 January 1988, at Northeast Harbor's Union Church, a ceremony was held in memory of Marguerite Yourcenar, whose ashes had been placed in the ground a few days earlier. She had arranged all the details in advance, and had wanted this service to correspond in all respects to the one she had organized for Grace Frick, in 1979. The pastor, though young, was the same one that had presided in 1979. He announced at the outset that "Marguerite Yourcenar having held her own convictions," the service would be somewhat unusual. The texts she had chosen were read: the Sermon on the Mount, from Saint Matthew 5; the first Epistle of Saint Paul, in 1 Corinthians 13; Saint Francis's Canticle of Living Creatures; two passages from the Chinese philosopher Chuang-Tzu; the Four Buddhist Vows; a poem by the nineteenth-century Japanese nun Rye-Nen:

> [Eighty-four] years have these eyes beheld the changing
> scenes of autumn.
> I have had time enough to admire the moonlight.
> Ask me no more:
> Only listen to the voice of pine and oak trees,
> when hardly any wind stirs.

After a reading of the lines that Michel de Crayencour had written on the death of Fernande, "We must not complain because this person is not anymore with us; we must rejoice that she has been with us so long," Walter Kaiser, a professor at Harvard, and Marguerite Yourcenar's translator and friend, delivered this eulogy:

Some days ago, in the lovely little hidden cemetery of Somesville, Jeannie, Dee Dee, Fuku, and I placed into the frozen earth all that physically remained of the great spirit we come to honor today. The day itself was chryselephantine, all gold and ivory, with a glittering sun shining in the bluest of skies above us and the earth beneath us mantled in deep, pristine, new-fallen snow. It was a day she would have loved. As we prepared her ashes according to her instructions, wrapping them first in a white scarf, placing them in an Indian basket of sweetgrass, covering them with a scarf bearing the Buddhist symbol of flying cranes, and then enveloping the basket with the white silk shawl she had worn the day she was made a member of the Académie Française, Fuku scampered about, playing silently in the powdery snow, performing, it seemed, a dance of celebration. Then, sensing that something serious was about to occur, he abruptly stopped and came to stand quietly beside the small grave into which we lowered the basket and strewed rose petals. As we stood there, I thought of the young French priest she describes whispering his last words, "*Satis, amice,*" in the Prairie of the Jesuits a mile or two to the south of Somesville, of Hadrian giving up his life peacefully in the July heat of Baiae, of Zeno's life ebbing out of his veins in his dark cell at Bruges, of Nathanael lying down in a hollow of the dunes on the island of Texel for his final sleep. In the breathless Maine cold that morning, a crystalline stillness hung in the bright air, so resonant that it almost seemed as if, for one brief instant, one could hear the music of the spheres. And so we committed her remains to this corner of the earth Marguerite Yourcenar loved so dearly.

They were only her bodily remains. She herself had long since achieved immortality—not merely that conferred by the Académie Française but the ultimate immortality she had guaranteed for herself through her deathless writing. For, so long as men and women ask themselves what it means to be a human being in this sublunary, transient world, Marguerite Yourcenar is one of the authors to whom they shall turn for an answer. It is the question she spent her entire life pondering; it is the question all her books strive to answer. And it is for the wisdom of that answer that her books will be read forever.

She had thought a great deal about death. Indeed, I can think of no other author in the world's literature who has more vividly depicted, again and again, the act of dying. But although, like Montaigne, she said that she "loved and respected those people who prepared for their own death," and although she once said that "death is the supreme form of life," she knew as well as Montaigne did that it is living that truly matters, not dying. She said shortly before her death: "One must toil and struggle to the bitter end, one must swim in the river that both lifts us up and carries us away, knowing in advance that the only outcome is to drown in the vastness of the open sea. But the question is, *Who* drowns? We must accept all the evils, cares, and afflictions that beset us and others, as we must accept our own death and the deaths of others, as a *natural* part of life. . . . We should think of death as a friend."

Once, a very few years ago, while talking about death, she mused in such a way as to give a sort of panoramic view of her entire life, and because of that— because it is about life, not about death, and about *her* life—I should like to read to you what she said then. "A friend of mine," she said,

> who was resuscitated after nearly drowning told me that the widespread belief that one sees one's whole life flash by in an instant is true. If so, it must be disagreeable at times. Greater selectivity is called for. But what would *I* like to see again? Perhaps the hyacinths of Mont-Noir, my childhood home, or the violets of Connecticut in springtime; the oranges my father cleverly hung from the branches in our garden in the Midi; a cemetery in Switzerland crushed by the weight of its roses; another buried in snow in the midst of white birches; and still other cemeteries whose names and locations escape

me, but that's of no importance. The dunes of Flanders and, later, of the Virginia sea islands, with the resounding roar of the ocean that has persisted since the beginning of time; the modest little Swiss music box that plays pianissimo an arietta of Haydn, which I turned on at Grace's bedside an hour before her death, when she had ceased to respond to word or touch. Or again, the huge icicles that form on the rocks here on Mount Desert, icicles that, in April, form channels for the melting snows that flow with a geyser's roar. Cape Sounion at sunset. Olympia at noon. Peasants on a road in Delphi offering to give their mule's bells to a stranger. The mass of the Resurrection in a Euboean village, after having crossed the mountains on foot during the night. The arrival one morning at Segesta, in Sicily, on horseback over trails that in those days were deserted and rocky and smelled of thyme. A walk at Versailles one sunless afternoon, or that day at Corbridge, in Northumberland, when, having fallen asleep in the middle of an archeological dig overgrown with grass, I passively allowed the rain to penetrate my bones at the same time it was penetrating the bones of the dead Romans. Some cats I picked up with the help of André Embiricos in an Anatolian village. Making angels in the snow. A mad toboggan ride down a Tyrolean hillside under stars full of omens. Or again, from more recent times and still hardly distilled enough to qualify as memories, the green sea of the tropics, stained here and there by oil; a triangular flight of wild swans en route to the Arctic; Easter's rising sun (which didn't know it was the sun of Easter), viewed this year from a rocky spur of Mount Desert high above a half-frozen lake hatched with fissures by the approach of spring . . .

I toss out these images at random with no intention of making them into symbols. And, doubtless, I would add a few beloved faces, of both the living and the dead, along with still other faces drawn from history or my imagination.

As that passage suggests, the experience of life in this world was, for Marguerite Yourcenar, vividly, perpetually rewarding and illuminating. Yet, for all that, her view of human existence was somber and grave. Like her character Valentina in "Anna, Soror . . . ," she seems to have "acquired early a singular gravity, and the calmness of those who do not even aspire to happiness." From her beloved Greeks, but even more from her own perception of experience, she knew that man's fate is inexorably tragic and that, as Job laments, man is born unto trouble as the sparks fly upward. She also knew, with Pindar, that man is ephemeral, but the shadow of a dream, and, with Hamlet, that he is but a quintessence of dust. She measured the transience of empires, the evanescence of love, and the perishability of earth itself. One felt that she agreed with Keats, that this world is a "Vale of Soul-Making," where our intelligence is transmuted into soul in the fiery alembic of pain and troubles. Equally pessimistic about mankind's future, given his ceaseless destruction of his environment and his failure to learn the lessons of the past, she cast a mournful eye upon what she called "the human document, the drama of man in his struggle with the familial or social forces that have made him and that, bit by bit, will destroy him."

At the same time, however, her infinite compassion for all created beings, man or beast, vegetable or mineral, and her radiant sense of the holiness of life itself, however brief and doomed, saved her from blank, nihilistic despair. Her ability to seize and savor the moment as it passed, in all its richness of detail, and her detached, organic view of the succession of those moments, which becomes the flow of history, gave her, if not precisely hope, at least a profound, suffusing acceptance. In her last great work, which she herself thought of as a kind of testament at the end of a lifetime of living and writing and which she once said to me would be a test of the reader's maturity, her protagonist Nathanael, shortly before his own death, meditates on what constitutes his identity as a human being. And as he does so, his meditation becomes a magnificent celebration of compassionate tolerance for all created things, a celebration of the essential brotherhood of all beings. Without any doubt, his words express Marguerite Yourcenar's final credo:

> But . . . who was this person he considered himself to be? . . . He didn't feel himself to be, as so many people do, a man as opposed to beasts and trees; rather, a brother of one and a distant cousin of the other. Nor did he particularly consider himself male in contrast with the gentler order of women; he had passionately possessed certain women, but, out of bed, his cares, his needs, his constraints of money, sickness, and the daily tasks one performs to live hadn't seemed to him so different from theirs. He had, rarely it is true, known the carnal brotherhood other men had shared with him; he didn't feel less a man for that. People falsify everything, it seemed to him, in taking such little account of the flexibility and resources of the human being, so like the plant which seeks out the sun or water and nourishes itself fairly well from whatever earth and wind has sown it in. Custom more than nature seemed to him to dictate the differences we set up between classes of men, the habits and knowledge acquired from infancy, or the various ways of praying to what is called God. Ages, sexes, or even species seemed to him closer one to another than each generally assumed about the other: child or old man, man or woman, animal or biped who speaks and works with his hands, all come together in the misery and sweetness of existence.

All came together, also, in her love. For the quality that most informs that passage in its profound expression of fraternity for all created things—the quality that, we may say, most informed her life—is a compassionate, empathetic love. There is a beautiful, ineffably moving sonnet by Robert Frost that I have never read without thinking in this regard of Marguerite. In it, he compares a certain woman to a tent of silk standing in a summer meadow, tied by ropes of love to everything around her, tied loosely but steadfastly, so that only by chance does one rope go more taut than another. I should like to read it to you now, knowing that as you hear it it will evoke her presence:

> She is as in a field a silken tent
> At midday when a sunny summer breeze
> Has dried the dew and all its ropes relent,
> So that in guys it gently sways at ease,
> And its supporting central cedar pole,
> That is its pinnacle to heavenward
> And signifies the sureness of the soul,
> Seems to owe naught to any single cord,
> But strictly held by none, is loosely bound
> By countless silken ties of love and thought
> To everything on earth the compass round,
> And only by one's going slightly taut
> In the capriciousness of summer air
> Is of the slightest bondage made aware.

Those of us who come together this afternoon to pay our final tribute of love and respect to this extraordinary human being who made such a profound difference in each of our lives—we are the lucky ones, we are what Stendhal called "the happy few." For it was our privilege to know her personally, to love her, and to be loved by her in return. That is a blessing that each of us shares and that the years will never diminish for us. A singular being of unsurpassable beauty and wisdom was, for a time, a part of our lives, and none of us has been left unchanged by the love she so prodigally gave us. In this world of Mount Desert, which she felt so intimately close to and where she made her home, her spirit will, I feel, forever range across its mountains and upon its shores, bestowing the benediction of her wisdom and affection upon this land. And as we say goodby to her today, I would utter for her the ancient Roman valediction that Hadrian himself would have known: *sit tibi terra levis, Margarita*—may the earth, this earth that you loved so dearly and so deeply, may the earth lie light upon you.

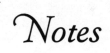

Notes

N o t e s

Introduction

1. Petite Plaisance was the home purchased by Grace Frick and Marguerite Yourcenar in the early 1950s on Mount Desert Island off the coast of Maine. It is now a museum of sorts, which can be visited by appointment during the months of July and August.—Trans.

2. "La Bienveillance singulière de Marguerite Yourcenar; un certain goût de la langue et de la liberté" [The Singular Benevolence of Marguerite Yourcenar: A Taste for Language and Liberty], interview with Josyane Savigneau, in "*Le Monde* des livres," *Le Monde,* 7 December 1984.

3. Marguerite Yourcenar, *Memoirs of Hadrian,* trans. Grace Frick (New York: Farrar, Straus, and Giroux, 1954), p. 122.

4. Marguerite Yourcenar, *Mishima: A Vision of the Void,* trans. Alberto Manguel (New York: Farrar, Straus, and Giroux, 1986), pp. 4–5.

5. The sealing protocol states that "this material is given to the Houghton Library on the following conditions: a) these papers must be kept *sealed* for a period of fifty years after my death; b) over the course of that period of fifty years, no one may be authorized to examine these papers. No copies may be made of them, and neither the contents nor even the existence of these papers should be made public."

6. This is an indirect reference to the French title of Marguerite Yourcenar's collection of novellas, *Comme l'eau qui coule* (Paris: Gallimard, 1982), which is literally "like water that flows." The English translation of this work is called *Two Lives and a Dream,* trans. Walter Kaiser (New York: Farrar, Straus and Giroux, 1987).—Trans.

7. The Bibliothèque de la Pléiade publishes very high-quality, critically annotated editions of the works of "great authors." National Public Radio book reviewer Alan Cheuse calls them the equivalent of the Library of America volumes in the United States. It seems, to me at least, however, perhaps because France is more a nation of readers than we are here in the United States, that more cultural prestige accrues to publication in the Pléiade than in the Library of America series.—Trans.

8. Jean Cocteau, *The Infernal Machine and Other Plays by Jean Cocteau,* trans. Albert Bermel (New York: New Directions, 1963), p. 54.

9. André Gide, *The Journals of André Gide,* trans. Justin O'Brien (New York: Alfred A. Knopf, 1947), pp. 18–19.

10. Yourcenar, *Two Lives and a Dream,* p. 224.

11. Yourcenar, *Memoirs of Hadrian,* p. 330.

Chapter 1

1. "Chronologie" [Chronology] in Marguerite Yourcenar, *Œuvres romanesques* [Prose Works] (Paris: Bibliothèque de la Pléiade, 1982).

2. Notaries in France perform several services that are the province of lawyers in America.—Trans.

3. Josyane Savigneau refers obliquely here, with the expression "*roman bourgeois,*" to Antoine Furetière's *Roman bourgeois,* published in France in 1666 and translated into English as *Scarron's City Romance* five years later. In marked contrast to the romantic tradition prevalent in narrative at the time, Furetière's *Roman Bourgeois* realistically depicted the lives and loves and lawsuits of members of the middle class.—Trans.

4. Marguerite Yourcenar, *Dear Departed (Souvenirs pieux),* trans. Maria Louise Ascher (New York: Farrar, Straus and Giroux, 1991), p. 22.

5. Ibid., p. 39.

6. Ibid., pp. 39—40.

7. Marguerite Yourcenar, *Archives du Nord* [Archives from the Nord], *Le Labyrinthe du monde II* [The Labyrinth of the World II] (Paris: Gallimard, 1977), p. 357.

8. Remembrances of Michel Fernand Marie Joseph Cleenewerck de Crayencour, related in Georges de Crayencour, "Marguerite Yourcenar de 0 à 25 ans" [Marguerite Yourcenar, Age 0 to Age 25], *Dossiers du CACEF* (Centre d'action culturelle de la communauté d'expression française [Center for Cultural Action of the French-Speaking Community]) 82—83 (December 1980—January 1981): 5.

9. Yourcenar, *Archives du Nord,* pp. 340—41.

10. Yourcenar, *Dear Departed,* p. 294.

11. Yourcenar, *Archives du Nord,* p. 359.

12. Ibid., pp. 360—61.

13. Ibid., pp. 367—68.

14. Letter to Daniel Ribet, a Lille attorney, 14 July 1968, Harvard Collection.

15. Georges de Crayencour, "Marguerite Yourcenar de 0 à 25 ans," pp. 6 and 7.

16. See the chapter "Les Miettes de l'enfance" [Scraps of Childhood], in Marguerite Yourcenar, *Quoi? L'Eternité* [What? Eternity], *Le Labyrinthe du monde III* [The Labyrinth of the World III] (Paris: Gallimard, 1988), pp. 201—28.

17. Letter to Georges de Crayencour, Christmas 1966, Georges de Crayencour Archives. "The book" became the three volumes of *Le Labyrinthe du monde.*—Trans.

18. Joseph is in fact the fourth given name of Michel René's son; it is the one Yourcenar chose to evoke her half brother: "We shall call him Michel-Joseph for short," she decided in *Archives du Nord* (p. 295). As is customary, Georges de Crayencour refers to his father with his first two given names: Michel Fernand.

19. Georges de Crayencour, "Marguerite Yourcenar de 0 à 25 ans," p. 7.

20. Yourcenar, *Archives du Nord,* pp. 179—80.

21. Ibid., pp. 183—84.

22. Yourcenar, *Quoi? L'Eternité,* p. 203.

23. Ibid., p. 206.

24. Ibid., p. 210.

25. Georges de Crayencour, "Marguerite Yourcenar de 0 à 25 ans," pp. 8—9.

26. Preliminary notes for *Quoi? L'Eternité,* Harvard Collection.

27. This is Yourcenar's original English.—Trans.

28. Marguerite Yourcenar, "En mémoire de Diotime: Jeanne de Vietinghoff" ("In Memory of Diotima: Jeanne de Vietinghoff") was published in *La Revue Mondiale* on 15 February 1929, pp. 413–18, and reprinted in its entirety, without modification, at the heart of the chapter titled "Tombeaux" ("Tributes") in the collection of essays *Le Temps, ce grand sculpteur* (Paris: Gallimard, 1983); *That Mighty Sculptor, Time,* trans. Walter Kaiser (New York: Farrar, Straus and Giroux, 1992).

29. Yourcenar, *Dear Departed,* p. 262.

30. Ibid., pp. 263–64.

31. Yourcenar, *Quoi? L'Eternité,* pp. 82–83.

32. Jeanne de Vietinghoff adopted the French spelling here, preferring it to Scheveningen, just as Yourcenar did later, a choice she explained on p. 123 of *Quoi? L'Eternité:* "Is it because of the gently drawn-out ending of this noun pronounced the French way (for Scheveningen in Dutch is just a noun like any other) that this beach has always been for me the archetype of all the beaches of the Nord?"

33. Yourcenar, *Quoi? L'Eternité,* pp. 78–79.

34. Interview with Egon de Vietinghoff, March 1988.

35. Ibid.

36. Yourcenar *Quoi? L'Eternité,* p. 127.

37. Preliminary documents for *Quoi? L'Eternité.*

38. "Apostrophes," Bernard Pivot's literary television program, Antenne 2, 7 December 1979. Similarly, when Jacques Chancel attempted to delve into the topic of nostalgia for a mother she had never known, while taping his radio interviews ("Radioscopie," France-Inter, 11–15 June 1979), Yourcenar gave the following response: "That sounds like a novel to me. It is possible, but why?"

39. "Apostrophes," Pivot's television program.

40. Yourcenar, *Quoi? L'Eternité,* pp. 127–28.

41. Ibid., pp. 304 and 253.

42. Ibid., p. 128.

Chapter 2

1. Yourcenar, *Quoi? L'Eternité,* pp. 153–54.

2. Yourcenar, *Archives du Nord,* pp. 346–47.
Saint-Loup, Rachel, and Monsieur d'Amercoeur are all characters in Marcel Proust's *A la recherche du temps perdu (Remembrance of Things Past).*—Trans.

3. Yourcenar *Quoi? L'Eternité,* p. 154.

4. Marcel Proust, *Remembrance of Things Past: Swann's Way (A la recherche du temps perdu: Du côté de chez Swann),* trans. C. K. Scott Moncrieff and Terence Kilmartin (New York: Random House, 1981), pp. 7, 13, and 32.

5. Preliminary notes for *Quoi? L'Eternité.*

6. Yourcenar, *Quoi? L'Eternité,* pp. 220–21.

7. Yourcenar, *Dear Departed,* p. 52.

8. Yourcenar, *Quoi? L'Eternité,* p. 221.

9. Ibid.

10. Ibid., p. 222.

11. Ibid., p. 224.

12. Ibid.

13. Georges de Crayencour, "Marguerite Yourcenar de o à 25 ans," p. 10.

14. Yourcenar, *Quoi? L'Eternité*, p. 22.

15. Ibid., p. 226.

16. One becomes an "officier d'Académie" by virtue of receiving the "palmes acadé-miques," a decoration for services rendered to education in France.—Trans.

17. Yourcenar, *Quoi? L'Eternité*, p. 274.

18. Yourcenar, *Archives du Nord*, p. 268.

19. Ibid., p. 271.

20. Ibid., pp. 271—72.

21. Letter to Georges de Crayencour, 21 September 1977, Georges de Crayencour Archives.

22. Yourcenar, *Quoi? L'Eternité*, pp. 31—32.

23. Georges de Crayencour, "Marguerite Yourcenar de o à 25 ans," pp. 9—10.

24. Yourcenar, *Quoi? L'Eternité*, p. 274.

25. Yourcenar, *Dear Departed*, p. 317.

26. "Apostrophes," Pivot's television program. Walter Kaiser's translation of this sentence (in French, "*Enfant, j'ai désiré la gloire*"), on p. 64 of the 1984 Farrar, Straus and Giroux publication of *Alexis*, is "As a child, I thirsted for fame." Since the same words, "*désiré*" and "*gloire*," appear both here and in the upcoming text, I have changed Kaiser's "thirsted" to "yearned" and his "fame" to "glory." "Fame! Hail to you whom I love and await!" seems too bald-faced an apostrophe for Yourcenar to indulge in, and "thirsted-for stormy winds" seems similarly inappropriate.—Trans.

27. Marguerite Yourcenar, "Ode à la gloire" [Ode to Glory], in *Les Dieux ne sont pas morts* [The Gods Are Not Dead], which appeared under the name Marg Yourcenar, R. Chiberre, editor (Paris: Editions Sansot, 1922).

In this and the other occasional translations of poetry to be found in this text I have followed what Susan Bassnett-McGuire has referred to in *Translation Studies* (London and New York: Methuen, 1980) as the "common practice of translating the French alexandrine into blank verse, since both have in common their pre-eminence as meters of classical theatre in their respective language systems" (p. 124).—Trans.

28. Yourcenar, "Les Rafales" [The Gusts], in *Les Dieux ne sont pas morts.*

29. See the chapter titled "Fidélité" [Fidelity] in Yourcenar, *Quoi? L'Eternité*, pp. 183—99.

30. Yourcenar, *Quoi? L'Eternité*, p. 304.

31. Cf. note 28, in chapter 1.

32. Yourcenar, "In Memory of Diotima: Jeanne de Vietinghoff," in *That Mighty Sculptor, Time*, p. 209.

33. Yourcenar, *Quoi? L'Eternité*, p. 209.

34. Ibid., p. 274.

35. Ibid., p. 210.

Chapter 3

1. The Comtesse de Ségur was a nineteenth-century author who wrote what are considered by many, Yourcenar among them, to be sticky-sweet, convention-ridden children's books.—Trans.

2. Remembrances of Michel Fernand Marie Joseph Cleenewerck de Crayencour, related in Georges de Crayencour, "Marguerite Yourcenar de o à 25 ans," p. 13.

3. Yourcenar, *Dear Departed*, pp. 298—99.

4. Yourcenar, *Quoi? L'Eternité*, pp. 265—66.

5. Ibid., p. 271.

6. Ibid., pp. 268—69.

7. Ibid., pp. 270—71.

8. Ibid., p. 271.

9. This "footnotes of history" translates *"la petite histoire,"* which Arthur Goldhammer has described as "the anecdotes, apocrypha and tattle whose omission [from formal historical accounts] unduly dignifies the past." See his review of Otto Friedrich's *Olympia: Paris in the Age of Manet*, which appeared in the *Boston Globe*, 22 March 1992, p. B40. —Trans.

10. Harvard Collection.

11. Yourcenar, *Quoi? L'Eternité*, p. 275.

12. Ibid.

13. Georges de Crayencour, "Marguerite Yourcenar de 0 à 25 ans," p. 12.

14. Yourcenar *Quoi? L'Eternité*, p. 277.

15. The poem she wrote for her governess, Camille Debocq, at Christmastime in 1915 is reproduced among the photographs included in this volume (see number 7); a copy of the text can be found in Appendix 1.

16. Yourcenar, *Quoi? L'Eternité*, p. 70.

17. Ibid., p. 69.

18. Yourcenar, *Archives du Nord*, pp. 237 and 238.

19. Unpublished letter to Jean Guéhenno, 7 March 1978. The "unpublished correspondence" consists of a collection of letters intended for the Harvard Collection that are temporarily housed at Editions Gallimard pending selection among them for publication.

20. Unpublished letter to Gabriel Germain, 15 June 1969.

21. See the "Chronologie" in Yourcenar, *Œuvres romanesques*.

22. Preliminary notes for *Quoi? L'Eternité*.

23. Matthieu Galey, *With Open Eyes*, trans. Arthur Goldhammer (Boston: Beacon Press, 1984), p. 30.

24. Ibid., pp. 14, 27, and 30.

25. Unpublished letter to Denise Lajoie, 26 March 1977.

26. Galey, *With Open Eyes*, p. 33.

27. Unpublished letter to Olga Peters, 20 May 1950.

28. Unpublished letter to Denys Magne, 15 April 1973.

29. Yourcenar, *Quoi? L'Eternité*, p. 151.

30. Ibid.

31. Ibid., p. 165.

32. Ibid., p. 166.

33. Marguerite Yourcenar Archives.

34. Letter to Georges de Crayencour, 31 July—3 August 1980, Georges de Crayencour Archives.

35. This dedication is in Yourcenar's original English. —Trans.

36. Yourcenar, *Archives du Nord*, p. 301.

37. "Apostrophes," Pivot's television program.

38. Galey, *With Open Eyes*, p. 34.

39. Yourcenar, "Aujourd'hui" [Today], in *Les Dieux ne sont pas morts*, pp. 89—91.

40. Yourcenar, "Le Travail" [Work], in *Les Dieux ne sont pas morts*, pp. 27—30.

41. Letter to Olga Peters.

42. Letter to Denys Magne.

43. *Alcools* by Guillaume Apollinaire, a preeminent, avant-garde literary figure of pre—World War I France, broke new artistic ground and influenced the schools of Dadaism and Surrealism.—Trans.

44. Letter signed M. de Crayencour, "Villa Loretta, Boulevard d'Italie, Monte Carlo," 18 July 1920, Plon Archives.

45. Letter signed M. de Crayencour, 27 September 1920, Plon Archives.

46. Letter signed Marguerite de Crayencour, 4 October 1920, Plon Archives.

Chapter 4

1. Unpublished letter to N. Chatterji, 17 July 1964.

2. "Crosscurrents" is Walter Kaiser's English translation of *"Remous,"* used in the postface of "A Lovely Morning" (*Une Belle Matinée*)," in *Two Lives and a Dream* (*Comme l'eau qui coule*), p. 227.—Trans.

3. Yourcenar, *Dear Departed,* pp. 234—35. Bracketed portion of text is my translation.—Trans.

4. This is Kaiser's English translation of *La Mort conduit l'attelage,* used in the postface of "Anna, Soror . . ." (*Anna, soror . . .*) in *Two Lives and a Dream,* p. 228. Margaret Crosland, on p. 120 of her *Women of Iron and Velvet* (New York: Taplinger Publishing Co., 1976), calls this text "Death Draws the Yoke."—Trans.

5. Yourcenar, *Two Lives and a Dream,* p. 228.

6. In the edition of *Anna, soror . . .* that appeared in 1981 at Gallimard, Yourcenar pointed out in her postface (pp. 132—33) that *"Anna, soror . . .* is but the partial prepublication of a collection that will, this time, be called *Comme l'eau qui coule,* a title that somewhat resembles *Remous,* but substitutes for the image of the ocean's fitful currents the image of the river or, sometimes, the torrent, now muddy, now limpid, that is life." Published in 1982, *Comme l'eau qui coule* comprises *Anna, soror . . .* (with a few modifications), *Un Homme obscur,* and *Une Belle Matinée,* the latter two texts having been published in a new Gallimard edition in 1985. All three texts were, furthermore, reprinted in the Pléiade edition of Yourcenar's *Œuvres romanesques.*

The published English version of the three short stories that make up *Comme l'eau qui coule* bears the title *Two Lives and a Dream.* Like its French counterpart, *Two Lives and a Dream* contains "Anna, Soror . . . ," "An Obscure Man," and "A Lovely Morning."—Trans.

7. "Chronologie" in Yourcenar, *Œuvres romanesques.*

8. Ibid.

9. "Radioscopie," radio program hosted by Jacques Chancel, France-Inter, 11—15 June 1979.

10. Yourcenar, *Memoirs of Hadrian,* p. 15.

11. Marguerite Yourcenar, "Carnets de notes de *L'Œuvre au noir*" [Reflections on the Composition of *The Abyss*], *Nouvelle Revue Française* 452 and 453 (September and October 1990).

12. Galey, *With Open Eyes,* p. 125.

13. Yourcenar, *Archives du Nord,* pp. 141—42.

14. Ibid., pp. 134—36.

15. Harvard Collection.

16. Yourcenar, "Anna, Soror . . . ," in *Two Lives and a Dream,* p. 185.

17. Ibid., p. 236.

18. Ibid., p. 170.

19. Ibid., pp. 236—37.

20. Yourcenar, *Dear Departed,* pp. 211—12.

21. Postcard to Camille Debocq, 19 June 1927, Gallimard Archives, Letot Collection.

22. "Kâli décapitée" was published in *La Revue Européenne* 4 (April 1928): 392—96 and was reprinted in *Nouvelles orientales* as part of the "Renaissance de la Nouvelle" [Renaissance of the Short Story] series directed by Paul Morand (Paris: Gallimard, 1938). It appeared again in *Œuvres romanesques,* pp. 1206—10.

Alberto Manguel's English translation, "Kali Beheaded," can be found in *Oriental Tales* (Farrar, Straus and Giroux, 1983), pp. 119—25.—Trans.

23. Marguerite Yourcenar, "Diagnostic de l'Europe" [European Diagnosis], in *Bibliothèque Universelle et Revue de Genève* 68 (June 1929): 745—52.

24. Alain Finkielkraut, *La Defaite de la pensée* [The Defeat of Thought] (Paris: Gallimard, 1987).

Finkielkraut's *Défaite de la pensée* is a meditation on what is seen as the degradation of culture, conceived as life entwined with thought, in the face of latterday notions according to which culture comprises everything from dunking one's buttered toast in café au lait to the greatest creations of the intellect.—Trans.

25. Paul Valéry, "The Crisis of the Mind," *Paul Valéry: History and Politics,* trans. Denise Folliot and Jackson Mathews (New York: Bollingen Foundation, 1962), p. 23.

26. Unpublished letter to Emilie Noulet, 20 November 1973.

27. Edmond Jaloux, "L'Esprit des livres" [The Spirit of Books], in *Nouvelles Littéraires,* 26 April 1929.

28. Yourcenar, "Diagnostic de l'Europe"; see the text in its entirety and the remarks added to it by Yourcenar in Appendix 2.

29. Postcard to Camille Debocq, 25 August 1928, Gallimard Archives, Letot Collection.

30. On 2 June 1952, Roger Martin du Gard would write to Yourcenar, who had sent him a copy of the second edition of *Alexis,* published at Plon: ". . . *Alexis,* with which I have reacquainted myself here in the little Sans Pareil edition, and which I was curious to read again, after *Hadrian.* (I understand perfectly why this book made such an impression on me in '29: for me, it is still equally distinctive, equally moving, and I recognize from beginning to end the pen that succeeded at imparting to the death of Antinous and to Hadrian's despair an *unforgettable* intensity. . . .)" Harvard Collection.

31. "Chronologie," in Yourcenar, *Œuvres romanesques.*

32. Marguerite Yourcenar, *Alexis,* trans. Walter Kaiser (New York: Farrar, Straus and Giroux, 1984), p. 92.

33. Galey, *With Open Eyes,* pp. 51—52.

34. Yourcenar, *Alexis,* preface, pp. ix—xi.

35. "Chronologie," in Yourcenar, *Œuvres romanesques.*

36. For this spelling of "Scheveningen," see note 32, in chapter 1.—Trans.

37. Yourcenar, *Quoi? L'Eternité,* pp. 141—42.

38. Yourcenar, *Dear Departed,* p. 316.

39. Ibid., pp. 315—18. The short story was titled "Le Premier Soir" [The First Evening] and was published in *Revue de France* 23 (December 1929): 435—49. It was awarded second prize by the review's subscribers (two thousand francs), behind René Bris for "Leçons d'anglais" [English Lessons]. The results were announced in the April 1930 issue.

40. Galey, *With Open Eyes,* p. 49.

41. Yourcenar, *Quoi? L'Eternité,* p. 142.

42. At the time of her father's death, in January 1929, Yourcenar was twenty-five and a half years old.

43. Galey, *With Open Eyes*, pp. 11—12.

44. From a notebook entitled "Notes sur 'Michel' pour servir à *Quoi? L'Eternité*" [Notes on 'Michel' to be used for *Quoi? L'Eternité*], which had already been used for *Archives du Nord*, Gallimard Archives. See the entire text in Appendix 3.

45. Yourcenar, *Quoi? L'Eternité*, p. 122.

46. Yourcenar, *Archives du Nord*, pp. 301—2.

47. Ibid., pp. 304—5.

48. Nonetheless, in a letter to Camille Debocq dated 7 July 1966, Yourcenar would note: "I did not see him again . . . except during one period, between 1929 and 1933, when my stepmother Christine had set up residence in Belgium, and that encounter was not a happy one." Gallimard Archives, Letot Collection.

49. Yourcenar is probably referring to Murad IV, the seventeenth-century Turkish sultan who ordered that his brother Bajazet be put to death. Racine's play *Bajazet* (*Bajazet*) was based on this historical episode.—Trans.

50. Yourcenar, *Archives du Nord*, pp. 306—7.

51. René Hilsum's account evoked Gallimard's refusal of the *Alexis* manuscript. In his biography of Gaston Gallimard (Paris: Editions André Balland, 1984), Pierre Assouline maintains to the contrary: "Thus that young woman of twenty-seven who in 1929 sent the manuscript of her first novel simultaneously to Gallimard and Hilsum, for she thought well of his books, received not even a response from the former and an enthusiastic note from the latter" (p. 206).

52. Interviews with René Hilsum, spring 1988.

53. Ibid.

54. "Radioscopie," hosted by Chancel.

55. Edmond Jaloux, "L'Esprit des livres," in *Les Nouvelles Littéraires*, 29 April 1930. Benjamin Constant is the author of *Adolphe* (*Adolphe*), about which see note 7 in chapter 5.

56. Paul Morand, "*Alexis ou Le Traité du vain combat*, par Marg Yourcenar" [*Alexis*, by Marg Yourcenar], in *Le Courrier Littéraire* 15 (April 1930): 158.

57. Yourcenar, *Two Lives and a Dream*, p. 237. (*Correspondance de Gustave Flaubert*, letter to Louise Colet of 23 December 1853, Bibliothèque de la Pléiade, vol. 2, p. 483; the translation here is Walter Kaiser's.)

58. Yourcenar, *Alexis*, p. 4.

59. Ibid., pp. vii—viii.

60. Gonzague Truc, "Marguerite Yourcenar: 1929—1938," in *Etudes Littéraires* (Canada) 1 (April 1979), a special issue devoted to Yourcenar and prepared under the direction of Yvon Bernier, pp. 11—27. Since his lecture was not published until its inclusion in this journal, the exact date of Truc's presentation is unknown. It has been situated between 1938 and 1939 and, in any event, took place before the publication of *Coup de Grâce* in May 1939.

61. Unpublished letter of Marguerite Yourcenar, 28 September 1977.

Chapter 5

1. Galey, *With Open Eyes*, p. 11.

2. Montpellier is a city in southern France where one of the finest French universities is located.—Trans.

3. Interview with André Fraigneau, 1989.

4. "Chronologie," in Yourcenar, *Œuvres romanesques.*

5. Galey, *With Open Eyes,* pp. 57 and 58.

6. Marguerite Yourcenar, *La Nouvelle Eurydice* [The New Eurydice] (Paris: Bernard Grasset, 1931), pp. 159—60.

7. This novel by Benjamin Constant, published in 1816, is considered a landmark work in the evolution of the novel of psychological analysis.—Trans.

8. Pierre Audiat, "L'Actualité littéraire," in *Revue de France* 6 (1 November 1931): 141—44.

9. Louis de Mondadon, "Revue des livres: Romans et nouvelles, *La Nouvelle Eurydice*" [Book Reviews: Novels and Short Stories, *La Nouvelle Eurydice*], in *Etudes* 210 (January 1932): 376.

10. Edmond Jaloux, "L'Esprit des livres," in *Les Nouvelles Littéraires,* 13 February 1932.

11. Marguerite Yourcenar, "Un Poète grec, Pindare" [Pindar, a Greek Poet], in *Le Manuscrit Autographe* 32 (March-April 1931): 81—91; 33 (May-June 1931): 88—97; 34 (July-August 1931): 92—102; 36 (November-December 1931): 95—98.

12. Marguerite Yourcenar, *Pindare* (Paris: Bernard Grasset, 1931).

13. Ibid., pp. 243 and 252.

14. Ibid., p. 261.

15. Ibid., pp. 269—72.

16. Yourcenar, *Pindare,* p. 284. For a discussion on the quotation from Alexis, see note 26 in chapter 2 regarding this translation.

17. Marguerite Yourcenar, *Le Dialogue dans le marécage* [Dialogue on the Marsh], in *La Revue de France* 12.4 (15 February 1932): 637—65.

18. Marguerite Yourcenar "Note sur *Le Dialogue dans le marécage*" [Note on *Le Dialogue dans le marécage*] dated December 1969, in *Théâtre I* (Paris: Gallimard, 1971), p. 176.

19. Ibid. Although it was staged very recently, after Yourcenar's death, in February 1988—she had agreed to it in 1987—this play, the very first, shows how little importance Yourcenar attached to dramaturgical necessities. J. L. Wolff, who mounted *Le Dialogue dans le marécage,* at the Théâtre Renaud-Barrault in Paris, did not conceal, during an interview, the problems posed for a producer: "It is a text of rare density, and I believe that we needed to flesh it out. Otherwise, we would have risked lapsing into poetry" (Interview with J. L. Wolff, given to Camillo Faverzani on 6 February 1988, reprinted in "Marguerite Yourcenar et la culture italienne" [Marguerite Yourcenar and Italian Culture] [doctoral dissertation, defended on 23 November 1988], vol. 1, p. 377).

20. Marguerite Yourcenar, "Sixtine" ("Sistine"), published in *La Revue Bleue* 22 (November 1931): 684—87, reprinted in *That Mighty Sculptor, Time.*

21. Yourcenar, "Note sur *Le Dialogue dans le marécage,*" p. 177.

22. Born in 1873 in southern Moravia, the philosopher and essayist Rudolf Kassner died on 3 April 1959. A friend of Rilke, Hofmannsthal, Gide, and Valéry, he became known through an essay entitled *Die Grundlagen der Physiognomik* [The Bases of Physiognomy], published in Leipzig at the beginning of the century. Two of his works have been published in French: *Eléments de la grandeur humaine* [Elements of Human Greatness] (Gallimard, 1931), and *Le Livre du souvenir* [The Book of Memory] (Stock, 1942). "Concerning us here is one of the highest and most noble minds of our time, and also one of those 'consciences' that are at once the adornment and the honor of an era," Marcel Brion would say about him.

23. Charles Du Bos (1882—1939) was part of the group at the *Nouvelle Revue Française,*

and he founded the review *Vigile* with François Mauriac in 1930. Notable works from his *œuvre* include the several volumes entitled *Approximations* [Approximations], collections of lectures, studies, and articles on literature, written between 1922 and 1937, as well as his *Journal* [Journal] (five volumes that appeared between 1948 and 1949, now in the process of being reissued).

24. A medical doctor, Gaston Baissette, who was born in Albi in 1900 and died on 5 November 1977, was the author of several essays and novels, notably *Le Soleil de Maguelonne* [The Sun of Maguelonne] and *Le Vin du feu* [The Fire's Wine] (Julliard). He published poems and short stories at a very young age. A contributor to *Cahiers du Sud,* he had, additionally, directed, in Toulouse, the *Cahiers de "Feuilles au Vent,"* whose first issue he devoted to the *Fantaisiste* poets.

Maguelonne is a French village in the commune of Villeneuve-lès-Maguelonne, in Hérault, situated south of Montpellier. During the second decade of the twentieth century, several young French poets, including Tristan Klingsor, Jean-Marc Bernard, and Tristan Derême, formed *Le Groupe fantaisiste.* Their aim was to inject a somewhat lighter spirit into French poetry.—Trans.

25. André Fraigneau, "Autour de Ariane et Thésée" [In the Ambit of Ariane and Theseus], preface to the special issue of *Cahiers du Sud* entitled "Retour aux mythes grecs" [Return to Greek Myths], no. 219 (August 1939): 59.

Gradiva, published in 1903 by the German writer Wilhelm Jensen, was made famous by the attention it received from both Sigmund Freud (see his *Delusion and Dream; an Interpretation in the Light of Psychoanalysis of* Gradiva, *a Novel by Wilhelm Jensen,* trans. Helen M. Downey [New York: Moffat, Yard and Co., 1917]) and the Surrealists. It concerns the awakening of Norbert Hanold, an archeologist devoted only to his research, to the sensual pleasures of life in the world.—Trans.

26. This is the French spelling of his name, which in Greek is Andreas Embirikos.

27. Patrick de Rosbo, *Entretiens radiophoniques avec Marguerite Yourcenar* [Radio Interviews with Marguerite Yourcenar] (Paris: Mercure de France, 1972), p. 146.

28. In *Le Voyage en Grèce,* Yourcenar published "Apollon tragique" [Tragic Apollo] (Summer 1935) and "Denière Olympique" [The Last Olympian Goddess] (Spring 1936). After being reworked, these texts were republished in the collection of essays *En pèlerin et en étranger* [Like a Pilgrim, Like a Stranger] (Paris: Gallimard, 1989).

29. Letter to Ethel Thornbury, 9 December 1954, Harvard Collection.

30. Unpublished letter to Denys Magne, 15 April 1973.

31. Marguerite Yourcenar, Afterword, *A Coin in Nine Hands,* trans. Dori Katz (New York: Farrar, Straus and Giroux, 1982), p. 170.

32. Ibid.

33. Galey, *With Open Eyes,* pp. 59 and 61.

34. Yourcenar, Afterword, *A Coin in Nine Hands,* 173—74. The bracketed portions of the text were left out of the English translation. I have inserted them here, as they directly pertain to the point being made in the text by Savigneau.—Trans.

35. Edmond Jaloux, "L'Esprit des livres," in *Les Nouvelles Littéraires,* 17 March 1934.

36. Louis de Mondadon, "Romans et Nouvelles: Marguerite Yourcenar, *Denier du rêve*" [Novels and Short Stories: Marguerite Yourcenar, *Denier du rêve*], in *Etudes* 221 (October 1934): 414.

37. Marguerite Yourcenar, *La Mort conduit l'attelage* ("D'après Dürer" [After Dürer],

"D'après Greco" [After Greco], "D'après Rembrandt" [After Rembrandt]) (Paris: Bernard Grasset, 1934). Cf. the preceding chapter.

38. Louis de Mondadon, "Revue des livres, Marguerite Yourcenar—*La Mort conduit l'attelage*" [Book Reviews, Marguerite Yourcenar—*La Mort conduit l'attelage*] in *Etudes* 223 (April 1935): 573.

39. Edmond Jaloux, "L'Esprit des livres," in *Les Nouvelles Littéraires,* 9 March 1935.

Chapter 6

1. *Les Charités d'Alcippe* was translated into English under the title *The Alms of Alcippe* (New York: Targ Editions, 1982) by Edith R. Farrell.

2. Interviews with Dimitri T. Analis, 1989.

3. Although I was unable to find either of these two passages from Jerry Wilson's journals in my reading, I did find passages quite similar to these: "She told about recovering in Athens from malaria when a friend insisted that she come with him on a three-month trip on the Black Sea. . . . [And about] seeing a peasant woman dressed in a dress made of skins with two kid goats stuffed down in her bosom—the beauty of that. It was during this trip that she wrote *Les Nouvelles orientales* dedicated to her compagnon [companion]."

4. André Fraigneau, *Les Voyageurs transfigurés* [Travelers Transformed] (Paris: Gallimard).

5. André Fraigneau, *L'Amour vagabond* [Vagabond Love] (1949; Monaco: Editions du Rocher, 1987), p. 100.

6. Interview with Jeannette Hadzinicoli, October 1989.

7. Yourcenar, *Archives du Nord,* pp. 151—52.

8. The Boeuf sur le toit was a Parisian night spot established in 1921 and owned by the author and playwright Jean Cocteau that catered to an international artistic clientèle, among whom were Picasso, Gaston Gallimard, André Fraigneau, Paul Claudel, Arthur Rubenstein, and André Gide, during the twenties and thirties.—Trans.

9. Galey, *With Open Eyes,* pp. 223—24.

10. Ibid., p. 226.

11. Marguerite Yourcenar, "Avertissement" [Foreword], *Feux* (Paris: Editions Grasset, 1936), pp. 9—10.

12. Marguerite Yourcenar, "Avertissement" [Foreword], *Feux* (Paris: Librairie Plon, 1957), pp. 1 3.

13. Marguerite Yourcenar, preface of *Fires* (*Feux*), trans. Dori Katz (New York: Farrar, Straus and Giroux, 1981), p. xxii.

14. Yourcenar, *Fires,* pp. 33—34.

15. Ibid., p. 35.

16. Ibid., p. 33.

17. Ibid., p. 4.

18. Ibid., p. 25

19. Ibid., p. 23.

20. Emilie Noulet, "Notes, *Feux,* par Marguerite Yourcenar" [Notes on *Fires* by Marguerite Yourcenar], in *La Nouvelle Revue Française,* January 1937, pp. 104—5.

21. Edmond Jaloux, "L'Esprit des livres," in *Nouvelles Littéraires,* 19 December 1936.

22. The French translation eventually became "Cavafy," after having been "Kavafis," for a long time.

23. Marguerite Yourcenar, "Présentation de Kavafis" [Introduction to Kavafis], in *Fontaine*, May 1944, pp. 38—40, followed by several poems.

24. Odette de Crécy was the *demimondaine* for whom the Charles Swann of Marcel Proust's *Remembrance of Things Past* cultivated a jaded and suspicious passion. She became Madame Swann. The passage quoted in the text is from p. 393 of vol. 1 of Marcel Proust, *Remembrance of Things Past.*—Trans.

25. Throughout their years together, Yourcenar and Frick noted down their daily activities, either in advance or after the fact, in a yearly engagement book, usually from New York's Metropolitan Museum of Art, that was kept next to the telephone in the front hallway of Petite Plaisance. I shall refer to these spiral-bound volumes alternatively as "calendars" and "daybooks."—Trans.

26. Letters from Nelly Liambey to Josyane Savigneau, dated 17 January 1989 and 22 June 1990.

Chapter 7

1. Marguerite Yourcenar, "Le Prince Genghi," reprinted with the title "Le Dernier Amour du prince Genghi" in *Nouvelles orientales* (Paris: Gallimard, 1938).

The English translation of this short story, "The Last Love of Prince Genji," can be found in *Oriental Tales,* trans. Alberto Manguel (New York: Farrar, Straus and Giroux, 1985), pp. 55—69.—Trans.

2. Dated 1932, and published on 6 February 1937 in *La Revue Bleue,* "Mozart à Salzbourg" [Mozart in Salzburg] was reprinted, with a considerable number of modifications made by Yourcenar in 1980, in the collection of essays *En pèlerin et en étranger,* pp. 91—97.

3. A reference, once again, to the aristocratic characters and milieus of Proust, in which Savigneau questions the quality and depth of Yourcenar's analysis.—Trans.

4. Editions NRF is used interchangeably for Editions Gallimard. When Gallimard started out as a publishing house in 1911, founded by André Gide, Jean Schlumberger, and Gaston Gallimard, creators of the *Nouvelle Revue Française,* it was called Editions de la *Nouvelle Revue Française.* It became Editions Gallimard in 1919.—Trans.

5. Note from Paul Morand to Emmanuel Boudot-Lamotte, 7 December 1936, Gallimard Archives.

6. Letter from Marguerite Yourcenar to Paul Morand, 25 January 1937, Gallimard Archives.

7. Letter from Marguerite Yourcenar to Emmanuel Boudot-Lamotte, 13 February 1937, Gallimard Archives.

8. The French here is *"impression de vague."* The word *"vague"* could be translated by either "vague" or "wave." Thus, *"impression de vague"* could refer to a "wave-like impression" or to an "impression of vagueness." It is more probable, given the aquatic context into which Yourcenar inserts this *"impression de vague,"* and since it is a question here of Virginia Woolf's *The Waves,* that she intended this *"vague"* to mean "vagueness" and so had to point out that she intended no double entendre.—Trans.

9. Unpublished letter to Barbara Kneubuhl, 8 June 1976.

10. Yourcenar's translation of Woolf's *The Waves.*—Trans.

11. The texts "Visite à Virginia Woolf" [A Visit with Virginia Woolf] (1937) and "Une Femme étincelante et timide" [A Sparkling and Timid Woman] (1972) were both reprinted under the latter title in the collection of essays *En pèlerin et en étranger,* pp. 107—20.

12. Yourcenar, "Une Femme étincelante et timide," in *En pèlerin et en étranger,* p. 116.

13. Ibid., p. 118.

14. Virginia Woolf, *The Diary of Virginia Woolf,* vol. 5, 1936–1941, edited by Anne Olivier Bell, assisted by Andrew McNeillie (New York: Harcourt Brace Jovanovich, 1984), pp. 60–61.

15. Interview with Florence Codman, March 1989.

16. Letter to Emmanuel Boudot-Lamotte, 16 November 1937, Gallimard Archives.

17. Letter to Emmanuel Boudot-Lamotte, 20 November 1937, Gallimard Archives.

18. Letter to Emmanuel Boudot-Lamotte, 16 November 1937, Gallimard Archives.

19. Letter to Charles du Bos, 16 November 1937, Jacques Doucet Collection, listed under reference number MS 23 976.

20. Letter from Charles Du Bos, 16 November 1937, Harvard Collection.

21. Letter to Charles Du Bos, dated 21–23 December 1937, Harvard Collection and the Jacques Doucet Collection.

22. Letter to Michèle Leleu, 27 November 1964, Harvard Collection.

23. Letter to Charles Du Bos, 27 April 1938, Harvard Collection and the Jacques Doucet Collection.

24. Marguerite Yourcenar, *Coup de Grâce,* trans. Grace Frick (New York: Farrar, Straus and Giroux, 1957), pp. 3, 10, and 21.

25. Ibid., pp. 18 and 19.

26. Ibid., p. 29.

27. Ibid., pp. 30–31.

28. Ibid., pp. 150–51.

29. Interview with Alix De Weck, November 1989.

30. Matthieu Galey, *Journal 1974–1986* (Paris: Editions Bernard Grasset, 1989), p. 92.

31. André Fraigneau, *La Grâce humaine* [Human Grace] (Paris: Gallimard, 1938), reprinted in 1989 by Editions du Rocher.

32. Yourcenar, *Coup de Grâce,* pp. 14–15.

33. Ibid., p. 37.

34. Ibid., p. 86.

35. Ibid., p. 72.

36. Ibid., p. 125.

37. Ibid., pp. 127–28.

38. In French, *"fric,"* pronounced as "Frick" would also be pronounced by a French person, is a slang word for money.—Trans.

39. André Fraigneau, "Propos romains" [Roman Remarks], *Les Etonnements de Guillaume Francoeur* [Guillaume Francoeur, Astonished] (1960; reprinted, Paris: Editions du Rocher, 1985).

40. Unpublished letter to Claude Chevreuil, 2 September 1963.

41. Yourcenar, *Coup de Grâce,* final, unnumbered, page of the preface (included in the 1981 printing).

42. Postcard to Charles Du Bos, June 1938, Jacques Doucet Collection.

43. Postcard to Charles Du Bos, 14 July 1938, Jacques Doucet Collection.

44. The text that precedes was originally written in English.—Trans.

45. Marguerite Yourcenar, preface to *Les Songes et les sorts* [Dreams and Destinies] (Paris: Editions Grasset, 1938), p. 8 and pp. 10–11.

46. Ibid., p. 11 and pp. 12–13.

47. Edmond Jaloux, "L'Esprit des livres," in *Les Nouvelles Littéraires*, 8 October 1938.

48. Ibid.

49. François Nourissier, "L'Olympe de Marguerite Yourcenar" [Marguerite Yourcenar's Olympus], *Le Point*, 8 December 1975.

50. Letter to Emmanuel Boudot-Lamotte, 6 January 1939, Gallimard Archives.

51. Galey, *With Open Eyes*, p. 188.

52. Letter to Jean Ballard, 5 June 1939, Harvard Collection.

53. "*Les petits papiers*" is a parlor game in which words written down willy-nilly by the various participants on scraps of paper are put together to form what generally turns out to be a hilariously incongruous sentence.—Trans.

54. "Retour aux mythes grecs," *Cahiers du Sud* 219 (Aug.-Sept. 1939): Preface by André Fraigneau, "Triptyque" [Triptych] by André Fraigneau, "Thésée" [Theseus] by Gaston Baissette, and "Ariane et l'aventurier" [Ariadne and the Adventurer] by Marguerite Yourcenar.

55. Letter to Jean Ballard, 18 June 1939, Harvard Collection.

56. *The Executioner* is one of the novels that made up Honoré de Balzac's vast social fresco of early-nineteenth-century France, *La Comédie humaine* (*The Human Comedy*). Specifically, it is one of the "Etudes Philosophiques," or Philosophical Studies.—Trans.

57. Edmond Jaloux, "L'Esprit des livres," in *Les Nouvelles Littéraires*, 5 August 1939.
Bajazet, produced in 1672, was based on an historical event that had taken place in Constantinople in 1638.—Trans.

58. Henri Hell, "Une Tragédie racinienne" [A Racinian Tragedy], in *Cahiers des Saisons* (Summer 1964): 294—95.

59. Unpublished letter to Henri Hell, 1 September 1964.

60. Marguerite Yourcenar, "Commentaires sur soi-même" [Self-Commentary], unpublished Gallimard manuscript. See Appendix 4 for the text in its entirety.

61. Gallimard Archives.

Chapter 8

1. Yourcenar, *Archives du Nord*, p. 305.

2. Yourcenar, "Commentaires sur soi-même."

3. Yourcenar, *Quoi? L'Eternité*, p. 278.

4. Letter to Jean Ballard, 1939, Harvard Collection.

5. Albrecht von Wallenstein, the commander of the forces of Emperor Ferdinand II during the Thirty Years War, was the subject of Friedrich von Schiller's dramatic trilogy *Wallenstein* (*Wallenstein*) (1798—99). After signal military successes that won him much imperial favor, Wallenstein became overly ambitious, got involved in a complicated series of intrigues, and was blind to the dangers he faced. He was murdered by one of his own lieutenants.—Trans.

6. Postcard to Lucy Kyriakos, which should be sealed, Harvard Collection. This postcard could not be obtained during my days of research at Houghton Library, in the spring of 1992.—Trans.

7. Now Hartford College for Women.

8. Letter to Emma Trebbe, 1 August 1959, Harvard Collection.

9. Letter from Constantine Dimaras, 25 November 1940, Harvard Collection.

10. Marguerite Yourcenar, "Forces du passé et forces de l'avenir" [Forces of the Past and Forces of the Future], in *En pèlerin et en étranger,* pp. 55—62.

11. The work in question here is *L'Anthologie de l'humour noir* [Anthology of Black Humor], printed in June 1940. Banned by Vichy-government censors, the work was reissued in 1951.

12. Letter from Jacques Kayaloff, 22 July 1941, Harvard Collection.

13. *Les Nouvelles Littéraires,* 22 May 1952, interview with Jeanine Delpech.

14. Letter from Jules Romains, 25 December 1951, Harvard Collection.

15. Vita Sackville-West, from her introduction to Anne Clifford Pembroke's *Diary of Lady Anne Clifford* (New York: George H. Doran Co., 1923), pp. xxiv-xxv, xxvi.

16. Letter to Jacques Kayaloff, 8 August 1941, Anya Kayaloff Archives.

17. Letter to Jacques Kayaloff, 7 December 1941, Anya Kayaloff Archives.

18. Letter to Jacques Kayaloff, 20 January 1942, Anya Kayaloff Archives.

19. The French explorer Samuel de Champlain named this island "L'Ile des Monts-Déserts" [Island of the Desert Mounts] when he discovered it in 1604; in English, the form is singular: Mount Desert Island.—Trans.

20. Marguerite Yourcenar, "Examen d'Alceste" [A Study of Alcestis] in *Le Mystère d'Alceste* [The Mystery Play of Alcestis], *Théatre II* (Paris: Gallimard, 1971), p. 99. This foreward reappears in part in the article entitled "Mythologies III, Alceste" [Mythologies III, Alcestis] in *Les Lettres Françaises* 15 (January 1945).

21. Harvard Collection.

22. Although in her conversation and her correspondence Yourcenar's language had suffered an inevitable contamination ("*'abortion'* [for *avortement*]; *'excitement'* [for *excitation*]; *'stage'* [for *stade*]; and *'components'* [for *composants*]"), in her books she succeeded at guarding against such slips. "In all of *Souvenirs pieux,* the respected French author Etiemble told her, "I found only one anglicism, *'exemplifier'* [exemplify]. What self-mastery this demonstrates."

23. "*Le Monde* des livres" [*Le Monde*'s World of Books], 7 December 1984. Interview with Josyane Savigneau.

24. This is Grace Frick's original English.—Trans.

25. This date, 1943, is used in the Pléiade's "Chronologie," whereas the preface of the play cites 1944, which is not likely.

26. The Wadsworth Atheneum.

27. Marguerite Yourcenar, "Carnets de notes, 1942 à 1948" [Notebooks, 1942—1948], *La Table Ronde* 89 (May 1955); reprinted in the collection of essays *En pèlerin et en étranger.*

28. Frederic Prokosch, *Voices: A Memoir* (New York: Farrar, Straus and Giroux, 1983), p. 234.

29. Letter to Gaston Gallimard, 26 August 1939, Gallimard Archives.

30. Prokosch, *Voices: A Memoir,* pp. 175—76.

31. Ibid., p. 309.

32. Ibid., p. 304.

33. Frick's entries in the calendars she kept, which can be consulted at Houghton Library of Harvard University, are often written half in English, half in French as is the case here.—Trans.

34. More often than not, as is the case here, Frick records the daily events of life with Yourcenar in the simple present tense.—Trans.

35. Roger Caillois was a French sociologist and important contributor to the analysis of the sacred.—Trans.

The first "Mythologies" text would be published in the January 1944 issue; this was the one that was reprinted, with certain modifications, in the collection *En pèlerin et en étranger* (see Marguerite Yourcenar, "Mythologie grecque et mythologie de la Grèce" [Greek Mythology and Mythology of Greece] in *En pèlerin et en étranger,* pp. 28–34).

Published in October of the same year, the text "Mythologies II," devoted to Alcestis, would constitute in part the preface of *Le Mystère d'Alceste* [The Mystery Play of Alcestis], published by Gallimard in 1971 (see Yourcenar, *Le Mystère d'Alceste,* pp. 81–161).

The texts *Ariane* [Ariadne] and *Electre* (*Electra*), lastly, published together in "Mythologies III" in the January 1945 issue of *Les Lettres Françaises,* would reappear respectively in the preface to *Qui n'a pas son Minotaure?* (*To Each His Minotaur*) and the foreword of *Electre ou La Chute des masques* (*Electra or The Fall of the Masks*) (see Marguerite Yourcenar, *Electre ou La Chute des masques* and *Qui n'a pas son Minotaure? Théâtre II* [Paris: Gallimard, 1971]).

Electra or The Fall of the Masks and *To Each His Minotaur* appear in Marguerite Yourcenar, *Plays,* trans. Dori Katz (New York: Performing Arts Journal Publications, 1984). Neither of the above prefatory works are included with Katz's translations.—Trans.

36. Marguerite Yourcenar, *Discours de réception de Madame Marguerite Yourcenar à l'Académie française* [Acceptance Speech of Madame Marguerite Yourcenar to the Académie Française] (Paris: Gallimard, 1981), pp. 14–15. Reprinted in the essay collection *En pèlerin et en étranger,* without the opening remarks and with the title "L'Homme qui aimait les pierres" [The Man Who Loved Stones], pp. 181–82.

37. This is Frick's original English.—Trans.

38. This is Frick's original English.—Trans.

39. Radio interviews with Chancel, "Radioscopie."

40. The front-page headline in *Le Monde* on 8 August 1945.

41. Yourcenar, "Carnets de notes, 1942–1948," in *En pèlerin et en étranger,* p. 175.

42. Harvard Collection.

43. Saint-Brendan was an historico-legendary figure who allegedly "discovered" America long before Columbus, during a sixth-century voyage.—Trans.

44. Letter to Jean Ballard, 4 September 1946, Harvard Collection.

Chapter 9

1. The first chapter of the third volume of Yourcenar's *Le Labyrinthe du monde* is titled "Le Traintrain des jours" [The Humdrum of the Daily Round].

2. Interview with Harold Taylor, February 1989.

3. Letter to Madame René Lang, 18 June 1957, Harvard Collection.

4. Interview with Charlotte Pomerantz-Marzani, March 1989.

5. Letter from Olga Harrington, Harvard Collection.

6. Perhaps it should be pointed out on Charlotte Pomerantz's behalf that Yourcenar also had several *good* things to say about her in this report.—Trans.

7. Letter to Jean Lambert, 14 May 1956, Harvard Collection.

8. A large number of letters in her unpublished correspondence attest to this.

9. Yourcenar, *Memoirs of Hadrian,* pp. 326–27.

10. Letter to Albert Camus, 14 November 1946, Gallimard Archives.

11. Letter from Gaston Gallimard, 3 April 1947, Gallimard Archives.

12. Letter to Jean Ballard, 14 February 1947, Harvard Collection.

13. Yourcenar, *Archives du Nord,* pp. 167–68.

14. Letter to Jeanne Carayon, 21 June 1974, Harvard Collection.

15. Regarding *To Each His Minotaur,* a "sacred divertissement in ten scenes," Yourcenar would point out, both in the Pléiade "Chronologie" and in the preface to this play, that the revision of the text had been done three years earlier: "... after the repair work done in 1944, the play was put aside, unfinished and neglected on account of other projects, for quite a good number of years; in 1956 or 1957, it was rewritten. . . . It then went back into its drawer, from which I have removed it only recently." *Qui n'a pas son Minotaure?* "Aspects d'une légende et histoire d'une pièce," in *Théâtre II,* p. 179.

This preface, Aspects of a Legend and History of a Play, unlike the play itself, has not been translated into English.—Trans.

16. As opposed to the wealthy Right Bank of the Seine in Paris, the Left Bank, home to thousands of university students, has been known as a crucible of social, political, and artistic ferment.—Trans.

Chapter 10

1. Galey, *With Open Eyes,* p. 113.

2. Marguerite Yourcenar, "Reflections on the Composition of *Memoirs of Hadrian,*" in *Memoirs of Hadrian,* trans. Grace Frick (New York: Farrar, Straus and Giroux, 1954), p. 326.

3. Letter to Joseph Breitbach, 7 April 1951, Harvard Collection.

4. Yourcenar, "Reflections on the Composition of *Memoirs of Hadrian,*" pp. 319–20.

5. Letter from Marguerite Yourcenar to Fasquelle publishers, 28 June 1926, private collection.

6. Yourcenar, "Reflections on the Composition of *Memoirs of Hadrian,*" p. 322.

7. Letter to Joseph Breitbach, 7 April 1951, Harvard Collection.

8. Yourcenar, "Reflections on the Composition of *Memoirs of Hadrian,*" p. 320.

9. Ibid., p. 328.

10. Unpublished letter to Olga Peters, 8 March 1950.

11. Galey, *With Open Eyes,* p. 114.

12. Yourcenar, "Reflections on the Composition of *Memoirs of Hadrian,*" pp. 324–25.

13. Ibid., p. 327.

14. Ibid., p. 328.

15. Ibid., p. 325.

16. Ibid., p. 340.

17. Yourcenar, "Carnets de notes, 1942–1948," in *En pèlerin et en étranger,* p. 170.

18. Yourcenar, "Reflections on the Composition of *Memoirs of Hadrian,*" pp. 342–43.

19. Unpublished letter to Olga Peters, 20 May 1950.

20. According to the 28 January 1950 calendar entry, which can be consulted at Houghton Library, it seems, rather, to have been "a radio broadcast of [the] Metropolitan [Opera], a very beautiful *Simon Boccanegra,* so that we had two Verdi in a week, both excellent."—Trans.

21. Letter to Georges de Crayencour, dated 31 July–3 August 1980, Georges de Crayencour Archives.

22. Ernest Renan was a nineteenth-century French historian and critic who practiced a

scientific approach to religion, literature, and history. He wrote a book on the future of science, a *Life of Jesus*, and the first volume of *The History of the Origins of Christianity.*— Trans.

23. Plon Archives.

24. Letter to Violet Paget, July 1883. Reprinted in the chapter "Sur Marius l'Epicurien de Walter Pater" [On Walter Pater's *Marius the Epicurean*], in Charles Du Bos, *Approximations* (Paris: Fayard, 1965), pp. 743–69.

25. Du Bos, *Approximations,* p. 746.

26. Galey, *With Open Eyes,* p. 116.

27. Ibid., pp. 117–18.

28. Ibid., p. 126.

29. Galey, *With Open Eyes,* p. 120.

Chapter 11

1. Samuel de Champlain, *The Voyages and Explorations of Samuel de Champlain,* trans. Annie Nettleton Bourne (New York: A. S. Barnes and Co., 1906), p. 84.

2. Galey, *With Open Eyes,* pp. 108–9.

3. Letter to Ethel Adrian, 30 July 1955, Harvard Collection.

4. "Une autre Marguerite Yourcenar" [A Different Marguerite Yourcenar], interview with Nicole Lauroy, in *Femmes d'Aujourd'hui,* 25 May 1982.

5. Letter to Ethel Adrian, 30 July 1955, Harvard Collection.

6. P. Pompon Bailhache, "L'Art de vivre de Marguerite Yourcenar, une leçon de sagesse sous un toit de bois" [The Art of Living According to Marguerite Yourcenar, A Lesson in Wisdom beneath a Wooden Roof], *Marie-Claire,* April 1979.

7. *Images d'Epinal,* from the capital of the département of Vosges in eastern France, are popular prints depicting traditional, if not melodramatic, scenes from French daily life as well as characters and events from songs, legend, and history. In their patriotic, rose-colored representation of things, they might be said to bear a certain similarity, despite having been around since the eighteenth century, to Norman Rockwell paintings here in America.— Trans.

8. Undated letter to Jacques Kayaloff, Anya Kayaloff Archives.

9. Letter to Jacques Kayaloff, dated December 1967, Anya Kayaloff Archives.

10. Letter to Natalie Barney, 15 June 1953, NCBC 2365, Jacques Doucet Collection.

11. Letter to Georges de Crayencour, 25 December 1973, Archives Georges de Crayencour.

12. Letter to Carmen d'Aubreby, 25 January 1959, Harvard Collection.

13. Letter to Jean Lambert, 23 September 1956, Harvard Collection.

14. "Marguerite Yourcenar s'explique" [Marguerite Yourcenar Explains Herself], interview with Claude Servan-Schreiber, in *Lire,* July 1976.

15. "Marguerite Yourcenar, une femme sous la Coupole" [Marguerite Yourcenar, A Woman underneath the Dome], part 1 of a conversation with Jean-Claude Lamy, in *France-Soir,* 5 March 1980.

16. Yourcenar refers here to Marcel Proust, who soundproofed the room in which he worked by lining it with cork while writing *Remembrance of Things Past.*—Trans.

17. Conversation with Jean-Claude Lamy, part 2 in *France-Soir,* 6 March 1980.

18. Bailhache, "L'Art de vivre de Marguerite Yourcenar."

19. Letter to Dr. Roman Kyczun, 29 June 1954, written "en route to Munich from Bad Homburg." Harvard Collection.

20. Bailhache, "L'Art de vivre de Marguerite Yourcenar."

21. Unpublished letter to Jeanne Carayon, 2 October 1971. The "works and days" above cites a title of Hesiod.—Trans.

22. Radio interview with Jean Montalbetti, Radio-Télévision Luxembourgeoise, 22 April 1978.

Chapter 12

1. Letter from Constantine Dimaras, 11 February 1951, Harvard Collection.

2. Letter to Joseph Breitbach, 7 April 1951, Harvard Collection.

3. Ibid.

4. Marguerite Yourcenar, "André Gide Revisited," in *Cahiers André Gide:* "Le Centenaire" [The Centenary] (Paris: Gallimard, 1972), pp. 21—44.

5. Unpublished letter to Jean Schlumberger, 15 August 1956.

6. Unpublished letter to Jean Schlumberger, 20 February 1962.

7. Letter to Constantine Dimaras, 8 July 1951, Harvard Collection.

8. Undated letter to Jacques Kayaloff, Anya Kayaloff Archives.

9. André Germain, *La Bourgeoisie qui brûle. Propos d'un témoin, 1890—1940* [The Burning Bourgeoisie. As Described by a Witness, 1890—1940] (Paris: Editions Sun, 1950), p. 237.

10. The illustrious *Institut de France,* located on the Quai Conti in Paris, comprises five academies, the most well-known of which is the Académie Française, whose purpose over the centuries has been the promotion and recognition of excellence in various fields of humanistic and artistic endeavor.—Trans.

11. Letter to Natalie Barney, 5 July 1951, NCBC (Natalie Clifford Barney Correspondence) 2353, Jacques Doucet Collection. All the correspondence exchanged between Yourcenar and Barney (from 5 July 1951 to 11 December 1969) is preserved at the Literary Library Jacques Doucet of the University of Paris, catalogued under reference numbers NCBC 2353 through 2408. Four of these letters (NCBC 2373 of 15 March 1954, NCBC 2389 of 5 June 1960, NCBC 2393 of 29 July 1963, and NCBC 2397 of 11 December 1963) are reprinted in the catalog entitled *Autour de Natalie Clifford-Barney* [Natalie Clifford-Barney and Friends], established in 1976 by François Chapon, the conservator of the Literary Library Jacques Doucet. Finally, seven letters exchanged with Frick are listed under reference numbers NCBC 2358, 2362, 2363, 2374—76, and 2395.

12. Marguerite Yourcenar, in the preface to *La Poudre de sourire* [Smile Powder], conversations between Marie Métrailler and Marie-Magdeleine Brumagne (Monaco: Editions du Rocher, 1982).

13. Letter to Jenny de Margerie, 27 August 1951, Harvard Collection. Montana is the name of a Swiss village above Sierre.—Trans.

14. Letter to Joseph Breitbach, 7 April 1951, Harvard Collection.

15. The prestigious Prix Femina, established in 1904, is awarded to a novel by a panel of women of letters. The prize-winning book is virtually assured of vastly increased sales, along with economic benefits for author and publisher. The "*Hadrian* affair" prevented *Memoirs of Hadrian* from receiving this prize, but *L'Œuvre au noir* (*The Abyss*) was to do so in 1968.—Trans.

16. Handwritten note from Jean Paulhan to Claude Gallimard, Gallimard Archives.

17. Gallimard Archives.

18. Ibid.

19. Letter to Roger Martin du Gard, 11 September 1951, Gallimard Archives.

20. Letter from Roger Martin du Gard to Gaston Gallimard, 24 September 1951, Gallimard Archives.

21. Letter from Marguerite Yourcenar to Jean Schlumberger, 19 September 1951; handwritten note from Jean Schlumberger to Gaston Gallimard, Gallimard Archives.

22. Note from Maurice Bourdel, 21 September 1951, Gallimard Archives.

23. Letter from M. Godemert to Marguerite Yourcenar, 24 September 1951, Gallimard Archives.

24. Telegram from Gaston Gallimard, 24 September 1951, Gallimard Archives.

25. Gallimard Archives.

26. Letters between Gaston Gallimard and Maurice Bourdel, between 8 October and 11 October 1951, Gallimard Archives.

27. Letter from Gaston Gallimard, 22 October 1951, Gallimard Archives.

28. Letter from Marguerite Yourcenar to Gaston Gallimard, 27 October 1951, Gallimard Archives.

29. Grasset Archives.

30. Letter to Claude Gallimard, 23 November 1951, Gallimard Archives.

31. Letter from Gaston Gallimard to Marguerite Yourcenar, 11 December 1951, Gallimard Archives.

32. Letter to Joseph Breitbach, 7 April 1951, Harvard Collection.

33. Letter from Constantine Dimaras to Marguerite Yourcenar, 18 August 1951, Harvard Collection.

34. Letter to Constantine Dimaras, 21 August 1951, from Evolena, Valais, Harvard Collection.

35. Jean Ballard, "*Mémoires d'Hadrien* par Marguerite Yourcenar" [*Memoirs of Hadrian*, by Marguerite Yourcenar], in *Cahiers du Sud* 310 (second half-year 1951): 493—97.

36. Letter from Jules Romains, 25 December 1951, Harvard Collection.

37. Thomas Mann, cited in Jacques Brenner's *Histoire de la littérature française de 1940 à nos jours* [History of French Literature from 1940 to the Present] (Paris: Fayard, 1978), p. 243.

38. Emile Henriot, "Mémoires supposés d'un empereur romain" [Supposed Memoirs of a Roman Emperor], in *Le Monde,* 9 January 1952.

39. Jeanine Delpech, "Instantané: Marguerite Yourcenar" [Snapshot: Marguerite Yourcenar], in *Les Nouvelles Littéraires,* 22 May 1952; Aloys-J. Bataillard, "Portraits d'écrivains: Mme Marguerite Yourcenar l'auteur des 'Mémoires d'Hadrien'" [Writers' Portraits: Madame Marguerite Yourcenar, Author of *Memoirs of Hadrian*], in *Gazette de Lausanne,* 16—17 February 1952.

40. Letter to Jacques Folch-Ribas, 4 March 1973, personal files.

41. Yourcenar, *Memoirs of Hadrian,* pp. 85—86.

42. Galey, *With Open Eyes,* p. 121.

43. Jacques Brenner, *Histoire de la littérature française.*

44. Galey, *With Open Eyes,* pp. 127—28.

45. Robert Kanters, *L'Air des lettres ou Tableau raisonnable des lettres françaises d'aujourd'hui* [The Way of Literature; or, A Reasonable Picture of French Literature Today] (Paris: Bernard Grasset, 1973), pp. 173—75.

46. Letter to Hélène Schakhowskoy, 10 August 1954, Jacques Doucet Collection.

47. For the Prix Femina Vacaresco, ten votes went to *Memoirs of Hadrian*, one vote to Marcelle Maurette, for *La Vie privée de Madame de Pompadour* [The Private Life of Madame de Pompadour], one to P. O. Martin, for *L'Inconnu nommé Napoléon* [The Stranger Called Napoleon], and one vote to Julien Luchaire, for *Boccace* [Boccacio]

48. The reason that Yourcenar refers to *amours, délices, et orgues* [loves, delights, and organs] as being famous is that this is the trio of words that all French schoolchildren learn to be masculine in their singular forms but feminine when used in the plural. As the rest of this sentence will show, she wishes, exceptionally, to use a masculine adjective to modify a plural *amours.*—Trans.

49. Letter to Madame Horast, 17 January 1957, Plon Archives.

50. Galey, *With Open Eyes*, p. 128.

51. Unpublished letter to Gabriel Marcel, 10 March 1968.

52. If Yourcenar's attitude had been what she claimed it was, there can be no doubt that Fraigneau, who is not above being caustic, would have drawn attention to it. Besides which, the rest of the letter to Gabriel Marcel shows how much Yourcenar wanted, given any opportunity, to get even with Fraigneau. Alluding to his attitude during the Second World War, and to his anti-Semitism, she goes so far as to attempt to determine the relative "merits" of Fraigneau, Sachs, and Montherlant . . . "I am not unaware that with regard to this point you would no doubt preach indulgence to me, and that I seem illogical, since I retain in spite of everything a certain sympathy for Maurice Sachs, whom I had known, though not extremely well, before 1939 and since I have not abandoned my admiration (with certain reservations) for Montherlant. But the situation of the tragi-comic character that was Maurice Sachs was very different, and beyond the fact that his horrible *Sabbat* (*Witches' Sabbath*) and his horrible *Chasse à courre* (*The Hunt*) attest to a picaresque genius I can't fail to appreciate, Sachs surely paid a high enough price for his vulgarities that we should be beyond condemning him for them today; I would prefer only to remember a boy as changeable as the weather, frivolous to the point of lunacy, but also capable of a curious ardor, as he was when I met him one last time in September 1939, at a Parisian café; he was enthusiastically Zionist that particular evening, and already limping due to the very sciatica that would cause him to remain in the back of a convoy and die on the roads of Germany. . . . As for Montherlant, despite all the clever tricks, and perhaps certain deceptions, it is the feeling of an ill-directed grandeur that dominates, for me, in his regard, and admiration for certain facets of the writer."

53. Ernst Jünger was a German writer whose work addressed social and political questions.—Trans.

54. Letter to Jean Ballard, 23 October 1952, Harvard Collection.

55. Letter to Natalie Barney, 15 October 1952, NCBC 2360, Jacques Doucet Collection.

56. Letter to Natalie Barney, 15 June 1953, NCBC 2365, Jacques Doucet Collection.

57. Galey, *With Open Eyes*, p. 128.

58. Founded in 1838, the *Société des gens de lettres* is a writers organization that protects and promotes authors' rights.—Trans.

59. Letter to Natalie Barney, 26 December 1952, NCBC 3264, Jacques Doucet Collection.

Chapter 13

1. Yourcenar, *Memoirs of Hadrian*, p. 178.

2. Letter to Natalie Barney, 15 June 1953, NCBC 2365, Jacques Doucet Collection.

3. Letter to Natalie Barney, 27 December 1957, NCBC 2386, Jacques Doucet Collection.

4. Yourcenar, *Memoirs of Hadrian,* p. 122.

5. Letter from Victoria Ocampo, 21 January 1951, Harvard Collection.

6. Letter to Jeanne Carayon, 3 June 1973, Harvard Collection.

7. Letter to Marcel Jouhandeau, 6 May 1954, Harvard Collection. Marcel Jouhandeau was a prolific novelist and essayist.—Trans.

8. This "preview performance" translates the French *la générale,* a final dress rehearsal, attended by invitation only, that provides an opportunity for both friends of the participants and members of the press to see the show before the première.—Trans.

9. Letter to Natalie Barney, 29 December 1953, NCBC 2370, Jacques Doucet Collection.

10. Madame Simone is the pseudonym of Simone (Benda) Porché.—Trans.

11. Letter from Grace Frick to Natalie Barney, 23 March 1954, NCBC 2376, Jacques Doucet Collection.

12. Yourcenar met Hélène Schakhowskoy in Paris in the early fifties, through their common friend Anne Quellennec: "I myself met Marguerite Yourcenar at the end of the twenties, as she was starting out, when she received a small literary prize for a short story, 'Le Premier Soir'; Marcel Prévost, who was responsible for this prize, was my cousin," Quellennec recalls. "I saw her again when she returned to Europe after the war, and we kept in touch until her death. It was in my home that she often met the publisher Charles Orengo, who remained, until he died, one of her friends and advisers."

13. Oppian, *Cynégétique,* translated by Florent Chrestien, original engravings by Pierre-Yves Trémois (Paris: Société des Cent-Une, 1955). Yourcenar's preface was reprinted, with certain modifications, under the title "Oppien ou les Chasses" ("Oppian, or the Chase") in the collection of essays *Le Temps, ce grand sculpteur.*

On p. 175 of Kaiser's translation of this work, titled *That Mighty Sculptor, Time,* Oppian's *Cynégétique* is referred to as *Cynegetica,* although the translation that I was able to find reference to was called *Cynegeticks.*—Trans.

14. Letter to Princess Hélène Schakhowskoy, 10 August 1954, the first of six letters from Yourcenar concerning the preface of Oppian's *Cynegetica,* indexed as Ms 22608 to Ms 22613 and kept at the Literary Library Jacques Doucet.

15. Marguerite Yourcenar, "Le Temps, ce grand sculpteur," in *La Revue des voyages* 15 (December 1954): 6—9; reprinted in *Voyages* (Paris: Olivier Orban, 1981); and republished in the volume of essays titled *That Mighty Sculptor, Time.*

16. "Les Spectacles, 'Electre' ou 'La Chute des masques'" [Theater, *Electra or The Fall of the Masks*], by Robert Kemp, in *Le Monde,* 11 November 1954.

17. Louise de Borchgrave, a Dutchwoman née Sloet van Oldruitebborgh, had married Robert de Borchgrave, brother of Solange, who was herself the wife of Michel Fernand Joseph, Yourcenar's half brother.

18. Ghislain de Diesbach, "Une Visite à Marguerite Yourcenar" [A Visit with Marguerite Yourcenar], in *Combat,* 21 February 1963.

19. Charles Orengo was an internationally known publisher and editor associated with several French publishing houses over the course of his career.—Trans.

20. Jerry Wilson notebooks, Harvard Collection.

21. Diesbach, "Une Visite à Marguerite Yourcenar," in *Combat.* Yourcenar's theater, in which one perceives that she had little interest in dramaturgy, seems to have been a secondary occupation for her. To Matthieu Galey, who reminded her of this, she responded: "Quantitatively speaking, yes. Qualitatively it remains to be seen. I sometimes enjoy myself in my plays as I might in a private preserve still largely free of intruders. ... I've always attached a considerable importance to voices. ... Few people to date have noticed the links between

my plays and my other, better-known works. The differences between them are differences of form only, not of substance" (*With Open Eyes*, pp. 154—55).

22. Letter to Florence Codman, 16 February 1956, Harvard Collection. "Willy" was the pseudonym of the flamboyant and ambitious Henry Gauthier-Villars, whom Colette married at the age of twenty. It was under Willy's tutelage and under his name that Colette wrote and published her early *Claudine* novels.—Trans.

23. Letter to Natalie Barney, 11 March 1956, NCBC 2385, Jacques Doucet Collection. Although the use, in this cite, of the supposedly generic "his" seems odd to many of us now, this was Yourcenar's habit, which I have adhered to throughout this book.—Trans.

24. Yourcenar, *Dear Departed*, pp. 44—45.

25. Ibid., pp. 41—43.

26. Letter to Julia Tissameno, 4 February 1957, Harvard Collection.

27. This text was republished under the title of "Ah, mon beau château" ("Ah, Mon Beau Château"), in the collection *The Dark Brain of Piranesi* (*Sous bénéfice d'inventaire*), trans. Richard Howard (New York: Farrar, Straus and Giroux, 1980).

28. Letter from Jean Cocteau, 28 July 1957, Harvard Collection.

29. Unpublished note to Madame Mikander, 17 January 1970.

30. Unpublished letter to Dominique Le Buhan, 23 December 1978.

31. Unpublished letter to André Connes, 23 November 1978.

32. "*Le Monde* des livres," interview with Josyane Savigneau, 7 December 1984.

33. Fernande de Crayencour's best friend from her school days, and later Michel de Crayencour's mistress, Jeanne de Vietinghoff was a prominent figure in the remembrance of Yourcenar's past that is chronicled, somewhere on the boundary of fiction and nonfiction, in the third volume of her autobiographical trilogy, *Le Labyrinthe du monde*, titled *Quoi? L'Eternité*.—Trans.

34. Letter to Jean Roudaut, 18 November 1978, Harvard Collection.

35. Letter to Louise de Borchgrave, 10 March 1957, Harvard Collection.

36. Letter from Gaston Gallimard, 13 September 1956, and response from Marguerite Yourcenar, 14 October 1956, Gallimard Archives.

37. Marguerite Yourcenar, "La Conversation à Innsbruck," in *Nouvelle Revue Française* 141 (September 1964).

38. Letter to Ethel Adrian, 7 September 1957, Harvard Collection.

39. Yourcenar had noted and underlined in a notebook this sentence of Natalie Barney's, from *Eparpillements* [Scatterings], a collection of aphorisms brought out by Sansot in 1910: "The most beautiful life is one spent creating oneself, not procreating."

40. Responses to a questionnaire presented by the review *Prétexte* 1 (September 1957).

41. Undated letter from Bernard Grasset to Maurice Bourdel, Grasset Archives.

42. Grasset Archives.

43. Letter to Natalie Barney, 12 August 1957, NCBC 2387, Jacques Doucet Collection.

Chapter 14

1. Marguerite Yourcenar and Constantine Dimaras, *Présentation critique de Constantin Cavafy, 1863—1933, suivie d'une traduction des* Poèmes [Critical Introduction to Constantine Cavafy, 1863—1933, along with a Translation of his *Poems*] (1958; Paris: Gallimard, 1978), pp. 10, 30, 32—33, 34, 41.

2. Letter to Natalie Barney, 26 June 1958, NCBC 2388, Jacques Doucet Collection.

3. Ibid.

4. Letter to Elie Grekoff, 27 August 1959, Harvard Collection.

5. Cf. chapter 5, "Nomadism of the Heart and of the Mind."

6. Yourcenar, Afterword, *A Coin in Nine Hands,* pp. 171—72.

7. Guy Dupré, "Marguerite Yourcenar, une revenante à découvrir" [Marguerite Yourcenar, Discovering a Returnee], *Arts* 19—25 (August 1959).

8. Letter to Natalie Barney, 1 January 1967, NCBC 2402, Jacques Doucet Collection.

9. The dedication to Jaloux appears once again in the Pléiade edition of Yourcenar's *Œuvres romanesques.*

10. Unpublished letter to Jean Lambert, 9 May 1974.

11. Letter to Balmelle, 2 April 1959, Harvard Collection.

12. Interview with Eugénio de Andrade, conversation recorded by Valérie Cadet, May 1990.

13. Unpublished letter to Jeanne Carayon, 27 April 1974.

14. Unpublished letter to Jacques Masui, 22 March 1975.

15. Letter to Jean-Louis Côté, 5 July 1979, Harvard Collection.

16. Unpublished letter to Niko Calas, 18 February 1962. Gustave Flaubert's *La Tentation de Saint Antoine* (*The Temptation of Saint Anthony*) (1874), inspired by Breughel's painting of the same name, concerns a saint in the desert recollecting instances of temptation in his life. It deals with issues of lust and philosophical doubt. Arthur Rimbaud's *Une Saison en enfer* (*A Season in Hell*), a work of both poetic and prose reflections that came out in 1873, also represents a retrospective spiritual self-examination.—Trans.

17. Unpublished letter to Denys Magne, 15 April 1973.

18. Marguerite Yourcenar, "L'Homme qui signait avec un ruisseau" [The Man who Signed with a Stream], *Nouvel Observateur,* 16—22 December 1983, reprinted in *En pèlerin et en étranger,* pp. 219—23.

19. Marguerite Yourcenar, "'Deux Noirs,' de Rembrandt" ["Two Negroes," by Rembrandt], "*Le Monde* des livres," 16 December 1988, reprinted in *En pèlerin et en étranger,* p. 78.

20. Marguerite Yourcenar, "Une Exposition Poussin à New York" [A Poussin Exhibit in New York], in *En pèlerin et en étranger,* p. 78.

21. "Perhaps there exists, in this painting by Velàzquez [*sic*], the representation as it were, of Classical representation, and the definition of the space it opens up to us" (Michel Foucault, *The Order of Things: An Archaeology of the Human Sciences,* translator unnamed [New York: Pantheon Books, 1970], p. 16).

22. Letter to Lidia Storoni, Yourcenar's Italian translator, 25 April 1960, from the Miramar de Malaya Hotel, Harvard Collection.

Calle Sierpes is a street in Seville. During Seville's *Semana Santa,* figures of a weeping Virgin Mary and the biblical episode of Christ's passion are paraded through the streets atop platforms borne by sandal-clad or barefoot penitents from all over Andalusia.—Trans.

23. Garcìa Lorca was shot by Franco's forces during the Spanish Civil War.—Trans.

24. Letter to Isabelle Garcìa Lorca, 10 May 1960, Harvard Collection.

25. Letter to François Augiéras, 16 May 1953, Harvard Collection.

26. Letter to François Augiéras, n.d., Harvard Collection.

27. Unpublished letter to François Augiéras, dated 9 June 1959, but more likely written on 9 June 1960 if one follows the logic of what is said.

28. Unpublished letter from François Augiéras, 21 June 1960, Périgueux.

29. Unpublished letter to François Augiéras, 28 March 1964.

30. Unpublished letter from François Augiéras, 16 April 1964.

31. Letter to Natalie Barney, 5 June 1960, NCBC 2389, Jacques Doucet Collection.

32. Letter to Jean Ballard, 11 December 1960, Harvard Collection.

33. Interview with Guy Le Clec'h, in *Nouvelles Littéraires,* 4 June 1971.

34. Patrick de Rosbo, *Entretiens radiophoniques avec Marguerite Yourcenar* [Radio Interviews with Marguerite Yourcenar] (Paris: Mercure de France, 1972), pp. 19–20.

35. "Marguerite Yourcenar s'explique," interview with Claude Servan-Schreiber, in *Lire,* July 1976.

36. Marguerite Yourcenar, preface to *Rendre à Caesar,* in *Théâtre I,* p. 16.
This preface was not translated along with the play itself.—Trans.

37. Letter to Jacques Kayaloff, 4 January 1961, Anya Kayaloff Archives.

38. Roger Vailland's *La Loi* (Paris: Gallimard, 1957) won the Prix Goncourt in 1957.

39. This is a reference to the game played by the Surrealists, called *le cadavre exquis,* which involved a group of people composing sentences at random, each participant providing only one element (subject, verb, complement) without knowing the others. The first sentence obtained in this manner was "The exquisite corpse will drink the new wine."—Trans.

40. Unpublished letter to Madame Calza, 18 April 1962. There seems to be no way of knowing to whom Yourcenar refers in mentioning a "foreign publisher." Perhaps she means Farrar, Straus and Giroux, but that's not certain.—Trans.

41. Letter to Miss Sibley, 2 February 1962, Harvard Collection.

42. Letter to Dr. Pals Kolka, 31 July 1962, Harvard Collection. (This letter, written originally in English, is available at Houghton Library.—Trans.) *The Grettis Saga* is one of the jewels among the Icelandic sagas. The text, which recounts the peregrinations of Grettir the outlaw hero, dates from the sixteenth century.

43. Letter to Lidia Storoni, Christmas 1962, Harvard Collection. Custine was a general of the French Revolutionary Wars, charged with treason and guillotined in 1793.—Trans.

44. Adrien Jans, "Marguerite Yourcenar: *Sous bénéfice d'inventaire*" [Marguerite Yourcenar: *The Dark Brain of Piranesi*], *Le Soir,* 3 January 1963.

45. Jacqueline Piatier, "Une Classique moderne, *Sous bénéfice d'inventaire* de Marguerite Yourcenar" [A Modern Classic, *The Dark Brain of Piranesi* by Marguerite Yourcenar], "*Le Monde* des livres," 19 January 1963.

46. Pierre de Boisdeffre, "Le Livre de la semaine" [The Book of the Week], in *Les Nouvelles Littéraires,* 3 January 1963.

47. Marguerite Yourcenar, *Nouvelles orientales,* 2d revised edition (Paris: Gallimard, 1963). Regarding this edition Yourcenar explains in her postscript that "[t]his edition of *Oriental Tales,* in spite of very many purely stylistic corrections, leaves the tales essentially as they were when they appeared for the first time in bookstores in 1938. . . . 'The Prisoners of the Kremlin,' a very early effort to reinterpret in a modern way an ancient Slavic legend, has been omitted as too obviously unworthy to merit repairs" (Yourcenar, *Oriental Tales,* trans. Alberto Manguel [New York: Farrar, Straus and Giroux, 1985], p. 145). Finally, the stories originally entitled "Le Chef rouge" [The Red Head] and "Les Tulipes de Cornélius Berg" [Cornelius Berg's Tulips] have respectively become "La Veuve Aphrodissia" ("Aphrodissia, the Widow") and "La Tristesse de Cornélius Berg" ("The Sadness of Cornelius Berg").

48. The work in question was *L'Incertitude qui vient des rêves* [The Uncertainty Coming from Dreams] (Paris, Gallimard), which appeared in 1956.

49. Unpublished letter to Roger Caillois, 24 February 1963.

50. Letter to Natalie Barney, 29 July 1963, NCBC 2393, Jacques Doucet Collection. A fragment of this letter was printed in an epigraph to the book that Jean Chalon devoted to Natalie Barney, *Portrait d'une séductrice* (Paris: Stock, 1976); *Portrait of a Seductress,* trans. Carol Barko (New York: Crown Publishers, 1979).

51. Unpublished letter to Suzanne Lilar, 19 May 1963.

52. Letter to Natalie Barney, 29 November 1963, NCBC 2396, Jacques Doucet Collection.

Chapter 15

1. Letter to Natalie Barney, 11 December 1963, NCBC 2397, Jacques Doucet Collection.

2. Letter to Natalie Barney, 30 March 1964, NCBC 2398, Jacques Doucet Collection.

3. Letter to Gaston Gallimard, 18 January 1964, Gallimard Archives.

4. Ibid.

5. Ibid.

6. Letter to Jacques Kayaloff, 13 May 1964, Anya Kayaloff Archives.

7. Greeting card dated December 1964, to Natalie Barney, NCBC 2400, Jacques Doucet Collection.

8. *Chansons de revendication* [Songs of Protest], trans. Sim Copans (Paris: Editions Lettres Modernes, 1965).

9. Marguerite Yourcenar, *Fleuve profond, sombre rivière, Les "Negro Spirituals," Commentaires et traductions* [Deep River, Dark River, Negro Spirituals, Commentaries and Translations] (Paris: Gallimard, 1966), p. 77.

10. Yves Berger, "*Le Monde* des livres," 27 March 1965.

11. Letter to Natalie Barney, 17 August 1965, Jean Chalon Archives.

12. Letter to Elie Grekoff, 27 January 1965, Harvard Collection.

13. Letter to Louise de Borchgrave, 10 March 1957, Harvard Collection.

14. Marguerite Yourcenar, *The Abyss,* trans. Grace Frick (New York: Farrar, Straus and Giroux, 1976), pp. 247–48.

15. Postscript of the 27 February 1967 letter to Natalie Barney, NCBC 2403, Jacques Doucet Collection.

16. Marguerite Yourcenar, "La Conversation à Innsbruck," in *Nouvelle Revue Française* 141 (September 1964): 399–419, and "La Mort à Münster," in *Nouvelle Revue Française* 149 (May 1965): 859–75.

17. Maître Marc Brossollet was the son-in-law of her previous counsel, Maître Mirat, who had died in 1959.

18. Telegram from Marguerite Yourcenar to Georges Roditi, May 1965, Plon Archives.

19. Letter to Natalie Barney, 27 February 1967, NCBC 2403, Jacques Doucet Collection.

20. Letter from Georges Roditi, 5 August 1965, Plon Archives.

21. Interview with Maître Marc Brossollet, March 1988.

22. Unpublished letter to Gabriel Germain, 27 October 1964.

23. Unpublished letter to Elemire Zolla, 11 October 1964.

24. Unpublished letter to Jean-Louis Côté, 28 December 1965.

25. Marguerite Yourcenar, "Présentation et traduction de quelques épigrammatistes de l'Epoque Alexandrine" [Introduction and Translation of Some Epigrammatists from the Alexandrian Era], *Nouvelle Revue Française* 167 (November 1966).

26. A reflection mentioned several times by Yourcenar; see especially her letter to Elie Grekoff, 13 December 1963, Harvard Collection.

27. Letter to Elie Grekoff, 15 December 1966, Harvard Collection.

28. Ibid.

29. Ibid.

30. Yourcenar, *Archives du Nord,* part 3, "Ananké" [Ananke], pp. 295—307.

31. Letter to Camille Debocq-Letot, 1 May 1961, Gallimard Archives, Letot Collection.

32. Letter to Camille Debocq-Letot, 7 July 1966, Gallimard Archives, Letot Collection.

33. Postcard to Camille Debocq, 25 August 1928, Gallimard Archives, Letot Collection. Glion is a hamlet near Montreux.—Trans.

34. Letter from Lucien Maury to Ahlenius, 22 December 1951.

35. Unpublished letter to Mrs. Kenneth B. Murdock, 19 August 1966. "Sixtine" ("Sistine") was published in *Revue Bleue* 22, 21 November 1931, pp. 674—87; it has since been reprinted in the collection of essays *That Mighty Sculptor, Time*, pp. 13—23.

36. Unpublished letter to Roger Lacombe, 8 February 1967.

37. Letter to Natalie Barney, 27 February, 1967, NCBC 2403, Jacques Doucet Collection.

38. Yourcenar had not been aware of this article, since she now only received the weekly edition of *Le Monde.* "I had a subscription to the daily edition of *Le Monde* for a year," she pointed out to Jacques Kayaloff (Letter to Jacques Kayaloff, 2 April 1967, Anya Kayaloff Archives). It was only because of the newspaper's routing problems, which often resulted in several papers arriving at a time, late, that she gave it up—"for they would pile up on the table, with the bands not even torn off." Which proves her concern with the news, in contrast to what certain people—and herself to a certain extent, at the end of her life—have attempted to substantiate. She even used the newspaper as a pedagogical tool, readily recommending it to young correspondents desirous of achieving expertise in their writing: "every week make yourself read a good newspaper written in excellent, 'contemporary' French, such as *Le Monde* in the weekly edition," she advised (Unpublished letter to Jean-Louis Côté, 29 July 1965).

39. "Sven Nielsen, un vendeur avant tout" [Sven Nielsen, Above All a Salesman], *Le Monde,* 15 March 1967.

40. Letter from Bernard Privat, 27 July 1967, Grasset Archives.

41. Letter from Bernard Privat to Charles Orengo, 8 August 1967, Grasset Archives.

Chapter 16

1. During the month of May 1968, French students, intellectuals, and blue-collar workers joined forces as never before to protest the sclerosis of the major institutions of French society. Barricades were erected in the streets of Paris, police and protesters clashed, factories were shut down. It was a time both of violence and, for progressives and the young, of hopeful visions of change.—Trans.

2. Galey, *With Open Eyes,* p. 134.

3. Gallimard Archives.

4. Unpublished letter to Jean Mouton, 7 April 1968.

5. "Passerelle (meaning footbridge) des Arts" is the old name for what is now the Pont des Arts over the Seine.—Trans.

6. The C.R.S., or Compagnies Républicaines de Sécurité, are elite mobile reserve units, under the jurisdiction of the Ministry of the Interior, that can be sent anywhere on French

territory to attend to such matters of public security as maintaining order in the face of student uprisings or dealing with natural disasters. With respect to the French protests of May 1968, their role might be compared to that of American National Guard troops at Kent State University in Ohio in the spring of 1970.—Trans.

7. Chalon, *Portrait of a Seductress,* p. 220.

8. Letter to Jean Chalon, 9 April 1976, Jean Chalon Archives.

9. This is my rendering of a well-worn slang expression of discontent with the suffocating regimen of French city life, "Métro-Boulot-Dodo," which rhymes and is literally something along the lines of "Metro-Job-Night-Night."—Trans.

10. Galey, *With Open Eyes,* p. 135.

11. Interview with Jean Chalon, in *Le Figaro Littéraire,* 20 May 1968.

12. Yourcenar, *The Abyss,* p. 177.

13. Daniel Cohn-Bendit was the twenty-three-year-old leader of the 800 students of the suburban Nanterre campus of the University of Paris who closed down the school on 2 May 1968, thus inaugurating "the events of May." Bernard Tapie was a government official.—Trans.

14. *Les Murs ont la parole, Sorbonne, Mai 68,* preface by Julien Besançon (Paris: Editions Tchou, 1968).

15. "*L'Express* va plus loin avec Marguerite Yourcenar" [*L'Express* Goes Deeper with Marguerite Yourcenar], in *L'Express,* 10–16 February 1969.

16. She would often refer those she spoke with to this sentence from her work: "One of the tragedies of European thought was that both the Right and the Left, from their differing perspectives, clung with a fierceness of sorts to quasi-theological conceptions of human nature."

17. Letter to Jacques Kayaloff, 17 November 1969, Harvard Collection.

18. Unpublished letter to Gabriel Germain, 11 January 1970.

19. Unpublished letter to Baron Etienne Coche de La Ferté, 9 September 1968.

20. André Billy, of the Académie Goncourt, "Marguerite Yourcenar: *L'Œuvre au noir*" [Marguerite Yourcenar: *The Abyss*], in *Le Soir,* 6 June 1968.

21. Patrick de Rosbo, "Une Rigueur prophétique" [A Prophetic Rigor], in *Les Lettres Françaises,* 12 June 1968.

22. Robert Kanters, "'L'Œuvre' de Marguerite Yourcenar" [Marguerite Yourcenar's "Opus"], in *Le Figaro Littéraire,* 14 June 1968.

23. Henri Clouard, "La Revue littéraire" [The Literary Review], in *La Revue des Deux Mondes,* 1 August 1968; José Cabanis, "Un Descartes sans 'cogito,' *L'Œuvre au noir,* de Marguerite Yourcenar" [Descartes without a "Cogito," *The Abyss,* by Marguerite Yourcenar], in *Le Monde,* 25 May 1968.

24. Edith Thomas, "Zénon, ou Le Drame de la pensée critique" [Zeno or The Drama of Critical Thinking], in *La Quinzaine Littéraire,* 1 July 1968.

25. Kléber Haedens, "Pourquoi oublier que la vie est aussi un bal?" [Why Forget That Life Is also a Ball?], in *Paris Presse,* 2 November 1968.

26. Jacques Brenner, "La Renaissance ressuscitée" [The Renaissance Revived], in *Le Nouvel Observateur,* 9 September 1968.

27. Letter to Charles Orengo, 1 August 1968, Harvard Collection.

28. Letter to Charles Orengo, 26 October 1968, Harvard Collection.

29. Along with the Goncourt, the Renaudot, the Femina, and the Interallié, the Médicis is one of France's main literary prizes awarded at the end of the year.—Trans.

30. Unpublished letter to Elie Wiesel, 20 July 1972.

31. Dominique Rolin, Académie Royale de Langue et de Littérature Françaises [Royal Academy of French Language and Literature]: "Séance publique du 22 Avril 1989; Réception de Madame Dominique Rolin" [Public Session of 22 April 1989; Reception of Madame Dominique Rolin]. Speeches of M. Jacques-Gérard Linze and Madame Dominique Rolin, Palais des Académies, Brussels.

32. Yourcenar, *The Abyss*, p. 166.

33. Marguerite Yourcenar, "Faces of History in the *Historia Augusta*," in *The Dark Brain of Piranesi*, p. 11.

34. Claude Mettra, "Les Explorations de Marguerite Yourcenar" [Marguerite Yourcenar's Explorations], in *Les Nouvelles Littéraires*, 27 June 1968.

35. Unpublished letter to Jean-Paul Tapié, 20 January 1969.

36. Marguerite Yourcenar, "Carnets de notes de *L'Œuvre au noir*," in *La Nouvelle Revue Française*, September-October 1990.

37. Ibid.

38. Unpublished letter to Ljerka Mifka, 1 August 1970.

39. Unpublished letter to Michel Aubrion, 19 March 1970.

40. "Marguerite Yourcenar parle de *L'Œuvre au noir*" [Marguerite Yourcenar Talks about *The Abyss*], interview with C. G. Bjurström, in *La Quinzaine Littéraire*, 16 September 1968.

41. Letter to Alexandre Coleman, 2 October 1976, Harvard Collection.

42. Unpublished letter to Ljerka Mifka, 1 August 1970.

43. Yourcenar, "Carnets de notes de *L'Œuvre au noir*."

44. Yourcenar, *The Abyss*, pp. 178–79.

45. Ibid., p. 177.

46. Marguerite Yourcenar, "Ebauche d'un portrait de Jean Schlumberger," in *La Nouvelle Revue Française*, 1 March 1969, pp. 321–26. Reprinted without modifications in the collection of essays, *Le Temps, ce grand sculpteur*, pp. 225–30.

The American translation of this essay, "Sketch for a Portrait of Jean Schlumberger," done by Walter Kaiser in collaboration with the author, can be found on pp. 210–15 of *That Mighty Sculptor, Time*. The passages cited above appear on pp. 211, 212, and 214–15. —Trans.

47. In France, on the eve of Epiphany, which marked the end of medieval Christmas celebrations, a coin or figurine is baked into a cake shared by everyone present. Whoever gets this charm in his or her piece of cake becomes the ruler of the feast.—Trans.

48. Letter to Henry de Montherlant, 6 January 1969, Harvard Collection.

49. All of these places are in southern France.—Trans.

50. Letter to Elizabeth Barbier, 18 March 1969, from the Hôtel des Comtes in Toulouse, Harvard Collection.

51. Letter from Jeanne Galzy, 30 October 1970, Harvard Collection.

52. Letter to Elizabeth Barbier, 18 March 1969, from the Hôtel des Comtes in Toulouse, Harvard Collection.

53. Rosbo, *Entretiens radiophoniques avec Marguerite Yourcenar.*

54. Letter to Patrick de Rosbo, 26 April 1969, Harvard Collection.

55. The *Index Librorum Prohibitorum* is a list of books that the Roman Catholic Church deems worthy of moral condemnation, be it in whole or in part, and thus prohibits its members from reading.—Trans.

56. Letter to Hélène Schakhowskoy and Anne Quellennec, 6 January 1970, Jacques Doucet Collection, MS 23 172.

57. Rosbo, *Entretiens radiophoniques avec Marguerite Yourcenar.*

58. Rolin, speech delivered to the Académie Royale of Belgium, "Séance publique du 22 Avril 1989; Réception de Madame Dominique Rolin, 22 April 1989.

59. Marguerite Yourcenar, "Séance publique du 27 Mars 1971, en présence de S. M. la Reine, Réception de Madame Marguerite Yourcenar: Discours de M. Carlo Bronne, Discours de Mme. Marguerite Yourcenar" [Public Session of 27 March 1971, In the Presence of Her Majesty the Queen, Induction of Madame Marguerite Yourcenar: Address by Monsieur Carlo Bronne, Address by Madame Marguerite Yourcenar], in *Bulletin de l'Académie Royale de Langue et de Littérature Françaises* 49.1, Brussels, Palais des Académies, 1971.

60. Monsieur Georges de Crayencour's archives relating to the correspondence received from his half aunt Marguerite Yourcenar consist of a hundred or so unpublished letters, cards, and inscriptions spread out over the period between 1964 and November 1987.

61. Letter to Jean Chalon, 9 July 1971, Harvard Collection.

62. Letter to Nabisco, 16 September 1971, Harvard Collection.

63. Unpublished letter to Ljerka Mifka, 1 August 1970.

64. Unpublished letter to Jeanne Carayon, 2 October 1971.

65. Unpublished letter from Jean Blot, 20 August 1971.

66. Unpublished letter to Jean Blot, 1 September 1971.

67. Unpublished letter to Jean-Louis Côté, 16 June 1973.

68. Unpublished letter to Marcel Lobet, 8 March 1973.

69. Cf. chapter 11, "Petite Plaisance."

70. Unpublished letter to Jeanne Carayon, 2 October 1971.

71. Ibid.

72. Yourcenar, "Carnets de notes de *L'Œuvre au noir.*" The Gruuthuse mansion, built in the fifteenth century, is now a museum housing collections of Flemish art; the *Béguinage,* built in 1245, is a retreat for secular nuns.—Trans.

73. Unpublished letter to Jeanne Carayon, 2 October 1971.

Chapter 17

1. Unpublished letter to Louise de Borchgrave, 25 April 1972.

2. In French, the word "*grâce*" is used in the expression "*grâce à qui,*" "thanks to whom" or "by the grace of whom" in English. The French word "*grâce*" also corresponds to the English "grace" in the various meanings of the latter.—Trans.

3. The English title of Molière's *Le Malade imaginaire* reveals what Savigneau is getting at here; it is called *The Hypochondriac,* trans. A. R. Waller, in *The Plays of Molière,* vol. 8 (Edinburgh: John Grant, 1926).—Trans.

4. Unpublished letter to Jeanne Carayon, 27 April 1974.

As Yourcenar quotes loosely from the French version of Molière's play, I cite loosely here from the Waller translation (p. 271).—Trans.

5. Rosbo, *Entretiens radiophoniques avec Marguerite Yourcenar.*

6. Unpublished letter to Jeanne Carayon, 20 August 1972.

7. Patrick de Rosbo, "Huit jours de purgatoire avec Marguerite Yourcenar" [Eight Days in Purgatory with Marguerite Yourcenar], in *Gulliver* 4 (February 1973): 30–35.

8. Letter to Marthe Lamy, 27 June 1973, Harvard Collection.

9. Once an abbey for women near Paris, Port-Royal was the center of Jansenist thought, a severe and controversial Catholic doctrine contrasted with that of the Jesuits, during the early seventeenth century.—Trans.

10. A château in the southernmost area of France near the Pyrenees that was one of the last fortresses held by the Albigenses, a Manichaean sect, in the thirteenth century.—Trans.

11. Patrick de Rosbo, "Marguerite Yourcenar en liberté surveillée" [Marguerite Yourcenar Free on Probation], in *Le Quotidien de Paris,* 25 April 1974.

12. Letter to Jeanne Carayon, 3 June 1973, Harvard Collection.

13. Ibid. The shift from the adjective "personal" to "private" in this passage from Yourcenar's 3 June 1973 letter to Carayon, which is also cited in chapter 13, "Balance," appears in Savigneau's text. The word used in the letter is *"personnelle."*—Trans.

14. Letter to Jeanne Carayon, 18 January 1976, Harvard Collection.

15. Letter to Jeanne Carayon, 8 April 1976, Harvard Collection.

16. Letter from Jeanne Galzy, 9 August 1975, Harvard Collection.

17. Chalon, *Portrait of a Seductress.*

18. Letter to Jean Chalon, 9 April 1976, Jean Chalon Archives.

19. Letter to Jeanne Carayon, 25 July 1976, Harvard Collection.

20. Letter to Jeanne Carayon, 31 August 1973, written from the Bar Harbor hospital where Yourcenar was being treated for a slipped lumbar disk, Harvard Collection.

21. Letter to Jeanne Carayon, 29 October 1973, Harvard Collection.

22. Both "magnetic fields" and "objective chance" are Surrealist terms, the former representing the English translation of *Les Champs magnétiques* (collaborative text by André Breton and Philippe Soupault), which was the first published instance of the technique of automatic writing, and the latter referring, in its least technical sense, to the importance of seemingly haphazard, coincidental events.—Trans.

23. Yourcenar, *Quoi? L'Eternité,* pp. 184–86.

24. Letter to Jean Chalon, 9 May 1974, Harvard Collection.

25. Letter to Jean Chalon, 29 March 1974, Harvard Collection.

26. Dominique Aury, "Marguerite Yourcenar, *Souvenirs pieux*" [Marguerite Yourcenar, *Dear Departed*], in *Nouvelle Revue Française* 259 (July 1974).

27. Letter to Jeanne Carayon, 14 August 1974, Harvard Collection.

28. Letter to Matthieu Galey, 14 December 1974, Harvard Collection.

29. Anya Kayaloff Archives.

30. Letter to Jeanne Carayon, 2 January 1975, Harvard Collection.

31. Letter to Jean Chalon, 7 February 1972, Jean Chalon Archives.

32. See Marguerite Yourcenar, "Le Tombeau de Jacques Masui" (1976), reprinted in the collection of essays, *Le Temps, ce grand sculpteur,* pp. 231–36; "Tribute to Jacques Masui," in *That Mighty Sculptor, Time,* pp. 216–21.

The collection of "Documents Spirituels" that Savigneau mentions in the text concerned matters relating, notably, to Eastern religious practices.—Trans.

33. Unpublished letter to Gabriel Germain, 8 May 1976.

34. Letter to Nico Calas, 26 September 1975, Harvard Collection.

35. Letter to Jeanne Carayon, dated 20–28 July 1976, Harvard Collection.

36. Letter to Jeanne Carayon, 19 February 1977, Harvard Collection.

37. Letter to Jeanne Carayon, 18 January 1976, Harvard Collection.

38. Ibid.

39. Henri Michaux, *Ecuador,* trans. Robin Magowan (Seattle: University of Washington Press, 1970), p. 40.

40. Letter to Jeanne Carayon, 23 March 1977, Harvard Collection.

41. Letter to Nobuyuki Kondo, editor in chief of the review *Umi,* 26 January 1969, Harvard Collection.

42. Galey, *With Open Eyes,* p. 87.

43. Marguerite Yourcenar, *Le Dialogue dans le marécage,* in *Revue de France,* vol. 12, no. 4 (15 February 1932). Reprinted in *Théâtre I,* pp. 173—201. See particularly in that edition, the "note sur *Le Dialogue dans le marécage*" [Note on *Le Dialogue dans le marécage*], written in December 1969, pp. 175—77.

44. These are both Nō plays of the Japanese Middle Ages.—Trans.

45. Marguerite Yourcenar, *Le Tour de la prison* [This, Our Prison] (Paris: Gallimard, 1991), p. 95.

46. Letter to Jeanne Carayon, 8 April 1976, Harvard Collection.

47. Galey, *With Open Eyes,* p. 197.

48. Ibid., p. 206.

49. Unpublished letter to Michel Aubrion, 19 March 1970.

50. Unpublished letter to Anat Barzilai, 22 September 1977.

51. Unpublished letter to Jeanne Carayon, 2 October 1971.

52. Unpublished letter to Father Yves de Gibon, 1 April 1976. Monsieur Homais, the pharmacist in Gustave Flaubert's *Madame Bovary,* is considered an archetype of the constantly speechifying, pretentiously free-thinking petty bourgeois.—Trans.

53. In the preliminary notes to *Quoi? L'Eternité,* one nonetheless sees how uncertain she still was at the end of her life: "Between the Hindu notion of Atman, of eternal wandering, and the Buddhist idea of an eternal passage, I shall never manage to choose, sensing all the while that these two notions opposed to one another no doubt merge into a whole somewhere out of our sight."

54. Conversation with François-Marie Samuelson, "Yourcenar: 'Il ne faut jamais être défaitiste'" [Yourcenar: "One Must Never Give in to Defeatism"], in *Le Figaro Magazine,* 31 October 1980.

55. Galey, *With Open Eyes,* p. 205.

56. Unpublished letter to Gabriel Germain, 13 June 1969.

57. Letter to Jeanne Carayon, dated 20—28 July 1976, Harvard Collection.

58. Rereading *L'Œuvre au noir* before its publication in the "Folio" collection, she changed "the suffering was worse as a result" to "the suffering should have been worse as a result" and commented: "which is not absolutely correct" (Letter to Jeanne Carayon, 8 April 1976, Harvard Collection).

59. Letter to Georges de Crayencour, 22 September 1977, Georges de Crayencour Archives.

60. Letter to Jean Chalon, 3 February 1977, Jean Chalon Archives.

61. Letter to Max Heilbronn, 17 April 1977, Harvard Collection. Galeries Lafayette is a major Parisian department store, along the lines of the American Macy's, that does a booming mail-order business and has branches in major cities throughout France.—Trans.

62. Unpublished letter to Suzanne Lilar, 16 March 1971.

63. Letter to Jeanne Carayon, 6 July 1977, Harvard Collection. The line from Rimbaud is Wallace Fowlie's translation from *Bateau ivre* (*The Drunken Boat*): *Rimbaud: Complete Works, Selected Letters* (Chicago: University of Chicago Press, 1966), p. 119.—Trans.

64. See especially the letter that Yourcenar sent to the newspaper *Le Monde* (2—3 March 1969), about "the seal hunt," as well as the texts "Bêtes à fourrure" ("Fur-bearing Animals") (1976) and "Qui sait si l'âme des bêtes va en bas?" ("Who Knows Whether the Spirit of Animals Goes Downward") (1981), reprinted in the collection of essays *That Mighty Sculptor, Time.*

65. Matthieu Galey, "C'est une reine Yourcenar ..." [Yourcenar, a Queen ...], an interview-portrait, in *Réalités* 345 (October 1974): 70–75.

66. Jean Duvignaud, "Marguerite Yourcenar: Les Avatars d'une hérédité" [Marguerite Yourcenar: Avatars of an Ancestral Heritage], in *Les Nouvelles Littéraires*, 27 September 1977.

67. François Nourissier, "Yourcenar dialogue avec le Temps" [Yourcenar Converses with Time], in *Le Point* 260 (12 September 1977).

68. Jacqueline Piatier, "Marguerite Yourcenar et la 'Légende des siècles'" [Marguerite Yourcenar and "The Legend of the Centuries"], in *"Le Monde* des livres," 23 September 1977.

Piatier refers to Victor Hugo's series of what were called "little epics," a book of poems published initially in 1859 but then added to and published in a collective edition in 1883. Vast in scope, *The Legend of the Centuries* covers the biblical period, the Middle Ages, the Renaissance, and deals with historical, legendary, and metaphysical issues.—Trans.

69. André Wurmser, "Marguerite Yourcenar de ces origines à nos jours" [Marguerite Yourcenar from Her Origins to the Present Day], in *L'Humanité*, 28 October 1977.

70. Dominique Fernandez, *"Archives du Nord,* de Marguerite Yourcenar. Promenade à fleur de peau" [*Archives du Nord* by Marguerite Yourcenar. A Superficial Stroll through the Past], in *Le Matin,* 30 September 1977.

71. Letter to Jeanne Carayon, 19 February 1977, Harvard Collection.

72. Letter from Claude Gallimard to Marguerite Yourcenar, 6 February 1977, Gallimard Archives.

73. Letter to Claude Gallimard, 18 February 1977, Gallimard Archives.

74. Letter to Georges Frameries, November 1977, Harvard Collection. See Georges Frameries, "La Vieille Dame et la mer" [The Old Woman and the Sea], in *L'Unité,* 14 October 1977.

75. Letter to Joseph Breitbach, 4 February 1977, Harvard Collection.

Images d'Epinal (see also note 7 in chapter 11) frequently consist of rather grandiose representations of historical figures not noted for their pacifism: Robespierre, Napoleon Bonaparte, General Boulanger, and so on, which may have something to do with what Yourcenar is saying here. In any event, she undoubtedly means to invoke the oversimplification of things that is perhaps the most noteworthy characteristic of *images d'Epinal.*—Trans.

76. There is still, on that spot, a hotel called the Saint-James, but it has nothing in common with the one Yourcenar and Frick knew.

77. Letter to Madame Heilbronn, April 1977, Harvard Collection.

78. Galey, *With Open Eyes,* note 1, p. 193.

79. Letter to Hélène Martin, 19 October 1977, Harvard Collection.

Chapter 18

1. Letter of 28 April 1978, Harvard Collection.

2. Marguerite Yourcenar, "Carnets de notes de *L'Œuvre au noir,*" in *La Nouvelle Revue Française* 452 and 453 (September and October 1990).

3. Letter to Louise de Borchgrave, 5 December 1978, Harvard Collection.

4. Letter to Anne Quellennec, 14 December 1978, Harvard Collection.

5. Letter to Georges de Crayencour, 14 July 178, Georges de Crayencour Archives.

6. Letter to Georges de Crayencour, 23 July 1978, Georges de Crayencour Archives.

7. For a discussion of the Quai Conti, see note 10, chapter 12, "First Renown."—Trans.

8. This is the title of one of the chapters in Galey's *With Open Eyes.*—Trans.

9. Marguerite Yourcenar, preface to *La Couronne et la lyre* [The Crown and the Lyre] (poems translated from the Greek) (Paris: Gallimard, 1979), pp. 9–40.

10. Galey, *With Open Eyes,* notably the chapter entitled "The Art of Translating," pp. 157–65.

11. Letter to Denise Lelarge, 25 September 1979, Harvard Collection.

12. Card to Denise Lelarge, 15 May 1979, Harvard Collection.

13. Matthieu Galey, *Journal 1974–1986* (Paris: Grasset, 1989), p. 183.

14. Jean-Paul Kauffmann, "Le Système Yourcenar" [The Yourcenar System], an interview-portrait in the guise of a lesson in the ABCs, in *Le Matin,* 10 June 1979.

15. Letter to Jean-Paul Kauffmann, 11 May 1979, Harvard Collection.

16. Letter to Georges Wicks, 12 March 1975, Harvard Collection.

17. See chapter 1, note 38.—Trans.

18. Letter to Georges de Crayencour, 28 May 1979, Georges de Crayencour Archives.

19. Mathilde La Bardonnie, "Une Semaine chez Marguerite Yourcenar: La Grande Radioscopie" [A Week with Marguerite Yourcenar: The Big Radio Interview], interview with Jacques Chancel, in *Le Monde,* 10 June 1979.

20. Jérôme Garcin, "Une Femme volubile" [A Voluble Woman], in *Les Nouvelles Littéraires,* 14 June 1979.

21. In the June 1990 issue of the monthly *Lire,* Bernard Pivot, evoking his memories from "Apostrophes," recalled the special program with Yourcenar broadcast in December 1979, then again at the time of her death: "Listening to Marguerite Yourcenar's responses, to those words that came out just exactly right, to those full, slow sentences, sinewy but still graceful and flowing—never before had I been so convinced that I speak poorly."

Bernard Pivot is noted for his eloquence.—Trans.

22. Monsieur Mt, "Yourcenar en son île" [Yourcenar on Her Island], in *Valeurs Actuelles,* 3 December 1979.

23. Bernard Poirot-Delpech, "Yourcenar à Apostrophes, 'Plénitude, voilà le mot'" [Yourcenar on "Apostrophes": "Plenitude, That's the Word"], in *Le Monde,* 9 December 1979. Although the subjunctive mood generally is very much alive and well in French, the construction quoted here is an example not of the present but of the imperfect subjunctive, which is very rarely used in spoken French. It might be said to have the same degree of unfamiliarity to the television viewer as this English usage, in which the old subjunctive "were" would today be replaced by "would be": "It were beyond my power to desist."—Trans.

24. Letter to Georges de Crayencour, 28 May 1979, Georges de Crayencour Archives.

25. Galey, *With Open Eyes,* p. 261.

26. Letter to Georges de Crayencour, 7 September 1979, Georges de Crayencour Archives.

27. Letter to Georges de Crayencour, 8 December 1979, Georges de Crayencour Archives.

28. Galey, *Journal 1974–1986,* p. 143.

29. Vassilis Alexakis, *Paris-Athènes* [Paris-Athens] (Paris: Le Seuil, 1989), p. 33.

30. Galey, *Journal 1974–1986,* p. 183.

31. Claude Servan-Schreiber, "L'Ordre des choses de Marguerite Yourcenar" [Marguerite Yourcenar's Order of Things], interview in *F. Magazine* 25 (March 1980).

32. Yourcenar, *The Abyss*, p. 11: "Who would be so besotted as to die without having made at least the round of this, his prison?"

33. Yourcenar, *Quoi? L'Eternité*, p. 278.

Chapter 19

1. Letter to André Lebon, 3 February 1980, Harvard Collection.

2. Jean d'Ormesson, born in 1925, is a prominent French author, journalist, and cultural figure. He has been editor in chief and a columnist for *Le Figaro* and the secretary general of UNESCO's International Council for Philosophy and Humanistic Studies. He became a member of the Académie Française in 1973.—Trans.

3. Press reactions to Simone de Beauvoir's *The Mandarins* cited by Julia Kristeva in "A Propos des *Samouraïs*" [On the Subject of The Samurais], an interview with Elisabeth Bélorgey, in *L'Infini* 30 (Summer 1990): 66.

4. She had this to say, moreover, to one of her correspondents: "As for losing weight, I've now done it. In the (nearly) six months that have gone by since Grace Frick's death, with the projects and the trips that have filled them, I have lost ten kilos, after the almost-total immobility of life during these last four or five years. I'm not complaining about it; one must tread as lightly as one can upon the earth" (Letter to Wilhem Ganz, 12 May 1980, Wilhem Ganz Archives). Ten kilos is approximately twenty-two pounds.—Trans.

5. Félicien Marceau is the pseudonym of Louis Carette, a prolific writer of fiction, drama, screenplays, and essays, born in 1913, and the winner of numerous prestigious literary prizes.—Trans.

6. Interview with Roger Straus, December 1988.

7. This incident made such a strong impression on Yourcenar that she relates it in *Quoi? L'Eternité:* "in less than an instant the biases to which Michel believed himself immune had welled up in his throat and spewed forth like some bitter bile. The same thing happened some years later, when he chanced to meet the rather shifty widow of an Israelite doctor he suspected, not without good reason, of performing abortions—that man who was revolted by anti-Semitism cried out: 'Dirty Jews!'" (p. 198).

8. Yourcenar, *Archives du Nord*, pp. 365–66. Edouard Drumont, 1844–1917, was a French politician and polemical writer who fought against the influence of big money, maintaining that Jewish holders of the latter were among the worst threats to French political and economic integrity. He wrote violent anti-Semitic diatribes and founded *La Libre Parole*, an anti-Jewish, rabidly nationalistic organization.—Trans.

9. Regarding the question of anti-Semitism, see the chapter entitled "Racism" in Galey, *With Open Eyes*, pp. 215–20.

10. Rosbo, *Entretiens radiophoniques avec Marguerite Yourcenar*, p. 106.

11. Thomas Gergely, "La Mémoire suspecte d'Hadrien" [Hadrian's Questionable Memory], in *Revue de l'Université de Bruxelles*, special issue devoted to Marguerite Yourcenar, March-April 1988, pp. 45–50.

12. Ibid., pp. 48–49.

13. Galey, *With Open Eyes*, p. 218.

14. Interview with Jean d'Ormesson, spring 1989.

15. Georges Clemenceau was premier of France from 1906—1909 and 1917—1919. His cabinet was widely viewed as playing an essential role in bringing about the Allied victory in World War I. When he lost the subsequent presidential election to Paul Deschenel, Clemenceau retired from politics to pursue his career as a writer. Jérôme Carcopino was an archeologist and an historian.—Trans.

16. Letter to Jacques Kayaloff, 6 December 1962, Anya Kayaloff Archives.

17. Letter to Jacques Kayaloff, 4 January 1961, Anya Kayaloff Archives.

18. Members of the Académie Française traditionally receive swords upon induction as part of their official regalia.—Trans.

19. Yasunari Kawabata, who died at his own hand in 1972, was an internationally acclaimed author of novels and short stories. He was the first Japanese writer to be awarded the Nobel Prize for literature. Miguel Angel Asturias, 1899—1974, was a Guatemalan poet and diplomat, as well as a winner, like Kawabata, of the Nobel Prize. He held a variety of diplomatic posts, including that of ambassador to France from 1966 to 1970.—Trans.

20. Letter from Roger Caillois to Jacques Kayaloff, 9 March 1971, Anya Kayaloff Archives.

21. Raymond Aron, 1905—1983, was an author, a sociologist, and a prominent conservative political commentator.—Trans.

22. Yourcenar articulated the conditions of her candidacy to the Académie Française in letters to Louis Pélissier, on 17 December 1977, and to Thérèse de Saint-Phalle, on 19 February 1978, Harvard Collection.

23. Regarding "historical footnotes," see note 9 in chapter 3, "Early Lessons."—Trans.

24. Letter to Jeanne Carayon, 8 April 1976, Harvard Collection.

25. Born in 1923, Michel Droit is a French author, journalist, and reporter for radio and television. He was a member of the French Resistance during World War II and is the only journalist ever to have interviewed Charles de Gaulle on television.—Trans.

26. Letter from Jean d'Ormesson, Harvard Collection.

27. Travel notebooks, Jerry Wilson, Harvard Collection.

28. This is my translation of Savigneau's French; I was unable to find the passage in Jerry Wilson's journal.—Trans.

29. Ibid.

30. Ibid.

31. Ibid.

32. The opera in question here is most likely Niccolo Piccinni's *Didon,* written in 1783.—Trans.

33. Raymond Barre, a prominent French politician of the Right, was prime minister of France under Valérie Giscard-d'Estaing from 1976 to 1981. At the time of Yourcenar's election, he was campaigning for the presidency of France.—Trans.

34. Letter from Katherine Gatch, 7 March 1980, Harvard Collection.

35. Harvard Collection.

36. Yourcenar had originally written: "illegal to have more than three children (sterilization after the fourth child)."

37. Notebook of Marguerite Yourcenar, Gallimard Archives.

38. See the text of this service in its entirety in Appendix 5.

39. Yourcenar, *Quoi? L'Eternité,* p. 278.

40. Marguerite Yourcenar, "*Deux Noirs* de Rembrandt" [Rembrandt's *Two Negroes*], in *En pèlerin et en étranger,* pp. 225—31.

41. The Marais is a particularly lovely, historic, and fashionable section of Paris, on the Right Bank.—Trans.

42. Yourcenar refers here to the Tantric *phurba,* used in a sacrificial ritual. It was I who gave her that wooden *phurba,* having bought it at the Tibetan museum on Staten Island in 1985. Thanking her on 3 November 1985, she wrote: ". . . what a joy and what a miracle it is, like everything that one does not expect."—Trans.

43. René de la Croix, Duc de Castries, born in 1908, wrote *The Lives of the Kings and Queens of France.*—Trans.

44. Maurice Rheims, who joined the Académie Française in 1976, is a French art critic.—Trans.

45. On that show, she talked about *Mishima: A Vision of the Void,* which had just come out, and about which Diane de Margerie had just written: "The essay furls around his *œuvre,* scrutinizing its so highly ambiguous lack of a message, enumerating all of the questions that the reader will not (ever) cease to ask on the subject of Mishima. . . . What seems most striking in these lucid pages, which give access to an incredibly diverse and complex *œuvre,* is that experience does not end up providing the prodigious creator, actor, and witness of his age that Mishima was with either consolation or hope. The encounter between that violent negation, which went as far as death, and the vital transmutation that the novelist Yourcenar has always performed by way of her own characters is fascinating" ("Sous le regard de Marguerite Yourcenar" [Under Marguerite Yourcenar's Gaze], in "*Le Monde* des livres," 2 January 1981).

46. Galey, *Journal 1974–1986,* p. 123.

47. Ibid., p. 126.

48. No less exceptional was the live television broadcast of the ceremony, on FR3. The program was produced by Maurice Dumay.

49. The *Chevaliers du Tastevin* are a Burgundian brotherhood of oenophiles whose induction rites are noted both for their ceremoniousness and for the abundance of wine with which they are celebrated.—Trans.

50. Galey, who has twice now mentioned tails in his Yourcenar-related journal entries, refers here, I believe, to the swords worn by the green-uniformed Academicians.—Trans.

51. Galey, *Journal 1974–1986,* p. 161.

52. Marguerite Yourcenar, "Discours de réception de Mme Marguerite Yourcenar à l'Académie française" [Marguerite Yourcenar's Acceptance Speech to the Académie Française] (Paris: Gallimard, 1981). The text in praise of Roger Caillois is reprinted under the title "L'Homme qui aimait les pierres" in the collection *En pèlerin et en étranger.*

53. The dictionary of the Académie Française exists to establish literary language.—Trans.

54. Galey, *With Open Eyes,* p. 221. On this topic she even expanded, curiously, to one of her correspondents: ". . . abortion . . . I don't like it very much, but these days it's a necessity; still I wish there were some kind of prayer ritual designed for the husband and wife who have eliminated a life—even wisely, even to avoid the worst of consequences. Needless to say, this wouldn't change the facts of the matter whatsoever, but it would make people think about the gravity of the act, and might dispose those involved to take less tardy precautions in the future" (letter to Odette Schwartz, 31 December 1977, Harvard Collection).

55. This French institution, which in 1799 replaced the former King's Council, is made up of specialists in finance, domestic affairs, public works, human services, and so forth, and

advises the government on matters juridical and administrative. It also serves as the supreme appellate court for citizens contending that they have been legally wronged by the administration.—Trans.

56. *Garçon de quoi écrire* [Waiter, Something to Write With], dialogue between Jean d'Ormesson and François Sureau (Paris: Gallimard, 1989), p. 89.

57. Christoph Ransmayr, *The Last World*, trans. John E. Woods (New York: Grove Weidenfield, 1990). Remarks gleened from various articles in the press.

58. Interview with William Styron, May 1990.

59. The Camargue is an area of coastal flood plain in southeastern France, in the delta of the Rhone, noted for its cattle, its sheep, the horses indigenous to the region, and its migratory birds.—Trans.

60. Philippe Sollers, *Women*, trans. Barbara Bray (New York: Columbia University Press, 1990), p. 412.

61. Galey, *Journal 1974—1986*, p. 183.

Chapter 20

1. According to all her friends, Yourcenar's intellectual vigilance remained intact, until her final illness. Her nurse and her doctors confirm that, prior to November 1987, she was neither senile nor delerious at any time. They do, however, point out that, between the summer of 1986 and the fall of 1987, she may have had some imperceptible strokes, and that her immense learning and her skill at manipulating her knowledge could have masked enduringly, no matter who her interlocutor, any very slight lapses of the mind.

2. Gallimard Archives.

3. Letter to Josyane Savigneau, 27 March 1986, Josyane Savigneau Archives.

4. Gallimard Archives.

5. It was during that year that the tombs of her maternal family were restored by a woman in Suarlée (Belgium).

6. Yourcenar, *Memoirs of Hadrian*, p. 16. Regarding Hadrian's meditation on pleasure, see also pages 12—16, beginning with: "The cynics and the moralists agree in placing the pleasures of love among the enjoyments termed gross, that is, between the desire for drinking and the need for eating, though at the same time they call love less indispensable, since it is something which, they assert, one can go without. I expect about anything from the moralist, but am astonished that the cynic should go thus astray."

7. Angelo Rinaldi, "Montherlant, soror . . ." [Montherlant, Soror . . . , a play on the title of the work under review, *Anna, soror . . .*], in *L'Express*, 23 October 1981. The Grand Prix de Rome is awarded by the French government to students excelling in the fine arts. It involves four years of study in Rome.—Trans.

8. Jean Chalon, "Yourcenar peintre pompier" [Yourcenar, a Pompous Painter], in *Le Figaro*, 11 September 1981.

Académie members are called "immortals."—Trans.

9. Jean Chalon, "Yourcenar toujours recommencé" [Yourcenar, As Ever, Renewed], in *Le Figaro-L'Aurore*, 11 June 1982.

10. François Weyergans, "En effeuillant la Marguerite Yourcenar" [Leafing Through the Venerable Marguerite Yourcenar], in *Le Matin* des livres, 24 November 1982. Molière's play *Les Précieuses ridicules* (*The Ridiculous Précieuses*) makes fun of women of affected manners and extravagant language.—Trans.

11. Gallimard Archives.

12. Marguerite Yourcenar, "That Mighty Sculptor, Time," in *That Mighty Sculptor, Time,* p. 57.

13. Danièle Sallenave, "Aux confins du monde et du temps" [On the Borders of the World and Time] in *"Le Monde* des livres," 25 December 1987.

14. This film—in which Yourcenar appears—was broadcast in November 1983 on French television (FR3) and won a prize as a documentary.

15. Preliminary notes for *Quoi? L'Eternité,* Harvard Collection.

16. Yourcenar, *Memoirs of Hadrian,* p. 24.

17. *La Voix des choses,* texts chosen by Marguerite Yourcenar, photographs by Jerry Wilson (Paris: Gallimard, 1987).

18. Interview with Marguerite Yourcenar, 15 November 1984. It was at this hospital that she met the young nurse, Monicah, who would accompany her on her trips in 1986.

19. *Les Charités d'Alcippe* (*The Alms of Alcippe*) had just been reissued by Gallimard in an elegant grey volume, and Yourcenar's collection of translations, *Blues et Gospels* [Blues and Gospels] had just appeared, with photographs by both Wilson and one of his friends, a much better photographer, Jean-Marie Grénier (Marguerite Yourcenar, *Les Charités d'Alcippe* [Paris: Gallimard, 1984]; *The Alms of Alcippe,* trans. Edith R. Farrell [New York: Targ Editions, 1982] and *Blues et Gospels,* texts translated and introduced by Marguerite Yourcenar, photographs assembled by Jerry Wilson [Paris: Gallimard, 1984]).

20. Along with Claude Gallimard and Maître Marc Brossollet, Guillou is her literary executor.

21. Letter to Josyane Savigneau, 27 March 1986, Josyane Savigneau Archives.

22. Yourcenar, *Oriental Tales,* p. 4.

23. She would be replaced by a little black poodle, Fu-Ku, bought by Yourcenar after returning from India, on 9 April 1985. Fu-Ku, for his part, would not be a traveler either. Yourcenar "shared" him with her secretary Jeannie Lunt, at whose home he now resides. Yourcenar provided for the dog in her will so that he would not be a financial burden to anyone.

24. Yourcenar, *Quoi? L'Eternité,* p. 187.

25. Letter to Georges de Crayencour, 7 November 1985, Georges de Crayencour Archives.

26. "Préface," *La Voix des choses,* p. 7.

27. From Petite Plaisance she wrote to Yannick Guillou: "I don't know if you have gotten any news about the latest developments in Jerry's situation. They are incredible: Three attempts at suicide, two of them in a sitting room at the Ritz (I hardly believe it myself!), landed him each time in the Sainte-Anne clinic, where he remains at this time. You can imagine how much all this upsets me, and also how powerless I am to do anything at all, especially since, though I am a little bit better, I am still very weak" (letter to Yannick Guillou, undated, Yannick Guillou Archives).

28. Yourcenar, *Memoirs of Hadrian,* p. 172.

Chapter 2 1

1. She who detested "letting herself go," showing herself to be weak or vulnerable, wrote nonetheless to Yannick Guillou: "Very dear Friend, your letter went straight to my heart. And this is not a hollow cliché. A letter like yours (and perhaps a dozen others) is proof that

one is not entirely alone. . . . Delivered, as you say. Delivered from the illness, such a deplorable one, but one made worse still by the labyrinth of inebriants, misunderstandings, and mirror games in which he was caught in the end. Delivered, I hope, from that too. I shall never forgive myself for not being there at the end, the state of my health being still too uncertain, but I don't believe my presence would really have made things much better. (He, at least, was faithful till the end, interrupting his treatment in Paris in order to come be with me during my operation)" (letter to Yannick Guillou, 23 February 1986, Yannick Guillou Archives).

2. Gallimard Archives.

3. Letter to Josyane Savigneau, 27 March 1986, Josyane Savigneau Archives.

4. She was supposed to have attended the final shooting in December 1987, which was the month of her death. The film came out in May 1988.

5. Interview with André Delvaux, December 1988.

6. Yourcenar, *La Couronne et la lyre,* p. 177.

I have translated Marguerite Yourcenar's French translation of Empedocles into English above. M. R. Wright, on p. 275 of *Empedocles: The Extant Fragments* (New Haven: Yale University Press, 1981), offers this English translation of the same passage: "For before now I have been at some time boy and girl, bush, bird, and a mute fish in the sea."—Trans.

7. An account of the relations between André Delvaux and Yourcenar, as well as a discussion of the work done by Delvaux on *L'Œuvre au noir,* appears in *André Delvaux, une œuvre, un film: L'Œuvre au noir* [André Delvaux, a Book, a Film: *The Abyss*] (Brussels and Paris: Editions Labor et Méridiens Klincksieck, 1988).

8. On 5 December 1979 in an interview with *Le Monde* on the subject of "freedoms and the state," François Mitterrand, then first secretary of the Socialist party, spoke of Zeno as a model of freedom: "Zeno is one of the most fascinating characters of modern literature. He seeks and he dies, apparently defeated but with a free, triumphant mind. In that regard I was very interested in the life and activities of the members of all those sects, surrounding Zeno, who, as is also the case today, had no other object than self-destruction, the sole preoccupation of each one of them being first of all to prove his brother wrong. Sectarianism, or antiliberty . . . Any dogma that attempts to validate itself by means of constraint kills man at the same time it kills freedom" (Philippe Boucher and Josyane Savigneau, "Les Libertés et l'Etat" [Freedoms and the State], interview with François Mitterrand, in *Le Monde,* 5 December 1979).

9. For this anniversary, Yourcenar had written to a friend of hers, Sister Marie-Laurence, a nun in Bruges, requesting that a mass be celebrated in Jerry's memory: "He asked me never to stop thinking about him. I am trying to execute this duty" (unpublished card to Sister Marie-Laurence, 7 February 1987). Similarly, she had had masses said in Grace's memory every year since her death.

10. Interviews with Christian Lahache, 1988.

11. The lecture would be put off until October on account of her health.

12. Yourcenar, *Dear Departed,* p. 26.

13. A few days later, on returning to France, Yannick Guillou wrote to one of his friends, the Italian harpsichordist Luciano Sgrizzi: "In no way did I get the impression from my last telephone conversation with the nurse that she was dying. When I arrived, I was told that her condition had worsened on Sunday the thirteenth, that since then she had refused all nourishment, and that they were giving her morphine. When I went into her room—no drips and no tubes anywhere in sight—her arms, which lay close to her body, and her face

were covered with red patches (an allergic reaction, they told me, to a drug), but her face seemed suddenly thirty years younger: with every wrinkle gone, and a distinction, a majesty, a luminous subtlety of features, her eyes half-closed, her mouth partly open, her tongue already black, the ends of her fingers blue. They had told her the night before that I was coming and she had tried to clap her hands. When she saw me, she moved her head slightly, and her eyes opened completely, and she smiled. . . . [S]he took my right hand and, gently, brought it toward her lips and kissed it. She also tried to speak to me but the words were garbled and I couldn't understand them. . . . It was eleven o'clock in the morning. . . . We came back, the nurse and I, early in the afternoon. She was in a coma. I got down on my knees at the foot of her bed and I prayed."

14. This is Arthur Goldhammer's translation of "*la chance qui consiste à ne pas être*" from p. 172 of Matthieu Galey's *With Open Eyes.* As Yourcenar goes on to say in this text, the word "luck," in good French, is a neutral one, thus her phrase does not imply that it would have been a blessing not to have been born.—Trans.

15. Yourcenar, *The Abyss,* p. 348.

16. Yourcenar, *Archives du Nord,* p. 14.

17. Ibid., pp. 372—73.

Appendix 2

1. *Numquid et tu . . . ?* is the title under which in 1922 André Gide, at the urging of Charles Du Bos, published a record of his experiences helping refugees during World War I. It concerns in large part his thoughts regarding Christian religious teachings. "*Numquid et tu . . . ?*" can be found on pp. 169—87 of the Justin O'Brien translation of volume 2 of *The Journals of André Gide* (New York: Alfred A. Knopf, 1948).—Trans.

Appendix 3

1. No doubt a reference to William II, the German emperor who presided over Germany's military build-up and colonial expansion and declared war on Russia and France in 1914.—Trans.

INDEX

Far from the Madding Crowd (Hardy), 167, 346

Farrar, Straus and Giroux, 222, 251. *See also* Straus, Roger

Farrell, Edith R., 473 n. 1

Fata Morgana (Breton), 143

Faux-Monnayeurs, Les (Gide), 209

Fayence, 237–38, 239, 310

Femmes. See *Women*

Fenton, William (Yourcenar's American lawyer), 306, 381

Fernandez, Dominique: review of *Archives du Nord,* 355–56

Feux. See *Fires*

Fichier parisien (Montherlant), 339

Finkielkraut, Alain: *La Défaite de la pensée,* 69, 469 n. 24

Fires (*Feux*): dedication of, 102; discussion of, 103–6; female narrator of, 103; importance of the senses in, 312; influence of Jean Cocteau on, 104; partial publication of, in *La Revue de France,* 103; prefaces of, 104; review of, by Edmond Jaloux, 89, 106; review of, by Emilie Noulet, 106; revision of, 243, 246, 247; role of myth in, 93, 103; role of Yourcenar's passion for André Fraigneau in, 98, 102, 105, 122, 404; sales of, 250; writing of, 98, 404

Fire That Consumes, The (*La Ville dont le prince est un enfant*) (Montherlant), 315

Flamand, Paul: roel of, in the Plon affair, 296

Flanner, Janet, 223

Flaubert, Gustave, 79, 177, 219; lecture on, 180; *The Temptation of Saint Anthony,* 486 n. 16

Fleuve profond, sombre rivière, 280, 281, 296, 348; early work on, 153, 272; review of, by Yves Berger, 281–82

Flexner, Hortense. *See* King, Hortense

Flies, The (*Les Mouches*) (Sartre), 151

Florence: 1923 trip to, 65; 1937 trip to, 118; 1958 trip to, 255

Folch-Ribas, Jacques, 219

Folle de Chaillot, La. See *Madwoman of Chaillot, The*

"Forces du passé et forces de l'avenir," 143

Foucault, Michel, 106, 266; *The Order of Things,* 486 n. 21

Fouchet, Max-Pol, 228

Fraigneau, André, 92, 100–101, 131, 172, 222–23; *L'Amour vagabond,* 101; comments of, on Yourcenar's work, 87, 94, 243, 302; *Les Etonnements de Guillaume Francoeur,* 126; exclusion of, from the Pléiade "Chronologie," 100; fascist sympathies of, 94, 140; *La Grâce humaine,* 124; *Julien l'Apostat,* 188; as a model for Erick in *Coup de Grâce,* 124, 357; reader's report of, on *Memoirs of Hadrian,* 188–89, 190, 220; *Le Roi fou et le solitaire,* 188; role of, in the publication of *Pindare,* 86–87; support of, of *Memoirs of Hadrian,* 207; *Les Voyageurs transfigurés,* 92, 100–101; Yourcenar's passion for, 97, 98–111, 118, 121; Yourcenar's split with, 124, 132. See also *Coup de Grâce; Fires*

Frameries, Georges, 356–57

Fräulein Margareta (governess of the Cartier de Marchienne family), 17

Freire, Carlos, 430

Freire, Héloïsa, 430

French Library (Boston), 318, 393

Freund, Gisèle, 341

Frick Gallery, 125, 126; 1981 visit to, 403

Frick, Grace, 112–34, 146, 195, 206, 322; background of, 116; birthplace of, 115; burial of, 373, 376; calenders and daybooks of, xi, 154, 172, 262, 329, 366, 373; cancer of, 156, 257–58, 260, 272, 273, 279, 322; cancer treatments of, 328–29, 353, 362; changing political views of, 173, 233; children's parties of, 145–46, 238; chronologies of Yourcenar's life, 10, 43; correspondence of, with Natalie Barney, 173, 233; death of, 2, 5, 272–73, 375; education of, 116–19; final illness of, 360–73; first trip of, to Europe, 96, 117; first meeting of, with Yourcenar, 96, 115–17; friendship of, with Florence Codman, 115–16; funeral service of, 373; hospitalization